A Military History of the
Modern Middle East

A Military History of the Modern Middle East

James Brian McNabb

An Imprint of ABC-CLIO, LLC

Santa Barbara, California • Denver, Colorado

Library of Congress Cataloging-in-Publication Data

Names: McNabb, James Brian, author.
Title: A military history of the modern Middle East / James Brian McNabb.
Description: Santa Barbara, California : Praeger, [2017] | Includes
    bibliographical references and index.
Identifiers: LCCN 2016047664 (print) | LCCN 2016058290 (ebook) | ISBN
    9781440829635 (pbk. : alk. paper) | ISBN 9781440829642 (ebook)
Subjects: LCSH: Middle East—History, Military—20th century.
Classification: LCC DS63.15 .M35 2017 (print) | LCC DS63.15 (ebook) | DDC
    355.00956—dc23
LC record available at https://lccn.loc.gov/2016047664

ISBN: 978–1–4408–2963–5
EISBN: 978–1–4408–2964–2

21 20 19 18 17   1 2 3 4 5

This book is also available as an eBook.

Praeger
An Imprint of ABC-CLIO, LLC

ABC-CLIO, LLC
130 Cremona Drive, P.O. Box 1911
Santa Barbara, California 93116-1911
www.abc-clio.com

This book is printed on acid-free paper ∞

Manufactured in the United States of America

The past is never dead. It's not even past.
— *William Faulkner*

Contents

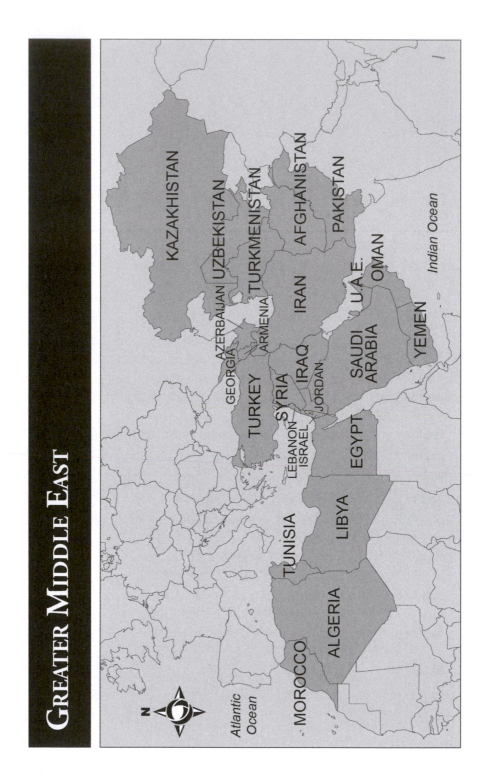

GREATER MIDDLE EAST

Introduction

The history of failure in war can almost be summed up in two words: too late.

—Douglas MacArthur[1]

In this book, my aim is to provide the reader with an increased understanding of the multitude of dynamics that have driven military events, issues, and outcomes within the Middle East during the modern era. While the modern era in terms of the Middle East traditionally begins with Napoleon Bonaparte's 1798 military campaign in Egypt, it is nearly impossible to understand today's Middle East without first analyzing the earlier history of the region. In doing so, the present becomes more readily understood as a, more often than not, consistent extension of past events. That the future will resemble the past is not the expectation; however, that events, patterns, and regularities that have driven behavior, issues, and outcomes over the centuries will weigh in on the creation of tomorrow is, in fact, a reasonable starting point. As such, and, in order to foster an increased understanding of both the contemporary and future eras, the volume will first explore and analyze the driving dynamics that continue to animate and influence political, economic, and military behavior within the modern Middle East.

This context or analytic foundation provides insight into a series of continuing patterns and regularities that have driven events in the Middle East from ancient times and into the modern era. Key themes and reoccurring patterns throughout history include the aggregation of power, a compelling and unifying ideology, and military effectiveness.

From these larger categories more specific dynamics arise such as universalism, perpetual war, asymmetric operations (*Flaechen-und Luecken*), psychological dislocation and ascendancy, and moving inside an opponent's OODA-Loop. While the pattern is simple and repetitive, the various dynamics, seemingly unrelated yet underpinning the pattern, can best be understood in a careful analysis of the historical trends. A core objective of the book aims at providing that contextual analysis, narrowing the domain, and in concentrating the focus on an extension of Harvard professor emeritus Samuel Huntington's "clash of civilizations" more narrowly defined in the present work as a "clash of universalisms" in an age of weapons of mass destruction.[2]

Since ancient times, the world's first great empires as seen in Mesopotamia (roughly present-day Iraq) and Egypt took form through the successful aggregation of power achieved by the successful control or influence of people, resources, trade, and trade routes. This pattern continued through the Middle Ages and into the modern world. In the twentieth century, the fall of one of history's great powers, the Ottoman Empire, led to the *disaggregation* of the combined power and military capability that had first influenced, then, later, dominated the Middle East, North Africa, the Caucasus, and parts of Europe for 400 years. With the final collapse of the Ottoman Empire in the aftermath of the First World War, a range of centuries-old animosities and frozen conflicts in the Middle East—effectively suppressed by Ottoman central power since at least the sixteenth century—began erupting within the region yet once again.

The eventual demise of the Ottoman Empire in the modern era was accelerated by challenges and pressures generated by a rising Western civilization. Following the Napoleonic campaign in 1798 and the expansion of Western influence, the politics and military affairs in the Middle East and the Ottoman Empire were significantly reforged by European powers and the United States. Finally under increasing Western and Russian economic and military challenges and, in the aftermath of the First World War, the Ottoman Caliphate was formally abolished in 1924. Thus, while some analysts argue that the instability in the present-day Middle East arising from the Arab Spring in 2011 was created by the United States and its Western allies by their introduction of military force into the region during the Persian Gulf War of 1991 in the Iraq War of 2003, the chaos and uncertainty began following 1924 as the Islamic world grappled with traditional authoritarian governments and culture in a rapidly modernizing world.

The conflict between traditional Muslim society and modernity accelerated late in the eighteenth century with the French introduction of liberty, equality, and, it is fair to say, their own brand of colonialism, following Napoleon's Egyptian campaign, rising to a crescendo with the final collapse of the Ottoman Caliphate in the wake of the First World War. Middle Eastern elite were faced with the same puzzling dynamics that had swept the continent during the French Revolution and which the Prussian war theorist, Carl von Clausewitz, had been tasked by his superiors to explain in what eventually became the seminal book, *On War* (1932).

> The French Revolution had taught him that a state's greatest source of political energy could be its people. This force, restrained when a society was parceled into mutually exclusive compartments of rank and professions, could be released by giving each individual scope to develop, by creating within him a sense of loyalty to the state, an identity of interests with its leaders, so that he would freely expend his energy for its sake. The state, Clausewitz put it, should breathe life into the individual human force ... Statesmen who ignored the political significance of passion, of the irrational, whether in governments, generals, or peoples, ran the risk of misinterpreting the modern world.[3]

The unleashing of the human spirit from the old authoritarian past in Europe, fueled with the arrival of democracy and individual liberty in the early modern era, drove politics and created a new energy on the early modern battlefield. This awakening that occurred in Europe and North America and made manifest in the French and American revolutions was not only a function of political liberty but also one of slipping the constraints of religious authoritarianism, as the religious wars in Europe created a new political dynamic with the new dominance of the secular, sovereign nation-state following the Treaty of Westphalia in 1648. In Western civilization a particular religion henceforth would not control the institutions of government, and all citizens were then empowered to decide for themselves what church, temple, or mosque they would or would not attend.

With the collapse of Ottoman power and its associated Caliphate came attempts by influential actors in the West to move modern Turkey onto a secular, sovereign pathway in order to align with the Western view of the modern political world. The attempts at creating a new, yet legitimate, political order led to instability and varying levels of violence and conflict. In a strategic sense, the struggle revolves around the unresolved question regarding the place of religion in public policy and as to Islam's position vis-à-vis the state. Operationally, the uncertainty, instability, and conflict have been exacerbated by legitimacy issues of any given government whether secular or Islamist, including inefficiencies, perceived incompetence, and outright corruption. In short, the struggle continues into the twenty-first century to replace premodern caliphal political structures and institutions with modern versions resting upon

as much or more political legitimacy coupled with the necessary authority and capacity to enforce order and stability.[4] The difficulty comes from
the multitude of stakeholders within the region with differing views on
what shape and form the new governments should have. The difficulty
in finding a way forward is also compounded by the international community's vast power and in a preference for the creation of new political
institutions within the Middle East that are not in direct opposition to
democracy, the rule of law, and human rights.

STRATEGIC SETTING

The Middle East as the geographical nexus between Africa, Asia, and
the Mediterranean has historically served as a key intersection of world
communications and trade. As a result, powerful interests, both internal
and external, to the region have competed and often clashed in their
efforts at vying for control and influence and, in many cases, attempts at
aggregating power. While the phrase "Middle East" has routinely been
utilized in Europe and in North America in the modern era, in formal
geographical terms the region is more accurately referred to as Southwest
Asia. However, the "Middle East" was adopted by the British in referenc-
ing their global activities extending to the Far East, as the region came to
designate a midpoint between the British home islands and the empire's
South and East Asian strategic interests.[5] In terms of international strategic and commercial activities, India, Southeast Asia, and China were
important components of the British Empire's global network and underpinned its ability to project power around the world. In that worldwide
enterprise, the Middle East served as a vital logistical link.

The midpoint transit status of the Middle East vis-à-vis Western
colonial interests was irrevocably altered in 1908 as the region's first
recoverable oil reserves were discovered by British petroleum engineers
in Persia (present-day Iran). Following this discovery the strategic importance of the region transcended British logistical interests, as industrial
and military requirements for energy in the modern era drove great
powers and their associated regional allies into an intense and often
deadly competition. With nearly 65 percent of known world oil reserves
and 20 percent of the globe's reserves of natural gas, the Middle East will
continue, into the foreseeable future, to be a vital region to both the
international political economy and the fortunes of nations. In addition
to critical economic issues, the Middle East, as home to the origins of
three of the world's great monotheistic religions—Judaism, Christianity,
and Islam—served and continues to serve as a center of gravity and acute
focus of attention for people attending temples, churches, and mosques
throughout the world.

Commercially, the Mediterranean, Red, Black, Arabian, and Caspian Seas command vital ports, trading centers, and critical sea lines of communications (SLOCs). The Strait of Hormuz, which leads south from the Persian Gulf and into the Arabian Sea, is among the world's most strategically vital waterways and presents a potentially critical choke point for seaborne trade. One third of energy products bound for international markets are dependent on reliable and unimpeded transport routes through the Strait. The U.S. Central Command (USCENTCOM), part of the U.S. Department of Defense and the combatant command with a focus on the Middle East, with arguably the most powerful military forces in the region has stated that should a nation such as Iran move to block the Strait in an effort at disrupting energy supplies to the world economy, it would take the United States and its coalition partners several weeks to reopen the vital waterway.

Both the disruption of energy supplies and the insertion of additional volatility and uncertainty into an already weak and tenuous global economy would have a significantly negative impact on the world's economic stability. Additional problems would accrue, at least in the short term, from the initiation of naval and military operations required to reopen the Strait. In sum, the Middle East is critically important to the people of the world for a variety of reasons, including those with a religious, economic, cultural, and military basis—as it has been for centuries.

ANCIENT BACKGROUND AND EVOLUTION TOWARD THE MODERN AGE

Written or recorded history arose as human beings began transitioning from hunter-gatherer groups into sedentary pastoral and agricultural settlements during the Neolithic or Agricultural Revolution (12,000–9,000 BCE). Given this historic shift in the nature of economic life within human communities, sedentary agriculturalists began creating methods for effectively recording weather cycles, the advantages and disadvantages of various growth nutrients, as well as storage and distribution issues. All of these advancements, including the creation of a written language and advances in organization, led to the ability to provide food for the community all year long, which in turn, provided the necessary time for cultural, artistic, and intellectual development. These events have rightfully led to the Middle East being referred to in the modern era as the "cradle of civilization," as the advances gave rise to the world's earliest civilizations, which arose in Mesopotamia (roughly present-day Iraq) and Egypt.

The accumulation of food through agriculture rather than hunting also required the ability to protect the fields and harvests from the more violent members of society as well as from those who still maintained a hunter-gatherer lifestyle and specialized in raiding and plundering activities. Certainly not all hunter-gatherer groups raided and pillaged others. In the transition from hunter-gatherer to sedentary agriculturalist, and with the advent of writing and recorded history, one finds the rudimentary beginnings of what has become known in the modern age as "asymmetric" military operations—usually violent conflict between one group that is heavily armed and another that is less well equipped.

Those who moved away from following the herds and hunting and those who refused to make a living raiding other human communities chose instead to cultivate the land and harvest crops. The crops, however, represented food to hungry raiders, who then used their advantages in surprise and speed to attack sedentary agricultural communities for food, manufactures, and slaves. The agriculturalists analyzed the situation and considered ways in which to offset the raiders' advantages. The question became, "How do we as a community neutralize the raiders' tactical strengths?" The answer became, "We build walls around our agricultural and trading settlements and man those walls to protect against attacks utilizing surprise and speed."

An opponent's military advantage, strength, or "solid" is analyzed for its weaknesses or "gaps." The resulting adjustment or development seeks to exploit those gaps or weaknesses. This process, essentially the core of modern-era asymmetric military operations, is known in the German language as Flaechen-und Luecken methods, or solids and gaps.[6] As related to tactics, the process is bypassing an enemy's strengths and in exploiting weaknesses "in between." In relation to military technology, the process of Flaechen-und Luecken does not necessarily indicate the possession of the "best technology" in a general sense but, rather, describes a process of striving for a relative advantage with a technology that neutralizes or bypasses the opponent's technological advantage.

The sedentary agriculturalists created walled settlements to offset the raiders' advantages, and these developed into the massive fortresses of the ancient Middle Eastern civilizations. In the ongoing process and pattern, raiders adjusted and developed counter technology such as siege craft and catapult bombardment implements. From about 10,000 BCE to the mid-fifteenth century the larger and more secure fortresses were able to withstand all but the most sustained and well-planned enemy campaigns, particularly when they were able to provision themselves while under siege. One of the greatest fortresses in the ancient world was Constantinople located on the site of present-day Istanbul in Turkey.

Constantinople had a series of walls extending for miles, skillfully constructed to dissuade all but the most persistent of attackers. Moreover, the inhabitants of the great city had the ability to receive supplies from the sea, which muted the ability for an enemy to choke surrender from a reduced population under siege. Thus, the transition from hunter-gathering to fortified trading and agricultural communities provided sustenance and security to the sedentary agriculturalists and their trading associates for thousands of years. However, by 1453, the Ottoman Turks had brought technology to the walls of the great city at Constantinople, which found gaps and weaknesses in the city's strengths.

Large bore cannon, such as the Ottomans' "Basilica"—a 27-foot (8.2 m) long cannon capable of firing a 600-pound (272 kg) stone ball more than a mile in distance (1.6 km)—made its appearance. The Basilica was built in Edirne, a city in present-day Turkey near the border with Greece and Bulgaria, and dragged by 60 oxen to the outskirts of Constantinople. Beginning on April 6, 1453, the Ottomans conducted a bombardment of the great fortress as part of a seven-week siege of what remained of the Eastern Roman Empire.

Constantinople fell on May 29, 1453, marking the end of a 1,500-year run of the Roman Empire. Ironically, while cannon and powder originated in the East, it was European founders who cast the cannon that eventually reached sufficient strength to batter down the walls of Constantinople. Many historians mark the date of the fall of Constantinople as the end of the late Middle Ages. Undoubtedly, it heralded the arrival of one of the most powerful empires in world history, including the domination of the Middle East by a tribe that had effectively aggregated power and overcome all challenges in its rise to world prominence. The Ottoman Empire stood for over 400 years.

While military effectiveness was vital in aggregating power throughout human history, so also was the establishment of a unifying ideology. The use of ideology toward the aggregation of political, economic, and military power is an important aspect of the story of warfare within the Middle East in both ancient times and in the modern era. The first known walled settlement in the Middle East is at Jericho, with an approximate date of establishment of about 9500 BCE. Somewhere in the vicinity of the late 1200s BCE (others argue 1550–1400 BCE), a little known tribe entered into the territory, which at the time was known as Canaan. The tribe came to be known as Hebrews and utilized a religion-based ideology. Recorded later in the *Book of Joshua* in the written *Torah* or *Tanakh* (alternatively, for the followers of Christ: the *Old Testament* of the *Bible*) is the account of how God "ordered" Joshua and his invading Hebrew army to attack the Canaanites in the land of Canaan (roughly present-day Palestine).

The Canaanite agricultural workers and merchants then living in the vicinity of Jericho did not attempt to fight the invading Hebrews but withdrew behind the safety of the city's walls. The Canaanites had lived in the region for centuries before the invasion and before Joshua and his Hebrew army came to claim the land for themselves, based on divine claims. The apparent justification for the attack was that "god" had decried that the land should go to Abraham's descendants. Thus "god" or "Yahweh" told Joshua, as recorded in the *Old Testament*, to "kill everyone," men, women, and children, in the city and take "all the silver and gold and the articles of bronze and iron sacred to the Lord and which must go into his treasury" (*Book of Joshua*, Chapter 6, Verse 17a and Verse 19).[7]

Similarly, the ancient Persians adopted a unifying ideology, which was religion-based. Somewhere in the range of 1500–1200 BCE, Zoroastrianism made its way into the region, which came to be referred to by those in the West as "Persia" and known in the present-era as Iran. Probably influenced by the singular deity of Brahmanism in India as found in the Hindu text, *Rig Veda*, Zoroastrianism argued that a singular, all powerful god, *Ahura Mazda*—rather than an assortment of gods as found in polytheism—had created the world that was divided into two parts: "Asha" and "Druj." Within Asha, obviously the realm under control of the existing authorities was order and truth. Within the realm of Druj—the designation attached to those not adhering to the prescribed order or foreign peoples, generally the barbarians—were disorder and falsity.

In the eighth century BCE, the Assyrian Empire (900–607 BCE) deployed a variant of Zoroaster's realm of truth and order (Asha) and utilized "Ashur" as the state god of the empire that purportedly possessed universal dominion and jurisdiction. Assyrian forces destroyed the northern Hebrew kingdom of Israel in 721 BCE (there were two Hebrew kingdoms at the time: Israel to the north and Judah directly south). Judah was conquered by the Chaldeans about a century later. Managing to regain power in Judah, the Hebrews, however, were subsequently forced to pay tribute to the Babylonian king Nebuchadnezzar, beginning in 600 BCE.

Problems erupted between Nebuchadnezzar and Judah (as Judah's leaders balked at continuing to make tribute payments), and Babylonian military expeditions were mounted in 597 BCE, 587–586 BCE, and 582–581 BCE. After the fall of Babylon in 539 BCE and into the reign of the Persian king Cyrus the Great, the Hebrews negotiated a return to the new Persian province of Judah. Prior to this time, while Yahweh had been the primary god of the Hebrews, they also recognized various regional and local deities. From the moment of return to Judah under Cyrus, the Jews publicly jettisoned the local gods and quietly proclaimed the universal jurisdiction of their one god.

In the same manner, the expansion of Roman power in the ancient world, and impacting events within the Middle East, was aided by the use of a unifying ideology. *Vera Lex* (or The True Law) was a principle that assured Roman citizens and Roman soldiers that they were on the right side of history since their ideology was the true and all-encompassing principle underpinning human civilization vested in divine purposes. So armed psychologically, Roman soldiers were convinced of the righteousness of their cause. Their performance in battle reflected this belief providing additional strength in trying times and finding sustenance in the secure knowledge that ultimately victory would be theirs.

The leaders needed to adjust to the culture and beliefs of the people and provide a unifying ideology to hold together what remained of Rome. In 312 BCE, Emperor Constantine I battled for control of the Western Roman Empire and met his opponent, Maxentius, at the Tiber River during the Battle of Milvian Bridge. Before the battle commenced, Constantine would later claim that the one true god had sent him a sign of a flaming cross in the sky with the message: "under this sign will you conquer." While Rome continued in various forms, over the next century its fortunes continued to recede.

Following the sacking of Rome in 476 BCE, the Eastern Roman Empire, Byzantium or the Byzantine Empire, continued with the baton of leadership in Anatolia and parts of the Middle East. By the seventh century CE, the Byzantine Empire (the Eastern Roman Empire) was besieged by the Turkic Avars in the Northwest—barbarian Slaves who had overrun the Balkans to the west and the Persian Sassanid Empire to the east and south. In 610 CE, the Byzantium emperor, Heraclius, offered a truce with the Turkic Avars, which was accepted.

His entreaties to the Persian Sassanid ruler were less well received. The Sassanid king, Khosrau II, responded to Heraclius in a scathing rebuke, wherein Khosrau stated that he was the master of the world, empowered by representing the one true god, and that Ahura Mazda (the one true god) was much more powerful than was Byzantium's Christ. Heraclius immediately and publicly disseminated Khosrau's response to his citizenry, which in their minds only confirmed the "evil" nature of the Sassanid Empire.

In 613 CE, the Sassanid Persians conquered the Byzantine province of Syria and occupied Damascus. In the summer of 614 CE, Sassanid troops under Khosrau entered Jerusalem and massacred its Christian population and removed the cross believed to have been the one upon which Jesus of Nazareth was crucified. The cross was taken by the Persians in an apparent display of the strength of their one true god versus the Byzantines' one true god and to leave no doubt in the minds of the people of the region who possessed the one true god. Regarding the nature of the entry of the Sassanid forces into Jerusalem in 614 CE, there is a continuing historical controversy regarding the nature and extent of an alleged Persian-Jewish alliance that brought the Sassanid army into the city.

Following the Persian conquest of Jerusalem, Khosrau, with Ahura Mazda in tow, attacked Byzantine forces in Egypt, subsequently occupied by Sassanid forces in 621 BCE. By 622 CE, Heraclius regained the initiative and placed crosses on his soldiers' shields and tunics and, under a banner of Christ, slowly began pushing the Sassanids out of formerly held Byzantine territory, including Egypt, Syria, and Jerusalem. On December 12, 627 CE, Byzantine forces under Heraclius defeated the Sassanid Empire at the Battle of Nineveh (present-day northern Iraq). And in 629 CE, Heraclius, in a lavish and highly orchestrated ceremony, personally returned the True Cross to the Holy Sepulchre in Jerusalem.

While the forces of Byzantium prevailed in the Byzantine-Sassanid War (602–628 CE), both the Byzantine and Sassanid empires were considerably weakened by the lengthy conflict. As the Arabs watched from their deserts and mountains, as a succession of empires fought competitors and opponents over multiple centuries, the events and what helped drive them did not go unnoticed. The use of symbols identifying all powerful deities for moral and psychological effect was a lesson learned by the Arabs who, had up until this point, allowed the proliferation of regional and local gods.

It was during the final years of the Byzantine-Sassanid War (602–628 CE) that Muhammad, the founder and prophet of Islam, was engaged in the formulation of a new religious and political orientation in the Arabian Peninsula. His revelations and teachings are codified in the main text of the Muslim religion, the *Quran*. Muhammad, of Arabic origin, is commonly believed to have lived between 570 CE and 632 CE. The date that Muhammad was reported to have received his first revelation is 610 CE, and he is believed to have founded Islam sometime after the first revelation, which the prophet reportedly received from the angel Gabriel. The first Islamic community was founded in Medina (present-day Saudi Arabia) in 622 CE. Thus, between 622 and 633 CE, the Arab tribes cast away the various regional gods and local deities and were united under a common flag possessing a unifying ideology.

In order to capture the imagination of the raiding Arab warrior in the seventh century and redirect his behavior toward tribal, kingdom, or caliphate territorial objectives, a new ideology was introduced and reflected the fundamental cultural traits of Arabia and North Africa. These highly maneuverable Arabian and allied expeditionary forces which conquered the Middle East and North Africa in the seventh and eighth centuries relied on an ability to aggregate power by building and maintaining coalitions that offered incentives reflecting the nature of the raiding cultures of both ancient Arabia and North Africa.

The term in Arabia for war was "harb" and was founded upon the belief that life was a constant struggle and contest for survival among a multitude of competing tribes. As long as there was life, so too would there be *harb*. Thus, this idea of war as a continuous process, as well as an established and accepted lifestyle, sharply contrasts with the West's concept of war, in which there is a beginning and an end with periods of peace in between. As a result, many difficulties in finding solutions to the problems of war and peace in Middle Eastern affairs have to do with a lack of understanding regarding the different perspectives on the nature of war, what it means, and how strategies and policies can be generated in mitigating its negative aspects.

For the founding generation of Islam, they incorporated Arabic culture into the new ideology. Since raiding and continuous struggle were part of the cultural fabric, the new ideology utilized these tendencies, traits, and preferences. The *Quran*, the revered book of Islam, effectively tied the new ideology into the Arabic culture of the seventh century when it stated that all warriors in the service of Islam would receive four-fifths of everything they capture from villages, settlements, and tribes which refuse to acknowledge the supremacy of the Muslim ideology (*Quran*, Chapter 8, Verse 41).

By 633 CE, Arab armies had been readied to conduct expeditionary operations and attacked the Sassanid Empire's political and economic center of gravity in Mesopotamia under Arab commander Khalid ibn Walid. In 634 CE, Khalid's forces attacked the Byzantine province of Syria. In 636 CE, Muslim forces defeated a weakened Byzantine army during the Battle of Yarmuk, and the Byzantines were forced to withdraw from the Levant to the western regions of Anatolia. Islamic Caliph Umar ordered the full invasion of the Sassanid Empire in 642 CE, and the conquest of the empire was completed in 651 CE.

These events led to the decline of the Zoroastrian religion in Iran and the imposition of the Muslim religious-political orientation. Within a century of its founding, Islamic armies had seized territory across the Middle East, taken Egypt, and swept across North Africa before being stopped in what is present-day France at the Battle of Tours in 732 CE by a Frankish army commanded by Charles "The Hammer" Martel.

An important aspect of Middle Eastern history that has also impacted the modern era is the nature of the tribes and tribal confederations operating north of the region in the steppe of Central Asia. These grassy plains gave rise to massive societies following the various herds and developing cavalry that was unparalleled in swiftness of movement, the range and lethality of their bows and arrows, or the courage of their mounted warriors. The main groups included the Turks and the Mongols. Throughout ancient history, those living in the sedentary agricultural communities in the Middle East were forced to defend against raiding campaigns launched from the Central Asian steppe.

Raiding parties would descend south from the steppe and embark on expeditionary campaigns against the trading and agricultural communities in the Middle East. With standing armies of their own as well as intelligence networks that extended into the Old Silk Road in Central and South Asia, the larger communities in the Middle East presented difficult targets for raiding parties which generally preferred attacking settlements less well guarded and defended. However, over time, the aggregation of power in Central Asia led to mounted armies capable of challenging the strongest empires of the Middle East and North Africa.

One will build the walls-of-the-Ruler to bar Asiatics from entering Egypt.

—Prophecies of Neferti[8]

However, before their eventual fall, the great civilizations within the Middle East developed their own standing armies not only to defend against attack at the walls but also to conduct proactive and preemptive campaigns against plotting enemies far from the gates of the home city. Ancient Persian ruler Darius fielded an expeditionary force that reportedly numbered in the hundreds of thousands and marched north into the Pontic-Caspian steppe region and conducted preemptive operations against steppe raiders (the Scythians), from 513 to 512 BCE. Unfortunately, for Darius, the steppe raiders refused to stand and fight and instead conducted harassing and asymmetric operations until the massive army was forced to withdraw south.

The Seljuk Turks began arriving in mass in the late tenth and early eleventh centuries CE in Persia where they established a powerful empire, occupied Baghdad in 1055 CE, and by 1071 CE routed the Byzantine forces then in power in Anatolia (present-day Turkey) at the Battle of Manzikert. After defeating the last remnants of the Eastern Roman Empire in eastern and central Anatolia, the Seljuk Turks' leadership believed what had once been held by Rome now rightly belonged to them. For this Turkish tribe, Rome was commonly pronounced "Rum," and "all that was Rum" now must, in their view, fall to their control.

The Seljuk Turks eventually established in Anatolia what they referred to as the "Sultanate of Rum." The ferociousness of the tribe and their desire for continuous expansion did not go unnoticed by the leaders of Western Christendom (roughly present-day Western Europe). Much has been written about what followed next and what would eventually be described as "the Crusades." In many instances, the narrative created and passed off as historical fact, generally in the nineteenth century with the rise of fundamentalism in the Muslim world, was that at the end of the eleventh century an imperial Western Europe under the cloak of Christianity attacked a virtuous and peaceful Muslim Middle East. The Seljuk Turks might have adopted Islam, but virtuous and peace-loving innocence were not attributes commonly applied by those familiar with the group and its murderous and plundering activities either in Central Asia or in the Middle East by the eleventh century CE.

Thus, while Islam can be a religion of peace and serve toward the betterment of mankind, it also served (as it continues to serve today) as a useful ideology for expansionistic and violent raiders. For the Seljuk Turks, as they descended from the open, often harsh, and wild terrain of Central Asia into Persia, it became expedient to adopt the ideology of the relatively advanced Persians whom they were in the process of subjugating and, upon successful conclusion of the conquering stage, would attempt to rule.

As the Seljuk leaders were planning operations to finish off what was left of "Rum," nobles and knights in Western Christendom were meeting with the Pope at the Council of Clermont in France in 1095. While the public discussions centered on the fact that the Seljuks had taken to killing any persons from the West attempting a pilgrimage to Jerusalem, the less visible story was one of military necessity. Since the Seljuks were intent on seizing all that was "Rum," the question essentially became for the Pope and the nobles and knights in attendance, "Do we fight them here, or over there?" The answer at the end of the Council was that soldiers, knights, and nobles from Europe would move against the Seljuks and attack them away from Europe.

The military operations during this time were known in the West as the "Wars against the Saracens" (Muslims). It was only later that the term "Crusades" was attached to the historical record. One of the reasons for the success of the "First Crusade" was the fact that most knew they had an enemy that was preparing to attack their own lands and were sufficiently motivated to fight to win. But perhaps just as important to the success of the First Crusade, was that the Seljuks had become Sunni Muslims and created significant animosity among the Shiite Muslims. This included the notorious Shia Nizari sect that had become known in the West as the "assassins."

When the First Crusade expeditionary campaign began deploying to the Middle East, the Nizari assassins simultaneously struck key Seljuk commanders essentially decapitating command and control at the outset. Moreover, the Seljuks made the classic military mistake of underestimating their enemy equating the knights and soldiers of Western Europe in the eleventh century with the dismal performance of the Byzantines during the Anatolian campaign where the Seljuks defeated them handily and drove them into headlong retreat at the Battle of Manzikert in 1071. Essentially, the First Crusade was against an enemy with few friends in the Middle East or anywhere else for that matter. Simultaneously, Western Christendom was animated by religious belief and a unifying ideology that was only surpassed by the military effectiveness of the knights, nobles, and soldiers of the First Crusade. The Seljuks were never again a viable force within the Middle East.

However, attempts at maintaining Western outposts (the crusader kingdoms as they are known to history) in the Middle East only served to provide a common foe for all the forces within the region who worked diligently in sending Western forces back to Europe. The successions of follow-on Crusades never equaled the success of the first, although Richard the Lionheart of England during the Third Crusade conducted an effective campaign ending in negotiations with the Muslim Kurdish commander Saladin allowing for Western access to Jerusalem and the holy sites.

The Ottoman Turks soon rose to the pinnacle of Middle Eastern power as they overwhelmed Constantinople in 1453. Apparently they too had designs on all that was "Rum" launching a seaborne invasion of the Mediterranean before being stopped during the Battle of Lepanto by Western fleets in 1571. By the mid-seventeenth century the Ottomans attempted a ground campaign against Europe but were finally stopped at the gates of Vienna in 1683.

Less known to history is the fact that when the barbarians sacked Rome in 476 CE, many of the books and scholarly works of the ancient Greeks and the Romans were shifted out of the region and ended up being guarded and preserved by intellectuals residing in the Middle East. Europe, following the collapse of Rome, entered into what many historians referred to as the "Dark Ages," as the learning and the cultural, philosophical, and scientific advancements of the ancients were unknown for a thousand years. By engaging in the Crusades, Western Christendom reconnected with these lost treasures, which made their way into Europe during the Renaissance. This rebirth of learning and the openness to the wider world gave rise to an advance in European culture and as ships sailed across the globe, brought wealth and increased knowledge from interaction with the Middle East, India, China, and other regions.

This process led to the Age of Exploration, the Age of Discovery, and proliferation of creativity and innovation that propelled Europe toward the Industrial Revolution and modern technology, essentially outpacing other regions of the globe. It also supplied Europeans with advanced military technology that was soon pushing forward with a unifying ideology toward the aggregation of power and control and influence over people, resources, markets, and trade routes. It was this aggregated power, unifying ideology, and military effectiveness that had stopped the Ottoman Empire at Lepanto and at Vienna in what were essentially defensive operations.

By the late eighteenth century, Europe and North America were sufficiently powerful enough to begin challenging for world supremacy, and a weakening Ottoman Empire presented itself as a valuable prize in the ongoing competition between European nations. Napoleon, unable to subjugate Britain for lack of the necessary naval capability, sought to cut off London from its access to India and China by moving against its interests in the "Middle East." His action into Egypt in 1798 began the traditional Western demarcation and the beginning of the modern Middle East.

Chapter 1

Napoleon's Egyptian Campaign and the Decline of the Ottoman Empire

With Napoleon's invasion of Egypt and the chain of events that followed, it was suggested, centuries of decline, inertia, and neglect finally ended and the Middle East rose, albeit awkwardly, to meet the challenges of modernity. The clock started ticking to mark this passage of Middle Eastern civilization from a previous era into the present.[1]

The voyages and land expeditions to the Middle East during the Crusades (or, conversely, the Wars against the Saracens) pulled back the curtain on a larger world than was previously known in Europe during the Middle Ages. With the infusion of the works of ancient Greece and Rome, new principles, new concepts, and new ways of investigating the empirical world soon animated society in Western Christendom. The divine right of kings would soon face scrutiny under the rediscovery of Greek philosophy and rational inquiry. The concepts inherent in *demos kratos*, or the people rule, would, over time, come to drive the aspirations and hopes of an expanding middle class. The desire for liberty would eventually drive the Americans and French to revolution, while British intellectual curiosity and the desire for empirical exploration would catapult the island nation into a leading role of the early Industrial Revolution.

With the landlines of communication and trade routes that characterized the Old Silk Road between Europe, the Middle East, and South and

East Asia monopolized by the Ottomans and their allies, in the fifteenth century, in terms of access to Asian markets, the European seafaring nations began exploring alternatives to the traditional overland trading routes. Accordingly, with the development of ocean-traversing technology and skills, the maritime trading nations in Europe increased their ability to expand trade and protect sea lines of communications (SLOCs). By the mid-eighteenth century, Britain had risen to global prominence by virtue of its prowess in sea power, trade, technological innovation, and military effectiveness. As London and Paris competed for control in North America and following the loss of its franchise within the original North American 13 colonies, Britain increased its involvement in India. In order to facilitate the movement of goods, Egypt became a key route of trade, extending from the Mediterranean, overland to the Red Sea, and on to South Asia.

By the late eighteenth century, the Ottoman Empire's control in Egypt was declining, as was its overall strategic position in the eighteenth century. The British, Russians, Habsburgs, French, and other powers in Eurasia and the Middle East were engaged in maneuvering for advantage in the event of the collapse of the Ottoman Empire.

> In 1776 the Baron de Tott submitted to Louis XVI a memorandum recommending that France acquire Egypt on the grounds that the disintegration of the Ottoman Empire was inevitable . . . In 1782 Joseph II of Austria suggested to Louis XVI that France should acknowledge that the Ottoman Empire was no longer capable of protecting itself and Louis should take advantage of that weakness and annex Egypt.[2]

The Mamluks had been provided significant levels of autonomy in administering Egypt as Ottoman vassals following their defeat in the Ottoman-Mamluk War (1516–1517).[3] However, by 1784, decades of mismanagement of agriculture coupled with conditions of drought had led to famine in Egypt followed by outbreaks of plague. Simultaneous to these events, the Mamluks had also stopped making the required payments to the Ottoman treasury. As a result, during 1786–1791, the Ottoman leadership tried unsuccessfully to bring their vassals in Egypt back under control.

Further west, the rising vitality and energy of the liberated people of France had overthrown the monarchy and were intent on spreading revolutionary ideals—along with acquiring new trading opportunities— and a young military commander, Napoleon Bonaparte, was meeting with success in the French campaign in Italy. The use of both diplomacy and military power that had been honed and expertly practiced by the French for centuries, coupled with the collective energy of a newly liberated people that the Prussians had come to refer to the energy of the French as *leidenschaft*, helped propel France toward continental leadership (along with a centuries-long tradition of military excellence) as a wide range of European states and principalities entered agreements with the new French government.

Nonetheless, the competition and conflict between France and the British monarchy continued unabated to the point where the British withdrew all Mediterranean naval ships, in October 1796, in order to protect the home islands from a potential invasion.

> ... Had it not been for Admiral John Jervis's defeat of the Spanish in the Atlantic off Cape St. Vincent in February 1797 and Admiral Adam Duncan's destruction of the Dutch fleet at the Battle of Camperdown in October, her [Britain's] enemies might have achieved a sufficient combination of force to achieve the necessary conditions for a Channel crossing.[4]

From a French strategic perspective, the end of the eighteenth century brought with it an opportunity to test the vacuum created in the Eastern Mediterranean by the withdrawal of the British fleet. More specifically, French control in Egypt would provide leverage in challenging British commercial interests in the Eastern Mediterranean and in cutting Britain's overland route to India via the Red Sea. If Napoleon could establish control in Egypt, the French would be in a position to more effectively challenge Britain's vast commercial interests in India, interests which helped finance British naval power projection. British naval power would have to be reduced, French military commanders believed (including Napoleon), before a channel crossing could be successfully mounted.

Given the weakness of the Ottoman Empire and the strategic position of Egypt in terms of British communications with its vast holdings in India, a campaign in Northeast Africa aimed at Cairo would degrade British trade and, eventually, British sea power. In fact, as early as the seventeenth century, King Louis XIV of France had proposed a canal linking the Mediterranean and Red Seas across the Egyptian Isthmus.

While France maintained what was generally considered the most effective land army in Western Europe—a martial tradition that had earlier blocked the Islamic invasion of Western Europe in 732 CE—Britain had concentrated on building what was arguably the most capable navy in the world. The French military successfully convinced the civilians in the French Directoire to make Cairo the objective, rather than London, at least for the time being. Thus, the invasion plans for Britain were shelved, and the strategy was to challenge British sea power by extending French power throughout the Mediterranean, which would undermine Britain's access to India. Following the establishment of a beachhead in Egypt, the objective was to leverage France's relationship with Tipu Sultan, then ensconced as the ruler of the Sultanate of Mysore and a hindrance to the British East India Company in South Asia. The French Directoire approved the Egyptian campaign on March 5, 1798.

As Napoleon gathered his expeditionary forces in Toulon, France, for the Egyptian campaign, he addressed the assembled troops on May 19, 1798:

> You have made war on the mountains, on the plains, and on the cities; it remains for you to fight on the seas ... The genius of liberty which made you, at her birth, the arbiter of Europe, wants to be genius of the seas and the furthest of nations.[5]

Napoleon's assembled force consisted of 40,000 soldiers, 10,000 sailors, 280 transport ships, 14 frigates, and 13 ships-of-the-line (64 to 120 guns). The French expeditionary force consisted of 31,000 infantry formed into five divisions, with each division having elements of cavalry (approximately 600 per division), artillery, and engineers (artillerymen and engineers totaling about 3,000). The artillery consisted of 171 assorted howitzers, mortars, and field guns firing shells, canister, and ball shot. Napoleon also brought a new weapon, a weapon which would factor into many modern-era wars and campaigns yet to come: *a printing press*, in this instance, an *Arabic* printing press, which he would use to help him communicate to the Arabs. When his forces arrived in Egypt in the summer of 1798, this marked the arrival of the first printing press in the Middle East.

One of his first messages using the press was a proclamation in Arabic to the inhabitants of Alexandria, Egypt, on July 1, 1798, stating that it was the intent of France to bring the blessings of liberty to the people of Egypt and to free them from the tyranny of the Mamluks. The printed proclamation, in Arabic, read in part: "... If Egypt is the Mamluks' farm, then they should show the lease that God gave them for it."

While Napoleon was intent on spreading the ideals of the Revolution in the Middle East and ultimately marching to the Indus River in India as did his hero, Alexander the Great, he like all great military leaders in history, whether operating in Europe, the Middle East, or Asia, needed to "incentivize" his military operations in such a manner that would motivate individual soldiers and in language they would understand. As his troops later prepared to disembark upon arrival in Egypt, he sent a message to his soldiers: "I promise to each soldier who returns from this expedition enough to purchase six arpents of land." Soldiers and warriors throughout history, whether Muslim, Christian, Hindu, Buddhist, or Jew, required incentives, whether it be a unifying religious-political ideology or immediate material inducement or, as in the case of the most successful armies in world history, both. Thus the French Revolution, not unlike the Roman expeditions or the Islamic expansionary campaigns of the seventh to seventeenth centuries, offered not only lofty, heroic, and "universally" valid ideals but also material reward.

On July 1, 1798, Napoleon's Army of the Orient, as the force was now being called, arrived off the coast of Alexandria, Egypt. Napoleon had brought with him, in addition to the Arabic printing press, a commission of scholars and scientists from L'Academie whose function was to examine all aspects of Egyptian history and culture while simultaneously sharing concepts arising from the Enlightenment regarding science, the arts, and self-government, for which they brought a substantial library. The proceeding interactions marked the introduction of Western modernity into the Middle East and the reciprocal movement of ideas (particularly about ancient Egypt) to European civilization. Nevertheless, Napoleon's Egyptian campaign (1798–1801) also has a less noble distinction in world history as being "the largest and most violent meeting between Western and Muslim Arab armies since the Crusades."[6]

The main objective was the city of Cairo, which had a population of approximately 300,000 and was along the Nile River (the longest river in the world). Napoleon understood that if he suffered significant delays in reaching it, his army might become victims to the great flooding that occurred in the river on a regular basis. Even on the relatively short journey to Alexandria, Napoleon's troops found that nomadic Bedouin tribesmen had filled many of the wells along the army's advance, and, as a result, the Army of the Orient was already parched and suffering from a lack of potable water. To add to the discomfort, the French were outfitted in wool uniforms and carried heavy packs in a summer environment where temperatures often rose to 115 degrees Fahrenheit. Moreover, French commanders mistakenly assumed that the population would welcome an army bringing them liberty from autocratic rule. The French military found themselves surrounded by a generally unwelcoming population, unprepared for the extreme heat, and suffering from a lack of food and water. Morale immediately took a turn for the worse.

> The first French units left Alexandria on July 3. They lacked sufficient horses ... and one division even had to leave its artillery behind. Napoleon sought to obtain horses and camels from local Bedouin leaders, but the sheiks in Cairo convinced the tribesmen to switch sides and they harassed the French along the entire line of march. The khamsin, the desiccating wind that blows up the dust of the Libyan Desert into great choking, blinding clouds, had begun ... Thirst quickly became the deadliest enemy ... Before the march was over, hundreds had died, some by their own hand.[7]

Hence, the campaign unfolded in both a harsher physical and harsher cultural environment than French planners had anticipated. While much of the Egyptian population was indeed in a state of relative political captivity under ruthless autocrats, the French were unable to effectively convey their message of liberty and the rights of man, finding themselves outmaneuvered in terms of messaging and communications by a merchant elite and ruling class well vested in the current status quo.

They were not interested in French achievements in liberal reform, science, the arts, or in French business establishing a presence in a society where a handful of powerful agriculturalists and wealthy merchants had long controlled commerce as well as Egyptian society.

The Egyptian elite, armed with a more expansive knowledge base regarding cultural fears and hopes, were better positioned for delivering an effective strategic narrative to the masses and outmaneuvered French efforts at proclaiming the benefits of liberty and equality. While Napoleon's use of an Arabic printing press was a pragmatic first step in the modernization and evolution of the Middle East and, over the long term, proved beneficial to the masses, the reality was that since most of the population was illiterate at the time of the French Egyptian campaign, it proved to be of limited value in furthering the realization of the immediate objectives of Napoleon's operations, which was to control the country, deprive the British access, and to sever London's lines of communication to India, followed by the invasion of Britain and the overthrow of the British monarchy.

Prior to departure from Alexandria, Napoleon divided his army sending some 12,000 troops with generals Dugua and Murat and the remaining forces from Kleber's command onto the town of Rosetta with orders to proceed south along the Nile after meeting up with a flotilla, which carried arms and supplies under Admiral Peree. Marching with Napoleon was the main body of 25,000 men, which took a direct route across the Beheira Desert to the village of Damanhur and then to El Rahmaniyah where both sections of the Army of the Orient would link up before proceeding to the main objective at Cairo.

While the Mamluk cavalry, inheritors of a tradition of excellence that had stopped the Mongol army at Ain Jalut in 1260 CE, was generally considered one of the finest (if not *the* finest) cavalry forces in the Mediterranean during the late Middle Ages, the Franks had assembled the finest infantry in the world as early as the eighth century CE and had maintained that status, arguably, for a thousand years (the Swiss and the Prussians, notwithstanding). Now, after having achieved complete surprise in terms of the Ottomans, the British, and the Mamluks, that infantry, now armed with muskets and artillery and commanded by one of the most successful generals in world history, suddenly appeared off the coast of Egypt, disembarked, and proceeded to march on Egypt's largest city. For the Ottoman-Egyptian army, the "Franks" had returned, and Napoleon had achieved the desired shock of surprise, including the psychological impact in the minds of enemy commanders and the individual soldiers. The initiative had been seized, and the enemy was forced to scramble in order to react to the next move.

Napoleon, failing with the strategic narrative in a foreign land, was now ready, however, to introduce the most proficient practitioners of nomadic steppe cavalry maneuver (the Mamluks) to the most proficient infantry army and practitioner of early modern-era warfare (a Napoleon-led French army). The Mamluks had paid a price by not adopting gunpowder weapons in their battles against the Ottoman Empire. The nightmare was about to be repeated with the arrival of the muskets and cannon of the French army.

Napoleon's desert-crossing force (100-mile march) reached the Nile on July 10 but not before threats of mutiny broke out in the desert on July 8 and 9, which Napoleon dealt with effectively and decisively. Arriving on July 10, Napoleon's vanguard led by Desaix's division came under attack by 300 horsemen under Muhammad Bey el-Elfi near El Rahmaniyah. Probably dispatched as a scouting or probing exercise, it would be reasonable to assume that el-Elfi was interested in whether Napoleon's force, after a 100-mile desert hike in 110 degree heat—in wool uniforms and heavy packs and weapons—would have suffered a debilitating loss in combat readiness. The French, however, repulsed the Mamluk's probing attack without loss, and Napoleon issued orders that the army would rest for two days, swim in the river, and enjoy any surrounding food supplies, which apparently included an ample amount of watermelon.

Now joined by the forces under Dugua and Murat, the combined Army of the Orient proceeded south on July 13, 1798, along the shores of the Nile after Napoleon received intelligence that Mamluk leader and joint ruler of Egypt Murad Bey's forces were in the vicinity of the village of Shubra Khit, eight miles south of El Rahmaniyah. At the Battle of Shubra Khit, Murad had perhaps 4,000 Mamluk cavalry and 10,000 peasant militia (or fellahin). Each Mamluk cavalryman carried two or three pistols, a short musket, javelins, and a scimitar sword (or two). The fellahin were armed with an assortment of more rudimentary weapons, including maces, clubs, spears, knives, and if one were fortunate, a sword. Mamluk river gun boats had arrived in the vicinity and were aligning to take on the French flotilla that had followed Napoleon's forces as well as lending fire support to Murad Bey's forces against the French army.

Napoleon's Army of the Orient, somewhat reduced since beginning the journey from Malta, still totaled nearly 27,000 infantry armed with muskets arrayed in five divisions. The French infantry were supported by nearly 2,500 artillerymen and engineers manning 171 assorted howitzers, mortars, and field guns, firing shells, canister, and ball shot. Napoleon's cavalry had been reduced by logistical difficulties in the transport and movement of horses, as perhaps as many as 30 percent of the 2,400 cavalrymen were now on foot, awaiting the capture of additional mounts. The Mamluks had committed only about a third of their forces when Murad Bey appeared with about 14,000 troops. About 30,000 Mamluk troops were taking up positions down the river at the capital city of Cairo.

Murad Bey's cavalry paraded out of gun range in order to display their colors and their valor. This went on for an extended period of time, and Napoleon ordered his band to strike up several French patriotic tunes while they waited for the Mamluk cavalry to do what they had done throughout history, charge the enemy after trying to intimidate them with parade maneuvers. After a rousing version of "La Marseillaise" in honor of the anniversary of Bastille Day, the French were soon at the height of patriotism and spirit. The Mamluks shortly thereafter initiated the expected cavalry charge. Napoleon's soldiers had orders to hold fire until the Mamluks came within 50 feet and then let loose with multiple volleys from muskets and field guns.

Napoleon's troops used multiple tactics and formations:

Depending on the engagement, the infantry were formed into columns for attacking in-depth, lines to concentrate firepower, or squares several ranks deep.

If a square was charged by cavalry, the outer ranks would kneel, those directly behind them would crouch, and the hindmost soldiers would remain upright.

The result was a fearsome and impenetrable wall of bayonets. Few horses could be induced to breach a mass of deadly 15 inch spikes.[8]

Murad Bey's forces, to their credit, charged the French battle squares again and again. Each time they were repulsed with significant casualties. After about 400 casualties and only a handful of French killed or wounded, the Mamluk-Egyptian forces withdrew and prepared to make a stand at the outskirts of Cairo. The result at the Battle of the Pyramids (defense of Cairo on June 21, 1798) produced the same result, however, with a greatly increased Mamluk-Egyptian casualty count. The Mamluk-Egyptian-Ottoman force (about 30,000) suffered thousands killed and wounded, with many drowning in the Nile River after being pushed back by the French.

After observing Mamluk attacks at El Rahmaniyah and Shubra Khit, Napoleon positioned cannon at the corners of his infantry battle squares, essentially taking away any advantage a cavalry force might enjoy by being able to attack the formation from the flanks or from the rear. In a classic instance of Flaechen-und Luecken, gunpowder weapons essentially eliminated the tactical maneuver advantage enjoyed and practiced for centuries by the nomadic steppe cavalry tribes, including the Mongols, the Turks, and the Mamluks. Now, as the early stages of the modern era unfolded, gunpowder weapons and infantry drill, organization, and discipline continued to eclipse the tradition of the heroic and gallant horseman as the ultimate arbiter of political, economic, and religious disputes.

Muscle, steel, arrow barrage, and courage combined with effective cavalry maneuver, long practiced by steppe warriors in Central Asia, the

Middle East, and North Africa, fell by the wayside as the modern era dawned at the end of the eighteenth century. Following Napoleon's operations along the Nile River in the summer of 1798, 700 years of Mamluk rule in Egypt collapsed.

After the successful conclusion of the Battle of the Pyramids, Napoleon and the French army marched into Cairo on July 25, 1798 (following the July 22 arrival of an advance element consisting of two French infantry companies and five officers). Murad Bey, who had been wounded in the face during the battle, fled to Upper Egypt, and his partner Ibrahim Bey, fulfilling the old adage that discretion was the better part of valor by waiting safely on the far side of the Nile during the climactic battle for Cairo, evacuated with the Ottoman viceroy along with the remnants of the Mamluk army to Syria. From Syria follow-on operations against the French could be coordinated. While Napoleon had served notice as to the proficiency of French arms by defeating Mamluk power within a month and capturing their capital city, the real campaign for Egypt was just beginning. Whereas Napoleon controlled the Nile Delta and Cairo, the Mamluks and their Bedouin allies controlled Upper Egypt, and the Ottomans were soon in consultation with the British to coordinate efforts against the French Army of the Orient.

After the Mamluk-Ottoman loss at the Battle of the Pyramids, the Ottoman Sultan asked other great powers for assistance. The Russian Czar, who sought Ottoman territory in general and the key port city of Constantinople in particular, offered Russia's assistance. He ordered Russia's Black Sea fleet to the Bosporus, and a combined Ottoman-Russian naval force began operating in the vicinity of Constantinople. Concurrently, the Sultan enlisted the aid of the British and the Austrians. While the 29-year-old Napoleon was maneuvering brilliantly on the battlefield, the revolutionary French government was being outmaneuvered in international politics and diplomacy.

In Cairo, Napoleon's forces found the streets deserted as many of the city's residents had fled. French troops instead were met with the sounds of wailing women drifting out to the narrow streets from behind closed doors and covered windows. Napoleon and his staff took up residence in Murad Bey's riverfront palace, but before he had a chance to savor his victory, he received word that his wife in Paris, Josephine, had been unfaithful. The dreams of conquest, glory, and the expected sounds of the cheering masses faded quickly in the dark—a darkness that permeated the spirits of the city's inhabitants in ways that the young French general found difficult to understand.

For the masses in Egypt, particularly those of Cairo, which had had most material things taken from them through Mamluk mismanagement, military coercion, and collective punishment, the French were taken aback at the dark mood and evident pain in the Egyptian people upon the institution of a French occupation. What the French did not comprehend was that the Mamluks had become part of Egypt and for 700 years had been the most formidable cavalry force in the Middle East. As such, there was comfort and solace in knowing that even if one were poor, one belonged to a nation, which was the defender of the true faith, proud warriors, generally believed to be the most capable man-for-man anywhere on the globe. Napoleon's army far from freeing the masses had destroyed the only remaining vestige available to a poverty-stricken and oppressed people, the idea that greatness was still part of their society and, as a result, nourished their soul with belief that greatness was part of themselves and their families.

The French had hoped, in addition to achieving their own objectives vis-à-vis the British monarchy, that their presence would empower the masses to take control of their society and, in doing so, free themselves from physical coercion and financial servitude by an elite few. Napoleon attempted to reform the government in Egypt and to highlight the need for educated, virtuous civil servants working for the public good. He directed his troops to tear down the walls and gates that guarded and sealed off Cairo's wealthier districts from the underclass. There was indeed greatness in the French ideals taken to Egypt in 1798. Unfortunately, great forces in Europe and the Middle East were combining to defeat this project in liberty, equality, and fraternity.

NELSON AND THE BRITISH NAVY FRUSTRATE NAPOLEON'S STRATEGY IN EGYPT

A week after the French occupied Cairo, Lord Nelson and his British naval task force appeared off the coast of Alexandria. French warships were anchored in shallow water just northeast of the city in Aboukir Bay in a line parallel to the shore. French Vice Admiral François-Paul Brueys d'Aigalliers believed he had positioned his ships close enough to the shore to prevent British warships from getting between the French line and the shore. Thus, the arrayed French warships, in combination, had nearly 500 guns facing the sea, as their commanders believed that would be the only direction from which an attack could be mounted. Brueys's fleet included 13 ships-of-the-line and 4 frigates; however, half of the Frenchmen serving aboard the vessels were under 18 years of age and most had never seen combat.

Boldness in war often initiates its own dynamic, creating opportunities that would not have been available without first seizing the initiative and "wrong-footing" the opponent in a dash of energy, speed, and decisive force. Such attributes had been part of the French army for centuries; they certainly were part of what made Napoleon one of the greatest military commanders in recorded history. However, the British navy had developed on sea what the French had perfected on land. Conducting military operations on the European continent offered interior lines from which to operate, and the French excelled in maneuver. However, the advantages offered in Europe were not available for a global French expeditionary force where SLOCs factored into operations. By the end of the eighteenth century, the British fleet sailed the world's oceans without peer.

On August 1, 1798, following a month in which French military power destroyed the Mamluk army in Egypt and sent the Ottoman viceroy in headlong retreat into Syria, the British naval task force consisting of 13 ships-of-the-line finally located the French fleet supporting Napoleon's land campaign. The British naval commanders were not aware of the configuration of the seabed between the French line of ships and the shore, but, they took a calculated risk and maneuvered half the British ships between the French and the shore. Once in position, Nelson's ships were able to open fire from two directions. Admiral Brueys's 118-gun flagship, the L'Oriente, took volley after volley, setting fires that eventually reached her powder magazine, which then created a massive explosion. Two French ships-of-the-line and two frigates were able to cut their cables and fight their way out to sea. By the time the battle was over, a day later, one French ship was at the bottom of the bay, three still floating but generally unrecognizable, and nine French warships captured.

The English were then in a position not only to patrol the coasts of North Africa and Egypt but also, having coordinated their efforts with the ruler of the Ottoman Empire, to traverse the entire eastern coast of the Mediterranean. It was said that "Napoleon did indeed have Egypt," but cut off from the sea, "Egypt actually had Napoleon." On September 11, 1798, Sultan Selim III of the Ottoman Empire declared war on France and formed an alliance with Britain, Austria, Russia, and Naples. Shortly thereafter, on October 21, the people of Cairo began rioting against the French.

Having received information that an Ottoman army was forming in Syria with the objective of attacking his forces in Egypt, Napoleon decided to strike first, and on February 6, 1799, commenced operations in Palestine as he proceeded north to Syria. With a force of 13,000 troops, Napoleon fought and overran enemy forces at El Arish (February 8–19), Gaza (February 24–25), and Jaffa (March 3–7), as he moved north toward the Syrian border. By mid-March, Napoleon laid siege to Acre and from March 17 to May 21 launched 7 assaults against the seaport fortress and dealt with 11 offensive operations from the city's besieged forces followed by the French temporarily halting the siege and withdrawing at the approach of a large army coming out of Syria. Napoleon then turned and attacked the approaching Ottoman-Syrian army at the Battle of Mount Tabor where he defeated and dispersed the force. He then resumed the siege of Acre.

Following the arrival of intelligence that a combined British-Ottoman fleet was planning on transporting a large Ottoman army for insertion into Egypt, Napoleon halted siege operations at Acre and returned to Egypt. In July 1799, the British-Ottoman fleet transported an 18,000-man Ottoman army and landed at Aboukir Bay. Napoleon promptly engaged this force in an attack mounted on July 25, killing or driving into the sea nearly 11,000 Turkish troops and taking 6,000 prisoners, including the commander of the force, Mustafa Pasha.

Following the victory at the Battle of Aboukir Bay, the French Directoire and other French leaders knew that Napoleon Bonaparte was too valuable a military leader for them to allow him to perish in the Middle Eastern theater surrounded by an overwhelming assortment of enemies and with the French unable to support or resupply his forces by sea. After the failure of French forces to take Acre, coupled with the siege of the French garrison on Malta (which would eventually fall to the British on September 5, 1800), and with the British cooperating with the Ottoman Empire, the French government knew that French control in Egypt, even if sustainable in the short term, would not create the conditions that would allow France to use it for launching operations in South Asia or in operations regarding succession issues of a crumbling Ottoman Empire.

Without the ability to challenge British naval supremacy in the Mediterranean Sea, with Britain's intent on protecting access to India through Egypt, and without a commitment of treasure and manpower that far exceeded that which French leaders were prepared to make at the time in the Middle East, France could not successfully and politically consolidate military gains in Egypt, Palestine, or Syria. If Napoleon's Egyptian campaign had proven anything (beyond his brilliance as an operational and tactical commander), it was that even with one of the most capable generals in history, commanding one of the finest armies in history, the political objective of leveraging tactical military supremacy in order to establish a liberal democracy within a culture fractured by years of autocratic rule was, at the time, strategically and operationally unsustainable.

Following operations at Aboukir Bay, arrangements were quietly made for Napoleon to return to France where he would be promoted first consul. On August 22, 1799, Napoleon unceremoniously, accompanied by a small contingent of aides and staff, left Egypt by sea. General Jean-Baptiste Kleber was named commander of the French forces that remained in Egypt. Kleber was tasked with an orderly evacuation of

French forces, but preliminary negotiations with the British were unsuccessful, and Kleber was forced to plan for continued military operations to protect French forces in Egypt. The French under Kleber successfully battled the Anglo-Ottoman coalition until 1800 when Kleber was assassinated in Cairo by a Syrian, and command of French forces was transferred to General Abdullah Jacques Menou, a French convert to Islam. Following the transfer of command, an Anglo-Ottoman invasion force surrounded French forces at Alexandria and Cairo. French army forces at Cairo surrendered on June 18, 1801, and Menou personally surrendered the Alexandria garrison on September 3. By September end, all French forces had been withdrawn from Egypt.

Following the departure of French forces from Egypt, Lord Nelson, the British admiral who helped sink French plans for the Middle East, observed at the time:

> I think their objective is to possess themselves of some port in Egypt and to fix themselves at the head of the Red Sea in order to get a formidable army into India; and in concert with Tipu Siab [Sultan of Mysore], to drive us if possible from India.[9]

Hence, the French objectives of establishing a foothold in Egypt to facilitate a move against Constantinople, the British in India, or both, were never reached. The actual results included the utter destruction of 700 years of Mamluk control in Egypt and the establishment of a vivid awareness within ruling circles in the Middle East as to how far the region had fallen behind European military capabilities and Western technology. Less apparent, but certainly not lost on an observant few, was the remarkable energy being generated by a revolutionary people under the banner of liberty, fraternity, and equality.

MEHMET ALI INTRODUCES MODERNIZATION AND REFORMS

In the years following the departure of French forces from Egypt in 1801, an extremely capable and ruthless leader rose to power in Cairo in the first decade of the nineteenth century. Kavali Mehmet Ali Pasha (the Ottoman version of the name; also known as Muhammad Ali in Arabic form) is widely considered to be the father of modern Egypt, as he was instrumental in reforming the Ottoman-Mamluk system and laying the foundations for a modernization process in the industry and the military. Mehmet Ali (modern Turkish) sought to reform both the economy and the Egyptian military, including the navy, by crafting it along the lines of the European model. Economically, he seized control of all aspects of the nation's economic life by monopolizing key sectors and demanding structural reforms. He also created new educational institutions in an attempt at transitioning Egyptian society from the medieval world of the Mamluks to the modern age. Militarily, he brought in French advisors and sent students to Europe to learn French in order to translate European military manuals into Arabic.

Mehmet was an ethnic Turk born into an Albanian merchant family on March 4, 1869, in the town of Kavala in Thrace (present-day Greece) and was eventually provided a position by his district military commander uncle with the rank of *Bolukbasi* (tax collector) in the Ottoman Eyalet of Rumelia. There he learned the nuances and craft of taxation, public administration, and leadership. Later, during Mehmet's rise to power in Egypt, he positioned himself as a champion of the people striving to overcome the cronyism and corruption of the Ottoman-Mamluk centuries-old system. This tactic effectively forestalled any sizable, popular opposition until he was able to consolidate his power within Egypt. In addition to a deft and capable hand at public administration, he gained valuable experience in military affairs, serving as an officer in the Ottoman military and eventually commanding an army in an unsuccessful bid at driving Napoleon from Egypt in 1799.

After being recognized as *Wali* (governor) of Egypt by Constantinople in 1805 and backed by the French, Mehmet systematically dismantled what remained of Mamluk power within Egypt, including the confiscation of feudal farms of the Mamluk emirs, while simultaneously stripping Cairo's religious institutions of some 600,000 acres of prime real estate holdings. Appearing to offer a gracious compromise to the then-reeling Mamluks, Mehmet invited their leaders to a feast in 1811 celebrating his son Tosu Pasha's appointment to lead the army being sent against the Saud-Wahhabi rebellion in Arabia. However, once his guests had arrived within the compound (Cairo Citadel), Mehmet ordered the gates locked and all Mamluks in attendance killed.

The Egyptian-Ottoman military in the opening years of the nineteenth century consisted of a wide range of ethnicities, including Circassian Mamluks, Albanians, Kurds, Greeks, and Egyptians. Only the Mamluks, Albanians, Kurds, and Greeks received training as military commanders, as Egyptian cadets were trained as noncombatants. By the 1830s, Egyptians were selectively trained for combat assignments but were not allowed to rise above the rank of major.[10] In similar fashion, when the Turks descended into Persia in the eleventh century, while they kept the educated and trained Persian bureaucrats in their administrations, they continued to rely on Turkish cavalry for military duty. Mehmet used educated Egyptians and imported European experts to establish schools and hospitals within Egypt, but he kept a wary eye on the Egyptian elite.

In the 1820s, Mehmet sent educational missions comprised of Egyptian students to Europe, resulting in the birth of the modern Arabic literary renaissance known as the *al-Nahda*. By 1835, Mehmet's government had established the first indigenous printing press in the Arab world (the Bulaq Press), which disseminated the official newspaper of the Mehmet Ali government. Within the military, he instituted reforms that came to be known as *Nizam-i Cedid* (new system) and *Nizam al-jadid* (new organization), essentially being instituted and organized with assistance from French and Italian officers recruited from Europe. The new system included men, equipment, and doctrine trained in the early modern European profession of arms. These reforms included remaking the Mamluk arms industry. Mehmet also built factories in Cairo that manufactured cannon and small arms. By 1830, the Egyptian arms industry was producing 1,600 muskets per month.[11]

For the growing Egyptian navy, Mehmet purchased finished warships from Italy and France, and they began arriving in Egypt in 1826. A shipyard was also established at Alexandria and, by 1830, had produced nine ships-of-the-line (100 guns each). During the same time period, Mehmet created a 100,000-man army, which, coupled with his growing naval capability, placed a relatively modern military and navy under his command—a military and naval capability that soon eclipsed that of the Ottoman Sultan in Constantinople. These developments were closely monitored in capitals throughout the Middle East and North Africa, eventually becoming a concern in both Europe and Russia. Britain's reliance on sea power, in particular, for defense as well as empire made the advancing capabilities of Mehmet's fleet, combined with significant French support, a growing concern in London.

At the beginning of the nineteenth century in Arabia, an Islamic fundamentalist group derisively called "Wahhabis" by their detractors, in conjunction with the House of Saud, began moving against Ottoman interests on the Arabian Peninsula and captured Mecca in 1802.[12] The Wahhabis then captured the Hejaz region in 1803, which eventually led to the Ottoman-Saudi War (1811–1818). The timing for the Wahhabi move against the Hejaz was propitious as the Ottoman Empire's main army was engaged in the Balkans in Europe putting down a series of rebellions. As Mehmet had finished dispensing with the Mamluk leadership at the Cairo Citadel, Ottoman Sultan Mahmud II (ruled 1808–1839) directed the Egyptian leader to deploy forces to Arabia to deal with the upstart Wahhabis.

Subsequently, in 1811, Mehmet dispatched a 20,000-man army, including a cavalry force of 2,000, under his 16-year-old son Tosu into the Arabian Peninsula where the Egyptian expeditionary force met heavy resistance at the Pass of Jedeia near al-Safra and was forced to withdraw to

Yanbu. Shortly thereafter, Mehmet reinforced the expeditionary army under Tosu, and at the end of 1811, the force conducted siege operations against Saud and his allies in Medina. After a successful, if not prolonged, conclusion at Medina, the Egyptian-Ottoman army proceeded to capture Jedda and Mecca and retook the Hejaz region from the House of Saud.

These campaigns, however, did not neutralize Saudi military capabilities, as they continued raiding and harassing Ottoman and Egyptian forces from the Central Nejd region. An irritated Mehmet dispatched another son, Ibrahim, who led an army into Arabia in the fall of 1816 and conducted a two-year campaign against the Saudis. These activities captured the Saudi capital of Diriyah in 1818, including most of the Saudi elite and their leader Abdullah ibn Saud, who was subsequently transferred to Constantinople and summarily executed.

After securing the Hejaz, Mehmet turned his attention to Africa and in 1820 dispatched an army of 5,000 troops under the command of his third son, Ismail (this time sending along a trusted military advisor, Abidin Bey), into the Sudan. These forces met fierce resistance from the warriors of the Shaigiya tribe. However, armed with modern weapons and tactics, Mehmet's army outgunned and outmaneuvered the Shaigiya and secured the Sudan, which served in expanding his ability to project power and influence into Ethiopia and Uganda. From this outpost, Mehmet's forces captured and made slaves of the inhabitants of the Nuba Mountains and western and southern Sudan. The defeated Shaigiya, in order to hold on to their lands, acquiesced as vassals and served in Mehmet's infantry regiment, the *Gihadiya* (in Arabic, *Jihadiya*). Mehmet and subsequent Ottoman-Egyptian rulers have been recorded in Sudanese history as being particularly brutal and repressive regimes, which eventually gave rise to the independence struggle in 1881 that featured the self-proclaimed Mahdi (Muhammad Ahmad).

While Mehmet was expanding his power and influence in Arabia and Africa, the Sultan in Constantinople, Mahmud II, was experiencing upheaval across the empire, particularly in his European provinces in the Balkans, Greece, and Macedonia. Ottoman losses during the Russo-Turkish War of 1768–1774 meant that the empire had ceded to Russia's vast lands in the Black Sea region and extending as far south as the Caucasus. In its European provinces, the empire was facing ethnic rebellion.

In Greece, the problem was particularly acute. Greek nationalists in the Roman principalities, in the Peloponnese, and in the Aegean Islands commenced insurgency operations during the Greek War of Independence (1821–1830), with the aim of liberating Greece from four centuries of Ottoman domination. From the perspective of the Ottoman Sultanate, Greece was a key province not only for its strategic position in the Balkans and the Mediterranean but also because much of the empire's shipping was Greek-owned and operated. Moreover, many of the key areas of the Ottoman Empire—Cyprus, Crete, western Anatolia, Macedonia, Thrace, and the city of Constantinople—had Greek majorities.

Sultan Mahmud II believed that Greece, being a conquered land, had been generously treated under the empire. He found it unconscionable that its inhabitants would now rise up in insurrection. In order to communicate his displeasure, in April 1821, he ordered Ottoman Janissaries (elite units within the Ottoman army) to seize the spiritual leader of the Greek Christian Orthodox Church whom he suspected of colluding with the rebels. As the patriarch of Constantinople (Gregory V) was leaving Easter Mass in full regalia, he was arrested and hanged on the spot from the cathedral gates and left there for three days. Following the third day, his body was dragged through the streets of Constantinople and flung into the Bosporus Straits.

While Mahmud was experiencing the slow unraveling of empire, by 1823 Mehmet's Nizam-i Cedid developed into a force of 24,000 officers and men, comprising six infantry regiments with five battalions of 800 men each—all armed with French muskets and trained in French infantry tactics. Mehmet deployed the first regiment on the Arabian Peninsula, the second in the Sudan, and the remaining four under the command of his son, Ibrahim in Morea in 1825 (southern Greece), following the urgent directive from Sultan Mahmud II to help quell the uprising in the empire's Greek territories now raging into their second year.

The Sultan's Ottoman army had been unable to suppress the Greek rebellion and Mehmet, whose Egypt was technically an Eyalet (province) of the empire but had achieved practical autonomy, realized there would be gains to be made by coming to Constantinople's aid. Sultan Mahmud II offered Mehmet the island of Crete in compensation for halting the rebellion and, in further negotiations, the Sultan also promised to grant the heartland of the insurgents, the Peloponnese, as a hereditary fief to Mehmet's son, Ibrahim. Mehmet would later argue that he was led to believe that, given Egyptian intervention against the Greeks, the position of Wali (governor) of Syria would also be made available to Mehmet or an appointee of Mehmet's choosing.

Consequently, in 1825, after receiving assurances of substantial reward, Mehmet sent four regiments (16,000 troops) aboard 100 transports escorted by 63 warships to quell the Greek rebellion. To the great consternation of the European powers, his Western trained and equipped army and navy had now been sent against the Orthodox Christian Greeks. In February 1825, the Egyptian ground forces, under the campaign commander, Ibrahim (Mehmet's son), overran the western region of the Peloponnese but were unable to secure the East where the Greek rebels were based at Nafplio. By this time the rebels were being led by a contingent of British and French officers, including Major Sir Richard Church, Colonel C. Fabvier, Admiral Lord Cochrane, and Captain F. A. Hastings.

Moving across the Isthmus of Corinth, Ibrahim's forces transited to the Greek mainland and captured the strategic stronghold of Missolonghi in April 1826. Greek forces then conducted guerrilla operations against the combined Ottoman-Egyptian armies, and Ibrahim turned to drastic measures such as burning crops and food supplies of the population in order to destroy the support and sustenance being provided to the insurgency. Ibrahim also brought Arab settlers into Greece in the attempt to dilute ethnic Greek influence while deporting hundreds of Greeks into slavery and sending them to work camps in Egypt.

Aligned against about 5,000 Greek fighters (whose partisan motto became "freedom or death") were the 16,000 Egyptian-Ottoman troops and 25,000 regular Ottoman army troops. In June 1827, the Acropolis of Athens, the last Greek fortress on the mainland, was overrun by Ottoman forces. Britain, France, and Russia, concerned about the military might being brought to bear on the Greeks and the scorched earth policy being conducted by Ibrahim, gathered in Britain and, in discussions which led to the Treaty of London in July 1827, sought to impose an armistice on the Ottoman Empire.

BATTLE OF NAVARINO

After initial negotiations failed with the Ottoman Sultanate, Britain, France, and Russia prepared to enforce the provisions of the Treaty of London through military action. In the summer of 1827, a large Ottoman-Egyptian fleet was being assembled in Alexandria for operations in the Greek theater, and Allied commanders sent a warning to Mehmet and Mahmud not to send the flotilla. The Ottoman-Egyptian leaders ignored what they believed to be meddling by the Allies into Sultanate affairs. As the fleet left Alexandria for Greece on August 5, 1827, the Ottoman leadership was finally in a position to finish off the remaining partisan rebel fighters and in putting an end to what had become known as the Greek War of Independence.

On August 20, 1827, Vice Admiral Sir Edward Codrington, commander of the Allied combined naval task force, received instructions from the Admiralty informing him that he was to impose and enforce the provisions of the London Treaty on both sides and to interdict the flow of reinforcements and supplies from Anatolia and Egypt to Ottoman forces in Greece. The application of military force against the

Ottoman-Egyptian fleet, the communication stressed, should be used only as a last resort. On August 29, the Sultanate formally rejected the Treaty of London's provisions, aimed at granting Greece autonomy while keeping the province within the empire. From September 8 to 12, 1827, the Ottoman-Egyptian fleet from Alexandria joined other Ottoman warships in Navarino Bay (present-day Pylos), located on the west coast of the Peloponnese peninsula in the Ionian Sea.

The Ottoman warships within the bay, in addition to imperial ships, were a combined force with warships from Algeria and Tunis as well as the Egyptian naval vessels. Ibrahim, Mehmet's son and in operational command of Egyptian-Ottoman forces, was contacted by Codrington and agreed to halt fighting until he received further instructions from his father who was involved in communications with the Western allies at his headquarters in Egypt. However, on October 1, the Greek rebels continued operations against Ottoman forces that had been ordered to temporarily stand down, leading Ibrahim to disregard his agreement with Codrington and in resuming attacks against the Greeks.

On October 13, Codrington was joined off Navarino Bay by French and Russian warships. While Codrington believed his combined fleet had the necessary firepower to destroy the Ottoman ships arrayed in Navarino Bay, his instructions were to impose the provisions of the treaty peaceably if possible. Therefore, he sailed his fleet into Navarino Bay in single column with the British in the lead, followed by the French, and then the Russians. Eleven Allied ships-of-the-line (average 70 guns each) and 9 frigates and 4 smaller warships, bringing to bear nearly 1,300 guns, all sailed boldly into the bay where 70 warships of the Ottoman Empire lay at anchor with more than 2,000 cannon at the ready. Adding to the Turkish firepower were the shore batteries, which were under Ottoman control.

The Ottoman fleet had taken a horseshoe or arc formation with three lines, and the ships-of-the-line anchored in the first wave. The Allied forces had superior firepower in that their cannon aboard the ships-of-the-line were 32-pound guns, as most of the cannon available to the Turks were 24-pounders. Additionally, while the Allies possessed 11 ships-of-the-line, the Ottomans had only 3 and, while the Turks had more than 70 ships, 58 were smaller vessels such as corvettes and brigs. Further still, the Allied crews, particularly the British and the French, had extensive combat experience during the Napoleonic Wars, while most of the Ottoman crews' only experience was in fighting smaller vessels. As if the superior firepower and superior gunnery expertise were not enough to tilt the odds in the Allies' favor, the Ottomans' ability to fight the Battle of Navarino was severely constrained by an additional and unforeseen development.

The Egyptian fleet present at Navarino Bay had largely been constructed or purchased with supervision by European naval officers, mostly French. The fleet had also been trained by a team of French officers under the overall direction of Captain J. M. Letellier,and these men served aboard the Egyptian-Ottoman warships as "shadow officers." On October 19, the day before the Battle of Navarino, French Rear Admiral De Rigny, serving with the combined Allied fleet, convinced the French officers to withdraw from the Egyptian fleet. They removed themselves to a smaller vessel in the bay and attempted to provide logistical advice to the Egyptians, but the damage to morale and effectiveness was significant. Most of the Ottoman sailors had been pressed into service (essentially forced conscription), and, as the French shadow officers withdrew from their crews, one can imagine the sadness some of the officers must have felt for these unfortunate and unwitting souls as powerful naval artillery prepared to open fire at them from point-blank range as well as the anxiety and fear that must have permeated the young Egyptian and Ottoman sailors.

At 2 p.m. on October 20, 1827, British Admiral Codrington aboard his flagship, HMS *Asia*, led his combined fleet into Navarino Bay. The Ottoman shore batteries guarding the entrance to the bay were ordered to hold their fire while Ibrahim Pasha sent a launch to Codrington's approaching vessel. The message from Ibrahim to Codrington was simple: "You do not have my permission to enter the bay." Codrington returned the Ottoman launch with his reply to Ibrahim: "I have come to give orders, not take them." Codrington continued on and, as his ships began to drop anchor at essentially point-blank range from the Ottoman fleet, a boat that had been lowered from the Allied ship *Dartmouth* proceeded in the direction of an Ottoman fire ship (a fire ship was a relatively small vessel loaded with flammable and combustible material in barrels mounted in the bow for use against an enemy target). The Ottomans opened fire on the approaching boat with musketry, and the exchanges escalated throughout the bay. In his communication with the Admiralty the following day, Codrington stated:

> I gave orders that no guns should be fired unless guns were first fired by the Turks; and those orders were strictly observed. The three English ships were accordingly permitted to pass the batteries and to moor, as they did with great rapidity, without any act of open hostility, although there was evident preparation for it in all the Turkish ships; but upon the *Dartmouth* sending a boat to one of the fire vessels, Lieutenant G.W.H. Fitzroy and several of her crew were shot with musketry. This produced a defensive fire of musketry from the *Dartmouth* and *La Syrene*, bearing the flag of Rear-Admiral de Rigny; that succeeded by cannon- shot at the Rear-Admiral from one of the Egyptian ships, which, of course, brought on a return, and thus very shortly thereafter the battle became general.[13]

Following two hours of battle, all Ottoman ships-of-the-line and most of the large Ottoman and Ottoman-allied frigates had been destroyed; after two more hours of fighting, the remaining Ottoman naval vessels had been sunk, scuttled, or set on fire. While no British, French, or Russian ships had been sunk, several ships had suffered significant damage; one Allied ship-of-the-line had 180 hull breaches (pierced by enemy cannon balls), while three Russian ships-of-the-line were essentially disabled, and three British ships, including Codrington's flagship, HMS *Asia*, were required to sail for England to immediately undergo repairs. The Allied fleet suffered 181 killed and 487 wounded, while the Ottoman fleet incurred losses exceeding 4,000 killed or wounded.

Word of the outcome of the battle reverberated throughout the maritime-oriented community that was Greece. People, in village after village upon hearing the news, rushed to the village squares, as church bells rang out and huge bonfires were lit on the mountain tops of the Peloponnese and Mount Parnassus in Central Greece. Demoralized Ottoman garrisons in the occupied zones made little effort to curtail the celebrations. The Battle of Navarino marked that final naval engagement between sailing ships with unarmored hulls and brandishing muzzle-loading, smooth-bore cannon. It also marked the first use in naval history of a steam-powered warship, as the relatively small Greek ship, the *Karteria* of the fledgling revolutionary navy, propelled by steam-powered paddles (as well as sails) made its appearance during the battle.

After suffering the devastating loss of essentially his entire navy and forced to withdraw his now unsupportable infantry from Greece, Mehmet demanded extra compensation for his losses from the Sultan. Mehmet demanded of the Sultan the Ottoman Eyalet of Syria in exchange for the loss of his navy. In Arabic, the region surrounding Syria is referred to as *Bilad al-Sham* (the Levant), and for centuries those in Mesopotamia, Persia, Anatolia, and Egypt sought to control it, as it possessed abundant resources as well as featuring the world's most ancient yet developed international trading communities centered on Damascus, Aleppo, and the Mediterranean coastal cities. Moreover, from Mehmet's perspective, possession of Syria would also provide a buffer zone against Ottoman power as well as a buffer zone against any foreign power that eventually seized control of Constantinople and Anatolia. With Egyptian military capacity based in Syria, it would also provide Mehmet with a possible staging area for direct operations against the Ottomans, should at some future time Mehmet decide to march on Constantinople.

For those same reasons, the Sultan refused Mehmet's demands. In response, Mehmet built a new navy, and on October 31, 1831, under Mehmet's son, Ibrahim, Egypt invaded Syria in the opening phases of the First Turko-Egyptian War. Ibrahim's forces quickly overran Syria except for the well-fortified port city of Acre, which required a six-month siege, before capitulating on May 27, 1832. However, the costs of the expedition required Mehmet to demand increases in fees and taxes from the Egyptian population, which created significant levels of domestic discontent with Mehmet's leadership. In addition to the domestic front, Mehmet soon realized the discomfort of the major European powers with his actions against Constantinople. The slow dissolution of the empire was unfolding as the Europeans and Russians moved to control or liberate key pieces of empire property. However, both the Europeans and the Russians did not wish to see Mehmet enthroned as the new Ottoman Sultan with control in Egypt, the Levant, Anatolia, and the key port cities that dotted the Eastern Mediterranean coastline between Asia Minor (Turkey) and North Africa.

After the fall of the stubborn port city Acre, Ibrahim took the Egyptian army into Anatolia and defeated an Ottoman army led by Reshid Pasha at the Battle of Konya on December 21, 1832. Sultan Mahmud II realized that, should Mehmet wish it, the Egyptian army could now march largely uncontested on Constantinople. Moscow, sensing opportunity, offered Mahmud military assistance and concluded the Treaty of Hunkar Iskelesi (Unkiar Skelessi) with him on July 8, 1833, to formalize the Sultan's acceptance. With the Russians seeking to continue their push south and in creating a greater Mediterranean presence by taking advantage of Ottoman weakness, the Treaty of Hunkar Iskelesi brought a sharp reaction from Britain and France. The treaty included a secret clause that opened the Dardanelles to Russia in time of war, while precluding its use by anyone else. Both nations negotiated the Convention of Kutahya between Mehmet and Mahmud II in May 1833, which stipulated that Mehmet would withdraw his forces from Anatolia and in return would receive Crete and the Hejaz (in Arabia) in compensation. Moreover, Ibrahim would be appointed Wali or governor of Syria in return for a yearly tribute payment to the Sultan.

Inhabitants of the Syrian Eyalet chaffed at their new Wali, uncomfortable with Egyptian policies at what they perceived to be excessive taxation, forced labor, a general disarmament of the population, and military conscription. A variety of incidents and uprisings began in 1834. On May 25, 1838, Mehmet informed the British and the French that he intended to declare independence from the Ottoman Empire and Mahmud II ordered his forces to advance into Syria. Ibrahim defeated them at the Battle of Nezib on June 24, 1839, and afterward, the Ottoman fleet defected to Mehmet. Mahmud II died almost immediately following the loss at Nezib and the defection of the Ottoman navy.

On July 15, 1840, Britain, Austria, Prussia, and Russia signed the Convention of London, which offered Mehmet hereditary rule in Egypt provided the North African country stayed in the Ottoman Empire and provided he withdrew from Syria and the coastal regions of Mt. Lebanon. Mehmet mistakenly believed that the French were prepared to side with Egypt and was consequently dismissive of British demands. Following this, British and Austrian naval forces blockaded the Nile Delta and shelled Beirut on September 11, 1840. On November 27, 1840, Mehmet agreed to the terms of the Convention of London and renounced claims over Crete, Syria, and the Hejaz. Also instituted in the 1841 agreement, to which France also reluctantly acquiesced, was the Anglo-Ottoman Commercial Convention of 1838, which abolished Mehmet's monopolistic control over Egyptian domestic and foreign commerce. Further diminishing Mehmet's power was a requirement in the agreement that compelled the reduction of the Egyptian army from more than 100,000 troops to no more than 18,000.

> From 1820–1840, Ali enjoyed the continuous support of France. Following his defeats of 1840–41, Ali and his successors never recovered from the effects of the European intervention, although his grandson, Ismail (1863–79) came closest to emulating the dynasty founder. Ismail's heavy borrowing at ruinous discounts and interest rates for his ambitious schemes of military, economic, and social modernization hastened his downfall. By the time of his dismissal in 1879, Britain and France were exercising a dual control over Egypt's finances under the authority of a public debt commission. After mounting crises beginning with the Urabi *coup d'etat* in September 1881, Britain backed into the occupation of Egypt the following July, without precipitating war in Europe. For more than sixty years thereafter, Whitehall decided the fate of the Egyptian army.[14]

From 1606 to 1826 the Ottoman Empire instituted efforts aimed at reforming its gunpowder weapons-brandishing medieval armed forces. In Persia, the problem was even more acute than that faced by Constantinople. The Shah during the time of the Qajar dynasty and continuing into the nineteenth century was forced to rely on militias that constantly required extensive negotiations as well as expensive promises all contributing to an extended mobilization process. For the Ottomans, Sultan Selim III attempted to reorganize the army (Nizam-i Cedid) in the late eighteenth century but met considerable resistance from a number of entrenched interests, most notably from the infantry units known collectively as the *Janissaries*. As a result of his attempts at modernization and reform, the Sultan was driven from power in 1807. His successor, Mahmud II, in November 1808, only months after becoming Sultan was faced with a revolt by the Janissaries rebelling yet again at plans toward modernizing the army. The Janissaries killed Mahmud's "grand vizier" Mustafa Bayraktar Pasha who had been ordered to spearhead the reform efforts and to modernize the Ottoman army.

These events, coupled with the difficulties experienced by a long line of predecessors, led Mahmud II to proceed with caution in his reform efforts. Eventually, however, on June 15, 1826, during the *Vaka-i Haryire* or "good incident," troops loyal to Mahmud II shelled the Janissary barracks in Constantinople, killing several thousand inside. The Janissary corps was subsequently dissolved and its provincial garrisons disbanded. The event is recorded and celebrated in Turkish history as the "auspicious event," which overcame a key obstacle and provided the opportunity to create that which eventually became modern Turkey.

THE RISE AND FALL OF OTTOMAN POWER

In the Middle Ages, the Ottomans created an empire through aggressive territorial expansion, a fairly sophisticated and organized system of taxation, a formidable military capability, and the utilization of a religion-based ideology for control and obedience. Once the forays into Europe had been blocked at the Battle of Lepanto in 1571 and outside Vienna in 1683, and, as a result, further imperial expansion and conquest thwarted, the Ottomans relied financially on agricultural production and the control of trade routes between the East and the West. However, the arrival of long-distance sailing ships and the rise of European shipping altered the traditional leverage enjoyed by the Ottomans in cooperation with their Mediterranean sailing contractors, the Venetians.

Since the Ottoman Empire traditionally controlled the overland Silk Road and commercial trade routes between Europe and Asia, they were able to dictate the terms of trade to both. Accordingly, the rest of Europe (minus the Venetians) sought options in order to mitigate the effects of this monopoly, leading eventually to the age of exploration and ocean-going technology. With the European voyages around the Cape of Good Hope at the southern tip of Africa, the Ottomans increasingly found themselves cut out of the lucrative spice trade from Asia to Europe and the Mediterranean world.

In addition to being limited in its trading influence in the Middle East and the Eastern Mediterranean during the eighteenth century, the Ottoman Empire also steadily lost territory in Eastern Europe to Austria and Russia. The empire found itself engaged on a number of fronts between 1568 and 1876 during the Russo-Turkish wars. During those wars, 11 conflicts, draining resources without replenishing the Ottoman treasury, were fought against an expanding and powerful Russian Empire. The Russian victory during the Russo-Turkish War of 1768–1774 secured vast stretches of land on the Black Sea north coast and brought territory as far south as the Caucasus under Russian control. The Russian army invaded the Balkans in 1806–1812, and by 1878, Russian troops came within 10 miles of Constantinople. For Western Europe, the prospect of a Russian-controlled former Ottoman Empire brought a concerted effort to limit Russia's Mediterranean influence and its relentless drive south toward warm water ports and control in Europe and in the Middle East.

In his book, *Guns, Sails, and Empires*, Carlo Cipolla argues that the development of gunpowder weapons and long-distance sailing ships enabled the Europeans to expand at the expense of the Muslim world in the sixteenth century.[15] This is an accurate, if not partial, portrayal of events. However, all too often the narrative developed characterizes Europe as pillaging and plundering its way through a peaceful, tolerant Middle East, North Africa, and Asia. The military history of the Middle East shows predatory behavior being engaged throughout the region, first by the nature of ancient kingdoms within the Middle East itself, taking control of the production of food and trade while financing sufficient military capability to enforce an elite preferred status quo. This was the case in ancient Mesopotamia and in Egypt. Asiatic nomadic cavalry descending into the region introduced a new mobility and maneuverability combined with the all too familiar savagery in keeping mass populations compliant in the fields, and focused on paying their taxes.

These new developments in mobility and maneuverability were not defeated by the West but rather by the introduction of gunpowder and gunpowder weapons that were first invented in China and spread across the Old Silk Road to the Middle East and Europe by the Mongols, eventually providing the Turkish tribes of the Ottomans the opportunity for bombarding the walls (and the inhabitants) of a trading city that stood unconquered for 1,000 years. It was not a Western plan or plot but the simple reality that the primary Ottoman motivation was to enrich themselves and their warriors as they proceeded in their campaign aimed initially at seizing all that was "Rum" (Roman world). Following the conquest of the last remnants of the Byzantine (Eastern Roman) Empire, the Ottomans immediately attacked into the Mediterranean where they defeated the seafaring and trading city-state of Venice in 1479, following a 15-year war.

The Ottoman Empire then turned east and attacked with gunpowder weapons in Persia followed by a pivot south, conducting operations against the Mamluks in Egypt. A series of wars then erupted against Vienna between 1540 and 1791 wherein the Ottoman Empire attempted to overrun European civilization. A Western fleet stopped further Ottoman advances into the Mediterranean at the Battle of Lepanto in 1571, and European ground forces, for all intents and purposes, halted their invasion of Europe at the Siege of Vienna in 1683. From 1500 to 1700, the Ottomans were using similar artillery and small arms as the Europeans; however, in the eighteenth and nineteenth centuries, a significant gap widened between the Ottoman Empire and Europe. The problem stemmed partly from the same type of issues the Russians faced by blocking the advancement in science and learning that the Europeans and North Americans embraced from the Renaissance (fourteenth to sixteenth centuries) to the Enlightenment (eighteenth century).

The West had finally seen the major religious wars come to an end with the signing of the Peace of Westphalia in 1648, which not only strengthened scientific inquiry but also codified the central position and power of the nation-state. Free to conduct experimentation and in possession of resources in which to support research and development, the West moved into the Industrial Revolution, which witnessed England, in particular, making historic gains in both civilian and military technology.

Conversely, in the Middle East in general and in the Ottoman Empire in particular, the inability to expand territory and seize resources with which to provide succor to one's warriors and with which other key elite in the establishment might avoid paying taxes was stalled by the obstinacy of the Europeans. The Ottoman Empire came into being by taking land and wealth via an overwhelmingly powerful military. "Conquer and tax" was a simple formula useful for centuries for most warlords in conjunction with their multiple purveyors of religious edicts, condemnations, and general authoritarian methods of behavioral control. Without the ability to expand territory and thus the tax base, which allowed the Sultan to provide warriors with lucrative *timars* from which they could enjoy revenue from a subservient people, the Sultan was faced with having to generate revenue from taxes on an expanding base of sales and marketing of goods and services, that is, international trade. The problem with this model of empire was, once again, the Europeans.

During the fifteenth through seventeenth centuries, the Ottoman Empire was arguably the premier military force in the world. It had managed, by virtue of its occupation of the key and strategic position of the former Byzantine Empire, to create a monopoly on the movement of trade between India and China, on the one hand, and Europe and the Mediterranean, on the other hand. The problem for the Ottomans' monopoly on trade arose when men began seeing the world as a globe rather than as a flat, immovable object. Thus, shedding the church's condemnation of Galileo and others who were intent on freely investigating the natural world, the West was able to escape the shackles of tradition and began embracing the dynamics that came from creativity and innovation. The result was a scientific revolution, which led to advanced technology and military supremacy.

The Ottoman Empire rested on a triad of capabilities. First, it evolved from the benefits of territorial expansion and in taxing those newly minted citizens. Second, its fortunes rested on massive tracts of land generally dedicated to agricultural production. And third, it benefited enormously from the control of trade routes between the East and the West. In terms of the first leg of the triad, its ability to expand had been frustrated by the Europeans. In the second, its control over the trade routes had been neutralized by ocean-going vessels and technology, which traversed the southern tip of Africa and into Asian markets. As such, by the eighteenth century, its fortunes had come to rely on its agricultural products and raw materials as its main economic asset. Its ability to control the terms of trade had vanished. A fourth leg had disappeared in the eighteenth century—military supremacy.

By this time, the European trading countries—Britain, the Netherlands, France, Austria, Germany, and, to a certain extent, Russia—through aggressive mercantilist policies had developed capital reserves that developing countries would require in order to modernize their infrastructure and reform their financial institutions. The Europeans, in stark contrast to the period between the fifteenth and early seventeenth centuries when the Ottomans reigned supreme militarily and financially, controlled the terms of trade.

Unfortunately, the Europeans conducted campaigns of predatory financial and military behavior in the same harsh and blatantly exploitative manner as its predecessors in the Middle East and in Asia. The blame for dismal economic conditions in the modern Middle East rests not with the West, East, North, or South. The blame rests on predatory schemes by corrupt and often incompetent leaders within the Middle East, acting in conjunction with dominant internal factions. Additionally, international actors, including states and private sector entities have, in many instances, undermined rational policies of growth and development by aligning with the corrupt and incompetent within the region.

In order to modernize in the early modern era, Mehmet Ali in Egypt and the Sultan in Constantinople needed foreign exchange (hard currency), and since the Europeans were now in a superior trading position, hard currency (and thus capital) was now in their hands. The Middle East had no other option other than a campaign aimed at economic, political, and educational reforms and a general modernization effort that would touch upon all aspects of society. However, since they lacked the capital, it had to come from loans from the rich European trading states. Those loans were granted, but they were granted by what could only be described as predatory mercantilists posing as international bankers. Accordingly, the Western bankers and their state supporters were prepared to make the loans for the modernized networks and systems that relatively advanced

European technology could provide; but the Middle Eastern borrowers would have to provide exclusive concessions to the European lenders for what essentially amounted to effective control of those strategic assets, such as railways, communication links, and factories.

As a result, Ottoman banks, mining companies, railroads, docks and warehouses, forestry enterprises, gas and water works, and so forth were all not only built by the Europeans but also subsequently owned by them. The British obtained significant shares in the Ottoman Central Bank, which they helped finance and create. France took control of the concession to run key railroads in the Ottoman Empire. The French also obtained tobacco rights and control of the docks in Beirut. The British took control of mineral rights in the city of Mosul, one of the premier trading posts of the old overland trading system in what is now present-day Iraq. The Russians pressed for and secured the rights to custom duties in Constantinople and in the Black Sea ports. Germany took control of the docks at Haidar Pasha (1899) and Alexandrette (1905) along with railway shares (Berlin-to-Baghdad aspirations) and various municipal transport monopolies.

> Even if the urge to develop the Ottoman economy had sharpened after 1840, that urge would have come too late. By then the Europe powers had, by concerted intervention, harnessed the Ottoman and Egyptian agricultural economies to the industrializing European economies, with the familiar pattern of the exchange of raw materials from the Middle East for industrial goods from Europe. As a result, in the Ottoman Empire even more than in Egypt the emergence of a domestic industry and of a Muslim middle class was checked. Instead, non-Muslim minorities and the enlarging European resident communities performed middle-class functions. The absence of economic reform in the Ottoman Empire thus closed the circuit of innovation. The rising secular educational system promoted primarily the interests of the new class of military officers, civil (imperial) servants, diplomats, and teachers who by 1870 formed a new urban educated elite. Their influence in domestic politics outlived the empire and indeed, Turkey's First Republic.[16]

By the end of the nineteenth century, the management of the state finances was largely being controlled by Europeans. The responsibility for these developments does not rest solely with the Europeans. In order to facilitate such a massive penetration of a state's economic assets, the cooperation of key Ottoman elite was necessary and was made possible partly by a desire to enrich themselves as they signed away control. This is not to say all Ottoman elite operated in this manner, nor is it to say all Western political and financial elite sought to plunder the empire.

But the people living in the Ottoman Empire, unbeknownst to them, had their economic wealth carted off by what might be characterized as modern pillagers and plunderers arising both in the Middle East and in

Europe. Prior to placing a blanket of blame on everyone in the West involved in nineteenth-century Ottoman and Egyptian economic affairs, it should be remembered that an enormous threat was posed to Western civilization by the rise of the Ottoman Empire and its vassals in Egypt. This was an enormously powerful and violent empire whose aim was to conquer and subjugate Europe and place the yoke of taxation upon its shoulders. This campaign was to be achieved not by negotiation, consent, or the virtuous example of exemplary leadership, but attained at the point of the sword, and later, by the general bombardment of a city's walls. To contribute in dismantling that threat from a purely defensive motivation certainly animated the decision making and behavior of many statesmen and bankers in Europe at the time. European military commanders were required to defend their people. If the bankers could take down most of the Ottoman's capability before a war had to be fought, so much the better.

The dynamics and the nexus between economic affairs and military operations have been ongoing for thousands of years, in Asia, in the Middle East, in Europe, and in the Western Hemisphere. Moreover, the process is not improved by burning down the town square, shooting the sheriff, or burning the bank. When the Egyptian people realized that the elite had essentially sold their country to the Europeans, they began, in a passionate and emotional fit, burning, looting, and killing. The process is improved by ordinary people becoming increasingly aware of the nefarious nature of many of these schemes and in shining the light of public awareness on the nature of those tactics, and then, holding those responsible to account. This requires reason over passion, wisdom over emotion, and education over ignorance. It required a new relationship between the rulers and the ruled. Napoleon and the French army, for all the havoc it wreaked during the Egyptian campaign, successfully served notice that the idea of a new relationship between ruler and ruled had arrived in the Middle East.

Chapter 2

The First World War and the Ottoman Succession

I look upon the people and the nation, as handed on to me, as a responsibility conferred upon me by God. And I believe, as it is written in the Bible,
that it is my duty to increase this heritage, for which one day I shall be called
upon to give an account. Whoever tries to interfere with my task, I shall
crush ... Let me assure the Sultan and his 300 million Muslims ... that the
German Emperor will ever be their friend.

—Kaiser Wilhelm II, 1913

While there was a general consensus within the Ottoman government
and military that Russia presented the most immediate and direct security challenge to the empire, the Ottoman leadership was divided prior
to World War I into two camps, regarding Germany on the one hand
and Britain and France on the other. However, Enver Pasha, who would
become the Ottoman's Minister of War and who had served as a military
attaché in Berlin, played an influential role in aligning Istanbul with
Germany. Six months before global war broke out, German General Otto
Liman von Sanders arrived in Istanbul in December 1913 as head of a
military delegation, intent on creating a greater interoperability between
the Ottoman and German militaries.

This close cooperation had begun much earlier in the late nineteenth
century, as the Ottomans began embracing the Prussian military model
and continued as they later began receiving training from the German
military mission. A two-year senior staff college—the Turkish War

Academy—had been reoriented along the lines of its German counterpart and Turkish corps, and divisional commanders received training from German instructors with a particular focus on training high-level Ottoman officers to make decisions on their own initiative.[1] Esat Pasha and Mustafa Kemal, two key Ottoman commanders during the Dardanelles campaign, were beneficiaries of this German military education and training.

Enver Pasha, in his efforts at modernizing the Ottoman military in the first decade of the twentieth century, had forced into retirement more than 1,300 regular army officers.[2] It was within this modernizing environment of high expectations and monitored performances that Esat Pasha rose ultimately to the command of Ottoman defenses on the Gallipoli peninsula during the Dardanelles campaign. Moreover, Mustafa Kemal, who would go on to become known historically as the father of modern Turkey in the years following World War I, displayed exceptional leadership in the counterattacks mounted by the Turks, as the Allies assaulted Ottoman positions in the Dardanelles.[3]

In the European theater, the Germans responsible for the actual implementation of the plan in August 1914 underestimated the size of the forces that would be necessary to accomplish quick victory in France. Accordingly, the western European theater did not transition to a quick and decisive outcome as hoped. Instead, it devolved into stalemate and trench warfare. One result of this impasse was that Britain and its allies, being stymied and deadlocked on the western front, sought to create advantage through maneuver and, given the constraints on European land operations at the time, opted to utilize its advantages in sea power, as British planners reviewed potential courses of action.

Following stalemate in the West and given that Germany now was intent on eliminating Russia from the war in order to more fully concentrate on France and Britain, the Allies decided that striking and eliminating the weakest link within the Central Powers, that is, the Ottoman Empire, would be a useful endeavor. The Ottomans, working in conjunction with Berlin, had effectively closed down the Dardanelles—the key straits linking the Mediterranean Sea and the Sea of Marmara. With this closure and the lack of control of the Bosporus Straits, came the inability of the Allies to resupply the Russian army, which, by January 1915, was under significant strain from relentless operations spearheaded by Germany. Britain and France considered the alternatives as the requests for assistance poured in from Moscow.

Britain and France were considering two separate courses of action. The first was a potential campaign that would involve an invasion of Schleswig-Holstein (Denmark) by sea, which would, at least theoretically, open the possibilities of supply to Russia via the Baltics. The second

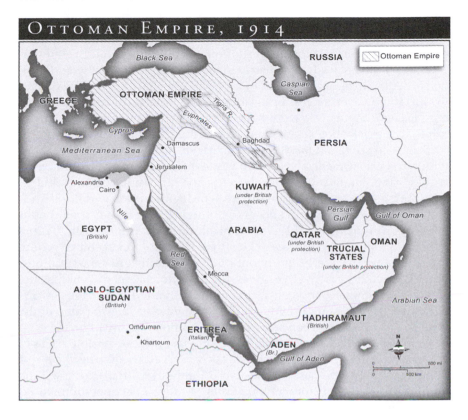

OTTOMAN EMPIRE, 1914

possibility under consideration, and one which was being advanced by a relatively young Winston Churchill who was serving as British Lord of the Admiralty, involved operations against the Ottomans in the Dardanelles, which would open up sea lines of communication from the Mediterranean to the Black Sea and help resupply the Russians from bases in the Eastern Mediterranean.

There were further advantages to be gained, in Churchill's view, by an effective Dardanelles campaign. In addition to resupplying Russia and keeping it in the fight—thus relieving pressure on the Allied lines on the western front—an attack threatening the Ottoman capital at Istanbul had the potential to reduce the threat being posed by Ottoman and German forces to Allied military units that were defending the Suez Canal—completed in 1869—and within Egypt itself.

Successful operations in the Dardanelles and into the Black Sea also offered the potential for convincing neutral Balkan states such as Bulgaria and Romania in joining the Triple Entente. With several promising associated benefits from a Dardanelles operation, the one potential and perhaps most strategically decisive outcome in terms of the war itself in "forcing the Straits" during a successful naval campaign operations would be in taking control of Istanbul and forcing the Ottomans out of the war. Even if that eventuality did not lead immediately to the end of hostilities, it would position the Allies to resupply Russia and control Anatolia, the Middle East, and the Black Sea. Given success in a Dardanelles campaign, in addition to forcing Turkey from the war would also provide substantial leverage in any future war termination negotiations with the remaining Central Powers.

Thus, Churchill and his allies at the British Admiralty, including those within the government, argued that while the upside of such a campaign would bring significant strategic benefits, the downside effects would be minimal, as the campaign planners would use older warships and, should they not meet with success in "forcing the Straits" they would indeed, given British and French control of the Mediterranean, be in a position to simply withdraw. The ships, in the worst scenario where many may be lost, were simply not critical for British naval operations. From Churchill's perspective, given the enormous level of benefits success would generate, and contrasted with the limited deleterious effects of failure, the decision to conduct the Dardanelles naval campaign at the beginning of 1915 was seen as prudent and rational as it was bold.

However, while the basic logic of the proposition was sensible enough, empirical reality in conditions of war soon served in altering the argument's original soundness. A study in Britain in 1907 had discussed the various difficulties in "forcing the Straits" as any naval operation would have to be supported by a ground force in order to consolidate any gains that a naval bombardment might bring. In short, the forts, the guns, and the firing positions would have to be placed under Allied control, lest Ottoman and German troop reinforcements and artillery be sent in as replacements. Additionally, mobile artillery and mortars were proving to be difficult in targeting for naval bombardment, and their effect on naval operations had proven worrisome. Given this, ground units would be useful in neutralizing the threat, both to the fleet and to merchant shipping. Further still, the presence of land forces would be necessary in obtaining needed supplies from the shore, without which the naval force would have to withdraw to home waters or, at the minimum, friendly waters in order to refuel and restock.

RUSSIA VETOES BRITAIN'S PLANS FOR A GROUND FORCE

Accordingly, the original British plan being presented was to be augmented and supported by a Greek army of three divisions, which would be tasked with securing Istanbul and in decapitating Ottoman command and control of the outlying coastal defenses. However, Russia vetoed the part of the plan where the Greeks, with support from Britain and France, would secure Istanbul. Moscow was undoubtedly mindful of the Crimean War, which was largely fought to insure that the Russians would not destroy the Ottoman Empire and seize control of the Dardanelles. However, this rejection by Moscow proved costly, as the Germans eventually forced the Russians, who were unable to receive support from its Triple Entente partners through the Dardanelles, out of the war in 1917.

Churchill, ignoring the ground force requirements identified by British military planners, eventually convinced Herbert Kitchener, secretary of state for war, that in the face of Russian objections over land operations aimed at Istanbul, a strictly naval operation should move forward in the Dardanelles. Subsequently, Churchill's plan for a naval operation-only was approved by the British War Cabinet at the end of January in 1915. With the benefit of hindsight, the following proposition can be advanced in regard to the events that surrounded the campaign: a serious strategic mistake on the part of the British high command was an attack on the Dardanelles and Gallipoli in which planning assumptions had underestimated the military effectiveness of the Ottoman army and the strength of the defensive positions it held. However, like many operations in British and French military history, the initial action, although unsuccessful, provided invaluable information and insight that informed follow-up action, which then was generally successful. This process of making operational and tactical mistakes and quickly transforming lessons learned for strategic success provides utility if, and only if, the men and materiel being sacrificed tactically are not critical for long-range success.

The first and most severe problem of the Allied action in relation to the Dardanelles and Gallipoli during World War I was in committing the cardinal sin of warfare: underestimating one's enemy. The unfortunate reality for Allied operations in the Middle East during the initial phases of the war was the tendency to underestimate the military capabilities of the Ottoman Empire. The Ottomans had continually fortified the entrance to the Straits for nearly five centuries, placing hidden batteries in the early modern era in the most inconvenient of places for opposing naval operations.

> Serious work on modern fortifications began in the late nineteenth century and resulted in a series of concrete and earth embrasured gun positions on both sides of straits. The fixed artillery for these positions was purchased abroad and was composed mostly of French and German 9- to 11-inch ordnance. Underwater minefields, search lights, and quick-firing light guns completed the defensive array. In the 20th century, anti-submarine nets and telephones were added.[4]

In the fall of 1914, Germany sent Vice Admiral Guido von Usedom—an expert in sea coast defenses—and 500 German specialists in coastal artillery, communications, military engineering, and mines to support Ottoman defenses guarding the Dardanelle Straits. This was immediately followed by an influx of additional German military hardware shipped to the Straits via Romania and Bulgaria. A few months earlier on August 2, 1914, after two warships—the *Sultan Osman I* and *Reshadieh*, built in British shipyards for the Ottomans—were confiscated by Britain, Germany offered the Ottomans two replacement ships from its navy. These were the battle cruiser SMS *Goeben* and the light cruiser SMS *Breslau*, two relatively older ships but both very powerful and capable warships. Later, upon commissioning within the Ottoman navy, the ships were renamed the *Yavuz Sultan Selim* and the *Midilli*.

The Allies were intent that these ships should never arrive in the Middle East and immediately set about to capture, or sink, both. However, the German navy successfully evaded these efforts, and the ships made their way to the Dardanelles where the Ottomans allowed them safe passage. This act confirmed for the Allies that a suspected secret pact made between the Ottoman Empire and the Central Powers two days after the outbreak of World War I in Europe was more than rumor. A neutral country, which the Ottoman Empire had claimed it was in the summer of 1914, would have been required by international convention to block movement of international military shipping through the Straits. This confirmed for London that the Ottoman Empire had, in fact, formally, if secretly, aligned with Germany.

In October 1914, the Ottomans formally closed the Dardanelles to Allied shipping, and on October 28, an Ottoman fleet led by the *Yavuz Sultan Selim*, now the most capable ship on the Black Sea, conducted attacks against Russian targets in and around the sea. However, the objective of the Ottoman ships, which was to destroy the Russian Black Sea fleet, was not realized and, following these attacks, Russia declared war on the Ottoman Empire on November 2, 1914. Britain followed with its own formal declaration of war on November 6. Prior to this British declaration of war, on November 3, Churchill ordered the first British attack on Ottoman positions in the Dardanelles, which was eventually carried out by the battle cruisers HMS *Indomitable* and HMS *Indefatigable* in concert with the older French battleships, *Suffren* and *Veritz*. Soon after, the Ottoman Sultan called for a jihad against the Triple Entente.

During the initial 20-minute bombardment on November 3, one round from Allied guns struck the magazine of the Ottoman fort at Sedd el-Bahr located at the southern tip of the Gallipoli peninsula, which upended 10 Turkish guns and served in killing 86. The total casualties during the brief encounter were 150, including 40 Germans. This engagement, however, created two important perceptual dynamics for both the Allied commanders and the commanders for the Central Powers. For the Allies, it falsely colored an overly optimistic picture of the ease Allied fleets might have in engaging shore defenses in any future naval bombardment. And, conversely, it served notice to Ottoman and German commanders that serious and immediate reinforcement of coastal defenses was needed.

These events were quickly followed by Ottoman ground operations against Russian forces in the Caucasus Mountains in December 1914 (Battle of Sarikamish). By January 1915, calls from Moscow for resupply by the British and French increased in frequency. It was at this time and under these circumstances that Churchill's naval action-only was approved by the War Cabinet. In February, British Admiral Sackville Carden led 15 ships of a combined Anglo-French fleet to conduct operations against Ottoman and German positions in the vicinity of the Dardanelles. However, before commencing the attack, Carden, in deteriorating mental and physical condition, passed command of the operation to his deputy, John de Robeck.

Subsequently, at 7:30 a.m. on February 19, 1915, two Allied destroyers were sent to probe the defenses of the Straits and, at 7:58, the Central Powers responded by opening fire with a 9.4-inch Krupp gun from Kumkale (Orhaniye Tepe battery). This was followed with the British battleships, *Cornwallis* and *Vengeance*, steaming forward to engage the batteries, with *Cornwallis* opening fire at 9:51 a.m. On February 25, following the initial probing operations, the Allied fleet entered the Straits themselves and were soon slowed by the presence of mine fields. On March 15, the British Admiralty authorized the combined naval task force to conduct an all-out naval bombardment of Ottoman forts and firing positions from inside the Straits. Once the shore batteries were silenced, mine-clearing operations could then move forward. In an area that was thought to have been cleared of mines, HMS *Inflexible* and HMS *Irresistible* moved forward but were both struck by mines.

By March 18, at a cost of only 118 casualties to Ottoman and German forces, the Central Powers managed to sink three battleships and damaged another with mines and inflicted 700 casualties on the Allied force. De Robeck then telegraphed the Admiralty that it would be necessary to have ground support prior to proceeding with further operations. The Allied naval task force eventually conducted three naval assaults between February 19 and March 18 deploying a battleship, 27 cruisers, 30 pre-dreadnoughts, 25 destroyers, 14 submarines, and an aircraft carrier (Ark Royal). During these engagements, the Allied losses included six pre-dreadnoughts sunk, one battle cruiser sunk, three pre-dreadnoughts damaged, one destroyer sunk, and eight submarines lost. Commanding the French contribution to the task force was Admiral Emile Guepratte, while the Ottoman forts and shore batteries were led by Ottoman officers Fuad Pasha, Cevat Cobanli, and Cihan Cildan Pasha.

The speed of change in terms of technology and the uncertainty of the impact and effects of those changes on warfare were evident in the decisions regarding the plausibility of success in a naval operation in the Dardanelles campaign. Churchill had written in 1911, "It should be remembered that it is no longer possible to force the Dardanelles, and nobody would expose a modern fleet to such peril." Yet, just three years later in 1914, as British leaders viewed with apprehension the destructive ability of German artillery on Belgian forts, Churchill was led to the conclusion that British naval gunfire had the capacity to destroy the Turkish forts operating in the Dardanelles.

RAPIDITY OF CHANGE IN TECHNOLOGY AND ITS DELETERIOUS EFFECT ON MILITARY PLANNING

If strategy is the effective alignment of ends with means, and given that the rapidity of change in terms of the capability of modern technology distorted one's understanding of what *means* could achieve, creating effective military strategy and doctrine in the modern age had become increasingly problematic. If strategy development and implementation were difficult for the political leaders and military commanders within the Western powers at the beginning of the First World War, one can imagine the difficulties and complexities faced by the leaders and military practitioners of the Middle East and North Africa in terms of both understanding and matching modern technology to effective military doctrine. The Germans in Turkey and the British in Egypt were conduits for both military thought and technology into the Middle East during World War I, with both Egypt and Turkey having sent officers to Europe for professional military education.

Beginning on April 25, 1915, in what amounted to the largest amphibious operation of World War I, 78,000 Allied troops organized as the Mediterranean Expeditionary Force (MEF) and came ashore on the Gallipoli peninsula with the intent of swiftly advancing eastward across the peninsula in order to neutralize Ottoman defenses and capture the Straits of the Dardanelles. However, hastily arranged Allied plans without adequate intelligence on terrain at the landing sites provided Ottoman forces strategic advantage, as they utilized positional defense in terrain unfavorable to the attackers. In more common parlance, the Allies, by underestimating their enemies, and failing to adequately prepare, disembarked from their ships and were immediately pinned down, as the defenders were familiar with the terrain and they were not.

Strong Ottoman counterattacks, led by outstanding officers such as Mustafa Kemal, and utilizing troops operating from the ridges above

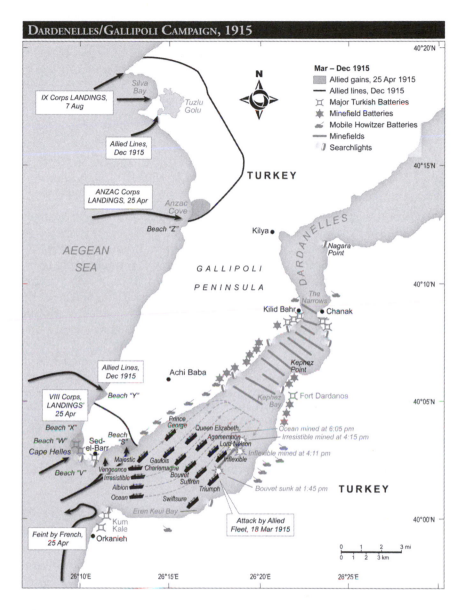

DARDENELLES/GALLIPOLI CAMPAIGN, 1915

40°20'N

Mar – Dec 1915
- Allied gains, 25 Apr 1915
- Allied lines, Dec 1915
- Major Turkish Batteries
- Minefield Batteries
- Mobile Howitzer Batteries
- Minefields
- Searchlights

Silva Bay

IX Corps LANDINGS, 7 Aug

Tuzlu Golu

N

Allied Lines, Dec 1915

40°15'N

TURKEY

ANZAC Corps LANDINGS, 25 Apr

Anzac Cove

Beach "Z"

Kilya

Nagara Point

AEGEAN SEA

GALLIPOLI

PENINSULA

The Narrows

40°10'N

Kilid Bahr · Chanak

Kephez Point

Allied Lines, Dec 1915

Achi Baba

VIII Corps, LANDINGS' 25 Apr

Beach "Y"

Kephez Bay   Fort Dardanos

40°05'N

Beach "X"

Beach "W"   Beach "S"   Sed-el-Barr

Cape Helles

Prince George

Ocean mined at 6:05 pm
Irresistible mined at 4:15 pm

Beach "V"

Queen Elizabeth
Agamemnon
Lord Nelson

Inflexible mined at 4:11 pm

Majestic   Gaulois
Vengeance   Charlemagne
Irresistible   Bouvet
Albion   Suffren
Ocean   Triumph
Swiftsure

Inflexible

Bouvet sunk at 1:45 pm   **TURKEY**

Eren Keui Bay

Attack by Allied Fleet, 18 Mar 1915

40°00'N

Kum Kale

Feint by French, 25 Apr

Orkanieh

0   1   2   3 mi
0   1   2   3 km

26°10'E   26°15'E   26°20'E   26°25'E

the Allied force, effectively blocked the Allied MEF from moving forward to their objectives along the ridges and shore of the Dardanelles Straits. Highlighting the difficulties faced by units of the MEF operating on Gallipoli, a British force landing at Cape Helles on April 25, 1915, was expected to advance six miles on the first day. On the second it would seize control of the Kilitbahir plateau overlooking the narrows. Instead, in eight months of fighting, the British never advanced more than five miles, and their first day objectives of Kirthia and the hill Achi Baba remained out of their reach. Pinned down for nine months and suffering tens of thousands of casualties (killed or wounded: 73,000 British, 28,000 Australians, 27,000 French, 7,400 New Zealanders, 4,800 Indians—with many more thousands becoming ill), the MEF withdrew.

> I did not know, to tell you the truth, that the Ottomans were nearly as good as they turned out to be.
>
> —British General Ian Hamilton, commander
> in chief (MEF Gallipoli, 1915), statement
> to the Dardanelles Commission.[5]

Gallipoli was the most successful Ottoman action of World War I as well as perhaps one of most consequential in terms of strategic effect overall. With the loss at Gallipoli, the Allies were unable to control the Dardanelles and without that control were unable to provision a faltering Russian Empire. Thus, given the MEF's inability to break through Ottoman and German defenses on Gallipoli, and given the failure of the Allied fleet in the Dardanelles Straits, Russia remained isolated. With Germany conducting a holding action along the western front, it was then able to continue its concentration on knocking Russia out of the war, which it accomplished in 1917. Germany then turned and unleashed its power on the western European front, and, as it made progress at the end of 1917 and early 1918, only the arrival of 1.5 million troops from the United States, coupled with the resupplying operations to Allied forces in Europe from America, eventually halted the German advance.[6]

ANGLO-INDIAN FORCES SURROUNDED AT KUT-AL-AMARA NEAR BAGHDAD

About the time the British were receiving reports regarding the Gallipoli catastrophe, an Anglo-Indian force was cut off and surrounded at Kut-al-Amara, a city about 100 miles south of Baghdad. From an Allied point of view, the news at the time across all fronts, including Europe and the Middle East, was, intermittently, both bleak and dismal. Quite remarkable, then, was the decision to redouble efforts, garner adequate resources, and press on. In April 1916, the effort, particularly across the Middle East, took on new energy and new direction.

In Mesopotamia, the Ottoman military posture was not as strong at the beginning of World War I as it had been in either the Dardanelles or in Palestine. London, however, was taking no chances when war broke out in August 1914, and, on August 25, they directed the India office to prepare a ground force to provide deterrence, security, and forward defense of the Persian oil fields and for several refineries and pipelines belonging to the Anglo-Persian Oil Company in the vicinity of Abadan Island in the North Persian Gulf. Toward these objectives, London also ordered the India office to secure the Shatt al-Arab estuary. Consequently, the 16th Indian Brigade Group led by Brigadier General W. S. Delamain was dispatched and arrived in Bahrain on October 23, 1914.

While the immediate objective was to secure Anglo-Persian Oil Company property and interests, India had communicated with British leaders its concern with the millions of Muslims within its borders and the expected call for jihad by the Sultan in Istanbul, should the Ottomans opt to align with German interests. London shared this concern as the loyalty of thousands of Indian Muslims serving in the Indian army might eventually prove problematic. Moreover, the Emir of Afghanistan had quietly stated that 50,000 soldiers were prepared to join in jihad, including an invasion of India. Thus, there was ample concern for strategic dynamics affecting not only Mesopotamia and the Persian oil fields but British control in India as well. Consequently, as the Ottomans attacked Russian targets in the Black Sea and closed the Turkish Straits to Allied shipping, and, following Britain's declaration of war against the Ottoman Empire on November 5, 1914, the 16th Indian Brigade Group was moved to Fao Peninsula in the Middle East on November 6, securing the Shatt al-Arab on the November 14.

Lt. General Sir Arthur Barrett, commander in chief of the Indian Expeditionary Force (IEF), directed Brigadier General Delamain of the 16th Indian Brigade Group to secure the city of Basra (southern Iraq) and to protect the transshipment port strategically located at the mouth of the Euphrates and Tigris Rivers. As directed, Delamain's 16th Group moved against and occupied Basra on November 22. Orders were then issued to provide a security buffer for Basra, and forces advanced north into Mesopotamia (present-day Iraq) and took control of Qurna on December 9. The ease with which these initial operations unfolded led the high command to underestimate the difficulties and complexities that permeated their next moves. The decision was made to move from Qurna to Baghdad with the full realization that the Allied force would have only two divisions within the II Indian Corps, the 6th and 12th Indian Divisions under Lt. General John Nixon, to take and occupy Baghdad.

From one perspective, the India office and British planners could be criticized for a complete breakdown in terms of the logic of strategy, that is, effectively matching ends with the means available to accomplish the stated objectives. Certainly their planning assumptions proved faulty and led to tactical difficulties. Yet, on an operational level, given the fact that the British had the wherewithal to follow up any lack of success arising from the conservative and somewhat limited two-division offensive, a failure would not be decisive. Moreover, should the two-division attack fail, an enormous amount of intelligence would be gathered as to the subsequent plans, strength, and mobility of enemy forces. Given the insight that would accrue at that time, Allied forces would be in a better position to gauge the necessary forces that *would* be required to ultimately prevail. Whether London actually believed Allied forces could secure Iraq with two divisions is unclear. However, what is clear is that two divisions were sent with that objective in mind.

The buildup of the two-division force took until April 1915, with Nixon replacing Barrett on April 9. In May, the IEF (D) began its movement forward toward Baghdad. In the movement north, Major General Charles Townshend's 6th Indian Division spearheaded the offensive. Townshend's division made consistent progress, taking Amara on June 3, Nasiriyah on July 25, and Kut-al-Amara on September 28, 1915, as the Ottomans were unprepared for the rapidity of Townshend's advance. However, the string of successes came to an abrupt end at Ctesiphon on November 21, as the Ottomans were able to finally marshal sufficient forces to stand, fight, and prevail. After being stopped at Ctesiphon, Townshend's 6th Indian Division fell back to Kut, and in the pursuit, the Ottomans managed to cut off all avenues of relief, as forces sent in support of the 6th were subsequently blocked from intervening. While Townshend managed to hold for several weeks, he eventually was forced to surrender on April 26, 1916.

> The British campaign in Mesopotamia began as a strictly limited operation. Excessive ambition led to disaster with the fall of Kut in April 1916. An advance to Baghdad in 1915 was indeed a failure in matching ends and means—the proverbial bridge too far ... The Mesopotamian Campaign brought the Indian army to a state of strategic overextension.[7]

At the beginning of 1916, these developments led to the British War Office assuming operational control in February from the India office and complete policy and management for the theater by July 1916. For six months, London prepared seven divisions that were then organized into two corps. This was followed by operations against Baghdad, which was captured in March 1917. Following the success in Bagdad, Britain waited eight months before taking Tikrit in November 1917. Tikrit operations were followed by a successful campaign against Mosul in October 1918. By the end of October 1918, the Indian army in Mesopotamia had grown in strength to 420,000 troops and Britain controlled Persia, Iraq, the Persian Gulf, and most of the key coastal regions of the Arabian Sea.

EGYPT AND THE SUEZ CANAL

Egypt and the Suez Canal were vital interests of the British Empire in the opening years of the twentieth century, as they established the maritime connection with India and provided invaluable basing for operations in the eastern Mediterranean Sea. After England and France, Egypt eventually became the largest British military base during World War I. Without access to the Suez Canal, a significantly larger British merchant fleet would have been required to move goods via the Cape of Good Hope located at the southern tip of Africa and into Asia. This shorter route to India, by ship to Alexandria and then overland to the city of Suez or the Persian Gulf, was more efficient—a 40-day journey compared to five months around the African Cape. And, without the canal, Britain's ability to power across the Mediterranean and into Asia would have been significantly reduced. Accordingly, from London's perspective, security of transit and power projection were essential objectives of the British presence in Egypt.

Germany viewed the ejection of Britain from Egypt as highly desirable in terms of its own ongoing objectives in developing control and influence in overseas markets and in accessing resources. The Ottoman Empire held a similar negative view of the British presence in Egypt and was quite displeased with both Britain and France for their intrusions into the Northeast African nation during the period, 1798–1914. Egypt, from a Turkish perspective, belonged to the Ottoman Empire. From the perspective of the Central Powers, Egypt represented a potential choke point for British power or, as some in Germany viewed it in the years leading up to World War I, Britain's "jugular vein."

During the nineteenth century, France and Britain had vied for control in Egypt, but with the rise and unification of Germany as well as the expansionistic foreign policy of Russia, both France and Britain soon realized the necessity of cooperation in the face of existential challenges arising at the end of the nineteenth and beginning of the twentieth centuries. When World War I broke out in August 1914, the units of the British army of occupation in Egypt were withdrawn and dispatched to France and replaced by the 42nd Territorial Division. In September, Major General John Maxwell assumed command of British forces in Egypt. Upon first arriving the new British commander assured the Egyptians that Britain would shoulder the burden of war and the defense of the canal.

However, by 1915, with so much preparation needing to be done to defend the canal, British officials began recruiting Egyptians for various tasks, such as digging trenches, building rail lines and water pipelines, and transporting supplies via camels. Eventually these workers came to be organized within the Egyptian Labour Corps (ELC) and the Camel Transport Corps (CTC). These groups grew to substantial numbers with one company in the CTC possessing 2,020 camels and 1,168 drivers. With a high turnover of drivers, the numbers constantly needed to be replenished, and British logistical services hired more than 170,000 Egyptians during the course of operations in the Middle Eastern theater during World War I. As word arrived that Ottoman forces were massing in Palestine for an attack on the Suez Canal, two divisions of the Indian army were sent to augment Maxwell's command in Egypt. Units of the Australian Imperial Force also arrived in late 1914 and began training for the defense of the British position in India. By January 1915, three fully trained divisions supported by a flotilla of warships were in place.

When the Ottoman Empire officially entered the war on the side of the Central Powers on October 31, 1914, Abbas Hilmi II—the head of government and the political leader in Egypt—declared his support for the Muslim Caliphate in Istanbul, which caused Britain to immediately move to dissolve the Khedive (monarch); declare a protectorate; and install Egyptian prince Hussein Kamel in the newly created position of Sultan of Egypt. On November 25, when First Lord of the Admiralty Winston Churchill proposed attacking the Ottoman Empire in the Dardanelles as a useful strategy for relieving pressure against Egypt and in protecting the Suez Canal, Alexandria was subsequently made the base for the MEF, which, under Ian Hamilton was to conduct amphibious operations against the Gallipoli peninsula. Cairo also hosted various Allied units preparing to storm the Dardanelles. As the Gallipoli and Dardanelles campaigns failed to achieve their objectives, hospitals within Egypt were set up to attend to the tens of thousands of Allied wounded during the fighting of 1915–1916.

In the first two years of the war, Egypt was threatened by Turkish forces operating in the Sinai, Gaza, and Palestine, and from the Libyan Desert to the west, where the Germans had succeeded in persuading the Senussi— the warrior Bedouin tribesmen of Cyrenaica—to rise against Britain. In the winter of 1915–1916, the Senussi, with German and Turkish money and arms, invaded Egypt, and the garrison at Sollum was quickly surrounded and forced to surrender. Britain established a special Western Desert Force and in operations mounted in January and February 1916 retook Sollum and drove out the Senussi. However, the Senussi continued raids and incursions into Egypt from the Libyan Desert, which required the British to maintain a large force on the western Egyptian border as a precaution.

In the East, two large attacks by Ottoman-German forces on February 3, 1915, and on August 3, 1916, were repulsed by British, Australian, and Indian forces. In the first attack, a Turkish army of 25,000, led by Djemal Pasha along with German advisor Kress von Kressenstein, left Beersheba in Palestine on January 15 and crossed 150 miles of the Sinai Desert without losing one person. The force was able to utilize pontoon bridges supplied by Germany for the attack on the Suez. The attack itself was mounted on February 3 and was repelled by Indian troops and a small British regular force supported by guns from British ships operating in the Suez Canal. Only one Ottoman unit managed to cross to the western side of the canal, which occurred under the cover of darkness.

Eventually, the Turks lost 2,000 men but occupied Sinai through February, causing the British to build up a major force in Egypt to defend the canal. For three years, Britain had to station more than 100,000 imperial troops in Egypt to protect the canal. While the largest numbers of troops were focused on conventional military operations, Britain and its allies utilized special forces and intelligence in Egypt and, eventually, in operations in Palestine and Syria. During the fighting in February 1915, a Gurkha force of 500 specially selected soldiers surprised the Turks at Tor east of the Suez on the 13th, with the aid of an Arab spy network managed by Lieutenant Colonel A. C. Parker (nephew of Lord Kitchener). Britain's countermoves against the Turk offensive aimed at Egypt included making contact with Arab leaders in western Arabia (the Hejaz) and the Sharif and Emir of Mecca.

Britain developed a dual strategy for Middle East military operations during World War I. The first aspect of this plan was an external strategy of invasion by conventional forces, ultimately sending forces into Mesopotamia (Iraq) and the Levant (Palestine, Syria). The second was an internal strategy of revolution supporting Arab nationalism directed by Britain's Foreign Office in the form of the Arab Bureau headquartered in Cairo. The most visible element of this strategy came to be personified by the heroic exploits of British army officer T. E. Lawrence (Lawrence of Arabia) detailed to the intelligence staff of the GOC Middle East (General Officer Commanding).

One more large conventional attack on Allied forces in Egypt took place on August 3, 1916, which was led by German General der Infanterie (equivalent to U.S. major general) Friedrich Kress von Kressenstein. Kressenstein's force consisted of 18,000 men of the Turkish Eighth Army, but the action was unsuccessful and the combined Ottoman-German force suffered losses of nearly 50 percent. The successful defense against Kressenstein's assault marked the end of the Central Powers' offensive operations against Allied positions in Egypt. Henceforth, the initiative passed to the British as they prepared to conduct operations against the Ottomans and Germans in the Sinai, Gaza, Palestine, and beyond.

In the fall of 1916, survivors of the failed Gallipoli and Dardanelles campaigns, that is, the MEF, were established in Egypt as part of the newly created Egyptian Expeditionary Force (EEF). General Archibald Murray took command of this force and proceeded east into the Sinai in clearing operations. These efforts were made more difficult by the presence of a railway that resupplied Ottoman forces in Palestine and in the Sinai. The EEF eventually built its own rail line extending from Egypt as well as a water line to support advancing Allied troops. The Ottomans attacked the British railway in the Sinai but were defeated at the Battle of Rumani on August 3, 1916, after which the British exploited the opportunity, pressing the initiative by attacking the remaining Ottoman positions in the Sinai and prevailing at the Battle of Magruntein during January 8–9, 1917.

ALLENBY TAKES COMMAND

Murray's EEF was then ordered into Palestine where it fought two battles at Gaza (March 26, 1917, and April 17–19, 1917). However, both battles found Allied forces facing stiff resistance, and the attacks failed in the objective of seizing Gaza and driving the Central Powers' forces out of the region. Nonetheless, with additional resources garnered and delivered by the new British Prime Minister, David Lloyd George, London was soon able to generate new life into the EEF, including a change in leadership. Following Murray's unsuccessful attempts at seizing Gaza in the spring of 1917, the British War Cabinet opted to replace him with General Sir Edmund Allenby, known as the "Bloody Bull," who arrived in Egypt in June 1917.

Empowered with new resources and new staff, Allenby set about reinvigorating EEF troop morale before recommencing operations against enemy positions in Sinai and Palestine. Concerned with reports that Britain was preparing to commit additional resources and renewed focus in the Middle Eastern theater, including Mesopotamia and Palestine, at the end of April 1917, Germany dispatched a military delegation headed by General Erich von Falkenhayn to Turkey arriving in May. The initial concern of the German military delegation was the British occupation of Baghdad, and it advised that a new army should be constituted to address this threat. Consequently, the new Seventh Army was established and based in Aleppo to counter British moves in Mesopotamia (Iraq). However, by September 1917, the greater concern was for the Ottoman presence in Gaza and Palestine, as the EEF was making preparations for getting underway. As a result, operations by the Seventh Army against the British in Mesopotamia were cancelled as Falkenhayn advised for a rapid redeployment of the army from Aleppo to Beersheba in Palestine. While the theory was sound, the practical application of the plan proved problematic as the limited Turkish rail network hindered its implementation. As such, very few of the Seventh Army's troops were in position before the British attacked during the Battle of Beersheba (October 31, 1917) and the Third Battle of Gaza (November 1–7, 1917).

Allenby brought a different style of leadership to Egyptian-Palestinian theater of operations than his predecessor. Unlike Murray, who had commanded the EEF from Cairo, Allenby frequently visited front line units and moved the Force's headquarters from Cairo to Rafah nearer to the front lines at Gaza. Allenby also reorganized the Force into a three, primary corps order of battle: XX, XI, and the Desert Mounted Corps. He was also convinced by the Arab Bureau of Britain's Foreign Office to utilize the Arab forces that had risen in revolt against the Ottomans and were then operating within Arabia. A remarkable British army officer detached to the Arab Bureau (British Intelligence), Major T. E. Lawrence, had found considerable success in working with Arab leaders in fomenting irregular operations, which ultimately caused the Ottoman and German leadership to station forces in response—forces which were badly needed elsewhere in the Middle East.

The Ottomans had called for *jihad* against the Entente Cordiale in the fall of 1914 in hopes of rousing support for the defense of the empire. Germany attempted to assist the Ottomans in this endeavor as it sent Kress von Kressenstein to Palestine, Oskar von Niedermayer to Afghanistan, Liman von Sanders to Turkey, and Wilhelm Wassmuss to southern Persia. Wassmuss, often referred to as the "German Lawrence," incited tribes to attack British interests, particularly its Persian oil pipeline, northwest of Ahwaz.

The British government, ever mindful of the power this campaign might have should it be allowed to successfully proliferate, sought the help of the Sharif of Mecca, Emir Abdullah Hussein, in countering the Ottoman call for jihad. The tribe that Hussein led, the Hashemites, was relatively weak, particularly in relation to Ottoman forces. But the alliance with Hussein was much more than a military-oriented alliance. The Hashemites were politically important within the Middle East for a number of reasons, including the fact that Hussein was seen as a descendent of the prophet Muhammad and regarded as the guardian or custodian of the holy cities of Mecca and Medina.

Allenby was facing two defensive lines in Palestine, which were vital to the Ottoman defense of Gaza and Jerusalem. The first included entrenchments that stretched 30 miles from Gaza to Beersheba. The Gaza-Beersheba line was complemented by the Jaffa-Jerusalem line that extended more than 50 miles. Thus, rather than attacking Gaza in frontal assault, as had been the focus of operations by the EEF under Murray, Allenby, the old cavalry officer that he was, sought to maneuver for position through flanking attacks. Thus, he saw the key to taking Gaza would be to first feign a direct attack and draw the forces and attention of the defenders' leaders at Gaza while sending a force in a flanking attack at unsuspecting Ottoman defenders that manned the lines in defense of Beersheba. Once Beersheba was in Allenby's hands, he was then positioned to threaten the left flank of the Ottomans' defensive line protecting its positions within Gaza. Once in such a position, Allenby could then move in three directions against Gaza itself.

Rumors circulated that the British were intent on attacking Gaza once again, but this time the operation would be centered on a naval amphibious landing north of Gaza and then descending down behind defenses. Additionally, British patrols routinely approached Beersheba every couple of weeks, expecting that when the actual attack was commenced, the Ottomans would at first believe it to be another scouting operation. Allenby wrote the following:

> When I took command of the Egyptian Expeditionary Forces at the end of June, 1917, I received instructions to report on the conditions in which offensive operations against the Turkish Army on the Palestine front might be undertaken in the autumn or winter of 1917 . . . The main features of the situation in Palestine were as follows: The Turkish Army in Southern Palestine held a strong position extending from the sea at Gaza, roughly along the Gaza-Beersheba Road to Beersheba. Gaza had been made into a strong modern fortress, heavily entrenched and wired, offering facility for protracted defense . . . I decided to strike the main blow against the left flank of the main Turkish position, Hareira and Sheria. The capture of Beersheba was a necessary preliminary to this operation, in order to secure the water supplies at that place and to give room for the deployment of the attacking force on the high ground to the north and north-west of Beersheba. It was, however, important in order to keep the enemy in doubt up to the last moment as to the real point of attack, and that an attack should also be made on the enemy's right at Gaza in conjunction with the main operations.[8]

The Ottomans had positioned nine infantry divisions and one cavalry division in the line protecting Gaza with a total force level of between 35,000 and 45,000 infantry, 1,500 cavalry, and 500 artillery guns. The British force was divided into three elements: the strike wing consisted of the Desert Mounted Corps, containing the Anzac and Australian Mounted Divisions and the 7th Mounted Brigade and XX Corps, with four infantry divisions and the Imperial Camel Corps Brigade. In total, it was a force of 47,500 infantry, 11,000 cavalry, and 242 guns. On the left of this striking wing was the British XXI Corps, containing three infantry divisions and two brigades for a total of 35,000 infantry, 1,000 cavalry, and 218 guns. Between the two main bodies of the EEF and protecting the gap between them was the Yeomanry Mounted Division consisting of some 5,000 cavalry troopers.

In order to facilitate the deception, an artillery bombardment of Gaza began on October 27, four days before the actual attack at Beersheba was scheduled to occur. The bombardment would last for six days, which included naval gunfire and was the largest artillery barrage of World War I, outside of France. On October 31, the British commenced the actual attack as two infantry divisions moved against the well-entrenched and well-defended southwest defenses of the town. The key to the attack, however, was in the flanking maneuver conducted by the 4th Australian Light Horse led by General W. Grant, who, in dramatic fashion, conducted one of the last successful cavalry attacks in the modern warfare.[9] By November 7, Gaza was under British control.

By November 14, the British took Junction Station, which effectively cut the Ottoman rail line into Palestine. From that point, the 75th Division—the last one formed during the war and consisting of Indian Gurkhas and British personnel from India—captured the road from Jerusalem to Jaffa. The key military geographic objective for the defense of Jerusalem, throughout history, has been the vital hill of Nebi Samwil, which from either defenders' or attackers' perspective was the key to the city. On November 21, the 75th captured Nebi Samwil, which then provided Allenby and the EEF the position from which the city of Jerusalem could be taken.

THE BRITISH AND THEIR ALLIES LIBERATE JERUSALEM

On December 8, 1917, Allenby dispatched the XX Corps for the final assault on Jerusalem. The following day, December 9, the Turkish army withdrew from Jerusalem and 400 years of Ottoman rule had come to an end. On December 11, Allenby made a dramatic and well-photographed entry into Jerusalem, choosing to walk instead of ride into the city through the Jaffa Gate. It was the first time since 1187 CE that Western forces controlled the historic city.

By the fall of 1918, the Ottomans fielded three armies with a total of 34,000 men defending a defensive line from the Eastern Mediterranean coast across the Judean Hills, the Jordan Valley, and to the Hejaz Railway. German General Liman von Sanders had replaced Falkenhayn and was in overall command. Under Allenby in Palestine were 69,000 men (57,000 infantry and 12,000 cavalry). The Turkish front line defenses were 3,000 yards deep, well-constructed, and protected by thin, barbed wire. The second line three miles to the rear was less prepared and consisted of strongpoints but not adequately connected in a consistent defensive line and unprotected by wire.

The Battle of Megiddo, September 19–25, 1918, was the climactic battle of British operations in Egypt and Palestine against German-led Ottoman forces during World War I. The name applied to Allenby's final offensive in Palestine was of course chosen for symbolic purposes, as scant fighting relative to other regions actually occurred in the vicinity of Megiddo. Symbolic, figurative, or literal, Allenby's cavalry did in fact advance past the ancient site of Megiddo, which served as the first battle in recorded history (1457 BCE).

Arrayed in front of Allenby were the Ottoman Eighth, Seventh, and Fourth Armies, with the Eighth nearest the Mediterranean coast, the Seventh in the middle of the Ottoman order of battle, and the Fourth on Allenby's right flank. Allenby's main focus was on the Seventh and Eighth Armies, commanded by Mustafa Kemal Pasha and Jeved Pasha, respectively. Once again, Allenby's ability to keep the enemy from ascertaining his striking plans forced Sanders to defend across the entire front, which left scant few troops in reserve.

By mid-September 1918, Allenby had positioned 35,000 infantry, 9,000 cavalry, and 383 guns on the western fifteen miles of the front line facing 8,000 infantry and 130 guns of the Ottoman Seventh Army. On the remaining 45 miles of the front, the British had 22,000 infantry, 3,000 cavalry, and 157 guns facing 24,000 men and 270 guns of the Eight and Fourth Ottoman Armies. However, 11,000 of those in the Fourth Army were east of the Jordan Valley, which when actual combat began effectively removed them from making effective contributions. Sanders had placed them guarding his left flank knowing that the "Bloody Bull" had a penchant for sweeping flanking maneuvers and often using his swift moving cavalry. Sanders, who had calculated so well in ascertaining British landing intentions during the Gallipoli campaign, now, with limited forces holding weaker positions, was a victim of British deception as to the actual plans of attack.

Allenby's battle plan was for his XXI Corps of five divisions to attack along the Mediterranean coast and force Jeved Pasha's Eighth Army to pull back along the line of the railway north to Tul Keram, followed by a move east to Messudieh Junction. Once this was accomplished, a gap would have been opened up along the coast through which Allenby planned on sending his Desert Mounted Corps. Once past the Ottoman lines it became incumbent upon them to ride north past the Judean Hills and arrive at the Plain of Esdraelon. Their objective was the capture of the Beisan and El Afule, which were key to controlling access to the rail link.

Once in control of Beisan and El Afule, the Desert Mounted Corps would have effectively blocked the escape route via rail for the Seventh and Eighth Ottoman Armies, at which point, the only alternative for retreat open to the Ottoman forces would have been east through the Jordan Valley. XX Corps was assigned the task of advancing parallel to the hills toward Nablus and in blocking the best passes into the Jordan Valley, thereby catching the retreating Ottoman units in a trap.

Allenby benefited from the British Air Corps' ability to maintain air superiority and in keeping German aircraft from conducting scouting missions. In a preliminary operation, the Air Corps dropped ordnance on Ottoman positions in Deraa (city in present-day Syria), which lent weight to Sander's opinion that Allied forces would conduct its main attack inland. Simultaneous to the air raid, Arab insurgent forces—among them T. E. Lawrence—cut the rail lines north, south, and west from Deraa, at which time Sanders transferred additional reserves east to address the rising threat. A second preliminary move occurred when the 53rd Division of XX Corps moved to engage Ottoman units east of the Judean Hills. This attack was to place the 53rd in position to maneuver once the actual main attack opened nearer the Mediterranean coast.

The main attack commenced at 4:30 a.m. on September 19, as Allied artillery opened fire for a brief, 15-minute barrage. The following infantry assault overwhelmed the outnumbered Ottomans in the first line. The 60th Division moving on the left of Allied advance gained 7,000 yards, nearly four miles, in the first two and a half hours shattering the first and second defensive lines and taking control of a bridge over the Nahr el Falik. The control of the bridgehead then allowed the cavalry to move forward.By the end of the first day's operations, XXI Corps had managed to seize most of the railway north of Tul Keram. As the Ottoman Eighth Army was attempting to withdraw through Tul Keram, it was struck from the air and engaged by the rapidly advancing 5th Australian Light Horse as well as the 60th Division, which had pushed forward 17 miles and secured Tul Keram. All cavalry units had met their expected objectives for the first day's operations and reached the outer perimeter of the Plain of Esdraelon and, by 2:30 a.m. on September 20, were advancing into the valley. The key objectives of El Afule and Beisan were captured later on September 20, securing the railroad in each region. Moreover, as the Allied cavalry swiftly advanced, it nearly succeeded in capturing General Sanders who had made his headquarters at Nazareth.

By close of the second day, the Turkish Eighth Army had essentially been destroyed and the Seventh was near collapse. With the railway blocked, its only chance of escape was east from Nablus down a road leading from Wadi Fara into the Jordan Valley. This position, however, was the objective of the Allied XX Corps, which had not enjoyed the same success as other Allied units. Thus, it was not where Allenby planned for it to be on the night of September 20 and morning of September 21, and the Ottomans began a successful evacuation from Nablus. However, they were then stopped by Allied airpower as Allenby's aircraft caught Ottoman forces on the road east of Nablus at a gorge. Bombing soon served to block the Ottoman passage through the gorge, and survivors scattered into the surrounding countryside only to be captured piecemeal in follow-on operations. Advancing Allied forces captured over 1,000 vehicles and 90 guns, which had been abandoned along the road.

Allied forces took 25,000 prisoners during and following the Battle of Megiddo. Less than 10,000 Turkish and German soldiers escaped and made their retreat north. British and Allied forces pressed the advantage and continued the pursuit of the retreating Central Power troops through the month of October. The EEF moved north toward the ancient city of Damascus (in present-day Syria). Sanders had placed Ali Riza Pasha Rehabi, an Arab general serving in the Ottoman army, in command of Damascus. Unbeknownst to Sanders, Ali was also the serving president of the Syrian branch of the Arab Secret Society and had been in contact with T. E. Lawrence.

BRITISH AND ARAB FORCES LIBERATE DAMASCUS

With the Ottoman military position in Palestine, Syria, and Mesopotamia collapsing at late autumn of 1918, the Arab Secret Society seized control in Damascus. On October 1, in a sequence preplanned by the commander of the EEF, the first troops of the Arab Revolt rode into the city followed on October 2 by Allenby's forces. During the month of October, Allied forces under Allenby seized Beirut (present-day Lebanon) on October 8; Tripoli on October 18, and the great trading city of northern Syria, Aleppo, on October 25. On October 30, 1918, with all lands outside of Anatolia (present-day Turkey) essentially lost in terms of the Middle East, Istanbul sued for peace and asked for an armistice. The Battle of Megiddo was certainly one of the best planned and executed British battles of the First World War and most certainly that which followed in the aftermath was historic in scale as Britain and France took positions of prominence across the Middle East in the wake of the collapse of the Ottoman Empire.

CRITICAL THINKING AND ADAPTABILITY IN MODERN WAR

Reforming the Ottoman military had been a pressing issue for successive Sultans for at least two centuries in the early modern era and in the lead-up to the First World War. An entrenched bureaucracy, backed by the powerful Janissaries and elite merchants who were quite content with the Ottoman status quo, successfully hindered the necessary reforms. Yet, the reforms needed for successful military operations in the modern, industrialized world went beyond the need to reorganize army units and train their leaders.

As was the case in many of the battles that took place during World War I, in any theater, battle communications with the front were generally broken in short order. Since nearly no battle plan survives, first contact with the enemy fully intact, those in the front lines are unable to receive new orders or benefit from new intelligence other than what they are generating on their own. Accordingly, while brilliant generals and field marshals construct plans that come from a career of experience and study, the original plan most often needs to be adjusted in the face of enemy action.

If, as was widely the case during the war, those at the front cannot communicate with the brilliance in the rear, they are then left to fend for themselves. It is the ability of these officers and men to adapt, adjust, and overcome. Conversely, it is their *inability* to do so that often factored significantly into the outcome of battle. It was, therefore, the intent of the Ottoman leadership to allow Germany to help develop *Auftragstaktik* at the general officer level and where appropriate, within its mid-level officer ranks. In the drill regulations of the infantry 1888, German commanders were told to tell subordinates *what* to do without insisting on *how* they did it. Due to the increased lethality of modern weapons, it was expected that greater force dispersion would be required. Given this, captains and lieutenants would often find themselves required to direct their units without orders from central command. As such, the nature of the decentralization of the modern battlefield created the necessity of developing initiative, critical thinking, and independent judgment at all levels.[10]

Yet, the ability to think independently, critically, and accurately in the midst of uncertainty, chaos, violence, and danger requires a culture that fosters, over a lifetime, a culture of innovative and courageous behavior. Accordingly, in order to be successful militarily in modern battle-space, traditional and authoritarian societies are faced with a dilemma: continue insisting on a compliant and submissive population producing military leaders incapable of fast and independent thinking or launch societal-wide reforms in the nature of education, socialization, and training, which will empower their commanders and decision makers to adjust quickly and effectively in the heat of modern-era battle.

In essence, the centralized power of the typical autocratic political regime within the Middle East will not simply have to reform in order to create modern democratic societies, rather, and perhaps more importantly, it will have to embrace change in order to defend itself in the modern battle-space. The centralized command structure with initiative and independent thinking suppressed in many of the armies within the modern Middle East will have to be overcome in order to prosecute effective military campaigns in the modern era. The need for military security will require changes in traditional society, which will, in turn, create the conditions leading ultimately toward greater political participation and greater democratization across the region.

This is not to suggest that Ottoman officers, had they been better at operating independently, would have prevailed over Allenby's forces during the campaign in Palestine during the First World War. It does suggest that given the realities of modern warfare, successful military officers will be forced to think in new and different ways and will benefit from being schooled in the science and art of critical and innovative thinking. The plight of the Mamluks in the face of a rising and technically proficient Ottoman army and their subsequent refusal to adapt to new weaponry and doctrine serve to illustrate the gravity of the situation for Middle Eastern cultures as the twenty-first century unfolds. Allenby's Middle East operations were instrumental in driving Ottoman and German forces from the Levant, the liberation of Arab lands from Turkish rule, as well as laying the foundation for the arrival of the Jewish people and the ultimate establishment of the state of Israel. As such, Allenby, the EEF, and the Cairo-based Arab Bureau's contributions to the creation of the modern Middle East are substantial.

MODERN WARFARE AND STRATEGIC ENDURANCE

In order to conduct modern, industrialized warfare at the great power level, the ability to generate and sustain strategic endurance had become, by the First World War, a prerequisite for success. Accordingly, the great powers, particularly Britain, France, Germany, Russia and the Ottoman Empire, maneuvered for control of those elements that contributed to strategic endurance: people, resources, markets, and trade routes. These crucial elements or components of aggregated power and the direction of that power for the obtainment of political objectives were certainly not new or unique to the modern world having animated world politics for centuries. What was new were the nature of energy, electricity, machining, and mass production, coupled with an exponential rise in the levels of lethality, range, and accuracy of rapid fire small arms and large bore artillery.

> Long lasting wars between great power coalitions in the modern age have been won by the side with the largest economic staying power and productive resources. In every economic category, the Anglo-American-French coalition was between two and three times as strong as Germany and Austria-Hungary combined—a fact confirmed by further statistics of the war expenditures of each side between 1914 and 1919: 60.4 billion dollars spent by the German-Austrian alliance as opposed to 114 billion spent by the British Empire, France and the United States together (and 145 billion if Italy and Russia's expenditures are included).[11]

Given the militarization of the various industrialized economies, as well as the mobilization of the entire populations for prolonged periods, the First World War came to be referred to as a "total war."

The militarization of societies, economies, and politics was the consequence. In the end, the war proved a contest of productive capacities; and the Allied victory was due to their material superiority, which by 1918 was insuperable.[12]

In order to form sufficient levels of aggregated power that would lead to a war-winning level of strategic endurance, Britain needed to borrow heavily (particularly from the United States and the banking syndicates in Europe) and was forced to make promises that were eventually difficult to honor. After the defeat of the Ottoman Empire and its Central Powers' allies, the promises that Britain had made in order to cobble together the winning coalition were, by 1919, beginning to color its postwar Middle East policy. Sharif Ali Hussein and his sons, Faisal and Abdullah, called for the promises made during the Hussein-McMahon correspondences to be honored by establishing an independent Arab state and to be placed under Hussein's control.

OTTOMAN SUCCESSION

To be sure, after bearing 500 years of Ottoman Caliphate power, which was aimed in the first centuries of its existences at invading European communities, the British and their closest allies had no intention of allowing the re-creation of a unified entity within the Middle East that was capable of moving, once again, toward the aggregation of power. The Hashemite belief that Britain would, after expending blood and treasure to end Ottoman rule in the Middle East, back the unification of all Arab lands, provide it with complete independence, and place it under their family's control, was, at its core, unrealistic.

Accordingly, the British and the French took steps to partition what remained of the Ottoman Empire, ensuring that each partitioned area and region remained sufficiently constrained and, theoretically, within the control of the victorious Allied powers. Unfortunately, the entire process of political and military administration in the post–World War I era was less than optimal and, given the level of animosity with which Western policies were met by local actors and coalitions of actors, led the areas under British and French control to a general state of anarchy with sustained conflict, rioting, and irregular warfare.

Nonetheless, while regional and local environments were marked with disunity and disarray, the strategic reality of the post–World War I era was that no entity within the Middle East possessed, in combination, sufficient aggregated power, a unifying ideology, and military effectiveness in order to effectively challenge the world system—a system largely constructed by a British-led Western Europe and one that eventually came to be led by the United States after World War II. British and French policies in the Middle East following the close of World War I were, in general, an operational and tactical failure. They were, however, a strategic success in that they removed the challenge that had existed to the West since at least the fifteenth century and one which blocked the overland movement of trade between Europe and Asia.

The process of disaggregation of Ottoman power was operationalized in the partitioning of the empire, most of which took place between October 30, 1918, and November 1, 1922. On October 30, 1918, the Armistice of Mudros brought the First World War to a close in the Middle Eastern theater of operations. Signed by British Admiral Somerset Arthur Gough-Calthorpe and Ottoman Minister of Marine Affairs Rauf Bey aboard HMS *Agamemnon* in Mudros harbor on the Greek island of Lemnos, the agreement granted the victorious Allied powers the right to occupy forts and military installations controlling the Straits of the Dardanelles and the Bosporus and the right to occupy "in the case of disorder," any territory within the empire that Allied commanders and statesmen deemed a threat to overall security. The signing of the armistice was proceeded by the entry of a French brigade into Istanbul on November 13, 1918, which coincided with the arrival of a combined Allied fleet (British, French, Italian, and Greek), with additional ground units embarked aboard ships. Less than two weeks later, Germany signed the armistice with the Entente officially ending hostilities of World War I.

The secret agreements and promises made during the war had been wide-ranging and had involved multiple parties. The discontent with the ultimate solutions to these, at times, overlapping and inconsistent agreements led to a mapping of the modern Middle East that insured, intentionally or not, a flare-up of friction between the various groups within the Ottoman Empire throughout the twentieth century. As early as March 18, 1915, the Constantinople Agreement, between Britain, Russia, and France—which anticipated the eventual breakup of the Ottoman Empire—promised Russia its long-sought goal of control over the Turkish Straits by providing Moscow with postwar control over Istanbul (provided that it remained an open and free port). This also included sizable territory in coastal Thrace and Asia Minor. In return for these concessions, Britain and France were to receive "spheres of influence," as new Middle Eastern political entities were created out of the ashes of the Ottoman Empire. The subsequent failure of the Dardanelles campaign and later collapse of the Russian Empire and its making a separate peace with Germany rendered the agreement invalid, particularly as the new Soviet government declared itself an enemy of all bourgeois capitalist states, with Britain and France featured prominently at the top of the list.

More of a lasting irritant toward a settlement, regarding the end of the First World War and the Ottoman succession, was what continued to undermine cooperation throughout the twentieth century: three highly problematic secret agreements. These were the understandings between the British government and the Sharif of Mecca (Hussein), which were encompassed within the Hussein-McMahon correspondences from July 1915 to March 1916; the Sykes-Picot Agreement between Britain and France in 1916; and the Balfour Declaration of November 2, 1917.

AGREEMENTS BETWEEN BRITAIN AND THE SHARIF OF MECCA

Sir Henry McMahon was the British high commissioner of Cairo (Egypt) and, as the British attempted to prod Hussein and his Arab followers to act in open revolt against the Ottoman Empire at the beginning of World War I, Hussein was as hesitant to be seen serving British imperial interests as he was in continuing in vassal status under the Ottomans. In order to entice the reluctant Hussein, Sharif of Mecca, McMahon, acting on behalf of the British government, pledged to work diligently in establishing an independent Arab state, under Hussein, once the Ottoman Empire had been defeated. The language was vague, however, as to exactly what territory that Arab state would encompass. Since the end of World War I, there have been substantial arguments that the British promised Hussein a unified Arab empire that encompassed Syria, Lebanon, Palestine, Jordan, Iraq, and parts of Saudi Arabia.

However, for Hussein to believe the British were going to fight a global war to end the threat from Germany and take apart a Turkish empire that had threatened Europe for centuries, as well as re-create a Muslim caliphate that would unify all Arabs across the Middle East to potentially face off against Europe once again, was simply unrealistic. Promises that were made in combat, under duress, as the Germans and the Ottomans bore down on British lines in Egypt, may have presented Hussein with a most opportune time to engage Henry McMahon in Cairo (and await a German-Ottoman assault), including a most propitious time to extract concessions in coercive negotiations. Nonetheless, Hussein and his sons Faisal and Abdullah eventually received leadership roles within their own kingdoms created in the new entities that became Iraq and Transjordan.

Part of the ambiguity and resultant difficulty lay with British military officers who served with the Arabs. T. E. Lawrence and Edmund Allenby, among others, sought, if not to insure, at least to promote Arab independence, with the thought that Arab soldiers had earned that right for their people. From an operational and tactical point of view, this was understandable, as several British general officers—in what became known as "liberation statements" as they arrived victorious in Jerusalem and Baghdad—argued any future settlement would have to be made with the consent of the population. This was, after all, the American belief, as President Woodrow Wilson championed the right of national self-determination. The idealism, while admirable, was tempered by empirical reality:

> Poor Wilson, he did not understand that lines which are not defended by bayonet, by force, by honor and dignity, cannot be defended by any other principle . . . Today the nations of the world recognize only one sovereignty: national sovereignty.[13]

SYKES-PICOT AGREEMENT AND THE BALFOUR DECLARATION

Also fanning the flames of the controversy was the secret agreement that the new leaders of Soviet Russia managed to release publicly, following the collapse of the Russian Empire. The Sykes-Picot agreement was made between Britain and France in May 1916, whereby they decided among themselves how the Ottoman Empire's holdings in the Levant, Mesopotamia, and Arabia were to be allocated and how, roughly, new borders should be drawn up. When the Bolsheviks in Moscow released this information to the Arabs following the collapse of the Russian Empire in order to embarrass the Western Allies and drive a wedge between Western and Arab societies, Arab leaders subsequently made entreaties to the Ottoman Empire to negotiate a better deal. As the Russians lost an empire in 1917 while simultaneously Western Europe expanded its influence in Ottoman-dominated territory, Moscow undoubtedly contributed to the conditions rendering Allied-Arab relations difficult and problematic for decades to come.

The third agreement that served to irritate the post-Ottoman Middle East and laid the foundation upon which many of the violent episodes of the twentieth century took place was the Balfour Declaration. The Balfour Declaration was an opportunity for the Zionists to consummate a Jewish political nation-state. From this perspective, ethnic-based nationalism served in establishing and maintaining the power of the centralized nation-state. Since the establishment of an international system based on the secular, sovereign nation-state following the Treaty of Westphalia in 1648 within Europe, international politics and business revolved, in large measure, around the power of the individual state and the alliances it was able to conclude with other states. The Zionists were European Jews, generally, who believed that creating a Jewish-based nation-state would be useful for their interests in politics, business, and security.

A key figure in the Zionist movement was Edmond de Rothschild. Rothschild was head of the richest banking family in Europe and one of, if not *the*, most important individual actors in global finance in 1917. As intelligence reports in 1917 began discussing the possible collapse of the Russian army on the eastern front and with the expectation that once Russia was knocked out of the war, Germany would be free to apply its might in the Western theater of operations, London began reviewing its options. As the war looked to be an extended affair and perhaps a fight to the death for the British Empire, an influx of capital would be needed in order to pay war expenses—particularly since the Americans were demanding up-front payments for the massive amount of supplies being sent to the British and French armies in Europe. The Zionists and their wealthy backers with their quest for a home in the Middle East were a potential and perhaps necessary source of revenue for British and French operations.

After private negotiations were conducted between Rothschild's financial group and Britain, Rothschild demanded that an official communication be generated for purposes of clarification and to avoid any future ambiguity. On November 2, 1917, acting on behalf of the British Crown, Britain's Foreign Secretary Arthur James Balfour wrote a letter to Rothschild, which became known as the Balfour Declaration:

> I have much pleasure in conveying to you on behalf of his majesty's government the following declaration of sympathy with Jewish Zionist aspirations, which has been submitted to and approved by the cabinet. His majesty's government view with favor the establishment in Palestine of a national home for the Jewish people and will use their best endeavors to facilitate the achievement of this object, it clearly being understood that nothing shall be done which may prejudice the civil and religious rights of existing non-Jewish communities in Palestine or the rights and political status enjoyed by Jews in any other country.[14]

PROMISES AND TERRITORIAL DEAL-MAKING

Displeasure erupted among the inhabitants of the Ottoman Empire, as the West attempted to reconcile these overlapping and, in some instances, contradictory promises and agreements. The most effective resistance was formed within Anatolia, as the plans for partition brought entry of foreign occupation troops into a land that had enjoyed elevated status within the Middle East for centuries. Moreover, Soviet involvement replaced Russian Empire's involvement, and as Moscow continued its information campaign to discredit the West and to destroy its post–World War I plans in the Middle East, the British were unable to control both sides of the Turkish Straits as envisioned. This particular British objective was also stymied by postwar partners, as French, Italian, and American high commissioners assumed responsibility for three of the four administrative zones established in Istanbul following November 3, 1918.

Nevertheless, for a brief period following the close of hostilities, the Turks were largely content to cooperate with the Allied powers in hopes that the perceived superior methods of government, science, and social justice that were heralded as Western culture might infuse Turkish life. As administrators and bureaucrats from the West arrived and positioned themselves, what the Turks experienced, in general, was not enlightened management but rather the same type of inefficiencies and corruption that had accompanied the last decades of the Ottoman Empire. The visions of superior administration gave way to the stark reality of empire assets being sold to the highest bidder, largely without regard for the public trust. The exalted position of the Ottoman Sultan was sullied, as citizens began to see Mehmed V (1918–1922) as merely a puppet of the Allied powers. As foreign troops arrived and as dismemberment through partition clearly became the policy focus, Turkish elements began forming units for resistance.

With Allied fleets operating freely in the seas and straits controlling coastal regions, Turkish national resistance elements withdrew into the interior of Anatolia toward what became the capital of modern Turkey: Ankara. Mustafa Kemal, the Ottoman officer who had distinguished himself at Gallipoli, led the Turks from the interior of Anatolia. The *Kuva-yi Milliye* (Turkish National Movement) was formed as the core political organization of the resistance, eventually giving rise to the Grand National Assembly. Backing Kemal and the National Movement in May 1919 were two army corps: XX Corps based in Ankara under Ali Fuat Pasha and XV Corps based in Erzurum under the command of Kazim Karabekir Pasha.

Secret political organizations, such as the *Karakol Cemiyeti* (Sentinel Association), sprang up across Turkey with the intent of joining the resistance. Kemal had exploited his earlier position as the inspector of the Ninth Army Troops Inspectorate, which provided him the task of overseeing the demobilization and disbanding of Ottoman military forces. Instead, he used his position to develop contacts that would later be utilized in fighting Allied intervention and attempts at occupation. Between 1918 and 1923, the Turkish resistance frustrated post–World War I Allied plans and succeeded in forcing the Greeks and Armenians out of Anatolia, while the Italians were never able to establish a presence in Turkey. The Kemal-led forces suppressed the Kurds, who were seeking their own independent state.

After the strategic victory over the Greeks on Sakarya in 1921 (where Kemal was wounded), the National Assembly bestowed upon Kemal the title of "Ghazi" or "Victor," which represented an exalted recognition once applied by the Turkish frontier cavalrymen who had founded the

Ottoman state. Years later, in 1934, after successfully establishing the modern Turkish state, the National Assembly would vote to provide Kemal an additional name-title: "Father Turk" or *Ataturk*. However, as resistance to Allied occupation grew after the close of World War I, London assigned the British Foreign Office to create plans that would neutralize Kemal and his followers' activities. On March 15, 1920, those plans were operationalized, as British troops began arresting members of Kemal's National Movement.

Kemal, who had received extensive education in the West, also studied British strategy during the Arab Revolt against the Ottomans. He devised a multipronged strategy that depended on political coordination, superior intelligence, a well-crafted information campaign, and the combat capabilities of the remaining Ottoman army units now under Kemal's control. The secret organizations now spanning the country provided the platforms for intelligence and propaganda as well as the formation of highly visible protests against occupation forces. Kemal's resistance, insurgency, and informational campaigns following the close of World War I, studied in detail, would likely generate valuable insight into twenty-first-century Middle Eastern insurgency and counterinsurgency (COIN) operations.

Kemal was quite active in his information campaign against not only the Allied occupation but also the government the Allies had installed in Istanbul. The information campaign was coordinated with staging mass meetings in low-profile venues in order to infuse the participants that they were part of an enormous undertaking with widespread support of most of the people. His group pursued two separate but complementary lines of communication in the information war: the first was directed at the citizens of the defeated Ottoman Empire, which argued that the Sultan and his government were puppets of the Western occupiers and that to resist him was to resist foreign occupation. The second message was aimed at the wider Islamic world, which argued that he and his forces were defending the true caliphate from Western aggression.

As a result, Kemal redirected the effective battle cry of the Arab Revolt, inspired by Lawrence and Hussein, for freedom from the Ottoman Turks to a reframed narrative that had him fighting the noble fight for "God" and the caliphate against the infidels. The Soviets' disclosure of the secret Sykes-Picot agreement in 1916 between Britain and France was an extremely poignant propaganda instrument in the hands of every group across the Middle East that sought to resist what had become framed as Western and Christian aggression against the virtuous and innocent Ottoman Empire. And, when the Balfour Declaration became widely known, the Western and Christian aggressors were then tied into the underhanded manipulations of the Jews of the world intent on stealing

Arab and Muslim land. It was indeed a powerful message crafted and delivered with precision, and now, coupled with modern communication devices such as the telegraph and modern print media, Kemal was enabled to orchestrate an effective information campaign that had the military backing of Ottoman armed units, many of which had exited the war completely intact. The telegraph was also invaluable to Kemal in terms of coordinating irregular and regular military operations across Turkey.

While the Armistice of Mudros in November 1918 had technically ended hostilities in the Middle East during World War I, the final details regarding the postwar settlement were to be decided in the follow-on discussions and formalized in a peace treaty. Unfortunately for the prospects of lasting peace, the agreement that was cobbled together, the Treaty of Sevres, on August 10, 1920, was rejected by the Turks. The Treaty of Sevres was signed by the Allied powers and representatives of the Ottoman government, which by the time of signing was nothing more than a diplomatic ghost. In the treaty, Turkey gave up all of its non-Arab provinces as well as parts of Anatolia. Simultaneous secret agreements among the Allies essentially created a blueprint for the carving up of much of what remained of the Ottoman Empire's holdings in Anatolia between the Greeks, French, and Armenians. The Dardanelles, Bosporus, and Istanbul would be part of an internationally administered region. The treaty never came into effect and, as the Kemalist revolt unfolded, it was disavowed by the Turks and fell by the wayside.

The French army occupied parts of Anatolia from 1919 to 1921, including key railways and communication links, coal mines, and the Black Sea ports of Zonguldak and Karadeniz Eregli, as well as within the occupation zones in Istanbul. France eventually withdrew from all these areas after the Accord of Ankara, the Armistice of Mudanya, the Treaty of Ankara, and the successor to the Treaty of Sevres—the Treaty of Lausanne.

At the close of the Great War, or World War I, as history soon redesigned it after the close of the Second Great War in 1945, the Egyptians were chafing against the British presence. During the Egyptian Revolution of 1919, violence was sparked by the forced exile of revolutionary leader Saad Zaghlul. Ultimate authority within Egypt at the end of World War I rested with the British Consul-General backed by the British army. Nonetheless, nationalist fervor, once limited to discussions among the nation's elite and educated circles, had, by the end of the First World War, spread to all segments of Egyptian society. With American President Woodrow Wilson championing freedom and self-determination in his "Fourteen Points," audiences across Egypt prepared for and demanded self-government.[15]

The British, who immediately began bringing troops home after the close of World War I, were not in a position either politically or financially to support the national aspirations of the region's people. America, which had only a token military presence in the Middle East, was not in a position politically or militarily to positively influence any democratization project in the postwar era. The idealistic calls demanding self-determination and democracy were admirable in the abstract, but empirically, and without concrete plans and necessary resources allocated for the establishment of rational means in achieving self-government, the effort soon devolved into a crisis of strategy, that is, the failure to align ends with means.

In the 1920s, as factions across Persia, including the Azadistan movement and Jangali movement, arose in the vacuum of central power, Reza Khan took his 3,500-man strong Persian Cossack Brigade to Tehran and seized the capital in 1921. Building the brigade to about 8,000 men, Reza conducted operations against various factions across Persia, including dissident movements in Tabriz, Mashad, and the Jangalis in Gilan and Simko. The Kurds were also targeted. The brigade was merged with the gendarmerie to form the core of the new Iranian army, which by the late 1920s approached 40,000 troops. This force allowed Reza Khan to remove the Shah, consolidate hold over Persia, and in proclaiming himself the new Shah. He established the Pahlavi dynasty, and Reza Khan took the name and title of Reza Shah. His son, the Shah of Iran, would be deposed by the arrival of the Iranian Revolution in 1979, marking the end of the monarchy and the installation of Shia Islamic theocracy.

With oil discovered in Persia in 1908 by an Englishman, Britain had taken extraordinary steps to secure its access to the reserves. The Anglo-Russian agreement in 1907 attempted to compromise on the long-standing disputes between the two empires in terms of Central and South Asia. As the Czarist and Ottoman regimes collapsed as a result of the First World War, Britain found itself, as it did across most of the Middle East at the end of the First World War, in a reasonably strong military position within Persia. The British Foreign Office attempted to capitalize on what Curzon had stated was an opportunity "to create a chain of vassal states stretching from the Mediterranean to the Pamirs and protecting not the Indian frontiers merely, but our communications with our further empire."[16] The difficulty in controlling factions across the Middle East and into Persia became increasingly acute, as Britain proceeded to reduce its military presence in the aftermath of World War I.

The Anglo-Persian Agreement of 1919 was aimed at providing Britain with substantial control within Persia, aimed at providing London with a controlling interest in that country's financial and military affairs. However, the nature of the negotiations and what had been agreed to become widely known, particularly that three Persians, the prime minister, the minister of finance, and the minister of foreign affairs, had all been bribed by the British. As the Bolsheviks took over in Russia, they announced good intentions toward Persia, swore off imperial ambitions, and roundly criticized the British. They then invaded Azerbaijan and northern Persia and provided support for Reza Shah who, after staging a coup, signed a Treaty of Friendship with Soviet Russia on February 26, 1921, followed by the denouncement of the Anglo-Persian Agreement of 1919.

THE IMPACT OF OIL

While oil was first discovered in Persia on May 26, 1908, it was not until 1925 that oil was discovered within Arab lands. Northern Iraq had been of strong interest for the Western geologists and petroleum engineers, particularly for the British, as they believed the region surrounding the city of Mosul held promise for sizable and recoverable petroleum reserves. The first recoverable oil discovered on Arab land was drilled in Kirkuk in 1925 about 100 miles southeast of Mosul (present-day northern Iraq). It would not be until 1938 that the first oil well was drilled in Saudi Arabia. There, near the city of Dammam on March 3, 1938, American engineers tapped the first commercially viable oil well after 15 months of drilling.

The enormous levels of petroleum reserves in Saudi Arabia eventually led to the kingdom becoming the most important oil-producing state in the world, particularly later as it surpassed the United States in production and as a series of oil price increases related to political events unsettled world markets beginning in the second half of the twentieth century. In addition to holding the world's largest petroleum reserves, the Kingdom of Saudi Arabia, strategically located in the Persian Gulf, is geographically a massive entity. The kingdom underwent two centuries of tribal wars in the unification of lands that, in the contemporary era, consists of 865,000 square miles—more than three times the size of Texas.

While the Arab provinces of the Ottoman Empire were largely created as proto-modern states with borders demarcated by the British Empire in consultation with various states and actors, much of the landscape was forged by factional infighting as various tribes and groups attempted to the fill the vacuum created by the collapse of the Ottoman Empire. While the Europeans were attempting to build modern, secular representative democracies, forces within Arabia beginning in the eighteenth century were attempting to resurrect the political, social, and religious environment of the seventh through tenth centuries. Neither agenda, the Western modernization and democratization project, nor the attempts at resurrecting the authoritarian Islamist religious past has, as of the early twenty-first century, met with lasting success.

In 1902, Abdul Aziz ibn Saud began operations aimed at taking back the territory lost in the nineteenth century to Ottoman-Egyptian forces. Sufficiently strengthened, Aziz was able to negotiate a settlement with the Ottomans and became their vassal in the Nejd. During World War I, as the British, the Sharif of Mecca, Hussein, and the Hashemite tribe were pushing the Ottomans back, Saudi forces remained largely out of the fight. After the war, the Saudis challenged Hussein and the Hashemites and took the Hejaz from Hussein, capturing Mecca in 1924 and Medina in 1925. Aziz renamed his realm the Kingdom of Saudi Arabia in 1932, and "Wahhabism" became ensconced as a state-sponsored and state-protected ideology in the twentieth century—within one of the wealthiest and most important energy suppliers, and, in one of the most critical regions in the world.[17] With trillions of dollars in oil revenue since 1938, this state ideology of Saudi Arabia has taken on a transnational life of its own and across the globe in the form of religious schools known as madrassas, in numerous governments such as Pakistan and in the multitude of "religious" fighters such as al-Qaeda, the Taliban, and the Islamic State of Iraq and the Levant (ISIL or ISIS).

THE IKHWAN: MEDIEVAL WARRIORS IN TWENTIETH-CENTURY ARABIA

Once in power and with a growing list of international customers, including the United States, the Saudi leadership sought to moderate its official position regarding armed and violent jihad and attacking, plundering, and, undermining their neighbors based on religious justification. This dilemma is illustrated in the case of the Ikhwan tribe. The Ikhwan brotherhood had become muwahhidun (Wahhabis) who had organized themselves into "Hujjar" or agricultural settlements geared for war. These fierce and highly skilled warriors provided the Saud-Wahhabi army with effective shock troops, as they conducted a campaign of conquest across the Arabian Peninsula, or conversely, dependent upon one's personal point of view, religious unification of the prophet's homeland in the modern era. In the post–World War I environment, the Ikwhan continued their nineteenth-century raids attacking Transjordan and the Hejaz in a series of actions between 1922 and 1924.

Since Ibn Saud sought the conquest of the Hejaz, which was then under his rival Hussein, the attacks by the Ikhwan on the Hashemites served Saud's purpose. However, following the Saud's conquest of the Hejaz in December 1925, he began attempts at reigning in the Ikhwan.

Nevertheless, Ikhwan leaders wanted to continue the expansion of Wahhabism into British spheres of interest, including Transjordan, Iraq, and Kuwait. Faisal al-Dawish of the Mutair tribe and Sultan bin Bajad of the Otaiba tribe, de facto leaders of the Ikhwan, complained that Ibn Saud had grown complacent and questioned his devotion to the muwahhidun cause and were angry with him for calling for the moderation of the raiding and plundering, which had brought wealth, prestige, and power.

As a result of the attempts by the Saudis to decrease the level of violence and attacks on neighbors, a rebellion involving the Ikhwan erupted, and they proceeded to conduct operations against settlements in Iraq and Kuwait. While the Ikhwan insisted that all infidels (non-Muslims) and misinformed believers (generally Shia Muslims) were legitimate military targets, the Saudis recognized that this perspective would eventually lead them into direct confrontation with the British. Thus, the Saudis began suppression operations against the Ikhwan with decisive action occurring during the Battle of Sibilla (March 29–31, 1929), marking the last major battle of camel raiders in Arabia.

Similar to the warrior spirit of the Mamluks aligning in challenge to the Ottomans, the Ikhwan aligned in challenge to the Saudis. The expectations of the Mamluks and the Ikhwan were also similar. For thousands of years disputes had been ultimately settled by a champion or a group of warriors aligning on the field of battle against an opponent or opponents in order to display their superiority in a physical confrontation. "To the victor, goes the spoils," was the defining, decisive, and operative concept.

This duel "writ large" was meant to be a contest of courage and physical as well as moral strength to determine the worthiness of the two combatants or the two combatant armies—a decision that would measure both the relative worthiness to prevail and in providing clear and unambiguous evidence of the strength to rule over a specific territory, a territory containing people, resources, markets, and trade routes. This twentieth-century battle between the Saudis and the Ikhwan was not completely dissimilar from the plight of the great warrior tribe of the Mamluks, first in facing the Ottoman Janissary arquebus (early gunpowder weapon) with sword and bow during the Ottoman-Mamluk War (1516–1516) and, then, when facing French muskets under the command of Napoleon Bonaparte in 1798.

A commitment to the old ways of fighting, a commitment to earlier tradition—of muscle and sword and of horse and bow—animated the behavior of the Mamluks as well as the Ikwhan. Both groups were brave, but both eventually paying an enormous price for insisting on fighting a battle without regard to the nature of evolution, of change, and, of technological and doctrinal innovation. At the Battle of Sibilla on March 29, 1929, the Saudis attacked first into the defensive battle array of the Ikhwan, followed by a feigned disorderly withdrawal. Sensing opportunity and seizing the initiative, the Ikhwan quickly launched an attack. However, as the Ikhwan moved in for the kill, Saudi warriors previously and discreetly positioned, opened up with British-supplied automatic weapons, and crushed the Ikhwan counterattack.

The Battle of Sibilla, the last of the great Bedouin battles, was the first time the Ikhwan had lost a major military engagement. Several other skirmishes took place between the forces of Ibn Saud and the Ikhwan throughout 1929 but none on the scale of Sibilla. By January 1930, the rebel leaders had been slain or imprisoned with the remaining Ikhwan warriors given the opportunity of joining the king's army. As a result, many were incorporated into regular Saudi units.

When Sharif Hussein was driven out of the Hejaz by the Saudi army in 1925, the British provided safe passage out of Arabia aboard an English vessel transporting him to Cyprus. Although Saud had not actively joined in the Arab Revolt during World War I, he was the recipient of a British subsidy beginning in 1916. With Hussein forced out of Arabia, the British made entreaties to Saud and proceeded to improve the relationship. In 1927, London, accepting reality, signed a treaty with him that recognized his control over the Hejaz as well as his leadership in Arabia.

To reward the contributions during the Arab Revolt against the Ottoman Empire as well as serving in constraining Saud's power, the British set up monarchies for the offspring of their former ally, Sharif Hussein bin Ali of Mecca. Since the French had treated Hussein's son, Faisal, rather brusquely in Syria, the British determined that he should sit on the throne in a newly created entity in Mesopotamia, which was called Iraq. The British also partitioned a portion of Palestine that lay east of the Jordan River, splitting it off from the land between the Jordan and the Mediterranean Sea (present-day Gaza, West Bank, and Israel). There they installed Faisal's brother, Abdullah, on the throne of what was called Transjordan. Since Transjordan was now detached from the Mandate that was called "Palestine," the British government insisted that this territory, which came to be called Jordan, was not to be subject to the Zionist project or Jewish migration.

While the British can be criticized for making extensive and at times conflicting promises during World War I, the commitment to Hussein, his family, and his tribe for fighting in the Arab Revolt was reasonably steadfast and not without considerable reward. However, two groups that found themselves left out of the newly created borders and proto-modern states were the Armenians and the Kurds. In order to placate the Turks and create an environment for moving forward in the postwar era, lands in Anatolia that were promised to the Armenians and the Kurds were never delivered. Both the British and the French had attempted to convince the United States to accept a mandate within Anatolia for the Armenian people. While President Wilson was open to the idea, the U.S. Congress refused to back it, just as it had refused to back the establishment of the League of Nations.

France had traditional ties with a portion of Syria, which was home to a Christian group, the Maronites, and had for centuries aided the Maronites in developing a network of schools, churches, factories, and trading posts. Once the Ottoman yoke had been dispensed with, this group sought to achieve a degree of autonomy that was now becoming politically possible. Toward these goals, Lebanese nationalists persuaded the Allies at the Congress of Versailles, the 1919 conference held to institute peace accords following the conclusion of World War I, to create a state centered on Mount Lebanon's Christian community, which came to be referred to as Greater Lebanon.

In terms of the 1920 British Mandate for Palestine, in 1914 there were about 700,000 people of which approximately 615,000 were Arab and about 85,000 were Jews, many of the latter having arrived in the Palestine area in the late nineteenth century and following the formal establishment of the Zionist organization in 1897 under Theodor Herzl. These figures would rise to a total population of 960,000 (806,400 Arab and153,600 Jewish) in 1929 and to a total population of 1,336,000 (961,920 Arab and 374,080 Jewish) in 1936.

The objective of the Zionists was "to create for the Jewish people a publicly, legally assured home in Palestine." At the Paris Peace Conference in 1919, Zionist and Arab representatives conducted discussions regarding the postwar settlement in the Middle East. The Zionist delegation was led by Chaim Weizmann, and the Arabs were led by Emir Faisal (Faisal I ibn Hussein). Faisal, Hussein's son, agreed to the establishment of a Jewish home in Palestine with a very important condition: that he be placed on the throne of Syria as well. Instead, Syria was given to the French under the auspices of a League of Nation's mandate, and Faisal withdrew his support for the Zionist project in Palestine.

While Jewish population in Palestine had doubled since the start of World War I, by 1929, this was cause for riots within the Arab community. Jewish settlers owned about 4 percent of the land in Palestine and about 14 percent of all agricultural land at a time when most of Palestine was rural and its economy and social structure were agriculture-based. Thus, Arabs began questioning how the Jews had acquired their land. Absentee landlords owned much of the land in the various villages in which the Arab Palestinians had lived. Jewish Zionists had purchased the land from these absentee landlords (who were mostly Arab) and proceeded to evict the Arab inhabitants from homes and villages where the Arabs had lived for generations.

Arab farmers who had tilled the soil for generations were removed from the land, and many headed to the cities to find work. There, they found that many industries had been bought by Jewish investors and businessmen, and many had policies of not hiring Arabs. Without income or job prospects, thousands of Palestinian Arabs ended up in refugee camps, where intense animosity arose toward the Jews. These camps became a breeding ground for fedayeen fighters (fedayeen, meaning "one who sacrifices himself"). As Arab unemployment drastically increased, so too did the violence directed at the Jewish people in Palestine.

Only in the aftermath of World War I and the Paris Peace Conference did the name "Palestine" apply to a clearly defined territory, and through the League of Nations it became the British Mandate for Palestine. When the Palestinian Arabs rioted in April 1920 and again in May 1921, it was the British government that was responsible for order in the Mandate. Accordingly, the rioting brought a strong reaction from British authorities, who tried to suppress the riots by bombarding villages from the air coupled with negotiations with noteworthy Arab Palestinians. This resulted in political concessions for the Arab population and in turn irritated the Zionist leaders. Eventually, underground Jewish groups engaged in violence that was directed at the more extreme Palestinian groups. The Zionist groups also conducted attacks against the British who attempted to maintain order in Palestine and who began slowing the rate of Jewish immigration into the Mandate.

In the following year, the United States issued the joint resolution of Congress, which gave formal U.S. acknowledgment to the ideal of a Jewish national home. The argument between the moderate Jews and the moderate Arabs focused on the scope in terms of the meaning of the Balfour Declaration (1917).

> The proper interpretation of a "National Home" for the Jews, as stated in the Balfour Declaration, according to Faisal, would be to provide for Jewish refugees a safe haven and shelter in Palestine, but not an independent and "purely Jewish government," which would result in dispossessing the Arab majority. Furthermore, Faisal's advice to the British government was to put pressure on the Zionist movement to accept this minimal interpretation.[18]

The Jewish position was an expansive rendering of the Balfour Declaration and one that argued under the terms of the Mandate that Britain's principal obligation was to facilitate the Balfour Declaration, pledging the "establishment of a national home for the Jewish people" and having no territorial restrictions whatsoever—neither east nor west of the Jordan River were to be placed on the Jewish national home. Of course, Britain maintained the partition of Palestine east of the river (Transjordan) was not subject to Jewish immigration vis-à-vis the Balfour Declaration. The operative parts of the Balfour Declaration read as follows:

His Majesty's Government view with favor the establishment in Palestine of a national home for the Jewish people, and will use their best endeavors to facilitate the achievement of this object, it being clearly understood that nothing shall be done which may prejudice the civil and religious rights of existing non-Jewish communities in Palestine, or the rights and political status enjoyed by the Jews in any other country.

Forcing people who had lived on the land for generations to depart through an eviction process and creating conditions that drove them into refugee camps would probably not meet the expectations of the British government that "nothing shall be done which may prejudice the civil and religious rights of existing non-Jewish communities in Palestine." Nonetheless, the fact remained that Arab Palestinians had lived under Ottoman rule for centuries and had never possessed a state that was called Palestine. In fact, Arabs had invaded the lands of the Eastern Mediterranean in the seventh century, killing inhabitants and reducing villages to ashes while simultaneously advancing the proposition that it was God's will that they should do so. Similarly, the Jews had marched on Jericho centuries prior to the Muslim invasions of the Middle East and North Africa and attributed their right to kill every inhabitant in Jericho and to "take all the gold and silver for the Lord's treasury" as divine will. At a minimum, both Arab and Jewish claims of seizing property and killing the inhabitants as being legitimate behavior because it is God's will to do so deserves, at the very least, closer scrutiny.

By 1929, Arab assaults on Jewish individuals and interests had reached new levels of violence, and underground Jewish groups responded in kind. In 1936, a general strike took place among the Arab workers in Palestine, and the situation had essentially turned into stalemate, violence, and anarchy. British authorities, now under fire from both the Arabs and the Jews, directed that an independent commission review the situation and make recommendations for the future of the Palestinian Mandate. In 1936, the British Peel Commission concluded that Arab-Jewish coexistence was impossible and recommended partitioning Palestine into Jewish and Arab areas. The Jews accepted this conclusion, while the Arabs did not. From 1936 to 1939, Palestinian Arabs were in open revolt against both the Jews and the British.

EXTREMIST GROUPS CHANNEL DISCONTENTMENT BY BOTH ARAB AND JEW

Although the British had consulted with noteworthy Arabs as they worked on the creation of the Mandate, scant attention was paid to the opinions of the average inhabitant. In its ongoing discussions with the leaders of the Arab Revolt during the war, London conducted discussions with Faisal and received his support for the Jewish national home construct in Palestine. However, Faisal informed the British that his acquiescence was contingent on his placement on the throne of the new Kingdom of Syria. Once the British opted to abdicate in favor of French control in Syria (Sykes-Picot agreement), Faisal withdrew his support for the Zionist project in Palestine.

As the French subsequently drove Faisal out of Syria, Faisal's brother announced his intention of marching on Damascus to remove the French and reinstall the Hashemite monarchy to "their kingdom." Abdullah at the head of an army of 2,000 moved toward what became Transjordan, and the British representative Sir Alec Kirkbride, with only 50 policemen at his service, inquired of his chain of command as to what action should be taken. The British high commissioner in Palestine, Herbert Samuel, told Kirkbride that it was unlikely that Abdullah would actually enter any areas under British control with a large force without first receiving authorization.

However, by March 21, 1921, Abdullah occupied the eastern area (east of the Jordan River) of Palestine. From the San Remo conference on April 25, 1920, where the principal Allied powers agreed to allocate territories of the Ottoman Empire into the three mandates of Iraq, Transjordan, and Palestine under British control to the establishment of the state of Israel in the post–World War II era, the Arabs objected to any agreement or attempted compromise regarding the presence of large numbers of Jewish immigrants in Palestine or in the establishment of a Jewish national home.

The case of Abd al-Rahim al-Hajj Muhammad serves to illustrate the predicament of many Arabs in the post–World War I era and the nature of their reaction to the influx of Western and Zionist influence. Prior to World War I, al-Hajj Muhammad worked in the fields of Palestine alongside his father and occasionally traveled with him throughout the region in the sales and marketing of their produce. He came to understand the concerns of others while simultaneously developing a network of contacts. When war broke out in 1914, he was conscripted into the Ottoman army and served in Beirut and Tripoli. His father passed away while he served in the military. After returning home, following the defeat of the Ottomans by the Western Allies, al-Hajj Muhammad already displeased with a world seemingly bent on its own destruction and at the hands of great powers and powerful individuals became further alienated by what he saw as coercive British policies in suppressing unrest and rioting within Palestine. His agricultural business eventually went bankrupt following the adoption of the Mandate of new economic policies, which in part imported wheat and other agricultural products at cheaper prices than that charged by the local farmers.

Later, during the 1930s, al-Hajj Muhammad established a base outside of Bal'a, near Tulkarm, and began training fighters to resist the British and Jewish agenda in Palestine. His recruits included former Ottoman soldiers as well as Arab Palestinians who believed they had been unjustly treated by the British and the Zionist presence. Under his direction, fighters launched attacks on British security personnel and on Jewish settlements. A key target for al-Hajj Muhammad were Zionist agricultural interests in Palestine, which included the orange orchards of the newly established Jewish settlements in the Wadi al-Hawarith west of Tulkarm. From his perspective, he directed attacks against Jewish targets that had taken over in the wake of World War I traditional areas of Arab and Muslim influence and against the security apparatus which supported them, including British security forces.

Even before the Palestine Mandate went into effect in September 1923, Arab leaders began organizing in order to resist the plan, and riots broke out in 1920 and 1921, causing the British to try to clarify the arrangement and to more carefully define what was meant by a "Jewish National Home." Arab leaders intent on keeping Western interests out of Palestine had circulated the story that the British and the Zionists would eventually install a Jewish-ruled regime that would take control of all that was in Palestine. Thus, the Churchill White Paper of 1922 attempted to clarify what was meant in the phrase "Jewish National Home." Rather than a ruling regime running rough shod over the Arabs in Palestine, the White Paper argued that "national home" was meant to create a culturally autonomous Jewish community and not to indicate that all Arabs in Palestine would now be coerced into living under Zionist rule. The envisioned plan was to create a binational but unitary Palestinian state in which Jews and Arabs might cooperate.

Within the White Paper there was also a discussion regarding the levels of Jewish immigration into Palestine. There was a segment of the Zionist community that believed "every Jew in the world" had a right to come to Israel and should any choose to do so, apply for citizenship within the nation. This was not what the British or even Rothschild had in mind. The White Paper stressed the concept of "economic absorptive capacity," which proposed that immigration would have to be limited in order to avoid overtaxing the resources of the region. Zionist representatives on the whole accepted the reality of this situation, while the extremists began planning to circumvent British policy. The Arabs, in general, continued to reject any proposal that allowed the Zionists to carve out territory and any proposal that did not grant independence to the Arab population in Palestine.

As the Zionist project in Palestine was met with hostility by the Arab population and as the British attempted to maintain peace and security while mollifying Arab apprehension, the Zionists began constructing security organizations to protect themselves. One of the first was the Haganah, created in 1920 and by 1948 became the foundation upon which the Israel Defense Forces were created. As the Arab Palestinians conducted operations against Jewish agriculture, elements of the early Haganah were created by Zionist leaders to protect Jewish farms and kibbutzim. Following riots in 1929, the Haganah's role was expanded and began taking the shape of a modern military rather than a patchwork of volunteers to stave off attacks on Jewish agricultural interests. Thus, it evolved from a largely untrained militia to an underground army.

In 1931, rejecting many Zionist leaders' attempts at negotiation and moderation (officially known as the policy of *havlagah* or restraint), elements within the Haganah left the organization and formed the Irgun Tsva'i-Leumi (National Military Organization). Within the policy guidelines of the havalagah, fighters had been instructed to only act in defense of communities and not to initiate counterattacks against the Arab fighters. This left the initiative in the hands of the opponent, and the leaders of the Irgun (pronounced "Etzel") refused to acquiesce in the face of deadly attacks from those that Irgun labeled as terrorists.

During the 1936–1939 Arab Revolt in Palestine, Haganah had increased its size to 10,000 regular fighters backed by 40,000 reservists. The British authorities, faced with increasing levels of violence from the Arabs, began closely coordinating security measures with the Haganah, which attempted to suppress the rioting and military operations with FOSH and later, HISH units.[19] The British did not formally recognize Haganah but cooperated with it by forming the Jewish Settlement Police, Jewish Supernumerary Police, and the Special Night Squads. The Special Night Squads were trained and led by Colonel Orde Wingate (British military intelligence), which conducted ambushes against individuals and groups of Arabs participating in the revolt.

Moderate forces on all sides—British, Arab, and Jewish—had to contend with the influence of the more extreme members of their coalitions. For the Muslim Arabs, Izz al-Din al-Qassam exemplified the more radicalized elements within their camp. Al-Qassam was a firebrand cleric who preached against a stagnant Islam in the years preceding World War I. He brought his message of mystical Sufi Islam to the ranks of farmers and local people within the villages and towns and preached the necessity of a revitalized understanding of Islam, which was capable of defending itself from Western colonialism through jihad. He served as a teacher at a Qadri madrassa (Islamic school) and served as the imam of the Ibrahim Ibn Adham Mosque. Al-Qassam's message was that moderation and negotiation were inadequate in achieving the desired ends of pushing the West and the Zionists out of the Middle East and that only resistance through jihad moving in accord with the power of Allah could achieve the aims of the Palestinian Arabs.

Al-Qassam and his militant followers conducted operations against the British as well as the Zionists. His preaching led to the formation, in 1930, of a group known as the Black Hand (*al-Kaff al-Aswad*). By 1935, he had recruited several hundred men and arranged military training for peasants as well as conducted various operations against Zionist and British interests. In November 1935, his group was believed to be responsible for the killing of a British constable, Moshe Rosenfeld, near Ein Harod. British security forces then pursued al-Qassam and his group of about dozen followers and eventually surrounded them in a cave near Ya'bad. There al-Qassam told his followers that it was necessary to die as martyrs, and they engaged the British in a firefight, which resulted in his and three other followers' deaths. Those five that were captured relayed the circumstances of his death, and the story spread like wildfire throughout the Arab Muslim community in Palestine. At his funeral in Haifa, thousands rushed past police forces intent on keeping the event under control. They were unsuccessful in that aim. The funeral of al-Qassam eventually led to the largest political gathering ever to assemble in Palestine with thousands in attendance. This added to the nationalist Palestinian mind-set that defined itself largely in negative terms: no compromise and no negotiations until the Jews are out and Palestinian Arabs are accorded complete independence. In the current era, the military wing of Hamas is named after al-Qassam: the Izz ad-Din al-Qassam Brigades.

As the revolt of 1936–1939 took place, al-Hajj Muhammad had utilized his extensive network of contacts and his understanding of the complex web of clan and tribal politics to build alliances within the middle classes of the major towns, well-educated elite, and clan elders to create a base of support and intelligence in which to conduct resistance operations against the British and the Zionists. In order to avoid detection, al-Hajj Muhammad did not lead a large body of fighters but instead relied on small, semipermanent bands of volunteer fighters, referred to as *fasa'il*, as they moved from one area to another, conducting various operations, usually under the cover of darkness against specific and well-defined targets. Thus, the age-old military strategy of combine-swarm-disperse served the asymmetric operational logic of revolutionary fighters facing a more powerful opponent. For the British and the Zionists, these of course were not independence-minded revolutionaries but rather murderers and terrorists who killed innocent men, women, and children in efforts aimed at discrediting the Western presence in Palestine.

Al-Hajj Muhammad was confirmed as the general commander of the revolt by the Damascus-based Central Committee of National Jihad in Palestine, in February 1939. In the process, he had developed enemies not only in Zionist and British circles but also within the competing Arab factions involved with the revolt. Al-Hajj Muhammad had refused to conduct political assassinations against local Arab leaders—a tactic favored by the al-Husayni family against those who attempted to compete with the al-Husayni family for power. At one point, al-Hajj Muhammad reportedly stated, "I don't work for Husayniya (*Husanyni-ism*), but for wataniya (*nationalism*)."

On March 23, 1939, as he returned to Palestine after receiving the official confirmation as the general commander of the revolt and after traveling with only a handful of aides and bodyguards, his entourage entered the village of Sanur, located between Nablus and Jenin. After being tipped off by unknown sources, a large force of British army soldiers surrounded Sanur. Villagers attempted to convince al-Hajj Muhammad to escape undercover. He refused and went out to confront the surrounding enemy with his small group. After he was killed, the British officer in charge of the operation, Jeffrey Motrin, placed a handkerchief over al-Hajj Muhammad's face in a sign of respect for the fallen rebel. Later Motrin would write, "Abdul Rahim [al-Hajj Muhammad] had a special respect among his people, and among us."

In order to address Arab concerns, a second White Paper was issued in 1939, which severely restricted Jewish immigration and distanced Britain from the original starting point of the Balfour Declaration—that of using its best endeavors for the establishment of a Jewish national home in Palestine—provided that the rights of the inhabitants were not infringed. As a result, the Haganah created the Palmach that began organizing illegal Jewish immigration into Palestine. Over 100,000 Jews were brought into Palestine via a special fleet of approximately 100 ships in 1939–1940. In 1940, as the British attempted to deport 1,800 illegal Jewish immigrants aboard the ocean liner *Patria* to Mauritius, a bomb planted by the Palmach was exploded in order to disable the ship's ability to maneuver; instead the bomb sunk the ship, killing 260.

As war once again engulfed Europe in 1939, Allied interests in securing energy supplies and blocking the Axis powers led by Germany, Italy, and Japan, from Middle Eastern resources, would soon trump concerns regarding the rise of both Jewish and Arab nationalism. Great power competition and global strategic concerns soon drove both Allied and Axis alliance behavior, as loyalty and military effectiveness of Middle Eastern partners soon overrode concerns for effective public administration in a region still mired in the instability and violent factionalism generated by the collapse of Ottoman central power.

Chapter 3

The Second World War

The bravest men can do nothing without guns, the guns can do nothing without plenty of ammunition, and neither guns nor ammunition are of much use in mobile warfare unless there are vehicles with sufficient petrol to haul them around ... In attacking our petrol transport, the British were able to hit us in a part of our machine on whose proper functioning the whole of the rest depended.[1]

—German Field Marshal Erwin Rommel Commanding,
Afrika Korps-Panzer Army Afrika

The Allied Middle Eastern theater of operations during World War II fell within the oversight of the British Middle East Command, established with headquarters in Cairo in June 1939. Egypt and the Suez Canal served as the geographical, strategic, and logistical center of the theater.[2] Additionally, the British Mediterranean fleet was based in Alexandria, Egypt. The area of responsibility (AOR) for the Middle East Command stretched 1,700 miles by 2,000 miles across North Africa and into the Middle East. Upon establishment in 1939, and as global war approached, a primary objective of the command was to coordinate three separate army commands located in Egypt, Sudan, Palestine, and Transjordan. As the war unfolded, the AOR included British Somaliland, Aden, Iraq, and the coasts of the Persian Gulf, with further responsibility being added later for Ethiopia, Eritrea, Libya, and Greece.

The geography of the North African campaign, particularly considering the mostly European-based combatants with their associated overseas allies, meant that nearly all materiel had to arrive by seaborne transport.

This fact provided Britain and its allies an immediate and sustained competitive advantage over Axis military operations in the Middle East and North Africa (MENA). For Axis operations in North Africa, shipments could only be off-loaded at three widely separated ports: Tripoli, Benghazi, and Tobruk, and each of these featured harbors that had limited capacity for handling freighters. Moreover, for much of the North African campaign, Tobruk, originally built-up by Rome, was under Allied control, as it had been taken away from the Italians and held by a stubborn group of mostly Australian soldiers. The logistical reality of limited port access by the Axis powers meant that only a few freighters at a time arrived in port, which, in turn, limited the convoy size and the volume of supplies and materiel delivered. When Germany arrived in force in 1941 and, under Rommel, drove into Egypt from Libya, limited supplies were required to move over vast distances to keep pace with fast-moving armored forces. These vulnerable and lengthy lines of communications and supplies—over open desert—provided Allied airpower with an array of vulnerable targets.

The strategic nature of the geography within the MENA region, serving as the nexus and crossroads of Europe, Asia, and Africa, compelled nations and groups throughout history to maneuver for control of sea and land routes in order to project power and influence. In the modern era, this interaction continued with greater speed, opportunity, and lethality, as the twentieth century brought four new dynamics to the historical contest. Electronic communications and devices drastically altered the conception of time and space, as the world became essentially a smaller place. Railway movement of goods and military power made the control of key rail links vital and in some instances critical to successful campaigns. Petroleum resources, fueling modern industry and military operations, became a modern-era dynamic in the struggle over control within MENA. While Alfred Thayer Mahan had touched upon the usefulness and even necessity of sea power for global influence, and Halford Mackinder illustrated that railroads would help circumvent traditional constraints on rapid movement of ground forces enabling, eventually, a power or group of powers to control the resources of Eurasia, the arrival of the airplane brought a new ability to offset the advantages of both traditional sea and land forces. They created a new dynamic and complex variable to the historical challenge of projecting influence and power over oceans and continents.

Moreover, in addition to the importance of MENA for global communications, secure bases in North Africa were sought for the purpose of providing the staging facilities for the Allied invasion of Axis-occupied Southern Europe, which was envisioned to complement Operation Overlord, the Allied landings in Normandy. Accordingly, Allied forces conducted Operation Torch in 1942 that entailed landings in Morocco and Algeria with the follow-on intent of invading Axis-occupied Europe by moving from secured bases in North Africa into Italy (Operations Husky, Avalanche, and Shingle), which would be complemented by an additional move into southern France during Operation Anvil-Dragoon. These operations would serve to complement the Normandy landings into northern France during Operation Overlord on June 6, 1944.

Since control of the air provided the opportunity (but not the guarantee) to control events on the ground and on the seas, the larger strategic objective for Allied commanders in the MENA region in the beginning years of World War II was to establish secure land-based air fields in which to project airpower across the Mediterranean and into Southern Europe. At the end of successful operations and the defeat of Axis forces in North Africa in May 1943 and in preparation for Operation Overlord, the invasion of Nazi-occupied Europe, Allied command was able to project airpower across the Mediterranean, the Middle East, and onto the European continent.

Initially, Adolf Hitler carefully avoided the mistakes made earlier in the century when Germany directly presented Britain and its allies with a challenge to its sea power. Moreover, he believed that North Africa and the Middle East should also not be afforded the opportunity to siphon off German military power needed for the critical campaign in Eastern Europe, in the form of a showdown with the Bolsheviks. As such, Benito Mussolini's Italy would have to be relied upon to control key bases within North Africa and neutralize and, if possible, destroy the British garrison and naval base in Egypt. Ultimately, however, the Italians under Mussolini were unable to provide Hitler with the needed control, and German troops were eventually siphoned off from European battlefields and sent to Libya to support the Italian army.

As originally conceived, Hitler's strategic objective, once he had subdued the Russians and linked up with Japan in Asia, would be in seizing or influencing the approximately 75 percent of global power as measured in people, resources, markets, and trade routes residing in Eurasia and, then, effectively challenging the British and their allies, should they prove unable or unwilling to peacefully acquiesce to a new reconfiguration of the international status quo. Two developments upset that strategic plan. First, the British were not intimated by Hitler's sudden pact with Joseph Stalin's Soviet Union. In fact, London quickly surprised the Fuhrer with its own sudden pact with Poland. Following these abrupt and startling developments, Hitler's strategic plan over time began slowly unraveling and would eventually condemn Germany, yet again, to a two-front global war.

And, once again, the resources of the United States, safely out of reach of the Luftwaffe, would serve to underwrite Allied strategic endurance and succeed in establishing the vital lifeline that, similar to the First World War, would keep Britain in the war. This was no act of charity on the part of the United States, as American leaders knew Britain and its navy was essential to the defense of the homeland, particularly until their own military, traditionally kept small during peacetime, could be mobilized and prepared to take on the Axis powers.

Within North Africa and the Middle East, operationally, events soon began to take a turn for the worse, as Mussolini, in possession of a massive military presence in terms of manpower, soon found that his army, on its own, was no match for Egyptian-based British and Commonwealth forces. As France reeled from the German assault in the spring of 1940 and, as it neared collapse, Italy declared war on France and Britain on June 10, 1940. Four days later, British forces crossed into Italian-held Libya and captured Fort Capuzzo on June 14, the same day German troops marched into Paris. In the wake of the French surrender, French North Africa (Morocco and Algeria) fell under control of the Vichy French government, which in collaboration with Berlin, essentially became vassals of the Axis powers until liberation in 1944 following the Normandy invasion.

As the summer heat began to subside, Mussolini prepared to move against the British in Egypt and, on September 8, 1940, gave the orders to invade. For the next three years, Axis forces would, alternatively, push east, and the Allies would push back, west. This cycle would continue in a series of advances and retreats, which came to be known in Allied soldier vernacular as the "Benghazi Handicap." Unfortunately, for the Italian forces under Marshal Rodolfo Graziani, the initial push into Egypt in September 1940 would essentially be their only advance of note in North Africa. The battle for control of Egypt was centered in Cyrenaica—a desert region in northeastern Libya just west of Egypt. Since the area was west of the British main bases, ports, and airfields in Egypt, they came to refer to operations in this region as the Western Desert Campaign.

MUSSOLINI ORDERS ITALIAN FORCES TO INVADE EGYPT

On September 13, 1940, 236,000 Italian troops under the command of Graziani invaded Egypt from Libya and quickly advanced about 50 miles to Sidi Barrani where Graziani called a temporary halt in order to establish a defensive perimeter and for consolidating lines of communication before continuing his army's advance. Facing these forces were 50,000 British and Allied troops based in Egypt.

In the fall of 1940, following Graziani's invasion of Egypt, British commanding general of the Middle East Command, Archibald Wavell, prepared for a counterattack against Italian forces. Winston Churchill, faced with dire circumstances on the home front as Germany prepared to assault the British Isles, clamored for action against the Italian invasion of Egypt. Churchill's concerns were strategic, while Wavell's perspective was operational. From an operational level Wavell wanted his troops—many just arriving from across the British Empire—to be better prepared and better supplied than they were at the end of the summer of 1940.

Strategically, Churchill and the War Office in London watched as Wavell fell back in the face of Italian advances in Ethiopia, Eritrea, and into Egypt from Libya. Operationally, Wavell considered his decisions to be consistent with "flexible containment," that is, conserving his forces by buying time in order to build up sufficient capacity to conduct a decisive counteroffensive campaign. In retrospect, Wavell's thinking was sound military judgment. Unfortunately, the exigencies of politics versus cautious and well-reasoned military strategy created friction between the two.

For Churchill, French North Africa to the west of the Egyptian-Libyan theater, now essentially in the hands of the Germans, was only a part of the problem, as neutral Vichy forces in Lebanon and Syria were no longer part of the British-French alliance, which had anchored the northern front of the Middle Eastern theater of war. Churchill was faced with the very real threat that those forces could begin direct military cooperation with German-Italian forces. This presented the possibility of a two-pronged attack against Egypt: from Italian Libya and from advancing Axis forces through Palestine. For Churchill, waiting to see how things turned out was not an option.

The British XIII Corps under Wavell laid the framework for Operation Compass, initially envisioned as a five-day expedition to force the Italians out of Egypt. It was intended to be brief because Wavell needed the 4th Indian Division to later move south to the East African theater and support operations in that region. On December 9, 1940, the first British offensive in the North African theater opened, as the Western Desert Force conducted a 60-mile march across the desert to cut off the Italian Tenth Army. Spearheading the attack was the British 7th Armoured Division, which pushed east, then toward the sea where, in conjunction with a motorized infantry division and a battalion of infantry tanks, they engaged and reduced a series of fortified positions that the Italians had constructed to defend the coastal plain.

The objective of the task force was to engage and dislodge forces then ensconced at the Italian garrison in Sidi Barrani located in western Egypt along the North African coast and about 50 miles east of the Libyan border. The British task force, executing a pincer maneuver against Sidi Barrani forced the surrender of five Italian divisions. From Sidi Barrani,

British commanders opted, given their success, to extend what was anticipated as a five-day raid into a full operational advance against Italian
troops in Libya.

After Operation Compass was launched, Wavell was somewhat aston-
ished about how quickly Italian forces retreated back into Libya.

> Wavell sensed an opportunity to destroy the Italian threat in Libya. The
> British continued to attack with their remaining forces even as the 4th Indian
> Division withdrew for their long trip south (approximately 2000 miles).
> Wavell reinforced the XIII Corps with the inexperienced 6th Australian Divi-
> sion as they arrived in theater. The relentless British pressure resulted in the
> capture of a number of Italian positions and cities in January such as Bardia
> on the 4th, Tobruk on the 23rd, and [the Australians took] Derna on the 30th.
> These successes brought the British thousands of Italian POWs, newly
> acquired territory, and a tremendous logistical problem. Wavell wanted to
> keep the pressure on the Italians here in order to hinder their operations in
> East Africa and the Balkans.[3]

While the individual Italian soldier was as brave as any other on World
War II battlefields, he suffered from deficiencies in training, equipment,
logistics, and leadership. Overall, British North African forces enjoyed
considerable advantages over their Italian counterparts whose significant
numbers could not overcome that which was lacking in overall combat
effectiveness as "... the Italian forces in North Africa had much more in
common with the Ottoman armies of 1917 that with the German armies
of 1940."[4]

It was the success of outnumbered British and Commonwealth forces
in quickly driving back Italian North African forces that brought the theater to Hitler's immediate attention. From a strategic perspective in
Berlin, if the Italians were unable to stand against the British in North
Africa, this may soon portend the arrival of Allied forces in Italy and then
a southern advance into the heart of Europe. Once again, Hitler's original
intent of avoiding war in the West until the East had been secured, and
avoiding the siphoning off German forces from the European theater into
North Africa and the Middle East until he was ready, was altered.
German forces would now have to be redirected to North Africa to support the Italians.

> The success of Operation Compass convinced Adolf Hitler to form a
> custom-tailored antitank division for service with the Italian forces in North
> Africa. With 115 antitank guns and sixty-nine tanks, this Obstacle Formation
> Libya (*Sperrverband Libyen*) was well-suited to the task of catching
> fast-moving tank units in ambushes. Within a few weeks of its arrival in
> Benghazi this curious organization would be joined by the other elements
> of the soon-to-be-famous Afrika Korps. The age of Allenby tactics had
> ended: that of Rommel tactics was about to begin.[5]

ROMMEL TAKES COMMAND

On the same day Benghazi fell to Allied forces (February 6, 1941), German Lieutenant General Rommel was appointed commanding general of the Afrika Korps. On February 7, what remained of the Italian Tenth Army surrendered, and Churchill ordered a halt to the British and Australian advance at El Agheila in order to allow troops to be redirected to defend against the Axis attack against Greece. One week later, on February 14, advance units of the Afrika Korps arrived in Libya and prepared to conduct Operation Sonnenblume against Allied forces in the Western Desert.

Rommel was sent to North Africa in February 1941 with orders from the *Oberkommando der Wehrmacht* (OKW), Hitler's immediate military staff—which later in the war experienced friction with a range of high-ranking officers within the German military—to assume a defensive posture and hold the front line against advancing Allied forces. The German high command wished to see a limited offensive toward Agedabia and Benghazi by May, with the intent for the establishment of conditions whereby Axis forces would be positioned for holding a line between the two cities. Rommel, however, saw things differently. In his estimation, such a line of defense would eventually prove problematic given that this would allow British forces to operate and maneuver in Cyrenaica. Rommel sought to take the initiative to drive Allied forces out of Libya, arguing that this was the best way to defend the Axis position within Libya, or what remained of it after Operation Compass.

Rommel avoided mounting a clearly recognizable offensive campaign and instead ordered units to probe the Allied positions for weaknesses. On March 24, 1941, Rommel sent the 5th Light Division with support from two Italian divisions in search of those weaknesses. His original intent was to await the arrival of the German 15th Panzer Division scheduled to arrive in May before conducting any sizable operations. However, the British had been significantly weakened through troop redeployments, following the success of Operation Compass, as London believed that the situation was under control in Libya and as the Axis powers launched an invasion of Greece (Battle of Greece or *Unternehmen Marita*, i.e., Operation Marita, April 6–30, 1941). Thus, Churchill by making this move weakened British forces, just as the Afrika Korps began probing for an eventual assault.

Weakened by the troop movements to Greece, British forces withdrew in the face of Rommel's probes to Mersa el Brega and began constructing defensive works. Rommel, unwilling to allow the British sufficient time to finish their construction projects, attacked. British General Wavell, overestimating the strength of the Axis forces, ordered a withdrawal from

Benghazi in early April to avoid being trapped by Rommel's thrust. As Rommel engaged the enemy and generated intelligence and insight, he came to the conclusion that the British were doing their best to avoid a decisive fight. Instead of a planned, limited probing action, he decided against waiting, while his army was being reinforced and opted to move immediately to offensive operations across Libya, with the intent of driving the British and Allied forces out of the Cyrenaica region.

Rommel ordered the Italian Ariete Armored Division in pursuit of the retreating British and Commonwealth forces while simultaneously directing the German 5th Light Division to attack Benghazi. The commander of the 5th Light protested the order, arguing that his vehicles were not prepared to commence offensive operations. Rommel is reportedly to have responded, "One cannot permit unique opportunities to slip by for sake of trifles." Rommel, who technically was subordinate to the Italian commander in North Africa—in this instance, General Italo Gariboldi—ignored repeated orders from the Italian to halt immediately. This was not unusual for the man who would become known later in the North African campaign as the Desert Fox. Previously, during the invasion of France, Rommel's 7th Panzer Division became known as the "ghost-phantom division," as most of the time neither the OKW nor members of Rommel's own staff knew where it was.

In short order, Benghazi was seized and Cyrenaica, as far east as Gazala, was in Axis hands by April 8. To the consternation of both the German and Italian high commands, Rommel's forces continued their attacks and by April 11 had encircled the key port of Tobruk on the Mediterranean Sea. Except for the stubborn Allied holdouts within Tobruk itself, Libya was cleared of Allied forces by April 15. Tobruk, with its ability to receive supplies from the sea, refused to fall. The Afrika Korps, conversely, had stretched its supply lines across Libya and were subject to frequent attacks by the British Royal Air Force (RAF). Tobruk was a highly desirable German objective, as without it supply lines would eventually be stretched hundreds of miles and be subjected to constant air interdiction by Allied aircraft.

Wavell made two unsuccessful efforts to relieve the garrison at Tobruk. These were Operation Brevity, launched May 15, 1941, and Operation Battleaxe, commenced on June 15, 1941. During Battleaxe, British Lieutenant General Noel Beresford-Peirse's XIII Corps, consisting of the 7th Armoured Division and the 4th Indian division, attacked Rommel's force made up of the 5th Light Division and recently reinforced by the 15th Panzer Division. Underestimating the strength of Rommel's army, British and Dominion forces nonetheless pushed forward for the relief of Tobruk. Key to the control of the terrain in the vicinity was the Hafid Ridge, Halfaya Pass, and the Italian-held Fort Capuzzo. The 4th Indian

Division swiftly secured Fort Capuzzo and fought off a spirited counterattack. However, the results of operations against Axis positions at Hafid Ridge and Halfaya Pass were less effective.

At both locations, Afrika Korps troops, in order to disguise their positions and lower their vulnerability, had emplaced and dug into the sand 88 millimeter (mm) antitank guns, which were arranged to trap British tanks as they approached. Arrayed in a U-shape, the 88s were not only buried in the sand, but tent fabric had also been placed on top of them. Even with field glasses the antitank gun's firing position looked like a sand dune. Rommel sent out light tanks to fake an assault on British positions, and, when British armor moved in to engage the light tanks, the tanks would feign retreat and lead the pursuing British armored units into the kill-zone trap.

Once British armor entered Halfaya Pass, the Afrika Korps' antitank units opened up with a rain of deadly fire. British troops came to refer to the Pass as "Hellfire Pass," as every tank, minus one, was hit. At Hafid Ridge, the British sought to engage Rommel's tanks; instead they were also met with lethal antitank gun and artillery fire. By noon on June 16, 1941, 75 percent of the 200 British tanks attacking at Hafid Ridge had been destroyed. By the afternoon, the Afrika Korps launched a counteroffensive. The 15th Panzer Division attacked the 4th Indian Division and then held Fort Capuzzo, and the 5th Light Division drove eastward in a flanking maneuver to come up on the British 7th Armoured Division's rear.

General Wavell ordered British Lieutenant General Alan Cunningham to withdraw immediately to avoid being overrun and encircled. With the failure of these efforts and following Battleaxe, Wavell was relieved by General Claude Auchinleck, commander in chief, India, who proceeded to reorganize the Western Desert Force into two strengthened corps, XXX and XII. This newly reconfigured and reinvigorated force was renamed the British Eighth Army and placed under the command of Cunningham.

With an infusion of armor and aircraft, the Eighth Army now had 770 tanks and 1,000 aircraft. Facing this army was Rommel's reinforced Afrika Korps, now under the umbrella of the new Panzer Group Africa, which he commanded. Panzer Group Africa consisted of the 15th Panzer Division, the 5th Light Division (which had been redesignated as the 21st Panzer Division), and the 90th Light Division. Included in Rommel's Panzer Group Africa were the Italian divisions, Ariete and Trieste (forming the Italian XX Motorized Corps), and three Italian infantry divisions. In all, Rommel faced the British Eighth Army with a Panzer Group that included 260 German and 154 Italian tanks.

Cunningham and the British Eighth Army commenced Operation Crusader on November 18, 1941, aimed at forcing a withdrawal of Axis forces and in relieving the siege at Tobruk. Pushing forward with the 7th Armoured Division, the British were successful in relieving the pressure from Axis forces on the Tobruk garrison by November 27. However the British, in contrast to Rommel, opted to send their armor into battle in what amounted to piecemeal fashion, while German doctrine operated on the principle embedded in the phrase: *Kleckern, nicht Klotzen!* or "concentrate, don't disperse."[6] As a result, the cost of the relief of Tobruk was significant, as on November 23, Rommel, aware of his numerical inferiority, launched a concentrated assault after massing his armor. The 21st Panzer Division, under attack from the Crusader offensive, held its defensive positions at Sidi Rezegh, essentially holding the British forces in place, while the 15th Panzer Division and the Italian Ariete attacked the flanks and enveloped the attacking Allied armor units, which were formed up on the British 7th Armoured Division. What ensued was one of the largest and most intense armored battles of the North African campaign, as the forward-moving British tanks of the 7th Armoured Division were surrounded and about two-thirds destroyed. Rommel deployed his tanks as a maneuver arm and rarely against other tanks. Antitank guns were the preferred option, as "tank tactics took the form of luring one's opponent to approach within range of one's own antitank guns."[7]

It was in France in 1940 as advancing elements of Rommel's 7th Armored Division were hit with a counterattack by 70 tanks of two British tank regiments, which drove into German infantry and antitank crews. In desperation, German 88mm flak guns, normally pointed upward for ground-to-air firing at Allied aircraft, were turned on the British tanks, marking the first time the 88s were used on ground targets. It would not be the last.

In North Africa, the 88s became an invaluable weapon against British armor, as did the concept of lightning war. Operationally, lightning war —blitzkrieg—was aimed at crippling an opponent's ability to generate combat power through maneuver and speed in time and space; yet, even more important was the psychological objectives that reflected Prussian General Clausewitz's early eighteenth-century observation that military operations were aimed more at killing the enemy's will to continue fighting than the physical killing of soldiers.[8] Thus the doctrine of blitzkrieg was as much of a psychological tactic as it was precision, maneuver warfare in time and space: seize, keep, and exploit the initiative; force the enemy to react to your movements; keep the enemy off balance; and strike with decisive force at weakness. The best lightning attack is one in which you achieve surprise, ideally penetrating into the enemy rear, suddenly instilling in the opponent that they are not only trapped but also unable to effectively respond to your next move. Thus, placing the commander and his forces on the horns of a dilemma, upon which, they are left with three options: retreat, surrender, or die.

On November 24, 1941, Rommel, sensing opportunity as the initial momentum of Operation Crusader stalled, counterattacked into Egypt and came up on the Allies rear with the objective of cutting supply lines and sending a lightning and foreboding message to the British and Commonwealth troops fighting in Libya that they had suddenly and decisively become trapped.

Rommel, in his response to the offensive drive of Operation Crusader, understood that the direct approach would entail operations aimed at defeating the Allied forces aligned in the vicinity of Tobruk (and Bardia). However, he also understood the limited numbers available to him in regard to such an undertaking. With a bold strike into Egypt and threatening Allied lines of communications and supply, Rommel believed that an attack in the rear would generate the psychological effect that would lead to the conditions undermining Allied troop morale and, as a result, break down the enemy's ability to generate combat power in Libya.

His objectives were achieved, as British field commander Cunningham opted to withdraw the Eighth Army to Egypt. However, upon being informed of this decision for withdrawal, the commander in chief of the Middle East Command and Cunningham's superior, General Auchinleck, arrived at the front from Cairo and canceled Cunningham's withdrawal orders. The effects that Rommel had managed to orchestrate in forcing Cunningham to order a withdrawal had been impressive. However, the reality (quickly grasped by Auchinleck and his staff) was that Rommel, after tangling with the British 7th Armoured Division, had only 100 operational tanks remaining.

As Rommel drove into Egypt, and as the Allied forces regrouped under Auchinleck's direction and began attacking Axis units and Rommel's lines of communication from Egypt to Libya, Rommel's chief of staff, Oberstleutnant Westphal, ordered the 21st Panzer Division to withdraw from movement toward Egypt and support the siege forces then aligned before Tobruk. By December 7, all German forces had retreated to Libya and moved expeditiously in a retrograde direction back to their original starting positions. By December 30, Rommel and Panzer Group Africa had fallen back to El Agheila, and the German-Italian garrison at Bardia surrendered on January 2, 1942. Operation Crusader marked the first victory over German ground forces by British-led forces in the Second World War.

By January 5, 1942, Rommel's forces received 55 additional tanks, and as supplies were being replenished, the Desert Fox and his staff were planning their next moves. The British had taken up strong defensive positions along a line running north to south in Libya, which came to be referred to as the Gazala line, as it extended south from the Mediterranean coastal town of Gazala. Nearest to Gazala and the coast was the 1st South African Division; extending south and in the middle position of the line was the 50th (Northumbrian) Division. Proceeding inland, the southernmost tip of the line was at Bir Hakeim, which was defended by the 1st Free French Brigade led by General Marie-Pierre Koenig.

Positioned eastward and behind the line were the British 1st and 7th Armoured Divisions, which were poised to maneuver and engage as a mobile counterattack force. The 2nd South African Division, then garrisoned at Tobruk, and the 5th Indian Division were held in reserve. Since Rommel had shown a penchant for strategic envelopment, that is, attacking the flanks and the rear of an enemy force, the Gazala line consisted of a series of Allied defensive positions formed into fighting squares or defensive boxes that were designed to enable the forces within them to defend against attack from all sides and angles. The intervals between the boxes were regularly patrolled, and massive minefields were established to limit Rommel's maneuver options.

THE BATTLE OF GAZALA AND THE FALL OF TOBRUK

British deception efforts were constantly being improved in the North African theater, and by the time of the Battle of Gazala (May 26, 1942–June 21, 1942), Rommel's intelligence reporting was inaccurate in its assessment that the Gazala line ended well north of Bir Hakeim. The Desert Fox was also unaware of the arrival of 167 U.S. Grant tanks armed with a 75mm gun and large numbers of 6-pounder antitank weapons.

However, Rommel's preferences for speed, surprise, and sudden shock meant that his own deception operations were extensive. British military intelligence informed Auchinleck in the spring of 1942 that the Axis forces currently arrayed against him totaled about 35,000 troops. The reality was that there were 55,000 German troops and 35,000 Italian troops at the time of the Battle of Gazala and the fall of Tobruk. While the Allies had reinforced their armor for a total of 843 tanks, so had the Germans and Italians, which now, combined, fielded 560 tanks.

On May 26, 1942, Rommel attacked first into the center of the Gazala line, and then in classic blitzkrieg fashion (and indirect approach) his motorized and armored forces attempted to outflank the line's defenses at the southernmost tip. For two days, stubborn Allied resistance inflicted heavy losses on Rommel's forces, while his tanks suffered losses in the 30 percent range. By May 28, he was forced into essentially a defensive posture, as British Commonwealth forces counterattacked with effect. His armored forces had succeeded in moving past the main Gazala line in their sweeping and flanking "right hook" only to find themselves nearly cut off and surrounded by British 1st and 7th Armoured Division elements.

However, three simultaneous events changed the battle: First, the Italian X Corps had successfully pushed through the Gazala line and cleared a path through the minefields, enabling the resupply of Rommel's forward armor units then being pummeled by a withering British counterattack. Next, his armor then linked up with the advancing Italian X Corps and moved to seize the initiative. Finally, on June 2, the German 90th Division reinforced by the Italian Trieste Division effectively surrounded the Allied strongpoint at Bir Hakeim (protecting the British left flank), which fell to the Axis on June 11. The British left had essentially collapsed, while Rommel's forward armored units were operating behind their main line of defense. Following the collapse of their left flank, the center of the British Gazala defensive line was essentially pierced, and Axis troops proceeded to pour through to link up with Rommel's tanks, which were then operating eastward of the Gazala line.

Rommel had learned important lessons when he served as an infantry officer during World War I. He later wrote, "The farther we penetrated into a hostile zone of defenses, the less prepared were the garrisons for our arrival, and the easier the fighting."[9] At the Battle of Gazala, Rommel's intent was to engage and defeat the British 1st and 7th Armoured Divisions, which served as key anchors of the British Eighth Army. By defeating the British Eighth Army, Rommel would be positioned to take Egypt and finish clearing North Africa. Tactically, Rommel's army at the Battle of Gazala led to what British soldiers referred to as the "Gazala Gallup"—a vigorous and lengthy retreat by the Eighth Army.

As Allied troops exited Libya, Rommel's forces approached the Allied garrison at Tobruk. Troops that had held the city for months in the face of earlier Rommel attacks now surrendered the city within 24 hours. The images of German dominance in North Africa had reached a compelling apex, and the Fuhrer made Rommel a field marshal. The reality of the situation was different than the images. Allied soldiers of the Eighth Army had managed to destroy much of Rommel's effective combat power during the Battle of Gazala. However, on June 26, Axis forces pressed into Egypt and encircled the Allied fortress at Mersa Matruh guarded by four Allied divisions. Over a period of 72 hours, three of those divisions managed to escape the encirclement. However, on June 29, the garrison surrendered and the Germans took 6,000 prisoners of war.

Earlier, on June 25, Auchinleck assumed direct control of the Eighth Army and opted to defend against Rommel's entrance into Egypt at a small railway link near the Mediterranean coast referred to as El Alamein. Since Rommel enjoyed wide, arc flanking movements, Auchinleck took up a position near the coast where the sea blocked Rommel from moving around the British right flank. El Alamein—also chosen as the British defenders' left flank—was protected by the massive Qattara Depression, which rendered movement by armored forces virtually impossible. The bill paid by Allied blood at Gazala left Rommel with only 13 operational tanks as he approached El Alamein. He wrote in his diary on July 3 that the momentum achieved by victories at Gazala and Tobruk had "faded away."

MONTGOMERY AND THE BRITISH EIGHTH ARMY CHALLENGE THE DESERT FOX

London, meanwhile, replaced Auchinleck as commander in chief, Middle East, with General Harold Alexander. The Eighth Army was to receive a new commander as well: Lieutenant General William Gott. However, before assuming command, Gott was killed in a plane crash. Subsequently, Lieutenant General Bernard Montgomery was assigned as general officer in command (GOC), British Eighth Army. After receiving resupply from Benghazi and Tripoli, Rommel commenced the attack on August 30, 1942, engaging Allied forces at the Battle of Alam el Halfa. Forced to attack directly into British defenses, hammered by Allied aircraft, and running low on fuel, Rommel withdrew on September 2. Luftwaffe aircraft that had supported the Afrika Korps during the spring of 1942 had been redirected to the Russian front.

The Fliegerkorps II that operated out of Sicily had wreaked havoc on Allied naval and merchant operations, as General Albert Kesselring's air forces provided for an increase in the flow of supplies reaching North Africa. Prior to the arrival of the Fliegerkorps II, 60 percent of Rommel's ordered and desperately needed supplies never made it to the Afrika Korps. With the Luftwaffe now largely absent, Rommel privately stated that without an infusion of airpower, North Africa and Egypt could not be taken and certainly could not be held. Germany's interdicting land-based airpower in the Mediterranean (largely Sicily-based) was forced in the summer of 1942 to fight elsewhere, and Rommel knew that without air support his ground operations were threatened not only from direct attack from tactical air but also in denying him badly needed reinforcements that would necessarily have to be transported across the Mediterranean Sea.

Thus, the obstinate defense by Soviet forces on the eastern front contributed to the conditions that enabled Allied forces in North Africa to seize the opportunity for victory over a very tenacious, modern, motorized, and armored field army, led by one of the most successful military commanders in the history of warfare. And, it was in 1942 that two battles and the commencement of Operation Torch by Anglo-American forces

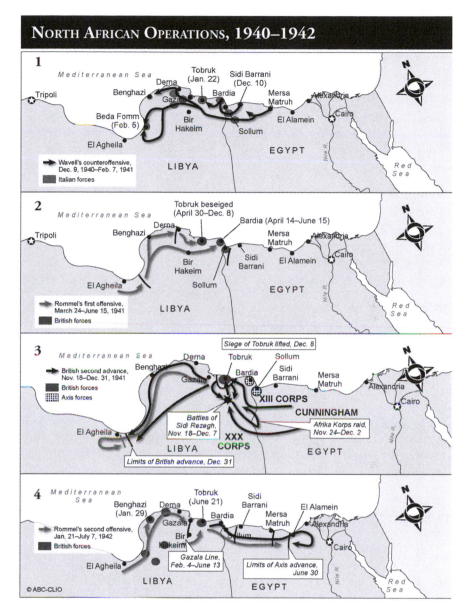

NORTH AFRICAN OPERATIONS, 1940–1942

1

Mediterranean Sea

Tripoli
Benghazi
Derna
Tobruk (Jan. 22)
Sidi Barrani (Dec. 10)
Bardia
Mersa Matruh
Alexandria
Gazala
Beda Fomm (Feb. 5)
Bir Hakeim
Sollum
El Alamein
Cairo
El Agheila
LIBYA
EGYPT
Nile R.
Red Sea

→ Wavell's counteroffensive, Dec. 9, 1940–Feb. 7, 1941
▪ Italian forces

2

Mediterranean Sea

Tobruk beseiged (April 30–Dec. 8)
Bardia (April 14–June 15)
Tripoli
Benghazi
Derna
Mersa Matruh
Alexandria
Bir Hakeim
Sidi Barrani
El Alamein
Cairo
Sollum
El Agheila
LIBYA
EGYPT
Nile R.
Red Sea

→ Rommel's first offensive, March 24–June 15, 1941
▪ British forces

3

Mediterranean Sea

Siege of Tobruk lifted, Dec. 8
Derna
Tobruk
Sollum
Benghazi
Sidi Barrani
Bardia
Mersa Matruh
Alexandria
Gazala
XIII CORPS
CUNNINGHAM
Cairo

→ British second advance, Nov. 18–Dec. 31, 1941
▪ British forces
▦ Axis forces

Battles of Sidi Rezegh, Nov. 18–Dec. 7
Afrika Korps raid, Nov. 24–Dec. 2
El Agheila
XXX CORPS
LIBYA
EGYPT
Nile R.
Limits of British advance, Dec. 31

4

Mediterranean Sea

Tobruk (June 21)
Sidi Barrani
El Alamein
Benghazi (Jan. 29)
Derna
Bardia
Mersa Matruh
Alexandria
Gazala
Bir Hakeim
Sollum
Cairo

→ Rommel's second offensive, Jan. 21–July 7, 1942
▪ British forces

El Agheila
Gazala Line, Feb. 4–June 13
Limits of Axis advance, June 30
LIBYA
EGYPT
Nile R.
Red Sea

© ABC-CLIO

marked the end of Germany's military initiative and a string of military successes enjoyed by Hitler's Third Reich. The two battles were the Battle of Stalingrad and the Second Battle of El Alamein. Operation Torch was the arrival of U.S. ground forces in North Africa to finish the destruction of Axis forces in Africa and prepare a southern axis of approach into

Nazi-occupied Europe, which eventually complemented the arrival of U.S. forces in Normandy on June 6, 1944.

Realizing that without airpower the North African Campaign would soon be lost, and understanding that American troops were preparing to join Allied troops for an invasion of Europe, the OKW transferred Rommel out of Africa to begin planning for continental defense. As a result, when the Second Battle of El Alamein began on October 23, 1942, Rommel had already departed. However, German General Georg Stumme, who had replaced Rommel, died of a heart attack in the early hours of the battle, and Rommel immediately returned to North Africa and retook command.

Under fierce Eighth Army attack, Rommel determined on October 29 that the situation, without German airpower, was essentially hopeless and requested that the German high command allow his forces to withdraw. Hitler personally responded with the infamous "victory or death!" message that, by the fall of 1942 and beginning of 1943, was being sent to more and more commands around the world. Rommel followed orders and stood fast. On November 4, Montgomery, reinforced with 300 Sherman tanks from the United States, ordered his armor to attack. His 500 tanks were met with 20 of Rommel's.

By midday on November 4, the Allied forces encircled the Italian XX Motorized Corps and by the late afternoon had completed its destruction. With the loss of this corps, Rommel now had a 14-mile gap in his defensive line, which the Allies immediately exploited by pouring armored and motorized units into. The Afrika Corps—at the time part of Panzer Army Africa—had two options: retreat or be strategically enveloped. Rommel ordered the army's withdrawal, and on the following day, after it had largely been completed, he received authorization from Hitler to withdraw.

THE AMERICANS ARRIVE DURING OPERATION TORCH

On November 8, 1942, the United States, working closely with Britain through the Combined Chiefs of Staff, launched Operation Torch, aimed at creating bases in French North Africa from which to defeat Axis military forces then operating in the vicinity of the Libyan-Egyptian theater. Operation Torch represented the first major American military undertaking in the African–Middle Eastern region, since U.S. Marines and the U.S. Navy battled the Barbary pirates early in the nineteenth century.[10] The operation, while a joint Anglo-American enterprise, marked the first major U.S.-led offensive operation against the Axis powers during the Second World War.

    While the planning involving the entry of U.S. ground forces against
the Axis powers had been ongoing, the timing of the actual amphibious
operations landing a combined Anglo-American force into French North
Africa was propitious. The German armed forces had just suffered two
of their greatest setbacks at the battles of Stalingrad and El Alamein, and
Hitler and the OKW then received news that the United States had transported its first army divisions into North Africa. The German high
command knew this development would probably be followed by U.S.
forces, combining with Allied troops in moving north across the Mediterranean Sea into Southern Europe.

    Stalin, dictator of the Soviet Union, early in the war, had been pressing
for the United States to open a second front against Germany by landing
in Western Europe to alleviate the enormous pressure Berlin had brought
to bear on the Soviet army, which was then defending on the Russian
front. American commanders were keen to enter the fight, but their counterparts in Britain were more cautious and eventually "slow walked" the
rising enthusiasm and clarion calls for U.S. troops to make a direct
approach into the Nazi-defended Atlantic Wall.[11] This view argued that
American troops would be largely untested with limited training, as they
moved to confront Germany's battle-hardened Wehrmacht, and should
they fail while suffering enormous casualties during the initial campaign,
the downside for morale and the continued commitment by an already
leery U.S. public would be substantial.

    As the British high command had watched firsthand as Germany
exploited in France and North Africa the speed, maneuver, and indirect
approaches into its blitzkrieg doctrine, the question was fairly straightforward: Why attempt a direct approach into the ensconced strength of a
waiting and ready opponent? The more viable strategy, it was argued,
would be to adopt an indirect approach, bypassing the strength of the
Atlantic Wall (the solid) and finding the "gap" that Churchill viewed as
being the southern approach to the continent, which he referred to as
the "soft under-belly of Europe." U.S. President Franklin Roosevelt came
squarely down on the side that argued for an indirect approach, providing U.S. soldiers and their field commanders more time to acclimate to
the realities of a ground war with Nazi Germany.

> On August 14, 1942, I received a directive from the Combined Chiefs of
> Staff. It stated that the President and the Prime Minister had decided that
> combined military operations be directed against Africa as early as practi-
> cable, with a view to gaining, in conjunction with the Allied forces in the
> Middle East, complete control of North Africa, from the Atlantic to the
> Red Sea ... My original directive from the Combined Chiefs of Staff envis-
> aged the attainment to our ultimate objective in three stages: first, the estab-
> lishment of firm and mutually supported lodgments in the area of Oran,

Algiers, and Tunis, on the North Coast, and of Casablanca on the West Coast; second, the use of those lodgments as bases to acquire complete control over all French North Africa, and, if necessary, Spanish Morocco; third, a thrust Eastwards through the Libyan desert, to take the Axis forces in the western desert in the rear and annihilate them. ... The aim was thus to insure communications throughout the Mediterranean, and to facilitate operations at a later date against the Axis on the European continent.[12]

Many U.S. strategists and commanders (including the Soviets) had hoped that a massive invasion aimed at northern France could be accomplished by 1943. Toward this end, three variants with the intent of conducting a massive amphibious operation into northern France were in the planning stages, including Operations Sledgehammer, Roundhammer, and Roundup. Instead, at the Second Claridge Conference held in late July 1942, the decision was made to adopt an indirect approach and to place the first American troops into French North Africa in late 1942 with Operation Torch.

In the early hours of the morning [0500] on 8 November 1942 approximately 90,000 Allied troops, mostly American, disembarked from their landing craft at various points in Vichy French-controlled Morocco and Algeria to begin America's first major offensive of the second world war, Operation Torch. Simultaneously, pro-Allied guerrilla fighters organized by General William J. ("Wild Bill") Donovan's recently formed Office of Strategic Services (OSS) sprang into action to assist invading forces. These men, who had been recruited and armed over the previous three months by OSS agents stationed in Vichy French North Africa, represented part of a new dimension in the field of American second world war military operations, a dimension which, in addition to guerrilla activities, included extensive espionage and intelligence work, especially in the field of assessing enemy motivation, and in the conducting of secret negotiations aimed at creating pro-Allied factions in either enemy or neutral countries.[13]

Operation Torch created three separate task forces: Western, Center, and Eastern, which conducted simultaneous amphibious operations that led to landings at locations near Casablanca, Morocco (Western Task Force—commanded by U.S. Major General George Patton), Oran, Algeria (Center Task Force—commanded by U.S. Major General Lloyd Fredendall), and in the close vicinity of Algiers, Algeria (Eastern Task Force—commanded by U.S. Major General Charles Ryder). The overall objective was to immediately push east and seize the Tunisian port and airfield complex of Bizerte and the capital city of Tunis. Once in possession of those objectives, the Allies would be positioned to conduct aerial bombardment of Axis positions on Sicily, protect Allied seaborne convoys, and attack Rommel's supply lines.

Within 24 hours, on November 9, Germany dispatched troops from Sicily to Tunisia. Realizing that the Allies were attempting to close in against Axis North African forces and place them between two pincers, that is, the British Eighth Army closing in on Rommel from the East, while the Torch invasion group drove in from the West. Axis commanders were attempting to reinforce the region around Bizerte and Tunis to avoid having German and Italian forces driven off the African continent. At the time, Rommel's forces totaled 78,000 troops but were in possession of only 129 tanks, and they succeeded in fortifying their positions in Tunisia before the pincer forces converged on their location.

As was originally expected, the first encounter of U.S. Army forces with Rommel's veterans resulted in defeat for the advancing Americans at the Battle of Kasserine Pass (February 19–24, 1943). After the debacle of Kasserine Pass, command of the U.S. II Corps was given to U.S. Major General George Patton. From that moment on, Montgomery's British forces essentially "elbowed" Patton's forces (and vice versa) for the opportunity to attack the retreating Axis forces. As near certain defeat approached, Rommel was moved out of Africa and installed in Europe to direct the expected amphibious assault into northern France. On May 13, 1943, as the British navy was waiting offshore from Tunisia in strength, and after U.S. and British forces had driven the remaining Axis forces to isolated pockets in the vicinity of Bizerte and Tunis, German Lieutenant General Hans-Jurgen von Arnim surrendered his forces. Nearly 240,000 Axis troops were taken prisoners, and 250 tanks, 2,330 aircraft, and 232 ships were confiscated. Overall, from 1940 to 1943, Britain suffered 220,000 casualties, while total Axis losses totaled more than 620,000, which included the loss of three field armies.

BRITAIN DEFENDS IN IRAQ

The British Western Desert Force and, later, the British Eighth Army relied considerably on Iranian and Iraqi oil to fuel military operations during the North African campaign. While major military clashes were occurring during the North African campaign, other military operations in the Middle East were beginning to undermine Britain's primacy in the region. In the spring of 1941, Axis intrigue in undermining Britain's influence in Iraq culminated in armed clashes during the Anglo-Iraqi War (May 2–31). During this conflict, the German Luftwaffe flew from airfields in Syria and Lebanon to attack British forces in Iraq. Under Vichy French control, Germany also used Syria and Lebanon to resupply Axis-aligned Iraqi forces. In response, Britain struck targets in both Syria and Lebanon during Operation Exporter (June 8–14, 1941).

Following the demise of the Ottoman Empire at the end of the First World War, the League of Nations designated Mesopotamia a "mandatory" administrative political entity. As a result, the region was referred to in the aftermath of the Great War as the British Mandate of Mesopotamia. With the rise of both Arab nationalism and Islamic fundamentalism in the two centuries prior to World War I, the population in Iraq was in no mood to move from Ottoman domination to British control. Recognizing this reality, Britain transitioned the Mandate (1920) into the Kingdom of Iraq, with nominal independence, in 1932.

However, given the strategic necessities brought on by global war in 1939, London moved toward the re-creation of the joint "RAF Iraq Command," which served as the umbrella group for the RAF, Royal Navy, British army, Commonwealth, and locally developed military units falling under the command of an RAF officer who served at the air vice-marshal rank. While the British Mandate of Mesopotamia officially came to an end in 1932, two years prior, in 1930, the Anglo-Iraqi Treaty was created permitting Britain to maintain a troop presence beyond the Mandate. As a result, RAF Iraq Command transitioned to "British Forces in Iraq," and their presence was kept to a minimum in terms of troop strength and confined to two RAF bases, RAF Shaibah, near the key Persian Gulf port of Basra, and RAF Habbaniya, about 50 miles west of Baghdad. Besides having a general presence in the land between the two rivers, Britain's interests in Iraq as World War II approached were in protecting its investments in the development of Iraq's oil reserves (at the time near Mosul and Kirkuk) and in maintaining a vital link in air communications between India and Egypt.

By 1937, however, Britain removed all but a small force to guard the air bases, as the nationalist sentiment grew in fervor. Following 1937, the government within Iraq assumed full responsibility for the internal security of the country. Italian intelligence operations within Iraq soon increased with the aim of undermining British influence. By March 31, 1941, as the war raged in Europe and North Africa, the regent of Iraq, Prince Abd al-Ilah, was made aware of a plot to overthrow the monarchy. The prince was subsequently whisked away to RAF Habbaniya and then transferred to the British warship HMS *Cockchafter*. Prime Minister Rashid Ali seized power April 3, 1941, in a coup backed by the "Golden Square," which became the collective name for three top-level Royal Iraqi Army officers and one top-level Royal Iraqi Air Force officer.

Ali's government was immediately recognized by Italy and Nazi Germany. Ali signed a secret agreement with the Italian ambassador that was intended to unite Syria and Iraq and nationalize all oil resources as well as provide the Axis powers three key fortified port facilities, with control for a radius of 20 miles. Iraq then cut off the pipeline of the British-controlled

Iraq Petroleum Company in Haifa, Palestine, and redirected oil to Tripoli in Lebanon, which was then under the control of the Vichy French regime. In a side deal with the Germans, Ali promised the use of all military facilities in Iraq, should the British be evicted successfully.

Ali then demanded that Britain remove all military personnel from Iraq. While Ali was initially supported by Rome, on April 17, 1941, he requested military assistance from Berlin, should Britain take any military action against his "National Defence Government." General Headquarters (GHQ) India dispatched the "Sabine Force," a brigade based in Karachi (present-day Pakistan), with orders to secure Basra and lend support as best as possible to the British forces at RAF Shaibah and RAF Habbaniya. However, upon landing in Basra on April 18, the brigade was captured by Iraqi forces. Britain then dispatched the 2nd Brigade of the 10th Indian Infantry Division, which arrived at Basra on April 29, along with the carrier Hermes and two cruisers.

Once apprised of Britain's decision to escalate rather than acquiesce, Ali mobilized the Iraqi army and air forces and ordered them to seize the RAF base at Habbaniya. By May 1, about 9,000 Iraqi troops and an assortment of armored cars, guns, and artillery threatened the base that housed fairly obsolete British aircraft, which was utilized primarily to serve as a cadet flying school with older biplane, World War I-era aircraft. Present at RAF Habbaniya were about 1,350 British personnel at the base (1,000 RAF and the 350-man 1st Battalion of the King's Own Royal Regiment [KORR]), in addition to approximately 1,200 Iraqi and Kurdish constabulary personnel. Nonetheless, Air Vice Marshal Harry Smart had only 35 airmen at the base who knew how to fly an airplane, with only three of those pilots having combat experience.

In the midst of the crisis, cables went back and forth with London, as Smart attempted to ascertain what was expected and what course of action the British high command was prepared to authorize. The contacts were with the foreign ministry rather than British military leadership, which gave rise to increased concerns within Iraq with the level of ambiguity in the communications coming from the diplomatic corps as to what London actually wanted. Smart sought something more definitive and if possible something directly from the British military high command, because each time he asked for guidance from his military superiors, he sensed no one wanted to take ownership of any military action, even in defense, within Iraq. Nevertheless, his determination finally required London to respond with concrete authorization to take military action when Churchill finally cabled back personally: "If you have to strike, strike hard."

Smart subsequently had the British ambassador in Baghdad issue a demand for the Iraqi troops to withdraw from the perimeter of the air base by 8 a.m. on May 2. However, apparently seeking the advantages of darkness and believing the Iraqis had no intention of withdrawing, Smart ordered his available aircraft to start engines at 4:30 a.m. Thirty minutes later, the RAF began attacking Iraqi positions that surrounded the air base. By day's end, each pilot had flown six bombing strikes against the entrenched forces. The 33 aircraft flying out of Habbaniya were soon joined with 8 Wellington bombers flying out of RAF Shaibah.

The Committee of Imperial Defense, now at war in Iraq, transferred command of land forces within the country to British Middle East Command from India and called on General Wavell to provide a relief force for the air base. The force established for entry into Iraq was called the "Habforce" (short for Habbaniya Force) and consisted of a British joint force, which immediately set out for the 535-mile journey from Haifa, Palestine, through Transjordan to Habbaniya on May 11. Remarkably, particularly given the primitive state of the equipment and paucity of trained airmen, the forces at RAF Habbaniya were able to neutralize the threat to the base before Habforce arrived.

At the beginning of May 1941, the Vichy French government and Germany signed the Paris Protocols, whereby Germany was able to send troops into French North Africa and Syria. This provided Berlin with the opportunity for setting up bases for projecting military force into Iraq and Iran and, in the case of Tunisia, for the purposes of challenging British control in Egypt. On May 6, Germany concluded an agreement with the Vichy French to release war materials, including aircraft, from sealed stockpiles in Syria and ship them to the Iraqi forces then fighting Britain. These arrangements included making available several airbases in northern Syria to Germany for transporting Luftwaffe aircraft to Iraq. From May 9 to 31, about 100 German aircraft and 20 Italian aircraft landed on Syrian airfields. In Syria, German aircraft were painted with Royal Iraqi Air Force markings. Between May 10 and 15, these planes flew into Mosul, Iraq, and commenced aerial attacks on British forces throughout Iraq.

On May 13, the first trainload of Axis and Vichy supplies from Syria arrived in Mosul via Turkey, and the Iraqis took delivery of 15,500 rifles, 6 million rounds of ammunition, 200 machine guns, 900 belts of ammunition, and four 75mm field guns with 10,000 shells. Two additional deliveries were made on May 26 and 28, which included eight 155mm guns, 6,000 shells, 354 machine pistols, 30,000 grenades, and 32 trucks.

With the dissipation of the immediate threat to RAF Habbaniya by late May, British leaders set their sights on Rashid Ali, who was then ensconced in Baghdad. Elements of the Habforce were combined with select units that had advanced on Habbaniya from Basra. The Habbaniya "Brigade" consisted of the Kingcol, which was reinforced with the 2nd

Battalion Gurkha Rifles, Indian army, assorted light artillery, and a group of RAF Assyrian Levies.

The brigade marched on Baghdad by way of Fallujah, which contained a key bridge over the Euphrates River. However, on May 22, the Iraqi 6th Infantry Brigade (Iraqi 3rd Infantry Division) counterattacked in the vicinity of Fallujah, with support from Italian light tanks (Fiat). British leaders moved in reserve forces to counter the attack and pushed the Iraqi 6th back. The following day, Luftwaffe aircraft attacked, and Allied and British positions in and around Fallujah were strafed by the *Fliegerfuhrer Irak*. German forces under such commanders as Rommel and Heinz Wilhelm Guderian had the ability to coordinate their attacks, effectively combining air and ground operations. However, beyond the German joint operations, when Germany attempted to aid other militaries such as the Iraqi army at Fallujah, attacks were not as efficiently coordinated, resulting in strikes that were not as effective as they otherwise might have been. For instance, as the Iraqi 6th counterattacked on May 22, and if the Fliegerfuhrer Irak had been directed to have flown in support at that time, the effectiveness of the counterattack would have been significantly amplified.

Instead, the 6th attacked without air support, and air attacks only took place after the Iraqi 6th had been driven back and had lost the initiative. While the Axis powers indeed had powerful militaries, their power projection capability vis-à-vis the British lacked a similarly robust forward presence and, in the British model, a forward presence aimed at conducting integrated and combined operations at the coalition level. This highlights a comparative advantage of the British Empire in relation to its competitors and its opponents. This advantage in the modern era arose from the ability of Britain to have trained with a variety of military forces around the world, as contrasted with the limited training for joint operations by Axis forces in the Middle East—outside of North Africa.

A strictly German battle against strictly British forces between 1940 and 1942 provided a competitive advantage to the joint German capability (panzers, infantry, artillery, air) of coordinating in a lightning-fast engagement or series of engagements (campaign). However, British military doctrine was not based on unilateral doctrine, that is, fighting alone. It had built and relied upon its worldwide strategic, multilateral, and competitive advantage in overcoming operational and tactical challenges. This required working closely with Commonwealth and Allied forces in combined joint operations. Thus, the Germans, try as they might, were unable to set the conditions in which the fight was simply a German versus Briton war—a war wherein London's coalition advantages would be neutralized.

Nowhere was this better exemplified than operations in the Middle East during World War II, as Germany simply did not possess the where-withal to coordinate, generate resources, and fight jointly as effectively as Britain did with its allies in North Africa or in the Middle East. This can be attributed to the inability of German armor to transit the English Channel, its inability to overcome the vastness of the Soviet Union, and the inability of the Luftwaffe to strike at the arsenal of democracy (America), which provided both British and Soviet forces the materials needed to stay in the fight much longer perhaps than otherwise would have been the case.

As the Habbaniya Brigade continued toward Baghdad, British Commonwealth (Indian army) forces in Basra began advancing north-ward toward the Iraqi capital. In two complementary operations launched on May 27, 1941, the "Euphrates Brigade" (20th Indian Infantry Brigade) in Operation Regatta moved north by road and riverboat up the Euphrates River, while the "Tigris Brigade" (21st Indian Infantry Brigade) transited by boat up the Tigris River during Operation Regatta. Seventy-two hours later, the 25th Indian Infantry Brigade (3rd Brigade, 10th Indian Infantry Division) landed in Basra and immediately proceeded north toward Baghdad. On May 29, Ali's National Defence Government collapsed, and Ali departed first to Iran and then proceeded to Berlin where he was greeted by Hitler as the head of the Iraqi government.

In order to neutralize Germany's efforts in establishing a military presence in Syria and Lebanon (which would give Berlin the ability to project military power into both Egypt and Iraq), Britain conducted the Syrian-Lebanon campaign (code-named Operation Exporter) from June 8 to July 14, 1941. Operation Exporter entailed a combined Allied force of British, Indian, Australian, Arab, and Free French, attacking Vichy French forces aligned with Germany in both Syria and Lebanon. Exporter called for four lines of advance by Allied forces: one moving on Damascus (Syria); a second advancing on Beirut (Lebanon) from forces originating in Palestine; a third against Ottoman forces in northern Syria and on Palmyra (central Syria); and the fourth advancing on Tripoli by Allied troops within Iraq.

By June 21, Allied forces occupied Damascus, and on the following day Hitler launched Operation Barbarossa—the invasion of the Soviet Union. Any additional support, materiel, or manpower Axis forces fighting in Syria and Lebanon had originally planned for would, henceforth, be quite limited, as Germany, locked in an existential struggle with the Union of Soviet Socialist Republics, that is, the Soviet Union (USSR), simply would not be able to properly supply its units fighting in North Africa *and* within the Middle East. By the second week of July, the Vichy French position with Syria and Lebanon had collapsed, and mass surrenders led to these forces being moved out of the Middle East. Of the 38,000 Vichy French taken prisoners, only about 6,000 opted to join the Free French led by Charles de Gaulle who flew into the region in late July 1941 to personally congratulate the victors. Shortly thereafter, Free French General Georges Catroux was installed as the military governor of Syria and Lebanon.

With the German push eastward during Operation Barbarossa, Britain believed that Hitler's aim, in addition to destroying the Stalin regime, was to take control of the agricultural land of the Ukraine, the oil fields located in Romania, and the Caspian (Baku, Azerbaijan) and once ensconced in the Caucasus, move south to control Iraqi and Iranian petroleum reserves. In the summer of 1941, while the Axis threat to Iraq and Syria had been significantly reduced, Rommel's forces in North Africa continued to threaten Alexandria, Cairo, and the Suez Canal. As the Third Reich attacked with massive force in Barbarossa and drove toward the Caucasus, London believed German forces had planned on utilizing the Turkish rail network to advance from both the Balkans as well as the Caucasus.

It soon became apparent that German forces under Friedrich Paulus on the Russian front, driving toward the Caucasus, desired to link up with German forces under Rommel, should he be successful in overrunning the British in Egypt and marching into the broader Middle East. The overall strategic hope was to then move toward India and link up with a Japanese empire that was pressing westward across Asia. In the summer of 1941, after the fall of France and after Britain took a savage aerial pounding by the Luftwaffe, the attack against the Soviets brought back memories of the Russians being knocked out of World War I and the full might of the Kaiser being turned westward on Britain and France.

During the Second World War, London began referring to the "Northern Front," which referred to a line of defense that Allied forces would take given a Soviet defeat at the hands of Germany. Such a defeat would lead to an expected surge of German troops descending into the Caucasus and threatening neutral Turkey and Iran. German leaders once again viewed the use of railways as an opportunity in circumventing British and Allied sea supremacy and allowing Berlin to rapidly project military power inland.

Thus, it became critical that the Soviet Union should be supplied sufficiently to avoid a repeat of the collapse of the Russian Empire, similar to what took place during World War I, which then allowed the Kaiser to turn his resources and attention toward the western front, in general, and toward Britain and France, in particular. In that campaign and following the Russian collapse, Germany was slowly making headway against Allied forces. The collapse of Russia immediately mobilized the United States. The presence of 1.5 million U.S. soldiers coupled with the massive influx of supplies countered the ability of Germany to place its entire focus and resources in the West. If the Soviet Union was knocked out in the current campaign, Britain feared that Germany's ability to project force across the Eurasian continent via rail would neutralize its traditional sea advantage. The acquisition of Middle East oil and cutting Britain's lifeline to India would be possible if the Soviets were unable to stand against the Wehrmacht. Accordingly, the Allied strategic imperative became: provide the Soviet army with sufficient resources for it to stand against Nazi Germany and open a second front in the West as soon as possible.

Following the German invasion of the Soviet Union, Britain and the USSR became formal allies. These developments led to a joint British-Soviet strategy toward the Caucasus and toward developing lines of supplies from the Middle East to Soviet-held territory in and around the city of Stalingrad. As a result, Iran became a focus for both of these policy imperatives. Reza Shah, ruler of Persia, changed the name to the Imperial State of Iran in 1935, in part to emphasize the Aryan heritage of the country. He did so with the undisguised desire to align Iran closer with Hitler's Germany and its own predilection for Aryan supremacy. Iran, significantly underdeveloped as the country entered the modern era, made major strides under Reza Shah who sought to improve and modernize infrastructure and transportation networks as well as establish modern schools and colleges. In these efforts, he needed Western assistance to access technology and the learning model that made such technology possible.

However, tensions had been strained with Britain since 1931 when the Shah cancelled a key oil concession (D'Arcy), which provided the Anglo-Iranian Oil Company exclusive rights to sell Iranian oil. Understandably, since it was British capital, technology, and oil expertise that extracted and marketed the oil, Britain believed it deserved the majority share of the profits. However, the 90 percent of the profits that London kept after petroleum sales and after the transactions moved through the British banking system served as an irritant between Tehran and London. By mid-1935, the Shah was increasingly leaning toward Germany for technology and modernization.

As World War II broke out, the Shah declared neutrality but practiced intrigue with the Axis powers. On July 19, 1941, and again on August 17, London sent diplomatic notes ordering the Iranian government to expel German nationals then in Iran, numbering about 700. Unable to convince the Shah through diplomacy to distance himself from the Third Reich, British and Soviet Forces invaded the Imperial State of Iran beginning on August 25, 1941. Final diplomatic notes declaring the commencement of military operations were delivered to the Shah's government on the night of the invasion by British and Soviet ambassadors. Those military operations (Operation Countenance) would continue until the fall of the Shah on September 1941.

On the night of the invasion, the Shah summoned both of the ambassadors from Britain and the Soviet Union and asked that if he sent the Germans home would the invasion be called off. Neither ambassador gave the Shah the clear-cut answer he sought. Frustrated and concerned, he wrote a letter to U.S. President Franklin Roosevelt:

> ... on the basis of the declarations which Your Excellency had made several times regarding the necessity of defending principles of international justice and the right of peoples to liberty, I beg your Excellency to take efficacious and urgent humanitarian steps to put an end to these acts of aggression. This incident brings into war a neutral and pacific country which has had no other care than the safeguarding of tranquility and the reform of the country.[14]

Roosevelt responded in a note diplomatically alluding to the dangers posed by Hitler's ambition to all regions of the globe, including North America, and the United States being actively involved in supporting those people and nations then resisting Hitler's military conquests.

As Germany invaded the Soviet Union in late June 1941, the apparent drive toward the oil fields in the Caucasus (Baku, Azerbaijan, in particular) and the Caspian Sea became a significant concern. Moreover, the Shah's Imperial State of Iran completed an 800-mile railway from the Persian Gulf port of Bandar-e Shapur (now Bandar Khomeini) to the Caspian Sea port of Bandar-e Shah in 1938, toward which the Germans had provided significant assistance in terms of engineering and rolling stock.[15] For the Allies, these harkened back memories of the drive to create a Berlin-to-Baghdad railway aimed at offsetting traditional British sea power supremacy and the creation of interior lines for the projection of land power into the Middle East.

During the joint Allied action taken against the Shah beginning on August 25, 1941, 40,000 Soviet troops descended into Iran from the North and marched on Tehran. On the same day, 19,000 British Commonwealth troops, mostly Indian brigades, and as part of Operation Countenance, entered Iran from various directions, with half moving straight for the oil fields in the vicinity of Ahwaz and airborne units moving into Abadan to protect the Anglo-Iranian Oil Company's refinery, then the largest in the world. A subsidiary goal of the combined action was to open a supply line utilizing the Trans-Iranian Railway in which to resupply the Soviet army, as it defended against Operation Barbarossa.

Within four days, and as Soviet and British troops backed by airpower rolled up Iranian defenses, the Shah issued an order to his armed forces to stand down and cease military operations against the invaders. On

September 17, 1941, the Shah abdicated and was eventually transported to South Africa where he passed away in Johannesburg in 1944. The Shah's son, the Crown Prince Mohammad Reza Pahlavi, took the oath after the abdication and became the new Shah of Iran. Under a separate agreement, the Soviet Union controlled northern Iran, Caspian ports, and the Iranian-Turkish border, while Britain's control included southern Iran, Persian Gulf ports, and the oilfields.

The United States began moving supplies to Stalin's army under the Lend-Lease Act of 1941. In 1942, Roosevelt proposed to Churchill that the U.S. Army become involved in the supervision of the 800-mile Trans-Iranian Railway. On August 22, 1942, Churchill responded in a cable to Roosevelt:

> I would recommend that the railway should be taken over, developed and operated by the United States Army; with the railroad should be included the ports of Khorramshahr and Bandar Shahpur. Your people will thus undertake the great task of opening up the Persian Gulf Corridor, which will carry primarily your supplies to Russia . . . We should be unable to find the resources without your help and our burden in the Middle East would be eased by the release for use elsewhere of the British units now operating the railway. The railway and ports would be managed entirely by your people.[16]

In the fall of 1941, the Trans-Iranian Railway was only capable of transporting about 6,000 tons per month. By the fall of 1943, U.S. Army engineers and contractors had expanded the railway's capacity to more than 175,000 tons of cargo per month.[17] Under the direction of the U.S. Army, Iranian camel paths were expanded into highways for trucks, and the railway, which had more than 200 tunnels, was reinforced and expanded in order to haul tanks and other heavy equipment over the mountains.

Between 1942 and 1945, more than 5 million tons of desperately needed supplies, including 192,000 trucks, and thousands of aircraft, combat vehicles, tanks, weapons, ammunition, and petroleum products were delivered to the Soviet army through the Persian Corridor.[18]

Chapter 4

The Cold War and the Establishment of Israel

This will be a war of extermination and momentous massacre which will be spoken of like the Mongolian massacres and the Crusades.

—Azzam Pasha, secretary, Arab League,
comments on Cairo radio following the
Israeli declaration of independence on May 14, 1948

The Arab-Israeli war that broke out in 1948 has not yet ended.

—Yoav Gelber, July 2009
Jewish Virtual Library

Since the Soviet army and air forces had grown to enormous strength in the closing years of World War II, the West sought to avoid a direct, conventional, armed confrontation. Instead, the view in the West was that internal contradictions and massive economic inefficiencies within the Soviet Union's political and economic system would eventually lead to its own collapse. Accordingly, given a containment of Soviet power, many experts argued that it would take somewhere in the range of a decade before such a collapse would take place (it actually took nearly 45 years). Based on these assessments as well as the massive Soviet conventional armed presence in Europe, Western leaders adopted the containment policies, which guided Western-Soviet relations during the Cold War and that eventually led to the establishment of the North Atlantic Treaty Organization (NATO) and the Southeast Asia Treaty Organization (SEATO).

In addition, U.S. and British strategic planners wanted to keep the Soviets out of the Middle East because the region contained the most defensible locations for launching a strategic air offensive against the Soviet Union in the event of a major war.[1]

In order to project land-based airpower from the Middle East, a third alliance was created in 1955 with the initiation of the Baghdad Pact, which led to the establishment of the Central Treaty Organization (CENTO). Originally, the treaty organization was going to be titled the Middle East Command (MEC), but Egypt, which the Allies were attempting to bring aboard, rejected that name and its British imperial connotations. As a result, Middle East Command was renamed the Middle East Defense Organization (MEDO). However, Egypt continued to balk at Western plans and eventually refused to join.[2] Its replacement, CENTO, excluded Egypt and at its inception in 1955 combined Iran, Iraq, Pakistan, Turkey, and Britain. In 1958, the United States joined CENTO's military committee. The original aim of the alliance was containing Soviet expansion by creating a pro-Western grouping along the Union of Soviet Socialist Republics' (USSR) southwestern frontier. This reflected Britain's earlier concern for the northern front during World War II, and in the postwar years, nations in this region were part of what Western statesmen and military commanders referred to as the *northern tier* defense area.

The treaty organization, however, lacked a unified command structure such as that which eventually contributed to the success of NATO. Additionally, it suffered from a reluctant United States, which demurred in taking too high a profile in the region while arguing that if it did so this would only play into the Soviet-inspired anti-Western propaganda campaign then permeating the region. Moreover, NATO members shared a similar vision that rested upon shared values in terms of human rights, democracy, the rule of law, and free market economics. One of the reasons for the success of NATO during the post–World War II Cold War era was a unifying ideology and common enemy, which provided the foundation for unity of purpose and unity of effort. Additionally, given the overwhelming power of the United States and its closest allies in the aftermath of World War II, NATO also benefited from a clearly defined unity of command. In contrast, CENTO was a grouping of dissimilarly disposed political, cultural, and economic actors, which made unity of effort, unity of purpose, and unity of command highly problematic.

Initially based in Baghdad (1955–1958), CENTO's headquarters moved to Ankara, Turkey, following Iraq's withdrawal from the organization in 1959. With the fall of the Shah of Iran in 1979 and with revolutionary Islamic clerics installing a theocracy shortly thereafter, Iran's exit from the alliance effectively removed Western access to bases within the country. As a result of the action by Tehran in 1979, the buffer zone of the northern tier nations that effectively contributed to the containment of Soviet expansionism now had a very large gap. It was the Soviet Union's intent on exploiting this gap in the western northern tier zone in the Middle East, and increasingly Iran became a target of Soviet intrigue. Ankara, conversely, anchoring the southeastern region of NATO, in addition to its service within CENTO, aligned Turkey as a key and vital member of the U.S.-led Western alliance, maintaining this defensive posture until the collapse of the Soviet Union in December 1991.

Nonetheless, both Iran and Turkey became key Cold War tension points and countries of contention following the demise of World War II Allied cooperation. In the Anglo-Soviet agreement signed in 1942, prior to moving forces into Iran, Soviet and British leaders pledged to remove all forces from the country within six months of the end of the war. The United States alone had 30,000 troops inside Iran by war's end, most of which were involved with transporting supplies and arms or the protection of the routes and infrastructure that were being sent during the war through the Persian Corridor to resupply the Soviets. U.S. troops in Iran, as well as British forces, were withdrawn in 1946.

As Anglo-American forces were preparing to exit Iran in the fall of 1945, Soviet forces in collaboration with the local Marxist party (the Tudeh) backed insurgents, which wrested control of Iran's northern territory of Azerbaijan and, in November 1945, announced the creation of Azerbaijan as an independent Soviet socialist republic within the USSR. This was followed a month later by Moscow's attempts to set up a similar entity within the Kurdistan region of Iran. In both instances, Soviet troops blocked Iran's army from entering these regions. In the middle of these postwar developments, Joseph Stalin's government reneged on its pledge to remove its troops—after the departure of U.S. and British forces—declaring that it would be leaving troops in the northern regions of Iran.

The events in the Middle East in the aftermath of the Second World War contributed to the growing distrust and general deteriorating conditions that ushered in the Cold War, as Britain and the United States applied political and economic pressure on Moscow and demanded that the Anglo-Soviet 1942 agreement be honored and Soviet troops removed from Iran. Along with Tehran's promise to consider Soviet requests for access to Iranian oil (in Baku, Azerbaijan), Western pressure ultimately convinced Moscow to honor its 1942 commitment and, in May 1946, Stalin removed most Soviet troops from Iran.

Russia with its historic expansionistic preference in controlling the Turkish Straits, followed in the twentieth century by the global designs of Stalin's Soviet Union, demanded in 1945 that Turkey return Kars and Ardahan, which had been ceded to Turkey in a 1921 treaty. Stalin further demanded that the Soviet Union be allowed to establish military bases

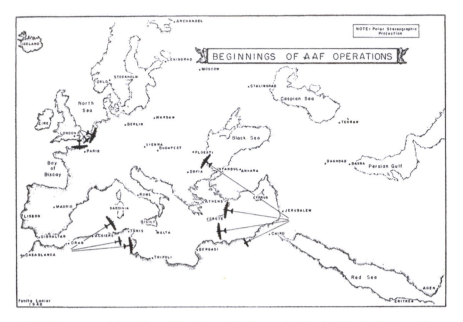

W. F. Craven and J. L. Cate, *The Army Air Forces in World War II. Volume Two: Europe: Torch to Pointblank, August 1942 to December 1943,* Washington, DC: Office of Air Force History, 1983, 2.

along the Turkish Straits and that Moscow be granted joint control of the strategic link between the Mediterranean and Black Seas. In the middle of these developments came the untimely and unfortunate death of U.S. President Franklin Roosevelt in the spring of 1945. This brought the presidency of Harry S. Truman into the burgeoning and increasingly conflictual Cold War era.

Stalin reportedly had admired Roosevelt, but he believed Truman was a weak replacement, and the relationship between the two leaders languished in comparison to the wartime partnership of Stalin and Roosevelt. As Stalin pressed the West in his attempts at claiming control of the Turkish Straits, Truman responded to the Soviet dictator's assertiveness by dispatching the U.S. battleship, *Missouri,* to the Straits in 1946. While Truman certainly did not possess the winning charm and physical presence of the aristocratic Roosevelt, he did possess one attribute that Roosevelt lacked and that ultimately persuaded Stalin to moderate his demands: atomic weapons.

Atomic weapons in the hands of the United States trumped charm and personality and eventually persuaded Stalin to moderate his geopolitical demands in the immediate aftermath of World War II. However, while the United States swiftly drew down conventional forces at war's end, the USSR continued to field enormous armies. The U.S. Army at the peak of its strength during the Second World War fielded 73 divisions and comprised 5.4 million troops. In May 1945, at the close of hostilities with Nazi Germany, the U.S. Army had consisted of approximately 3.5 million men configured in 68 divisions within Europe alone and were supported by 149 air groups. In a breathtakingly swift program of demobilization, one year later, in the spring of 1946, only 400,000 American troops remained on the continent. Globally, the U.S. Army had been reduced from a combined 8 million men to 1 million, while the air forces moved from more than 200 air combat groups to less than 50.[3] The drawdown in U.S. troop strength that followed the end of World War II represented the "most rapid demobilization in the history of the world."[4]

However, coupled with nuclear weapons and a global network of allies, troops, and intelligence, Western control of the northern tier of the Middle East had, by 1946, created an effective buffer in blocking Soviet expansion, providing strategic air basing, and insuring Western access to Middle Eastern oil reserves. As 1947 approached, the traditional strong British presence in the Eastern Mediterranean was being undermined by the budgetary constraints. The costs of two world wars and the impending loss of India began taking its toll on Britain's ability to fund its global commitments.

On February 21, 1947, the British ambassador in Washington, DC, delivered a communication from London to the U.S. government outlining the need for Britain to end its support and commitments in the Eastern Mediterranean. Since Soviet intrigue and "revolutionary" activities, that is, attempts at undermining governments friendly to the West, were ongoing in both Greece and Turkey, it was generally understood between the two governments that such a withdrawal would almost certainly lead to a communist takeover in both countries. And, once ensconced in the Turkish Straits and in Greece, the Eastern Mediterranean as well as Egypt would soon be controlled by Stalin.

The United States traditionally demobilized following war, not wanting to bear the cost of a large-standing military, either financially or as potentially threatening personal liberty. It also kept its overseas commitments to a minimum, seeking to avoid what President George Washington had warned were intractable problems arising from foreign intrigue and entanglements. However, just as A. T. Mahan's thesis regarding global sea power drove the expansion of the U.S. Navy and overseas commitments in the early years of the twentieth century, the Second World War increased the U.S. focus in North Africa, the Eastern Mediterranean, and within the Middle East itself.

TRUMAN DOCTRINE

In the 1930s and 1940s, Roosevelt and Ibn Saud developed a strong working relationship, and U.S. oil, by 1947, had become the most prominent player in the world's largest oil fields located inside the Kingdom of Saudi Arabia. In 1945, the United States secured agreement with the Saudi king to base aircraft on a long-term basis at Dhahran. The strategic requirements for the defense of the region, from an Allied point of view, meant that if Britain needed to reduce its footprint in the region, the USSR should not be permitted to fill any vacuum created as the British withdrew. While strategic logic compelled the United States to take the baton from Britain and shore up Western interests throughout the region, Britain had theater concerns as well.

> The world war had vastly weakened Great Britain. By 1947, the country no longer had the resolve to deal with the dilemma in Palestine: the Zionists demanding statehood, at least in part of the country, and the Palestinian Arabs demanding all of the country as their indivisible patrimony ... The additional embarrassment of having to fight illegal immigrants, most of them Holocaust survivors, and the trauma of continuous Jewish terrorist attacks finally persuaded Whitehall to throw in the towel. In February 1947 Foreign Secretary Ernst Bevin announced that Britain would terminate its rule and hand over the Palestine problem to the United Nations.[5]

As a result of the totality of post–World War II developments, on March 12, 1947, U.S. President Truman went before the U.S. Congress and delivered a speech outlining the need for the United States to step forward and relieve the British in the Eastern Mediterranean, or, alternatively, face the undesirable outcome in which the West conceded Greece and Turkey and, given the loss of influence in these two key countries, the additional probable loss of Egypt to Stalin. Truman's task was difficult given the tradition of the United States in terms of demobilization and a general attempt to avoid foreign intrigue far from its shores. Accordingly, further entanglement and further expense were not something America's representatives in the U.S. Congress in 1947 were prepared to readily embrace. Truman's request for $400 million to support Western interests in Greece and Turkey and to engage overseas after the close of the war would significantly alter the traditional American foreign policy orientation.

Nevertheless, in what became known as the Truman Doctrine, the United States committed itself to provide security in the Eastern Mediterranean, as Britain was forced to withdraw. This role eventually expanded, placing the United States in a position as the guardian and financier against the Soviet Union's quest for global domination and, in doing so, changed the fundamental U.S. relationship with the rest of the world.

While the specific intent on March 12, 1947, was Greece and Turkey, the Truman Doctrine ultimately expanded U.S. efforts and support within Iran and Saudi Arabia. In October 1950, Truman wrote to King Saud that "the United States is interested in the preservation of the independence and territorial integrity of Saudi Arabia. No threat to your Kingdom could occur which would not be a matter of immediate concern to the United States."[6]

> Up through 1947, American exports of oil exceeded imports. But now the balance shifted; in 1948 imports of crude oil and products together exceeded exports for the first time. No longer could the United States continue its historical role as supplier to the rest of the world. Now it was dependent on other countries for that marginal barrel, and an ominous new phrase was being heard more often in the American vocabulary—"foreign oil."[7]

As the United States made preparations for moving in support of Western interests in Greece and Turkey, the United Nations accepted the Palestine file from Britain and, in February 1947, appointed a commission of inquiry, the UN Special Committee on Palestine (UNSCOP), to make recommendations.[8] Given the intractability of Arab-Jewish discord, the committee recommended eventual partition of Palestine into two states. Under the recommendations, the towns of Jerusalem and Bethlehem were to fall under international supervision, as both shared significant meaning to more than one of the three religious groups: Judaism, Christianity, and Islam.

When these recommendations were forwarded to the UN General Assembly, the assembly made adjustments, including reducing the size of the recommended Jewish state to 55 percent of Palestine (Arabs would hold 45 percent). The assembly then voted to approve the plan along the following lines: 33 votes in favor (Western Europe, the United States, the Soviet Bloc, and most of Latin America), 13 votes against (mostly Arab and Muslim countries), and 10 abstentions, including Britain and China. The Zionist leadership, including David Ben-Gurion, the chairman of the Jewish Agency Executive (essentially the Yishuv government), and Chaim Weizmann, considered the most prominent of the Zionist political leaders, accepted the terms and conditions. However, the right wing of the Zionist movement rejected the compromise and demanded sovereignty over the entire region that encompassed ancient Israel.

For the right wing of the Zionists, a modern Jewish state was entitled to all that was the ancient Land of Israel, and the justification, apparently, was that "God had given it to us." Joining in a vote against this proposition were the Arabs—spearheaded by the Palestinian Arab leadership. Unfortunately, this grouping not only rejected the hard-line Zionist view of the Middle East but also rejected any compromise regarding "their" land. The vote was "no" just as it had been in 1937 when the Peel

Commission recommended only 17 percent of Palestine be allotted for the establishment of a Jewish national home. The Peel Commission's recommendation would have provided more than 80 percent of Palestine to the Palestinian Arabs—a Palestine that was never an Arab nation-state but, rather, an Ottoman Turk province for nearly 500 years. And, before that, it had been a land that was overrun by plundering Arab raiders coming out of medieval Arabia and operating under the cloak of religious justification.

Self-interest, emotionalism, unbridled passion, and pride on both sides of the Arab-Israeli issue, were, in the first instance, a massive impediment toward moving to a comprehensive solution and settlement in 1947. In the second instance, the self-interest, emotionalism, unbridled passion, and pride were stoked into a white hot reactionary fire by those seeking to exploit the undisciplined emotionalism for ulterior motives, rationally calculating how best to manipulate these characteristics to enrich themselves and their followers. These elements existed across the spectrum of religion and were not confined to Muslims, Jews, or Christians. The manipulation of religious passions for material and narrow self-interest on the part of nefarious elite has been a key driver of events in the Middle East and North Africa since recorded history first began nearly 5,000 years ago.

Thus, the responsibility for the eruption of war in 1948 between the Arabs and Jews rests with a clash of ideologies. On November 29, 1947, the UN General Assembly passed the Partition Resolution (No. 181), which then led the leaders of the Palestinian Arabs to incite rioting, violence, and chaos. The settlement following the First World War, which was rejected outright by Arab leaders, insured that fully 80 percent of Palestine would be controlled by the Palestinians and Arab inhabitants. But now, following the Second World War, as the offer became only 45 percent, the Arab leadership, both within Palestine as well as the wider Arab world, rejected once again any compromise and apparently decided that the Jews would certainly not live in peace in the other 55 percent.

There would be no peace while Jews possessed "Arab" land. Forgotten were the raiding parties coming out of Arabia in the seventh century, which had taken the land by force. Forgotten were the Turks that had taken the land by force, from the Arabs, and had been in control of the land for 500 years, until British, Australian, and Indian troops aided in the destruction of Ottoman power. Apparently, the victorious Western allies from the perspective of many in the region had no standing or say on the dispensation or administration of former Ottoman provinces, which their societies paid for with blood and treasure, all the while, empowering and working in conjunction with Arab and other Middle Eastern indigenous forces.

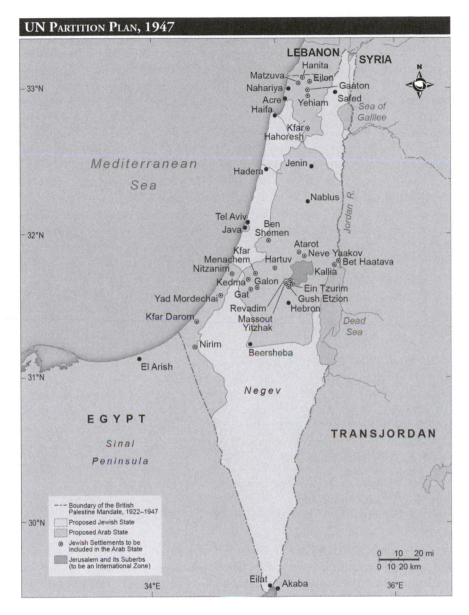

UN PARTITION PLAN, 1947

Most certainly there were errors in Western judgment regarding the dispensation and administration of the former Ottoman territories. Adding to the animosity was the manner in which the partition issue was managed. Prior to the actual vote on November 29, Britain announced (on September 20, 1947) that it would begin withdrawing from Palestine. The Zionists immediately moved into the areas vacated by the British which, ultimately, would fall under their 55 percent—*even before the vote was consummated* within the General Assembly. Thus, they moved into land that was not legally theirs and then later claimed legitimacy by pointing to a vote in the UN General Assembly. This ignited a storm of protest and resistance, as Zionists took over 5 Arab (and mixed towns) and nearly 200 mostly Arab villages. Approximately, 250,000 to 300,000 Palestinians and other Arabs fled to Palestine's Arab sectors or were forced into refugee status in other neighboring countries.

On November 30, one day after the UN vote authorizing partition, Arab militants ambushed two civilian Zionist/Jewish buses near Petah Tikva, about six miles east of Tel Aviv, murdering seven passengers. Concurrently, Arab snipers began firing at civilians from positions in Jaffa and hitting innocent pedestrians in Tel Aviv. The same day, the Husseini-led Arab Higher Committee (AHC), arguably the Palestinian Arabs' ruling body at the time, ordered a general strike throughout Palestine.

WAR FOR ISRAELI INDEPENDENCE

In April 1948, the British had withdrawn the 6th Airborne Division, and the Haganah (the forerunner of the Israeli Defense Forces [IDF]), simultaneously, launched several large-scale operations across the country aimed at degrading the combat capabilities of various Palestinian militias. By May 1948, Zionist paramilitary units were going door to door, conducting forcible expulsions of all Arabs living in the vicinity of key roads and Jewish communities.

> These refugees were sometimes literally deported across the lines. In certain cases, IDF [Israeli Defense Forces] units terrorized Palestinians so as to hasten their flight, and isolated massacres took place that might have expedited the flight.[9]

After forcing the departure of these Palestinian Arabs from their villages, Jewish paramilitary groups then demolished buildings and homes with the objective of insuring that they would never be able to return. Between 1947 and 1949, over 700,000 Palestinians out of a prewar population of 1.3 million were uprooted from their homes and dwellings in what eventually became the State of Israel. Israeli leaders at the time argued that while partition and independence would bring internal problems such as the Palestinian revolts during 1936–1939, such actions would not bring attack from neighboring Arab states. And, even if such a remote possibility were to occur, Zionist leaders believed that the international community would be compelled to enforce the vote taken in the General Assembly regarding partition. Both of these assessments proved inaccurate.

Within the various Arab capitals in the spring of 1947, concern developed that the Zionists were moving to control all of Palestine (i.e., the ancient home of the "Land of Israel") and would not be content with the allotted territory. Given that the right wing of the Zionists had demanded *all* of Palestine and those Jewish paramilitary groups were going door to door evicting Palestinian families, the matter quickly developed into a heated debate in Arab countries with millions demanding action from their governments. Arab governments, many aligned with the West, were faced with an unsettling scenario of massive influxes of refugees inflaming the anger of citizens within their nations to do something about it. In this highly charged and emotionally ridden environment, on May 14, 1948, Israel declared its independence and, as the British Palestine Mandate expired on May 15, neighboring Arab armies attacked the new State of Israel.

The first to strike was Egypt in the form of an air attack on Tel Aviv using Spitfire (Mk Vc), Dakota (C47), and Short Stirlings aircraft. These were followed by a ground force invasion from several directions. Syria sent 4,000 troops into northern Israel from the East, complementing a Lebanon force of 2,000 in four infantry battalions with artillery and armored cars that descended and attacked in the north of Israel. Iraq attacked westward south of the Golan, with approximately 9,500 soldiers arrayed in four infantry brigades accompanied by an armored car battalion, while Jordan attacked Jerusalem in a pincer movement, utilizing a force of about 6,000 centered upon 4,500 Arab Legion troops configured in two mechanized brigades deploying Marmon-Herrington armored cars (Mk IVF 2-pounder gun and a Browning machine gun) and artillery (towed 25-pounders).

An Egyptian force of 10,000 was split into two columns—one proceeding into the Gaza Strip while the other moved northeast across the Negev past Beersheba. Saudi Arabia contributed troops and placed them under Egyptian command. The Egyptian force was commanded by Major General Ahmed Ali al-Mwawi and consisted of 5 infantry battalions, an armored battalion with British Crusader, Light Tank Mark VI, and Matilda tanks, a battalion of 16 25-pounder guns, and a battery of 8 6-pounder guns, a medium machine gun battalion, and supporting forces. In support of the ground advance, the Egyptians also utilized 15 fighter aircraft (British Spitfires) and 5 bomber/transports (Dakotas and Short Stirlings), which moved into the Sinai. U.S. M4 Shermans (medium tanks) were deployed as well, starting in the summer of 1948.

Israel met the invasion with nearly 50,000 fighters, about half of which were regional forces trained to defend their specific locales. In a more organized and centrally commanded grouping, 20,000 soldiers were aligned in six Haganah brigades, with an additional 6,000 in what were described at the time as elite forces in three Palmach brigades. The centralized forces within Israel at the time and those that later would become the IDF were lightly armed and lightly trained in possession of 33,000 rifles and submachine guns and 1,500 machine guns. The forces were also armed with 850 light mortars, 85 antitank weapons, 4 tanks, and 400 to 500 of what could be charitably called armored cars (homemade).

THE FORMATION OF THE IDF

As Ben-Gurion proclaimed Israel's independence and the establishment of Israel as a sovereign nation-state on May 14, 1948, his first directive was in the formation of the IDF, which over the next half century would become one of the world's premier military organizations. The Israeli Air Force, over time, earned a reputation as being among the world's elite and, as some would argue, the best in the world. Not surprisingly, this characterization of being the best in the world was not widely shared within the ranks of either the U.S. Navy or the U.S. Air Force.

The IDF was formed initially from the Haganah and Palmach and officially came into existence on May 31, 1948, but since it was declared the only legal armed force in Israel, its leaders took steps to bring other armed organizations under its control as well. A modern nation-state, at least theoretically, has a legal monopoly on the organization, control, and application of organized violence within its borders. Given this principle, the Stern Gang and Irgun were brought under the control of the Israeli central government during the fall of 1948. Additionally, IZL (Irgun Zevai Le'ummi or National Military Organization) and Lehi (Lohmanei Herut Israel or "Fighters for the Freedom of Israel") were eventually dissolved, and individual members, who chose to, joined the IDF by November 7, 1948.[10]

The Arab-Israeli War of 1948 (or alternatively, the War for Israeli Independence, depending upon one's perspective) was an unsophisticated, largely infantry skirmish fought with World War II infantry weapons. Of the Arab forces, only the British-trained and armed Arab Legion, which managed to capture the West Bank and eastern Jerusalem, performed with any aplomb; although, certainly there were Arab soldiers and commanders that served with distinction. The Syrians engaged, fought a handful of minor skirmishes, and then went home. The Egyptians, whom the Arabs had hoped would be the most effective beyond the Arab Legion, found campaigning in the modern era problematic and turned in suboptimal performances.

They did, however, manage to wrench Gaza out of Israel's hands, temporarily. In contrast, the Israelis benefited from a more unified command that led soldiers in an existential battle of national survival. As a result, the commitment to the outcome was much higher in the ranks of the IDF than most of the Arab formations. The Arabs were further constrained by a loose grouping of disparate forces attempting to coordinate military operations in an environment characterized by a lack of synergy, unity of effort, and unity of command.

Even more telling upon the outcome was the nature, once again, of the conditions that had established the framework in which the outcome of the war was decided. For instance, most Arab armies had come to depend on the British for supply of arms, munitions, and spare parts. In May 1948, the UN Security Council slapped an arms embargo on all parties involved with the hostilities. For the Arabs, this created significant problems, since they relied on overt and legal supply from largely British and French sources.

For Israel, which had developed an underground network to circumvent British control within Palestine in the late 1930s and into the 1940s, it was prepared to draw from illicit sources the arms and supplies required to conduct a drawn-out campaign. Thus, the longer the war continued, the better Israel fared in terms of logistics and supply in relation to the Arab attackers. The lack of sustained and consistent military power projection and strategic endurance were deficiencies that plagued Middle Eastern militaries throughout the modern era, as no Arab army could sustain itself 50 miles beyond its borders in the twentieth and into the twenty-first centuries.

Consequently, the Arab forces attacking Israel in May 1948 sought a swift and decisive victory. However, a knockout punch in the early weeks of the campaign eluded the attacking armies, and the war only provided the Zionists the opportunity in honing their skills, organization, and arms and in spreading central government power throughout the newly minted country. The Arab-Israeli War of 1948 did not destroy or even weaken the new State of Israel; it merely strengthened it through a baptism of fire.

For many in the Arab world who found their armies constrained by an arms embargo, the lesson had been clear: it was time to look for new suppliers for arms and munitions. In the second half of the twentieth century, the Soviet Union would attempt to fill that gap. While the United Nations negotiated two separate cease-fires, armed conflict continued throughout 1948 and into 1949. By the time the fighting had ended, Israel had taken 80 percent of the original British Palestine Mandate. Moreover, as the original UN Partition Resolution had authorized a second Palestinian state, following armed conflict in 1948, no independent Palestinian Arab state had been created. In fact, land not held by Israel was in the hands of Egypt (Gaza) or Jordan (West Bank). A series of armistices was reached by Israel with Egypt (February 24, 1949), Lebanon (March 23, 1949), Jordan (April 3, 1949), and Syria (July 20, 1949). However, the technical state of war was never resolved. While some refer to the war as the Arab-Israeli War or the War for Israeli Independence, for the Palestinian Arabs, the war came to be referred to as *al-Nakba* or *the catastrophe*.[11]

From an Israeli standpoint there are at least two separate lenses through which to view the war. First, the 1948 war was the most costly of all Israeli wars, with fatalities exceeding 6,000. Given a Jewish population in the Yishuv of approximately 630,000, the casualty figure represented about 1 percent of the Israeli population. The inaccurate assessment that Israel might experience internal unrest upon a declaration of independence but not an attack from external actors was not the only problem that arose. The Yishuv leadership had assumed that Western powers would feel obligated to defend the UN Partition Resolution through the powers of the Security Council. At the time the Soviet Union had backed the Partition Resolution and generally supported the new State of Israel. Therefore, most of the Yishuv felt comfortable that the Arabs would be sufficiently deterred from initiating any hostilities. Ben-Gurion was the exception and understood that nothing was assured.

Another view was slightly more optimistic:

> ... the war for independence was, at least in certain respects, Israel's most successful campaign against the Arabs. It was the only contest in which Israel succeeded in translating a military victory into a political settlement; one that survived for eighteen years.[12]

Among the Arabs, however, the defeat of their objectives during the 1948 war with Israel left a general sense of disillusionment, particularly within Egypt. This also led to the establishment of the Free Officers Movement that blamed the poor showing of the country on the pervasive corruption by the king, his court, and the military officer corps. The overall charge, however, was that of an overreliance on British influence allowing a corrupt regime and its military officers to continue their hold on power within Egypt.

With India achieving independence from the British Empire and with the creation of Muslim Pakistan on August 14, 1947, nationalism was pervasive around the world. In Egypt, it had reached a fever pitch. The flames of Arab nationalism were also being fanned (and in some instances ignited and doused with gasoline) by the "revolutionary" Soviet Union in the decades following the Second World War in an attempt to undercut the West's postwar influence in the region.

THE EGYPTIAN REVOLT

By 1951 the British position in Egypt was essentially in free fall, as nationalistic police officers turned against the government and began harboring and aiding a growing Egyptian insurgency led by fedayeen resistance fighters. Attacks against British and government interests engulfed and moved beyond the main cities of Cairo and Alexandria and the historically stable Suez Canal Zone. In January 1952, a coordinated bombing took place near Ismailia directed against British shipping and other Western interests. In the attack, several British soldiers were killed. British troops responded, eventually chasing the attackers into the city where the fedayeen fighters found refuge in police barracks. After British officers explained the situation to the Egyptian police commanders, the police refused to allow the British to make any arrests. A British negotiator was summoned and entered the discussions, but, after he was killed, the British troops attacked and eventually killed 50 Egyptian policemen and wounded 100 more.

When word began to spread, which portrayed the fedayeen as brave and patriotic fighters being unjustly pursued by the imperial and anti-Egyptian British, rather than providing an accurate account of what actually transpired, that is, indiscriminate bombing of civilian targets followed by running and hiding, Egypt erupted into riots and chaos. The Free Officers Movement initiated rioting in Cairo and, from there, inflamed passions spread across Egypt like wildfire. By the summer of 1952, the entire country was a tinderbox. It was then that the revolutionaries acted. The Egyptian Revolution of 1952 began on July 23 with a military coup led by the Free Officers Movement. The coup was led by Egyptian army officers, including Muhammad Naguib and Gamal Abdel Nasser who removed King Farouk and established a "republic."

Apparently both the United States and the Soviet Union were providing intelligence to the coup plotters in hopes of making inroads toward influence with any post-British new government. This intelligence identified key Egyptian command, control, and communications posts within the military and within the internal security ministry. The Free Officers Movement also had persuaded several police organizations to participate in the coup, and on July 23, 1952, these units arrested key participants in the royal Egyptian government. Remarkably, only about 90 Egyptian army officers, all of whom were drawn from the junior ranks, engineered the government takeover. The people of Egypt awoke to a 7:30 a.m. broadcast on July 23, which marked the first communication to the nation from the revolutionaries. The announcement was read by Anwar El-Sadat, a Free Officers Movement member and future president of Egypt.

... Egypt has passed through a critical period in her recent history characterized by bribery, mischief, and the absence of governmental stability. All
of these were factors that had a large influence on the army. Those who
accepted bribes and were thus influenced caused our defeat in the Palestine
war [Arab-Israeli War of 1948]. As for the period following the war, the
mischief-making elements have been assisting one another, and the traitors
have been commanding the army. They appointed a commander who is
either ignorant or corrupt. Egypt has reached the point, therefore, of having
no army to defend it. Accordingly, we have under-taken to clean ourselves
up and have appointed to command us men from within the army whom
we trust in their ability, their character and their patriotism. It is certain that
all Egypt will meet this news with enthusiasm and will welcome it.[13]

Following the coup, the British presence outside the Suez Canal was
swiftly reduced, and the revolutionaries attempted to chart a nonaligned
course between the West and the Soviet-led Warsaw Pact. The Warsaw
Pact was an alliance that included countries aligned with Moscow's interests, although some, such as Yugoslavia, tended to be much more
independent-minded than the Soviet Politburo would have preferred.
Seeking nonalignment, Cairo was pursuing a balanced approach. While
these efforts were theoretically sound, the practicality of the matter
clashed with the abstract as it meant the new, "revolutionary"
government of Egypt had virtually no fully committed supporters for its
survival among the world's great powers. Empirical reality and the
nature of international politics soon forced the issue.

Since many in the Egyptian military believed the West in general, and
the British, in particular, let them down when they applied an arms
embargo during operations against Israel in 1948, a door of opportunity
was opened for the Soviet Union, and it provided Moscow the ability to
ship arms into the country. And, although Egypt attempted to moderate
Soviet influence, this development of aligning Egypt with Moscow served
to disturb not only the British but also the French who had significant concerns of communist encroachment against its interests in North Africa and
the Middle East. For the British and the French, it appeared the United
States was working in conjunction with the Soviets to edge them out of
the Middle East. Perhaps it was not an inaccurate or unrealistic assessment.

THE SHAH, SOVIET INTRIGUE, AND
MOSSADEQ IN IRAN

While the Egyptian Revolution was unfolding and aimed at eliminating the British presence, events within Iran were taking a different turn,
although the rise of nationalism animated the political landscape there
as well. Reza Shah Pahlavi moved the country into the modern age by

instituting a range of reform policies, including building industry, transportation and education and advancing women's rights. This made enemies in both the agrarian-land holding class as well as the traditionally conservative ranks of the Shia Muslim clerical establishment. Following the departure of the Shah during the Second World War for aligning with Nazi Germany too closely for the interests of either the British or the Americans, his son, Mohammad Reza Shah Pahlavi, assumed the throne. Somewhat weak and prone to vacillation, he was outmaneuvered by a coalition of traditional and nationalistic forces aligned with Mohammad Mossadeq who became prime minister of Iran in 1951.

Mossadeq had ridden to popularity on an anti-British platform and had promised to nationalize the Anglo-Iranian Oil Company (AIOC) upon becoming prime minister. Once he assumed the office, Mossadeq moved to nationalize the AIOC, much to the consternation of both Britain and the United States. With the loss of India in 1947, the AIOC and the Suez Canal were arguably the two most valuable foreign assets of Britain. Thus, the Iranian problem arose in the midst of the Egyptian Revolution and as Britain reeled from the expenses and loss of its own manpower from the Second World War. Initially, British Prime Minister Clement Attlee and U.S. President Truman took a hopeful approach toward the Mossadeq government, believing that a freely elected government was a vast improvement over the authoritarian regimes that had been the tradition in Persian and Iranian history. However, Mossadeq wanted to be free to establish any foreign relations he deemed necessary, including a closer relationship with the Soviet Union.

> It is of critical importance to the United States that Iran remain an independent and sovereign nation [arguably not as sovereign or independent as this, at the time classified report, would lead one to believe], not dominated by the USSR. Because of its key strategic position, its petroleum reserves, its vulnerability to political subversion, Iran must be regarded as a continuing objective of Soviet expansion. The loss of Iran by default or by Soviet intervention would a) Be a major threat to the security of the entire Middle East, including Pakistan and India; b) Permit communist denial to the free world of access to Iranian oil and seriously threaten the loss of other Middle Eastern oil; c) Increase the Soviet Union's capability to threaten important United States-United Kingdom lines of communication.[14]

As negotiations unfolded over the status of the AIOC, Mossadeq's government conceded that payment was due for the investments Britain had made in insuring the company's success. However, an impasse arose between the parties as both Britain and the United States demanded that an additional clause be placed in any agreement. The stipulated clause and a precondition for transferring control of the AIOC to Mossadeq's government would require the establishment of an international

marketing organization made up of British, American, and Dutch personnel who would purchase all Iranian oil and market it in the international
system. This demand heralded the Allies' intent on minimizing Moscow's involvement within Iran and the expectations of Soviet behavior
aimed at the penetration of Iranian energy markets.

In the middle of these discussions, in October 1952, Mossadeq opted to
expel all British diplomats, including all identifiable undercover intelligence officers.[15] This development then increased the ability for the
Soviets to expand operations within Iran and, in consequence, immediately changed the dynamics of the negotiations for the U.S. government.
Earlier, the Truman administration had held the view that Mossadeq represented the most effective barrier to a communist takeover of Iran. At the
beginning of 1953, however, the new Eisenhower administration held a
different view regarding the likelihood of a) the establishment of Jeffersonian democracy under Mossadeq in Iran and b) the extent and nature of
Soviet intrigue, than that held by the previous administration.

In Britain, Attlee was replaced with Winston Churchill, and Dwight D.
Eisenhower had selected John Foster Dulles as secretary of state, the
brother of then Central Intelligence Agency (CIA) director, Allen Dulles.
John Foster Dulles was strongly anticommunist, referring to it as "Godless terrorism."[16] Between December 1952 and February 1953, Churchill
and Eisenhower made a concerted effort to resolve the AIOC/Iranian
issue through diplomacy. Having failed, Eisenhower instructed his
secretary of state in March 1953 to generate plans for the overthrow of
the Mossadeq government. The CIA generated preliminary plans, and
in April it was decided that it would work with the British Secret Intelligence Service (SIS) for conducting covert operations aimed at deposing
Mossadeq. A joint U.S.-U.K. unit was established on the island of Cyprus
in the Eastern Mediterranean, tasked with the operational planning necessary for the overthrow of the Iranian government. This operation,
code-named, "TPAJAX Project," was authorized and directed by a U.S.
presidential executive order to "... cause the fall of the Mossadeq
government; to reestablish the prestige and power of the Shah and to
replace the Mossadeq government with one which would govern Iran
according to constructive policies." By the mid-1950s, the U.S.-Soviet
rivalry, referred to as the *Cold War*, was raging across the globe and
impacting events throughout the Middle East.

NASSER SEIZES THE SUEZ CANAL

Three years after the overthrow of Mossadeq, on July 26, 1956, Egypt's
Nasser nationalized the Suez Canal. Soviet-inspired, this action provided

Nasser effective oversight of the main flow of oil between Western Europe and the Middle East. Moreover, it provided the former Egyptian army officer leverage over Britain's or the United States' ability to surge military capability through the canal in support of Western-friendly oil producing states in the Middle East. Earlier it had been a subsidiary goal of what the Kaiser had hoped to obtain as the result of World War I, as the German leader believed the canal would serve as a useful "choke point" for strangling the British Empire and curtail its ability to draw resources from India and project power into the Middle East.

With the loss of India in 1947, the strategic value of the canal (as well as the Eastern Mediterranean—hence, the notification to the United States leading to the establishment of the Truman Doctrine in 1947) to Britain had lessened. Nevertheless, petroleum and petroleum products continued to be a vital national interest for Britain, France, the United States, and the entire Western world. Japan, a key—or perhaps better stated, *the* key—U.S. ally in Asia following the Second World War, was also highly dependent on oil imports, which provided nearly 90 percent of Japanese domestic needs.

A month before Nasser had seized control of the Suez Canal, the French met secretly with the Israelis and shared a conviction that Nasser and his Soviet supporters were partly responsible for the instability that had gripped Algeria. Moreover, both the French and the Israelis at the time believed that Nasser had essentially opened the door for Soviet military involvement in Egypt. And, once ensconced in Egypt, the Soviets would then be positioned to engage in undermining Western influence in Africa and the broader Middle East.

On the face of it, one might observe that Nasser was simply empowering the average Arab or Muslim to overcome the excesses of Western imperialism. This was certainly true to the extent that the colonial empires (Britain, France, and Italy in North Africa and the Middle East) fell away following the Second World War and that the masses were at least offered the opportunity to take control of their own political systems. However, three questions arise: 1) Are the masses of people sufficiently educated to participate in a type of governing system that requires tolerance and the protection of minority rights? 2) Do they have sufficient access to objective information in order to effectively monitor their government? and 3) Do they possess the technical prowess, managerial skill set, and belief in the rule of law (as opposed to the rule of individuals) necessary for the effective operation of a modern democratic system? The process of democratic transitions and consolidation requires that it be managed with some degree of order to avoid chaos, conflict, and the manipulation of the emotions and passions of the people by the narrow self-interests of those seeking to enrich themselves and their cronies at the people's expense. This applies equally to the great powers who, under the guise of freedom or revolution or democracy, allow their own economic or geopolitical special interests to undermine the general well-being of a population.

In an era of great change, and after nationalizing the Suez Canal, Nasser subsequently appealed to the United States to supply him with weapons. The Eisenhower administration, however, demurred, influenced partially by the objectives of the 1950 Tripartite Declaration, which attempted to moderate the introduction of arms into North Africa and the Middle East after the close of the Second World War. The declaration pledged that the governments of France, Britain, and the United States would seek to moderate tensions within the Middle East by restricting the sale of arms.

Consequently, Eisenhower instead came back to Nasser's government with a pledge of resources to back the construction of the Aswan Dam. However, wanting to secure weapons and weapons systems, Nasser decided then, instead, to accept an offer by the Soviet Union to supply him with arms. An incredulous Eisenhower administration then cancelled its support for the Aswan Dam, which then incited Nasser to seize the Suez Canal, stating at the time that Egypt, once in possession of the canal, would generate sufficient transit fees to build the dam on its own. On August 23, 1956, in an effort to solve the impasse, the British and French offered a compromise wherein the canal would be administered by a company owned by all the countries that depended on the canal for transit. This was rejected by the Nasser government.

It was in this environment that Nasser opened the door for the introduction of Soviet military equipment and advisors into the Mediterranean, North African, and Middle Eastern regions. It was also in this environment that plans were made to stop him. Nasser attempted to moderate the level of influence afforded to Moscow, as he sought to remain "nonaligned" in his foreign policy. For the West however, this was a distinction without a difference. The British subsequently joined the French and Israelis in compiling operational planning aimed at taking back the Suez Canal and removing the Nasser regime from power.

For the Israelis, their concerns included the naval blockade Nasser applied to the Straits of Tiran, essentially cutting sea access for the Israeli city of Eilat in the Gulf of Aqaba east of the Suez Canal. Moreover, terrorist attacks on Israeli civilians and other national interests were being launched from Gaza and through the Sinai Desert. The Arab-Israeli War of 1948, although ostensibly concluded, continued asymmetrically, in the ghazi forms of guerrilla and terrorist attack. In consequence to the adverse developments, the Israeli government coordinated with the French and British in formulating options to neutralize the new threats. The Allied operational plan for retaking the Suez Canal and creating conditions in which the Nasser government would fall was initially called "Hamilcar." However, this subsequently transitioned into Operation Musketeer, which placed Britain in command of joint British-French operations, with British General Charles Keightley serving as operational commander and French Vice Admiral Pierre Barjot serving as his deputy.

The Anglo-French operation included air-ground-sea forces of approximately 45,000 British personnel and 34,000 Frenchmen, 200 British and 30 French warships, 7 aircraft carriers, more than 70 merchant vessels, hundreds of landing craft, and 21,000 British and French vehicles. All told, with combat and supporting units, the mobilized joint task force was made up of more than 100,000 soldiers, sailors, airmen, and marines, although the actual combat forces moving to seize the Canal Zone numbered about 7,000. The operational plan called for an Anglo-French landing at Alexandria followed by an advance on Cairo, while the Israelis would move against the Egyptian right flank through the desert. However, the landing site was moved from Alexandria to Port Said in what was called Operation Musketeer Revise. Understanding the potential for repercussions in moving against such a high-visibility target that the Suez Canal represented, Nasser began initiating defensive re-posturing, as he moved half of his Sinai forces west of the canal.

Shortly after 2 p.m. local time on October 29, 1956, four North American P-51 Mustang fighter aircraft, using their propellers and wing tips, cut overhead telephone lines (command and control), utilized in linking 30,000 troops of the Egyptian 3rd Infantry Division and Palestinian 8th Division with their subordinate units. In response to Operation Musketeer, the Israelis had devised Operation Kadesh, which sought to complement the Anglo-French action against the Suez, but with the further objectives of removing the Egyptian blockade of the Straits of Tirana, clearing out the fedayeen fighters then ensconced in Gaza, and providing a buffer zone in the Sinai.

The strategic military weakness of Israel then, as it is today, was that it did not possess strategic depth. Strategic depth in British operations in North Africa in World War II allowed them to use territory to burn up Italian and German fuel (and armor) and to keep the battles that accomplished this away from the British naval base at Alexandria, the capital at Cairo, the Nile River Delta, and the Suez Canal. Israel, in possession of only a sliver of property, did not, and does not, have this luxury. Any legitimate state (and Israel's legitimate right to exist has been affirmed on numerous occasions and in numerous forums and institutions, including the United Nations and the U.S. Congress) has the right to defend itself against an attack from external sources. By extension it has the right to defensible borders. If its neighbors conduct regular or irregular military operations against it, those neighbors' lands are subject to defensive acts, including military operations in which they may forfeit the owner-ship of those lands. Since Israel was under attack from Gaza and the Sinai, it sought to undermine those conducting and supporting those attacks.

Under such conditions and without strategic depth that provides the necessary terrain for a military strategy of "defense-in-depth," a nation does not have the luxury of time in awaiting an attack. It is forced to move proactively against an expected attack and, in Operation Kadesh, Israeli leaders sought to establish the Sinai as an additional buffer zone. There-fore, in addition to supporting the Anglo-French move on the Suez and the operations aimed at opening the Gulf of Aqaba to its shipping into the Red Sea (freeing up the city of Eilat), the Israelis through Operation Kadesh sought to destroy Egyptian military capabilities in the Sinai.

About an hour after the P-51s cut the Egyptian lines, 10 Israeli brigades invaded Egypt and advanced across the Sinai toward the Suez Canal. On October 29, 1956, Israeli paratroops (IDF) dropped east of the town of Suez. On October 30, additional paratroops dropped east of the Mitla Pass, and troops began crossing the border at Qussaima.

> ... Two battalions of Colonel Ariel Sharon's 202d Parachute Brigade— roughly 3,000 men riding in M3 half-tracks, French-made AMX-13 tanks and 100 trucks received from France only three days earlier—stormed into Egyptian territory. Sixteen low-flying Israeli Douglas C-47 Dakota trans-ports and their escort of 10 British-built Gloster Meteor jets rumbled over-head. Having evaded radar detection, the camouflaged Dakotas rose to 1,500 feet about 18 miles east of the canal. At 4:59 PM, the first of 395 para-troopers of the 202d Brigades 1st Battalion leaped into space to land unop-posed just east of the strategic Mitla Pass. The invaders dug in at the granite-flanked eastern entrance to the pass to await the arrival of Sharon's column, churning across more than 105 miles of sun-baked desert toward them. The link-up came at 10:30 PM the following day.[17]

On October 31, British Royal Air Force jets attacked targets in and around Cairo and struck Egyptian air assets at the Cairo International Airport. Behind Sharon's vanguard, other Israeli units followed, and in the course of the next week moved swiftly 134 miles down the Sinai Mediterranean coast, attacking fedayeen fighters in Gaza, while also advancing down the eastern side of the Gulf of Aqaba as well as the western perimeter of the Gulf of Suez. In a lightning strike that combined air and ground operations during Operation Kadesh, the IDF managed to achieve operational surprise.

Part of the prearranged plan within Musketeer-Kadesh was that the Anglo-French joint force would hold until Israel engaged Nasser's forces with the intent of not publicly appearing to be engaged in a coordinated British-French-Israeli operation. Thus, the Anglo-French joint task force would appear surprised and dismayed by the eruption of Israeli-Egyptian fighting near such a key waterway as the Suez Canal. In accord with the prearranged script, the British and French through the United Nations would demand that fighting in the area of the Canal Zone cease within 12 hours or they would be forced to intervene for the security of transit.

However, as with most military operations shrouded in the proverbial Clausewitzian "fog of war," things did not unfold exactly as planned. Before the 12-hour ultimatum expired, a French destroyer as well as Israeli air and naval forces fired on the Egyptian frigate *Ibrahim al-Awal*, with the Israeli units capturing the frigate and towing it to port where apparently it then became part of the Israeli navy. Egypt swiftly accepted the UN call for a cease-fire on November 2, 1956. Israel's Ben-Gurion accepted the next day. However, since Egypt immediately and unexpectedly complied, British and French leaders told Israel to withdraw its acceptance, as this would circumvent the entire plan. Accordingly, the Israeli government then attached unacceptable conditions upon Egypt for it to militarily stand down.

As a result, Allied airstrikes continued, although Israeli units halted on a line 10 miles from the Suez Canal. The necessary synchronized coordination required by the operational concepts of Musketeer-Kadesh during the 1956 Suez Crisis was, in a word, bungled. Other aspects of Allied military operations, nonetheless, achieved operational objectives as laid out in the planning process. Of particular importance to the Allied and Israeli air campaign was the destruction of newly supplied Soviet Mikoyan-Gurevich MiG-15 jet fighters and Ilyushin Il-28 jet bombers that were brought into Egypt by Nasser. While the MiGs were evacuated to Jordan and Saudi Arabia, Allied air strikes destroyed Nasser's new jet bombers. Eventually, the Allied air attacks, conducted over a period of 48 hours, dropped 1,962 bombs in 18 attacks on 13 targets and destroyed 260 Egyptian aircraft.

Following what essentially amounted to the destruction of the Egyptian air force, Allied forces conducted a series of airborne assaults coordinated jointly with amphibious operations. On November 5 and 6, British paratroops landed west of Port Said, as French paratroops landed south of the key Mediterranean port at the northern end of the Suez Canal. Also on November 5, the IDF captured the strategic city of Sharm el-Sheikh located on the southern tip of the Sinai Peninsula and the key to lifting the blockade at the Straits of Tiran and the Gulf of Aqaba. The occupation of Sharm el-Sheikh marked the end of the Israelis' Operation Kadesh. By November 7, Anglo-French units had succeeded in controlling the canal from Port Said to Ismailia.

In the middle of all these, Soviet Foreign Minister Nikolai Bulganin and Soviet Premier Nikita Khrushchev sent written notes and cables of admonishment to Allied leaders threatening Soviet attacks on London, Tel Aviv, and Paris, using "rocket weapons," and stridently warning that continued operations against Nasser risked leading the great powers into a "third world war," including a strike "that may threaten the very existence of Israel." In response to the diplomatic maneuvering taking place among veiled threats of global and perhaps, nuclear war, on November 1, 1956, the UN General Assembly voted for a cease-fire that was to go into effect one week later. On November 21, the first UN peacekeeping troops landed at Port Said, and two days later British and French forces began their withdrawal from Egypt. By December 22, 1956, as the remaining British troops withdrew, Britain ended 74 years of occupation of the Canal Zone. Three months later, in March 1957, the IDF withdrew from the Sinai.

EISENHOWER DOCTRINE

In the wake of the Suez Crisis, the United States undertook a commitment to keep the Straits of Tiran open, in general, to Israeli shipping, in particular. As the Soviet Union continued with its attempts at penetration into the Middle East, on March 9, 1957, the U.S. government announced what came to be known as the Eisenhower Doctrine in which the United States pledged economic and military aid to any Middle Eastern nation requesting assistance in response to coercive or other unwanted activities on the part of the USSR.

On February 1, 1958, the United Arab Republic was formed, uniting Egypt and Syria, which lasted only until 1961. Nasser insisted that a strong central government be located in Cairo and that political parties within Syria be abolished. Nasser also demanded the removal of Syrian army influence from politics. Damascus's trading and merchant elite, in one of the oldest and most successful trading cities in the world, soon began to chafe at the communist-inspired view of rigid central control of both politics and economics. However, discontent within the commercial sector eventually combined with displeasure within the Syrian officer corps, and rebellious army units marched on Damascus in 1961 and restored Syrian independence from Cairo.

A few months after the United Arab Republic came into being, seismic political shifts occurred in Iraq and in Lebanon in July 1958. In Iraq, the Hashemite dynasty, which had brought King Faisal I to power in 1932 with British support, had attracted the ire of Nasser and the Soviets by joining with the British in the Baghdad Pact alliance in 1955 (to oppose further Soviet encroachment into the Middle East). For Nasser, the Baghdad Pact was simply the West attempting to block his objectives toward consolidating power across the Arab world. In what came to be known as the *14 July Revolution*, King Faisal II of Iraq and his family were murdered and a group mirroring the Egyptian example of "Free Officers" executed a coup.

Simultaneous to the Iraqi developments, conflict was also taking place in Lebanon. In July 1958, civil war broke out between Muslims and Maronite Christians. Nasser was displeased with pro-Western President Camille Chamoun, a Christian, for not breaking relations with the West during the Suez Crisis in 1956. Lebanon's Muslim population (in general) sought to join Nasser's United Arab Republic, while the Christians sought continued ties with the West. Following the 14 July Revolution in Iraq, and not wishing to see a repeat in Lebanon, U.S. President Eisenhower authorized Operation Blue Bat on July 15, 1958, which entailed the first application of the Eisenhower Doctrine.

The objective of Blue Bat was to support Chamoun's government against internal strife and to dissuade Egypt and Syria from interfering either covertly or openly with military support. Toward these objectives, the United States sent 14,000 military personnel (8,509 army and 5,670 marine) to secure the Beirut International Airport, located a few miles to the south of the city, Beirut's port, and the approaches to the city. These forces were supported by a naval force of 40 ships and 40,000 sailors and marines.[18] Subsequently, the presence of U.S. forces stabilized the situation for Chamoun's government and, by October 25, 1958, Eisenhower withdrew American troops.

On March 24, 1959, the new Iraqi government repudiated the Baghdad Pact, which effectively ended the organization's viability. Britain, in an informal agreement with the United States, then organized CENTO, which included Turkey, Iran, and Pakistan. By 1961, the Kurds in northern Iraq who had been promised increased autonomy by Iraqi leader Qasim attempted to establish independence from Baghdad. The struggles that followed came to be known as the First Kurdish-Iraqi War of 1961–1970, or the Barazani Rebellion. In June 1963, Syria joined Baghdad in its war on the Kurds, an ethnic group whose people lived (and still live) in the territory that became modern Syria, Turkey, Iran, and Iraq. Syria responded to the Kurds' desire for independence by joining the Iraqi military campaign and, in sending aircraft, armored vehicles, and a 6,000-man force. Even into the twenty-first century, the Kurds have been unable to establish political independence over their home territory, which they have inhabited continuously for thousands of years.

As the new Iraqi regime opted out of the British-led Baghdad Pact, oil-producing states within the Middle East began cooperating to gain increased leverage over Western oil companies. In a further sign of "Western distancing," as Western oil companies arbitrarily lowered the price paid for Middle Eastern oil, regional producers formed Organization of Petroleum Exporting Countries (OPEC) during meetings in September 1960. This would later (in January 1968) give rise to the Organization of Arab Petroleum Exporting Countries (OAPEC), which paralleled OPEC but included only Arab producers. When war came to the region in 1967—the Six-Day War—10 Arab countries announced an oil embargo on Britain and the United States, accusing the two nations of supporting Israeli attacks on Arab nations. This marked the first concerted effort by OPEC to use oil as a political and economic weapon. The boycott was short-lived, however, ending in August 1967 and without appreciably impacting Western economies. Later, following the October war of 1973, OPEC actions against the West became more pronounced, and oil exports, as a political tool, gained in effectiveness.

The Arab Common Market was formed in 1964 and consisted of Egypt, Iraq, Jordan, and Syria (Libya and Sudan joined in 1977), which sought to promote inter-Arab trade and development. Also established in 1964 was the Palestine Liberation Organization (PLO), seeking the establishment of an independent Arab Palestinian state within the boundaries of the former British Mandate. The PLO refused to accept the legitimacy of the State of Israel and instead focused on armed "resistance" operations (guerrilla activities) against the Jewish state.

Instructive as to the actual Western point of view with regard to the developments within the region are the comments of then British Labour Party Foreign Secretary Michael Stewart to representatives of the Israeli government in 1966:

> We see no prospect that the Arabs will be willing to make peace on terms which you can accept in the foreseeable future, or any means of compelling them to. You must be realistic about the strength of Arab feeling on this. You must also recognize that it is important to Western interests—which are extremely important to you own survival—for us to maintain tolerable relations and some influence with the Arabs. You must not, therefore, expect us to take sides, or to appear to take sides, with you against the Arabs. For our part, we will see that you are able to acquire weapons for your defense; and, as you know, the Arabs are well aware that they cannot attempt to destroy Israel without taking on the United States Sixth Fleet. In return, we expect you to co-operate in preventing the dispute coming to a boil, by acting with restraint, and by maintaining a reasonable relationship with the United Nations, so that, if you have to be helped it can be done under United Nations cover. We understand the difficulties of your position, but the law of possession, the preservation of the status quo works markedly in your favour.

Stewart also provided a stark message to the Arabs:

> You have lost a diplomatic war, took to arms, lost a military war, and have been losing a cold war ever since. Some day you will have to come to terms

with the reality and face the consequences of this, instead of wasting your substance and energies in this fruitless pursuit of what you might have got twenty years ago. There is no prospect that Israel will make any substantial concessions now or in the future, and there is no prospect of your being able to force them to; sooner or later you must swallow your pride and settle for the status quo with (American) compensation for the refugees. Meanwhile you are your own masters. We shall not compel you to make peace and we shall oppose any attempt by either side to upset the status quo by the use of force.[19]

From a British post-imperial perspective, an existing status quo provided stability and order upon which economic and social progress became possible. That postimperial perspective also understood the need for change and growth. "British policy was based around the preservation of the status quo. It was extremely desirable that change in the Arab world was ordered and gradual. British policy since 1962 had been strongly aligned with the conservative monarchies—such as Saudi Arabia and Jordan—against Nasser's Egypt."[20]

Status quo powers within the region in the early 1960s included Saudi Arabia, Jordan, the oil emirates in the Gulf, Iran, and Turkey (a NATO member). The Soviets, conversely, had an abiding interest in sponsoring "socialist" Arab regimes and insurgencies attempting to circumvent the existing Western-Arab-Turk-Persian regional status quo. During the Iraq revolution in 1958, the British-affiliated Hashemite monarchy was overthrown by socialist intrigue and a coup d'état sending shock waves throughout the region, particularly within the capitals of the countries supportive or aligned with Western democracies. With the union of Egypt and Syria that same year creating the United Arab Republic, Turkey and Israel both found themselves with "revolutionary" Arab states on their respective borders.[21] In Israel's case, a Soviet-inspired socialist state was not only on its border; it was, in fact, flanked by Soviet-influenced and Soviet-militarily-supplied states.

BRITISH-FRENCH INFLUENCE ECLIPSED
BY U.S.-SOVIET COMPETITION

As French and British colonialism withered in the Middle East during the years 1955 to 1967, it was replaced by a burgeoning U.S.-Soviet rivalry for influence.[22] Juxtaposed with these strategic Cold War dynamics was the economic element where the share of Middle Eastern oil in total world production from 1950 to 1973 rose from 17 percent to nearly 40 percent. While the United States had domestic reserves and global trading capacity to provide some respite from the growing importance of Middle Eastern oil, Japan and Western Europe, key U.S. allies, were and remain highly dependent on oil imports from the region, with Western Europe requiring some 60 percent of its needs to come from abroad. Japan's vulnerability was much greater—dependent on imports for about 90 percent of domestic consumption.

In 1955, Russia offered arms to the largest and most important oil producer in the Middle East, Saudi Arabia, following the death of King Ibn Saud in 1953. Crown Prince Faisal, the Saudi premier and foreign minister at the time, confirmed the offer and the kingdom's refusal of it.[23] In the preceding month, the announcement was made of the Soviet-Egyptian arms deal, which provided the USSR the opportunity at circumventing the Baghdad Pact and in establishing itself within what Napoleon had called the most important nation in the world—Egypt.[24] This became known as the Cairo-Czechoslovakia arms deal where Cairo sent cotton and the Soviet client state, Czechoslovakia, sent arms and munitions. Also in 1955, Moscow opted to provide Egypt with an experimental nuclear reactor. This transpired a few days after the United States concluded a similar agreement with Israel.

As Moscow pushed into the Middle East, the West pushed back in central Europe. In 1956, the Soviets were faced with the most significant challenge to their rule as antigovernment uprisings in Budapest, Hungary, were regarded in Moscow as a direct threat to their position in Eastern Europe. Forced to respond militarily in central Europe, Moscow soon watched as British, French, and Israeli troops moved against its new ally in Cairo—Nasser—during the Suez Crisis.[25] Only by threatening nuclear war, did the Soviets manage to motivate Washington into calling off the activities of its Allies.[26]

The Soviet Union's push into Egypt and Syria brought the Cold War and nuclear weapons into the complex web of relationships within North Africa and the Middle East. The difficulty in establishing a stronger Russian presence in the Muslim world was not in its "revolutionary socialism" brand, but rather in the accompanying metaphysical principles that for Karl Marx, Friedrich Engels, and Vladimir Lenin were both atheistic and materialistic in orientation. This created difficulties for Arab and Muslim revolutionary leaders' intent on exploiting the Cold War rivalry in pursuit of their interests in both politics and economics. After Moscow threatened nuclear war during the Suez Crisis in 1956, the United States became less inclined toward its earlier policies of caution and constraint regarding weapons and arms moving into Israel.

> In 1960, reports began emerging that Israel was constructing a nuclear plant in Dimona. In 1966, the news of the plant's existence was confirmed and Nasser began warning that Egypt would launch a preemptive attack if Egypt had the slightest reason to believe that Israel was on the verge of manufacturing atomic weapons.[27]

In 1960, Israel's continued assertive stance in terms of expanding the boundaries of its land and its control over resources led to the Rotem Crisis. Border tensions with Syria developed into armed confrontation in February and March 1960, and Egypt responded by sending forces to the Israeli-Egyptian border. With the establishment of the United Arab Republic (union between Egypt and Syria), in February 1958, Israel-Syrian disputes now involved Egypt and, by extension, the Soviet Union. By late 1959, disagreements over Israeli cultivation rights on the eastern shore of Lake Galilee brought action by the Syrian military. Syria's leadership viewed the issue as one more encroachment upon Arab rights by the Jewish state and directed the military to shell IDF positions with heavy mortars. As a result, an Israeli policeman was killed and two others injured.

To avenge this, the Israeli Golani Brigade conducted Operation Hargol (Cricket), attacking Syrian soldiers in the village of Lower Tawafiq, killing 9 and wounding an additional 15. Syria then responded by deploying two reserve brigades, an artillery regiment and a tank brigade to the Syrian-Israeli border. In solidarity, Nasser ordered Egypt's light footprint in the Sinai reinforced as the 2nd Infantry Division and the 4th Armored Division were quietly moved across the Suez Canal and into the desert in late February 1960. By February 27, the Egyptian army had positioned all three of its armored brigades and six infantry brigades in the Sinai near the Israeli border, as Syria deployed seven brigades to the border area in the north. From the United Arab Republic military staffs' point of view, they now had Israel in a pincer vise and awaited, in anticipation, the political orders for it to be crushed.

As the Egyptian forces moved stealthily into the Sinai unbeknownst to the Israelis, U.S. intelligence captured the moves with overhead imagery. This early warning was subsequently provided to the Israeli leadership who directed their own flights (Israeli Air Force Sud-Ouest Vautour IIB 33 "Big Brother" aircraft) to monitor developments. Quietly and rather surreptitiously, Egypt had positioned 500 tanks and SU-100 tank destroyers directly across from about 25 Israeli tanks. In consequence, chief of the IDF general staff, Rav Aluf Haim Laskov, recommended to the Israeli political leadership a massive mobilization of reserves and preparation for an imminent invasion from at least two axes of advance—from the north (Syrian attack) and from the south (Egyptian attack).

The Israeli prime minister rejected this request and instead limited the call-up to 7,000 reservists while simultaneously ordering regular army units to take up positions opposite the threatening invaders. The IDF sent the 1st Golani Brigade and the 7th Armored Brigade into the northern Negev near the Rafah opening and directed the 35th Paratroopers Brigade and the 37th Mechanized Brigade to deploy to the Ktzi'ot region.

By this time, word of the Egyptian and Syrian movements had been circulating, and Nasser had hoped that his actions would cause widespread panic within Israel itself. Instead, the Israeli media, working under government orders, kept the crisis secret.

Nevertheless, Israeli leaders were as sufficiently concerned as they were militarily unprepared and realized that a negotiated solution would have to be pursued in order to avoid a military escalation of the crisis. The political leadership, accordingly, sought to resolve the issue within the United Nations and turned to diplomacy to avoid an unexpected war. The crisis was subsequently resolved through negotiation and each side demobilized. However, in Egypt and throughout the Arab world, the incident received extensive coverage and was portrayed as a great victory for Nasser and the armies of the United Arab Republic. For Nasser, it was a useful public diplomacy gambit and, coming on the heels of the Suez Crisis, further burnished his credentials as, arguably, the most effective and influential leader in the Arab world.

From the perspective of the leadership in Tel Aviv, the Rotem Crisis was a wake-up call for both the IDF as well as the Israeli intelligence community, which failed to provide warning of developments that posed, potentially, an existential threat to the nation. As such, the crisis provided lessons to both Israel's political leadership and Nasser himself. For the national government in Tel Aviv, it was an opportunity to better prepare for future attempts at intimidation and to improve military readiness and early warning, which placed Israel in a compromised position, described by Rabin in a note on February 25, 1960, to Israeli Air Force Commander in Chief Ezer Weizman: "We've been caught with our pants down. During the next twenty-four hours everything depends on the air force."

Since the IDF was surprised and generally unprepared in February 1960, Ben-Gurion's refusal to escalate the crisis with a massive mobilization, instead seeking to de-escalate the tensions, was probably the most propitious path for Israel's foreign policy. For Israel's political leadership the lesson was twofold: 1) be prepared to compromise if necessary for the survival of the state; and 2) let us take proactive steps in order to avoid such predicaments in the future. Accordingly, early warning systems and increased human intelligence collection were part of the new strategy. The event also instilled in Israel's political, military, and intelligence communities an increased preference for coordinating with the Americans.

Lessons from the Rotem Crisis of 1960 were different for Nasser. For the Egyptian leader, there was benefit from a "swaggering" use of force, particularly in a highly publicized manner in which he achieved political results leading to new levels of adulation throughout the Arab world. He, unfortunately, brought the "lessons learned" into 1967 where similar actions performed during the Rotem Crisis only served to a) exacerbate a delicate situation, b) paint him into a corner, and c) ultimately cost him the leadership of the Arab world as well as his air force.

Much farther way from the tensions on the Israeli borders, in the south of the Arabian Peninsula, a group of pro-Nasser officers in September 1962 overthrew the conservative Yemen regime of King al-Imam Badr. The attempt on Badr's life having failed, the deposed king promptly declared war on the new regime plummeting Yemen into civil war. In October, Nasser decided to send Egyptian troops to support the Yemeni rebels turned government bureaucrats.[28] However, by 1967 with no resolution in sight, with more than 70,000 Egyptian troops in Yemen, and, as Nasser began seeing his reputation among the Arabs dissipating, the Egyptian president began contemplating a face-saving exit strategy. By April 1967, a row between the Syrians and Israelis seemed to present an effective solution to his problem as well as a chance to reinvigorate his sagging standing as the leader of the Arab world.

Chapter 5

Arab-Israeli Conventional Operations, 1967–1973

> The 1967 Six Day War was indeed lightning war of the kind whose effects we experienced everywhere in 1940 but this time compressed within a limited timeframe never before realized.[1]

> The 1967 Arab-Israeli [Six Day] War is the only major war fought in the 20th century where the whole war was essentially decided by a single battle on a single day.[2]

With the British slowly winding down its military commitment in the Middle East in the 1960s, the United States increased its support for the security of Israel, while the Soviet Union continued funneling weapons and weapons systems in an effort to undermine both Israeli and the Western presence in the region. Considering that Israel was surrounded by hostile states, the military hardware provided by the United States was a necessary adjunct to the defensive needs of the Jewish state. America committed itself toward supplying Israel with sufficient technology to insure that the Israeli Defense Forces (IDF) and the Israeli Air Force (IAF) maintained a "qualitative edge" vis-à-vis its potential challengers across the Middle East.

Yet, there were aspects of Israel state policy in terms of its relations with its neighbors that often unnecessarily fanned the flames of Arab anger and placed U.S. leaders in difficult positions.

> In 1953 Israel launched an ambitious project to pipe water from the upper Jordan around the West Bank and on to the Negev desert. By 1956 Israel

had resumed the diversion project which eventually made the flow of the lower reaches of the river too saline to serve the needs of the Kingdom of Jordan . . .[3]

At the Cairo summit, January 13–17, 1964, the Arabs adopted a counter-diversion project where the Authority was to draw up plans to divert the Jordan River at its source, thus preventing Israel from exploiting the river for its own ends.

The Israeli government decided that the best way to put an end to the Arab counter-diversion scheme was to destroy the counter-diversion equipment. On November 13, 1964, Israel launched a massive air strike against the Syrian counter-diversion sites wrecking Syria's engineering equipment.[4]

In 1980, a commission established by the UN Security Council Resolution 446 of 1979 concluded that Israel's water policies had violated Security Council decisions and the Fourth Geneva Convention of 1949 . . . In 1998, of the total water supply of the West Bank, 56 percent was flowing west for consumption in Israel proper, leaving 24 percent for some 200,000 set-tlers and 20 percent for over 2,000,000 Arabs.[5]

In addition to the scarce resource of water in the Middle East, the scarce resource of arable land often became a subject of dispute, and ultimately, war.

Moshe Dayan, Minister of Defense during the Six Day War, called the decision to capture the Golan Heights on the final day of the war one of the worst mistakes of his political career. "The capture of the Golan Heights was unnecessary. Look, we can speak in terms of 'the Syrians are scoundrels, they should be screwed, now's the time' and so forth, but this is not policy. You don't screw the enemy because he's a scoundrel but because he threatens you, and the Syrians on the fourth day of the war were no threat to us." Dayan attributed the Israeli decision to attack the Golan Heights to political pressures exerted by settlers of Israel's Jordan Valley, especially on then Prime Minister Levi Eshkol, who himself hailed from Degania (a kibbutz located south of the Sea of Galilee). The settlers were motivated, according to Dayan, by narrow considerations: "The delegation (of settlers) that came to convince Eshkol to attack the Heights . . . thought about the land on the Heights . . . They did not even try to hide their greed for that land. That's what guided them."[6]

I know how at least 80 percent of the incidents began there . . . It would happen like this: We would send a tractor to plow someplace where nothing could be done, in the demilitarized zone, knowing ahead of time that the Syrians would start shooting. If they didn't shoot, we would tell the tractor to go on, until the Syrians got annoyed and [began] shooting.[7]

Moshe Dayan rose to hero status within Israel for bravery and leadership while aiding in the creation and defense of the Jewish state and following the 1956 and 1967 Arab-Israeli Wars. The above observations were made after the Six-Day War had ended. The following discusses how it began and how it was conducted.

> On April 5, 1967, Rabin notified Eshkol of the intention to cultivate some disputed parcels of land near the Syrian border and "let him understand" that the expected Syrian reaction might eventually lead to the use of air power ... The Syrians opened fire at 0940 and starting shelling settlements at 1152. At 1214 the authorization to use the Air Force was given. Israeli air strikes ceased about 1400 and were resumed at 1525 only after the Syrians launched a heavy artillery bombardment of Kibbutz Gadot at 1145.[8]

On April 7, 1967, in the skies above the Sea of Galilee, Israeli and Syrian air force fighters clashed in a major engagement, resulting in the downing of six Syrian aircraft. Israel followed up the air victory with two IAF jets buzzing the city of Damascus (i.e., flying fast and low).[9] In the Arab media, the incident was portrayed as 130 Israeli jet fighters brazenly buzzing the capital city of Syria after invading Syrian air space and attacking innocent Syrian aircraft.[10]

During these Israeli-Syrian clashes, Gamal Nasser of Egypt, for many months prior, had been watching his reputation suffer, as a result of the inconclusive nature of his intervention in Yemen—although Egypt had deployed tens of thousands of troops and had been in occupation of the country for years. In Yemen, forces aligned with Nasser attempted to undermine the British, which responded by supporting a war of attrition against occupying Egyptian troops.[11] In the face of rising criticism over Nasser's failure to support Syria against the Israelis, the king of Jordan stated publicly that Nasser was "hiding behind UN Emergency Force (UNEF) skirts," then operating as peacekeepers in the Sinai. Although five years of fighting in Yemen had left the Egyptian army in a reduced state of readiness, Nasser believed that by showing the flag and through a threat of force Israel could be dissuaded from moving against Syria and, once having accomplished this (again, as he did during the Rotem Crisis of 1960), he would show the Arab world that he alone was capable of constraining Israeli behavior.

Nasser had his own timeline in mind for what was about to transpire—the envisaged threat of force and the follow-on negotiations leading to his desired political settlement. However, the original plan rarely survives intact after first contact with an opponent or enemy. For Nasser, on May 13, 1967, his government was informed (erroneously, it would later turn out) by the Soviets that Israel had mobilized 13 IDF brigades for deployment on the Syrian-Israeli border.[12] This report followed in the wake of a series of early warnings from the Soviets, beginning on April 29, 1967, that Israel was massing on the border.[13] In response, on May 14, Nasser issued the order for general mobilization, and Syria followed his lead by placing its forces on high alert. At this time, the U.S. Sixth Fleet increased its alert status, and Soviet vessels from the Black Sea Fleet entered the Eastern Mediterranean through the Turkish Straits. On May 16, Nasser ordered UN peacekeeping forces out of the Sinai, as two Egyptian infantry divisions accompanied by 200 tanks began making their way to form up with the single division already there.

> Israel mobilized 60,000 to 70,000 reservists in mid-May in response to the Egyptian build-up. Once it had done so, Israel needed a relatively quick solution to the crisis, as its economy could not afford the absence of so many workers for any length of time.[14]

Nasser then ordered the Gulf of Aqaba and the Straits of Tiran closed to Israeli shipping on May 22, 1967, knowing full well that Israel's leaders would consider this an act of war. "Egypt's remilitarization of Sinai and re-imposition of blockade over the straits of Tiran in May 1967 had given rise to many attempts at explanation."[15] The publicly stated explanation was made by Nasser himself at a press conference on May 28, 1967: "We intend to open a general assault on Israel. This will be total war. Our basic aim is the destruction of Israel."[16]

On May 30, the king of Jordan traveled to Cairo where he and Nasser signed a mutual security pact that placed the Jordanian military under Egyptian command. This was quickly followed by Iraq joining the alliance and moving troops into Jordan on May 31. Although Nasser's United Arab Republic had fallen apart in 1961, he concluded an alliance with Syria in November 1966. In the middle of the May crisis, Nasser accused Israel of aggression toward Syria, threatened military action while declaring a state of emergency, and simultaneously moving several divisions close to the Israeli-Egyptian border in the eastern Sinai.

At the level of mobilization on the part of all the parties by the end of May, along with the public rhetoric made by some that served to narrow their options and even paint them into a corner, particularly Nasser, one would have been foolish not to be prepared for all-out war. In many respects, the events prior to the initiation of the 1967 Six-Day War were similar to those leading up to the First World War, where leaders sought to frighten their opponents by the "swaggering use" of military force while not actually wishing to fight a global war. The tactic was to bring a situation to crisis levels by ratcheting up the public rhetoric, mobilizing the military, and placing your opponent(s) in a position of either fighting or acquiescing, with the belief that your opponent would see the costs of war far outweighing the costs of a negotiated settlement.

While Nasser ratcheted up the noise and military pressure, he felt comfortable that the crisis would not necessarily lead to armed conflict. Nasser had pinned his hopes on statements made by the United States following the Suez Crisis of 1956. The United States had promised Israel that if it stood down from combat operations during the 1956 crisis, it would, in the future, insure that access to the Israeli port of Eilat would be maintained through the Straits of Tiran. The United States informed Israeli leaders that it understood the need for Israel to maintain freedom of action by keeping unilateral options open to insure free navigation, but that Israel, in any future crisis, should allow the United States to deal with any issue regarding a blockade in the Straits of Tiran in international diplomacy and at the United Nations. Accordingly, Washington acquiesced to the fact that Israel had the right to act militarily if necessary but with the caveat of only acting militarily after the United States took international action to insure free passage through the Straits of Tiran.

As a result, Nasser believed that by imposing a blockade on Israeli shipping, even though Israel's leaders claimed such action to be *casus belli* for war, he would show himself in the Arab world to be, once again, fearless in the face of Israeli threats and the one leader who could force the Israelis to behave themselves, all the while knowing (believing) that the United States would be required to step in before Israel could launch any unilateral action. He would then negotiate a settlement insuring that Israel would not attack Syria in exchange for lifting the blockade. All in all, it was a grand scheme for the Egyptian president and, ostensibly, for the leader of the Arab world.

The problem with Nasser's strategic logic was that the Soviets were wrong—or were providing erroneous information for ulterior motives—about Israel's plan to invade Syria, and Israel had no intention of being humiliated again by the Arab leader, as happened during the Rotem Crisis in 1960. Compounding the problems for Nasser's plans for adroitly managing the issue, regional events spun out of his control during the first week of June in 1967. On June 4, 1967, a national unity cabinet in Israel received a briefing on military developments deemed by the IDF, AMAN, and MOSSAD leaders as essential for understanding the crisis. This briefing went on for seven hours, and, after it ended, the Israeli prime minister authorized Operation *Moked*, the IDF battle plan that laid the foundations for a rapid and decisive victory during the Six-Day War.

Two of the most critical vulnerabilities of the State of Israel in 1967 were the lack of strategic endurance and limited strategic depth. One of the reasons David Ben-Gurion hesitated in the full mobilization of IDF reserves during the Rotem Crisis of 1960 was directly related to how critical those individuals were to the proper functioning of the Israeli economy. As we have seen, in order to sustain the economic production necessary to conduct extended modern industrialized war in the twentieth century, it was necessary to have sufficient numbers of people who could both work and fight. If you were required to pull your people away from work in order to deploy for a fight, that fight could not be extended without serious disruptions in the economy.

Thus, one needed sufficient numbers for warfare as well as for economic production. Limited in population, Israel lacked the numbers for effective strategic endurance. Admittedly, by the time of the 1967 Six-Day War, both the United States and Britain were sufficiently disposed to ensure the survival of the Jewish state that, if necessary, they would have been prepared to augment any deficiencies in troops and materiel in an extended and/or existential fight. This vulnerability led to two policy implications for Israeli national strategy: 1) fight with an intent to win quickly, and 2) do not alienate the United States and Britain.

The territory that Israel occupied in 1967 was quite limited. Flying over the state in airplane would take about four minutes. With hostile neighbors surrounding Israeli borders, an armored attack on an unsuspecting Israeli population could be mounted from multiple directions with the State of Israel overrun in a very brief amount of time. Thus, to allow an enemy to seize the initiative and to conduct a surprise air attack followed by a coordinated ground campaign posed an existential threat to the nation. This threat forced Israel to adopt strategies and policies, which made it appear on the regional and world stage as overly aggressive and militaristic, exactly what its opponents within the region had intended by refusing to make peace.

In World War II, the Soviet Union had used its vast spaces to chew up Adolf Hitler's advancing armies, buying time by grudgingly trading space. Britain used the same tactic to frustrate Erwin Rommel's attempts at taking control in Egypt. As such, the vastness of the Soviet Union and North Africa provided strategic depth in defense. Israel could not adopt such a defense-in-depth strategy and, to avoid being overrun, had to anticipate not only an enemy's mobilization, preparation, and alignment for battle, but also had to be successful at solving one of the most difficult of all military intelligence problems—understanding an enemy's or potential enemy's intent.[17]

EGYPT'S "PLAN KAHIR"

Conversely, the Egyptian army—the most powerful of the Arab armies at the time and the one that Israeli intelligence was most concerned with following the Cairo-Czechoslovakia 1955 arms agreement through which Egyptian cotton would be traded for Soviet-arranged weapons and supplies—adopted a contingency plan for mobile defense-in-depth in the Sinai. Egypt's "Plan Kahir" called for drawing the IDF deep into the Sinai Peninsula, and once Israeli forces had arrived inside a triangle defined by

Suweitma, Bir Gifgafa, and Jebel Libni and moved beyond their culminating point, Egyptian forces would envelop and destroy the attackers. This would in part be accomplished by massed Egyptian firepower in the form of antiarmor guns and an armored strike force waiting patiently and quietly in the rear to mount a counterattack against the tiring troops and their overextended lines of communication.

For the Egyptian high command and their Soviet supporters, given the infusion of Soviet MIG fighter jets into the Egyptian Air Force (EAF), the IAF would not be able to gain air supremacy nor air superiority.[18] Thus, Plan Kahir was going to inflict decisive defeat upon the IDF in many ways not dissimilar to the plight of the German army in both the Soviet Union and in North Africa. Kahir, however, smartly conceived and well thought out, unfortunately misread key dynamics that provided for Allied success in World War II. The problem for the Egyptians and their Soviet supporters was that while control of both the sea and the air were ultimately in the hands of the Allies during most of World War II, during the Six-Day War neither Egypt nor the Soviets would be able to maintain air or sea superiority.

As events unfolded in May 1967 taking the Arabs and Jews on a collision course to war, Nasser still had not been briefed on the specifics of the Egyptian war plan. At a final briefing, Nasser disapproved of the plan's specifics, arguing that it would be politically unpalatable to allow Israel to take territory in the Sinai. Instead he ordered his military chief, Amer, to move his forces forward and, if necessary, meet IDF forces at the border. In many respects, the Six-Day War was a reflection of the military and political dynamics animating the Second World War, as the strains and pressures between the strategic and operational levels of war once again factored into events unfolding in 1967.

> By the 1967 war the IDF was capable of conducting rapid maneuver warfare into an enemy's rear with large armor formations supported by an air force.[19]

> The superior Israeli planning effort improved the chances for victory against an enemy coalition with overwhelming numerical advantage.[20]

OPERATION MOKED

Strategically, the Arab nations and Israel shared common general objectives in their approach to security. Leaders of modern nation-states attempt to insure the security of the state by maximizing freedom of action while minimizing threats—particularly those of an existential nature. After their experiences during the 1948 Arab-Israeli War when the Israelis found themselves surrounded by the armies of hostile states and, in the case of the Rotem Crisis, with a superpower (Union of Soviet

Socialist Republics [USSR]) backing those hostile militaries, Israel's view on war in 1967 was to prevail or lose the state. Therefore, while the IDF was fully focused on winning, or die trying, this complete commitment to victory was not shared by the Arab armies facing it during Operation Moked in 1967.

Overall command of the IDF during Moked fell to General Yitzhak Rabin (chief of staff, IDF), while the IAF was led by Major General Mordechai Hod. The operational war plan called for surprise air strikes against EAF jet aircraft before they could get airborne. Once the EAF was neutralized, Israeli ground units would launch lightning strikes against the Egyptian army divisions, which had advanced into the Sinai Desert and were, by the end of May 1967, threatening Israel's southern borders. If the plan unfolded as generally expected, Israel would knock the Egyptians out of the war within a week and turn to face hostile forces that may or may not then attempt to attack Israel on their own.

Accordingly, enemy air forces capable of striking homeland cities became the first concern. In 1967, Egypt, Syria, Iraq, and Jordan had between them 450 fighters and nearly 100 bombers. The air component of Operation Moked (English: Operation Focus) was based on a plan conducted by the Luftwaffe on June 22, 1941, during Operation Barbarossa, which sent German aircraft in a surprise preemptive strike to destroy much of the Soviet air force before it could launch.[21] Similarly, Operation Moked aimed at achieving air superiority within six hours through the destruction of the EAF aircraft on the ground.

> In 1966, the Israelis developed a runway demolition bomb, weighing 154 pounds and creating a crater five meters wide and one and a half meters deep. The bomb was dropped from an altitude of one hundred meters and slowed down by a parachute that would simultaneously activate a rocket that would propel it through multiple layers of runway.[22]

The IAF was concerned first with Soviet-supplied MiG-21s and TU-16 and IL-28 bombers, which became the initial targets, followed by airfields and air defenses. Toward these objectives:

> The Israelis committed their entire air force (minus eight fighters on home combat patrol and four on runway alert) in a bid for air superiority on the first day of the 1967 war ... this was an instance where a single battle was decisive.[23]

At 7:45 a.m. on June 5, 1967, 180 IAF attack aircraft and bombers (Ouragans, Mysteres, Super Mysteres, Mirages, and Vautors) took off in cells of four heading out into the Mediterranean Sea. The only Arab military radar station to monitor these flights was in Amman, Jordan, whose personnel, based on the manner in which they took off, formed up and the heading taken, believed them to be aircraft from the U.S. Sixth Fleet.

Shortly thereafter, the first wave of IAF strike aircraft descended to an altitude of 30 feet, turned south and southeast and headed for the Egyptian airfields at Mach 1 (approximately 750 miles per hour [mph]). The initial targets, the jet aircraft that had been supplied by Moscow, were located at four airfields in the Sinai, three along the Suez Canal, six in the Nile Delta, and five in Upper Egypt.

> What made an effective strike-first and gain air superiority plan possible was superior comprehensive intelligence including base locations, aircraft types, munitions, fuel supplies, data on pilots, operational training capabilities, radar sites, regional control centers and aircraft scrambling procedures.

The intelligence and information obtained in support of Moked was extensive. In Egypt, between 7:30 a.m. and 8:30 a.m. radar personnel would be at the end of their shifts, getting ready to leave, some tired, and many having breakfast. Personnel for follow-on shifts were coming to work, many stuck in traffic. During that time as well, there was a gap in Egypt's combat air patrol (CAP), as aircraft were landing and before replacements became airborne. This same dynamic was exploited on December 8, 1941, during the Pacific campaign in the Second World War, when the Japanese nearly destroyed the entire U.S. air fleet on the ground within the Philippines.

The IAF could refuel, rearm, and preflight an aircraft within eight minutes, and this could be accomplished eight times a day for every strike and fighter aircraft. Each IAF aircraft took off with a maximum bomb load and conducted four to five sorties a day. Planes returning from action radioed in ahead of time any problems or special needs enabling ground crews to obtain the right tools and parts and be organized to effect results quickly. Israeli pilots flying missions during the Six-Day War were instructed to spend only seven minutes over their targets before breaking off and heading home. All of these efficiency efforts maximized mass, speed, and lethality, as delivered in the opening hours of Moked. Achieving the indispensable element of surprise as well in the first hour, IAF strikes against Egyptian targets involved three waves of IAF aircraft. While the first wave was attacking its targets, a second wave was already halfway to the target area. This pattern was followed by a third wave then taking off from home airfields.

Interestingly, the IAF had taken a page from Soviet armor doctrine, which argued that upon assault by artillery, enemy forces would be neutralized for about three minutes before regaining positions and composure enabling it to fight back. Within those three minutes, Soviet tanks would then launch an assault on the opposing forces that had been pelted with the initial artillery barrage. A three-minute window of opportunity, however, requires a complex, combined-arms approach relying on a highly synchronized attacking force. The IAF delivered just such a performance on June 5, 1967, as the Moked air plan gave the EAF only a three-minute respite between attacks. In just three hours, the IAF destroyed 300 of the EAF's 340 aircraft. Very few in the Egyptian command structure wished to be the one bringing the president such bad news. As a result, Nasser would not be told that his air force had been destroyed until eight hours after it occurred.

Once the IAF air operation had destroyed the threats to Israeli cities and airfields, Hod then diverted his pilots to support the IDF's armored advance. On the fifth and sixth day of the war, the IAF also attacked land and air forces of Jordan and Syria and the Iraqi air force.

Number of Aircraft Destroyed—per Country—1967 Six-Day War

Egypt: 338 aircraft
Syria: 61 aircraft
Jordan: 29 aircraft
Iraq: 23 aircraft
Lebanon: 1 aircraft
Israel: 19 aircraft (only 3 to enemy action)

Following the noon hour on the first day of Operation Moked (June 5), the IAF had air supremacy over Egyptian, Jordanian, and Syrian air space. The same meticulous attention to detail was applied to ground operations as well. The Soviets had supplied the Egyptians with tanks (T34, T54/55) and armored personnel carriers, and while the Russian military had traditionally been among the best in the world, they were neophytes in terms of desert warfare. They brought in armor that was watertight in order to ford the many rivers of Europe. They also supplied personnel carriers that could operate in a chemical-biological warfare environment. In both instances, the vehicles sealed tightly. In the heat of the desert, this became intolerable. The Soviets were also used to fighting where they had rail access. Thus, they moved their armor via railway to the theater, offloaded, advanced a few miles, and fought. In 1967, this logistical luxury was not available to the Egyptians.

On the Israeli side, no IDF tank (Centurions, Pattons, Super Shermans) was left without a transporter for movement toward the actual frontline deployment area. Contrast this with the Egyptian military, which did not possess a single transporter. Soviet tanks, unloaded in ports, in Port Said or in Alexandria, transited via rail to El Arish and El Kantara and moved on their own tracks to deployment areas. Accordingly, Egyptian armor located west of the Suez Canal traveled through hundreds of miles of desert under their own power to take up fighting positions.[24] Moreover, Egyptian tanks operated along the roads, which made them attractive targets for IAF aircraft. Israel planted spies in Arab territory, who offered advice such as suggesting to plant trees to provide shade for soldiers in the field during operations to protect against a glaring sun. Arab armies planted such trees, only to find that it allowed the IDF to target their forces easier in open terrain.

The IDF had figured out that a well-maintained tank could be expected to operate for approximately 100 hours of actual combat driving before it began requiring minor repairs or, in some instances, a major overhaul. Accordingly, the IDF transported the tank to the battle and closely monitored its hourly expenditure. After-action reports indicate that the Israeli tanks fought for 60 hours in the Sinai, 50 hours in Jordan, and 40 hours in Syria during the Six-Day War. Conversely, the Egyptians drove their tanks hundreds of miles just to reach the battle zone and then engaged in combat driving. Accordingly, they were faced with a heightened rate of breakdowns.

In conjunction with the initial air strikes on June 5, IDF Southern Command ground forces moved to assault Egyptian forces arrayed near Gaza and in the heart of the Sinai Desert, as they pressed forward to the Suez Canal. At 8:15 a.m. on June 5, 1967, in the headquarters of the Southern Front, IDF Brigadier-General Yeshayahu Gavish sent the message *Sadin Adom* (Hebrew for "red sheet"), which served as the prearranged signal for launching the Israeli preemptive attack on Egypt. Three division-size task forces (or *Ugdahs*) started engines and proceeded in the direction of the Egyptian forces in the Sinai. Positioned on the right flank of the advancing Israeli army and organized into one of three Ugdahs were two armored brigades with 250 tanks, a brigade of paratroopers advancing in armored personnel carriers (half-tracks, mostly World War II vintage), and a reconnaissance force (nearly a brigade).

The forces on the Israeli right totaled somewhere between 15,000 and 20,000 men and were commanded by Brigadier-General Israel Tal who moved to engage the Egyptian 7th Division and 20th Palestinian Liberation Army (PLA) Division located in the vicinity of Khan Yunis, Rafah, and the coastal road to El Arish. While the 20th PLA Division (Gaza), led by Major General Mohammed Abd el Moneim Hasni, had been reinforced with Egyptian artillery and fielded about 50 Sherman tanks, combat readiness and overall combat effectiveness of the 20th was low. The Egyptian 7th Division was located just south of Gaza, ensconced in defensive field fortifications but hastily organized and sent quickly into the Rafah-El Arish region.

Brigadier-General Ariel Sharon's division (Ugdah) consisted of about 15,000 men and 150 tanks organized into an armored brigade, an infantry brigade, a paratroop brigade, six artillery battalions, and a reconnaissance unit. Facing Sharon to the Southeast in the Abu-Ageila-Kusseima area was the Egyptian 2nd Division, "a good division but commanded by an inept political appointee."

The third Ugdah multitask force, or division, was commanded by Brigadier-General Avraham Yoffe and consisted of 12,000 men and approximately 200 tanks. Supporting Southern Command were also three independent IDF units: the force opposite Gaza contained 7,000 men, the independent brigade as Kuntilla had 4,000 troops, and the unit at Eilat had slightly less than 2,000 men. The total combat strength of Gavish's Southern Command was more than 70,000 men and approximately 750–800 tanks. The Egyptians covered the area at Kuntilla-Nakhil (Operation Kuntilla) with the 6th Mechanized Division, commanded by Major General Abd el Kader Hassan and reinforced with a tank brigade. The 6th, generally considered one of Egypt's premier combat units, was led by a highly regarded military commander.

In the heart of the Sinai was the Egyptian 3rd Infantry Division (Jebel Libni-Bir Hassan region), which was a reserve division led by an incompetent political appointee, Major General Osman Nasser. Backing up the 6th Mechanized Division, also in army reserve, was an armored task force, which was essentially a reinforced armored brigade, located east of Bir Hassan and west of Lussan. Most likely, the unit with the highest level of combat readiness of all Egyptian forces in the Sinai was the 4th Armored Division, which was well led (Major General Sidki el Ghoul, commanding) and held in strategic reserve. Under the direct control of General Headquarters (GHC) Cairo, the Egyptian 4th Armored Division was deployed in the Bir Gifgafa region.

Supporting Egyptian objectives in the Sinai were also smaller-sized units. An independent infantry brigade had been moved to the recently occupied positions at the strategically important city of Sharm el-Sheikh located at the southern point of the Sinai Peninsula, and, at the nexus of the Gulf of Suez, the Red Sea, and the Gulf of Aqaba. During May 1967, three quickly organized mobile reserve infantry brigades had been rushed to defend at Mitla and Giddi, the two strategic passes from the Sinai to the Suez Canal itself. The total ground component of Egyptian forces in the Sinai at the end of May 1967 was about 100,000 men fielding 930 tanks, 200 assault guns, and 900 artillery pieces. These forces were subordinate to the Sinai Front Command, led by General Abd el Mushin Murtagi and his field commander, Lieutenant General Salah el din Mohsen.

The Egyptian operational plan, Kahir, had hoped to trap IDF forces in the desert once they had advanced into the triangle marked by Bir Gifgafa, Jebel Libni, and Suweitma (east of Bir Thamada) and moved beyond their culminating point (an advancing force that has been overextended beyond supply and lines of communication, mechanical breakdowns, and general exhaustion). The difficulty of creating seamless connectivity and unity of effort between the strategic and operational levels of war created problems for the Egyptians in late May and early June 1967, as Nasser refused to follow the carefully planned Egyptian operational construct. As a result, the Egyptians themselves were caught in an IDF triangle marked by Nakla, Mitla Pass, and Bir Gifgafa. There they were forced into retreat.

FOUR PHASES OF THE GROUND CAMPAIGN

The ground component of IDF operations in the Egyptian theater under Operation Moked had four phases based on the assumption that in order to prevail in a ground campaign against Egyptian forces, the IDF would have to break through those forces as they defended a limited number of key passes through the Sinai. The first phase consisted of a two-pronged advance into the Egyptian front lines led by Tal's division along the Rafah-El Arish (near the Mediterranean), coastal axis and, to the south, Sharon's drive on Abu-Ageila-Um Katef. The second phase was dependent upon opportunity expected to develop as a result of Tal's and Sharon's attacks, envisioned that Yoffe's forces would be directed either between Tal and Sharon's divisions or farther to the south to attack at the second Egyptian line near Jebel Libni while the independent brigade would attack at Kuntilla serving more as a diversionary maneuver.

In the third phase, and the one that reversed the "triangle trap," the armored units of Tal, Sharon, and Yoffe were to be concentrated in a general triangle marked by Nakla, the Mitla Pass, and Bir Gifgafa. The fourth phase followed with an advance to the Suez Canal and southward for the capture of Sharm el-Sheikh. By midnight on the first day, the spearhead of Tal's IDF forces, the 7th Armored Brigade, led by Colonel Shmuel Gonen, arrived at El Arish having advanced 40 miles. The lightning advance continued for an additional 48 hours, as Gonen and the IDF 7th Armored Brigade became the first Israeli ground units to reach the canal.

Sharon was tasked with taking Abu Ageila as the main entry point (this key site was part of operational planning in both 1956 and 1967) for transiting the Sinai toward the canal and leading to the cities of Egypt. The IDF engaged in operational deception (OPDEC) and convinced Egyptian commanders that the main effort would be south of Abu Ageila between Qusaymah and Kuntilla. As a result, the Egyptian commander of the 2nd Division, Major General Sadi Naguib, moved his command post from Abu Ageila to Qusaymah. This OPDEC was effective as, once the war began, he was out of position when the main attack took place at Abu Ageila.

Sharon had come up through the ranks as a paratrooper but opted to use an American strategy being used in Vietnam during the mid-1960s, which utilized "air mobility/air assault," or the use of helicopters, to insert troops onto objectives, rather than parachuting troops into battle. He ordered one of his paratrooper battalions to assault Egyptian artillery positions that manned the ridge at Um Katef and which were prepared to fire down upon any IDF advance on Abu Ageila. The battalion went in at night and caught the artillery units and supporting infantry in a surprise attack. Word quickly spread to the frontline Egyptian infantry that IDF troops had arrived to the rear of their positions and were in the process of neutralizing their artillery support. This, coupled with the trickling but electric news that Egyptian airfields (also in their rear) were being struck by the Israeli air force, added to the sudden shock resulting from the realization of being surrounded by enemy forces—forces that, reportedly, were destroying two key components, which infantry relied upon, artillery and air support.

> Ideally, the Israeli's opening moves would be rapid, unpredictable, violent, and disorienting, throwing the Egyptian high command into a temporary state of confusion concerning the Israeli intent.[25]

On June 5 and 6, both Tal and Sharon drove forward in breakthrough advances, according to plan. Joffe's division was subsequently ordered to advance between Tal and Sharon, and the second line of Egyptian defenses was engaged in the vicinity of Jebel Libni. Overwhelming the defenders, IDF commanders then huddled to ascertain how to maximize the remarkable success of the ground attacks. The consensus was to race to the Suez, arriving ahead of the retreating Egyptian forces. Accordingly, IDF units then proceeded through the Giddi and Mitla passes east of the Suez Canal and positioned them to engage the retreating Egyptian forces before they could safely transit the canal and find sanctuary on the west side. Remarkably, IDF ground units completed their assigned tasks in the Sinai theater and drove the Egyptian defenders into headlong retreat in four days.

Thus, Israeli armor and tanks operating on the Egyptian front during the 1967 Six-Day War completed their missions within 96 hours. Considering that IDF doctrine projected that tanks could be expected to operate for 100 hours before probable maintenance issues arose, the expedited manner in which actual operations were conducted highlighted Israel's army's "time discipline" and combat effectiveness of its forces during the Six-Day War. IDF armor units, engaged on the Jordanian Front during the Six-Day War, concluded operations in three days. On the Syrian Front (Golan Heights), where IDF forces fought perhaps as many as 1,400 attacking enemy tanks, IDF operations took six days. The entire Arab-Israeli War of 1967, the Six-Day War, lasted 132 hours and 30 minutes.

EGYPTIANS AND SOVIETS SEARCH FOR GAPS IN THE IDF SOLID

In the years after the advance into the Sinai, the IDF's tank force took on an exalted and near mythical status, as the belief persisted that the armor could force its way through any barrier or Arab armed force. The lessons from Rommel campaigns—that antitank guns were effective in neutralizing massed tank assaults—had not yet found wide acceptance within the IDF armor units. This bravado, while quite useful for morale and unit cohesion, also created a vulnerability that would later be exploited by the enemies of Israel. As Rommel had known and practiced, advancing armor was vulnerable to infantry utilizing antitank weapons; this would also present a costly lesson for the IDF that would arrive later in the 1973 Arab-Israeli War—the October War; from the Israeli perspective, the Yom Kippur War; and from the Arab view, the Ramadan War.

However, boldness in war often creates its own dynamics as well as opportunities, and the swift advance of the IDF ground units in 1967 was certainly a testament to the bold audacity of Israeli commanders and their soldiers as well as their willingness to engage constructively in "managing chaos." While the Egyptians would bounce back from the travesty that occurred in the Six-Day War, in terms of readiness, organization, doctrine, and tactics, they simply were not trained nor adequately prepared and equipped to deal with an Israeli army and air force armed with modern weapons, practicing modern doctrine, and fighting for their very survival. The refusal of Nasser to listen to his military commanders compounded the problem. The Israeli movement through the Egyptians was swift, as armored and mechanized IDF units fought with support from the IAF transiting the Sinai to the Suez Canal, awaited the withdrawing Egyptian formations, and engaged them as they retreated.

The combined arms offensive (armor, infantry, and close air support) during the ground campaign of Operation Moked was one of the most impressive maneuver warfare victories conducted during the twentieth century. Both air and ground campaigns combined to make the Israeli victory during the first week in June 1967, which was, many would argue, one of the most successful campaigns in world military history. IDF General Dayan, while serving as the minister of defense, was the principle architect behind Moked, incorporating the lessons of the Arab-Israeli War of 1948 and the Suez operation in 1956 as well as a vast array of knowledge and understanding of both ancient and modern warfare.

The rapid collapse of Soviet trained Egyptian armored forces in the Middle East war in June of 1967 remains a puzzle. In less than 60 hours, the numerically inferior Israeli forces routed two enemy brigades, and up to a dozen armored artillery regiments ... Of the 1,100 tanks and self-propelled armored assault guns committed by the Egyptians in the Sinai and Gaza sectors, almost 800 were either destroyed or captured intact ... in what was truly one of history's decisive armored battles.[26]

The IDF strategic plan was to focus on Egypt, destroy its ability to project military force, and remove Nasser as a threat, particularly his Soviet jet aircraft. However, since an Egyptian (Riad) was now in command of King Hussein's military, the entreaties that Israeli diplomats sent to the king that if he stayed out of war, Israel would not attack, fell on deaf ears. As the IDF conducted operations against Egypt, Jordan opened up with long-range 155 millimeter (mm) artillery and began targeting Israeli airfields. Egyptian military commander in chief Amer then dispatched a message to Hussein, falsely stating 75 percent of the aircraft the IAF had sent against Egypt had been shot down and urging him to move forward in attack.

The king moved forward and Jordanian forces (essentially the British-trained Arab Legion) joined the fracas but were forced to withdraw, as IDF units overran the Old City of Jerusalem and the West Bank in ongoing skirmishes on June 7. Jordanian aircraft (Hawker Hunter jets), which had been bombing Israeli targets, were caught on the ground refueling at Amman and Mafraq and destroyed. Those 22 fighter-bombers represented the extent of the Jordanian Air Force, which, following June 8, essentially ceased to exist. IAF aircraft also targeted the Syrian and Iraqi airfields from which attacking Arab aircraft were launched and eliminated those runways and aircraft presenting a threat. In one final action, IAF aircraft bombed Damascus and drove Syrian ground forces out of the Golan Heights on June 9.

On June 10, Soviet Premier Alexei Kosygin picked up the "hotline" to the White House that had been installed in both the Kremlin and in the executive mansion in Washington, DC, following the Cuban Missile Crisis in 1962. The Soviet leader conveyed that "grave consequences" would erupt if Israel were to be allowed to continue to attack and that the Soviets were prepared to take all "necessary action ... including military" if Israel did not halt at the Golan Heights and continued to advance into Syria.[27] Following this exchange, U.S. Secretary of Defense Robert McNamara recommended to President Lyndon Johnson that he send the U.S. Sixth Fleet into the Eastern Mediterranean as a precaution. Later that day, Israel halted Operation Moked, which was followed by an accord whereby all sides agreed to a UN cease-fire.

USS *LIBERTY* REFUSES TO SINK

Remarkably, the U.S. naval vessel, USS *Liberty*, was attacked by the IAF and Israeli Navy on June 8, 1967.[28] However, on June 5, several days prior to the Israeli surprise attack, the *Liberty*—a communications intelligence vessel under dual control of the U.S. Sixth Fleet and the Defense Intelligence Agency (DIA)/National Security Agency (NSA)— was ordered to conduct signals intelligence operations off the coast of the Sinai in the Eastern Mediterranean.[29] At 2 p.m. on June 8, *Liberty* was engaged by Mirage jet aircraft of the IAF, which attacked the U.S. ship with 30mm cannon and rockets. After the Mirages emptied their available ammunition into the *Liberty*, two IAF Dassault Mysteres arrived with napalm ordnance, and following the strike, the ship caught fire. The Mysteres aircraft then strafed the ship with cannon.

The Dassault attack was followed by the arrival of IDF naval torpedo boats, which attacked the *Liberty* by firing five torpedoes, of which one hit and caused a 39-feet gap in the ship's hull. The ship remained afloat. During the attacks, the *Liberty*'s crew called repeatedly for assistance from U.S. Sixth Fleet command. While two separate flights were eventually ordered to render assistance, higher U.S. authorities recalled each. The official position in Washington and in Tel Aviv was that the *Liberty* was mistakenly attacked by Israel, which was, after all, engaged in a rather complex combat operation. Thus, it is plausible that this is exactly what occurred. Conversely, the strategic logic of the Cold War demanded U.S. national command authority be prepared for a dangerous escalatory response from the Soviet Union, as Israel attempted to destroy Arab air forces (MiG jet fighters and Tupolev bombers) and take control of the Sinai Desert.

If the Soviets had decided to escalate the situation by stating its client state in Egypt, now under aggressive attack from Israel, had asked for its direct military intervention, the United States would need legal cover in responding to any moves made by Moscow. Or, additionally, should Israel find itself on the losing end of Operation Moked and find itself in a position of being overrun by Arab armies, the United States would also need to provide the American people with a rationale for direct military intervention in defense of Israel. A U.S. naval vessel that had been sunk could, depending on the unfolding scenario, be attributed, as needed, to the Soviets in the first instance, or to the Arabs in the second.

With civilizations in the balance, in terms of a U.S.-USSR scenario escalating into a general strategic nuclear exchange, or, even the prospect of Israel being overrun and destroyed, the United States needed to be prepared to respond. While the sinking of a U.S. naval vessel would have been seen as a tragedy by the national command authority in Washington (the Johnson administration), the aftereffects of not being prepared to respond during the Six-Day War might have been astronomical, as the Soviets may have attempted to move in force toward the oil resources of the Middle East, probably insuring a direct U.S.-Soviet military confrontation.

However, the lightning success of the IDF mitigated the need for the United States to respond. For Moscow, Nasser's Egypt was never fully committed to allowing the Soviet Union the complete access into the Middle East that it sought. Nasser's strategic objective was in creating an Arab bloc controlled by Egypt, leading the Arab world and allowing it to more effectively interact with world powers.[30] This meant keeping its distance from both the United States and the USSR. Thus, Moscow was not fully committed to Nasser's survival.

From the Suez Crisis of 1956 to the 1967 Six-Day War, the Egyptian military had been supplied in an ad hoc manner, drawing differing weapons and weapons systems from a number of sources. This was the result of a weapons procurement process directed at establishing political connections within the West as well as in the Soviet Union. This process brought a varied array of weapons but an array largely unrelated to any comprehensive attempt in creating combat effectiveness through the establishment of sound, effective military doctrine. The question left unanswered was how this multitude and disparate array of arms could be unified in supporting a rational and consistent military strategy in time of war. In sum, there were numerous weapons and weapons systems, many unrelated with no single conception of how they tied together through unity of effort and produced deliverable combat effectiveness on the battlefield.

Following the travesty that was the 1967 war for Egyptian leaders, the Egyptian military listened more closely to their Russian advisers and worked more intelligently on creating an effective plan for utilizing weapons and weapons systems. The results were evident later, in the 1973 Arab-Israeli War.

REVOLUTIONARY WAR BECOMES "LEGITIMATE RESISTANCE OPERATIONS"

Modernity and modern war were significantly influenced by the arrival of the steam and combustion engines as well as other advances such as advanced metallurgy, precision machining, and electricity. Less obvious has been the impact of the clock. Traditional societies only recently transitioning from the late Middle Ages can purchase planes, artillery, or automatic weapons. However, the difficulty arises in embracing the discipline of time and the choreographed and coordinated combined arms approach incorporating modern technological advances. The highly synchronous and highly disciplined manner in which Israel conducted a surprise and combined-arms attack during the Six-Day War pointed to the fact that the IDF had been successful in embracing the use of time and effectively integrating it into doctrine, which exploited

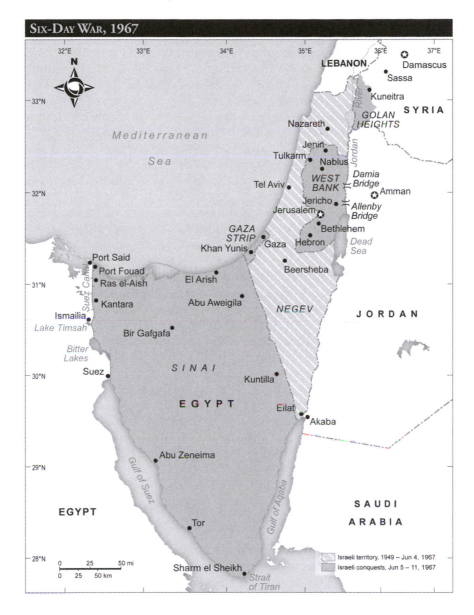

SIX-DAY WAR, 1967

and utilized modern implements of war. As a result, they stole a march on the Egyptians and their centuries-long tradition of cutting-edge military proficiency. This would change in the years following the 1967 war.

After the loss, Egyptian leaders were forced to review all aspects of the country's defense posture and its military personnel.[31] However, with its military in disarray immediately following the Six-Day War, Nasser was forced to readjust his aims of destroying Israel and instead scaling back his timeline for leading the Arab world to the global prominence it once enjoyed centuries ago. At the Khartoum Summit in August 1967, Arab leaders met and declared their famous three "No's"—until all territory taken from them by Israel in the 1967 war was returned. Thereafter, Arab policy would be based upon *no negotiations, no recognition, and no peace.*

Following the Six-Day War, Israel possessed all of historic Palestine (Land of Israel), including a united Jerusalem. It had also increased its ability to defend in depth. In November 1967, the UN Security Council Resolution 242 demanded the "withdrawal of Israeli armed forces from the territories occupied in the recent conflict." The Arabs held firmly to the three No's.

Since Arab armies, even when combined, were too weak to confront Israel militarily, and since Arab political leaders were unwilling to make peace, they opted for the age-old stratagem of "ghazi warfare." It was a type of warfare conducted on the fringes: in ancient times, raids and plundering along the borders, and in modern times, guerrilla and terrorist activities. As Egypt's strongest supporter was the Soviet Union, from 1955 to 1973, ghazi warfare became "glorious popular revolutionary war"—after significant departures of Soviet personnel in the late 1970s, "legitimate resistance operations." This was, in fact, the mantra being fed by Moscow to the Viet Cong in the mid-1960s as well. Thus, in the Middle East it was referred to as a condition of "no war—no peace." The objective was to conduct guerrilla and terrorist activities aimed at applying constant pressure on the target, without igniting or engaging in a conventional war. The aim was to subject the opponent to a "death by a thousand cuts" or, in more modern vernacular, to weaken the enemy, while your own side prepared itself for a showdown when the time was right.

Accordingly, Egypt conducted what became known as the War of Attrition (1967–1970), in which Egyptian armed forces avoided engaging in major conflict with the IDF and instead opted for commando raids, artillery fire, and the occasional air strike. Resources were also funneled to "resistance operations," being conducted by various groups such as the Palestinian Liberation Organization. The overall objective of the War of Attrition was to impose "an unacceptable cost on Israel for the continued occupation of the Sinai Desert."[32]

While these efforts were ongoing, the Soviet Union became the main supplier of Egyptian arms; and Israel, whose main supplier through the 1967 war was France, now turned to the United States and stepped up its military support of the IDF. In response to Nasser's embrace of Moscow, the United States committed itself to maintaining a "qualitative edge" for the IDF in relation to surrounding hostile Arab armies. High-performance fighter aircraft (A4 Skyhawks and F-4 Phantoms), transferred from the United States, provided Israel the capability for conducting long-range air strikes throughout Egyptian territory.

Egypt's leaders were subsequently infuriated with these "high-tech" transfers, driving them closer to the Soviet Union, which then began supplying Egypt with mobile SA-3 (SAMs—surface-to-air missiles), which provided Cairo the capability for intercepting low-altitude jet aircraft. Along with the Soviet systems came Soviet technicians who subsequently became extensively involved in the Egyptian air defense network. Moscow also began providing high-performance aircraft, as MiG-21 were sent along with a limited number of Soviet pilots. By June 1968, the EAF included 110 MiG-21s, 80 MiG-19s, 120 MiG-15/17s, 40 SU-7Bs, and 50 IL-28 and TU-16 bombers. Soviet instructors trained both Egyptian and Syrian pilots. In 1968, the United States transferred 48 Douglas A-4H Skyhawks to Israel and, by 1969, an additional 50 F-4E and 6 RF-4 Phantoms were flying under the IAF emblem. Along with Sidewinder AIM-9 air-to-air missiles, the United States also dispatched electronic countermeasure (ECM) equipment, jammers, and chaff dispensers to deal with the Soviet systems.

During the years that followed the Six-Day War, frequent low-level aerial clashes occurred, as the IAF attempted to suppress ensconced and fortified Egyptian artillery and air defense sites. Egyptian military operations during these years fell into four stages: From June 1967 to August 1968 in what was referred to as the "Defiance" stage, Egypt worked on the reconstruction of its armed forces following the devastation of the Six-Day War and focused on the defense of the western side of the Suez Canal. In the "Active Defense" stage (September 1968–February 1969), Egyptian forces began the selective shelling of IDF positions on the eastern side of the canal in an effort to disrupt IDF attempts at consolidating its defensive positions. During this stage, the Egyptians began formulating plans for crossing the Suez and attacking IDF fortifications. In the "War of Attrition" stage (March 1969–August 1970), the Egyptians

> ... projected day and night raids into the Sinai that would eventually reach company strength. This was augmented with constant exchanges of artillery fire across the canal and imbued the Egyptian fighting soldier with a sense of confidence. Harassment tactics also included Egyptian frogmen who were to sink transports at the port of Eilat. (This action occurred in November 1969 and again in February 1970 and was the catalyst for using high-pressure water to breech the Bar-Lev Line.) As a result of the ceasefire, a fourth stage was developed and labeled "No War, No Peace" (August 1970–October 1973).[33]

By the spring of 1970, Israel was looking for ways to increase the costs to Egypt for its ongoing military actions against the IDF in the Sinai. In the summer of 1970, the IAF conducted deep-strike missions into Egypt aimed at economic targets.[34] On July 30, 1970, there was a direct Soviet-Israeli air battle that resulted in five Soviet aircraft downed and no Israeli losses.[35] Shortly after this encounter, Egypt and Israel agreed to a cease-fire, ending the War of Attrition in August 1970. Israeli casualties during the war were 700 dead and 2,700 wounded, with Arab losses estimated to be about four times higher.

In September 1970, Nasser died of a heart attack and was succeeded by Anwar Sadat who came to power with a promise to the Egyptian people of a "battle of destiny" with Israel. After taking office, Sadat visited the Soviet Union and requested advanced aircraft and air defense systems sufficient to challenge and defeat the IAF. Moscow refused the request for sending high-performance air-superiority and long-range strike air-craft, telling the new Egyptian leader to focus instead on a new strategy using existing airpower, weapons, and platforms toward regaining con-trol of the Sinai Desert. Moscow convinced Sadat that any plan aimed at the destruction of Israel would necessarily bring in the United States. Given the likely implications of an Egyptian strike into the heart of Israel, the Soviets were not prepared to risk nuclear war for the destruction of such a small state. Moreover, by 1970, a less hostile relationship had developed within U.S.-Soviet relations; consequently, the "detente" that arose between the two superpowers diluted the Arab world's ability to use U.S.-Soviet Cold War friction in playing one side against the other.

As 1970 came to an end, Sadat proclaimed that 1971 would become the "year of decision" if diplomacy failed to dislodge Israel from the Sinai. Simultaneously, he and other trusted senior Egyptian commanders were moving to reduce incompetence and corruption within the officer corps. Their efforts were directed at reducing the political posturing and politi-cal intrigue within the Egyptian military and sought instead to create a military focused toward winning on the battlefield and in the skies. Sadat's team initiated a wholesale "housecleaning" of the officer ranks from the general staff down to unit commanders and eliminated those motivated chiefly by personal advancement (and enrichment) at the expense of national policy.

Eventually, Sadat began to publicly distance himself from the Soviets in order to minimize the perception within Egypt and the wider Arab world of an Egyptian president serving as Moscow's puppet. Additional-ly, in July 1972, unhappy with Moscow's continued refusal to provide the advanced weaponry (both ground and air-based systems) needed to defeat the IDF in the Sinai, Sadat took the drastic step of expelling some 20,000 Soviet personnel then operating in Egypt. However, by the end of the summer, he had provided Moscow continued access to Egyptian maritime facilities. In October 1972, Sadat met with his senior military leaders and informed the group that he intended to pursue a military campaign against Israeli forces then arrayed within the Sinai. Following Moscow's advice, however, he also reiterated the need to avoid a general war with Israel and to avoid any action that would bring in the United States. Sadat explained that once the Soviets signed off on the approach, new weapons allowing for a limited campaign would be forthcoming.

The Egyptian Minister of War General Sadeq was opposed to any major combat operations against the IDF, arguing the Egyptian military was simply unprepared and ill-equipped to take on Israel in a large, conventional military campaign; particularly since the IAF continued to maintain air superiority if not complete supremacy. Consequently, Sadeq was replaced with General Ahmed Ismail who supported Sadat's plan. In February 1973, in light of these developments, Moscow revisited its decision regarding a light armament footprint within Egypt and acquiesced to Sadat's demands for advanced arms.

Two and a half years prior and following the Israeli downing of five MIG jet fighters piloted by Soviet crew on July 30, 1970, the Soviet Union began gradually developing an interlocking air defense shield utilizing SAMs. While the Americans brokered a cease-fire following the IAF downing of the Soviet-piloted aircraft, Moscow moved 45 SAM launchers within range of the Suez Canal. In response, the United States equipped the IAF with ECM equipment and "Shrike" and "Wall-Eye," air-to-surface guided missiles to counter the SAM systems.

THE SADAT CONCEPT

While the increasingly sophisticated nature of the Egyptian air defense network concerned IDF commanders and intelligence analysts, the belief was that defensive systems did not warrant an air campaign followed most likely by IDF ground forces to destroy the sites, which quite possibly would force the Soviets to respond militarily as many of their technicians and advisors would be in the middle of both the air and ground operations. The Israeli view of the matter came to rest on what was called the "Sadat Concept." In the IDF's view, Egypt under Sadat would have to obtain new long-range weapons, including surface-to-surface missiles and deep-strike bombers to threaten Israel itself (to deter Israel from utilizing its own Jericho I missiles) as well as an influx of air-superiority fighters before challenging the IDF in the Sinai.

> The aftermath of the June 1967 war also led to a more rigid approach to Israeli strategic thinking which was increasingly dominated by an outlook known as the "concept." In its most straightforward form, the concept stated that Syria would not attack without Egypt, while Egypt would not

attack Israel until it had achieved air parity with Israel. Conveniently, Egyptian air parity with Israel seemed elusive and perhaps unobtainable.[36]

In the spring of 1973, disagreements developed within the Central Intelligence Agency (CIA) with some warning of an increasing likelihood of an Egyptian attack regarding its frustration of the IDF presence in the Sinai, while others rest assured this would not develop based upon the continuing viability of the "Sadat Concept." In the third week of September 1973, King Hussein of Jordan, flew his own helicopter to Tel Aviv and secretly warned Israeli leaders that an attack was imminent. Israel's Prime Minister Golda Meir called in her closest advisors in the first week of October and inquired as to the expectation, likelihood, or even the possibility of a military strike. The "Sadat Concept" had convinced the leaders of Israeli military intelligence (AMAN) that an attack would not be forthcoming. General Eli Zeira, head of AMAN, dismissed the claims of those arguing that an attack from either Egyptian or Syria was imminent.

For Zeira, Egypt would avoid war until it received aircraft capable of attacking IAF bases in Israel as well as taking possession of surface-to-surface missiles with the accuracy and range necessary for deterring the IAF from attacking targets throughout Egypt, including cities. The cumulative assessment from the U.S. intelligence community was that Egypt, while making a high-profile show of it with its "Tahir 41" maneuvers being conducted in late September and early October 1973, would refrain from challenging IAF air dominance.

On September 30, 1973, the same day that Sadat passed the pre-arranged signal to the Syrians (code word: BADR) to commence military operations against Israel, Zeira received word from the MOSSAD (Israel's version of the CIA) that a reliable human intelligence source (HUMINT) warned that Tahir 41 would end in an actual canal crossing. However, Zeira waited until the following morning before passing along this information to IDF Chief of Staff Elazar and Minister of Defense Dayan. Two days before the Egyptians and Syrian attacked, Israel became aware of Soviet personnel hastily making exits out of Egypt. In a further meeting with Meir, Zeira stated that the Russians mistakenly believed the Egyptians were going to attack.

Without strategic depth or strategic endurance, Israel depended on frontline regular IDF ground forces, backed by IAF command of the air, to hold off an enemy attack long enough for the IDF reserves to be mobilized and swiftly deployed into battle. Those reserves were essential to the Israeli economy, and, thus, the fighting could not be extended without significantly harming the overall fortunes of the country. Given this, the IDF would have to defeat any attack swiftly and get back to work. The key time frame for Israeli security was the first 48 hours of any military crisis, which was the required time for call-up, mobilization, and deployment of reserve forces.

Most in the national security organizations within Israel in 1973 assumed that MOSSAD and AMAN would be able to know in advance if a strike was imminent. Thus, national leaders would have time to mobilize the reserves and defend the country. Just as the U.S. intelligence community failed in warning American national decision makers in December 1941 regarding the impending attack against Pearl Harbor, Israeli intelligence failed in its mission of alerting Israel's national decision makers of a surprise attack by Egypt and Syria in October 1973.

The responsibility for this lapse rested chiefly with the leader of AMAN who was apprised by multiple sources, including MOSSAD, that an attack was imminent. Zeira was finally convinced just 10 hours before the attack was initiated and the mobilization began.

> Only a last minute warning by Israel's most important intelligence source in Egypt, Ashraf Marwan the late President Nasser's son-in-law and close adviser to Sadat—prevented a complete surprise. Marwan met the chief of MOSSAD Zvi Zamir in London 16 hours before the onset of war to warn him of the impending attack. The warning reached Israel at 4 AM, ten hours before the firing commenced. Mobilization began five hours later as the first reserve forces were arriving at their bases when the shooting starting.[37]

The attackers waited until the Jewish holiday of Yom Kippur when national broadcasting was limited. However, this also meant that most IDF reserve personnel were spending time at home with their families and were unable to be reached by phone. Those 10 hours were crucial and provided IDF personnel critically needed time to reach the battlefield on the Golan Heights, just as Syrian units had overwhelmed Israeli forces through numerical superiority and were preparing to descend into Israeli cities (IDF reserves constituted 80 percent of the Israeli army's ground forces). While the director of AMAN deserves criticism for the early warning lapse, it should also be noted that Egypt engaged in a very clever deception campaign leading up to the 1973 October War.

By the time of the October War, the IAF's inventory included 127 F-4 Phantoms, 162 A-4 Skyhawks, 35 Mirage IIICs, 15 Super Mysteres, and 40 Neshirs (Israeli copy of the French Mirage V). Egypt's air force included 210 MiG-21s, 100 MiG-17s, 80 SU-7Bs, and 30 TU-16 bombers. At the time Algeria, Libya, and Iraq operated 105 fighters then serving under Egyptian command. Syria's air inventory included 200 MiG-21s, 80 MiG-17s, and 30 SU-7Bs. Syrian air defense also included the interlocking range capability of an integrated network consisting of SAM-2s, SAM-3s, SAM-6s, and SAM-7s.

Sadat's campaign plan in October 1973 was called Operation BADR. The Egyptians understood that they would not be able to wrest air superiority away from the IAF by engaging in air-to-air combat maneuvering (ACM or dog fighting). The question then became: How does Egypt protect any ground forces moving across the Suez Canal and engaging the IDF positioned at the Bar-Lev Line as well as the expected counterattack from IDF forces moving in support across the Sinai? The answer was: deploy an integrated air defense network of SAMs that will send up a "rocket wall" depriving IAF aircraft from operating at will over the designated area. The designated area in this instance would be in and around Suez Canal and the Bar-Lev Line.

With the construction of the integrated air defense network, the Egyptians were prepared to, if not neutralize, at least constrain Israeli airpower. The question then arose: How do we offset the effectiveness or IDF armor and prevail on the ground, even with IAF airpower sufficiently moderated by "the rocket wall"? The answer came from Rommel's playbook during World War II. Rommel never sought to deploy tank against tank if it could be avoided. The tank's purpose was to rapidly maneuver in order to exploit vulnerable areas of an enemy's position, punch through, and allow follow-on forces to overwhelm the enemy by moving swiftly through the exposed gap. Given the presence of enemy armor, the preference for Rommel's Afrika Korps was to send guns against tanks and trap them in fields of interlocking fire or, if time and circumstance did not provide opportunity in setting up a "hell-fire pass" scenario, through the superior range of the antitank guns vis-à-vis the tank itself.

Thus, in considering overcoming superiority both in air and on land, the Egyptians and their Soviet advisors came up against the traditional Flaechen-und Luecken military puzzle. Given the presence of a solid (or superior capability), how does one effectively overcome the challenge this presents? The ability to find a solution to this puzzle often determined the outcome of battles, campaigns, or wars and, in some rare instances, the fate of civilizations. The answer that consistently solved the puzzle was found in bypassing the strength of the solid and instead aiming for the gap or gaps (or, vulnerabilities in the solid), followed by the effective exploitation of the gap within the solid.

Thus, in October 1973, the Egyptians sent "guns" against Israeli tanks or, more precisely, antitank guided missiles (ATGMs) against tanks. Operation BADR marked the first used of ATGMs in large combat operations. As the Egyptians launched their attack, included in the force that crossed the Suez Canal to engage the IDF on October 6, 1973, were 5,000 infantrymen armed with Soviet-supplied "SAGGER" ATGM systems in their backpacks. The SAGGER ATGM utilized a 5.7-pound warhead capable of penetrating eight inches of armor at ranges of nearly two miles. The missile was optically sighted and electronically guided by wires, which trailed behind the projectile allowing the operator to steer the missile all the way to the target.

The Israeli tanks were overall superior to the mix of Egyptian tanks in 1973. Moreover, the "tankers" of the IDF had developed a tradition of bravery and excellence extending from operations in 1956 and 1967. In certain respects, these attributes, then and now, contribute(d) to the combat effectiveness of a military group or formation. In other respects those attributes, unconstrained by clearheaded thinking, result in one of the most prolific destroyers of men and armies, that of underestimating one's enemy. Egypt's armored units fielded over a thousand tanks of their own, but these were a mix of Soviet T-62s, T-54s, and T-55s, and of those only 200 were the newer T-62s. The T-62 was the only tank in the same class as the IDF's armor in terms of range, firepower, speed, and protection. In modern warfare, range and accuracy often determined the tank-on-tank battle outcome.

OPERATION BADR: YOM KIPPUR WAR

The Egyptians conducted military maneuvers along the western side of the Suez Canal under the guise of "Tahir 41" and, as IDF observers watched from the eastern side of the canal, the Egyptian soldiers moved about rather leisurely, often taking off shirts and sunbathing, some fishing, all with the orders to appear unconcerned with any upcoming dangers. Word came from military intelligence (AMAN) that IDF observers at the Suez were not to attack at that time. At 1:55 p.m., on October 6, 1973, and as reservists in Israel waited orders, the quiet was shattered by a massive Egyptian (2,200 guns) artillery barrage against IDF positions in the Sinai and a Syrian artillery bombardment of IDF positions then in occupation of the Golan Heights. About 50 minutes later, Egyptian ground units began crossing the Suez Canal, while Syrian armor pushed forward to drive the IDF units off the Golan Heights.

At the Suez Canal, Israel had built a 22-meter high barrier to defend its occupation of the Sinai. In defense of the Bar-Lev Line were regular IDF troops formed as the Sinai 252 Division and led by Major General Albert Mendler. This was the only major Israeli ground force in the Sinai. While the division had at its disposal about 300 tanks, only 3 were actually forward deployed and in position at the time of the Egyptian assault. Additionally, the Bar-Lev Line had about 75 operational artillery pieces and a few hundred infantrymen in position with an additional 15,000 troops near the Suez Canal, all in varying levels of readiness.[38] According to the Israeli defensive plan (DOVECOTE), should an attack occur, 600 tanks would reinforce Division 252. However, these were tanks of reserve armored divisions, and as the Arab artillery bombardment opened on the Golan and in the Sinai, many of these IDF reserve units were just gathering at their respective mobilization stations. As a result, it would be 40 hours before their presence could make a difference on the battlefield.

During the first 18 hours of Operation BADR, Egyptian forces sent 90,000 troops and 850 tanks across the Suez Canal, which proceeded to roll over IDF forces manning the Bar-Lev Line. The Israelis had constructed a massive sand barrier on the eastern side of the Suez Canal in order to slow any Egyptian advance. The first Egyptian troops crossed the canal in rubber boats, and combat engineers used high-pressure water pumps and hoses to cut passages through the sand berms in strategic locations. The rubber boats would eventually transport 32,000 Egyptians across, while 5,500 crossed inside tanks, armored vehicles, trucks, amphibious vehicles, and jeeps on floating platforms transiting Lake Timsah and Bitter Lake. Another 1,500 moved across the Suez using light pontoon bridges, with 61,000 troops and heavy armor moving across specially designed heavy pontoon bridges.

> Egypt's ability to deploy a seven division force on the Israeli side of the Suez hinged largely on the new Russian heavy pontoon bridge. This high-speed heavy assault bridge, designated Model TPP was supposedly designed by the Russians to cross the Danube and Rhine Rivers. The Egyptians constructed 14 bridges across the Suez and were able to keep 5 to 7 of them operational despite heavy IAF attacks. The Egyptians used smoke to cover the bridges . . . The Israeli's, without the benefit of the sort of sophisticated weaponry used by the U.S. in Vietnam, had problems pin-pointing the bridges for destruction.[39]

The breach and subsequent crossing of the canal was a well-planned and well-executed operation, with the loss of only 5 combat aircraft, 20 tanks, and 280 men. At the most critical phase of Operation BADR, the canal crossing, Egyptian artillery kept up its bombardment of IDF positions east of the canal, while specially designed infantry units moved forward with light weapons and ATGMs and kept IDF personnel suppressed within their bunkers at the Bar-Lev Line. Critical to Egyptian operational plan, the IAF's attempts at bombing the bridges and Egyptian ground units were halted after the air defense network shot down 14 Israeli jets.

As predetermined within the planning of Operation BADR, Egyptian forces advanced eight miles east of the canal and then halted. From the positions they now held, Egyptian ground forces were, generally, protected by the air defense network from IAF air strikes.

> During the night, the three brigades of Division 252 attempted to join the besieged Bar-Lev Line Forts. Most of the tanks were hit by anti-tank weapons of which the Egyptians made extensive use of. With only a few

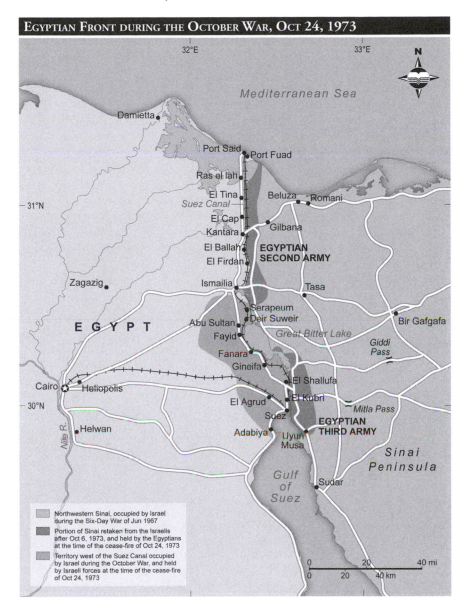

EGYPTIAN FRONT DURING THE OCTOBER WAR, OCT 24, 1973

exceptions, the Israeli tanks could not assist the forts. By the morning hours of October 7, the extent of the catastrophe on the Suez front had become evident: Most of the forts had fallen and the rest were encircled and many of the soldiers who had manned the forts had either been killed or taken prisoner. In the night fighting, the Sinai Division lost about two-thirds of its 300 tanks and was left with 103 tanks to hold off the Egyptian advance until the reserve army arrived. By Sunday morning 90,000 soldiers, 850 tanks and thousands of other fighting vehicles were already deployed in territory that less than 18 hours earlier had been held by the IDF.[40]

By the end of the first day, Israel was facing a military catastrophe in the Sinai Desert. By the end of the second day, on the Golan Heights, the vastly outnumbered regular IDF forces, fielding about 175 tanks, had been pushed back by a massive Soviet-style frontal assault along the 36-mile Syrian-Israeli border spearheaded by over 1,200 advancing Syrian tanks and backed by more than 1,000 artillery pieces and supporting airpower. The evening of October 7, 1973, was a dark moment in the short life of the State of Israel and one which brought dread to the political and military leaders of the Jewish state. Meir reportedly stated that should this indeed mark the end of the Jewish state, she would not care to go on living in the aftermath of such a failure.

In the Sinai, Israeli "tankers" advanced and charged ahead, attacking without adequate artillery, air, or infantry support in attempts at rescuing comrades then encircled at the Bar-Lev Line. Unlike the Egyptian soldiers in 1967 who retreated en masse at the sight of Israeli armor, this time, Egyptian soldiers stood and fought. In one instance, 22 Israeli armored reserve tanks attacked advanced elements of Egyptian forces on October 8 and were engaged by Egyptian infantrymen armed with SA-3 SAGGER ATGMs. By the time the Israeli column broke off the attack, only six IDF tanks remained operational. And by the time the 1973 war came to a close in the third week of October, about 500 IDF tanks would be destroyed. During the action in the first two days of combat, Major General Shmuel Gonen, commander, IDF Southern Forces, radioed to headquarters: "It's not the Egyptian Army of 1967."[41]

NEAR DISASTER ON THE GOLAN

On the Golan Heights, the situation became critical during the first 48 hours. Israel had seized the Golan Heights from Syria during the 1967 war, as its geographical location dominated the Hula and Jordan River valleys and Lake Tiberias (Sea of Galilee). Accordingly, the control of the Golan Heights allowed Israel to defend its water sources. Prior to the war, IDF Brigade (Barak) 188, positioned on the Golan Heights, had been reinforced by Brigade 7 (7th Armored Brigade). Combined, the two brigades fielded 177 tanks supported by 2 infantry battalions and 11 artillery batteries. On October 6, these forces defended against a force of 600 Syrian tanks supported by 80 artillery batteries.

The Syrian objectives during the 1973 October War included retaking the Golan Heights and seizing control of the Jordan River bridges. As BADR commenced, Syrian commandos were transported on helicopters on October 6 to Mount Hermon where their objective was the capture of a key IDF intelligence listening post, which was successfully seized, along with sensitive Israeli surveillance equipment. Forty-eight hours later on October 8, the IDF's elite Golani Brigade attempted but failed in retaking Mount Hermon. While the United States had attempted to ensure that the IDF had a qualitative edge over its enemies, the Syrians had Russian night technology in their tanks, which the IDF did not have at the time. With better night fighting equipment, the element of surprise, and numerical superiority, almost 75 percent of the tank crews in the IDF's 7th Armored Brigade were killed or wounded in the first four days of the war. The 188th Barak Armored Brigade suffered even greater rates of loss.

> In the early hours of the second day of the war the southern section of the Golan Heights was broken and the fifteen tanks remaining with Brigade 188 could not halt the Syrian advance. It was at this stage that the first reserve troops started climbing up the Golan to engage the enemy combatants. This blocked the Syrian's westward advancement. The Syrians reached Kfar Nafah in the late morning—at about the same time the first IDF reserves arrived there. In the ensuing tank battle, which lasted more than three hours the Israel tank teams drove back the Syrians. By Sunday evening the IDF had accumulated sufficient forces to prevent any additional Syrian achievements on the Golan and the Israeli command began preparing for a counter-offensive—scheduled to begin Monday October 8.[42]

On the second day of the battle on the Golan Heights front, the rigidity of Syrian command and control made its presence known on the battlefield. Syrian field commanders wishing to deviate from the operational plan were required to leave the front lines for consultation with the high command in Katana nearly 25 miles away. As events unfolded in rapid succession during combat, the decision-making process within the Syrian military, particularly the time lag between decision and implementation on the battlefield, could not match the speed of events on the ground. Consequently, a lack of tactical flexibility at the brigade and regimental level sufficiently constrained any opportunity for deviation from the operational plan.

As success was being made against IDF forces defending in the southern Golan Heights sector on the second day of the war, Syrian armored units in the north, instead of hammering away at the now nearly paralyzed IDF 7th Armored Brigade, would have been better served by pressing south and reinforcing the success of the attack in the southern Golan Heights and maximizing the opportunity for a breakthrough. Syrian field commanders wanted this adjustment, but by the time an

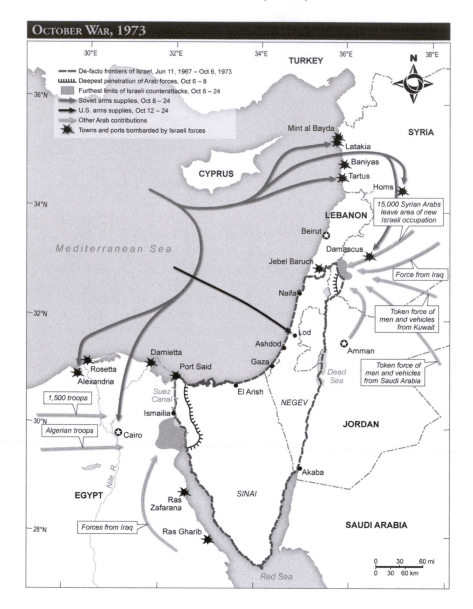

OCTOBER WAR, 1973

- De-facto frontiers of Israel, Jun 11, 1967 – Oct 6, 1973
- Deepest penetration of Arab forces, Oct 6 – 8
- Furthest limits of Israeli counterattacks, Oct 8 – 24
- Soviet arms supplies, Oct 8 – 24
- U.S. arms supplies, Oct 12 – 24
- Other Arab contributions
- Towns and ports bombarded by Israeli forces

officer was sent to Katana, received permission for the "deviation from plan," and returned, events and opportunity had passed the Syrians by. As U.S. General Douglass MacArthur famously observed in an earlier time: "All military disasters can be summed up in two words: too late."

For Israel, however, the reserves arrived in the nick of time. While the 10 hours of advance notice fell short of the expected 48 hours in order to mobilize the reserves, those 10 hours proved crucial and weighed heavily on the outcome of the 1973 October War. Israeli leaders, once they grasped the nature of the Egyptian advance in the Sinai and realized that the Egyptian army was holding its position about eight miles east of the Suez Canal rather than marching on Tel Aviv, turned their focus on the Syrian front. The Syrians had planned on seizing the Golan Heights within 24 hours and had intended to work with Moscow in acquiring a UN-sponsored cease-fire before the IDF reserves could make their presence known on the battlefield. This expectation and the assumption upon which it rested ultimately proved incorrect.

As the Israelis counterattacked in the afternoon of October 8, Hafez al-Assad, the Syrian ruler, realized that he had not achieved control of the Golan Heights within 24 hours and that he would now be faced with the combined strength of an Israeli army that, when fully mobilized and deployed, fielded over 300,000 soldiers. Assad was also perturbed at the Egyptians who, at the time, were holding safely under their air defense umbrella a few kilometers east of the Suez Canal. Egyptian leaders had led Assad and his military leadership to believe that the operational plan for the Egyptians was *Granite I*. Granite I was a previously held war plan that envisioned seizing the strategic Mitla and Giddi passes followed by the retaking of the entire Sinai.

For Assad, this scenario would have tied down IDF forces, both regular and reserve if necessary, for an extended period of time, as they battled Egyptian forces for control over the entire Sinai. Now Assad received word that this indeed was not what Sadat had in mind and that his actual plan was to remain under the cover of the air defense screen and begin negotiations. If Syrian forces had seized control of the Golan Heights within the expected 24 hours, both Syrian and Egyptian negotiators working in conjunction with the Russians would have been better positioned to move forward as expected at the United Nations in achieving a cease-fire while negotiations continued.

However, the Israelis, now apprised that Sadat intended to stand pat near the Suez Canal, turned the focus and might of its reserves on Syrian units in the Golan Heights. As the IDF began its counterattack on the Golan Heights on October 8, Sadat secretly signaled to U.S. Secretary of State Henry Kissinger that he wanted postwar negotiations leading to a permanent settlement with Israel. Sadat understood that without air superiority over the Sinai the probability of retaking the desert would be minimal at best. Thus, his goal in applying military force during Operation BADR was in changing the facts on the ground sufficiently in order to induce (or, perhaps more accurately, coerce) Israel into giving the Sinai back to Egypt in order to obtain a peace settlement. The objective for Israel in seizing the Sinai in the first place was to provide strategic depth, or a buffer zone, against a hostile Egypt. If peace could be arranged between the two nations, there would be less need for the defensive buffer zone.

MUTUALLY ASSURED DESTRUCTION

The overall objective of course is what Carl von Clausewitz argued as the purpose of war—to destroy the will of your opponent and his or her soldiers to carry on, to resist, and to avoid being compelled to fulfill your will. As Liddell Hart observed, one seeks to achieve this psychological dislocation through indirect methods before commencing the kinetic attack.[43] And, as Sun Tzu argued, you seek to engage an army that has already been defeated by steps you have taken prior to the actual battle.

Frightening one's opponent sufficiently to disrupt his or her ability to make sound decisions or degrading his or her morale and courage in such a fashion as to cause him or her not to be at his or her physical best before commencing the actual attack dates back to the earliest eras of organized warfare. However, in the modern age permeated with nuclear weapons as well as other weapons of mass disruption and destruction, the traditional and age-old military strategy presents a dilemma. With the advent of nuclear weapons came the reliance on the concept of deterrence in lieu of combat with weapons of mass destruction. As the United States, followed by the Soviet Union, obtained these weapons, it became increasingly clear that an actual battle involving thermonuclear devices would very likely end up destroying both parties engaging in a strategic nuclear war. The scenario of such an event became known as mutually assured destruction (MAD), which arguably had a deterrent effect on the initiation of direct, great power war while leading both protagonists to find alternative options for solving the issue or conflict.

At its core, effective nuclear deterrence relies on three conditions: the physical ability to deliver a nuclear strike on an opponent (even after absorbing a surprise first strike—referred to as second-strike capability), the will to carry out such an action, and that those who you are seeking to deter are fully aware you are in possession of capability and will. These three core characteristics of deterrence rest upon a significant assumption. This assumption leads to the expectation that those you are seeking to deter are rational decision makers. The term "rational" as utilized within deterrence theory refers to a decision maker who possesses the ability and tendency for ranking his or her preferences starting with the "most desirable" option—or the one with the greatest "utility" for the decision maker. The rational decision maker then extends other options in a ranking from the most preferred to the "least desirable" choice or option. The ultimate decision then becomes a function of that option, which best aligns with their policy preferences combined with their view of their ability to achieve it.

During the Cold War, the United States and the Soviet Union rationally avoided that option that would, in all likelihood, entail MAD. The difficulty in the traditional military strategy of seeking to achieve the psychological dislocation of an opponent through sudden panic and helplessness induced by the use of military force to achieve surprise places that opponent, by intent, in a state of mind less rational than he or she would otherwise be. In a modern era characterized by nuclear arms, effective deterrence relies on the opponent's ability to remain rational and to understand the implications of what the use of nuclear munitions might entail.

> Although Israel is not a fully declared nuclear power, virtually all serious academic analysis both in and outside of that country assumes that there has been a strong Israeli nuclear weapons program for decades. Most major studies of the 1973 war suggest that Israel had or probably had some sort of nuclear option that it could have gone forward with in the event of an existential threat . . .[44]

Once a war has begun and given that the two sides have access to nuclear weapons (through their own inventory or an ally), that which keeps the conflict from "going nuclear" (or, if it does, to limit the lethality of the exchange) is the concept of "intrawar deterrence."[45] This proscription again rests upon the concept of rationality. In sum, traditional military strategies aimed at sending an opponent into a state of sudden shock followed by a sense of panic and desperation may ultimately serve to undermine the effectiveness of rational deterrence in an era of thermonuclear weapons.

> The 1973 war is a particularly valuable example of the dangers of rapid military escalation that, according to many plausible sources, involved serious Israeli consideration of nuclear weapon use.[46]

> This will be a battle of destiny . . . Now the time has come for a decision . . . the time has come for a shock.[47]

> The sudden onset of a new war that began with a series of Arab battlefield victories deeply disoriented some Israeli leaders and appears to have pushed some into serious consideration of a nuclear solution. This outcome appears to have been avoided by the ability of Israeli leaders to discuss the threat in an open, professional, and democratic fashion which in this case allowed the most reasonable voices to come to the fore. The decisive Israeli battlefield victory of October 14 eliminated the need for Israel to consider nuclear weapons use, although the Egyptians then faced defeat themselves and signaled that they also had serious options for escalating the war.[48]

As Israel recovered from the sudden shock of the first two days of the October War, it began a massive counteroffensive against the Syrians on the Golan Heights. Sadat was pressed hard by the Syrians to come out from under his air defense network and engage the Israelis in the Sinai, as he had promised the Syrian leadership he would do under Granite I. Sadat, in order to relieve the pressure being mounted on Syrian forces on the Golan Heights, opted to attack in the Sinai and moved out from under the cover of his Russian-supplied air defense network over the strenuous objections from his military commanders, including Lieutenant General Shazly.

Here, once again, the friction between the strategic and operational levels of war made itself known. Militarily, it was highly problematic to attempt ground operations while the IAF maintained air superiority over the Sinai beyond the range of the air umbrella in position near the canal. Egyptian ground forces moving in an open desert while their opponents controlled the skies, invited military defeat. Political objectives drove this decision, and Sadat opted to engage in the open desert without adequate air cover. Perhaps the honor of the nation was at stake; perhaps his conscience would not allow him to hide under the air defense umbrella after promising the Assad government that he would be vigorously prosecuting a campaign across the entire Sinai Desert.

For whatever reason, the Egyptian army was ordered to advance eastward and engage the Israeli army in an effort at drawing reserve IDF reinforcements away from the Syrian front. The problem was not simply lack of air cover, but that the original plan that had been meticulously planned, trained for, and executed did not include this new twist. The new orders sent the Egyptians to engage in battle that their own field commanders strenuously opposed and the troops had not received extensive preparation for. Phase II of the 1973 October War (wherein Sadat moved his forces out from under their air protection) mirrored the political decision of Nasser in 1967 to ignore the meticulously planned, gamed, and trained operation plan to await the IDF inside the Sinai and move confused Egyptian forces to the Israeli-Egyptian border.

In the face of the Arab setbacks, on October 9, Moscow initiated a weapons and supply airlift to both Egypt and Syria. On the same day, the IAF bombed the Soviet Cultural Center in Damascus, killing several Soviet diplomats. On October 10, the IAF achieved air superiority over the Golan Heights, and IDF ground units commenced their counterattack. As the IDF drove back Syrian forces, Prime Minister Meir agreed on October 11 to a limited offensive that would place the Israeli army close enough to Damascus to threaten the Syrian capital with long-range artillery. On October 12, the IAF attacked the Soviet merchant ship *Ilya Mechnikov* in the Syrian port of Tartus. On October 13, the IDF achieved the positions Meir had approved on October 11 and placed 175mm guns within range of Damascus, subsequently opening fire on its airport. Also on October 13, the United States initiated Operation Nickel Grass, "The U.S. airlift to Israel lasted 33 days (October 13 to November 14), and transported a total of 22,497 tons of military material with an estimated 5,500 tons being transported by Israeli civilian aviation."[49]

On October 14, Egyptian forces launched a major offensive in a drive to reach the strategic passes in the Sinai located at Mitla and Giddi some 30 miles east of the Suez Canal. The Egyptian offensive included 1,400 tanks and pushed forward toward the key passes. What remained of the IDF defenses (Sinai Division 252) at the Bar-Lev Line had fallen back deep into the Sinai Desert and awaited reserve reinforcements. As those reinforcements arrived, the IDF counterattacked against the advancing Egyptian forces, this time with close air support from the IAF. After the destruction of 250 Egyptian tanks, the IDF forced the Egyptian army into general withdrawal. While all of this was going on, U.S. Navy's A-4 Skyhawks were transferred to Israel, quickly painted with IAF colors and emblem, and sent into battle.

> In October 1973, U.S. forces—including the Strategic Air Command—were placed on heightened alert in response to possible Soviet military intervention to keep the Israelis from destroying the surrounded Egyptian Third Army. During the crisis, Kissinger sent Soviet leader Brezhnev a message stating that the introduction of Soviet troops into the region would represent a violation of the recently signed Agreement Between the United States of America and the Union of Soviet Socialist Republics on the Prevention of Nuclear War. The implication of Kissinger's message was obvious ... the introduction of Soviet troops could have led to a nuclear faceoff between the Cold War antagonists.[50]

Late in the evening on October 15 and extending into the early morning of October 16, IDF forces led by Sharon, pushing westward, crossed the Suez Canal. Sharon's and other IDF forces moved swiftly in attacking a range of Egyptian targets on the western side of the canal, including key SAM and anti-aircraft artillery (AAA) sites. This action opened up a 15-mile gap in Egypt's air space. On October 16, Sadat issued a warning that Egyptian missiles were "on their pads, ready with one signal to be fired into the depth of Israel." Egypt, at the time of the 1973 October War, had German-designed *al-Kahir* surface-to-surface missiles and Soviet-supplied Scud missiles. Eventually Sadat fired Scuds in the direction of Israel and at the bridges, allowing the IDF to cross the canal at will. The Soviet Scud was a highly inaccurate ballistic missile, and aiming them at a bridge was highly problematic. At least two, perhaps three, Scud missiles were fired on October 22, with the intent of destroying pontoon bridges spanning the canal. None landed on target.

On October 22, a Soviet freighter passed through the Bosporus Straits and arrived in Alexandria, Egypt, three days later. At press conferences held by both Kissinger and U.S. Secretary of Defense James Schlesinger, the ship was believed to be carrying nuclear weapons.[51]

> Two brigades of Soviet Scud surface-to-surface missiles each equipped with a nuclear warhead are now in position east of Cairo poised to strike Tel Aviv and other Israeli population centers.[52]

By this time the IDF had moved swiftly in a strategic envelopment aimed at trapping those Egyptian forces operating in the Sinai. On October 23, a UN-sponsored cease-fire went into effect but quickly unraveled as Israeli Major General Avraham Adan's division drove south, reaching Suez city in the evening of October 24, after an extensive firefight occupied the city. With the combined successes of the counteroffensive, the IDF had essentially cut off the Egyptian 2nd and 3rd armies that had originally sought to take the strategic passes in the Sinai Desert to avoid just such a predicament they now faced. Kissinger worked assiduously to reestablish a cease-fire, which was accomplished on October 25.[53] During his negotiations with the Egyptians, Kissinger worked to convince Sadat to break with the Soviet Union and establish relations with the United States.

Chapter 6

British Military Withdrawal, the Iranian Revolution, and the Iran-Iraq War

Those who study jihad will understand why Islam wants to conquer the whole world. All the countries conquered by Islam or to be conquered in the future will be marked for everlasting salvation. Islam says: kill all the unbelievers just as they would kill you all.

—Ayatollah Ruhollah Khomeini, 1942

Let our position be clear: An attempt by any outside force to gain control of the Persian Gulf region will be regarded as an assault on the vital interests of the United States of America, and such an assault will be repelled by any means necessary, including military force.

—U.S. President Jimmy Carter, State of the Union Address, January 23, 1980

The British began withdrawing military forces from the Persian Gulf in 1971, looking to the United States for additional presence and to reduce overall costs as the price of victory in two world wars and the loss of India in 1947 took its toll. For the Americans, costs of the Vietnam War coupled with the funding for President Lyndon Johnson's "Great Society" social programs in the 1960s forced the United States to abandon the gold standard while simultaneously accelerating the printing of money—all of which essentially became a process of issuing "IOUs" (promises to pay later) to cover deficit spending. U.S. President Richard Nixon, seeking to limit American casualties after the Vietnam War and to reduce financial costs of overseas commitments, sought the assistance of powerful actors within the Middle East to safeguard the movement of oil out of the Persian Gulf. As a result, Nixon turned to the government of Mohammad Reza, the Shah of Iran, to offset costs and to share the burden of insuring Western access to the region.

> Nixon departed from the Johnson administration and supported a Iranian primary role in the Persian Gulf region—Johnson favored a balance of power between Iran and Saudi Arabia as a means of ensuring security in the Gulf. With British withdrawal of forces "East of Suez," the Nixon Doctrine posited U.S. support for regional allies to uphold the peace rather than direct U.S. involvement. Nixon found the Shah to be "decisive, confident, strong, kind, and thoughtful ..."[1]

At the strategic level, the Nixon Doctrine envisioned three key elements for use in the Middle East. The first was that Iran would be militarily reinforced with U.S. weaponry, trainers, and intelligence-security specialists as it took on the role of chief advocate and enforcer for U.S. strategic (block the Soviets from regional penetration) and economic (keep the oil flowing at reasonable costs) interests. The second was the United States would need to be able to rapidly project military force into the Gulf should Iran require backup, particularly in the face of any challenge arising from the Soviets. Accordingly, the U.S. military began conceptualizing how a new Rapid Deployment Force (RDF) would be organized and prepared for overseas contingencies and deployment. The third recognized that Saudi Arabia, in possession of the world's largest oil reserves, would continue to receive assurances that the U.S. military would respond with the full toolkit regarding any attempt to undermine the stability within the kingdom or from an external threat.

To shore up the northern tier defense of the Middle East, the Nixon administration reached out to Pakistan. In 1971, Islamabad renewed its active participation in Central Treaty Organization (CENTO) and began coordinating more closely with Iran. Henry Kissinger, Nixon's national security advisor as well as secretary of state, worked with the British to provide air force facilities at both the Indian Ocean's strategic island of Diego Garcia and the Masirah Island off the coast of Oman. Iran, newly empowered and essentially deputized by the United States, soon began shoring up Western interests. For instance, in 1971, Tehran seized the key islands located in the Persian Gulf near the vital choke point of the Strait of Hormuz, the Greater Tunb, the Lesser Tunb, and Abu Musa.

With U.S. and British tacit support, Iran took control of the islands to forestall them falling into the hands of Gulf region's radicalized groups such as the Popular Front of the Liberation of Oman and the Arab Gulf (PFLOAF). For the Arabs, calling it the *Persian* Gulf was a stark contradiction to the historical record. Additionally, the singling out of the Shah of Iran by American leaders did not sit well with many of the Arab states, particularly Saudi Arabia, which had traditionally been a strong and reliable U.S. ally in the Gulf. However, this disagreement was tempered by the realization of the threat posed by the Soviets and their ongoing strategy of undermining Western interests while expanding their influence and control within Arab, Iranian, and Kurdish societies.

Throughout the 1950s, 1960s, and into the 1970s, Western-oriented conservative (both Arab and Persian), Middle Eastern monarchies, many aligned with the Western world, attempted to shore up their security and interests against Soviet-inspired "revolutionary" movements and instability. While the Soviet's and Gamal Nasser's reputations suffered in the Middle East in the wake of the 1967 Six-Day War, Moscow continued to have considerable influence in both Egypt and Syria. As both Cairo and Damascus exploited the Palestinian issue for leverage against Israel and the West, the Soviets were indirectly in support of the Palestine Liberation Organization (PLO) and its "revolutionary" and "resistance" methods and objectives, which included terrorist activities and asymmetric military operations.

Frustrating Moscow's plans, Egypt, now without Nasser and his Soviet entourage, soon joined the Hashemite Kingdom in moving toward peaceful relations with both the West and Israel. As the United States worked to ensure the free flow of oil in the Gulf, Anwar Sadat in Egypt used his military operations during the 1973 October War to achieve political results. By instilling Egyptians with a sense of pride with their military's overall performance in 1973, Sadat created the conditions in which peace with Israel became possible. In October 1977, Sadat made an historic visit to Israel and worked to advance his nation's interests in arriving at a workable solution to three long decades of war.

Following Nixon in the White House, U.S. President Jimmy Carter mediated a series of meetings at the U.S. presidential compound at Camp David in the U.S. state of Maryland where he and Sadat were joined by the prime minister of Israel, Menachem Begin. In September 1978, the trio signed the Camp David Accords. The main points of the agreement included the withdrawal of Israel from the Sinai and the establishment of normalized relations between Israel and Egypt. On March 26, 1979, a formal peace treaty between Egypt and Israel was signed. The following day, the Arab League expelled Egypt and transferred its headquarters from Cairo to Tunis. Nevertheless, on December 10, 1979, Sadat and Begin were jointly awarded the Nobel Peace Prize.

PALESTINE LIBERATION ORGANIZATION

Conventional military operations aimed at the destruction of Israel subsided after the combined failures during wars in 1948, 1967, and 1973. There were hopes of Soviet intervention by many Arab leaders in their aims of seeing the Jewish state banished from the region. Frustrating these plans, America's involvement in the defense of Israel only grew stronger during the period of 1948–1973. Egypt, arguably in possession of the most capable conventional military force within the Arab world, distanced itself from the Soviet orbit and by 1979 made peace with Israel. Arab hopes of a conventional military campaign to destroy Israel dissipated with Egypt's decision. Asymmetric operations, irregular warfare, and terrorism came to dominate the agenda of the enemies of Israel.

The PLO, from its creation in 1964 by Ahmed Shukeiri, and pursuing the objective of destroying the Jewish state by following "the path of holy war (al-jihad)" and erecting a Palestinian one in its place, was angered by the peace process between Egypt and Israel. Having been largely driven from Jordan into Syria, the group, its various subunits, and supporting elements eventually transitioned into Lebanon where the central government found it difficult to maintain order and stability given the presence of a myriad of factions and groups. Ungoverned spaces in the Middle East and North Africa having been spawned by the inability of central governments to control their territory have traditionally provided a fertile repository for guerrilla and terrorist sanctuary. Lebanon, experiencing a civil war between 1975 and 1990, provided such a repository for the PLO. From its position in Lebanon, the PLO soon began launching attacks against Israeli civilians and other targets of opportunity within and, external to, the Jewish state.

The asymmetric operations conducted by the PLO and its affiliated groups included the hijacking of civilian passenger aircraft, bombings, and hostage-taking. One of the more high-profile operations was conducted against Israel at the 1972 Summer Olympics in Munich. Eight members of the Palestinian group "Black September" (in memory of the Kingdom of Jordan's operations against them) armed with AKM assault rifles and grenades broke into the Olympic Village, which housed athletes from around the world, and took several of Israel's competitors hostage. The attackers were part of the Palestinian fedayeen and came from refugee camps in Lebanon, Syria, and Jordan. Their objective was to trade nine seized Israeli athletes and coaches for 234 Palestinian and non-Arabs who had been captured or arrested and imprisoned in Israel. The list of those to be freed included two imprisoned members of the German Red Army Faction.

The venue of the Olympic Games provided a global stage for the attackers to have their demands broadcast around the world, and, during the crisis, television coverage insured that the hostage-taking became a topic for international discussion. Unfortunately for the Palestinian cause, world reaction to masked gunmen seizing innocent participants at a deeply honored historical event such as the Olympic Games created significant outrage and animosity on a global scale rather than the hoped-for outpourings of deep feelings for the plight of the Palestinians.

The members of Black September rode on a bus to the airport and demanded an aircraft in which to depart with their hostages. However, instead of a flight crew, the Boeing 727 jet was operated by six armed members of the German security forces dressed as crew members. In the ensuing gun battles, all of the Israeli hostages were killed along with a West German police officer. Of the eight Black September hostage-takers, five were killed and three were taken prisoners. Subsequent after-action reports led German officials to create structures and processes in order to better coordinate antiterrorist operations. Among those reforms was the establishment by West Germany of an elite counterterrorism unit, GSG-9, specifically organized and trained for dealing with terrorist-related incidents.

On June 27, 1976, an Air France passenger jet, which originated its flight to Paris in Tel Aviv and had 248 passengers, was hijacked by seven members of the Popular Front for the Liberation of Palestine–External Operations (PFLP-EO). The jet was diverted to the airport at Entebbe, Uganda, where the authoritarian leader of the country, Idi Amin, welcomed its arrival as well as the hijackers. The objectives of the PFLP-EO included the release of 40 Palestinian prisoners and 13 others incarcerated in four additional countries.

In response, 100 commandos of the Israeli Defense Forces (IDF), acting on information supplied by MOSSAD, flew 2,500 miles aboard IAF transport aircraft and conducted Operation Thunderbolt aimed at obtaining the release of the hostages and killing or capturing the "terrorists." Amin, a "revolutionary leader" in Uganda, had several Soviet-built MiG fighter jets parked at the Entebbe Airport. In the ensuing fighting, 15 MiG-17s and MiG-21s (some reports claim 30 MiGs) were destroyed. All hijackers, 3 hostages, and 45 Ugandan soldiers were killed. Five IDF commandos were wounded and the unit commander, Lieutenant Colonel, Yonatan Netanyahu, was killed. Netanyahu was the older brother of Benjamin Netanyahu who later became Israeli prime minister. Amin, upon learning that Kenyan officials had provided help to the Israelis during Operation Thunderbolt, had several hundred Kenyans then residing in Uganda killed.

OPERATION LITANI

On March 11, 1978, a group of Palestinian fighters embarked in two rubber boats from Lebanon and landed on the Israeli coast followed by attacks on Israeli civilians. After landing on the coast, the group hijacked a bus and a car and proceeded to the outskirts of Tel Aviv where they were eventually interdicted by IDF personnel. However, 37 Israeli civilians were killed along with 9 of the Palestinian fighters. In response, 48 hours later on March 14, 1978, 25,000 IDF soldiers moved into Lebanon as part of Operation Litani, in which the main objective was to create a buffer zone by pushing anti-Israeli elements north from the Litani River and away from the Israeli border. Operation Litani, which ended up killing 2,000 Lebanese and Palestinian civilians, represented the largest IDF military action since the 1973 October War.

As a result of the operation, nearly 300,000 refugees were created, as the population withdrew to avoid IDF operations and the armed clashes with the terrorists (or freedom fighters) that fought back and were driven mostly to the outskirts of Beirut. More than 75 percent of those driven from their homes were Lebanese who, in all likelihood, had little or nothing to do with the terrorists who had arrived in the rubber boats. In southern Beirut, in the coming years, these angry and disenfranchised people became part of the environment from which Hezbollah ("Party of God"), a Shiite terrorist group sponsored by Syria and Iran, would spring years later.

U.S. President Carter, during his peace negotiations at the time, worked for the inclusion of the status of the West Bank and Gaza Strip in the negotiations, as the Jordanians and Palestinians had been invited to take part in the process. However, both the government of Jordan and the PLO rejected the talks out of hand and refused to attend the meetings. Carter also brought to his presidency a near singular focus on human rights around the world. While admirable in a perfect world, in doing so, given the political and military dynamics at the time, he alienated several key governments that had been backed traditionally by the United States due to their strong stance regarding Soviet intrigue and expansionism. Under Carter, the key South American nation of Brazil essentially cut off military-to-military relations with the United States because of what it believed to be internal meddling by the Carter administration. The Carter administration's insistence on political reforms within Iran, without considering the strategic dynamics impacting the internal and external environment, led to an unraveling of government control and the seizure of government within Iran by radical Islamist militants. The "revolutionary" regime remains in place today, and the democratization and advancement of human rights that Carter sought have, unfortunately, delivered a series of setbacks under the authoritarian theocracy of the Islamic Republic of Iran.

DESTABILIZATION OF IRAN

Carter threatened to cut off military aid to several key U.S. allies, including Iran, that supported American efforts against the Union of Soviet Socialist Republics (USSR). The Carter administration stipulated that the Shah needed to improve his human rights record, or U.S. aid, including military assistance, might be terminated. The Shah attempted to satisfy Carter's demands by loosening authoritarian control, which in turn gave rise to protests, strikes, and general instability and unrest. This instability and unrest created the conditions eventually leading to the fall of the Shah's government. Many analysts and historians have argued that the United States should not have been involved, in the first place, with any dictatorial regime engaged in suppressing the legitimate rights and aspirations of people. However, others have argued that in allowing the country to descend into chaos under the guise of "democratization" created the conditions in which a more suppressive and more authoritarian regime seized power.

In response to Carter's threats, the Shah's government in Iran released 357 political prisoners in February 1977, and public demonstrations began against the Shah in October 1977. With the ongoing public demonstrations springing up across the country, an organization of writers and publishers sought increases in free speech, which was followed by a group of 64 lawyers calling an end to military tribunals. Another group of lawyers began publicizing the activities of SAVAK (Iranian secret intelligence service, with police powers under the Shah, which received U.S. support and advice during the initial years of its establishment). Business people demanded less intrusion and more freedom from government controls. Between August and December 1978, strikes and demonstrations effectively paralyzed the country. People began taking to the streets, believing that the government was under siege and unable to maintain control. Instead of an orderly transition to a more open and tolerant society, Iran became a hotbed of passions and anger. The Shah and his sister, Princess Ashraf, who both had developed a propensity toward a high-profile lifestyle of extravagance, along with their American supporters within the country, soon became the focal points of the ensuing violence.

The instability created within Iran and fanned into flames by American policy presented the Soviet Union with an opportunity in undermining a key Western ally. Moreover, the harsh suppressive methods of the Shah's authoritarian regime insured the creation of significant dissatisfaction within the country, particularly among the Islamic Shi'a fundamentalists. Iranian clerics and other leaders who had been exiled from Iran ramped up their already steady complaints about regime behavior and instructed their followers to incite violence and instability.

It was not simply that the Shah was harsh and oppressive that drove anger toward his policies. The Shah, as his father Reza Shah before him, had attempted to bring Iran into the modern world, to minimize elite control over land, to industrialize, to expand opportunities in education, and to improve the rights of women. Many of the fundamentalist clerics, now allied with a privileged land-holding elite, wanted no part of the modern world or any part of the Shah and his modernizing but simultaneously oppressive and increasingly secular regime. The Shah and Carter found themselves outmaneuvered by powerful domestic factions within Iran, which found encouragement if not outright intelligence support from those in the Warsaw Pact.

IRANIAN "REVOLUTION" AND THE TAKING OF HOSTAGES

Revolutionary groups began attacking police stations and other state security facilities throughout the capital city of Tehran, capturing weapons and armories. As the chaos spread, mass defections occurred within the ranks of the security and military services, including the top commanders of the imperial guards. When it became apparent that the country had been lost, the Shah and his family left Iran on January 16, 1979. Following the Shah's departure, his nemesis, Khomeini, having been in exile for 14 years, returned to Iran on February 1, 1979. On February 11, the Supreme Council of the Armed Forces met and drafted a statement of neutrality that was read on state radio on the same day. This event signaled to the people of Iran that neither the Shah's regime nor the follow-on government of Shapour Bakhtiar of the dissident National Front had the backing of the security institutions or the military. By default, this left the country in the hands of the militant Islamist forces led by Khomeini.

Over the next several months, revolutionary elements consolidated their hold over the country as 500 military officers of general officer rank were executed, while thousands more at the mid-grade level were arrested. The Shah and his family found temporary sanctuary in Egypt but were later granted entry into the United States on "medical grounds." This decision by the Carter administration brought the level of scorn and condemnation heaped upon the United States by the revolutionary media propaganda machine in Iran to new heights.

On November 4, 1979, just as the Shah landed in New York, a group of Iranian radicals, aligned with the "Muslim Student Followers of the

Imam's Line," breached the walls of the U.S. embassy in Tehran, overwhelmed the small security force, and took 66 U.S. diplomatic and other personnel hostage. In America, the incident became known as the Iran hostage crisis and lasted from November 4, 1979, until January 20, 1981, and was featured nightly on U.S. national broadcast news programs, for 444 days. In Iran, the incident was referred to as the "Conquest of the American Spy Den."

As the hostage crisis remained unresolved for an extended period, and as Iran demanded the return of the Shah for prosecution (as well as an expected execution), the United States, under the Carter administration, refused. Within the United States came a growing chorus of voices demanding that the president take decisive action to free the hostages. Carter's secretary of state, Cyrus Vance, consistently, throughout the entire ordeal, counseled against taking any military action. As negotiations continued to fail, Carter began considering military options. While he had promoted human rights and was a strong advocate of peaceful international relations, he was also a former naval officer educated at the U.S. Naval Academy at Annapolis, majoring in engineering. On November 12, 1979, Carter authorized the formation of a planning group (Joint Task Force— JTF 1-79) to create operational plans for the rescue of the hostages at the U.S. embassy in Tehran. The planning went forward under the code-name "Rice Bowl," with Major General James B. Vaught in command.

OPERATION EAGLE CLAW AND THE LACK OF JOINT-INTERAGENCY COORDINATION

Two planning assumptions soon animated the initial discussions of JTF 1-79. The first was a consensus that in order to succeed the ground rescue force would have to be placed at its final assault position with total surprise. This consensus factored significantly into the actual operational phase of the action (code-named: Operation Eagle Claw) in that it required a complete radio and communication blackout throughout the entire operation. Unfortunately, this requirement had unintended consequences, as it impaired the operation's ability to adjust to new information (particularly weather) and to help the operators overcome the fog and friction of war, which subsequently interfered with operational intent arising from tactical development.

The second element that was adopted by JTF 1-79 (Rice Bowl) was that the relatively newly created "Delta Force" with Colonel Charles Beckwith in command would be the ground force rescue team. Delta at the time was a small, elite U.S. Army unit of 120 men trained as an all-purpose counterterrorist strike group.

But Delta Force did not have the means either to get to Iran or to make a clandestine approach to the American Embassy. The United States had a glaring lack of centralized command that could conduct a turn-key operation having under its control all the necessary support elements—air transport, intelligence, logistics, and combat air support. The government had to improvise, calling on units from various services. All these disparate units of the operation never held an exercise as a whole.[2]

Interagency cooperation throughout the U.S. government, particularly between the U.S. Department of Defense, U.S. State Department, and the U.S. Central Intelligence Agency (CIA), was limited in 1979. In fact, up to the late 1970s, cooperation among the services *within* the Department of Defense was also quite limited. This inability to operate seamlessly across services constrained America's ability to conduct effective joint military operations. Moreover, beyond the Defense Department, the inability for separate governmental agencies to cooperate effectively and jointly reduced U.S. efforts at bringing all elements of American power to bear on a range of difficult and seemingly intractable issues.

In late 1979, while Rice Bowl tasked the CIA with lining up logistical and informational requirements within Iran itself, the movement of Delta into Iran would be accomplished by assets under control of the U.S. Defense Department. However, once in-country, CIA-arranged Iranian trucks would be required to move Delta clandestinely into the inner urban areas of Tehran itself. Once this aspect of the plan surfaced—that the U.S. military would be required to rely on the CIA for a critical operational element of Eagle Claw—American military commanders quietly voiced concerns. Subsequently, former U.S. Special Forces officers were sent clandestinely into Tehran by the Pentagon to confirm up-front aspects of Eagle Claw that would be handled by CIA.

As the operators were brought in to prepare for the execution aspects of Rice Bowl-Eagle Claw, U.S. Army Colonel Charles Beckwith (Delta commander) asked that 10 helicopters be placed at his disposal. The U.S. Navy responded by saying that eight was the "maximum number that could be put in the hangar bay of the USS *Nimitz* without taking away other aircraft that were normally stationed there." Later after the action, the Defense Department formed the Holloway Commission to examine all aspects of Rice Bowl-Eagle Claw (Admiral James L. Holloway was a retired U.S. chief of naval operations). The commission found "that in a condition of non-war twelve helicopters could have been used and that no factors, either operational or logistical would have prevented the launching of eleven helicopters from the *Nimitz*."[3]

Access to Masirah Island off the coast of Oman negotiated by Kissinger during the Nixon administration became a key logistical hub for the hostage rescue attempt. Six Lockheed C-130 Hercules U.S. Air Force (USAF) aircraft would lift off from the island and transport Beckwith and Delta into Iran. A group of U.S. Army Rangers would fly from Egypt into Iran and secure an obsolete air base at Manzariyeh southwest of Tehran for the eventual extraction of the hostages. Delta would fly into Iran to the rendezvous at Desert One, essentially a dirt road in the Great Salt Desert, where the force would move from the C-130s to U.S. Navy's RH-53D helicopters chosen for their extended range. Accordingly, on April 24, 1980, eight RH-53D helicopters, two less than what Beckwith requested, lifted off from the deck of the USS *Nimitz* operating in the vicinity of the Persian Gulf and headed to a remote road serving as an airstrip in the Great Salt Desert of eastern Iran near Taba.

The helicopters came from a naval antimine squadron used primarily for minesweeping in the ocean, and, since the terrain would be ground rather than sea, naval pilots were replaced with marine pilots. Unfortunately, the marines were qualified in CH-53s rather than the RH-53D naval version. When warning lights eventually came on reporting malfunctioning systems and a problem with cracks in the rotor, the marines, not realizing that navy doctrine for those advanced aircraft allowed for continued operation, reported that a number of helos were not capable of continuing.

Inside Iran, a massive dust storm arose (referred to locally as a "haboob"), causing problems with equipment and visibility. Nevertheless, had the marine pilots been provided secure communications in which to report and to receive updates on the nature of equipment and weather, they would have been able to move through the warning lights as well as the localized nature of the dust storm. As it unfolded, Beckwith was informed that three RH-53Ds had been disabled and, as a result, he now had only five operational helicopters, one less than the minimum required according to the operational plan. Following this, he requested and received authorization from the White House to abort Operation Eagle Claw. After receiving word to stand down and as the helicopters were maneuvering in close proximity to the C-130s at Desert One, one of the helicopters collided with a Hercules C-130 on the ground causing the fuel bladder-laden C-130 to explode. In the ensuing disaster, eight U.S. servicemen were killed (along with an Iranian civilian whose group happened upon Desert One) and two U.S. aircraft were destroyed.

Eagle Claw originally envisioned Delta flying via helicopters at night from Desert One to a position 50 miles southwest of Tehran and linking up with trucks with Iranian markings that would have been provided by the CIA. Delta would then have moved surreptitiously through the streets of Tehran to the U.S. embassy. Once there and achieving tactical surprise, Delta, according to the plan, would have then quickly assaulted (in a silenced mode) and overcome the hostage-takers. Once the hostages were recuperated, Delta, with hostages in tow, would transition via trucks to a prearranged site at a local stadium where helicopters awaited to extract and fly them to the awaiting USAF C-141s and MC-130s guarded by U.S. Army Rangers at the Manzariyeh Air Base. From Manzariyeh, the air flotilla would fly to Egypt and to safety.

After the failed attempt of the rescue became public, with Carter accepting full responsibility, the American hostages were moved from the embassy and scattered across Iran in an effort to frustrate any future bids at securing their freedom. By mid-1980, further negotiations had gone nowhere. However, the Shah had departed the United States in December 1979, weeks after the hostages were taken and his return to Iran demanded as a condition for their release. The Shah traveled to Egypt where he was granted asylum, thereby changing the nature of the negotiations for the hostages' release. The United States was able to argue in the negotiations, "How can we release him to you in exchange for our hostages? We don't have him." Six months later, the Shah's death was announced on July 27, 1980.

THE SOVIETS ARRIVE AT THE IRANIAN BORDER

> Throughout the late 1970s and the 1980s, the objectives of U.S. strategy in the Gulf were to maintain access to the area's petroleum resources, keep the Soviets out, and improve political stability in the region. During the early part of this period, the principle perceived threat was the Soviet Union. The fear was that the Soviets would exploit regional instability and possibly U.S. engagement elsewhere to grab the oil resources of the Middle East. With the fall of the Shah of Iran in early 1979, the threat became more complex.[4]

In the midst of the Iranian Revolution, the Soviet Union decided to push south and invade the eastern neighbor to Iran, Afghanistan. Discussions within the Kremlin regarding sending Soviet forces began in earnest in early 1979. Soviet leader Leonid Brezhnev summoned the chief of the Soviet General Staff, N. V. Ogarkov, and informed him that the Soviet Politburo, ruling committee of the USSR, had reached a preliminary decision for a temporary introduction of Soviet forces into Afghanistan and told him to prepare 75,000 to 80,000 troops. This was the first Ogarkov had heard of this proposal. With a look of amazement, he responded that 80,000 troops would not be able to stabilize the situation in Afghanistan. Apparently, Ogarkov used the adjective "reckless" to describe his view of the decision. Dmitri Ustinov, the Soviet defense minister at the time, cut him off in mid-sentence with the sharp admonishment: "Are you going to teach the Politburo? Your duty is to carry out your orders."

Moscow had long envisioned having military bases within Afghanistan, seeking actively in the mid-nineteenth century to undercut British influence in India. The Soviet KGB observed and provided intelligence to the Kremlin leadership that Afghanistan's borders with Iran and Pakistan, even in the mid-twentieth century, were practically open and that having a strong position within Afghanistan would allow Moscow to project power and influence into both Iran and Pakistan. If the Soviet Union could project effective power and influence into Iran, it would then have the opportunity to project power and influence into the Persian Gulf and the Middle East. Finally, if Moscow could project power into Pakistan, it would then have the opportunity of having greater influence for obtaining a prize it had sought for two centuries—a dominant position within India itself—while simultaneously distancing the key South Asian country from Western influence. Thus, great strategic opportunities waited the Politburo. However, a relatively small, unruly group of Afghani tribesmen stood in the way.

In April 1978, Afghan communists supported by leftist army commanders overthrew the largely unpopular and authoritarian government of Mohammad Daoud and announced the establishment of the "People's Democratic Republic of Afghanistan." Moscow quickly moved to establish close relations with the newly installed regime led by Nur Mohammad Taraki who had stated his intent of bringing "socialism" to Afghanistan. The Taraki regime attempted to move strongly in suppressing any dissent aimed at undermining the government. However, the strong-arm tactics quickly alienated most of Afghanistan's population as well as the army. While the terror campaign conducted against its opponents created problems, the most damning for the Taraki regime was in introducing a series of social and economic reforms, which were in direct opposition to the religious and cultural values of Afghanistan's highly conservative, Muslim, tribal society. Afghan leaders swiftly reacted and declared a jihad against "godless communism" (using the phrase from one of the original Cold War warriors, John Foster Dulles, who served in the Eisenhower administration). By August 1978, the Taraki government faced open revolt with segments of the army that joined in the rebellion. By September 1979, Hafizullah Amin managed to seize power and ordered Taraki arrested and killed.

In response, Soviet premier Brezhnev in November 1979 ordered 4,500 Soviet combat advisors along with strike aircraft (both fixed-wing and rotary) into Afghanistan to conduct operations against forces working in opposition to Moscow's interests. In December, Moscow massed elements of the 40th Army (consisting of mostly Central Asian troops) along the Afghanistan border. On December 24, 1979, Soviet airborne forces, including KGB and GRU special units dressed in Afghan army uniforms, were inserted into Afghanistan joining up with previously positioned Soviet personnel on the pretext that the Afghan government had invited it to help against an unnamed external threat. Airborne and special units quickly took control of major government, military, and media buildings in Kabul and surrounded the Tajbeg Presidential Palace.

Relying on mechanized tactics operating with close air support, Soviet forces quickly took control of Kabul and, with a special assault force (Spetsnaz or Soviet army special forces), attacked the presidential palace and killed Amin and immediately installed Barak Kemal as an acceptable replacement. Kemal positioned himself as a devoted Muslim and Afghan nationalist, and about 50,000 Soviet forces occupied major cities and controlled major transportation hubs and roads. Afghan forces opposed to the Soviet intervention, unable to confront the more powerful Soviets in conventional military operations, soon resorted to guerrilla warfare, with the primary goal of avoiding defeat, staying in the field, and, through "death by a thousand cuts," (conducting attrition operations against the Soviets) outlasting the occupiers in a Southwest Asian version of ghazi warfare.

CARTER DOCTRINE

Moscow's sudden invasion of Afghanistan, given the turmoil in Iran, angered the Carter administration, which had worked assiduously to improve relations with the Soviet Union. On December 28, 1979, Carter publicly denounced the Soviet invasion as a "blatant violation of accepted international rules of behavior" and followed three days later when he accused the Soviet leadership of lying about its motives for intervening. On January 3, 1980, Carter asked the U.S. Senate to delay consideration of the strategic arms limitation agreement known as SALT II. Less than a month after the first Soviet troops rolled into Afghanistan, Carter, during his State of the Union address (January 23, 1980) to a joint session of Congress, laid out what became known as the Carter Doctrine, which very publicly proclaimed that the United States would respond with all necessary force to forestall any attempt by hostile forces to seize territory within the Middle East.

The Soviet invasion also convinced Carter of the urgent need to move forward with the creation and deployment of the RDF.[5] Carter also directed the CIA to begin formulating covert assistance programs for the Afghan *mujahedeen* while also directing the USAF (July 25, 1980) to expand the American targeting list of both Soviet conventional and nuclear forces.

The Reagan administration (1981–1988) expanded the CIA's role in arming and supporting the Afghan mujahedeen. Shoulder-fired "stinger" missiles were used against Soviet helicopters and aircraft, and, by the time of the Soviet withdrawal in 1988–1989, the CIA had armed and supported approximately 300,000 rebel fighters. While this effort contributed to the ultimate defeat of the Politburo agenda and in driving Soviet forces from Afghanistan, later, as the United States faced an Al-Qaeda and Taliban partnership, the strengthening of the mujahedeen fighters served in creating problems for the United States and the West. The Soviet campaign in Afghanistan was the largest and lengthiest Soviet military action during the Cold War and represented the largest military commitment since World War II. It was also arguably one of the most costly in terms of treasure, manpower, and prestige—both domestic and international.

> One high-ranking member of the KGB later confessed, "We made two major errors of judgment: we overestimated the willingness of the Afghan army to fight, and we underestimated the upsurge of the Afghan resistance."[6]

The U.S. support that was generated for the anti-Soviet mujahedeen represented the main paramilitary operation of what became known as the Reagan Doctrine.[7] From 1946 to 1983, U.S. policy revolved around containing the Soviet Union and frustrating its desired expansionistic agenda. U.S. President Ronald Reagan believed that while containing Soviet power was necessary, it was not sufficient. For Reagan, the power of the USSR should be "rolled back." Toward this policy objective, in 1983, the Reagan administration issued National Security Decision Directive 75 (NSDD-75), aimed at diminishing Soviet power and influence.

NSDD-75, drafted by Reagan's National Security Council, contained three core principles. The first was aimed at applying external pressure on the Soviets through military power and geographic positioning. The second was focused on internal pressure within the Soviet Union itself through the initiation of U.S. economic policies that would transition the USSR toward "a more pluralistic political and economic system in which the power of the privileged ruling elite is gradually reduced."[8] The third principle was to engage the Soviets in diplomacy where negotiations could be leveraged in consolidating and exploiting any gains achieved by the first two principles.

> Implementation of U.S. policy must focus on shaping the environment in which Soviet decisions are made both in a wide variety of functional and geopolitical arenas and in the U.S.-Soviet bilateral relationship . . . Soviet calculations of possible war outcomes under any contingency must always result in outcomes so unfavorable to the USSR that there would be no incentives for Soviet leaders to initiate an attack . . . . . . In the Third World, Moscow must know that areas of interest to the U.S. cannot be attacked or threatened without serious U.S. military countermeasures.[9]

As the Soviets battled Afghan forces in an attempt to control the government in Kabul during the early 1980s, westward of Iran with the

Khomeini regime still holding American hostages in Iran, on September 1980, Saddam Hussein launched an Iraqi invasion of southwest Iran seeking to control the oil-rich and mainly Arab-populated region of Khuzestan. In the light of these developments, and as the United States increasingly began reviewing military options, Tehran reentered negotiations with Washington, with Algeria acting as mediator. The hostages were formally released into U.S. custody after the signing of the Algiers Accords, just minutes after the new U.S. president, Reagan, was sworn in.

IRAN-IRAQ WAR

Iraqi leader Saddam saw both threat and opportunity with the Iranian "revolution." The Sunni Gulf states—Saudi Arabia, United Arab Emirates, Qatar, Oman, Bahrain, Kuwait—along with Western powers were concerned about potential attempts by Shi'a Iran to sow discord in the region and beyond. By moving against the clerics in Tehran, Hussein envisioned strong backing and substantial reward. Khuzestan, a primary target of Hussein in September 1980, was a Persian Gulf province of Iran and served as the center of its oil industry. In March 1979, unrest broke out in areas inhabited by Arabic-speaking people, Turcomans, and Kurds. In May 1979, the "revolutionary" regime of Khomeini directed its forces to open fire on the demonstrators in the key city of Khorramshahr, which sought independence from the ongoing revolutionary turmoil that permeated Tehran. Baghdad was supportive of the mainly Arab Khuzestan population and sought to have the province, eventually, becoming part of a greater Iraq.

Khomeini, once ensconced in power within Iran, set about undermining the government in Baghdad as well as working to suppress uprisings within Iran. Years earlier, Khomeini had found refuge in the Shiite region of southern Iraq after being driven from Iran by forces under the control of the Shah (SAVAK security services) and with backing from its main international supporter, the United States. As the exiled and bitter Khomeini increased the anti-Shah rhetoric from southern Iraq, the Shah asked Saddam to deport Khomeini who eventually shipped the Ayatollah off to France.[10]

While Khomeini had developed a strong personal dislike for Saddam, he was even more opposed to what Saddam's party, the Ba'athists, represented. The secularization and Westernization of Arab and Muslim society, which Khomeini accused Baghdad of being party to, brought a flurry of reciprocal and antagonistic acts between the Iranians under Khomeini and an Iraq led by Saddam. During the first half of 1980, Radio Iran's increasingly strident verbal attacks on the Ba'ath Party of Iraq were meant to turn the Shiites against the Sunnis within Iraq and to foment an Iraqi revolution. Khomeini made personal speeches that were broadcast into Iraq calling on Iraqi Shiites to overthrow the Iraqi government.

More particularly, Khomeini wanted to secure the troubled Iranian Khuzestan region by creating internal problems for Saddam that would serve in diverting his attention and focus from an effort aimed at undermining Iranian revolutionary rule. Khomeini was also intent on controlling the key southern Iraqi port city of al-Basra as well as Shiite holy sites located in Karbala and al-Najaf.[11] Saddam, with the passing of Egypt's Nasser, sought to seize the mantle of Arab leadership and, in his mind, become the modern-day manifestation of the ancient Mesopotamian king, Nebuchadnezzar.[12]

As Radio Iran broadcast anti-Ba'athist programming into Iraq, Saddam countered by having Iraqi radio stations broadcast into Khuzestan, encouraging Arabs and Baluchis alike to revolt against the Iranian government in Tehran. Iraqi television based in Basra showed Khuzestan as a part of a new Iraq—renamed as the new *Nasiriyah* province—and renamed all cities in Khuzestan with Arabic names.

A few years earlier, in 1975, Iraq and Iran had been in conflict over a variety of issues. Iran was supportive of the Kurds in northern Iraq regarding their bid to create an independent homeland apart from Iraq. On March 6, 1975, Iran and Iraq signed the Algiers Agreement following an OPEC summit in Algeria in which Iran agreed to stop supporting the Kurdish rebels in return for Iraq relinquishing its claim to the full possession of the Shatt al-Arab—a waterway that extended from the confluence of the Tigris and Euphrates Rivers into the Persian Gulf. As Iran successfully maneuvered itself into control of half the waterway by exploiting the Kurdish issue within Iraq, Saddam, who as vice president was in charge of the negotiating team, became thoroughly displeased with Iranian coercive diplomacy.

When Khomeini took power four years later, he reinstituted support for rebel elements throughout Iraq, with a particular focus and assistance to Kurdish separatists and Iraqi Shiite underground movements. His words, broadcast into Iraq, were, "Wake up and topple this [Ba'athist] regime in your country before it's too late."[13]

The charges of impropriety and aggression flew between Baghdad and Tehran. Between March 1979 and September 1980, Iran claimed that it had endured 434 attacks by Iraqi artillery, infantry, and armored forces as well as 363 violations of its air space. Iraq countered by arguing that it had experienced 544 violations of its borders and air space. Later as large-scale, conventional war broke out, Iraq claimed that it was not the aggressor or the initiator of the Iran-Iraq War (1980–1988), begun on September 22, 1980, but that the war actually had begun on September 4,

1980, when Iran had shelled Iraqi towns and villages along the middle of the border line between the two countries.

While Khomeini hoped to spark unrest and instability within Iraq, Saddam was counting on the Arab inhabitants within Khuzestan to rise up and fight with his forces if he opted to invade. As the Iran-Iraq War progressed, neither Saddam nor Khomeini was able to convince large numbers of the inhabitants of the other nation to fight on their respective sides. Some would later argue that it was an instance of nationalism superseding religious affiliation. Perhaps. Or, alternatively, it was an instance where people were unconvinced with the respective arguments of why they should leave their homes and families, be transported to another region, and kill or be killed in the name of someone else's nationalistic pride and someone else's religious interpretation of God's will or in the pursuit of someone else's economic objectives.

By mid-September 1980, Saddam announced that Iraq was unilaterally abrogating the 1975 treaty between Iraq and Iran and that the Shatt al-Arab was returning to complete Iraqi sovereignty—a move Iran completely rejected. On September 22, 1980, Iraqi T-62 tanks (Russian-built and Russian-supplied) of the 6th Iraqi Armored Division crossed the Iranian border and proceeded to the Khuzestan Province. While Saddam was not a trained military commander and had never been a soldier, he had been briefed on the 1967 Six-Day War and the 1973 October War.[14]

What he had hoped to duplicate in his campaign against Iran was complete surprise, which contributed to the conditions that allowed the Israeli Air Force (IAF) to destroy the Egyptian Air Force on the ground in June 1967. Moreover, through lightning advances and maneuver, he sought to replicate the Egyptian success in October 1973, as they swiftly moved across the Suez Canal and took only a predetermined amount of territory, which they then held successfully against the IAF's counterstrikes by placing that territory under the protection of a "rocket wall." The rocket wall, of course, consisted of a barrage of surface-to-air missiles (SAMs) supplied by the Soviet Union. Simultaneously, the Israeli armored counterattack was neutralized by Soviet-supplied antitank guided missiles. The Egyptians then engaged the Israeli leadership in successful negotiations, which returned lost land from the 1967 Six-Day War.

Thus, the core of the operational campaign plan the Iraqi military utilized in the opening stages of the Iran-Iraq War was from the 1967 and 1973 conventional wars against Israel. For Saddam, after replicating those conditions, he would then be in a position to negotiate the return of complete sovereignty over the Shatt al-Arab. Accordingly, the objectives of the Iraqi military campaign into Iran in September 1980 were limited, as was the expected time frame for achieving those ends. Saddam sought the complete reversal of the terms of the Algiers Agreement and the return of the Shatt al-Arab waterway to Iraqi control and the immediate halt to Iranian agitation and support to revolutionary groups and activities within the country.

A third objective was controlling Khuzestan or, minimally, insuring that Tehran could not use the oil-rich province's resources to sponsor revolutionary activities across the Middle East. He also believed, mistakenly, that once his army had moved into Khuzestan, the Arabic-speaking citizens would rise up and greet his army as liberators. Hence, he would either succeed in taking control of the oil resources in the province or make sure the revolutionary government in Tehran would not be able to use those resources against his interests, that is, if Saddam was forced to withdraw, he planned to have his forces destroy the oil infrastructure. And, finally, Saddam assumed he could achieve his objectives in two weeks, again attempting to replicate the lightning success of the Israelis in the Six-Day War.[15]

While Saddam achieved surprise with his advance into Iran, moved into Khuzestan, and captured several villages and small towns—he even managed to capture the strategic city of Khorramshahr after intense hand-to-hand combat—he accomplished little else. At the same time as the Iraqi 6th Armored Division's drive into Iran, MiG-21s and MiG-23s of the Iraqi Air Force attempted to knock out the Iranian Air Force in a surprise attack, hitting air fields at Mehrabad and Doshen-Tappen, both near Tehran, as well as Tabriz, Bakhtaran, Ahvaz, Dezful, Urmia (Urumiyeh), Hamadan, Sanandaj, and Abadan.

Following the initial air and ground assaults and six days into the war, on September 28, Saddam called for a cease-fire and issued a set of demands (similar to Egypt's Anwar Sadat in the 1973 October War), which Tehran promptly rejected. The first problem for the realization of Saddam's plan was that the Iranian Air Force, unlike the Israeli accomplishment in 1967, had not been knocked out in the first strike. Moreover, it was the United States that had been supportive of the Iranian Air Force from 1971 until the overthrow of the Shah at the end of the decade. As such, Iranian jets were parked under specially strengthened hanger canopies as well as within reinforced concrete bunkers, and many rode out the initial Iraqi air strike. Additionally, the bombs the Iraqi Air Force dropped on Iranian air fields did not succeed in rendering the runways inoperable for an extended period as had occurred during the Israeli air strike against Egypt in June 1967. Where the bombs did hit, the Iranians quickly succeeded in repairing the damage within hours and, by the second day of the war, Iranian pilots were able to mount limited counterattack sorties.[16]

Additionally, the ability to mesh operations seamlessly in an integrated joint or combined arms approach, which eluded the Americans' special operations effort during Eagle Claw, provided the IDF with an operational edge in 1967—but shown to be lacking in 1973—and also eluded the Iraqi armed forces in their initial efforts against the Iranians. A further mistake, also made by the Israelis in the 1973 October War, was in not understanding the nature of Erwin Rommel's armor tactics during the desert war in North Africa.[17]

> The Iraqis repeated the mistake of the Israelis in the Yom Kippur War [1973 October War] on the Suez Canal front relying on tank units instead of combined arms teams.[18]

IDF doctrine in the 1967 and 1973 wars was tank-on-tank battle with scant reliance on infantry. However, the Israelis enjoyed the advantage of air superiority in 1967 and, over most of the Middle East in 1973, which Saddam failed to achieve in September 1980. Arising out of the adoption of the assumption of achieving air superiority in the opening hours of the campaign, came the reality that Iraq had not planned to provide adequate air defenses for its own vital oil facilities.

In consequence, with the Iranian refusal to negotiate and the inability of Saddam to march on Tehran and force the Khomeini government's capitulation, the war bogged down into an extended war of attrition, which Iraq was not prepared to engage in. Trenches sprang up, and with the use of chemical weapons (CWs), came gas masks. At some points along the front lines, the scene resembled the western European front during the First World War.

Included in Saddam's government's mistaken assumptions was the belief that Iran's military would not be able to respond effectively given the degraded state of the Iranian officer corps. Khomeini's revolutionary government, as mentioned, had executed 500 general officers and purged about 10,000 officers from Iran's army, with many arrested and jailed. Moreover, the fact that America was forced to withdraw military support for Iran as the Shah was expelled led Iraqi leaders to believe that a range of parts necessary for the proper functioning of the Iranian military would not be available should armed hostilities break out.

Hence, the assessment was that the Iranian military had been deprived of its leadership as well as its logistical lifeline to the United States. Based on these dynamics, an assessment was made that Iran was in a weakened state militarily, void of competent combat commanders, and experiencing rebellious eruptions from a variety of displeased and displaced constituencies throughout the country. Unfortunately, for Saddam's regime underestimating one's opponent brings with it an enormous negative downside and is rightly considered the cardinal sin of military intelligence. This calamity eventually assisted in undermining the Third Reich under Adolf Hitler in Germany during the Second World

War, and it befell Iraq under the political and military leadership of a strategically challenged and militarily untrained Saddam.

Adaptability and flexibility on the part of the Iranian leadership eventually circumvented Iraq's early advantages. As Saddam's forces invaded Khuzestan Province and as Iran suffered from an initial lack of strategic, operational, and tactical leadership, Khomeini was convinced by his advisors to immediately welcome back thousands of Iranian military officers. Iraq was not able to capitalize on this early disarray as, in the first years of the war, Saddam involved himself in all details of planning and execution, while the suboptimal results reflected his lack of formal training and strategic, operational, and tactical experience as a military commander. The only thing that kept things from deteriorating or spiraling out of control for Iraq was the fact that the revolutionary religious zealots under Khomeini, fearful of the resurgence of U.S.-trained Iranian military in Iran, demanded to be involved in all details of planning and execution as well.

However, political and ideological correctness, combined with regime loyalty, were measurable metrics for high-level service in the Iranian military rather than military competence in the latter years of the Shah's reign as well as in the first two years of revolutionary Iran. Within Iran, Khomeini and his ideologues demanded oversight over military decision making. Later, as it became apparent that the clerics who knew how to overthrow a country's government did not know how to conduct a successful modern military campaign, professionally trained Iranian military officers regained positions of responsibility for military operations.

These adjustments eventually resulted in Iran seizing control of the strategic Fao Peninsula. Unfortunately, following these initial successes, Khomeini then stepped in again and directed the Iranian armed forces to invade Iraq, which the Iranian professional officer corps had rejected out of hand and as being ill-advised. Once the Iranians adopted objectives that included an invasion accompanied with regime change within Iraq, as the Iranian officer corps feared, the U.S. military and the American intelligence community were, in short order, directed by U.S. President Reagan to step in and stop the Iranians from achieving their objectives.

However, before the war was concluded in 1988, tens of thousands of Iraqis and Iranians would die. The first phase of the war, as hostilities erupted into open warfare in September 1980, was largely under the control of Saddam and the Iranian clerics, with Saddam managing to push about 50 miles into Iran and then, according to plan, and attempting to replicate the success of the Egyptians during the initial phases of the 1973 October War with Israel, tried to engage the Iranians in negotiation. The Iranian clerics in rejecting Saddam's entreaties responded by sending 100,000 Iranian volunteers to the front, arriving in November 1980.

The ages ranged from 12 to 70, and instead of adequate training and weapons, the Iranian clerical leaders provided them with sets of plastic and cardboard keys to wear around their neck. The keys were said to be "keys to heaven," and the new, largely untrained fighters were told that to perish in battle fighting for the Ayatollah was the same as fighting for Allah. By fighting for Allah, the soldier was assured a place in heaven.

> Only an ideologically motivated army like ours ... [and only an ideology like ours] is capable of mobilizing the people for a long war of attrition which we plan to wage until the Iraqi regime falls.[19]

While the Iranian clerical leadership inherited a reasonably well-trained and equipped armed services upon seizing power, after a series of executions, purges, and imprisonments, by the fall of 1980, those services were drastically reduced. After Iraq invaded and the threat to clerical rule in Iran shifted from internal to external sources, it took months to begin repairing the damage done to the Iranian armed forces and to reincorporate the ousted military officers into its ranks. To bridge that gap and to buy needed time, the Iranians created and fielded the Pasdaran, a paramilitary group also referred to as the Iranian Revolutionary Guard (IRG), and within the Pasdaran, the Basij militia.

It was within these ranks that human wave attacks were launched against entrenched Iraqi armor and artillery, with minefields being cleared with the elderly and the young walking through them. Hojjat el-Eslam Salek was head of the Basij militia and stated that Iran was engaged in a new "Islamic warfare" where the superior Iranian population would prevail over time in the face of the corrupt, godless Ba'athists. The military reality beyond the ideological bravado, however, was that the Iranian masses were sent into battle lacking sufficient training and tended to congregate indecisively on the battlefield, which, in turn, insured a high casualty rate.

During the Iran-Iraq War, Iraqi leaders as well as international military advisors underestimated the ferocity of Iranian foot soldiers stoked with a revolutionary fervor similar to the energy of leidenschaft, which arose during the French Revolution. In massed infantry assaults of 1,000-man human waves, the teenagers and old men attacked into the teeth of Soviet-supplied Iraqi armor and artillery. As a result of the revolutionary fervor, coupled with incompetent military leadership on both sides in the early months of the war (and the Soviet-supplied arms and supplies to Iraq as well as the eventual Western support for Iraq), the Iran-Iraq War was the longest conventional war of the twentieth century lasting from September 22, 1980, to August 20, 1988, and cost more than 1 million casualties.

While CWs made their appearance on the battlefield during the Iran-Iraq War, a nuclear threat also arose. Prior to the war, Iraq established a rudimentary nuclear program in the 1960s and by the mid-1970s was intent on expanding it by acquiring a nuclear reactor. The French and Italian governments turned down a request from the Iraqis to sell them a plutonium-producing reactor. However, the French opted to provide a research reactor (Osiris-class) and a smaller accompanying Isis-type reactor along with the provision of 72 kilograms of enriched uranium (93 percent). The agreement was signed in November 1975. Following this accord, the construction of a 40-megawatt light water reactor was initiated in 1979 at the Al Tuwaitha Nuclear Research Facility outside of Baghdad, with the main reactor referred to by the French as Osirak. In July 1980, France shipped to Iraq approximately 12.5 kilograms of highly enriched uranium (HEU) to fuel the reactor. This was one of six expected deliveries for an expected 72 kilograms. Under the agreement, no more than two HEU fuel loadings, or 24 kilograms, could be inside Iraq at any one time.

Prior to the outbreak of war in September 1980, Iran had created contingency plans for destroying Iraq's reactor. However, a direct attack was believed to be unwise by several specialists, and Iran instead eventually developed plans for destroying the accompanying research laboratories, the reactor control building, and training facilities. The Osirak nuclear reactor in Iraq was protected by a lone SAM-6 missile battery, three Roland missile batteries, and 40 antiaircraft artillery positions consisting of 23 millimeter (mm) and 57mm radar-guided guns. To overcome Osirak defenses, Tehran crafted Operation Scorch Sword, which entailed an air strike on the Iraqi nuclear facility. At dawn on September 30, 1980, eight days after Iraq crossed the Iranian border and moved on Khuzestan, four Iranian F-4E McDonnell Douglas Phantom jets were sent to strike the nuclear facilities located near the city of Tuwaitha about 10 miles southeast of Baghdad. This attack marked what many analysts called the first "preventive" use of force against a nuclear reactor and only the third attack on a nuclear facility in history. In the middle of a war and in the heat of combat, the concepts of preemption and prevention, generally utilized to indicate the use of force in initiating a military campaign in conditions of peace, become less meaningful in describing military action and the use of force in the midst of a war. The strike at the nuclear facilities near Tuwaitha caused only minor damage.

Since the Iranian Operation Scorch Sword did not disable the Iraqi nuclear facility, on June 7, 1981, eight IAF General Dynamics F-16A fighter/attack jets took off from Etzion Air Base in Israel, with six McDonnell Douglas F-15As in support during Operation Opera. The IAF F-16As were loaded each with two unguided Mark-84, 2,000-pound, delay-action, gravity bombs. Of the 16 Mark-84s released, at least 8 hit the nuclear facility. Saddam, in expressing his displeasure at a successful Israeli operation against his country, eventually executed the officer, Colonel Fakhri Hussein Jaber, in charge of that sector of air defense (Iraq's Western Air Defense Zone) as well as all officers under his command above the rank of major. The nuclear facility was to be rebuilt; however, France pulled out of further negotiations in 1984, after world opinion condemned all involved, including the Israelis, the Iranians, and the Iraqis. Later, during air operations in the Gulf War (1991), the USAF completed the destruction of what remained of the facility.

GULF OF SIDRA AND QADHAFI'S "LINE OF DEATH"

In the same year the Israelis destroyed the Iraqi nuclear facility (1981) the Soviets placed a nuclear reactor in Libya. In the North African nation of Libya about a decade earlier, as the Soviet-inspired and sponsored "revolutionary" fever permeated the Middle East, 70 army officers and enlisted men led by a 27-year-old captain by the name of Muammar al-Qadhafi overthrew the monarchy and established the Revolutionary Command Council (RCC) on September 1, 1969. Qadhafi declared that his revolutionary forces had established a "republic" in Libya, as he turned to the Soviet Union for increased assistance. On October 11, 1973, Libya notified the U.S. State Department that the Gulf of Sidra, located on Libya's Mediterranean coast, was to be henceforth considered a closed bay and a part of Libya's territorial waters. Qadhafi proclaimed a line of death for anyone or any nation attempting to enter within the new boundaries without first seeking his approval.

Under international practice the opening for a closed bay could not be more than 24 miles, while the Gulf of Sidra opening that Libya was now claiming was over 300 miles across. The U.S. ambassador to Libya was withdrawn in 1973, and the United States officially refused to recognize this claim on February 11, 1974. The U.S. Navy subsequently received orders to conduct freedom of navigation (FON) exercises in the vicinity of the Gulf of Sidra.

On December 2, 1979, a mob apparently inspired by the Iranian seizure of the U.S. embassy in Tehran one month before attacked and burned the U.S. embassy in Tripoli. On September 16, 1980, a Libyan fighter aircraft engaged a U.S. EC-135 reconnaissance plane over the Mediterranean and fired an air-to-air missile that missed the American aircraft. This was followed the next year with Moscow placing the nuclear reactor in Qadhafi's Libya. And on May 6, 1981, in response to the deteriorating U.S.-Libyan relations, the United States ordered the Libyan diplomatic mission in Washington, DC, closed, and Libyan personnel were ordered to return home.

About three months later, on August 19, 1981, two Libyan SU-22 Soviet-built fighter aircraft approached U.S. aircraft operating in the Mediterranean Sea, and one SU-22 fired an AA-2 "Atoll" (Soviet) air-to-air missile in the direction of two U.S. Navy F-14 "Tomcat" fighter jets attached to the aircraft carrier USS *Nimitz*. The Tomcats evaded the missile and abruptly maneuvered to engage the SU-22s. Once in position, both Tomcats fired AIM-9L Sidewinder air-to-air missiles subsequently downing the attacking Libyan fighter jets. Shortly after the August 19 incident, U.S. news reports stated that Libyan "hit squads" had entered the United States to assassinate Reagan. And as tensions rose, on October 15, 1981, the United States deployed two airborne warning and control system (AWACS) aircraft to Egypt to patrol the Egyptian-Libyan border area.

The U.S. Navy conducted an exercise beginning on January 23, 1986, in the Mediterranean north of the Gulf of Sidra. Between February 11 and February 15, U.S. and Libyan aircraft had more than a dozen encounters without shots being fired. However, on March 24, 1986, Libya fired six SA-5 high-altitude, long-range, low-speed SAMs and two SA-2 low-altitude, short-range, high-speed SAMs at U.S. aircraft, all failing to hit their targets. American Vought A-7 Corsair II attack aircraft from U.S. carriers operating in the vicinity of Libya knocked out the SA-5 batteries and returned four hours later to strike the targets again when the SA-5 installations resumed activity. During the engagements, a Grumman A-6 "Intruder" aircraft engaged four Libyan attack boats as they approached U.S. ships.

Following these events a terrorist bomb exploded at the La Belle nightclub in Berlin on April 5, 1986, killing three people, of which, two were off-duty U.S. army personnel. More than 200 were wounded, including 60 U.S. citizens. At a press conference on April 9, President Reagan said there were significant signs and evidence that led the U.S. government to conclude that the Libyan government was responsible for the attack. On April 15, 1986, 100 U.S. aircraft, including USAF F-111s based in the United Kingdom, and carrier-based A-6, A-7, and F/A 18 and F-14 aircraft, supported by communications, reconnaissance, and electronic warfare aircraft and refueling tankers, attacked two military complexes, two air bases, and a port in Libya.

Intelligence sources within Libya reported that 70 people were subsequently killed, including Qadhafi's infant daughter. Two USAF officers were killed when their F-111 was shot down. Later on April 15, apparently in a reprisal strike, Libyan patrol boats fired two missiles at a U.S. Navy communications station on the Italian island of Lampedusa—both, however, missing their targets. In a message broadcast to the American people following the April 15 raid against Qadhafi's regime, Reagan cited intercepted radio messages between Libya and the Libyan embassy in east Berlin that had discussed the April 5th Berlin nightclub bombing.

Later that year, on December 21, 1988, a bomb exploded on a U.S. Pan Am civilian jet airliner (Flight 103) en route from London to New York, killing all 244 passengers and 15 crew on board—with an additional 11 killed on the ground in Lockerbie, Scotland. Two Libyan intelligence agents were subsequently indicted for the downing of the plane. The UN Security Council passed three resolutions that placed sanctions on Libya until it surrendered the two agents involved in the bombing of Pan Am Flight 103 in 1988 and the French UTA Flight 772 in 1989. Libya subsequently surrendered the two individuals on April 5, 1999, and the United Nations suspended the sanctions on the same day. However, U.S. sanctions against Libya remained in place.

ASSAD, THE MUSLIM BROTHERHOOD, AND THE HAMA MASSACRE

While conflict raged in Iran, Lebanon, Afghanistan, and in the skies off the Mediterranean coast of Libya, in the early 1980s, during the Hama Massacre in Syria (February 2–February 28, 1982), tens of thousands of people perished in one of the greatest single acts by any Arab government against its own people in the modern Middle East.[20] After the Syrian invasion of Lebanon in 1976, Sunni Islamists fought the Syrian government forces. By 1979, the Muslim Brotherhood began guerrilla operations in multiple cities across Syria targeting military officers and government officials. On June 26, 1980, the Muslim Brotherhood and other affiliated Islamist factions attempted to assassinate Syrian President Hafez al-Assad. At an official Syrian state reception for the president of Mali, a machine-gun burst from a would-be assassin barely missed Assad, and as the Syrian president was scrambling to avoid being hit, he was forced to kick away a hand grenade that had also been thrown in his direction.

Surviving with only slight injuries, Assad immediately turned his fury against jailed Islamists giving the order for the immediate execution of over 1,200 prisoners, who were killed while still in their cells at Tadmor prison. By July 1980, the Syrian Ba'athist government outlawed membership in the Muslim Brotherhood, making it a capital offense. Nearly two years later as Syrian soldiers were searching for suspected guerrillas in the city of Hama, they came across the hideout of Abu Bakr (Umar Jawwad) —a high-level guerrilla commander. Bakr immediately called for help, and soon thereafter rooftop snipers were killing Syrian soldiers who had besieged the building Bakr was in. As the government summoned reinforcements, Bakr gave a prearranged signal for a general uprising to begin within the city.

Mosque loudspeakers that normally were used to call the population to prayer now called for jihad against the government, and hundreds of Islamist guerrillas answered the call with prearranged plans to attack the homes of government officials and Ba'ath Party leaders. These rebel forces also overran police posts and ransacked local armories and weapon supply depots. By sunrise on February 3, 1982, 70 leading Ba'athists had been assassinated during the attacks, and the Islamists declared Hama a "liberated" city. In response, Assad dispatched his brother, Rifaat, who commanded the Defense Companies (Syrian Special Forces). These units were subsequently joined by other elite military groups, including the *Mukhabarat* (Arabic for military intelligence service) agents and, after attempting to enter the city and being met with significant resistance, ringed the town and proceeded to shell the city with artillery and aircraft. The bombardment went on for three weeks. While the troops and security personnel surrounded the city, tunnels that ran under the "old city" of Hama had diesel fuel pumped into them and then set ablaze in an attempt at killing those who had taken refuge below ground. Syrian government forces stationed Soviet-supplied T-72 tanks at the entrance-exits of the tunnels, and as people fled the underground burning fuel, they were killed by tank machine guns and supporting troops.

After a 27-day siege, government troops entered the city and conducted follow-up operations. Following the Hama Massacre, the Muslim Brotherhood's Syrian presence was reduced to insignificant levels. Amnesty International placed the death count between 10,000 and 25,000 residents of Hama. The Muslim Brotherhood members, many who had fled to Iraq and Jordan, claimed that at least 40,000 had been killed by government forces. Iran's Khomeini, a Shiite Muslim, offered only mild condemnation of the massacre, as he sought to maintain Iran's alliance with Assad's Alawite minority-run government.

Assad's forces had also entered Lebanon and, in collaboration with Iran, were in active support of PLO operations against Israel. After the IDF had withdrawn from Lebanon following Operation Litani in 1978, the UN Security Council authorized the creation of the UN Interim Force-Lebanon (UNIFIL) and deployment to the border in order to confirm IDF withdrawal and to provide assistance to the government of Lebanon in reestablishing governance and stability. Israel assisted friendly factions within Lebanon in an attempt at neutralizing the PLO's ability to use Lebanon as a springboard for attacks into the Jewish homeland.

Tel Aviv's main ally became the Christian Maronite Phalange Party whose military was commanded by Bashir Gemayel. Gemayel shared the Israeli objective of removing all insurgent elements of the PLO from

Lebanon, particularly those staging operations along the Lebanon-Israeli border. Working in close cooperation with Tel Aviv, his fighters began receiving military education and training within Israel, with select individuals attending the IDF Staff and Command College. In order to reduce Syria's and the PLO's ability to use Lebanon as a base of operations against Israel, Tel Aviv sought to install a pro-Israel Christian government in Lebanon.

On December 20, 1981, the Israeli cabinet received a briefing on an IDF plan called Operation Big Pines, which envisioned an IDF invasion of Lebanon up to the Beirut-Damascus highway where Israeli forces would link up with Maronite forces. The conflict between Israel and the PLO intensified with cross border incursions by both the IDF and PLO forces between 1980 and 1981 in direct violation of UN Security Council resolutions. Those incursions and violations were monitored and recorded by UNIFIL. Although armed fighters steadily increased with estimates placing the number of armed PLO fighters in Lebanon in the range of 15,000 to 18,000, the Israeli cabinet declined to approve the operation.

While individual incidents occurring between Lebanon-based Palestinian fighters and the IDF continued into 1982, it became apparent to Israeli political leaders that Lebanon had become not only a staging ground for the PLO but also an occupation zone of the Syrians. For Tel Aviv, the threat was increasing—not necessarily from the Lebanese themselves—but from those who sought to use Lebanese soil to engage in attacks on Israel. Beginning on June 1, 1982, the IAF conducted extensive air strikes against PLO bases and ammunition depots along the Mediterranean coast.

ISRAEL INVADES LEBANON

On June 4, 1982, the Israeli cabinet authorized a large-scale ground operation in which the IDF would invade Lebanon and attempt to drive out elements that were posing the threat. Two days later, the IDF invaded southern Lebanon in Operation Peace for Galilee, planned under the supervision of Ariel Sharon, which essentially revolved around three objectives: 1) expel the PLO from Lebanon; 2) remove significant Syrian influence from Lebanon; and 3) install a pro-Israeli Christian government.

Involved in the operation were five IDF divisions as well as two reinforced brigade-size units, which jointly fielded about 78,000 troops, 1,240 tanks, and 1,500 armored personnel carriers. Moving with considerable dispatch, the IDF was able to seize and maintain the overall initiative, although mechanized and armored columns found the narrow roads within Lebanon, both in the cities and in the mountain passes, difficult to traverse often creating bottlenecks, which made IDF units easy targets for Syrian and allied jihadists' combined arms tactics.

Learning lessons from the 1973 October War, the Syrian army established 20 Commando Battalion, which was comprised of 50 hunter-killer teams of 4 to 6 men in each team. These teams were specifically created to engage Israeli mechanized units and tanks. A typical team consisted of two shooters and two loaders armed with rocket-propelled grenades (RPGs) and antitank guided missiles (ATGMs). Two other soldiers were armed with SA-7 SAMs (man-portable air defense systems [MANPADs]), shoulder fired. Their main tactic was to wait until IDF mechanized and armor elements entered a narrow city avenue or town road then firing at the lead unit disabling it while also taking out the rear vehicle and thus trapping the column.

The hunter-killer teams were working in conjunction with Syrian attack helicopters consisting of Soviet supplied Mi-25s and French-built Aerospatiale Gazelle SA-342 helicopters firing AS-12 antitank missiles and a French-German ATGM referred to as "HOT" (similar to the U.S. TOW wire-guided missile). Once the hunter-killer infantry engaged and effectively stalled the advance of IDF units, the attack helicopters would then engage from the air. The problem for ground units and aircraft engaging the Israeli army was the IAF.

About a year before Operation Peace for Galilee, on April 28, 1981, IAF F-16 fighters providing air cover for Christian militiamen in Zahle, Lebanon, from 117 squadrons based at Ramat David Air Base shot down two Syrian helicopters. On April 29, Damascus immediately deployed three SAM-6 SAM batteries to Lebanon's Bekaa Valley, marking the first Syrian deployment of Soviet-supplied SAMs into Lebanon. For Israeli leaders and commanders, this was viewed as a violation of a tacit Syrian-Israeli agreement regarding the Syrian presence within the country. The introduction of this capability also threatened the IAF's ability to conduct unimpeded reconnaissance flights across Lebanon.

Sensing a significant escalation and a subsequent increase in risk to Israeli national security, the deployment of SAM-6 systems into Lebanon altered the strategic calculation for Israeli leaders. Subsequently, on December 14, 1981, Israel officially annexed the Golan Heights, which had been captured from Syria during the 1967 Six-Day War. This act was considered by Syrian President Assad to be a declaration of war. Thus, both Israel and Syria considered the other side's behavior by the end of 1981 tantamount to acts of war.

For the Israelis, part of the rationale for Operation Peace for Galilee was to remove both the Syrian influence as well as the SAM batteries, which had taken such a toll on the IAF during the 1973 October War. Following the losses incurred by the IAF over the Suez Canal, Israel had worked on overcoming the effectiveness of SAM networks on IAF tactical air operations. During the 1982 Israeli invasion of Lebanon, the IAF conducted Operation Mole Cricket 19, which saw for the first time in modern history a Western air force effectively engaging and destroying a Soviet-built SAM network. Two days after the ground assault began, Mole Cricket 19 was launched on June 8 to destroy the SAM sites in the Bekaa Valley and to establish air superiority over Lebanon.

During the first attack, 17 of 19 Syrian SAM sites were destroyed, including batteries and radar sites. Twenty-nine Syrian Air Force (SAF) fighters were also shot down during the first attack, as they attempted to intercept the attacking IAF F-16As and F-15As. All IAF aircraft returned safely. The following day, the IAF destroyed the two remaining SAM sites, and Syria lost an additional 35 fighters (MiG-21s and MiG-23s—mostly ground attack versions with only a handful of the MiG-23M air-to-air models available to the SAF) without inflicting losses on the attacking IAF aircraft. The two engagements, involving approximately 90 IAF aircraft and 100 SAF aircraft, were one of the largest air battles since the Second World War and the largest jet engagement since the Korean War. Due to IAF air dominance during the engagement, the action became known as the "Bekaa Valley Turkey Shoot."

ISRAEL'S U.S.-SUPPLIED QUALITATIVE MILITARY EDGE

The qualitative edge the United States had promised Israel in the 1960s was clearly in evidence during Mole Cricket 19. McDonnell Douglas (now Boeing) F-15s and General Dynamics F-16s, both of which were flown by the IAF during the 1982 invasion, were specifically designed for air superiority. Both fighters possessed superior acceleration and maneuverability at combat speeds (in excess of Mach 2), which was provided by a thrust-to-weight ratio greater than one that provides the following air combat maneuverability capability: the thrust provided by the airplane's engines exceeds their takeoff weight allowing the jet to accelerate even as it maneuvers or climbs.

Additionally, both the F-16 and the F-15 jets were fitted with superior radars, which worked in conjunction with outstanding cockpit visibility providing the pilot and, in instances of double-seat configured aircraft such as the F-15D, the crew a competitive advantage in detecting an opponent before the enemy was aware of their presence and in the swift delivery of undetected shots. The accuracy and lethality of those undetected missile shots were improved by the high performance and reliability of the U.S.-made AIM-7F Sparrow radar-guided missiles, AIM-9L Sidewinder infrared-guided missiles, and the computer-aimed 20mm cannons.

The AIM-9L featured an "all-aspect capability" allowing it to be launched at an opposing aircraft not only in head-to-heat air combat but also from any angle which, in turn, eliminated the requirement of maneuvering behind an enemy to fire it. The Syrians in comparison were relying on 1960s Soviet technology in the form of the vintage AA-2 "Atoll" and were significantly disadvantaged, as they engaged IAF pilots flying U.S.-built fighter jets. In short, Israeli pilots flying U.S. combat aircraft could strike an opponent before the enemy knew he was being targeted. This fact created significant morale problems for Arab air forces, utilizing Soviet aircraft, and ordered to fly combat missions against the IAF.

The Bekaa Valley air battle in June 1982 was the first to involve the use of modern AWACS aircraft, which saw the IAF utilizing the U.S.-built Grumman E-2C Hawkeye. AWACS is essentially airborne radar that can assist in "vectoring" fighters to their targets as well as orchestrating overall air battle management and engagement. The E-2C that was deployed by the IAF in 1982 possessed an APS-125 radar mounted in a "dish" shaped "listening" structure above the fuselage. Mounted on the E-2C, it was capable of scanning 3 million cubic miles of air space. Additionally, it could monitor over 200 aircraft simultaneously while also managing up to 130 separate air-to-air engagements at distances of up to 250 miles.

Further still, the E-2C included an ALR-59 passive detection system that tracked radar signals 500 miles away effectively doubling the Hawkeye's early detection range. This capability enabled the IAF to detect Syrian aircraft immediately upon takeoff and to ascertain how many enemy aircraft were inbound and from what direction. The IAF also exploited the advanced avionics aboard the F-15, which when positioned in a standoff mode of the engagement was capable of serving as a "mini AWACS" in assisting in the monitoring and managing of the air battle.

The overall IAF AWACS air-to-air engagement capability allowed it to vector its fighters into "blindside" attacks on Syrian aircraft, which were equipped with only nose- and tail-threat warning receivers to warn pilots of a missile attack. As such, SAF pilots were denied any advance warning of a missile attack by the IAF's all-aspect AIM-9Ls or AIM-7Fs, with the latter capable of being fired well beyond visual range. The IAF aircraft could fire shots at its Syrian opponents often undetected from launch to impact, which, in turn, denied the Syrians any opportunity to evade or return fire.

In the modern age, as command, control, and communication became known as "C3" (and later as "C4" with the addition of computers), modified Boeing 707s were equipped with standoff jammers capable of disrupting several enemy frequencies, effectively jamming Syrian communications and radar systems cut off SAF MiGs from ground control, and leaving them isolated and vulnerable to AWACS-directed attacks from F-15s or F-16s. To protect their own C3 against Syrian electronic countermeasures (ECMs), Israeli fighter aircraft were equipped with ECM pods, including the indigenously produced EL/L-8200 series, which provided protection against ground-based and airborne radar threats.

For the first time, in 1982, the IAF relied on remotely piloted vehicles (RPV) or "drones" to fingerprint surface-to-air radar providing key information to Israeli countermeasures. When the actual air battle began, drones were used as decoys to simulate electronically the radars' signature of full-size strike aircraft—a tactic utilized for the purpose of manipulating Syrian air defense personnel into activating their SAM target acquisition and tracking radars. In doing so, the IAF was able to identify a variety of targets for the AGM-78 Standard anti-radiation missile (ARM) and AGM-45 Shrike air-launched ARMs that followed.

ANCIENT ANIMOSITY, MODERN WEAPONS, AND GHAZI WARFARE

In possession of air superiority, the IDF was able to overcome large ground-based challenges to its presence in Lebanon in the summer of 1982. While the IDF was able to prevail in major combat operations, the reality of occupation in often hostile regions of Lebanon created problems that could not be overcome with conventional military superiority. In August and September, more than 14,000 PLO combatants were evacuated from Lebanon, many transitioning to Tunisia with their leader, Yasser Arafat. On August 23, 1982, the man who had worked with the Israelis, Gemayel, and leader of the Christian Maronite Phalangist (Kataeb) Party became president of Lebanon. He was assassinated on September 14, 1982, by a bomb planted by Habib Shartouni, an individual affiliated with the Syrian Social Nationalist Party, killing Gemayel and 26 others at the party's headquarters.

After Gemayel's murder, a group of about 150 fighters aligned with the Christian right and Israel, referred to as the "Young Men," was sent into a refugee camp so militant and radicalized that neither the Lebanese army nor the IDF opted to conduct operations within it. Apparently, IDF forces encircled the Shatila camp near the Sabra neighborhood to keep PLO operatives from leaving while the Young Men went on a killing spree, joined by follow-on groups of various fighters who had been told that the PLO was responsible for the death of Gemayel, eventually murdering between 1,000 and 2,000 individuals then inside the camp. The wholesale slaughter included women and children.

International condemnation for all involved was widespread. In some respects, the slaughter resembled ancient tactics of various groups operating in the Middle East. In those instances, the commander, emir, shah, or sultan—the supreme leader—would ceremoniously announce to his assembled forces that the slaughter of the inhabitants of a particular village, town, or city would begin at a specified time and then conclude at a future predesignated moment, usually the following morning, which served in initiating a night of terror, rape and slaughter—all very solemn, all very official, except perhaps, to the victims. Apparently, from approximately 6 p.m. on September 16, 1982, until 8 a.m. on September 18, 1982, a widespread, two-day massacre took place within Lebanon in the modern Middle East.[21]

The Young Men were a group recruited by Elie Hobeika, the Lebanese forces intelligence chief. The slaughter in the Shatila refugee camp was widely understood to have taken place under the direction of Hobeika. Hobeika's own family, including his fiancée, had been murdered by Palestinian militiamen and their Lebanese allies during the Damour massacre of 1976. Apparently, the Damour massacre was in response to the Karantina massacre of Palestinians and Lebanese Muslims by Christian militants, which occurred in the same year. Later, on January 24, 2002, Hobeika would be killed by a car bomb in Beirut, shortly before testifying about the 1982 Shatila massacre.

PEACEKEEPERS AT RISK: LEBANON (1982–1983)

When word reached Washington, DC, regarding the horrendous savagery of the massacres in late September 1982, President Reagan dispatched a 1,200-member Multinational Peacekeeping Force into Lebanon. This force was made up of U.S., French, and Italian military personnel, and its objective was to aid the Lebanese government in establishing an end to the Lebanese Civil War that had been raging since 1975. Specifically, the force was meant to aid in brokering a cease-fire between the Christian, Druze, and Muslim factions. However, Syrian and Iranian influences (including Soviet intrigue) viewed this as an unwelcome intrusion and had no desire to see Western forces, particularly U.S. troops, meet with any success in Lebanon.

On April 18, 1983, a delivery van laden with 2,000 pounds of high explosives crashed through the lobby door of the U.S. embassy in Beirut and detonated its bomb. Sixty-three people were killed, including 32 Lebanese employees, 14 visitors, and 17 Americans (including 8 CIA officers). A group that called itself the Islamic Jihad Organization took responsibility. Later, investigations would reveal that this group eventually became affiliated with a new group, Hezbollah (Party of God), and in the bombing of the American embassy received assistance from the Syrians with approval and financing from senior Iranian officials.

In August 1983, militia groups opposed to the U.S. and European presence began shelling U.S. Marine posts near the Beirut International Airport with mortars and rocket fire. These militias viewed the U.S. presence as supportive of the Lebanese army whom they were fighting in the southern suburbs of Beirut. On August 29, 1983, 2 marines were killed and 14 wounded during an attack. This prompted the Reagan administration to allow the marines to return fire. On September 25, 1983, the USS *New Jersey*, a battleship first deployed at the close of World War II, arrived off the coast of Lebanon and with its 16-inch guns (406mm) was positioned to increase the ability of the Multinational Force to protect itself from incoming fires.

One month later, a suicide bomber drove a truck laden with 2,500 pounds of high explosives into a four-story building at the Beirut Airport where U.S. Marines were headquartered. In what was reportedly, at the time, the most powerful nonnuclear explosion in history, the force of the blast lifted the building off its foundations into the air before collapsing in a heap of rubble and human remains. Two hundred and twenty U.S. Marines, 18 U.S. sailors, and 3 U.S. Army soldiers perished in the attack. Two minutes later, an additional terrorist drove a truck laden with explosives into the basement of a nearby barrack, which housed French paratroopers, killing 58. The Islamic Jihad Organization (i.e., Hezbollah, Syria, Iran) claimed responsibility for both blasts.

On November 28, 1983, the *New Jersey* fired 11 16-inch rounds at Syrian/Druze antiaircraft batteries that had been targeting U.S. reconnaissance aircraft. On February 8, 1984, the *New Jersey* fired 300 16-inch shells at Syrian/Druze and Shiite positions in the hills overlooking Beirut. About 30 of those landed on a Syrian command post in the Bekaa Valley east of Beirut, killing the commanding general of Syrian forces in Lebanon and several other senior officers. Later in the year, U.S. forces, including its coalition partners in the Multinational Force, withdrew from what were generally considered indefensible positions within Lebanon.

In the midst of the upheaval in Lebanon, seven American hostages were seized and held within the country. The Reagan administration worked to free these hostages and through intermediaries, opened discussions with the Iranians. Apparently, the Iranians wanted weapons to use against the Iraqis in return of the U.S. hostages. However, with an arms embargo levied against the Iranian regime, no weapons could legally be provided to Tehran by the U.S. government. Simultaneous to the hostage situation in Lebanon, the Reagan administration was intent on supporting the anti-Marxist fighters in Nicaragua popularly referred to as the "Contras." The Contras were actively resisting the Soviet-inspired intrigue and armed violence and other various Latin American leftist groups, which were in direct and indirect support of the "Sandinistas," a guerrilla group attempting to take control in Central America.

However, constraining the Reagan administration were laws that prohibited supplying material support, or weapons, to the Contras. The U.S. Congress had enacted the Boland Amendment, which made it illegal to provide support to the Contras. Reagan administration officials concluded that the hostages needed to be freed and the fighters blocking the communists in Central America needed U.S. help.

During the secret negotiations, Iran expressed an interest in U.S.-built HAWK (SAMs) and U.S.-built TOW (antitank, antiarmor missiles) weapon systems.[22] The eventual covert arrangement had Israel shipping the weapons clandestinely to Iran, with the United States replenishing IDF stocks. The money from Iran would then be clandestinely rerouted to the Contras. This plan, however, became known to members of the U.S. Congress, which then sent a team of investigators to follow up.

Ultimately it was deemed that the sale of weapons to Iran was not a criminal offense, but charges were filed against five individuals within the administration for supporting the Contras. However, since the Reagan administration refused to declassify specific documents that Congressional investigators needed for effective prosecution, the more serious charges were ultimately dropped. Eleven officials were eventually indicted and convicted on lesser charges related to the Iran-Contra affair/scandal. Some of these convictions were vacated on appeal, while the remaining individuals were pardoned by President George H. W. Bush in the final days of his presidency.

OPERATION RAMADAN

Prior to the Iran-Contra affair, and, as the Iran-Iraq War moved into its second year, on July 11 and 12, 1982, Iran initiated Operation Ramadan, which engaged Iraqi artillery and tanks that were, at the time, dug in and serving as stationary firing platforms on the front lines. This was then followed on July 13 by an infantry assault by more than 100,000 Pasadaran and Basij forces conducting human wave attacks. By July 16, 1982, Iranian forces had pushed to within eight miles of the key Iraqi southern city of Basra. Nevertheless, Iraqi forces were now fighting on their own soil, as Iranian counteroffensives had forced their withdrawal from Iran. The Iranian waves were subsequently met with strengthened resistance and sustained artillery, tank, and machine-gun fire. The decision by the Reagan administration to provide assistance for the defense of Iraq served in improving the morale of both the Iraqi leadership and its military commanders. In public, Washington gradually abandoned its often-stated policy of neutrality and noninvolvement in favor of a tilt toward Iraq.[23]

To support the human wave assault, Iran sent to the front several regular army divisions, including the 16th, 88th, and 92nd Armored Divisions as well as the 21st and 77th Infantry Divisions. In defense, Iraq concentrated three armored divisions—the 3rd, 9th and the 10th—which blocked the Iranian advance with significant casualties on both sides. The Iraqi 10th Armored Division was so badly mauled that following the battle it was disbanded and troops and tanks were dispersed and assigned to other units. Operation Ramadan became one of the largest land battles since World War II, pitting 175,000 Iranians against 90,000 Iraqis. Of these forces, 60,000 were killed in action (KIA), 80,000 were wounded in action (WIA), and another 20,000 taken as prisoners of war (POWs).

While the battle was technically an Iranian tactical victory, the more important strategic impact on the outcome of the war relegated the Iranian assault to the level of being an indecisive engagement. The effect of the battle was that while the Iranians maintained their siege of Basra, they lacked the command and control as well as the logistical capability to sustain offensive operations, sustain the initiative, and push forward. Iraq, now defending home territory with word that assistance from the United States was on its way, had a 5-to-1 advantage in combat-ready soldiers and armor. It was Khomeini who had decided upon the invasion of Iraq as well as the seizure of Basra. Khomeini believed that Iranian will, energy, and fervor and God's favor would overcome the godless Ba'thists. These are, indeed, powerful elements on the field of battle but insufficient without sound military leadership and strategy. Operation Ramadan, unfortunately, had been initiated against the advice of the Ayatollah's military officers.

In Khomeini's view, the strategic concept was sound enough—should Iran be able to take Basra and incite a general insurrection within the Shiite majority in southern Iraq, Baghdad would be forced to fight on two fronts, as Iran was actively sponsoring the Kurdish rebellion then under way in northern Iraq.[24] In short, it seemed quite a reasonable strategy to the Ayatollah. As the Prussian General Helmuth von Moltke (the Elder) famously stated, "Strategy is the easy part, the difficulty lies in execution." Or as is commonly cited in Western military literature, "Amateurs focus on strategy, experts focus on logistics." For Operation Ramadan, Iran's logistical structure and capacity at the time were unable to support the Ayatollah's strategy.

While the clerical establishment demanded the invasion of Iraq, they at least listened in part to the Iranian military's advice. During Operation Ramadan, and having taken lessons from Rommel's armored experiences as well as the lessons from Egyptian-Soviet operations in 1973, Iranian military officers created RPG teams to attack Iraqi tanks. Unfortunately, supplies were limited, and each of the deployed teams was only able to take three grenades with them into battle. However, while tactical expertise made its way onto the battlefield on the side of Iran, and as Iranians paused in the advance to dig in for defensive purposes and to consolidate their gains, Iraq sent Soviet-supplied Mi-25 helicopters along with French-built Aerospatiale Gazelles armed with Euromissile HOT against the columns of Iranian mechanized infantry and tanks, as Saddam's military was receiving advice from a team of East German advisors, which advocated deploying hunter-killer teams of helicopters.

However, while the Iraqis had held the advantage for the first two years of the war, Tehran, by drawing on superior numbers and a "revolutionary fervor," took and held the initiative after 1982 and kept the Iraqis pinned back on their own soil. Moreover, while Iranian human wave attacks without air cover proved lucrative targets for Iraqi artillery, Iraqi leaders and their regional and international supporters became significantly concerned about losing the campaign for the defense of Basra. This fear led Baghdad to use CWs. Mustard gas and nerve agents (Sarin in particular) were delivered against attacking Iranian waves by nondescript small aircraft based near Baghdad and mounted with dual-use aerial spraying equipment, which normally delivered insecticides upon fields of crops. Massive casualties resulted with about 15,000 Iranians killed in each "human wave" offensive they undertook.

Thus while the emboldened Iranians pressed their attack into Iraq, and as the war extended past two years, the Iraqis turned to the Soviets for resupply and maintenance of the weapons and weapon systems previously supplied. Europe and the United States were also providing chemical precursors (dual-use) that could be "weaponized." With its back to the wall, and fearing that it would be overrun by its inability to counter the overwhelming numbers involved in the Iranian human wave assaults, Baghdad managed to stop the Iranian advance by combined arms attacks, which included chemical munitions—weapons that had not been used previously in any major war since the Second Italo-Abyssinian War (1935–1936).

By the sixth year of the war, Khomeini finally arrived at the conclusion that Iranian "will" in the form of human wave attacks could not defeat an Iraqi combined arms approach featuring artillery, tanks, machine guns, minefields, attack helicopters, and jets, providing close air support, and utilizing chemical munitions. He decided to rely on the professional advice of Iranian military officers who had served under the Shah. In the fall of 1985, these officers were provided the opportunity in planning and executing their own operation without interference from the Iranian clerical establishment or the revolutionary zealots in the paramilitary organizations (Revolutionary Guards, i.e., Pasadaran and Basij militias).

The plan was not to attempt to seize Basra in a direct assault but rather in using a campaign or series of engagements to arrive at clearly specified and politically derived strategic objectives. Thus, *Wal Fajr 8* (Operation Dawn 8) was conceived for the purpose of capturing the Fao Peninsula in the Shatt al-Arab and, from there, conducting follow-on operations aimed at taking the key southern city of Basra. Operation Dawn 8 was launched on February 9, 1986, as Iranian forces conducted an amphibious assault in boats across the Shatt al-Arab waterway. Iranian forces first feigned an attack on Basra, which pulled in Iraqi defenders before launching the amphibious assault against the peninsula. Iraqi forces on the peninsula were unprepared for the surprise move, and Iran was successful in placing what amounted to about a division-size contingent on the peninsula.

Operation Dawn 8 was arguably the most successful Iranian operation of the Iran-Iraq War, as the possession of the peninsula cut Iraq's access to the Persian Gulf via the Shatt al-Arab, forcing it to rely on Kuwait to ship its oil into the world market. Three days later, Iraq launched a counteroffensive, which failed. Saddam was forced to dispatch one of his best commanders, General Maher Abd-Rashid, and the best Iraqi combat formation, the Republican Guard, to take back the peninsula.

On February 24, 1986, Rashid's Iraqi forces attacked with a ferocious intensity, killing more than 30,000 Iranian troops in approximately four days. However, the Republican Guard suffered 10,000 dead, and despite the concerted use of hundreds of tanks, massed artillery, helicopter gunships, and an extensive bombing campaign by the Iraqi Air Force, Rashid failed to retake the Fao Peninsula. With the success of Operation Dawn 8 and the failure of the Republican Guard to retake the peninsula, the Gulf monarchies, particularly Kuwait and Saudi Arabia, became extremely concerned regarding the potential for Iran to control Shiite-majority southern Iraq and the possibility to export its revolutionary activities across the Middle East.

In an effort to isolate the Fao Peninsula and Basra from Baghdad's control, Iran launched Operation Karbala 5 on January 9, 1987, which became the largest engagement of the war and generated massive levels of casualties on both sides. By 1987, Basra, enduring years of rocket fire, aerial bombardment, and shelling, including massed human wave infantry assault, was a ghost of its former self. Essentially 2 million civilians had fled the city, with about 100,000 remaining by the time of the Karbala 5 attack. Iraq had created a vast array of defensive fortifications around the Basra area. In one location, the Iraqis had created an artificial lake about 30 kilometers long and 1,800 meters wide, which came to be referred to as "Fish Lake," mostly due to the fact that extensive shelling of the area had killed thousands of fish that were floating odorously about.

Beyond the water boundaries that Fish Lake, the Hawizeh Marshes, and the Shatt al-Arab waterway provided, Iraqi engineers constructed five lines of defense as one approached Basra, including an array of mine-fields, a network of trenches, concrete bunkers, barbed wire with each of the five lines backed by radar-guided artillery, and ground attack aircraft including helicopters—all capable of delivering conventional or chemical munitions. The Iraqi leadership called it their "wall of steel."

During Karbala 5, Iraq lost 50 to 60 jet aircraft—about 10 percent of its air force, many from the lethal effects of Iranian SAMs such as the imported Swedish RBS 70 shoulder-fired MANPADs. As the attack unfolded, Iraq commenced bombing Iranian supply routes with CWs. When Iranian attacks broke through four of the five defensive lines, Saddam responded by personally firing the commander of the 3rd Corps, Major General Tali Khalil Arham al-Dhouri, who was responsible for Iraqi operations in the southern sector and the defense of Basra. Saddam also ordered the arrest of several lower-ranking officers who he believed had performed poorly and had them marched before a firing squad and, summarily, shot.

Iraqi Republican Guard units launched a counterattack on January 28 and in the ensuing battles claimed killing more than 60,000 Iranians. The Iranians countered that they had destroyed 81 Iraqi brigades and battalions, 700 tanks, 1,500 other vehicles, 80 aircraft and 250 antiaircraft guns and inflicted more than 20,000 casualties. As the Republican Guard pressed its attack, Iran continued shelling Basra, at one point hitting a petrochemical plant, which released a poisonous cloud of toxic gas that floated southwest of the city.

Iran retaliated with a succession of attacks in what Khomeini had decried would be the final battle for victory. On February 22, 1987, as the Iranians pushed forward with about all that they could muster in the southern sector, the Iraqis lured the attacking IRG infantry (Pasadaran and Basij paramilitaries) into carefully constructed kill zones, pinned them down with direct fires, and annihilated them with massed artillery. By the spring of 1987, Iranian leaders publicly declared the end to human wave attacks.

Kuwait was especially concerned with the Iran-Iraq War, since at its height Iranian troops were essentially only about 10 miles from its border. This led to increased support for Saddam and increased calls for consultations with Western governments, particularly the United States. Eventually the United States reflagged a number of Kuwaiti tankers with the American flag to ensure their passage out of the Persian Gulf and into world markets. President Reagan was hesitant to take this step, realizing it would most likely bring the U.S. Navy into the ongoing conflict between Iran and Iraq, as U.S. warships moved in defense of the U.S.-flagged tankers. What ultimately convinced him was an agreement the Soviet Union had reached with the Kuwaitis, since it seemed to them that the Americans were stalling. Signed between the Soviets and the Kuwaitis on March 2, 1987, the agreement stipulated that reflagging was to begin within 10 days of the signing.

OPERATION EARNEST WILL

As the deal was to take effect within 10 days, the Reagan administration was sufficiently motivated for approving the Kuwaiti request and subsequently moved within 5 days, closing a deal to reflag the Kuwaiti tankers with an American flag, thereby co-opting the Soviets.[25] The Kuwaiti tanker fleet at the time consisted of 22 ships, and the United States placed its flag on 11 tankers. The reflagging and follow-on naval convoying activities became part of Operation Earnest Will, which lasted from July 24, 1987, to September 26, 1988—the largest naval convoying of ships since the Second World War. Any attack on such flagged ships could be treated as an attack on the United States and would provide the legal basis for military retaliation.

Such support neutralized a key point of leverage the Iranians had over Saddam by virtue of its successful military operations aimed at blocking the Shatt al-Arab waterway—stopping his ability to generate revenue by the export of oil. The Kuwait-U.S. move ensured an Iraqi stream of revenue for the duration of the war and served to frustrate the Iranian leadership and its desire to see the war conclude on its terms. In short, the United States, by conducting Operation Earnest Will, moved to internationalize the Iran-Iraq conflict, placing the Iranian leadership on the horns of a precarious dilemma: escalate and be faced with a military conflict involving the United States and its associated allies, or accept that Iraqi oil will make it into the international marketplace, ensuring that Baghdad continued to have a steady stream of revenue to continue fighting. The escalation of what became known as the "tanker war" during the Iran-Iraq conflict was actually under way prior to the initiation of Operation Ernest Will, as Iraq attacked Iranian tankers, including the key oil terminal at Kharg Island, in 1984. Iran responded by attacking tankers carrying Iraqi oil from Kuwait followed by a precipitous escalation that began targeting any tanker belonging to Gulf countries supporting Iraq.

Within the Gulf, on May 17, 1987, an Iraqi F1 Mirage jet *reportedly* (at the height of the Iran-Contra scandal, which had become public in

November 1986) misidentified the USS *Stark* (FFG 31)—a Perry-class frigate—and fired two "Exocet" AM39 air-to-surface missiles (range of 40 miles and each carrying a 352-pound warhead, both jet and missile French-built), which killed 37 and wounded 21 aboard the *Stark*. The United States publicly considered this act to be a mistake, as the Iraqis at the time were engaging a nearby Iranian warship.

Further dangerous escalatory moves occurred during the Iran-Iraq War when Iran began mining Gulf waters to interdict ships moving in support of Iraq. The USS *Samuel B. Roberts* (FFG-58) was hit by an Iranian mine on April 14, 1988, 65 miles east of Bahrain, with the resulting explosion ripping a massive hole in the ship's hull. The United States responded by launching Operation Praying Mantis—its largest action involving surface warships since World War II—four days later when it attacked two Iranian frigates (*Sabalan* and *Sahand*) and fired on Iranian oil platforms in the Sassan and Sirri oil fields.

As the United States increasingly targeted Iranian naval vessels, facilities, and oil areas, on July 3, 1988, the USS *Vincennes* operating in the Gulf mistakenly (apparently) believed an Iranian F-14 (a U.S.-built—and supplied earlier to the Shah—Grumman high-performance fighter jet) was flying into the region over the Strait of Hormuz where the ship was engaged in a hostile environment. With no response from the Iranian civilian aircraft and after repeated attempts by crewmen aboard the *Vincennes* to communicate with the jet, the ship fired a SM-2 missile in defense only later (apparently) finding out the aircraft was actually a European-built Airbus A300B2 and was a civilian airliner (Iran Air Flight 655). The attack killed 290 passengers and crew, including 66 children.

To increase the costs to Iran for rejecting Iraqi offers of a cease-fire, Iraq began targeting Iranian cities in 1984, with attacks by aircraft (Soviet-supplied Tu-22 Blinder, Tu-16 Badger strategic bombers, and MiG-25 Foxbat and SU-22 Fitter attack fighters used for smaller and short-range targets). Then, later in the war, Iraq turned to indiscriminant Scud-B (Soviet-supplied ballistic missile) surface-to-surface missile attacks. Iran responded by purchasing Scud missiles and fired them at Iraqi cities. Iranian use of ballistic missiles in attacks against Iraq was generally limited in number, as Iran preferred artillery shelling of civilian targets (particularly Basra and Iraqi border towns and villages) during the phase of the Iran-Iraq War. These operations came to be collectively referred to as the "war of the cities."

The United States did not wish to see the "revolutionary" forces of Iran overrun Iraq; given such an outcome, Tehran would not only be in a position to threaten Saudi Arabia and the largest oil reserves in the world but would also position itself to link up with its Alawite allies in Damascus and its various proxy groups then forming in Lebanon. Should the clerics in Tehran be successful in taking control in Iraq and Syria, they would then have interior lines of communication and direct access to the Mediterranean Sea and be positioned to project instability and intrigue into Europe and beyond.

Once achieving these geostrategic objectives, Iran would immediately be able to threaten traditionally stalwart U.S. allies, including Israel, Kuwait, and Jordan, as well as Saudi Arabia. These allies would have been subjected to either direct military attack, guerrilla operations (including terrorist attacks), and a barrage of information and propaganda aimed at undermining stability and order or a relentless campaign utilizing a combination of all these tactics. U.S. leaders understood the strategic ramifications to regional allies as well as to the international financial system if the radical clerics in Iran were able to control Middle Eastern oil, the vast Muslim populations in the region, and the key communications link the Middle East effectively represented in connecting Asia, Africa, and the Mediterranean worlds.

As a result of these key dynamics and the recognition of the implications for the security of the United States and its allies around the world, in the margins of a classified report that was provided to U.S. President Reagan in advance of an expected massive Iranian offensive in the spring of 1988, Secretary of Defense Frank C. Carlucci had written simply, "An Iranian victory is unacceptable."[26]

As early as 1982, after two years of war between Iran and Iraq, the United States had arrived at the conclusion that the Iraqi military would not be able to achieve Saddam's goals of seizing and holding Khuzestan while simultaneously demanding Iranian acquiescence for the abrogation of the Algiers Agreement and the return of the Shatt al-Arab waterway to complete Iraqi sovereignty. In order to forestall an Iraqi defeat, as Iran mounted its human wave attacks in the second and third years of the war, the United States began aiding Baghdad through the normalization of relations that had been stalled since Iraq had embraced Soviet influence in the 1960s and 1970s.

The United States also provided economic aid, operational intelligence regarding battlefield developments, and weapons through clandestine CIA operations.[27] As early as 1979, Saddam had allowed the CIA to open a facility in Baghdad for closer consultation, as radical forces seized control within Iran.[28] By the second year of the war, President Reagan directed the Pentagon to forestall an Iraqi defeat using all available legal means. The U.S. Defense Intelligence Agency (DIA) built a high-tech facility in Baghdad, which provided a direct downlink to receive satellite photography and other intelligence, surveillance, and reconnaissance (ISR) imagery, signals, and human intelligence (HUMINT) data.

As Khomeini refused to accept any settlement except the dismissal of the Ba'athist regime in Baghdad, which would have allowed him to essentially take control of the Shiite region in southern Iraq, the United States stepped up its discreet but direct military assistance to change his strategic calculus.

> A continued failure by Baghdad to exploit its many military advantages over Iran will mean that Iraq will suffer additional military setbacks and probably lose the war over the long-term. Iraq's strategy to outlast Iranian resolve to bring down the Ba'athist regime—will not work unless Baghdad substantially raises the cost to Iran. Only a change to a much more aggressive posture designed to preempt Iranian offensives and cripple Iran's economy would turn the war around.[29]

By late 1987 and early 1988, U.S. military and intelligence personnel were involved with planning day-to-day strategic bombing strikes against Iranian military targets for the Iraqi Air Force. Moreover, U.S. military personnel were providing tactical military advice to the Iraqis on the battlefield and, when warranted, finding themselves alongside Iraqi troops fighting at the border and at times within Iran itself. In addition to the tactical assistance, more than 60 DIA officers were secretly providing detailed information on Iranian deployments. CIA and other U.S.-affiliated organizations arranged the delivery of weapons and weapon systems along with munitions such as the Mark-84 gravity bomb that arrived from inventories within Saudi Arabia. While Iraq had accepted Soviet weapons and weapon systems (tanks, aircraft, SAMs, etc.) in the 1960s and 1970s, with tens of thousands of Iranian personnel on Iraqi soil during the Iran-Iraq War by the mid-1980s, it was open to U.S. support, and the United States was open to provide the necessary military support to avoid an Iranian takeover of the country.

The Soviets had a long and generally effective tradition of exploiting military equipment exports and supplies as a way of extending its influence into a target country. Later, when the targeted country needed spare parts, ammunition, advisors, and the like, it became dependent on the Soviets for supplying the needed material. To dilute the ability of the Soviets to gain leverage around the world, particularly in the developing world, the United States initiated a plan referred to as "Bear Spares" (Soviet "Bear" as a symbol of USSR might), where the United States provided spare parts, supplies, and ammunition for Soviet hardware to countries that sought to reduce their dependence on Moscow for defense and security needs.

Within the Middle East, along with success in Egypt, Syria, and Iraq, the Soviet KGB (State Security and Intelligence Service) for several decades had worked toward penetrating the Shiite clergy in Iran. When the

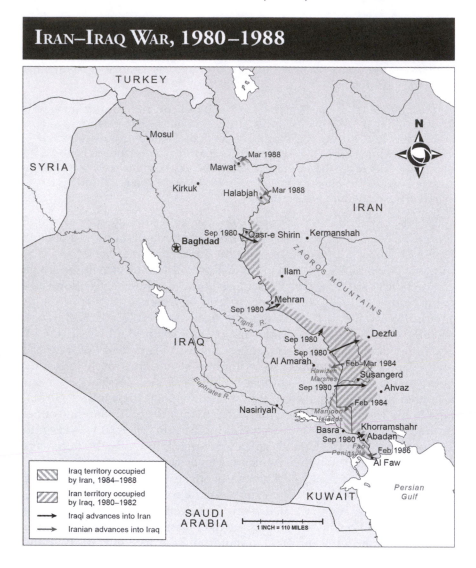

IRAN–IRAQ WAR, 1980–1988

Iranian Revolution occurred in 1979 and Khomeini came to power, the Soviets, who had been supplying Iraq to offset the U.S.-aligned Shah, suspended arms sales to Iraq with the intent that since the United States had effectively been expelled from Iran, they would then be positioned for making great strides in becoming the dominant player within Iran. Thus, KGB Director Yuri Andropov convinced Soviet leaders Brezhnev and Alexei Kosygin to place an arms embargo on Iraq and curry favor with

Tehran. However, by cutting off Saddam in favor of currying favor with Tehran, Baghdad became more inclined to develop closer relations with the United States.

Part of the increased American support for Iraq was unconventional warfare training subsequently provided to select Iraqi security and military personnel by U.S. Army Special Forces at Fort Bragg, North Carolina. The main focus was in preparing for an outcome in which Iran was successful in overrunning Iraq, and irregular warfare operations would have to be conducted against an occupying army. Iraqi helicopter pilots, traveling on Jordanian passports, also received training in the United States. By the last year of the Iran-Iraq War (late 1987 to early 1988), the United States was actively supporting Iraqi operations in order to frustrate Iranian attempts at taking control of Basra and southern Iraq.

American support for Iraq soon began altering the Iranian leadership's strategic calculus. Iran was increasingly aware that the United States was determined to block its objectives within Iraq and quite prepared to commit sizable resources in order to accomplish this. This commitment provided a new level of confidence inside Iraq dissipating the expectation within Iran that a continuation of the war would force the Iraqi elite to demand a new government in Baghdad. As a result, by January 1988, Iran was planning for one last massive offensive to settle the issue over Basra. U.S. satellite imagery identified Iranian troop movements toward a critical gap in Iraqi defenses, which Tehran intended to exploit and overwhelm with its 1988 spring offensive. Instead, Iranian forces were hit first by an Iraqi offensive in April 1988, dubbed Operation Blessed Ramadan.

It was reported that Iraq had first used CWs against human wave attacks in 1984. However, during the last 18 months of the war (1987–1988), Iraq employed about 70 percent of all chemical munitions that were utilized during the war. Under orders from Saddam, and apparently with at least tacit approval by the U.S. government, the Iraqi military employed mustard gas, Sarin (GB), Tabun (GA), and Cyclosarin (GF) against Iranian attempts to overrun Iraqi cities. Sarin, Tabun, and Cyclosarin are lethal nerve agents, and the utilization of these chemicals as weapons in military operations stand in violation of international accords and the laws of war.

The use of these agents, however, does not stand in isolation, as the Islamic Republic of Iran was sponsoring illegal and deadly attacks on a range of non-military targets spanning not only the Middle East but across the globe. Moreover, the Iranian regime had summarily executed tens of thousands within Iran after seizing power through armed insurrection. Following this murderous path to power, Iran was then in the process of attempting to spread its idea of government across the Middle East, including the eventual aim of destabilizing Saudi Arabia and seizing the world's largest oil reserves. The decision by the United States to oppose this expansionary, violent, and terrorist-centered agenda rested on a pragmatic assessment that the Iranian regime posed significant risk to its allies within the region, the loss of which would eventually negatively impact American national security and that of its allies in Europe and in Asia. Japan itself was reliant on imports of oil, mostly coming from the Middle East for 90 percent of its needs. In Europe, the figure reflecting dependence on Middle Eastern oil was in the 60–70 percent range. Traditionally reliant on allies in both times of peace and in times of war, the protection of those allies and their interests was a vital national security concern for the United States. In short, from the perspective of national security officials in Washington, DC, in 1980 and 1981, Iran would have to be blocked in its attempt at overrunning Iraq and expanding its influence and military power across the Middle East. This was a clear and present danger to the vital national security interests of the United States in that those interests depended on economic vitality for strategic endurance and the ability to protect allies in the Western Hemisphere, Europe, Asia, and within the Middle East. Necessary action taken regarding national self-defense is protected under both international law and the UN Charter and does not require UN Security Council's approval prior to engaging such a threat.

As previously mentioned, the Carter Doctrine stated the intent of the American government to block any attempt by outside forces or those hostile to the United States to seize control of Middle Eastern oil resources. All necessary means to defeat such threats to the national security of the United States, according to the Carter Doctrine, would have included all military options, including the use of nuclear weapons or other weapons of mass destruction. However, in taking action during the Iran-Iraq War, the Reagan administration was enforcing much more than the security of Saddam's government in the mid- to late 1980s.

With the Soviet Union's invasion of Afghanistan, which placed more than 100,000 Soviet troops within striking range of Iran's eastern border at a time when the Iranian Revolution sparked, burned, and proliferated into the Iran-Iraq War, the stability of the Middle East was perched in a fairly precarious position by the mid-1980s. U.S. President Reagan and his national security team determined that Iran could not succeed in spreading its power across the Middle East, just as the Soviet Union could not be allowed to exploit the turmoil and move with force into the Persian Gulf region. The combination of events created a significant realignment of U.S. strategic doctrine. Prior to the Iranian Revolution and the Soviet invasion of Afghanistan, the United States had committed itself to defending only Europe and Japan with a full military commitment, including nuclear weapons, if required. This meant that America would respond to any Soviet military aggression against Western Europe or Japan with the full range of military options, including tactical and strategic nuclear weapons, if necessary. With the advent of the Carter Doctrine in 1980, the two full military commitments would henceforth include a third—the Middle East.

> The United States reacted to Soviet troop movements on the border of Iran by informing the Soviet Union that they would defend Iran in the event of a Soviet invasion ... [Carter national security advisor] Brzezinski characterizes this recognition of the Middle East as a vital strategic region on par with Western Europe and the Far East as a fundamental shift in U.S. strategic policy.[30]

Thus with the drive of Iranian soldiers into Iraq and the Soviet Union ensconced to the east of Iran in Afghanistan, the United States essentially became committed to insuring that the forces of Khomeini did not overrun Iraq and, in doing so, pose a direct threat to Saudi Arabia and the oil reserves of the Middle East. As a result of the Middle Eastern security, stability, and the continued flow of oil to the United States, American and allied assistance enabled the Iraqi armed forces to preempt Iran's spring offensive. Beginning in April 1988, and extending to the Iranian acceptance of a cease-fire in August 1988, four major battles were conducted that were well planned, well executed, and featured combined helicopter (air assault-air mobile) operations and amphibious landings, with close air support in an integrated, combined arms approach. At the beginning of 1988, Saddam acquiesced and allowed professionally trained Iraqi commanders, working in conjunction with the U.S. military and the U.S. intelligence community, to direct and coordinate the campaign that served in ending the Iran-Iraq War.

Starting with Operation Blessed Ramadan, in conjunction with the conventional military arms, the Iraqis deployed CWs, including nerve (Cyclosarin, Tabun) and blister (Mustard) agents, against Iranian command and control facilities, artillery positions, and logistical points. Three less intensive follow-on battles were conducted that utilized a similar combined arms approach. After first gaming, rehearsing, and conducting exercises for the operations, Iraqi forces launched successful attacks against Iranian forces at Fish Lake and Shalamjah regions near Basra, and they recaptured the oil-rich Majnum Islands.

Further north, in the last major engagement of the war prior to the August 1988 cease-fire, Iraqi armored and mechanized forces drove the Iranians back into Iran and in the process captured large amounts of armor and artillery. Following the Iraqi counteroffensive, with the costs to the Ayatollah and his regime having risen sufficiently, the government of Iran finally agreed to terms. The Iran-Iraq War ended when Iran accepted UN Security Council Resolution 598 leading to an August 20, 1988, cease-fire.

THE COST OF WAR LEADS TO AN INVASION OF KUWAIT

The Iran-Iraq War, fought in many instances similar to World War I, was the costliest and bloodiest conflict since the Second World War.

> The Iran-Iraq War from 1980 to 1988 was characterized by mutual regression to a World War I model, as the adversaries found it impossible albeit for different reasons to sustain the high-end matrices of the early stages. Barbed wire and poison gas, bayonet charges, suicidal human-wave assaults, notably by Iran's youthful Basij, suggested a king of de-modernization through attrition, which was common in long-running, mid-level conventional conflicts between adversaries with limited industrial or technological bases.[31]

Iraq invaded Iran with the intent of securing territorial claims to the Shatt al-Arab, building prestige in the eyes of the Arab world (thus picking up the baton of leadership that was lost with the death of Egypt's Nasser), and creating the conditions that would lead to the fall of the Ayatollah and his government—a government that was actively promoting Shiite and Kurdish rebellions within Iraq. But Saddam mistakenly believed he could replicate the Israel success during the 1967 Six-Day War. Accordingly, he attacked for a week and then called for terms, which were immediately rejected by Tehran, partly out of revolutionary and religious fervor but also due to the fact that Saddam had failed to destroy the Iranian Air Force in a surprise attack during the first few hours of the war. He also miscalculated the will to fight among the civilian population, both young and old, as well as the tepid response to his invasion by Arab residents in the Khuzestan Province.

In addition to the physical suffering, the war cost at least $200 billion (USD) directly, and another $1 trillion (USD) indirectly. The Iran-Iraq War, which accomplished little, essentially impoverished both nations. However, Saddam exited the war with a string of victories that had brought the clerical leadership in Iran to the bargaining table. As a result of Western, Soviet, and Middle Eastern allies' resupply, his forces by war's end were arguably the most powerful in the Middle East, excluding the Israeli armed forces. Deeply in debt as a result of the lengthy war and with a military by war's end conducting effective combined arms combat, Saddam soon began making demands of his neighbors and the international community. The Iran-Iraq War saddled Saddam's Iraq with an $83 billion war debt. His neighbors, particularly Saudi Arabia and Kuwait, balked at providing significant relief from that debt, which only served in irritating Saddam believing they owed him for saving their regimes by withstanding the Iranian counterassault. Saddam, angered and likely affected by the constant stress that was generated in an existential struggle for eight continuous years during war with Iran, then entered into a serious of miscalculations, which proved much more costly than the war debt arising from the Iran-Iraq War.

Chapter 7

The Establishment of USCENTCOM, Iraq's Invasion of Kuwait, and Operation Desert Storm

You may fly over a land forever; you may bomb it, atomize it, pulverize it and wipe it clean of life—but if you desire to defend it, to protect it, and keep it for civilization, you must do this on the ground, the way the Roman Legions did, by putting your young men into the mud.

—T. R. Fehrenbach, *This Kind of War*

The Rapid Deployment Joint Task Force (RDJTF), created during the Carter administration to enable a surge in U.S. military power in the Middle East during crisis situations, evolved into the U.S. Central Command (USCENTCOM) on January 1, 1983, under U.S. President Ronald Reagan. The Command's central geographical position between Europe and Asia (U.S. European and U.S. Pacific Commands, respectively) created an area of responsibility (AOR) encompassing the Middle East and Central Asia.

USCENTCOM's first objective was to deter and, if necessary, defeat a Soviet attack aimed at the turbulent developments that engulfed Iran. The ability to swiftly surge forces into the Middle East through a joint and unified command was viewed as both increasing the deterrent effect and, should deterrence fail, providing the logistical structure and operational framework that would enable the integration of air, naval, and ground forces for the purposes of successful warfighting.

By the fall of 1989 and with the Soviet Union under Mikhail Gorbachev working in an increasingly cooperative capacity with the United States, U.S. leaders revisited the threat analysis for the Middle East. By November 1989, CENTCOM planning under U.S. Army General H. Norman Schwarzkopf considered the greatest threat to Persian Gulf security was most likely instability resulting from an aggressive Saddam Hussein who would aim the newly empowered Iraqi military at one or more of his neighbors. Moreover, since Saddam believed that the British had arbitrarily created Kuwait out of ancient Mesopotamian lands, and since he thought of himself as a modern-day Nebuchadnezzar with Kuwait part of the realm, CENTCOM assessed in November 1989 that an attack on Kuwait or the United Arab Emirates might be forthcoming and such a scenario should be reviewed, analyzed, and planned for. An invasion of Saudi Arabia by Saddam was also a scenario under review at the time, although this was believed less likely than an attack on Kuwait or the United Arab Emirates, as any venture by Iraq into Saudi Arabia would compel the United States to react with military force.

As a result of the new regional dynamics—the Soviets being perceived as less of a threat by the United States coupled with an increasing probability that Saddam would attempt to engage in coercive negotiations with his Sunni neighbors to such an extent and in such a manner that would possibly require a U.S. military response—a full-scale plan was scheduled by CENTCOM for publication in July 1990. In the interim, Schwarzkopf's staff created an adjunct plan for a command post exercise, Internal Look 90, scheduled for July 23–28, 1990. Internal Look 90 was an effort aimed at examining the full OPLAN and related issues and "validating operational and logistical support concepts."[1]

> Although the actual conflict was relatively brief (1991 Persian Gulf War), preparation for war began almost two years ago when USCINCENT [CENTCOM commander] determined the Iran-Iraq conflict had altered the balance of power in Southwest Asia. As a result of that conflict, Iraq emerged the victor with the 4th largest military in the world and the most threatening and powerful force in the region.[2]

While in possession of a vast military machine that had been built up in the last year of the war, Saddam's Iraq had exited the nearly nine-year war with Iran with a significant and perhaps debilitating level of debt of $83 billion (USD). Of this, about $40 billion was owed to Western institutions and the remaining $43 billion was owed to Arab countries—$17 billion to Kuwait and an additional $26 billion to the Saudis. The annual interest on the combined Iraqi debt alone consumed nearly one-third of Iraq's revenue from oil. The acute nature of this problem was compounded by the fact that the price for a barrel of oil had fallen from $38 to less than $10 in the mid-1980s, as the United States in conjunction with the Saudis pursued a path of "rolling back" Soviet power by effectively decreasing the Union of Soviet Socialist Republics' (USSR) revenue from the sale of oil. The Saudis, coordinating efforts with the Reagan administration, increased production of oil to the point of flooding the market and, as a result, drove down the price per barrel, as traded on the international market.

Saddam had taken exception to the policy of driving down the price of oil, which, in effect, decreased his revenue from the sale of oil. In response, he began threatening both the Saudis and the Kuwaitis for their contributions in the overproduction of oil. Adding to Saddam's irritation with the Kuwaitis was the fact that they had taken to directional drilling (slant drilling) into the Rumaila oil field where only a fraction of the land containing the oil field was owned by Kuwait, with the vast majority of the oil reservoir underground and within land owned by Iraq.

From Saddam's point of view the overproduction of oil that had led to depressed prices was being accomplished in part through the theft of Iraq's oil by the Kuwaiti monarchy. In response, he demanded that Kuwait forgive his war debt and make a $10 billion payment as restitution for the costs of oil taken from Rumaila. Kuwait countered by offering $9 billion but did not agree to completely cancel the war debt.

Iraq was suffering in the aftermath of a long and costly war, and the Iraqi economy was in shambles in two critical areas. The first was related to infrastructure that had been badly damaged directly by war and indirectly by Baghdad's inability to reinvest and maintain the country's infrastructure. Second was the rapid declining value of the currency, the Iraqi dinar. Within Iraq, by 1989 inflation was running at an annual rate of 50 percent, which meant that each year the Iraqi dinar lost half its value. In such conditions, keeping one's wealth or savings in the Iraqi national currency was economically irrational. The dismal state of infrastructure coupled with declining revenues and a general devaluation of the currency injected great domestic financial uncertainty within the country, which eventually extended into external capital markets.

SADDAM'S IRAQ SEEKS COMPENSATION FOR DEFENDING THE OIL-RICH SHEIKDOMS

Into this deteriorating economic climate came 200,000 demobilized Iraqi troops at the end of the Iran-Iraq War, looking for work and finding scant opportunity to support themselves and their families. In 1989–1990, a financially stressed Iraq was creating the necessity for a rapid demobilization of hundreds of thousands of more troops into a war-torn economy. For Saddam both, or either, Kuwait and Saudi Arabia were going to provide financial relief; or, he was going to use the massive army to seize what he believed was owed to him. Saddam and his closest advisors knew that demobilizing hundreds of thousands of more soldiers and releasing them into a war-torn Iraqi economy was a recipe for instability.[3] Demobilizing into a depressed economy was not an option for Saddam and his inner circle. Either he created a military confrontation and kept the soldiers on the job while coercively managing to obtain financial relief, or, he obtained the necessary financial relief peacefully. The latter did not materialize. Saddam, refusing to demobilize into a war-torn economy without financial relief, opted for war.

Adding to Saddam's consternation was a significant territorial dispute arising from British support of the al-Sabah family following the First World War. The territory, through agreement with the ruling dynasty of the al-Sabah family, became a protectorate of the British Empire in 1899. However, it was previously a part of the Ottoman Empire's Basra province, which led Iraq to claim it as part of its territory. Modern Iraq was made up of 18 provinces, and Saddam generated a propaganda campaign that claimed Kuwait would soon become Iraq's 19th province.

London drew the Kuwaiti border between the al-Sabah kingdom and Iraq in 1922 essentially making Iraq landlocked. As a result, modern Iraq was essentially constrained in its access to the Persian Gulf. This is one of the reasons the Shatt al-Arab waterway was so important to Iraq in the lead-up to the Iran-Iraq War, as it provided Persian Gulf access for Iraq from the southern port city of Basra.

In 1990, Iraq demanded access to the Persian Gulf through the Kuwaiti islands of Bubiyan and Warbah. The seemingly recalcitrant and ungrateful nature of Kuwaiti, Saudi, and Emirati (UAE) responses to his demands frustrated Saddam who believed each of those nations owed him and the Iraqi armed forces for stopping revolutionary Iran from expanding across the Middle East and overrunning their kingdoms. The same logic brought him to the conclusion that the West and the United States owed him as well for frustrating Iranian revolutionary attempts at seizing Mecca and Medina in Saudi Arabia and, in the process, taking control of the world's largest oil reserves. Frustrated in his demands, in mid-July 1990, Saddam directed a fully propagandized diplomatic campaign against Kuwait, the United Arab Emirates, and the United States. In response, Kuwait placed its forces on full alert and prepared to defend its capital, Kuwait City.

On July 23, 1990, Iraq moved 30,000 troops to the Iraq-Kuwait border, and U.S. naval and marine forces operating in the Gulf were placed on alert. The United Arab Emirates requested U.S. aerial refueling support to enable its air force to increase combat air patrols over critical facilities and territory. The United States responded with Operation Ivory Justice on July 24, 1990, by dispatching two Boeing KC-135 Stratotankers and a Lockheed C-141 Starlifter with support equipment and personnel arriving on the same day. Northrup Grumman E-2C Hawkeye airborne warning and control system (AWACS) radar aircraft and two U.S. Navy frigates were also sent to the northern Persian Gulf in a show of support for U.S. allies. Sent partially as a signal to Saddam that the United States would back its Gulf allies, the limited nature of the deployments simultaneously attempted to moderate any sense of impending escalation.

The consensus within U.S. intelligence as well as within the State Department was that while Saddam had put forces into position enabling him to conduct a large military operation against Kuwait, any such action would most likely be limited in duration and scope. The key Kuwaiti oil pumping rigs accessing the Rumaila oil field were one and four kilometers from the border with Iraq. Thus, the U.S. leadership came to believe that Saddam was presenting a very public "swaggering" use of force meant to extract concessions from the Kuwaiti government. If Saddam was unable to negotiate a satisfactory agreement, it was widely believed that he might even push several kilometers into Kuwait and occupy the oil rigs that had been extracting oil from the Rumaila oil field, although that was believed to be an extreme measure. Much of the reporting and analysis argued that while possible, an all-out invasion and complete occupation of Kuwait would be unlikely due to the severity of an expected U.S. and allied response.

On July 25, 1990, Saddam met with the U.S. ambassador to Iraq, April Glaspie, who in attempting to lower the temperature and downplay any desire for the United States to become embroiled in military hostilities stated, "We have no opinion on Arab-to-Arab conflicts such as your border disagreement with Kuwait." Saddam misread this as an act of acquiescence on the part of the United States and, at least, an implicit "green light" for him to come to some agreement with the Kuwaitis. Ms. Glaspie's view on concluding an arrangement with Arab neighbors, it could safely be said, differed from Saddam's view of concluding an arrangement with neighbors in general and his conception of how to go about ending a border disagreement with Kuwait, in particular.

IRAQ INVADES KUWAIT

To the chagrin and extreme displeasure of regional and world leaders, at 10 p.m., on August 1, 1990, the operations officer of Kuwait's 35th Brigade was notified of an impending Iraqi invasion and ordered to place the brigade on alert and to prepare to defend the country.[4] Two hours later at midnight on August 2, two Iraqi armored divisions accompanied by one mechanized division (the three divisions of Iraq's Republican Guard Corps) advanced into Kuwait. With the assistance of prepositioned Special Forces, in addition to those arriving by helicopter, the Iraqi troops assaulted government positions and facilities. At 12:30 a.m. on August 2, the 35th Brigade received information that the Iraqis occupied Al Ratkaj, and by 1 a.m. the Republican Guard was in occupation of all frontier boundary centers in the North.

Prior to the Iran-Iraq War, Saddam and his staff originally conceived of and deployed the Republican Guard for internal security purposes, a modern-day *Praetorian Palace Guard*, but during the conflict with Tehran, the Iraqi leadership transitioned the Guard into a full corps and utilized it as their main striking force during offensive operations. The two premier Republican Guard divisions were the Hammurabi Mechanized and the Medina Luminous Armored. The Hammurabi Division consisted of two mechanized and one armored brigade, and the Medina Division consisted of two armored and one mechanized brigade. Iraq's armored forces utilized Soviet-supplied T-55 and T-62 tanks that were deployed during the Iran-Iraq War; however, the Republican Guard now featured Soviet T-72 tanks (about 1,000 in service with the Guard in the summer of 1990) with a 125 millimeter (mm) smoothbore gun with a laser range finder, ballistic computer, and infrared night-vision equipment. The mechanized brigades utilized Soviet-supplied armored personnel carriers such as the BMP-1 (73mm gun and AT-3 missile) and the BMP-2 (30mm gun and capable of firing the AT-4 and 5 missile).

At the time of the Kuwaiti invasion, Iraq had 955,000 men under arms making it the fourth largest army in the world, with an additional 650,000 personnel in paramilitary forces. The Iraqi armed forces fielded 4,500 tanks, 490 combat aircraft, and 3,000 artillery pieces. Facing this massive threat, Kuwait's military consisted of only four brigades plus the Amiri Guard and the Commando Battalion. The limited nature of Kuwaiti armor consisted of British-supplied Chieftain, Vickers, and four M-84 (Yugoslavia variant of the T-72) tanks. Mechanized units utilized an assortment of Soviet-supplied BMP-2s, U.S.-supplied M113 armored personnel carriers, and Saladin armored cars. In contrast to Iraq's million man army, the Kuwaiti military consisted of 16,000 men grouped into three armored and one mechanized brigade, supported by one understrength artillery brigade.

Within 72 hours of launching its invasion of Kuwait, Iraq had moved into Kuwait with 120,000 troops and 850 tanks and was in effective occupation of the country. The United States immediately sought to surge forces for the defense of Saudi Arabia but found the Saudi leadership unconvinced that Saddam would be foolish enough to attempt an invasion of the Kingdom of Saudi Arabia. The leaders of Saudi Arabia as well as their counterparts in Washington understood the sensitivity of the Arab and Muslim world should foreign non-Muslim soldiers arrive in force in the lands near the holy places of Mecca and Medina. Because of these sensitivities and the low probability in the minds of Saudi officials that Saddam would attempt to use military force against the kingdom, the king of Saudi Arabia was hesitant to grant a request from the United States to send defenders against a possible invasion by Saddam.

In response to this understandable hesitancy, U.S. President George H. W. Bush dispatched his secretary of defense, Richard Cheney, and chairman of the Joint Chiefs of Staff, Colin Powell, to personally brief Saudi King Fahd ibn Abdul al-Aziz. Cheney presented Fahd with U.S. satellite imagery of Iraqi forces arrayed on the kingdom's border. Comprehending that the threat was indeed real, Fahd agreed to the U.S. request to deploy forces to Saudi Arabia to deter Saddam from invading Saudi territory. However, Fahd disagreed with the U.S. plan to position American forces around vital oil and infrastructure only and requested that the United States, if it were invited in for the defense of the kingdom, prepare to defend the entire kingdom and not just the oil fields and infrastructure such as pipelines and ports.

OPERATION DESERT SHIELD

By August 7, 1990, Cheney had returned to Washington and briefed President Bush that Fahd and the United States had reached an agreement for the utilization of American military forces for the defense of the kingdom. The president swiftly ordered U.S. combat forces to deploy to the Gulf, and, shortly thereafter, Cheney issued a directive assigning USCENTCOM the mission to deter and, if necessary, defeat any Iraqi aggression aimed at Saudi Arabia.

> Shortly after Cheney released his directive, the Joint Chiefs of Staff issued the first DESERT SHIELD deployment order to two F-15 squadrons, Maritime Pre-positioned Squadrons 2 and 3, based on the islands of Diego Garcia and Guam; two carrier battle groups; the ready brigade of the 82d Airborne Division; and an airborne warning and control system (AWACS) unit. Cheney's directive unleashed what became the most concentrated and complex projection of American military power since World War II. Such a massive deployment, however, would not be easy ... Fortunately, during the INTERNAL LOOK exercise the command and its components had examined the requirements for responding to Iraqi aggression in the Middle East. That exercise provided the component commanders a chance to review their plans and requirements and to lay the foundation for subsequent planning.[5]

As a result of the Iraqi threat in the summer of 1990, U.S. air, naval, and ground forces were dispatched to the Middle East under Operation Desert Shield, with the eventual aim of positioning sufficient U.S. and coalition forces in the theater to defend Saudi Arabia. Following the surge positioning U.S. and coalition forces in blocking positions at the border, and should diplomacy fail in convincing Iraqi forces to withdraw from Kuwait, a second follow-on buildup was envisioned and aimed at augmenting forces previously deployed. The follow-on forces would be configured for an offensive ground campaign enabling the United States and its coalition partners to militarily compel the exit of Saddam's forces from Kuwait, if necessary.

The United States maintains a myriad of ground, naval, and air forces capable of deploying anywhere in the world within days. On such unit is the ready brigade of the 82nd Airborne Division based at Fort Bragg, North Carolina. The ready brigade (always on standby and prepared to deploy within 18 hours of orders) of the 82nd Airborne Division (2nd Brigade was designated as the ready brigade in August 1990) began moving out on August 8, completing its deployment to Saudi Arabia on August 14.

By the end of the first week of Desert Shield, more than 4,000 U.S. Army soldiers had deployed to Saudi Arabia on 106 aircraft. These troops were supported by 15 AH-64 Apache attack helicopters, 8 OH-58 Kiowa

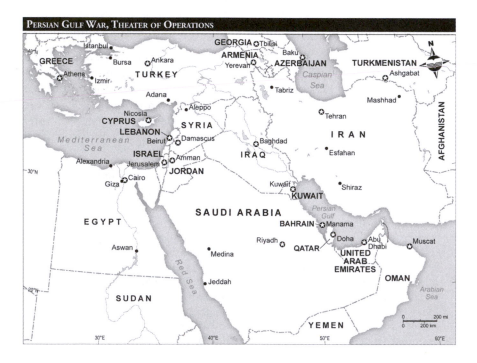

observation helicopters, 18 M551 Sheridan armored reconnaissance/airborne assault vehicles (AR/AAVs), 56 TOW antitank missile systems, 2 multiple launch rocket system (MLRS) launchers, and 12 105mm towed howitzers. As impressive as the airborne brigades of the 82nd were (and are), the fact on the ground—the relative correlation of forces in August 1990—was such that should the heavy armor of the three Iraqi Republican Guard divisions attack the assembling U.S. forces (4,000 U.S. troopers lightly armed versus approximately 100,000 Iraqi troops with heavy armor), the battle would have presented the United States with quite a challenge.

Nonetheless, troopers of the 82nd realized that they were being positioned to give Saddam pause in his deliberations regarding a cost/benefit analysis of a potential move into Saudi Arabia. Many referred to their initial vulnerability lightheartedly, stating that their relatively small numbers were there to serve as a "speed bump" for advancing Iraqi forces. For the Bush administration and top Pentagon leaders, the more accurate metaphor was that the 82nd's presence served as a "trip wire" that, once crossed by Saddam, would "let loose" a series of unpleasant and violent responses.

The instruments of those potential responses were swiftly dispatched to the region as 48 F-15 Eagles from the 1st Fighter Wing at Langley Air Force Base in Virginia landed in Saudi Arabia within hours to cover the arrival of U.S. ground forces. These aircraft were soon joined by 36 F-15s from the 36th Tactical Fighter Wing based in Bitburg, Germany, landing at Al Kharj Air Base about an hour's drive south of Riyadh. Simultaneously, the USS *Eisenhower* carrier battle group moved from the eastern Mediterranean to the Red Sea, while the USS *Independence* carrier battle group, then in the Indian Ocean, was ordered into the north Arabian Sea.

The U.S. Air National Guard (ANG) was also tasked for duty during Desert Shield and quickly responded, joining the active duty F-15s at Al Kharj Air Base when the 169th Fighter Wing of the South Carolina ANG deployed 24 F-16 Fighting Falcons. The fighters of the South Carolina ANG were augmented by 24 F-16s of the New York ANG's 174th Fighter Wing based at Syracuse. As President Bush authorized the activation of American military reserves on August 22, active duty heavy (armored and mechanized) ground forces began landing in the theater, as a brigade of the I Marine Expeditionary Force (I MEF) was quickly positioned in the vicinity of the key Saudi port of Jubayl.

By the third week of August, lead elements of the 101st Airborne (Air Assault) Division as well as the 24th Infantry (Mechanized) Division began disembarking near Dhahran. With these heavier forces came additional Apache attack helicopters, M2 Bradley fighting vehicles, and M1A1 Abrams tanks (including the 216 M1A1s deployed by the 24th Infantry

Division). In September and October, follow-on American forces arrived, including the 1st Cavalry Division and the 3rd Armored Cavalry Regiment. London sent the British 7th Armoured Brigade and the 4th Armoured Brigade (under 1st U.K. Armoured Division HQ) to join the I MEF in defense of the main road leading to Jubayl. Paris dispatched the 6th French Light Armored Division, which was placed for the defense of the left flank of the allied position within Saudi Arabia. In the Persian Gulf itself, the 4th Marine Expeditionary Brigade (MEB) was positioned aboard U.S. Navy ships ready to conduct amphibious operations in support of CENTCOM objectives. Within 90 days, CENTCOM had moved sufficient forces into the theater that arguably altered Saddam's cost/benefit strategic calculus sufficiently as to dissuade the Iraqi leader from any previous thoughts he may have been entertaining regarding the acquisition of the Saudi territory.

The rapid deployment of surge forces into Saudi Arabia during the summer and fall of 1990 was one of the most remarkable logistical feats in world history. U.S. service and coalition partner personnel attached to support and logistical operations in all of the services were critical to the massive movement of men and materiel that provided the deterrent effect generated during Operation Desert Shield. Overall they found the government of Saudi Arabia when it came to (low visibility) material support an effective and willing partner—certainly the world-class ports and air facilities made a herculean task more manageable.

> On 10 September King Fahd verbally committed his nation to provide comprehensive support, although the details remained unclarified until mid-October, when the Department of Defense sent a negotiating team into Saudi Arabia. Instead of concluding a contract or international agreement with the Saudis, the team reached an understanding which became a de facto agreement. That was done to prevent bureaucratic delays and to make giving a gift from Saudi Arabia to the United States as easy as possible, while addressing the Kingdom's continuing desire to avoid formal ties. Saudi Arabia agreed to pay all costs of all contracts entered into by U.S. forces as of 30 October 1990 and backed up its promise with a check for $760 million that a very nervous American officer carried back to New York for deposit.[6]

While the U.S. Air Force (USAF) was the essential key for the immediate insertion of airborne forces and tactical airpower into the crisis zone, prepositioned stocks of equipment aboard army supply ships were critical for the early success in surging forces and materiel into Saudi Arabia to deter an Iraqi attack.

> Four ships that had been anchored off the coast of Diego Garcia brought rations, cots, tents, blankets, and medical supplies, as well as refrigerated trailers, reverse osmosis water purification units, forklifts, and tactical

petroleum terminals. Those ships, which had been stocked and positioned so they could support an expeditionary force such as the one now deploying, arrived at Saudi Arabian ports on 17 August. They bought time for [Army logistics commander] Pagonis to put into operation a more formal logistics system. "There was no doubt about it," Pagonis later said, "We would have never made it if we did not have those four Army pre-po ships."[7]

Cooperation with the British for the use of the island of Diego Garcia also enabled fighter and bomber aircraft to be prepositioned and in providing and projecting immediate airpower into the Persian Gulf. American *forward presence* made possible the rapid positioning of ground, naval, and air forces in response to the invasion of Kuwait. While forward presence and prepositioning were critical in the early stages of the crisis, sealift became crucial for the overall success of Operations Desert Shield and Desert Storm, as it carried 90 percent of the cargo needed for both the operations.

However, by November 1990, the United States, its allies, and coalition partners realized that while Saddam had been dissuaded from continuing his advance into Saudi Arabia, the impressive buildup had not convinced him to withdraw from Kuwait. On November 8, chairman of the Joint Chiefs of Staff, General Powell, and CENTOM commander, General Schwarzkopf, informed Secretary of Defense Cheney that if national policy regarding the Kuwaiti crisis was to evolve from deterring an invasion into Saudi Arabia to one that required the ejection of Iraqi forces from Kuwait, the coalition would need to be militarily reinforced. In a public address, President Bush announced that since Saddam refused to withdraw, the United States in coordination with its coalition partners would surge additional forces into the Gulf, enabling offensive operations to militarily compel Iraq to leave Kuwait.

Accordingly, heavy ground forces based at Stuttgart, Germany, would join with the 1st Infantry Division (Mechanized) and augment the forces then in place in the Kuwaiti theater of operations (KTO). Thus, the U.S. VII Corps' 1st and 3rd Armored Divisions, the 2nd Armored (Forward), and the 2nd Armored Cavalry Regiment were ordered into the Middle East in November 1990. Joining U.S. ground forces, the British 1st Armoured Division (having moved inland from the Jubayl road) and the 6th French Light Armored Division were the Egyptian 3rd Mechanized Division and the Syrian 9th Armored Division. All were in the theater and on the ground in Saudi Arabia by December 1990.

Thirty-four nations (in the broadest sense, in terms of political or economic support, at least 50) contributed to the remarkable coalition coordinated by U.S. Secretary of State James Baker III, although many contributed with constrained numbers of troops, materiel, and other resources.[8] The coalition was the largest the world had seen since the Second World War, eventually deploying 737,000 troops in the KTO, including 190 naval vessels and 1,800 aircraft. U.S. forces included 532,000 troops, 120 ships, and 1,700 aircraft. These forces lined up against roughly 545,000 Iraqi troops in the KTO aligned in 8 Republican Guard divisions (110,000 troops) and 36 additional divisions. By the end of the 1991 Gulf War (Desert Storm), 42 Iraqi divisions were rendered combat ineffective.

Key U.S. allies, Japan and Germany, while not sending troops, contributed $10 billion and $6.6 billion, respectively. As U.S. armor traditionally stationed in Germany for the defense of Europe transitioned into the Middle East during Operation Desert Shield, Germany stepped up to fill gaps in European defense created with the movement of U.S. heavy divisions off the continent. While both Japan and Germany were constrained in contributing troops for overseas contingencies from both historical and constitutional reasons, Japan was also able to contribute much needed minesweepers for Persian Gulf duty. Both Saudi Arabia and Kuwait supported Operation Desert Shield/Storm with $16.8 billion and $15 billion, respectively. The Kingdom of Saudi Arabia was also a no-cost host for all incoming coalition forces, providing 4,800 tents, 20 million meals (and bottled water to the coalition located throughout the entire theater), and 20 million gallons of fuel per day.

For Hosni Mubarak's contribution of Egyptian troops, the United States forgave Egypt's $7.1 billion in debt. The Soviet Union under Gorbachev worked in conjunction with the United States in supporting both diplomatic and military efforts in the United Nations and in the international arena. The historic change in policies instituted by Gorbachev's USSR (Glasnost, Perestroika, i.e., new openness, restructuring their economy, and reaching out to the West) aided U.S. efforts significantly vis-à-vis Saddam's Iraq and created the conditions for greater international cooperation regarding the Middle East. Cooperation with Moscow during Operations Desert Shield and Desert Storm made things possible that at other times during the Cold War probably would not have been achievable. Certainly the United States would not have removed heavy divisions positioned to defend against a Soviet invasion in Europe in earlier years.

Soviet cooperation was particularly in evidence in the UN Security Council where, between August 2 and November 29, 1990, 12 resolutions were passed that concerned the Iraqi invasion of Kuwait. UN Security Council Resolution 678, passed on November 29, authorized members to use "all means necessary" to enforce previous resolutions with a deadline for Iraq's withdrawal from Kuwait on January 15, 1991. The resolution served as the UN authorization for the use of force against Iraqi forces in Kuwait in the follow-on to Operation Desert Shield: Operation

Desert Storm. On January 12, 1991, the U.S. Congress confirmed its support by voting to provide the president's authorization should the use of force against Iraq become necessary to achieve the goals as set out in the resolution.

There were a wide variety of contributors to the advances made by the U.S. military in the 1980s, including President Reagan, who as president made a point of revitalizing the armed forces of the United States both materially and, through an effective leadership campaign, rebuilding morale. It was this rejuvenated and retooled military that would engage Saddam's forces in early 1991. While there were a multitude of strategic and operational thinkers that improved the American military following the Vietnam War, space constraints here would narrow coverage to three representative views and approaches.

WARDEN AND BOYD: INSIDE-OUT, STRATEGIC PARALYSIS, AND THE OODA-LOOP

Many of the key officers and Department of Defense officials in 1991 had spent a significant portion of their careers, if not directly in-theater, at least grappling with the many complexities of the Vietnam experience. A vocal critic of the attrition that marked the Vietnam War, USAF Colonel John A. Warden III, argued for an "inside-out" air strategy during the planning stages of Operation Desert Storm. The United States prosecuted "Rolling Thunder" during the Vietnam War, which was used as a signaling device to influence a negotiated settlement to the war. The gradualism and attritional aspects of the Rolling Thunder air campaign, particularly as the war ended badly for the United States, became a source of irritation for airpower advocates within the United States.

CHECKMATE AND INSTANT THUNDER

Warden's group in the Pentagon, referred to as "Checkmate," was created in the planning directorate of the Air Staff. Warden and Checkmate referred to the new thinking by attaching the phrase "Instant Thunder" to emphasis the preference for a decisive use of airpower rather than a gradualist approach. The group was set up following the close of the Vietnam War and tasked to analyze options regarding the use of airpower, including the evaluation of vulnerabilities and high-payoff concepts, and provide pragmatic concepts in order to guide and inform campaign planning.[9] The operational design was to avoid the politically correct "signaling" and attempts at shaping negotiating behavior of Rolling Thunder and instead provided the air campaign blueprint for massive, rapid, and precisely delivered attacks against Iraqi centers of gravity. Victory, from this perspective, would be achieved by delivering a state of *strategic paralysis* to an opponent. This involved striking swiftly through airpower at an enemy's command centers and communications, radar, and power generation facilities.

> To summarize the major aspects of our working definition, strategic paraly-
> sis is a military option with physical, mental, and moral dimensions which
> intends to disable rather than destroy the enemy. It seeks maximum pos-
> sible political effect or benefit with minimum necessary military effort or
> cost. It aims at rapid decision through a "maneuver-battle" directed against
> an adversary's physical and mental capability to sustain and control its war
> effort in order to diminish its moral will to resist.[10]

In doing so, the aim was not only to destroy the military and political leadership's ability and will to carry on but also to cut them off from their deployed armed forces. Once cut off from headquarters, the fractions of the enemy's forces now without centralized command and with their own ability to communicate drastically reduced would then be destroyed should they refuse to accept surrender demands. What became known as USAF Colonel John Warden's Five Rings—leadership, system essentials, infrastructure, population, and fielded military—presented a targeting package for prevailing in "deep battle" and recognizing the contribution each ring brought to the nation's ability to prosecute a war.

DOMINANT BATTLESPACE KNOWLEDGE

Within the Soviet Union, discussions revolved around as "deep battle," which recognized the increased ability of air mobile troops to attack deep into the rear echelons of an enemy's battle array, including headquarters. For Warden, the United States had already displayed with rapid effective-ness its ability to conduct air mobile-air assault actions during helicopter operations in Southeast Asia. Warden, however, anticipated precision strike weapons, along with U.S. advantages in avionics and aerospace engineering, information warfare, and dominant maneuver. Thus, the Revolution in Military Affairs (RMA) that evolved in the years leading up to Desert Shield and Desert Storm brought the ability to gather real-time, all-weather information continuously to formulate what came to be referred to as dominant battlespace knowledge (DBK). DBK involved relaying automated target information of operational plans into a recog-nizable network in which it could then be utilized.

While electricity, steam, and internal combustion engines drove many advances in military arms at the beginning of the twentieth century, one of the major advancements at the end of the century was the computer microchip—the incredibly shrinking and smaller sizes produced even greater capacity for computing systems onboard, in the air, in space, and on the ground. Combined with guidance systems, these advances produced a range of precision-guided munitions (PGMs) imbued with unprecedented accuracy and lethality, which made significant strides in delivering strategic paralysis to the Iraqi leadership and the deployed forces during offensive operations in the KTO in 1991. PGMs became more widely used during U.S. operations in Afghanistan in 2001 and in Iraq in 2003.[11]

The RMA preceding the Persian Gulf War of 1991 led to other innovative ideas, including those of another USAF officer who served in Korea and Vietnam, seeking to exploit U.S. technological advantages in time. Air Force Colonel John Boyd introduced the "OODA-Loop"—observe, orient, decide, and act—with two primary objectives. The first manipulates time to create ambiguity and generate uncertainty, confusion, panic, and chaos—to shatter cohesion, produce paralysis, and bring about collapse. Boyd's OODA-Loop shares certain aspects of Warden's Five Ring approach in that it also seeks to generate strategic paralysis. The collapse Boyd refers to is the second objective that seeks the collapse of the opponent's will to resist and to fight on. These objectives are achieved by "getting inside" an adversary's OODA-Loop.

> Boyd's thoughts on strategic paralysis are process-oriented and aim at psychological incapacitation. He speaks of folding an opponent back inside himself by operating inside his observation-orientation-decision-action (OODA) loop. This severs the adversary's external bonds with his environment and thereby forces an inward orientation upon him. This inward focus necessarily creates mismatches between the real world and his perception of that world.[12]

Given that the OODA-Loop models the process by which an individual (or organization) receives input, processes that information, and then reacts to the information or event, getting inside the adversary's OODA-Loop refers to the ability of receiving accurate input regarding situational awareness faster and more accurately than one's opponent, followed by swift decision making and taking action more quickly than the opponent or organization. Thus, you see, decide, maneuver, and shoot faster than the enemy.

Superior situational awareness afforded by advantages in battlespace information technology provides the pilot or military (or naval) commander a competitive and decisive advantage. Boyd's experience of air combat between Russian MiGs and U.S. F-86s in Korea led to the creation of the F-16. Its chief designer stated, "Time is the dominant parameter. The pilot who goes through the OODA cycle in the shortest time prevails because his opponent is caught responding to situations that have already changed."

The key is superior agility in moving through the OODA-Loop, and Boyd defined it as existing where one side in a conflict or in a competition is more agile than its opponent if it can "change the situation more quickly that the other side can update its orientation." When one side has this capability, Boyd argued, he or she has the ability to *operate inside an opponent's OODA-Loop*. Accordingly, agility "depends on keeping one's orientation better matched to the real world than one's opponent during times of ambiguity, confusion, and rapid change, when the natural tendency is to be disoriented."[13]

For Boyd, however, the most determining factor for an opponent's OODA-Loop speed is neither methodologies nor tools, but *culture*. This reflects the tendency of Western culture in fostering innovation, creativity, and problem-solving skills; whereas in traditional authoritarian societies, as found in Russia and in the Middle East, there is a tendency for inculcated obedience, uniform thinking, and centralized control.[14] In sum, isolate the authoritarian—a decision maker, airman, soldier, marine, or sailor—and put him or her head-to-head with an individual who was raised, educated, and trained in a society that fosters independent thinking and problem-solving skills, and you obtain a decidedly competitive advantage in the air, on the sea, and on the ground.

The inside-out strategy of Warden and the idea of strategic paralysis shared with Boyd in knocking out command and control in the initial phases insured that airpower would dominate the early phase of the air *and* land battle, as it contributed to strategic paralysis across enemy formations. Attacking swiftly with great accuracy and lethality and maintaining that tempo also served to disorientate, confuse, and destroy good order and discipline and, as a result, produced a negative impact on the opponent's will to fight. Once the initial attacks had taken their toll through a process known as the "preparation of the battlefield," the ground offensive, if necessary, was then launched.

General Schwarzkopf, U.S. commander in chief, Central Command (USCINCCENT), and a U.S. Army general, was open to Checkmate's perspectives regarding the use of airpower. In August 1990, following Iraq's invasion of Kuwait, Colonel Warden, along with the Air Staff's director of plans, Major General Robert M. Alexander, presented the concepts within Instant Thunder to Schwarzkopf at MacDill Air Force Base in Tampa, Florida. Schwarzkopf accepted the plan as a basis for further refinement and expansion and sent Warden and a small contingent from Checkmate to Riyadh, Saudi Arabia, to brief Lieutenant General Charles Horner (USAF), director of the Joint Forces Air Component and Schwarzkopf's deputy (Forward) in the Gulf.

Within his headquarters, Horner then created a special planning group (SPG) of about 30 officers, which became known as the "Black Hole" due to the rigor that was applied to operational and information security. Led by Brigadier General Buster Glosson (USAF) and aided by Colonel Tony Tolin and an original member of Warden's Checkmate planning group in the Pentagon, Lieutenant Colonel David Deptula, the broad outline envisioned by Warden was detailed into specific master attack plans (MAPs) and air tasking orders (ATOs).

ARMY JEDI KNIGHTS

In mid-September 1990, Schwarzkopf assembled a group of officers within CENTCOM that was designated J5-Special Planning Group (CCJ5-SPG) for operations in the KTO. The officers were graduates of the Army School of Advanced Military Studies (SAMS) in Fort Leavenworth, Kansas—referred to as "Jedi Knights" within army circles. The SAMS curriculum at the time of the Kuwaiti crisis was based on AirLand Battle, and the CCJ5-SPG became part of the joint operations, CENTCOM Plans and Policy Directorate and Combat Analysis Group, which were tasked with developing and analyzing courses of action for the overall ground offensive plan.

In addition to the military doctrine and strategy that underpinned operations during Desert Storm (and also arising in the wake of the Vietnam experience) was what came to be known as the Weinberger Doctrine. Caspar Weinberger served as secretary of defense under President Reagan and, in 1984, put forward six major tests that he argued should be considered when contemplating the use of U.S. combat forces abroad.[15] These tests became popularly known as the Weinberger Doctrine:[16]

> *Test One*: The United States should not commit forces to combat overseas unless the particular engagement or occasion is deemed vital to our national interest, or that of our allies.
>
> *Test Two:* If we decide it is necessary to put combat troops into a given situation, we should do so wholeheartedly, and with the clear intention of winning.
>
> *Test Three:* If we do decide to commit forces to combat overseas, we should have clearly defined political and military objectives.
>
> *Test Four:* The relationship between our objectives and the forces we have committed—their size, composition, and disposition—must be continually reassessed and adjusted if necessary.
>
> *Test Five:* Before the United States commits forces aboard, there must be some reasonable assurance we will have the support of the American people and their elected representatives in Congress.
>
> *Test Six:* Finally, the commitment of U.S. forces to combat should be the last resort.

The U.S. military that was deployed to the KTO in 1990–1991 and the leaders who sent it as well as the commanders who would lead it had, in general, transitioned from the bleak aftereffects of the Vietnam Syndrome to a firm commitment toward winning, and winning through the intelligent application of military force. The clearly defined political objective that military force would be used to support was the ejection of the Iraqi military from Kuwait and the reestablishment of the prior government's authority. The military objective, so conceived and framed, then led to the recognition that the Iraqi Republican Guard divisions were the foundation of Iraq's invasion and subsequent occupation of Kuwait. The three most powerful Republican Guard divisions in the KTO were identified as centers of gravity of the combat capability, which enabled Iraq to take and hold Kuwait. In short, without the Guard's presence, other Iraqi formations would find it nearly impossible to stand and fight in the face of a coalition offensive ground campaign.

Thus, Schwarzkopf and his staff took Warden's original conception in Instant Thunder and understood that by striking command and control in a decisive air campaign strategic paralysis of the enemy was possible. However, CENTCOM also adjusted the original conception that did not focus on immediate attacks on enemy ground units, and by the time the air campaign of Desert Storm was initiated, Iraqi Republican Guard units came under intensive air bombardment. While command and control of an enemy's armed forces was a center of gravity, Schwarzkopf also elevated Iraqi Republican Guard units as important centers of gravity within the KTO. CENTCOM and U.S. national command authority (NCA: the president and his top national security personnel, including the secretary of defense) effectively integrated air and ground concepts into a joint operational plan. This would include coordinated activity across the federal government.

The Bush administration argued that Saddam's move to control Kuwaiti oil not only posed a direct threat to the U.S. economy (and thus national security) and the security of trusted and critically important allies, but the invasion—if allowed to stand—also threatened international peace and stability. As the military buildup took place from August 1990 to January 1991, members of the Bush administration worked both private and public diplomacy and laid the necessary political groundwork in order to achieve its objectives. By mid-January 1991, Bush, his White House communications team, and key members of the U.S. Congress (as well as the James Baker-led State Department) had convinced the American public of the need to take military action against Iraq.

Concurrently, the administration won a vote in Congress that underscored this support and was able to leverage this political framework toward the creation of a coalition of nations that was unprecedented, particularly when one considers the range of support that encompassed the Arab and Muslim world, the Soviet Union, and constituencies around the world. The difficult but necessary groundwork, as envisioned by the Weinberger Doctrine, had been completed and was supported by a new and reinvigorated military doctrine embedded within U.S. strategy and tactics. A massive and reinvigorated American military, partly established during the Reagan administration, resourced by the U.S. Congress and the American people, supported by a world-class defense industrial base had, by the first of January 1991, been deployed to the deserts of Saudi Arabia.

OPERATION DESERT STORM

The U.S.-led coalition's offensive military action in January 1991 against Iraqi forces arrayed in the KTO, designated Operation Desert Storm, unfolded in four phases:

Phase I—*Strategic air campaign*
Phase II—*Air supremacy in theater*
Phase III—*Battlefield preparation*
Phase IV—*Offensive ground campaign*

Using night-vision goggles and infrared radar to navigate, nine U.S. Army Apache helicopters and one Black Hawk helicopter lifted off from Saudi Arabia at 11 p.m. on January 16, 1991, joined up with USAF search-and-rescue helicopters, and proceeded into western Iraq, as part of the vanguard of the strategic air campaign of Desert Storm. At approximately 2 a.m. on January 17, the Apaches locked on to their targets—two early warning intercept stations—and engaged with Hellfire missiles. The objective was to create a corridor into Iraq in which USAF jets could safely transit, as they moved to strike targets in the KTO and throughout Iraq. As the helicopters completed their mission and turned to head back to Saudi Arabia, simultaneously, more than 100 USAF aircraft passed overhead and through the gap opened by the Apaches in the Iraqi early warning network.

The Desert Storm air war may be divided broadly into four chronological stages: the body blow delivered on the first night of the war, 17 January, and continuing through the first 24 hours; the next two weeks of the campaign, when the effort focused on gaining air superiority and continuing the strategic air campaign; the next three weeks or so, when emphasis shifted to the task of cutting off the Iraqi forces in the Kuwaiti Theater of Operations (KTO) and reducing their effective fighting strength through continuous bombardment of their positions, in preparation of the ground campaign. These phases had considerable overlap: for example, attacks against Iraqi ground force positions in the KTO began on the first night, and the strategic campaign continued, albeit at a lower level of effort, through-out the final weeks of the war.[17]

Two and a half hours after the Apache helicopters lifted off, at 1:30 a.m. on January 17, nine U.S. Navy warships, including the guided-missile cruiser *San Jacinto* (CG 56) operating in the Red Sea and the guided-missile cruiser *Bunker Hill* (CG 52) in Persian Gulf waters opened fire with tomahawk cruise missiles directed at Iraqi targets. These initial strikes marked the first combat launch of the tomahawk. During these initial operations (on January 19) USS *Louisville* (SSN 724), submerged in the Red Sea, fired the first submarine-launched tomahawk cruise missile in combat history.[18]

At about 3 a.m., television networks (broadcast and cable) interrupted their regularly scheduled programming to report U.S. strikes against command and control targets in Baghdad. With a well-synchronized strike aimed at the destruction of early warning sites by raids and Navy-launched cruise missiles, coalition air forces caught the Iraqi leadership completely by surprise. About 90 minutes later, and recovering slightly from the initial shock, Iraqi leadership ordered the firing of "Scud" ballistic missiles at both Saudi Arabia and Israel. At distances beyond 175 miles, the Soviet-supplied Scud was highly inaccurate and prone to breaking up in flight, making its military effectiveness marginal.

However, coalition leaders, both political and military, were concerned that Saddam would send canisters of nerve gas or biological agents with his Scuds, creating a weapon of terror that would far exceed the missile's conventional military value. However, the Scuds that he fired in the 1991 Persian Gulf War, reportedly, did not contain chemical or biological weapons. The United States had deployed Patriot antimissile batteries to the KTO and to Israel. The presence of the batteries relieved some anxieties in both Saudi Arabia and Israel. However, the actual military effectiveness of the Patriot system and the results actually achieved were less than portrayed at the time. For instance, Iraq fired eight Scuds into Israel on January 17, 1991, and none was successfully intercepted by Patriot missile systems.

Nevertheless, the overall performance of U.S. technological systems was impressive. American electronic warfare systems overwhelmed Iraqi command and control in the initial stages of air operations, as U.S. and allied forces swiftly established air dominance over Iraq and Kuwait while knocking out command and control facilities and air defense networks, destroying Iraqi aircraft on the ground, and driving the rest into hiding or internment in Iran. In expectation of an amphibious assault by U.S. Marines positioned aboard ships off the coast of Kuwait, and in an effort to raise the costs of war to the coalition, the Iraqi leadership began pumping oil into Gulf waters on January 19, as pumps were activated and valves opened at the Ahmadi loading complex. Oil entered Gulf waters at a rate of 200,000 barrels (8.4 million gallons) per day.

Having established air supremacy (CENTCOM announced aerospace supremacy on January 27, 10 days after the air phase began), coalition airpower then concentrated on lines of communications of Iraqi forces within the KTO. However, on January 29, Iraqi leaders—Saddam, Izzat Ibrahim al-Douri, and Salah Aboud Mahmoud—caught CENTCOM by surprise when 1,500 troops in three battalions briefly invaded Saudi Arabia at the coastal town of Khafji, engaging elements of U.S. Marine Forces Central Command (MARCENT) and Arab Joint Forces Command-East (JFC-East) at several points along the Saudi-Kuwaiti border.

Over the next 36 hours, the marines, joined by Saudi and Qatari troops, engaged the Iraqis in skirmishes that resulted in the marines losing three armored vehicles, while a USAF AC-130H gunship supporting the marines with ground fire was shot down by an Iraqi infrared surface-to-air missile (SAM), killing 14 airmen. Marine combat units armed with TOW missiles, operating jointly with coalition forces and backed by additional airpower, destroyed 24 Iraqi tanks and 13 armored vehicles. Thus, the Iraqis were driven decisively back and forced to make a hasty and ignominious retreat from Saudi Arabia. The Battle of Khafji represented the first significant ground action of the Gulf War and, with the Scud missile launches, the only major Iraqi offensive action of the war.[19]

As the marines and coalition forces drove Iraqi forces back from Khafji, Iraqi commanders prepared to conduct a preplanned counterattack utilizing elements of the 1st and 5th Mechanized Divisions augmented with armor from the 3rd Armored Division. As Iraq prepared to launch the counterattack, coalition airpower delivered a series of debilitating blows to the massing Iraqi forces. Two of the Iraqi objectives in invading Saudi Arabia and attacking Khafji were to seize the initiative and to force the coalition into an early ground campaign. Iraq managed to hold Khafji for 36 hours before being driven back across the border on February 1; however, undeterred by the surprise Iraqi move, CENTCOM continued on its own time schedule.

SADDAM'S STRATEGY

Saddam sought to fight the war on his terms, wherein he could sacrifice large numbers of troops and armor in generating American casualties rather than allowing the coalition to dictate the timing and conditions of combat. The Iraqi leadership realized that given the West's vast superiority in aerospace, control of the sea, high-tech weaponry, and information systems, a conventional arms matchup with an American-led coalition could not be won without exploiting asymmetric advantages. Thus, gaps and solids (Flaechen-und Luecken) factored into Iraq's prewar analysis. Saddam and his staff were planning on creating effects to attack the American people's willingness to support the Desert Storm, splitting the coalition by involving Israel, and playing for time in which to negotiate terms that favored his interests.

There were a number of factors contained within this analysis from which Iraq's eventual strategy sprang. Foremost was Saddam's assumption that the United States would be unable to maintain an army in the field in the face of thousands of casualties. Thus, the cost of liberating Kuwait would exceed that which the U.S.-led coalition would be willing to pay; as Saddam observed, "Yours is a nation that cannot afford to take 10,000 casualties in a single day."[20]

Baghdad was correct in its initial reading of American sentiments regarding casualties. An opinion poll in early January 1991 showed a strengthening of U.S. support for military action against Iraqi forces in the KTO, with 63 percent in favor compared with 55 percent in early December. However, when asked if such action were to come with 1,000 American casualties, only 44 percent expressed a willingness to support such an approach. When asked if military action were to be accompanied by 10,000 troops being killed, only 35 percent expressed approval.[21]

Accordingly, Saddam was not only preparing to fight a military campaign, but he also was preparing to wage a public diplomacy campaign to impact political dynamics within the United States. Toward this, Iraq's battle array in the KTO was organized for a maximum ability to generate American casualties rather than in an explicit expectation of tactical or operational military victory. Similar to the leaders of North Vietnam and their proxies in the South, the Viet Cong, Iraq's political leaders were essentially prepared to risk significant losses tactically in order to achieve a strategic victory when the American public tired of mass casualties, a seemingly never-ending war, and in response could be expected to turn against the war effort, forcing U.S. leaders into negotiations and an eventual withdrawal of American troops.

Iraqi forces in the KTO were arrayed for in-depth defense and had constructed a series of defensive sectors that would prove inviting for a coalition ground attack. Saddam had learned in the Iran-Iraq War from European and American advisors how to create kill zones in which to funnel attacking waves of Iranian infantrymen. In the KTO, in 1990 and 1991, Iraq created berms or ridges of bulldozed sand and combined with ditches—some filled with oil—barbed wire, and other antitank obstacles hoped to trap coalition ground forces, as they attempted to attack into the arrayed Iraqi defenses.

The Iraqi leadership had positioned its first line of infantry to channel attacking forces through a number of break points along the front, which would be pre-sighted and then saturated with Iraqi artillery bombardment as enemy forces entered. Once channeled according to plan, the Iraqi second line of heavier forces would be used to isolate and counterattack. The third line consisted of the operational reserve, as three Republican Guard divisions would then maneuver to the appropriate point(s) in the Iraqi defenses and move in for the kill once enemy positions were exposed, weak points in extended lines were established (culminating points reached), and coalition counterattack reserves were committed to a line of approach.

Iraq's army had grown tenfold during the war with Iran, and in the KTO by January 1991 were some 36 combat divisions, with 400,000 to 450,000 troops fielding approximately 4,000 tanks, 2,800 armored personnel carriers, 3,000 artillery pieces, and 800 aircraft, in addition to the 8 Republican Guard divisions and their approximately 110,000 troops. The massive size was protected by a series of carefully engineered protective barriers along the border from the Persian Gulf to the eastern border of Kuwait. The Iraqi strategy depended on coalition forces attacking in a direct approach, something CENTCOM commanders had originally prepared to do. By early October 1990, American commanders along with their supporting planning staffs opted to forego this strategy and bring in additional forces allowing not only for direct assault into the Iraqi battle array and defenses (which would serve as a holding attack—freezing Iraqi forces in place) but also in conducting an indirect approach (flanking maneuver and attack), which required deception operations leading the Iraqis to believe the main attack would be mounted directly into Kuwait from Saudi Arabia, with a supporting amphibious assault upon the coast of Kuwait from shipborne marines.

U.S. AND COALITION LEADERS COUNTER SADDAM'S STRATEGY

Schwarzkopf, his "Jedi Knights," air and naval planners, along with other elements of U.S. intelligence, by the fall of 1990, were able to ascertain the intent of the Iraqi operational plan. Similar to the strength of Alexander the Great who was able to swiftly discern an enemy's plan in advance and just as swiftly produce a counterplan to defeat it, CENTCOM was able to create a strategy that would minimize coalition casualties.[22] Borrowing from Ulysses Grant's Vicksburg indirect approach during the American Civil War, coalition ground units would maneuver out into the Iraqi desert in a "left hook" to the west of the KTO, sidestepping the Iraqi kill zones and then close for an eastward attack on a line of least expectation. Operational deception (OPDEC) was critical for maintaining the element of surprise as to the true intent of the coalition's strategy. Aiding in this endeavor and contrary to the media coverage of the Vietnam War, the U.S. government kept close control over media reporting during Operations Desert Shield and Desert Storm.

Instead of being drawn in by Iraq's Khafji ploy, U.S. and coalition forces continued to "prepare the battlefield," and within three weeks, coalition air forces knocked out 33 of 36 bridges along the Iraqi supply lines and degraded Iraq's ability to ship food, spare parts, ammo, and other critical commodities from 20,000 to 2,000 tons per week.[23] The logistical degradation of an arrayed army before commencing offensive operations paralleled the British approach for the ultimate defeat of Erwin Rommel's Afrika Corps in Egypt, Libya, and Tunisia during World War II. By the fourth week of the air phase of the Desert Storm offensive, the main focus was in shaping the battlefield for imminent ground operations, as coalition air forces attacked troop concentrations and associated support facilities.

With a marine force offshore Kuwait and the initial allied troop buildup in the eastern part of Saudi Arabia—directly across from Kuwait—Saddam and his generals believed that the main thrust of the ground assault would come from eastern Saudi Arabia, coordinated with an amphibious assault into Kuwait from ships in the Persian Gulf. Highly visible, open media and very public amphibious rehearsals persuaded the Iraqi command to commit four divisions to protect against an amphibious assault launched by U.S. Marines. While allied commanders aided and abetted this subterfuge through a disinformation campaign (part of the OPDEC plan), a massive shift from eastern to western Saudi Arabia by the XVII Airborne Corps and the VII Corps was clandestinely underway.[24] This massive movement of men and materiel was completed by the third week of February 1991.

> From left to right (west to east) stood the French 6th Light Armored Division, the U.S. 101st Airborne Division, the U.S. 24th Infantry Division (Mechanized), and the U.S. 3d Armored Cavalry. The U.S. 82d Airborne Division held a position behind the French. The VII Corps presented a front of five divisions and one separate regiment. From left to right stood the U.S. 1st and 3d Armored Divisions, the U.S. 1st Infantry Division, the British 1st Armored Division, and the U.S. 1st Cavalry Division (Armored). The U.S. 2d Armored Cavalry screened the boundary with the XVIII Corps on the left.[25]

While phases one through three of Desert Storm were being accomplished, the U.S. government attempted, through a flurry of diplomatic activity, to convince Saddam to withdraw from Kuwait. Baghdad, on February 15, made an offer in which it would depart from Kuwait provided that coalition forces would also leave the KTO, pay Iraq's war debts (Iran-Iraq War), and induce the Israelis to pull out of the West Bank. The Bush administration rejected Baghdad's terms. As diplomacy was nearing a dead end, the Soviets attempted to construct an acceptable compromise wherein their long-time client, Saddam, could be tempted to withdraw.

By February 20, Saddam had accepted the fact that he would be withdrawing from Kuwait minus any inducements from Kuwait or coalition forces. The one caveat was that "once" a cease-fire agreement was reached, Saddam would be provided 21 days to withdraw. Coalition political leaders and military commanders understood this to be an effort to draw out the Iraqi occupation of Kuwait allowing for any number of mishaps to occur that would impact the ability to hold the coalition together or the will and desire to maintain the huge military presence within Saudi Arabia. Baghdad and Moscow were reaching for the time-tested strategy as found in many political and commercial negotiations: when faced with strength—stall, wear down the opponent in order to force a change in his or her original demands while utilizing time to gather valuable information useful in undermining the opposition's position, and, if possible, work to split the opposition.

While Iraqi Foreign Minister Tariq Aziz was still in Moscow and after demanding a 21-day period in which to withdraw, Iraq began setting fire to Kuwaiti oil fields. President Bush rejected the Soviet-assisted compromise and warned Saddam that he should withdraw from Kuwait by noon on February 23 or face a ground assault. Receiving no response to the demand, at 1 a.m. on February 24, 1991, orders were issued to subordinate commands by Schwarzkopf's staff: *execute order for ground offensive operations* (Phase IV).

Coalition forces were arrayed in three basic sectors. For illustrative purposes, they can be categorized as sectors one through three, although Schwarzkopf's staff did not refer to them as such. Nearest the Persian Gulf coast was one sector, in the middle of the coalition battle array was the second sector about 100 miles from the coast, to the east of sector one. The third sector was east of the second. This line of arrayed coalition forces extended some 300 miles from the coast (sector one) of the Persian Gulf into the Saudi Arabian desert (sector three). As Saddam's generals expected a direct attack into Kuwait from sector one assisted by an amphibious assault from shipborne marines, they arranged their forces accordingly and braced for a direct assault; as mentioned, U.S. OPDEC brilliantly facilitated this basic misunderstanding. While all eyes were on the Kuwait-Saudi border, CENTCOM surreptitiously shifted forward elements of XVIII Airborne Corps and the VII Corps further east and away from the Kuwait-Saudi border.

On February 24, 1991, the United States and coalition forces attacked in the areas where the Iraqis expected to be attacked, involving maneuver and fire from both sector one and sector two. This action froze Iraqi forces in place in defense of sector one—at the Kuwait-Saudi line. Unknown to Iraqi commanders was that this was a holding action and not the main attack. In sector three, the XVIII Airborne Corps conducted a wide-ranging, flanking maneuver, undetected by the Iraqis, sweeping left in what came to be known as the "left hook." After moving north relative to the Saudi-Iraq border, XVIII Airborne Corps swung back east and headed to a position behind Iraqi forces arrayed in the KTO. Its job was to isolate Iraqi forces within the KTO, prevent reinforcement from Iraq, and prevent the expected retreat by Iraqi forces from the KTO once the main thrust had taken its toll.

AMERICAN AND BRITISH ARMOR

The main thrust of Operation Sabre (essentially the AirLand campaign following the initial air operations of Desert Storm) was to come from the second sector or the middle of the coalition array in Saudi Arabia. In the middle was the U.S. VII Corps consisting of five heavy divisions and four separate field artillery brigades. This heavy formation was to attack north with one overriding directive: destroy the Iraqi Republican Guard. The VII Corps, commanded by Lieutenant General Frederick Franks Jr., was augmented with the British 1st Armoured Division and was the recipient of the heavy U.S. formations pulled out of Germany when President Bush decided in late October 1990 that an overwhelming and decisive U.S. ground campaign would be required to drive Saddam from Kuwait. Along with the British 1st, two key U.S. heavy formations arriving in the theater from Germany were the 1st and 3rd Armored Divisions. These three divisions (what Franks called the "three fists" of the assault) were joined by other storied and premier U.S. formations: 1st Infantry Division (Mechanized), 1st Cavalry Division (Armored), 2nd Armored Cavalry Regiment, and the 11th Aviation Brigade.[26]

AMERICAN AND FRENCH FORCES EXECUTE THE "LEFT HOOK"

In sector three and tasked with executing the left hook, the XVIII Air-borne Corps, commanded by U.S. Lieutenant General Gary Luck, con-sisted of other American divisions, brigades, and regiments with a long tradition of combat excellence: the 82nd Airborne Division, 101st

Airborne Division (Air Assault), 24th Infantry Division (Mechanized), 3rd Armored Cavalry Regiment, and the 12th and 18th Aviation Brigades. The XVIII Airborne Corps was augmented with the French 6th Light Armored Division. In sector one, along the eastern one-third of the front, three commands were instituted. Directly east of VII Corps (on its right flank) in sector one were three individual commands: Joint Forces Command-North (JFC-North) made up of formations from Egypt (4th Armored Division, 3rd Mechanized Division, 20th Special Forces Regiment), Syria (9th Armored Division, a special forces regiment participating in an operational reserve capacity), and Saudi Arabia (five independent brigades and smaller units—Saudi Arabia also contributed the second largest air force within the coalition). JFC-North was under the command of a Saudi Arabian general, Lieutenant General Khalid ibn Sultan.

Also in sector one and to the right (east) of Khalid's JFC-North was the second individual command: the I MEF, commanded by Lieutenant General Walter Boomer and consisting of the 1st and 2nd Marine Divisions. The marines were augmented with the 1st (Tiger) Brigade of the Army's 2nd Armored Division. To Boomer's right (east) was the third individual command of sector one: JFC-East (eventually the first units to enter a liberated Kuwait City—albeit via courtesy of the armed forces of the United States and its many coalition partners and supporters, including the Kingdom of Saudi Arabia), which held the extreme right or eastern flank of the coalition line and extended to the Persian Gulf coast opposite the Kuwait-Saudi border. Saudi General Khalid led this command as well, which was made up of units from all six members of the Gulf Cooperation Council (in addition to Saudi Arabia and Kuwait, contributing forces and support were the United Arab Emirates, Bahrain, Qatar, and Oman).

The ground assault began on the 24th Infantry Division with Major General John Tilelli Jr.'s 1st Cavalry Division feinting north up the Wadi al Batin (alluvial fan or "dry wash"), which ultimately drew the attention of five Iraqi divisions. This feint, about 100 miles inland from the Gulf coast, was coordinated with an attack by the marines and the Army's Tiger Brigade in sector one whose ultimate objective was to join with Arab forces and take Kuwait City. Along with the Arab units and as the U.S. Navy demonstrated with the 5th MEB offshore, these actions froze Iraqi units in place, while the XVIII and VII Corps conducted the clandestine flanking movements to the Iraqis' western (right) flank.

Supporting attacks are often timed in order to deceive an opponent as to an army's true intention regarding the main attack. Since resources are usually limited, supporting attacks are generally constrained to one attack. However, during Desert Sabre, three supporting attacks were conducted. The 1st Cavalry Division, the marines, and Tiger Brigade as well as the Arab allies all hit the Iraqis to hold them in place and to deceive them as to the actual direction of the main assault. As a result, Iraqi commanders were faced with attack from three widely separated points requiring them to begin the defense of the KTO by dispersing combat power and logistical capability.

> A demonstration, a feint, three supporting attacks, an economy-of-force measure to isolate—guard if you will—the battlefield, and a main attack that featured a penetration early on and in itself was an envelopment [along with a fleet of allied ships off the coast] . . . The Iraqis dug four divisions in along their seaward flank specifically for the purpose of defending against amphibious assault, and, as many more heavy divisions were postured in a way that they might quickly intercede when the marines came across the beaches. Instead, once the ground war began and was well underway, the 5th MEB landed behind enemy lines and became an operational reserve for the supporting attack.[27]

After briefly engaging up the Wadi al Batin, the 1st Cavalry withdrew and swung west to catch up with the VII Corps where the 1st Cavalry's follow-on mission was to serve as the VII Corp's operational reserve. In the far west, the French 6th and the American 101st started the massive Western envelopment maneuver by simultaneously conducting a ground assault aimed at securing the coalition's left flank and an air assault to establish forward support bases deep in Iraqi territory. Simultaneously, the VII Corps would breach the Iraqi line at its far west end, driving 100 miles north to al-Busayyah, Iraq, prior to pivoting eastward with one of the primary objectives of the ground campaign, that of engaging and destroying the Republican Guard and then moving into position to take control of the northern half of Kuwait.

The XVIII Airborne Corps would be maneuvering on an axis of advance that would allow it to cover the VII Corps' left flank while maintaining the ability to isolate the KTO from the rest of Iraq, as it conducted air assault missions at considerable range, speed, and surprise—outflanking Iraqi forces in the KTO and preventing their reinforcement. An essential part of XVIII Corps' envelopment maneuver to isolate the battlefield and cut off escaping Iraqi forces from the KTO was the role of the 24th Infantry Division (Mechanized) in blocking the Euphrates River valley to prevent Iraqi forces in Kuwait from escaping north. Once achieving the blocking position, and in coordination with the 3rd Armored Cavalry Regiment, the 24th Infantry Division was to engage and contribute to the destruction of the Republican Guard.

While the 38-day air campaign degraded Iraqi forces in the KTO during the lead-up to the ground campaign, VII Corps contributed its own efforts at battlefield preparation, as 17 cannon battalions and 3 MLRS separate batteries dispensed and delivered 14,000 rounds of cannon artillery and 4,900 MLRS rockets by G-Day on February 24. These attacks were primarily aimed at Iraqi artillery and, in coordination with the air campaign, destroyed much of the artillery of the first echelon of the Iraqi infantry in defense of the KTO.

In the AOR of the VII Corps was, in the first line of Iraqi defense, the 25th, 26th, 27th, 31st, and 48th Infantry Divisions. Within this first line were prepared defenses consisting of berms, multiple trench lines, wire obstacles, minefields, and "fire trenches" filled with crude oil, which were constructed with the objective of being set afire as the enemy attacked. Positioned behind the first line of infantry and defensive fortifications and serving as a tactical reserve was the Iraqi 52nd Armored Division consisting of three brigades: 52nd Armored, 80th Armored, and the 11th Infantry (Mechanized). The third layer of defense was manned by the Iraqi "Jihad" Corps consisting of the 12th and 10th Armored Divisions as well as the Iraqi 2nd Armored Corps made up of the 17th Armored Division and the 5th Mechanized Division.

In preparation for the surprise flanking movement ("left hook"), CENTCOM moved elements of the XVIII Airborne Corps and the VII Corps westward. Since the air campaign along with U.S. information operations had largely "blinded" Iraqi command and control, this maneuver went undetected until it was too late. On G-Day (February 24), the XVIII Airborne Corps began moving its lead elements 190 miles north into Iraq and then proceeded northeast and east to control east-west communications along Highway 8 and block routes leading from Basra into the KTO. This was mirrored by the move north and then a turning movement east by VII Corps. Similarly, as there is often friction between the strategic and operational levels of war, it also occurs between the operational and tactical levels. The Desert Storm/Desert Sabre operational concept called for surprise and swift movement in order to a) disrupt command and control, b) neutralize capability of Iraq's missiles and weapons of mass destruction (WMD), and c) first trap, then destroy what was considered a center of gravity of Iraq's combat effectiveness within the KTO, the Republican Guard.[28] Schwarzkopf provided a straightforward explanation of what center of gravity meant to him:

> ... that thing if you destroy it, you destroy his [the opponent's] ability to wage war. The centers of gravity were Saddam Hussein himself because of the highly centralized leadership. I don't mean personally destroyed. I mean the ability to function. Number two, the Republican Guard. And number three, his chemical, biological, and nuclear capability. It doesn't take a genius to figure out that if these things are gone, his ability to wage war is for all intents and purposes, finished.[29]

While Iraq boasted a massive army (fourth largest in the world at the time of Desert Storm/Sabre), 34 of 51 Iraqi divisions consisted of poorly trained conscripts essentially armed with decades-old armor technology (T55 Soviet-supplied tanks as well as Chinese Type 59 and Type 69). The vast majority of the estimated 1,000 "more modern" T72 Soviet-supplied tanks in the Iraqi army were in the eight Republican Guard divisions. As coalition forces attacked into Iraq and Kuwait on the ground after a 38-day pummeling from the air (including messages in Arabic air dropped and directing Iraqi soldiers how to safely surrender) followed by a massive artillery and rocket barrage, many Iraqi conscripts defending in the front lines understandably opted to surrender. Many of those did not found themselves buried in their trenches and fortifications as U.S. and British armor rolled over them; of the three Republican Guard divisions that anchored Iraq's order of battle in the KTO (and whose destruction was VII Corps' main mission in Desert Sabre), two, along with various other Iraqi units, stood and fought. The two that were unable to withdraw without suffering extensive losses were the Medina Luminous Armored Division and the Tawakalna Infantry (Mechanized) Division.

CENTER(S) OF GRAVITY AS THE OPERATIONAL OBJECTIVES

Thus, Schwarzkopf's operational plan—similar to the two militaries that contributed most to the development of operational art in the mid-twentieth century, that is, the Germans and the Soviets—was designed to destroy the center(s) of gravity of an opposing force or forces. A key center of gravity is that which provides a force its ability to generate combat power and effectiveness. For Iraq in the KTO, following the degradation of command and control, the center of gravity was the Republican Guard, and its destruction became a primary objective of the operational plan. Schwarzkopf as the operational commander had to synchronize directives from his superiors who operated at the strategic level of war (America's NCA: in this instance the Bush administration and Pentagon leaders) with that of clear directives to his tactical commanders such as Lieutenant General Gary Luck of the XVIII Airborne Corps, Lieutenant General Fred Franks of the VII Corps, Lieutenant General Walt Boomer of the I MEF, and Lieutenant General (Saudi Arabia) Sultan ibn Khalid of the Joint Arab Commands (North and East).

The XVIII Airborne Corps, which focused on rapid movement based on air mobility through the use of helicopters (air assault) as well as paratrooper operations (airborne), predictably moved according to plan (and in a manner Schwarzkopf had come to expect), as it quickly took up positions to isolate the battlefield and cut off any reinforcements. Schwarzkopf had been trained originally as a paratrooper. During the Vietnam War with only one major U.S. Army airborne operation—Operation Junction City—air mobile-air assault (helicopters rather than parachutes) became more prevalent in U.S. Army operations, and Schwarzkopf adapted accordingly. As a result, he was oriented toward speed, maneuverability, and surprise—generally from the air. Armor, however, possessed additional cultural propensities and attributes that were as necessary for its type of high-intensity combat in terms of success. The VII Corps, made up of heavy armor, had an orientation and culture for prevailing in intense combat and like air mobile-air assault viewed rapidity of movement as an essential tactic but not the only sine qua non ("without which, not" or a necessary condition) of winning the battle tactically, which often required the ability to prevail toe-to-toe and steel-to-steel with opposing heavy formations. Accordingly, the VII Corps heavy divisions were raised and trained during the Cold War to face Soviet armor in a European slugfest. In short, air mobility and armor, while sharing many of the same concepts in waging war, differed at a fundamental level in what it took to defeat an opponent given their respective areas of specialization.

During Desert Sabre, Lieutenant General Franks, commanding the VII Corps, was more cautious and deliberate in his advance than theater and operational commander, General Schwarzkopf, was comfortable with. For Schwarzkopf and the operational plan, it was essential that both the XVIII Corps and the VII Corps through rapidity of movement and maneuver cut off the escape of the Republican Guard divisions in the KTO. Less known publicly was the planning assumption of Schwarzkopf and his Jedi Knights that had been informed by the Israeli ground operation during the Six-Day War. CENTCOM understood the mechanical and maintenance necessity of observing that armor during combat conditions can operate for about 100 hours before increasing the probability, significantly, for breakdowns and maintenance issues. Just as the Israelis concluded armor operations in the Sinai Desert in 96 hours, Schwarzkopf established 100 hours as the preferred (not necessarily required) outer time parameter for the ground assault during the Persian Gulf War in 1991.

The VII Corps' main attack commenced at 3 p.m. on February 24 and ended 89 hours later with a cease-fire at 8 a.m. on February 28. Within that time frame, the VII Corps drove 260 kilometers, destroyed 1,350 Iraqi tanks, 1,224 armored personnel carriers, 285 artillery pieces, 105 air defense systems, and 1,229 trucks, and took 22,000 Iraqi soldiers prisoners. The cost to the VII Corps was 47 soldiers killed in action, 192 wounded, 9 M1A1 Abrams tanks destroyed with 4 damaged, 14 Bradley fighting vehicles destroyed with 9 damaged, and 2 helicopters destroyed with 3 damaged.[30]

While the Republican Guard Tawakalna Infantry (Mechanized) and Medina Armored Divisions were essentially destroyed during Operation

Desert Sabre, a gap in the planned encirclement resulted in the escape of the famed Republican Guard Hammurabi Armored Division. Lieutenant General Franks's VII Corps movements became a function of tactical developments rather than the operational plan.

Since the United States and its coalition partners were in possession of a preponderance and some would argue an insurmountable level of military superiority (considering the combined resources of the coalition nations, an overwhelming technological capability, control of aerospace and the sea, and fighting in the open desert with incredibly well-trained and well-led soldiers, sailors, airmen, and marines), any prospects of an operational defeat at the hands of a Saddam-led army were minimal at best. For all his bravado and rash statements, Saddam knew militarily he was in for "the mother of all battles" and was hoping to forge a political situation through the manipulation of propaganda and media, featuring U.S. casualties and the expected entry of Israel into the conflict resulting in the fracturing of the coalition as Arab members were forced to abandon support for attacks on Iraq (rather than being confined to the liberation of Kuwait). From there, Saddam would be positioned to negotiate his way to more favorable circumstances and the creation of a narrative allowing him to proclaim victory in the Iraqi media.

The theatrics and media manipulation aside, militarily, and at all three levels of the continuum of war (strategy, operations, and tactics), the odds did not favor a successful outcome for Saddam. Outclassed in aerospace and in Gulf waters, his traditional advantage in heavy armor over regional competitors would not be present during ground combat in February 1991. The main battle tank (MBT) for U.S. armor units in VII Corps was the M1A1 Abrams, which could produce speeds in the 50-mile-per-hour (mph) range and fire with its thermal imagery and laser range finder accurately and lethally out to about 3,000 meters. The premier tank fielded by the Republican Guards during Sabre was the T-72 with a firing range of about 1,500 meters but could not accurately fire (on the same level as the Abrams) while moving. However, there was a variety of other motorized and mechanized equipment that moved with U.S. armor, which could only achieve speeds of approximately 30 mph. This, in turn, reduced the Abrams' ability to maintain top speeds for any lengthy and massed movement.

TACTICAL DESERT MANEUVER

Moreover, U.S. armor specialists found that in war game activities and rehearsals, 12 mph was an optimal speed for an M1A1 Abrams MBT to advance in terms of maximizing both accuracy and in keeping the armored "battle box" formation composed of various field equipment together and synchronized. More specifically, the 12-mph speed for the Abrams tank was one of several smoothly riding interfaces between gear ratios, which provided for optimal firing stability. While there were additional smooth riding points at faster speeds, the 12-mph interface was preferable for linear formations of unlike vehicles in a brigade or a battalion in order to facilitate movement cohesion during an advance. Moreover, controlled speed maximized the opportunity to exploit the superior range of the Abrams, as one preferred to fire when an enemy T-72 was in range (3,000 meters); yet, with the Abrams out of range of the enemy's gun (1,500 meters). Moving too fast in an Abrams with enemy armor buried in the sand to offset thermo imagery advantages by the American crew, one could happen upon a T-72 at 1,200 meters before actually sighting the tank. Thus, speed had to be carefully calibrated in order not to forfeit the competitive advantage in range, accuracy, and lethality.

> Because the M1A1 rode smoothly at that speed [12 mph] its gyro-stabilization was optimized and the tank could fire accurately while moving—this yielded yet another operational capability unheard of in earlier wars: the uninterrupted advance of a great mass of armor firing accurately on the move into a defender who could not hope to achieve the same range or accuracy even from fixed or surveyed positions.[31]

For the first time in history, massed forces were able to coordinate movement through Middle Eastern deserts, to include night maneuver and converge on targets in achieving tactical surprise. The Global Positioning System made possible by U.S. satellites operating in space created a military capability that was unknown to Iraqi commanders during Desert Sabre. This advantage was apparent during the Battle of 73 Easting on February 26, when nine M1A1 Abrams and 12 Bradley fighting vehicles of the U.S. 2nd Armored Cavalry Regiment were tasked with scouting and establishing contact with the main Republican Guard defenses in order to provide battlefield intelligence to headquarters.

The three squadrons of the 2nd Armored Cavalry Regiment came across forward elements of the Tawakalna Infantry (Mechanized) Division of the Republican Guard Forces Command (RGFC) not by road but by crossing the desert. The commander of the Republican Guard units, not knowing the Americans could navigate the desert using satellite signals, and at night, had expected the United States to utilize the roads in their advance. As such, he positioned his forces to defend against an approach via the only road available.

> The Iraqi commander thought it ideal ground from which to defend. Unaware that the American units had received global positioning systems,

he assumed they would move along roads to avoid becoming lost in the featureless desert, thus he organized his defense along the road by fortifying the village with anti-aircraft guns (used in ground-mode), machine guns, and infantry. The defense was fundamentally sound. He took advantage of an imperceptible rise in the terrain that ran perpendicular to the road and directly through the village to organize a "reverse slope" defense on the east side of that ridge. He built two engagement areas, or kill sacks, on the east side of the ridge, north and south of the village, emplaced minefields to disrupt forward movement and dug in approximately 40 tanks and 16 BMPs (infantry fighting vehicles) about 1,000 yards from the ridge, and destroy U.S. forces piecemeal as they moved across the crest.[32]

Coming out of the desert from a direction the Iraqi commander did not think possible, U.S. forces caught the Republican Guard units (Tawakalna Division) by surprise. "In just 23 minutes E Troop destroyed approximately 50 T-72s, 25 armored personnel carriers, 40 trucks and numerous other vehicles, without suffering any casualties."[33]

In addition to the other technological advantages offered by the American Abrams MBT (Chobham armor, low profile, speed, range, and accuracy) was the depleted uranium high-performance M829A1 Service Sabot tank shell. U.S. crews used only training rounds in war games and rehearsals. Operation Desert Sabre was the first time they were allowed to utilize the Sabot tank shell. Any trajectory expectations for ranging the round that occurred during training fell by the wayside, as U.S. crews found the Sabot to be straight and flat as it was fired at their targets. Given that U.S. tanks could acquire and hit their opponents operating Soviet-supplied T-72s at 2,500 to 3,000 meters while the T-72s' maximum range was 1,500 meters, Iraqi tank crews opted to strategically position their tanks in ambush, burying much of the tank in earth with only the turret visible to reduce the thermo-imaging capability of the American tanks.

IRAQI ARMOR TACTICS

The preferred option for Republican Guard tank crews was to position their tanks on the downward rise of terrain, which blocked the Americans' ability to optically range (see and target) forward. Thus, the U.S. tanks would move forward, climbing the slight rise without being able to detect the Iraqi tanks, which for a critical few minutes would be below the Americans' line of sight yet targetable by the Iraqi armor laying in ambush. Once the United States arrived at the crest of the rise and was prepared to descend along the downward slope, the Iraqis who had previously positioned their tanks between 500 and 1,500 meters from the crest would have the opportunity of firing first—prior to the Abrams range finder acquiring the now firing T-72. The sand surrounding the

T-72, essentially burying the tank in sand except for the turret and gun, served to mask the thermal signature being emitted by the tank and its crew.

This tactic used quick speeds being generated by the Abrams to the advantage for the Iraqis, as U.S. armor moved swiftly forward on a rise without first detecting the presence of buried tanks. As the United States moved across the crest, the Iraqi gunners opened up. Thus, since the Iraqis intended to exploit the Americans' penchant for speed, U.S. armor commanders found that a useful remedy to these traps was to proceed with caution while seeking to establish, in advance, the Iraqi ambush positions. This often required working jointly with Apache gunships and USAF A-10 close air support jets (Warthogs) as well as with surveillance aircraft and other equipment providing overhead imagery. When in doubt, a default position was relying on the established optimum speed for large formation advances and firing: 12 mph, which allowed the United States and their allies to carefully scout forward. Conversely to what armor units had learned in training and rehearsals, Schwarzkopf and his staff's operational design was less concerned about losing a limited number of tanks than about losing the Republican Guard as a whole if the left hook did not trap them in the KTO. And to trap the Guard in the KTO would require speeds faster than 12 mph, particularly since CENTCOM planning assumptions included the need to keep armor operations under 100 hours.

Thus, at the strategic level, U.S. policymakers did not wish to allow Saddam to escape with his fangs intact (the Guard's armor). This would only invite further strategic and operational problems in the not too distant future enabling Saddam to survive in a post–Desert Storm Iraq as well as keeping within his tool kit the military capacity for future operations against Saudi Arabia. For Franks, in command of the VII Corps, an additional operational planning assumption was important as well—the need to keep American casualties to a minimum. Franks's assumption was not only tactically and morally sound but also that, at the strategic level, limited U.S. casualties would limit Saddam's ability to use the casualties to discourage the American public. Schwarzkopf and his Jedi Knights obviously sought to keep U.S. and coalition casualties to a minimum as well.

Within the different levels of the continuum of war (strategy, operations, tactics), ideally one seeks to maximize unity of effort. In reality, as was the case with Desert Storm, there is a propensity for friction and significant disagreement regarding assumptions, methods, and how to arrive at the initially agreed-upon aims.

At the operational level, one seeks to organize, maintain, and execute with the commander's intent (Schwarzkopf) as laid out in the operational design or campaign plan. As combat intensifies, previously constructed plans in some briefing room away from the battlefield seem less relevant to the troops and their commanders now under fire. However difficult, tactical execution (Franks) must align with the theater or operational goals, which in turn are aligned with strategic intent and aims. While it may seem at times illogical to follow strategically derived objectives usually generated by civilian political leaders, one needs to keep in mind that even Carl von Clausewitz recognized this main operative principle regarding the conduct of war: "War is a continuation of policy by other means." Those policies, theoretically, have been rationally derived, and thus, the conduct of war must adhere to rationally designed state policy. If it does not, it has the tendency to devolve into unrelated chaotic violence unaccountable and unhinged from its original rational purpose.

In short, there is, or ought to be, a strong preference for tactical leaders in following the operational plan or design as laid out by the operational or theater commander. It becomes incumbent on tactical commanders subordinate to the theater commander to closely adhere to the plan. However, in the Western tradition, and adding to the difficulties, there is also a preference for instilling in tactical commanders an ability for independent decision making on the dispersed battlefield, which in turn generates swiftness of decisive action by allowing flexibility and adaptability contributing to commanders and troops' ability to operate inside an opponent's OODA-Loop. While the Western tactical commander, trained for adaptability, flexibility, and the ability to execute effectively (Auftragstaktik), within the fog and friction of war, is positioned to outperform his or her opponent(s), such independent mindedness can also move beyond the parameters of the operational plan. This is why the communication of the operational commander's original *intent* is critical in achieving unity of effort and unity of command while allowing tactical subordinates needed flexibility.

BATTLE OF AL-BUSAYYAH

These dynamics were clearly on display in the run-up to and action in the Battle of al-Busayyah (Iraq) on February 26, 1991. The operational plan for VII Corps in Desert Sabre called for bypassing pockets of resistance in the timely pursuit, entrapment, and destruction of the Republican Guard. The VII Corps, as planned, would push north 100 miles to the town of al-Busayyah then pivot eastward and seek out and destroy the Guard. However, upon approaching al-Busayyah, the commander of the U.S. 1st Armored Division (subordinate command of Franks's VII Corps), Major General Robert Griffith, realized his line of march, as he approached al-Busayyah in the afternoon of February 25, and took his command directly through the town.

While the town had been strafed and rocketed previously by Apache gunships, al-Busayyah remained actively defended by Iraqi infantry supported by tanks and mechanized armor (Soviet BMPs) still in defensive positions and with orders to protect the town as it served as the headquarters of the Iraqi 26th Infantry Division. Realizing the operational plan was to bypass such an obstacle, Griffith consulted with his superior, General Franks, and requested time to reduce the town in order to enable the 1st Armored to proceed without leaving a force (however small) in its rear to potentially disrupt supply and lines of communication back to bases in Saudi Arabia. Franks concurred with Griffith's decision. On the morning of February 26, the 1st Armored fired 1,500 artillery shells and 350 rockets at the Iraqi positions. The surviving Iraqi soldiers obstinately refused to surrender. At the core of the defenders was an Iraqi Special Forces battalion that, in coordination with a regular Iraqi infantry battalion, two armored brigades, and one company of T-55 tanks, remained ensconced in their positions although in a somewhat reduced state following the 1st Armored artillery and rocket barrage.

Schwarzkopf, famous throughout the U.S. Army for a temper that brought him the moniker "Stormin Norman," was none too pleased. Griffith, now under orders from Franks, who had received pointed directions from Schwarzkopf to move forward, left a small tank force to deal with the obstinate Iraqi defenders, as U.S. airpower was brought to bear on an approaching Iraqi relief column aiming to reinforce the defenders at al-Busayyah. The Iraqi relief column never made it.

The tension and friction between the three levels of war are present even among the most competent of political leaders, strategic-level military commanders, and their operational and tactical commanders. An advantage for the coalition during Operation Desert Shield/Desert Storm/ Desert Sabre was the level of experience and competence of the political leadership of the United States coupled with the unparalleled military proficiency of the officers and men (and women) who served in the coalition. The level of competence and experience was mirrored by the British, French, and within the ranks of many of the Arab coalition partners.

Franks and Schwarzkopf remained at odds and offered dueling accounts in the years that preceded Desert Storm/Desert Sabre.[34] The U.S. system with the expectation of the primacy of the operational plan and commander's intent juxtaposed with a strong preference for flexible, independent decision making among both senior and junior officers was the main cause of the friction rather than either of the two outstanding U.S. commanders, who, in pursuing their duty as they had been trained, brought about one of the most remarkable ground campaigns in either American or world history.

In the end, over a period of 43 days of offensive operations, Desert Storm/Desert Sabre rained destruction upon Saddam's armed forces. Forty-two Iraqi Divisions were either destroyed or degraded to the point of being unable to conduct combat operations. Additionally, the entire Iraqi navy was sunk, and 50 percent of Iraqi combat aircraft were destroyed or forced into Iran, while 82,000 Iraqi troops were taken prisoners.

When the air operations started I had 39 tanks. After 38 days of the air battle I had 32 tanks. After 20 minutes against the 2nd Armored Cavalry Regiment, I had zero tanks.[35]

The success of allied forces in Operation Desert Storm convinced the Soviets that integration of control, communications, electronic combat and delivery of conventional fires had been realized for the first time.[36]

Arab forces, in an apparent nod by the Americans toward public diplomacy, were the first to enter a liberated Kuwait City, as thousands of Iraqi forces attempted to escape north along Highway 8 only to be met by strafing and bombing runs conducted by coalition aircraft. As the images of the carnage made it into the international media with the headlines of "the highway of death," President Bush called a halt to combat operations. The coalition ground campaign, Operation Desert Sabre, lasted from February 24 to February 28, when a cessation of hostilities was declared by coalition forces, for a total of 114 hours.

It never appeared in the press or in public discussions, but the Israeli finding in the 1967 Six-Day War—that armor combat operations have about 100 hours' window of opportunity before maintenance issues and expected breakdowns begin to interfere perceptibly with operations—was part of the planning assumptions. This is not to say that this dynamic was solely responsible for constraining U.S. armor to 100 hours of combat drive time. With the escape north of the Hammurabi Republican Guard Division and the open media coverage of the carnage along the "highway of death," as conscripted Iraqi young men facing strafing runs by coalition aircraft tried to escape from the KTO, U.S. NCA believed the time was right to end the bloodshed.[37]

Moreover, there was concern within the coalition that operations that extended beyond the original UN mandate of removing Iraqi occupation troops from Kuwait would lead to a fracturing of the unity that had thus far been achieved. The remarkable unity of the vast coalition of nations in support of Desert Shield and Desert Storm was a fundamental strength for combat operations, and many considered it a center of gravity for both campaigns. The Iraqi leadership rightly sought to degrade and neutralize this center of gravity. Additionally, while the coalition enjoyed world-class harbor facilities and a massive logistical effort to maintain a coalition that numbered in the hundreds of thousands, the fact remained that by chasing the fleeing Iraqi army north into Iraq itself would have reduced supply capabilities and opened up vulnerabilities, as combat forces became extended and quite possibly fractured the coalition.

> Logistic units were hard pressed to keep up with the rapid pace of maneuver units. Both logistics structure and doctrine were found wanting in the high temp offensive operation. HET and off-road truck mobility were limited, and MSRs into Iraq few and constricted. Had the operation lasted longer, maneuver forces would have out run their fuel and other support.[38]

On a daily basis the supply and logistical requirements of Desert Storm/Desert Sabre were 62,500 cases of Meals-Ready-To-Eat (MREs), 9 million gallons of water, 4,800 fuel tankers with 5,000 gallon capacities, and 450 tractor trailer loads of other supplies. By the end of Desert Storm/Desert Sabre, U.S. forces alone (532,000 personnel) consumed 95,000 tons of ammunition and 1.7 billion gallons of fuel.

CEASE-FIRE AND THE DISCUSSIONS AT SAFWAN

It became a strategic-level decision endorsed by the president that the campaign against Iraqi forces in the KTO should be terminated upon the successful conclusion of a cease-fire agreement. For the United States, the nature of war termination involving the 1991 Persian Gulf War (Desert Storm/Desert Sabre) created problems that would have to be sorted out in the future. First, politics and war, as much as many would prefer to see these two subjects separated, cannot be excluded from one another. It is, therefore, preferable to have a close synchronization of national policy making, diplomacy and finance-economics with battlefield operations. This is not to advocate that politicians, diplomats, and bankers direct armies in the field or even weigh in on operational or military strategy.

However, if the United States had created a team of diplomats that was prepared to engage in negotiations after the coalition had ejected Iraqi forces from Kuwait, General Schwarzkopf would not have gone into the cease-fire discussions without instructions from the NCA. The team of diplomats would not have been isolated at the U.S. State Department but would have been part of the coalition team being provided briefings by intelligence and military specialists as to operational and tactical developments. These individuals would also be apprised of developments related to statecraft as well as receiving instructions from the executive branch. Yet it was left to the operational military commander to negotiate the cease-fire agreement. Schwarzkopf settled for the presence of two Iraqi generals when he called for a high-level meeting at the Iraqi Safwan airfield just over the border from Kuwait. Saddam later boasted that Bush yielded in the war, not Iraq, as the Iraqi leader had never requested terms.

In any event, Schwarzkopf prepared for the discussions at Safwan without detailed instructions from either the NCA or State Department. The first problem arose when he was informed by his staff that Safwan, although previously reported that the airfield had been taken by Franks and VII Corps, had not, in fact, been taken. Schwarzkopf and Franks apparently had difficulties in the communication process as Desert Shield/Desert Storm/Desert Sabre unfolded. This was quickly remedied. Upon receiving orders from Schwarzkopf to take Safwan, elements of VII Corps succeeded in swiftly securing the base, although, upon arriving, U.S. forces were faced with obstinate Iraqi commanders. Exasperated, the American officer in charge refused to enter into negotiations, as the Iraqis hoped that by stalling, help would soon arrive. The American officer reportedly stated, "Leave by 1600 or we will kill you." Negotiations having concluded, the Iraqis opted to depart the area.

On March 3, 1991, Schwarzkopf met with the Iraqi generals at Safwan airfield and discussed the nature of the cease-fire. As the Iraqi delegation initially balked at the terms of the U.S.-proposed cease-fire, eyewitness accounts state that a flight of four Apache helicopter gunships flew low over the tent where the meeting was being held. Apparently, the Apaches had had a devastating impact during the course of the war on Iraqi

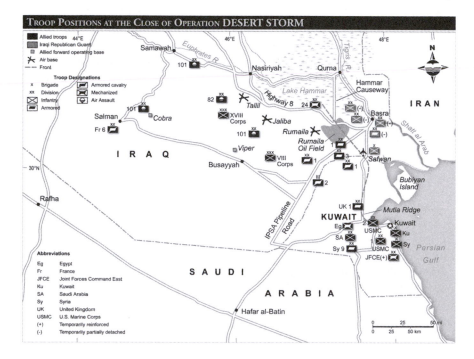

ground forces. After the Apache flyby, the two Iraqi generals reportedly dropped their hesitancy and became more agreeable. Perhaps it was not completely void of value to have Schwarzkopf in the lead of the cease-fire negotiations.

In terms of the cease-fire itself, allied forces would remain in defensive positions, and Iraqi forces would be allowed to withdraw (without equipment or supplies). No Iraqi aircraft would be allowed to operate in areas near U.S. forces. However, Schwarzkopf agreed to allow the Iraqi military to fly helicopter gunships. The Iraqi generals were apparently surprised at this concession, and one reportedly asked, "So you mean even helicopters that are armed can fly in the Iraqi skies?"[39] Affirmative, was the reply.

Here, unfortunately, began a series of missteps that allowed Saddam to remain in power for another dozen years. Following the cease-fire agreement, President Bush sought to incite the people of Iraq to rise up and overthrow Saddam's regime. Many attempted to do so, believing American help would be forthcoming. It was not. Saddam's military and security forces (including the Republican Guard) used helicopter gunships in suppressing the uprisings, which occurred mostly in the Kurdish regions in the North and in the Shiite regions in the South. If Bush wanted to create a strategic policy of supporting the Iraqi people in terms of a general insurrection, his administration should have shared this with its operational commander prior to Schwarzkopf engaging in cease-fire arrangements—a heads-up that would have allowed him to think through the implications of allowing the Iraqi military to suppress its people by engaging population centers with helicopter gunships.

> The untidy end to the conflict showed that it is not enough to plan a war. Civilians and military officials must also plan for the peace that follows.[40]

A synchronization of all elements of national power, "MIDLIFE" (military, intelligence, diplomatic, law enforcement, information, finance, economics), is as much required in war termination as it is in the general exercise of statecraft and national policy. President Bush had addressed the people of the United States after Iraq invaded Kuwait in the summer of 1990. In that address, he presented U.S. national policy goals:

> Four simple principles guide our policy: we seek immediate, complete, and unconditional withdrawal of all Iraqi forces from Kuwait. Second, restoration of Kuwait's legitimate government to replace the puppet regime. Third, security and stability of Saudi Arabia and the Persian Gulf; and fourth, safety and protection of the lives of American citizens abroad.[41]

This proclamation followed in the tradition of the Carter Doctrine presented in January 1980, in which the United States considered the security of the Persian Gulf to be in the vital interest of the nation. Following the Carter Doctrine, first the Rapid Deployment Force, then CENTCOM, consolidated under Reagan provided the tools in which to enforce national policy. Containment instituted under Harry S. Truman and shored up under Dwight D. Eisenhower for the long haul positioned the United States under Reagan to institute rollback policies, which led to the willingness on the part of the Soviet Union to end confrontation and create a more constructive dialogue. For decades, the United States was constrained in its ability to influence events in the Middle East due to the threat of Soviet military intervention. This threat was dissolved by the time the UN Security Council began deliberations regarding Iraqi aggression against Kuwait in the summer of 1990. For Saddam, who traditionally relied on Soviet military equipment and power, now found himself exposed on both the regional and international stage.

The Bush administration then, through an expansive diplomatic campaign, aligned the United Nations and the regional players for a finely tuned and highly synchronized coalition effort. However, the president as well as his operational commander, Schwarzkopf, failed in the achievement of what both considered a necessary outcome of Operations Desert Storm and Desert Sabre—the destruction of the Iraqi Republican Guard in the KTO. It was not only helicopter gunships that allowed Saddam to crush the uprisings in the years that followed the close of the 1991 Persian Gulf War but also the RGFC that remained an effective force for Saddam's continuing control of Iraq through the suppression of its people and later when Saddam sent the Republican Guard south to intimate Kuwait and Saudi Arabia. This was acutely on the mind of Schwarzkopf as well as of the president in the weeks leading up to the ground phase.

> The first thing that we are going to have to do is, I don't like the word "decapitate," so I think I will use the word "attack," leadership, and go after his command and control. Number two, we've got to gain and maintain air superiority. Number three, we need to cut totally his supply lines. We also need to destroy his biological and nuclear capability. And finally ... we need to destroy, not attack, not damage, not surround—I want you to destroy the Republican Guard. When you are done with them, I don't want them to be an effective fighting force anymore. I don't want them to exist as a military organization.[42]

The Hammurabi Armored Division of the Republican Guard—a key target of Operation Desert Sabre that escaped the grasp of Schwarzkopf and Franks—was sent back to within 12 miles of the Iraq-Kuwait border, where on October 3, 1994, Saddam used the Hammurabi Armored as well as the al Nida Division, also of the RGFC, along with 40,000 other troops assigned to the Basra southern sector of Iraq, in an attempt to coerce the United States into dropping the oil sanctions that had effectively barred Baghdad from selling it on the open international market. Kuwait responded by deploying most of its 16,000-man army to the border. U.S.

President Bill Clinton (who succeeded Bush as president in 1993) and his Secretary of Defense William Perry spent much of their time dealing with Saddam's intransigence regarding sanctions, violence against the Iraqi citizens, and his refusal to honor the terms of the cease-fire agreement signed at Safwan in 1991.

In order to protect the Kurdish population in the North and the Shiites in the South, the United States and international allies imposed no-fly zones above northern and southern Iraq.[43] Saddam spent much of the 1990s resisting the imposition of the no-fly zones and in refusing to co-operate with UN inspectors attempting to ascertain the nature of his chemical, biological, and nuclear programs. During an expected visit by former U.S. President Bush to Kuwait, on April 14–16, 1993, Kuwaiti security personnel discovered evidence that Saddam's intelligence service had placed a small van loaded with 180 pounds of high explosives, detonators, timing devices, and other bomb components in an assassination attempt. Kuwait apprehended 14 suspects and eventually sentenced 6 to death (5 Iraqis and 1 Kuwaiti). One of the Iraqis testified that the Iraqi government was behind the plot.

The United States dispatched Federal Bureau of Investigation (FBI) and other intelligence personnel to Kuwait to ascertain the facts in the case and to conduct an independent investigation. Those sent reported on June 24, 1993, that the Kuwaitis had solid reasons and evidence in convicting the six and attributed the attempted plot to Iraqi intelligence operating under orders from Saddam. On June 26, the USS *Peterson*—a Spruance-class destroyer operating in the Red Sea—and the USS *Chancellorsville*, a Ticonderoga-class cruiser on station in the Persian Gulf were ordered by President Clinton to fire tomahawk cruise missiles (20 feet in length, with a 1,000-pound high explosive warhead, 550 mph flying 50 feet off the ground, and a 700-mile range) in response. Twenty-three missiles were launched and 20 landed on target: the headquarters building of the Iraqi intelligence agency responsible for the Kuwait assassination plot. Three days later, a U.S. F-4G "Wild Weasel" fired a high-speed, anti-radiation missile (HARM) at an Iraqi radar in response to threatening moves against U.S. aircraft patrolling the UN-approved southern no-fly zone over Iraq.

As early as 1991 and 1992, the UN Security Council described Iraqi behavior as material breaches of the cease-fire agreements. On December 27, 1992, the United States shot down an Iraqi jet that had violated the no-fly zone in southern Iraq. Following this, Iraq deployed 8 SA-3 and 12 SA-2 antiaircraft missile launchers in the no-fly zone and operated them in a manner threatening coalition aircraft patrolling the zone.

Operation Vigilant Warrior was part of the U.S. response to Iraq's violation, which envisioned sending 350 additional combat aircraft coupled with 18,000 members of the 1st MEF and 16,000 troops of the 24th Infantry (Mechanized) Division. An additional 156,000 troops were placed on alert. All of this was in response to Saddam's movement of the Hammurabi and al Nida Republican Guard Divisions, which joined 40,000 other Iraqi troops in the vicinity of Basra and the Iraq-Kuwait border.

> Iraq has not fully complied with the terms of the ceasefire agreements that followed the expulsion of Iraqi forces from Kuwait in early 1991. Several Iraqi violations of ceasefire provisions have resulted in brief military confrontations between Iraq and the United States, supported in some cases by other allied forces. Iraqi violations prompting a U.S. military response have fallen into four general categories: obstruction of UN weapons inspection teams, involvement in international terrorist acts, failure to abide by the air exclusion zones imposed by the allies over parts of Iraq, and troop movements that could threaten Kuwait or internal targets of repression by the Iraqi government.[44]

By 1997, international support for use of force against Saddam had eroded sufficiently so that only when the Iraqi regime threatened Kuwait did U.S. diplomats find any interest in taking action.[45] Iraq refused to allow U.S. or British citizens to be members of the UN inspection teams, and by January 16, 1998, Saddam threatened to expel every UN weapons inspector irrespective of nationality, unless all sanctions against Iraq were eliminated within six months. The United States continued to fly air patrols over Kurdish Iraq in the North and Shiite Iraq in the South. And, on occasion Iraqi surface-to-air systems would lock on to coalition aircraft and in some instances fire a missile at the overhead aircraft. Remarkably no coalition aircraft were shot down by the SAMs, although allied aircraft flew patrols protecting Kurds and Shiites over a period of years.

In the midst of this environment, and as the United States stood increasingly alone in the Middle East, terrorist attacks aimed at America and Americans began proliferating and took on a brazenly new level of violence and lethality against U.S. interests in the region and around the world.

Chapter 8

Containing Saddam, Jihad in Afghanistan, and Terrorist Attacks on the U.S. Homeland

Jihad is central to the Muslim perception of the world, dividing it into *dar al-Islam* (abode of Islam) and *dar al-harb* (abode of war) which is destined to come under Islamic rule. Jihad purifies the *dar al-Islam* and is the tool to shrink and eradicate the *dar al-harb*. As a doctrine, the aim of jihad is clear: to establish God's rule on earth by compelling non-Muslims to embrace Islam, or force them to accept second-class status, if not eradicate them altogether.[1]

Since the September 11 attacks, America is safer, but we are not yet safe. We have done much to degrade al-Qaida and its affiliates and to undercut the perceived legitimacy of terrorism. Our Muslim partners are speaking out against those who seek to use their religion to justify violence and a totalitarian vision of the world.[2]

Iraq formally accepted the terms of the cease-fire on March 3, 1991, which required international inspection teams' unfettered access to all sites and facilities across Iraq for the identification and eventual destruction of Saddam Hussein's chemical, biological, and nuclear programs, including delivery systems and ballistic missiles with ranges beyond 150 miles. In support of these objectives, the UN Security Council enacted Resolution 687 describing the steps toward the elimination of Iraq's programs, systems, and weapons, which included the creation of a special commission, UNSCOM, to inspect all facilities with the caveat that all weapons and weapons-related research and components were to be turned over to UNSCOM inspectors. On April 6, 1991, Iraq accepted the terms of UN Security Council Resolution 687.

At the end of the Gulf War (1991), Iraq formally admitted to 280 tons of mustard gas, 75 tons of Sarin, 500 tons of Tabun, 1,481 chemical artillery shells and bombs, and 30 chemical Scud warheads. They did not disclose how much was destroyed during the war. Two days later, the European Union (EU) and the United States enacted a no-fly zone code-named Operation Provide Comfort in northern Iraq for the protection of the Kurdish minority against acts of reprisals and in the expectation of the U.S. government that internal forces within Iraq would attempt to oust Saddam in the months following the end of the 1991 Gulf War. The United States also ordered Baghdad to cease all military activities in these northern regions. The Kurds, with Iranian encouragement, had rebelled against Baghdad, and the Iraqi central government responded with bombing and strafing attacks from the air against civilian targets, which included the use of chemical weapons.

On August 26, 1992, the allies imposed a no-fly zone code-named Operation Southern Watch over the southern region of Iraq in order to protect the Shiites. The Shiites while representing the majority population in Iraq (relative to the Sunnis and the Kurds) were underrepresented in the Ba'athist regime under Saddam, and after exhortations by American politicians following the Gulf War aimed at having the Shiites rise up against Saddam's regime, the United States sought to provide air cover. Similar to the Kurdish situation in northern Iraq, the government in Baghdad had traditionally and at times violently suppressed what it deemed to be rebellious acts or intentions by the Shiites in the South.

Saddam sought to blur the issue of the invasion of Kuwait and split the coalition by arguing that part of the rationale was in generating leverage to compel the West to force Israel in making concessions to the Palestinians. In doing so, Saddam and his planners hoped to frame the struggle with Kuwait in such a way that other Arab leaders who may have been considering the issue of intervention on behalf of the Kuwaitis by joining the U.S. coalition during Desert Storm would find it difficult to align against Saddam's plan to "benefit" the cause of the Palestinians at the expense of the Zionists. This attempt failed on two levels. First, the United States and its coalition partners were able to generate an effective counter media campaign utilizing established and well-controlled media "pools" whereby U.S. authorities were able to oversee the unfolding strategic narrative. This media effort arose from lessons learned during the Vietnam War in which Ho Chi Minh, General Vo Nguyen Giap, and others outmaneuvered the United States not on any battlefield but in the capture and formulating of a strategic narrative that exploited the freedom afforded to America's media. This barrage of information and images in support of the communist enterprise in Vietnam reduced the will of the American people in terms of their support for an ill-defined and, at times, ill-conceived American strategy in Southeast Asia in the late 1960s and early 1970s.

A multitude of Arab states sent forces to reverse Saddam's invasion and, following Desert Storm, Syria accepted the principle of direct dialogue with Israel for peace.[3] Although it was a productive turn of events, the negotiations failed to result in a peace treaty. President George H. W. Bush pressed Israel to conduct negotiations with the Palestinians and the Arab states in an attempt at moving the peace process forward. Israeli Prime Minister Yitzhak Shamir agreed but refused to participate if the Palestine Liberation Organization (PLO) was to be included and declined to have Palestinian independence or statehood as formal topics on the agenda. The negotiations took place during the multilateral Madrid Conference, on October 30–November 1, 1991.

As with many of the Palestinian-Israeli negotiations and meetings, the failure to produce results led to increasing levels of frustration. As was a common pattern, the United States was pressed to initiate talks between the Palestinians and Israelis ostensibly to reduce tension over the issues.[4] For a short period this indeed led to a decrease in tension—until the end of the talks, which invariably led to some degree of disappointment. This, in turn, raised the tension levels along with the proclivity for violence. The extreme positions within the Palestinian camp that demanded the dissolution of the State of Israel served to undermine any attempts at accommodation, while Israel found itself repeatedly unable to reach an accord or compromise by the demands of those within the Jewish state demanding that Israel "must" expand until it acquired all the territory that encompassed the ancient "Land of Israel." The hard-line factions within both the Israelis (and their external supporters) and the Palestinians (and their external supporters) were better at undermining peace than were the moderate factions within both groups at establishing a just and lasting peace.

Following the failure of the Madrid Conference in 1991, the PLO was faced with challengers who believed that it had become insufficiently violent in its operational methods, and Hamas (Islamic Resistance Movement) and Islamic Jihad began agitating for the mantle of Palestinian leadership. The PLO, founded in 1964 for the specific purpose of the liberation of Palestine through armed irregular struggle, had apparently become overly sedate for the militant Islamist factions and their wealthy supporters. The United States and Israel had designated the PLO a terrorist group; however, following the Madrid Conference they dropped it from the terrorist list. Islamic Jihad, or originally the Egyptian Islamic

Jihad (EIJ), was responsible for the assassination of Egypt's President Anwar Sadat, who had the temerity of making peace with Israel.

The Palestinian Islamic Jihad (PIJ) was founded in 1981 with the primary objective of the destruction of the State of Israel and the establishment of a sovereign Islamic Palestinian state within the geographical borders of pre-1948 Mandatory Palestine. The PIJ rejects any compromise and any negotiated peace process with Israel, believing that a Palestinian state can only result from the use of force. The armed wing of the PIJ is the Al Quds Brigades, which receives direct support from Hezbollah and Iran. Both Hamas and the PIJ were offshoots of the Muslim Brotherhood, which briefly took control of Egypt in June 2012.

COLLAPSE OF THE TURKESTAN MILITARY DISTRICT AND THE SPREAD OF VIOLENT JIHAD

The Madrid Conference was cosponsored by the United States and the Soviet Union and marked one of the last official Middle East-related acts of the Union of Soviet Socialist Republics (USSR). By the end of December 1991, the Soviet Union collapsed and a massive immigration of Jews from the USSR brought 700,000 additional Jews into Israel. With the collapse of the Soviet Union came the collapse of the Turkestan Military District, which projected Soviet power throughout the soft geographical "underbelly" of the USSR and encompassed the Muslim nations of Central Asia that at the time were socialist republics contained within the Soviet Union and under the control of Moscow.

These states—Uzbekistan, Kazakhstan, Kyrgyzstan, Tajikistan, and Turkmenistan—came into being by Soviet decree. In the "non-Slavic south" of the former Soviet Union, under the control of the Turkestan Military District for 70 years, a vacuum was created in the 1990s with the dissolution of the USSR, and militant Islamist groups believed that an opportunity to erect a regional caliphate in the space of the collapsing Soviet military district had arrived. And, of course, the mujahedeen and their supporters in the Soviet-Afghan War in the 1980s claimed that it was Allah who had struck down the Soviet Union by means of the resistance in Afghanistan. And it was Allah who would now insure a caliphate be established in Central Asia. Moscow moved quickly to establish the Commonwealth of Independent States (CIS)—a loose grouping of the former Soviet republics—in an attempt to fill the gap and vacuum of power, as the Turkestan Military District ceased to exist on June 30, 1992.

However, in 1992, the Russian-backed government of Tajikistan was driven from Dushanbe (the nation's capital) by the Islamic Renaissance Party (IRP). The West, in addition to China, became concerned that militant Islamist groups might sweep into power throughout Central Asia, ultimately creating a regional caliphate in what was referred to by professional geographers as the "non-Slavic south" of the Soviet Union, or Muslim Central Asia. This worry led China to enter negotiations with Kazakhstan in 1994, as both countries were concerned that with the fall of the USSR and the weakness of Russia, the immediate aftermath would lead to instability in Central Asia on China's back door. These negotiations were conducted under the auspices of the "Shanghai 5," a group founded on April 26, 1996. The original Shanghai 5 consisted of China, Kazakhstan, Kyrgyzstan, Russia, and Tajikistan and eventually evolved into the establishment on June 15, 2001, of the larger Shanghai Cooperation Organization (SCO).

Iran and India are both observer nations within the SCO, with Iran seeking full membership, which, if consummated, could theoretically provide Russian and Chinese military protection to Iran. The introduction of Chinese or Russian troops into the Middle East would circumvent U.S. efforts of the last half century and run directly and diametrically opposed to the principles and spirit of the Carter Doctrine. Through 2015, China and Russia have been cautious toward bestowing full-member status to Iran.

The weakness of post–Soviet Russia's position in Muslim Central Asia also worried the Soviet-era authoritarian leaders of the Central Asian republics. The raging civil war in Tajikistan convinced the leaders of Kazakhstan, Kyrgyzstan, and Turkmenistan to sign North Atlantic Treaty Organization's (NATO) Partnership for Peace (PfP) in 1994, with Uzbekistan joining in 1996 and Tajikistan signing on in February 2002. This did not extend NATO Article 5 protection to PfP members (an "attack against one is an attack against all"—collective protection for all full members), but it did allow for training and rotation of forces into the Central Asian republics to act as a deterrent against Islamist forces.

THE TALIBAN IN AFGHANISTAN AND THEIR LINKS WITH ARAB MILITANTS

Along with the raging civil war in Tajikistan, fighting was raging within Afghanistan. The Soviet-Afghan War (1979–1989), in which the United States along with partners Saudi Arabia and Pakistan provided support to the mujahedeen against the USSR, had ended with the withdrawal of Soviet forces in 1989. This was quickly followed by a civil war (1989–2001) where the forces of the mujahedeen aligned with various factions to fight for control over Afghanistan. By 1994, the Taliban (*talib*—student/*Taliban*—plural) had garnered sufficient resources from Pakistan and Saudi Arabia to enable it to go on the offensive in factional infighting within Afghanistan.

The Taliban began attacking local warlords and generated a growing following fostered by its military success and the pledge to clean up Afghanistan, enforce God's will, and end corruption. After taking Kandahar in late 1994, the Taliban captured a large supply of modern weapons, including fighter aircraft, tanks, and helicopters. By September 1996, the Taliban occupied Kabul and had taken approximately 80 percent of the country while one of its more powerful opponents, the Northern Alliance, under Ahmad Shah Massoud, had control of the northern 20 percent.

It was during this time that the leadership of the Taliban expanded its links with Arab Islamist militants who previously aided a wide variety of anti-USSR mujahedeen factions against the Soviets and made common cause with the Middle Eastern group led by Osama bin Laden's al-Qaeda, allowing them to set up training bases in Afghanistan. In 1997, Pakistan, Saudi Arabia, and the United Arab Emirates recognized the Taliban as the legitimate government in Afghanistan. While Pakistan's exact role in the rise of the Taliban remains unclear, Pakistan understandably had, and continues to have, a strong interest in the degree of stability of its neighbor to the west. As a result of this concern, Pakistan upon becoming an independent nation in 1947 developed significant levels of influence within Afghanistan, which could then be leveraged to constrain attempts by external powers to control the region or in internal groups hostile to its interests taking power. However, its greatest concern was any increase of influence within its western neighbor by its chief rival residing to the east: India.

Al-Qaeda leader Laden was the son of a Saudi construction company billionaire, Mohammed bin Awad bin Laden, and studied at a Saudi university until 1979 (age 22), when he opted to join the mujahedeen in Pakistan for the purpose of fighting the Soviets in Afghanistan. In 1988, at age 33, bin Laden formed al-Qaeda (Arabic for the Base). The Central Intelligence Agency (CIA) had maintained a database of individuals and tribes catalogued for the purpose of undermining the Soviet occupation of Afghanistan during the Soviet-Afghan War, which was also referred to as "The Base." It is not clear at this time whether the CIA database directly or indirectly influenced the decision of bin Laden to describe the new organization as *the Base*.

When Saddam invaded Kuwait, bin Laden offered to bring forces into the Kingdom of Saudi Arabia to protect the holy sites. The monarchy refused his offer and instead turned to the United States, which served to anger bin Laden, as the "infidels" would now be allowed to defend Mecca and Medina or possibly occupy the lands surrounding the holy cities. As bin Laden subsequently involved himself in undermining the legitimacy and stability of the government of Saudi Arabia, the Saudi king eventually was compelled to banish bin Laden from the kingdom. Bin Laden then sought refuge among fellow radical militants in the African nation of the Sudan. Under the combined pressure of the United States and Saudi Arabia, Sudan forced his departure in 1996, and bin Laden (then 39) settled in Afghanistan. He was an incensed and angry individual in terms of the Saudi monarchy and its strongest supporter, the United States, and he was heir to a personal fortune from family inheritance estimated at about $300 million.

After establishing a base within Afghanistan, bin Laden took to issuing *fatwas* (declarations of war) against the United States for a number of reasons, the most prominent of which was the continuing presence of U.S. personnel within Saudi Arabia (albeit in drastically reduced numbers from the days of Desert Storm). The jihadists had drawn great inspiration from their victory over Soviet forces in Afghanistan; in their minds it was Allah who foreordained their success. Moreover, with the fall of the USSR in December 1991, they were looking forward to establishing a Muslim caliphate upon the ashes of the Soviet Turkestan Military District in largely Muslim Central Asia. Subsequent moves by the United States and NATO allies (including Turkey), working in conjunction with the authoritarian leaders of the Central Asian republics such as the NATO PfP program, put a halt to the desired Islamist expansion and, by doing so, created increased levels of animosity at the West in general and the United States in particular. Added to the increasing levels of disenchantment with America was the rapid and decisive outcome of the 1991 Persian Gulf War (Desert Storm/Desert Sabre) whereby the Muslim victory over the Soviet Union was eclipsed by the rapid defeat of what had become (arguably) the most powerful Arab army in the Middle East by Western arms.[5]

SADDAM RENEGES ON 1991 GULF WAR CEASE-FIRE AGREEMENTS

In Iraq, although Saddam had committed to allowing full access to his weapons programs as a condition of the cease-fire, he subsequently reneged on that pledge and began offering Russia increased involvement in Iraq's oil and defense sectors. Without such cooperation and without full access, given a continuing pattern of Iraqi subterfuge and deceit, the United States under the Clinton administration adopted the position that the only way it was going to find out the status of any weapons of mass destruction (WMD) projects or weapons inventory was to remove the regime from power. The U.S. government, under President Bill Clinton, came to the conclusion that regime change was necessary in Iraq.

U.S. concerns included what Saddam's government was working on and what it had achieved in terms of WMD, and, with the obfuscation and general non-cooperation with UN weapons inspectors on the part of the regime, there was no way in establishing any reasonable degree of confidence what was, in fact, going on within the country in terms of WMD. However, the overriding and most compelling concerns were the chemical munitions supplied to Iraq, surreptitiously by the United States and the West during the Iran-Iraq War. The status of this inventory and its ultimate destruction compelled the United States to either establish with certainty or, given the refusal of the regime to cooperate, assist the establishment of a new government, which would provide access to establish an accounting as to the exact inventory and other WMD clandestine programs.

In the aftermath of the Gulf War and throughout 1991 and 1992, Iraq resisted efforts by UNSCOM to fully inspect the sites that needed to be carefully scrutinized. From Saddam's perspective, the oil embargo had to be lifted. For the United States, it wanted Saddam's complete co-operation regarding WMD, as agreed to in the 1991 Gulf War cease-fire accords, or it wanted Saddam ousted. In January 1993, following the loss of the U.S. presidential elections of Bush to Clinton, Iraq began military incursions into the demilitarized zone between Iraq and Kuwait and increased its military activity in both the northern and southern no-fly zones. On January 19, 1993, U.S. President Bush, on his last day in office, ordered a tomahawk cruise missile strike on the Zaafaraniya Nuclear Fabrication and Industrial Complex in the Baghdad suburbs, in a strike that also targeted other military facilities.

One month later, a Ryder rental van was driven by, at the time, unknown terrorists into the basement (B-2 level) of the North Tower of the World Trade Center in New York City on February 26, 1993. Inside the rental truck was a 1,300-pound bomb of complex design. The munition was a urea nitrate-hydrogen gas-enhanced bomb, with aluminum, magnesium, and ferric oxide particles surrounding the explosive. The charge utilized nitroglycerin and ammonium nitrate dynamite and included three tanks of bottled hydrogen configured in a circular framework around the main charge. This served to enhance the fireball and the afterburn of the solid metal shrapnel particles.

The use of compressed gas cylinders was similar in design to the bomb detonated during the 1983 Beirut barracks bombing, which killed 220 U.S. Marines and 21 other American service personnel. Both of the attacks (the 1993 World Trade Center truck bombing and the 1983 Beirut barracks truck bomb attack) used compressed gas cylinders to create fuel-air and thermobaric bombs, releasing more energy than conventional high explosives. Only once before the 1993 World Trade Center terrorist attack had the Federal Bureau of Investigation (FBI) recorded a bomb using urea nitrate—this occurred in the Iran-supported 1983 attack on the Marine barracks. The group that ultimately formed into Hezbollah (under Iranian influence) carried out the attack.

The attack on the World Trade Center in 1993 was led by Ramzi Yousef, and financing for the operation had been funneled to his group by Yousef's uncle, Khalid Sheikh Mohammed, who later served as the principal architect of the September 11, 2001, terrorist attacks in New York and at the Pentagon. The intent was for the detonation to bring down the North Tower, and, as it collapsed, the hope was that it would then crash into the South Tower bringing it down as well. While the blast sent smoke up 93 floors, killed 6 people, and injured 1,000 more, the North Tower did not fall. However, the massive blast caused significant structural damage. Yousef had spent time at al-Qaeda training camps in Afghanistan, and planning for the attack in February 1993 had begun in 1991.

Two months later after the attack in New York, on April 13, 1993, Kuwaiti security personnel uncovered a plot by Iraq's intelligence service (*Jihaz Al-Mukhabarat Al-Amma*), known as the Mukhabarat, to assassinate both former President Bush and the Emir of Kuwait. Sixteen individuals were subsequently arrested in Kuwait, and the U.S. government dispatched both FBI and CIA officers to ascertain the validity of the charges. Two individuals confessed to being involved in a plot sponsored by the Mukhabarat, and U.S. Attorney General Janet Reno and CIA Director R. James Woolsey presented formal reports to U.S. President Clinton.

Clinton subsequently authorized a cruise missile strike on the headquarters of the Mukhabarat. On June 26, 1993, 23 tomahawk cruise missiles were launched by the USS *Peterson* (DD-696) and the USS *Chancellorsville* (CG-62) at the Mukhabarat complex in the Mansour district in Baghdad, with 16 of the missiles landing on the buildings, 3 missing their mark and hitting a residential section (killing a dozen civilians), and 4 unaccounted for.

In 1993, secret negotiations were underway between a group of Israeli academics and PLO officials, in which an interim body, the Palestinian Authority (PA), was created for the purpose of conducting limited government operations in part of the occupied territories in a phased attempt leading to a permanent peace settlement. These arrangements became part of the 1993 *Oslo Accords* where the PA was given control over some West Bank cities, but Israel's military maintained control over 60 percent of the West Bank itself. In 1993, Israeli Prime Minister Yitzhak Rabin and PLO Chairman Yasser Arafat publicly shook hands at the behest of President Clinton on the Oslo Accords. This was followed in 1995 by Israel and the PLO signing the Oslo II agreements under which Israel passed security control to the PA in parts of the occupied territories.

For his commitment toward peace in the Middle East, Rabin was assassinated by Jewish ultranationalist, Yigal Amir, on November 4, 1995.

In Iraq, Saddam continued with his deceptive and general noncooperative behavior with UNSCOM inspection teams and by the fall of 1994 argued that Iraq had fulfilled all requirements of the cease-fire accords and was in complete compliance with applicable UN Security Council resolutions. Saddam then demanded that the oil embargo that had been in place since 1990 (Desert Shield) be lifted or, minimally, that a firm timetable for removal be established. Simultaneously, he threatened to halt all cooperation with UNSCOM inspection teams and began deploying elite troops near the Kuwaiti border. In response, President Clinton authorized Operation Vigilant Warrior, as the 1st Brigade of the 24th Infantry Division (Mechanized) based at Fort Stewart in Georgia was deployed drawing prepositioned equipment in Kuwait. Upon arrival of the 1st Brigade and as other U.S. military units made preparations for getting under way (October 1994), Iraq subsequently withdrew its forces from the vicinity of Kuwait. Saddam had tested the new and relatively young U.S. president.

THE BOJINKA PLOT

In what became known as the "Bojinka plot," a massive, multiphased terrorist operation was planned in 1994 to be executed in the first months of 1995 by Yousef and Sheikh Mohammed. The al-Qaeda–affiliated terrorists sought to almost simultaneously detonate bombs on 11 airliners flying from Asia into the United States (which would have killed about 4,000 individuals), kill Pope John Paul II, and crash a plane into CIA headquarters in Langley, Virginia. Funding for the operation came from bin Laden and Wali Khan Amin Shah, an Afghan. The plot had to be abandoned after police in Manila happened upon an apartment, which contained explosives, computers, and documents. While Yousef and Sheikh Mohammed escaped from the Philippines to Pakistan, Yousef was later arrested in Islamabad, Pakistan, on February 7, 1995. Amin Shah was arrested in Malaysia in December 1995.

Yousef eventually received a sentence of 240 years in prison for his part in the 1993 World Trade Center bombing. The Bojinka plot's failure led Sheikh Mohammed to the belief that explosives were risky to have around, and when he resurrected the multi-plane terrorist operation for September 11, 2001, he opted to use the aircraft as missiles rather than coordinating and housing explosives aboard. Sheikh Mohammed, known in law enforcement and counterterrorism circles as KSM, was eventually arrested in Rawalpindi, Pakistan, in 2003 and charged with being the architect of the 9/11 attacks.

In the Middle East, on July 1, 1995, in response to UNSCOM evidence, Iraq admitted for the first time that it possessed an offensive biological weapons program but officially denied it had moved toward "weaponization." It was about this time, the summer of 1995, the unity of the UN Security Council regarding sanctions and inspections in Iraq began to diminish, as Russia pushed for an end to what they believed to be a highly intrusive inspection and sanction regime. Some analysts suggested that Russia was interested in "getting in on the ground floor" for commercial opportunities in a post-sanctions Iraq.

In support of the U.S. position, Israeli intelligence reported in July 1995 that Iraq was attempting to purchase missile guidance systems (gyroscopes) from a Russian export company. On November 10, 1995, with the assistance of Jordanian and Israeli intelligence, UNSCOM inspectors intercepted 240 Russian gyroscopes and accelerometers en route from Russia to Iraq. And, on December 16, 1995, Iraqi scuba divers operating under the directions of UNSCOM dredged the Tigris River near Baghdad and found 200 additional Russian-made missiles, instruments, and components.

ATTACK ON U.S. PERSONNEL AT THE KHOBAR TOWERS

On June 25, 1996, a converted gasoline tanker truck filled with two tons of high explosives (equivalent to 20,000 pounds of TNT) was driven to Khobar, Saudi Arabia, where it was eventually parked in front of the Khobar Towers, an eight-story residential complex that housed U.S. Air Force (USAF) personnel from the 4404th Wing (Provisional—air rescue and fighter squadrons) as well as other nationalities. The detonation of the tanker bomb on June 25 created a crater in front of the Khobar Towers, 85-feet wide and 35-feet deep. Nineteen USAF personnel were killed and 498 additional individuals of various nationalities were wounded.

Saudi intelligence argued that it was the work of Hezbollah and Iran. Others came to believe that it was the work of al-Qaeda and bin Laden. In the recognition of the need to provide greater security for U.S. personnel in Saudi Arabia, foreign military personnel were moved from Khobar to the more remote and highly protected Prince Sultan Air Base near Al Kharj in central Saudi Arabia, about 70 miles from Riyadh. In late 2003, France pulled its personnel out of Saudi Arabia and brought them home. At the same time, the United States and Britain moved their personnel out of Saudi Arabia and relocated them to Al Udeid Air Base in Qatar.

In May and June 1996, UNSCOM supervised the destruction of Iraq's main production facility of biological warfare agents at Al Hakam. In northern Iraq on August 31, 1996, and to the dismay of the U.S. government, Saddam moved three armored divisions, allegedly at the

invitation of one Kurdish faction, into the Kurdish city of Irbil and pro-
vided support for one Kurdish group, the Kurdistan Democratic Party
(KDP), against another, the Patriotic Union of Kurdistan (PUK), as the
KDP pushed the PUK east into Iran. Many analysts viewed this as a bra-
zen attempt by Saddam to reassert his control over the largest city in Iraqi
Kurdistan.

Four days later, on September 3, 1996, the United States launched
Operation Desert Strike, a series of cruise missile attacks on Iraqi targets
in Kut, Iskandariyah, Nasiriyah, and Tallil, in response to Saddam's move
into the Kurdish region. After the United States began striking targets
during Desert Strike, Iraqi forces were quickly withdrawn from the
Kurdish enclave. However, news reports following the events in August
and September 1996 stated that the Iraqi move toward north was aimed
at disrupting a U.S. covert operation aimed at toppling the Iraqi regime.
Perhaps the best metric that something indeed was compromised was
the fact that the United States subsequently evacuated nearly 6,000 people
involved in an array of humanitarian and intelligence programs.

On January 1, 1997, as Operation Provide Comfort, the no-fly zone over
Kurdish enclaves in the North, came to an end, Operation Northern
Watch was launched by the United States, United Kingdom, and Turkey
to continue the protection of the Kurds above the 36th parallel. On
March 26, 1997, U.S. Secretary of State Madeleine Albright delivered a
speech at Georgetown University, in which she conjectured that Iraqi
sanctions would probably not end until and unless Saddam was replaced.
Many observers, particularly in the international community, viewed this
publicly stated position as counterproductive in getting the Iraqis to cooperate with UNSCOM. However, it served as a diplomatic signal to the
Iraqi regime that time was running out for Baghdad's complete cooperation in terms of its cease-fire agreements and the WMD file.

On September 13, 1997, an Iraqi military officer assigned by the Iraqi
government to travel with an UNSCOM team attacked a UNSCOM
weapons inspector onboard a UNSCOM helicopter, as the inspector was
attempting to take photographs of the unauthorized movement of Iraqi
vehicles at a site designated for inspection. Four days later, while waiting
for access to the site, UNSCOM inspectors witnessed and captured on
videotape Iraqi guards moving files, burning documents, and dumping
waste cans into a nearby river. At the end of September, UNSCOM
inspected a "food laboratory" and, as one of the inspectors entered the
building through the back, encountered several individuals attempting
to run out through the back carrying suitcases. Upon inspection, it was
revealed that the suitcases contained logbooks for the creation of illegal
bacteria and chemicals. The letterhead of the documents came from the
Office of the President (Saddam) and the Special Security Office (SSO).

BIN LADEN DECLARES WAR ON THE UNITED STATES, ISRAEL, AND THE WEST

In February 1998, bin Laden signed a fatwa, declaring war on the West and Israel. In May 1998, al-Qaeda released a video that declared war on the United States and the West. Also in 1998, Saddam refused to allow U.S. or British citizens to be part of the inspection teams and demanded a halt to U.S. U2 surveillance flights, as Russia offered to replace the U.S. flights with Russian aircraft. On August 5, 1998, Saddam suspended all cooperation with UNSCOM teams.

August 7 marked the eighth anniversary of the arrival of U.S. troops in Saudi Arabia during Operation Desert Shield in 1990. On August 7, 1998, trucks with ammonium nitrate–based bombs utilizing oxygen tanks and gas canisters were used in terrorist acts against U.S. embassies in Dar es Salaam, Tanzania, and Nairobi, Kenya. Eighty-five were killed in Dar es Salaam and 213 killed in Nairobi (where an additional 4,000 were wounded). Bin Laden stated that the sites had been targeted because of the U.S. invasion of Somalia. Al-Qaeda worked with elements of the EIJ (Ayman al-Zawahiri) in arranging the bombings. President Clinton responded publicly by ordering Operation Infinite Reach, a series of cruise missile attacks on targets in Sudan and Afghanistan on August 20, 1998. A less public response as part of Infinite Reach was the president's directions to the CIA and U.S. Special Operations community to prepare plans to undermine Taliban rule in Afghanistan and to drive al-Qaeda from their safe haven.

The August 5 announcement by Saddam that he was suspending all cooperation with UNSCOM teams was met on September 29, 1998, by the U.S. Congress passing the "Iraq Liberation Act" (HR 4655), which formally codified the U.S. objective of removing Saddam from power and replacing the dictator with a democratic government. On October 31, 1998, HR 4655 was signed into law.

In an historic step toward the resolution of the Israeli-Palestinian conflict, on October 23, 1998, the PA agreed to remove clauses from the PLO charter that called for the destruction of Israel. On that day, Clinton met with Israeli Prime Minister Benjamin Netanyahu, PA President Arafat, and King Hussein of Jordan in the signing of the Wye River Peace Accords. The agreement established a preliminary plan for the gradual transfer of the West Bank to Palestinian control and the release of 750 Palestinian prisoners.

On November 13 and 14, President Clinton ordered air strikes on Iraq in preparation for Operation Desert Thunder but halted the order at the last minute as Saddam agreed to cooperate with UNSCOM. On November 18, UNSCOM teams returned to Iraq, which was subsequently followed on November 23 by Saddam ending all cooperation with the inspection teams. On December 13, 1998, Clinton again approved air strikes. Between December 16 and 19, Operation Desert Fox was carried out, hitting 100 Iraqi targets with 415 tomahawk cruise missiles and 600 laser-guided bombs. The United States and Great Britain followed this 4-day, 70-hour operation with a sustained bombing campaign that would eventually last two years, regularly conducting air operations against Iraq's missile factories, command centers, and airfields in an effort to disrupt Saddam's attempt at rearming. During a UN Security Council meeting on December 21, Russia, China, and France called for lifting the eight-year oil embargo on Iraq. The United States reiterated its position and intent on vetoing any such effort.

After establishing the complicity of bin Laden and al-Qaeda for the 1998 embassy bombings in East Africa, the U.S. government demanded that the Taliban turn over bin Laden to American custody on November 14, 1999. The Taliban refused, and the United States, operating through the United Nations, froze all Afghan foreign assets and tightened the preexisting embargo on Afghanistan. The country, by the end of the 1990s, was 80 percent under Taliban control while the Taliban's enemy, the Northern Alliance, held about 20 percent of the northern region of Afghanistan. At the end of the year, on December 17, 1999, UNSCOM was replaced in Iraq by the UN Monitoring, Verification, and Inspection Commission (UNMOVIC).

After the fall of the Soviet Union and the demise of a strong bipolar international structure (with one pole based on the United States and NATO and the other pole centered on the USSR and the Warsaw Pact), a multitude of previously frozen conflicts around the world ignited and by the time of the Clinton administration were raging in a number of areas. As such, Clinton was faced with a different international environment than was Reagan and sought to uphold American values and interests in the face of erupting and proliferating regional violence but not marked by the immediate threat of nuclear destruction at the hands of the Soviet Union.

Throughout the late 1990s, the United States was locked into a low-intensity conflict with al-Qaeda and, as the year 2000 approached, al-Qaeda operatives planned to conduct a series of terrorist acts to mark the arrival of the "millennium." Their plans and attempted bombings became known as the Millennium Plot. Targets included Los Angeles International Airport (LAX), the USS *The Sullivans* (DDG-68), and four sites in Jordan, each foiled by the alert action of law enforcement. The plot against the U.S. Navy ship failed when the boat filled with explosives sent to strike *The Sullivans* sank before reaching its intended target.

SPECIAL ACTIVITIES DIVISION PERSONNEL ARRIVE IN AFGHANISTAN

In March 2000, a CIA Special Activities Division team went into Afghanistan with the objective of capturing senior al-Qaeda leaders. However, key U.S. leaders and administrators were uncomfortable with the operation and after the CIA station chief in Pakistan called Langley Air Force Base to express his disapproval, the operation was called off. In July 2000, President Clinton invited PLO Chairman Arafat and Israeli Prime Minister Ehud Barak to Camp David to conclude negotiations on the unresolved Israeli-Palestinian issues and to create what was called in the field of international diplomacy a "final status agreement."

It was at Camp David in the summer of 2000 that the distance between the two sides' positions as well as the unwillingness of either to compromise became increasingly clear. Israel would not withdraw from land seized during the 1967 Six-Day War and return, as demanded by the Arab world, to pre-1967 borders. It would appear from subsequent behavior that the results of a war were only applicable if the Arabs and the Palestinians won and received in total what they desired; otherwise initiating a war and losing, in their view, had no consequences. Part of the results of losing a series of wars to the Israelis was that Israel kept sending settlers into areas that, prior to the initiation of war, were under Arab control. After the Second World War and the establishment of the State of Israel in 1948, the U.S. and international community-backed plan of insuring 80 percent of the territory of Palestine was controlled by Palestinians was rejected by the Palestinians. Instead they opted for war and after a series of armed clashes between 1948 and 2000, the Palestinians found themselves then in possession of 20 percent of the land.

The continuous acts of violence have not strengthened the Palestinian position and instead serve mostly to allow for further Zionist territorial encroachment. Accordingly, in the case of East Jerusalem with its then 175,000 Jewish settlers would remain, from Tel Aviv's point of view, solely under Israeli control. Further, Tel Aviv would annex settlement blocs in the West Bank, containing 80 percent of the 180,000 Jewish settlers. Finally, Israel would not accept legal or moral responsibility regarding the "right of return" of the Palestinians that had become, through choice of Israeli coercion, refugees in the Arab-Israeli dispute—a dispute that in the summer of 2000 had been ongoing for more than 50 years (1948–2000). The Palestinians insisted on Israel's departure from the West Bank and the Gaza Strip as well as turning over East Jerusalem and the recognition of an independent Palestinian state in those territories.

AL AQSA INTIFADA

A few weeks after the disappointing outcome of Camp David II, frustration over the perceived failure of the peace negotiations to create a Palestinian state led to the outbreak of the Al Aqsa Intifada in September 2000, which flared until 2005 with the Israeli withdrawal from the Gaza Strip. Shortly after the initiation of what became known as the "Second Intifada" in September, the USS *Cole* (DDG-67) entered the harbor of the historically key port of Aden, Yemen, on October 12, 2000. From 1967 to 1990, Aden had been the capital city of the People's Democratic Republic of Yemen, also called South Yemen, a client state of the Soviet Union. Forces in North Yemen fought those in the South in wars that erupted in 1972, 1979, and 1982. In May 1990, the countries temporarily united but the ongoing rivalries drove the country into civil war in 1994. Yemen, situated along the border of southern Saudi Arabia and with its strategic position along both the entrance to the Red Sea and the Suez Canal as well as serving as a commanding port to the Arabian Sea, became a battleground for al-Qaeda and Iranian intrigue following the demise of the Soviet Union.

As the USS *Cole* was taking on fuel in Aden's harbor, a small boat maneuvered next to the ship's hull and detonated a bomb, tearing a hole 40 by 40 feet in the side of the American ship. Seventeen sailors were killed and 39 wounded in the attack that was later determined to be the work of bin Laden's al-Qaeda network. Less than one month later, George W. Bush (George H. W. Bush's son) was elected president of the United States, winning a close election over Democrat and vice president under Clinton, Al Gore.

By early 2001, the United States was in the middle of planning operations to remove the Taliban and drive al-Qaeda from its latest sanctuary. In June, al-Qaeda merged with the Ayman al-Zawahiri-led EIJ. The EIJ had attempted to kill Egyptian President Hosni Mubarak in 1995 but found themselves ejected from their sanctuary in the Sudan. In February 1998, bin Laden and al-Zawahiri had cosigned the fatwa against the United States. And by 2001, the architect of the planned Bojinka plot, Sheikh Mohammed (KSM), had been tasked by bin Laden and al-Zawahiri to strike into the homeland of the United States. KSM decided that explosives were problematic in that they required purchasing, transporting, and housing prior to even making it to a target site. This created risk and vulnerability that eventually led to the undermining terrorist planning and operations in the Philippines during the Bojinka plot. Instead KSM opted to use hijacked airplanes as missiles.

SEPTEMBER 11, 2001

After months of planning with a relatively modest investment of approximately $500,000, 19 hijackers of mostly Saudi nationality took control of four U.S. civilian airliners and crashed them into the twin towers of the World Trade Center in New York and into the Pentagon in Washington, DC. Two jet airliners—American Airlines Flight 11 and United Airlines Flight 175—were flown into the North and South Towers of the World Trade Center. At 8:46 a.m. (ET), Flight 11 struck the North Tower followed at 9:03 a.m. (ET) by Flight 175 striking the South Tower. Minutes later, at 9:37 a.m. (ET), American Airlines Flight 77—flown by a hijacker—crashed into the Pentagon. At 9:59 a.m. (ET), the South Tower of the World Trade Center collapsed into a pile of rubble. At 10:03 a.m. (ET), United Air Lines Flight 93, under control of al-Qaeda hijackers, crashed into a field near Shanksville, Pennsylvania, as passengers and crew struggled to retake the aircraft from the hijackers. These acts probably saved hundreds of lives, if not thousands, as the hijackers of Flight 93 were prevented from carrying out their plot. At 10:28 a.m. (ET), the North Tower of the World Trade Center collapsed in similar fashion as the South Tower minutes before. All told, 2,996 people were killed in the air and on the ground.

Bin Laden and al-Zawahiri initially denied any al-Qaeda involvement in the attacks on the U.S. homeland on September 11, 2001. However, on December 13, 2001, the Pentagon released a videotape, in which bin Laden was shown at a dinner with associates in Afghanistan on November 9, 2001, saying the attacks on September 11 exceeded even his most "optimistic expectations." Later, in 2004, bin Laden finally publicly claimed responsibility for the attacks. In the Middle East immediately following the attacks, Saddam proclaimed to the international media that the attacks represented "the operation of the century."

There was more than $250 billion in damages to the U.S. economy compared to the al-Qaeda's cost of $500,000 for the planning and execution of the terror attacks on the American homeland. This does not include the hundreds of billions in costs that the United States incurred in subsequent

Table 8.1 Strategic Economic Impact of the Terrorist Attacks on September 11, 2001

$128 billion	Estimated economic loss during the first two to four weeks after the World Trade Center's collapse in New York as well as the decline in airline travel over the next few years
$60 billion	Estimated cost of the World Trade Center's site damage, including damage to the surrounding buildings, infrastructure, and subway facilities
$40 billion	Value of emergency antiterrorism package approved by the U.S. Congress on September 14, 2001
$15 billion	Aid packages passed by Congress to bail out the airlines
$9.3 billion	Insurance claims arising from the 9/11 attacks

operations in Afghanistan and eventually in Iraq (nor the pain and suffering of all who were affected on 9/11 and during U.S. operations in Afghanistan and Iraq). Prior to the September 11 attacks, terrorism was thought of within American society as mostly individual events committed largely by radical groups in remote and faraway regions. The people of the United States were *shocked* on September 11, 2001—shocked by geographical proximity of the attacks and shocked by the horror suffered by the multitudes of innocent civilians at the hands of a sinister group of murderers claiming to be men of God.

> We do not disassociate Islam from war. On the contrary, disassociating Islam from war is the reason for our defeat. We are fighting in the name of Islam. Religion must lead to war. This is the only way we can win.[6]

According to Islamic law, there are at least six reasons why bin Laden's barbaric violence did not fall under the rubric of jihad:[7]

1. Individual and organizations do not declare jihad, only states can.
2. One cannot kill innocent women and children conducting a jihad.
3. One cannot kill Muslims in a jihad.
4. One cannot fight a jihad against a country in which Muslims can freely practice their religion and proselytize Islam.
5. Prominent Muslim jurists around the world have condemned these attacks on September 11, 2001, and their condemnation forms a juristic consensus (*ijma*) against bin Laden's actions. This consensus renders his actions as un-Islamic.
6. The welfare and interest of the Muslim community (*Maslaha*) is being harmed by bin Laden's actions, and this equally makes them un-Islamic.

The cloak of religious authority had traditionally provided many rogue groups such as the modern variants their main centers of gravity from which they generated both combat and political power. In the modern age with a literate public and a vibrant social media in the West, this has become less opaque and often reveals the true nature of many of these modern versions of the classic raiding and marauding groups—the selfish pursuit of earthly pleasures, vain glory, and power wrapped in a cloak of God. Following the attacks on September 11, 2001, U.S. President Bush, with support from the U.S. Congress, authorized the CIA and U.S. Central Command (USCENTCOM) to begin operations against the Taliban and al-Qaeda inside Afghanistan. Two days before the strikes, the Taliban had killed the leader of the Northern Alliance, Massoud, who was then cooperating with the United States and against the Taliban and al-Qaeda. In 2001, Massoud and the Northern Alliance, in control of about 20 percent of Afghanistan, had about 12,000 regular fighters and 10,000 militiamen (65 tanks and armored vehicles, 3 cargo planes, 8 transport helicopters, and about 25 older short-range Soviet ballistic missiles and U.S. stingers) to the Taliban's 50,000 regular fighters and about 40,000 militia (including 650 tanks and armored vehicles, 15 combat planes, 40 cargo planes, SA-7s, and U.S. stingers), which were in effective control of about 80 percent of the country.

The killing of the extremely popular and charismatic Massoud by the Taliban on September 9 only served to energize the Northern Alliance and directed their anger against the Taliban and their Arab guests (bin Laden and al-Qaeda). The Northern Alliance, in 2001, included Uzbek forces under the command of General Dostum, Tajik forces of former President Rabbani, and the Shiite Hazaras led by Haji Mohammad Mohaqiq.

OPERATION ENDURING FREEDOM

Following the September 11 attacks, President Bush demanded the Taliban extradite bin Laden and other al-Qaeda leaders to America. The Taliban responded that they had asked bin Laden to leave the country but declined to extradite him without evidence of his involvement in the attacks on 9/11, although they were open to review any evidence the United States might have. On September 12, the CIA briefed President Bush on a potential operation that had been in the planning stages for the overthrow of the Taliban. Included in the presentation was a pledge to have Special Activities Division officers on the ground and working with the Northern Alliance within two weeks of the plan's authorization.[8]

The initial military objectives of the war, which would be commanded by U.S. Army General and CENTCOM Commander Tommy Franks (designated Operation Infinite Justice—then changed to Operation Enduring Freedom [OEF] out of deference to Muslim sensitivities that "Infinite Justice" resides within the will of Allah alone), were laid out by President Bush in his September 20 address to a joint session of Congress and his October 7, 2001, address to the nation. The objectives were:

1. Destruction of terrorist training camps and infrastructure within Afghanistan;
2. Capture of al-Qaeda leaders;
3. Cessation of terrorist activities in Afghanistan.

The first U.S. forces on the ground, a CIA seven-man contingent designated, the Northern Alliance Liaison Team (NALT), landed on Afghan soil in a CIA-owned Soviet-built helicopter via a U.S. staging base constructed at Karshi Khanabad Air Base (referred to by U.S. personnel as "K2") in Uzbekistan on September 26 and met up with Northern Alliance forces in the Panjshir Valley.[9] In mid-October, in support of CIA's Operation Jawbreaker, an additional Special Activities Division team

(Directorate of Operations—covert paramilitary group) arrived south of Mazar-e Sharif.[10] By the beginning of November 2001, roughly 100 CIA officers (including Near East Division officers trained and experienced in culture, languages, and contacts) and 350 Army Special Forces were on the ground in Afghanistan and preparing to bring the war to the Taliban and their al-Qaeda guests by coordinating U.S. airpower with the thousands of infantrymen of the Northern Alliance.[11]

In support of OEF, the American nuclear-powered aircraft carrier USS *Kitty Hawk* steamed 7,000 miles at "flank" (maximum) speed to establish a forward operating base for U.S. SOF. The air war commenced on the night of October 7, 2001, as OEF began with an aerial bombardment of preplanned targets in and around Herat, Shindand, Shibarghan, Mazar-e Sharif, and Kandahar. Five USAF B-1B bombers and 10 B-52s operating out of Diego Garcia in the Indian Ocean, 25 USN F-14 and F/A-18 fighters launched from the USS *Enterprise* and the USS *Carl Vinson* in the North Arabian Sea, and two USAF B-2 Stealth bombers flying from Whiteman Air Force Base, Missouri, in the continental United States conducted the opening night attacks. The attack aircraft were supported by accompanying F-14 and F/A-18 fighter sweeps and by electronic jamming of enemy radar and communications transmissions by USN EA-6B aircraft.

OPENING A NEW FRONT IN THE MIDDLE EAST

By the summer of 2002, influential members within the Bush administration were pressing for a campaign to remove Saddam from power. The intense focus that had been the hallmark of the early success in OEF would soon be dissipated (along with the priority for resources), much to the chagrin of several military commanders and international partners. General Franks and his staff at CENTCOM were privately displeased—or perhaps the term better capturing the general's perspective would be "exasperated"—with certain high-level officials' decision within the Bush administration to initiate a second front in Iraq prior to a successful finish in Afghanistan.

Accordingly, OEF can be thought of as two separate campaigns. From October 7, 2001, to the close of Operation Anaconda in late March 2002, the United States had fought exposed formations of Taliban and al-Qaeda forces—OEF I. Following the summer of 2002, OEF took the form of both counterinsurgency and counterterrorism operations—OEF II. In the middle of the two operations, the United States launched Operation Iraqi Freedom (OIF) on March 20, 2003. The decision by the president to initiate operations against Iraq necessitated that the U.S. military transitioned to what essentially amounted to a holding action against the

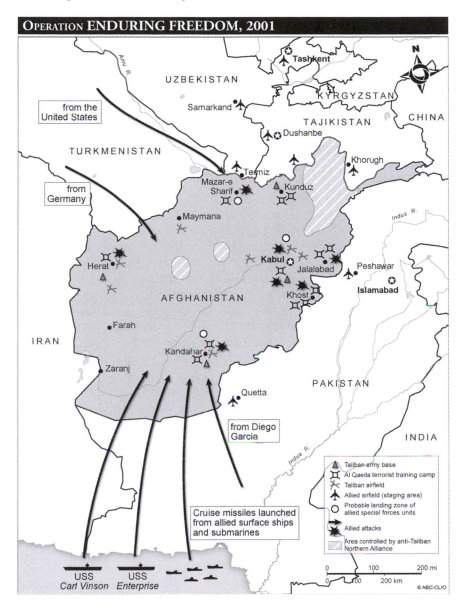

OPERATION ENDURING FREEDOM, 2001

insurgency in Afghanistan, while it took down the regime of Saddam. Major combat operations designed to topple Saddam's government were swift and decisive, similar in results to the rapid takedown of the Taliban and al-Qaeda in Afghanistan.

However, OIF, like OEF, consisted of at least two parts. Part one (OIF I) was the rapid takedown of a conventional (albeit with remarkably "un"conventional speed and maneuver) military offensive campaign, while part two (OIF II) forced the United States to conduct extensive insurgency campaigns in both Iraq and Afghanistan, simultaneously rebuilding the institutions of government (state-building) in both countries. The dual campaigns diverted resources and focus and required the United States and its allies to find solutions without first fully comprehending the problems. The analogy of the man searching for "a black hat, in a dark room—which isn't there" seems apt.

Concurrently with the state-building requirement, the United States attempted to reconcile factions into accepting the creation and presence of a larger national entity (nation-building) in both countries. Moreover, in addition to the requirements of both nation- and state-building, the U.S. Department of Defense was engaged in a violent insurgency campaign directed by former Iraqi military commanders and intelligence officers from Saddam's Ba'athist regime, leveraging superior knowledge of in-country terrain, both geographical and human.

In certain respects, the United States and its allies were victims of their own military success. The dominant American military performances during Operation Desert Storm in 1991 and OEF I (October 2001–April 2002) drove U.S. enemies in Iraq and Afghanistan to avoid fighting pitched conventional battles against the U.S. military. If the performances turned in by the United States during Desert Storm and OEF I could be characterized as the "solid," then insurgent and terrorist strategies were adopted by its opponents in both Iraq and Afghanistan in an attempt to exploit the "gaps" or vulnerabilities of that solid.

Asymmetric warfare, falling within the Flaechen-und Luecken strategic perspective, is that which becomes unequal, disproportionate, or irregular and attempts to exploit an opponent's weaknesses and vulnerabilities rather than attempting to fight in a manner, time, and place that allow the opponent to maximize combat power, including the ability to generate effects sufficient in achieving desired results during conflict. Asymmetric operations can occur in at least two ways. The first would entail two equally powerful combatants who attempt to exploit each other's weaknesses and avoid attacking into an enemy's strength. A powerful combatant may opt to forgo an attack in a direct approach and instead bypass an enemy's prepared defensive array by conducting an indirect approach that strikes at weakness. Thus, even during combat involving symmetrical opponents, where strength can be described as a rough parity between the two sides, asymmetric operations are often the preferred strategy.

When one is relatively weak and the opponent strong, such as the case in OEF I, one side may opt to avoid being pummeled in conventional

operations and opt for asymmetric means, wherein the weaker opponent—
in this instance the Taliban and al-Qaeda—attempts to use a strategy to
offset his or her own deficiencies in quantity and quality. Instead of fighting on an open battlefield, where one is exposed to superior airpower and
precision-guided munitions (PGMs), the tactic is to fight "among the people."[12] Such was the nature of the conflict in OEF II and OIF II. In a war
conducted by insurgents and terrorists among the people, America's
conventional and kinetic relative superiority is degraded and, in many
cases, unable to be brought to bear on an enemy as he or she hides among
the people. Given the required restraint by laws of war instituted by
European and North American armies, their respective enemies exploit
the gaps within those strategies. Other militaries, including that of Russia
and Bashar al-Assad in Syria, often refuse to allow insurgents or terrorists
to find sanctuary within the civilian population and conduct bombing
campaigns wherever their opponents hide, largely in contravention to
the laws of war.

War among the people is asymmetric and essentially entails violent
conflict between a formal military and an informal, less-equipped, less-
supported, often undermanned, but determined and resilient opponent.
Unable to achieve a decisive conventional military victory vis-à-vis the
stronger side, the insurgent or guerrilla attempts to achieve military
victory through a mixture of covert and clandestine means to inflict
sufficient damage upon the stronger side to impact its will to carry on.
This amounts to raising the costs incurred so that they exceed the
expected benefits.

Once the insurgent, guerrilla, or terrorist has been able to alter the
stronger opponent's decision calculus regarding costs and benefits, what
ultimately finishes the will to continue, that is, acquiescence or capitulation, becomes a function of the essence of strategy itself: to convince an
opponent that he (or she) will not be able to achieve his or her aims.
The stronger country, tired of the insurgency and with the home population
calling for either victory or withdrawal, realizes victory is not possible without killing nearly everyone they are trying to save or influence. Given such
conditions, withdrawal often becomes the only rational option; hence, the
Soviet decision for withdrawal from Afghanistan in the late 1980s and the
U.S. withdrawal from Iraq in 2011—although the United States opted to
reengage within Iraq as Islamic State in Iraq and the Levant (ISIL), or *Daesh*,
moved on Baghdad in the spring of 2014.

What brought a reliance on insurgent and terrorist campaigns in the
Middle East and Afghanistan was the inability to achieve aims on
the conventional battlefield. The pattern dates back centuries within the
Middle East and South Asia and occurred when conventional weaknesses
required the prosecution of ghazi warfare. In the modern era, the Arab

armies' inability to overrun Israel in 1948, 1956, 1967, and 1973 led to the establishment of the PLO and the conduct of an asymmetric or unconventional paramilitary campaign aimed at undermining the Jewish state and at reclaiming perceived lost lands.

Following March 2002, the Taliban and its supporters in Pakistan and within al-Qaeda opted to pursue a violent insurgency aimed at increasing the costs sufficiently to the United States and its European allies to warrant a withdrawal, which ultimately led to the eventual return of the Taliban and their allies. While OEF I delivered a massive setback to the aspirations of the hard-core Islamists in creating a Central Asian caliphate in the space of the former Soviet Muslim republics, it nevertheless remains as key component of the worldwide expansion objectives of the revolutionary and singularly violent fundamentalists. Thus, in their minds, the war does not end until they have won. If they are not powerful enough to stand and fight in the open, they then fight from the shadows, hiding among the people. Such individuals, according to the finest traditions of secular Arab culture, do not deserve to rule, which has been the case in Western history as well. While primitive, both traditions certainly aided in the establishment of the most competent security and military conditions of the day, leading toward a more stable and honor-based political environment.

The sustained competitive advantage in warfare enjoyed by the United States and its ability to provide Israel with a qualitative advantage in military technology have been the main factors that have frustrated the fundamentalists' expansionary goals and made them two of the most prominent targets for vetting their frustration. Conversely, the military superiority of the United States and its vast array of allies has kept massive levels of warfare minimized, particularly through the Cold War era.

U.S. military superiority has kept Arab- and Muslim-initiated armed conflict since 1973 (with the exceptions of Desert Storm, OEF, and OIF) within the domain of ghazi or unconventional warfare. The most frustrating aspect of this imbalance in military capabilities, for the Arabs and Muslims, is that it does not lend itself readily for quick purchase. If the military capability and effectiveness of the United States was simply a function of high-tech weaponry and systems, the trillions of petrodollars that have been generated in the last half century would have, at the very least, closed the gap in measurable ways. It has not.

INNOVATION AND TRANSFORMATION IN MILITARY TECHNOLOGY AND THOUGHT

Peter Drucker (Austrian American), who is acclaimed in many circles as the most prominent management thinker , writer and teacher of the twentieth century, was involved in a range of ideas, concepts, and practices in the managerial arts.[13] One of the most important was in terms of the managerial imperative for fostering an institutional and corporate environment infused with a culture of creativity and innovation. He says, "Cutting edge managers must install within the company culture the ability to rapidly abandon yesterday … [and] the best way to forecast the future, is to create it." In these ideas are concepts that marked a part of Drucker's vision for both management and society. Organizations and society, in general, that embrace change and create a more productive and just future became part of Drucker's graduate seminars at Claremont Graduate University in California during the last 25 years of the twentieth century.

This did not mean that a company, organization, or nation-state was required to eliminate or disregard its finest traditions or principles. It simply meant that it was a primary responsibility of management, or a primary responsibility of political leaders of a nation, to instill within the people a predilection for searching for new and better ways of doing things. This willingness to embrace change would create an essential competitive advantage for modern and successful firms and organizations. This has been a fundamental competitive advantage of Western civilization in general and a force multiplier for the military of the United States in particular.

In 2015, the U.S. Department of Defense posted a discussion of the transformation process on its website:

> Transformation is foremost a continuing process that does not have an end point. It is meant to create or anticipate the future. Transformation is meant to deal with the co-evolution of concepts, processes, organizations, and technology. Change in any of these areas necessitates change in all. Transformation is meant to create new competitive areas and new competencies. It is meant to identify, leverage, and even create new underlying principles for the way things are done. Transformation is meant to identify and leverage new sources of power. The overall objective of these changes is simply— sustained American competitive advantage in warfare.[14]

With the crumbling of the Soviet Union, the United States stood supreme and was able to direct its cutting-edge and, some would argue, revolutionary military toward evicting Saddam from Kuwait. The United States had utilized advanced weaponry integrated with effective doctrine and applied in battle by skilled military commanders and soldiers, sailors, and marines during Desert Storm. The organizational process within the U.S. defense community and industrial base was such that, even in the face of great success conducting operations in the Persian Gulf, the search continued following Desert Storm for new and better ways of doing things. Following Desert Storm, the United States moved forward in developing new technologies and examining how best they might be integrated in effective doctrine. Then in 1998, U.S. Navy Vice Admiral Arthur K. Cebrowski cowrote an article with John J. Garstka, "Network-Centric Warfare: Its Origins and Future," published in the U.S. Naval Institute's journal, *Proceedings,* in January 1998.

> We are in the midst of a revolution in military affairs (RMA) unlike any seen since the Napoleonic Age, when France transformed warfare with the concept of levenZe en masse ... Here at the end of the millennium we are driven to a new era in warfare. Society has changed. The underlying economics and technologies have changed. American business has changed. We should be surprised and shocked if America's military did not ... Arising from fundamental changes in American society and business, military operations increasingly will capitalize on the advances and advantages of information technology.

In understanding this revolutionary transformation to network-centric warfare, it is useful, as it is with most issues on war, to glance back on key issues discussed by Carl von Clausewitz. Fundamental to his inquiry regarding the nature of war were the questions: What seems to be present in war irrespective of time or place? Are there dynamics that one can expect to have to deal with whether one fights at Thermopylae or Tora Bora? And if there are, can we find a way of dealing with it, in advance, that will provide us an advantage over an opponent? Clausewitz identifies four elements that are timeless dynamics of the phenomena of war: danger, exertion, chance, and uncertainty.

For Clausewitz, *uncertainty*—an ever-present dynamic of war—brings with it the continuous and vexing presence of a "fog" that obscures the facts and complicates both decision making and action:

> War is the realm of uncertainty; three quarters of the factors on which action is based are wrapped in a fog of greater or lesser uncertainty ... Since all information and assumptions are open to doubt and with chance at work everywhere, the commander continually finds that things are not as expected ... uncertainty and fog continually impinge on our decisions.[15]

On the twentieth-century battlefield, or in the twenty-first-century battlespace, the commander finds that his plans have been set back by enemy action as a result of events that were not foreseen in planning. Intelligence reports are often wildly inaccurate, and decisions involving matters of life and death need to be made, often without knowing with any precision as to what is actually happening. Thus, the commander ends up taking action on what can only be described as his or her and his or her staff's best guess. Given the inevitability of the presence of this phenomenon, or this "fog," one would opt to maximize one's own ability to deal effectively with it while simultaneously seeking to insure one's opponent's "fog" remains thick, dense, and as opaque as possible.

In Desert Storm, the United States and its coalition partners went after command and control in order to cut the communication links from headquarters to deployed forces. This also cut the link from intelligence gathered by those deployed forces and degraded their ability to communicate back and to keep headquarters apprised on the developing situation. Taliban and al-Qaeda commanders were the victims of strikes on command and control during OEF as well. The forces in the North were cut off from command and then routed. This was repeated in the South, as U.S. and coalition forces drove the Taliban from what amounted to their geographical center of gravity, that is, the area surrounding the city of Kandahar.

Imposing a ceaseless and enduring fog upon enemy commanders, the United States and its coalition partners were also able, through new developments in information technology, to shorten the sensor-to-shooter cycle, operating once again inside the opponent's OODA-Loop.

> The greatest tactical innovation of the war [Enduring Freedom] was a unique air-land partnership that featured unprecedented mutual support between allied air power and ground-based SOF teams . . . Global communications connectivity and the common operating picture that was made possible by linking the inputs of UAVs [unmanned aerial vehicles] and other sensors enabled a close partnership between airman and SOF units and shortened the time from identification to successful target attacks. Such networked operations are now the cutting edge of an ongoing shift in American combat style that may be of greater revolutionary potential than the introduction of the tank at the beginning of the 20th century.[16]

The development of PGMs and the evolution of intelligence sensors, command and control systems "networked" together, along with SOF forces on the ground utilizing the state-of-the-art technology then linked or "networked" with airmen firing PGMs with both air and ground integrated with the command element for real-time interfacing for effective battle management, including battle assessment and decision making. Overhead satellites, UAVs, and onboard cameras all served to supply commanders with a picture of what was happening in real time.

Thus, network-centric warfare has become a military doctrine aimed primarily at leveraging for military advantage superior information technology by computer networking sensors, commanders, and shooters. It simultaneously seeks to a) move inside an opponent's OODA-Loop, providing the ability to maintain the initiative and force an opponent to react to your battle operations, and b) reduce the effects of fog and uncertainty.

Operations in Afghanistan between October 2001 and April 2002 delivered what could be described as a strategic blow to both the Taliban and al-Qaeda. However, while both were now down, neither was completely out, as the terrorists and their supporters were dispersed but not permanently defeated. Still, it was a remarkable feat for the CIA, the U.S.

military, and the capable infantrymen of the Northern Alliance. The remote and inaccessible mountain caves and ravines, which for centuries had provided sanctuary for those who bravely fought enslavement by evil empires as well as those who fought against being killed or imprisoned for their activity as raiders, pillagers, and plunderers, had now, through technology, come within reach of both the evil empires and the great civilizations.

Adding to the unfinished business in Afghanistan were U.S. NCA (Bush administration-Pentagon) orders to prepare for operations to effect regime change in Iraq by spring of 2003. From the close of the 1991 Gulf War until the September 11 attacks, Saddam had consistently refused to honor the conditions of the cease-fire that had ended the war. By 2000, and two years after the Clinton administration publicly declared U.S. policy to be aimed at regime change in Iraq, Saddam had openly begun welcoming Vladimir Putin's Russia's return to involvement in Iraq's defense establishment and its oil sector as had the Soviets been involved decades earlier.

While post–Soviet Russia, under Boris Yeltsin, had attempted to adopt Western traditions by moving toward democratization and economic liberalism, internal and external dynamics derailed the move for greater openness and a quest for more cooperative foreign policy. With the rise of Putin, Russia, by the end of 2002, was once again attempting to undermine the position of the West within the Middle East in an effort to claw its way back to a position of world prominence. Saddam, desperate for sanctions relief and the elimination of arms inspection teams from Iraq, saw in Putin's Russia an opportunity to achieve both. Moreover, since the United States had publicly declared in 1998 it would henceforth support a change in the Iraqi political leadership, Saddam and his government probably viewed the embrace of Putin as the only viable option for remaining in power—however slight the chance might be.

Extremely concerned regarding the nexus between terrorist attacks aimed at America and WMD, the Bush administration was less inclined following 9/11 to allow a continuation of the status quo with Saddam's rhetoric and behavior. The invitation by Saddam for Putin to reinstall Moscow's influence within Baghdad and the Middle East was one more reason that regime change in Iraq was necessary, at least from the perspective of many of the senior leaders in the Bush administration.

> In April 1991 the UN Security Council linked removal of Iraqi sanctions to Saddam Hussein's verifiable accounting for all his weapons of mass destruction and acceptance of a monitoring regime to insure, in perpetuity, that he did not recreate these capabilities ... The Security Council consensus may have been strong when the inspections resolution was written, but the will of the council decayed from that day forward ... Russia was pushing Saddam's case. Moscow worked to put more compliant inspectors on the

inspection teams. It constantly challenged the credibility of inspector assessments and helped shift the burden of proof onto the inspectors. It was also clear Moscow aided Iraq in preparing for so-called surprise inspections. Iraq paid well for the help. Among documents published in the Iraq Survey Group's 2004 report on Iraq's WMD program (informally known as the Duelfer Report) was a complete list of oil allocations given by Iraq under the UN's Oil-for-Food program to a range of beneficiaries. Included were many senior Russian officials and offices, e.g., the Presidential Office and the Ministry of Foreign Affairs ... According to key Saddam lieutenants these allocations and other direct cash payments produced the desired effect.[17]

Thus, Iraq, aided by Russia, circumvented the inspections regime meant to confirm Saddam's compliance or noncompliance with the cease-fire conditions following the 1991 Persian Gulf War. This process involved direct and indirect payments from Iraq to key Russian officials involved in decision making at the United Nations, the Russian Ministry of Foreign Affairs, and the presidential office—all with key input regarding Iraqi sanctions following the Gulf War.

Saddam also knew some Council members would not agree to military actions against him. This confidence was borne out in December 1998, when UNSCOM reported that after years of effort, it could not complete the tasks given to it by the Security Council under the conditions Iraq permitted. The Council could not agree on a response that would compel Iraqi compliance and U.S. President Bill Clinton (with support from Britain) ordered a limited four-day bombing campaign. That was all. Oh, and the inspectors left and Saddam did not let them back until November 2002 when the build-up to war was clear.[18]

The United States and its allies had sought a full accounting of Iraqi WMD inventories and programs, as Saddam, in their view, had gone "rogue" and the allies did not know what his regime was pursuing or had in its possession. To end the 1991 Gulf War, Saddam pledged to provide a full accounting and allow inspectors sufficient access to ascertain for themselves those programs and holdings. However, from the end of the war until March 2003, Saddam attempted through subterfuge and deception to frustrate those attempts. By 1998, UN Security Council consensus on demanding that full accounting was unraveling with Russia actively promoting Saddam's interests in order to reestablish Moscow's control in the key Middle Eastern country.

Following the attacks on September 11, U.S. President Bush initiated a "global war on terrorism" (GWOT) and, borrowing from Reagan's effective characterization of the USSR as the "evil empire," described three countries as part of an "axis of evil"—Iraq, Iran, and North Korea. The Bush administration then sought and received authorization from Congress for the use of force against Saddam.

Chapter 9

The Iraq War and the Rise of the Islamic State in the Middle East

If the war continues long enough—this is the theory—the dog succumbs to exhaustion and anemia without ever having found anything on which to close his jaws or to rake with his claws.[1]

A government that is losing an insurgency is not being out fought, it is being out governed.[2]

On March 20, 2003, the armed forces of the United States under President George W. Bush, with an affirmative vote from the U.S. Congress, launched Operation Iraqi Freedom (OIF) for the stated purpose of eliminating Saddam Hussein's inventory and programs regarding weapons of mass destruction (WMD).[3] While the threat from WMD inventories and programs took center stage in the lead-up to war with Saddam, it was the stated policy, beginning with the Clinton administration, of the United States to effect regime change and remove Saddam from power in Iraq. Four countries provided troops during the initial offensive campaign phase of OIF: the United States (248,000), the United Kingdom (45,000), Australia (2,000), and Poland (194); while 36 other countries eventually contributed troops following the close of major combat operations during the third week of April 2003.

Two concepts are relevant in an analysis regarding the decision for war taken by the Bush administration against Saddam's regime in Iraq:

preemptive and *preventive* war. To preempt with military force is legitimate under international law in cases where an opponent or enemy has decided upon military action and an attack is either under way or very credibly imminent. In such circumstances, a nation-state about to be attacked rationally acts, first, in self-defense. In short, if you are about to be attacked, rather than absorb the blows passively, you opt to strike first. The circumstances for preemptive war are less controversial than those involving a "preventive" use of force under international law.[4]

In acts of legal preemptive war, you are not only about to get hit, but it is also quite obvious to any rational, objective viewer that this is what is happening. In such circumstances, military action is justified by self-defense, as prescribed by Article 51 of the UN Charter. However, "preventive war" has become the subject of intense debate in international politics and law, as it is considered by many to be a *discretionary* use of force.

In preventive war, the enemy is positioning itself to strike but has not committed forces for an actual attack. However, you have information or intelligence that a decision for war will be taken when the conditions are propitious for the attacker; nevertheless, an authorization for an immediate strike has not been made. Not wishing to allow the potential attacker the opportunity to create or await favorable conditions for a future strike, you strike first. Since future intentions are difficult to forecast, preventive war contains a greater level of ambiguity than do those actions of a preemptive nature. Moreover, if nation-states widely pursued policies of striking first in terms of their perceptions of future threats, this would increase not only the likelihood of increased levels of war but also the likelihood of misperceptions leading to armed conflict.[5] Any nation opting for preventive war moves onto thin ice relative to international legal authority for the use of force. As such, there is a limited margin for error when national leaders opt to justify the use of force by claims to preventive war.

Following the use of military force by the United States against Saddam's Iraq, a wide range of individuals, groups, and governments scattered across the Middle East and in many quarters of the international community claimed that the Bush administration's use of force as a preventive act was blatant aggression and, as such, illegal under international law. However, the legal justification for the use of military force against the regime in Iraq was based neither on preemptive nor a preventive use of force but rather on Saddam being in material breach of UN Security Council's (UNSC) resolutions. Under such circumstances, if Iraq was found in material breach, military action would then be justified under international law. Saddam's regime was found, by the UNSC, to be in material breach of UNSC resolutions.

In refusing to cooperate with the United Nations regarding WMD, Saddam created the conditions wherein the international community was unable to establish with any clarity his compliance or noncompliance with the terms ending the Gulf War in 1991. Moreover, during the Clinton administration, Saddam routinely moved large formations of armor into the southern Shiite sections threatening those in the South as well as moved forces to intimidate and threaten the Kurds in northern Iraq. At one point, Saddam positioned forces for another attack on Kuwait but was deterred by counteractions taken by the U.S. military.

While several White House spokesmen brought up the phase "imminent threat" in reference to dangers posed by Saddam's regime, the U.S. government did not argue that a use of force against Saddam was an act of self-defense, authorized explicitly under Article 51 of the UN Charter.[6] Thus, while much commentary was carried on by pundits in high-profile press events condemning the United States for an anticipatory or preventive use of force against Iraq, the U.S. government argued that military action was explicitly authorized by UNSC Resolution 678, as Saddam's government was found to be in material breach of previous UNSC resolutions.

The United States, in the lead of a coalition of allies, undertook military operations against Saddam during OIF, sending a force of approximately two divisions into a county of 26 million people with the geographic size of France or California.[7] There were varying perspectives regarding the necessary force levels for such a major undertaking. The ground force component commander, Lieutenant General David McKiernan, expressed his view this way:

> I will tell you unequivocally that the force I had as the ground component commander as of G-Day [beginning day] were the forces I asked for and were sufficient to do the mission that I was given.

The problem for McKiernan was that when he started (G-Day) forces may have been sufficient for the initiation of OIF, but planning also assumed that follow-on forces would be needed as the campaign unfolded, and McKiernan's command's success required a consistent and unimpeded flow of the follow-on forces to meet the developing force requirements necessary for success in the campaign. Thus, when McKiernan stated that he had sufficient forces for the mission assigned, this included forces that were not there on G-Day but would be surged into the theater as required.

> In terms of force flow, if you fight a campaign on a model that you are going to employ the front end of the force while simultaneously deploying the rest of the force, there is a large imperative that the flowing of the rest of the force has to be near perfect . . . I'm saying that the flow was not a continuous

flow in all cases. There were gaps in time when we were still waiting for additional capabilities to be introduced into the fight up in Iraq.[8]

Instead of operating with assumptions aligned with the Weinberger Doctrine that had met with significant success in Operation Desert Storm and required overwhelming decisive force, the model that was used in OIF was to commit the most economical level of force possible with additional numbers being surged in as required. The hope was that there would be success with the minimal force that was utilized initially and, by prevailing quickly, accomplish two goals: 1) conserve the follow-on forces for future contingencies and 2) expend the least amount of money possible.

Taking a slightly different perspective and, by the time of OIF, largely free from the constraints of active duty—the need for subordinate support for national command authorities (NCA) in a time of war—was four-star Army General Barry R. McCaffrey who commanded the 24th Infantry Division (Mechanized) during the 1991 Gulf War:

> In my judgment, there should have been a minimum of two heavy divisions and an armored cavalry regiment on the ground—that's how our doctrine reads.[9]

In the lead-up to OIF, the chief of staff of the U.S. Army, General Eric Shinseki, told the Senate Armed Services Committee on February 25, 2003 (one month before the commencement of the operation), that several hundred thousand soldiers would be needed in Iraq when post-hostilities control was factored into the decision calculus regarding necessary troop strength.[10] His estimate was more than double that of key Bush administration officials. Two days after Shinseki testified before the Senate Armed Services Committee, Deputy Defense Secretary Paul Wolfowitz countered the army leader's position in testimony delivered to the House Budget Committee:

> Some of the higher-end predictions that we have been hearing recently, such as the notion that it will take several hundred thousand U.S. troops to provide stability in post-Saddam Iraq, are wildly off the mark. It is hard to conceive that it would take more forces to provide stability in a post-Saddam Iraq than it would take to conduct the war itself.[11]

Shinseki had served in the U.S. peacekeeping mission in Bosnia, following major ethnic clashes in the former Yugoslavia. During that mission, the Pentagon had estimated that a good guide for stabilization and peacekeeping force requirements was for the presence of at least 1 soldier for every 50 Bosnians. Using that metric, Iraq would have required 300,000 troops to both win and then contain the situation during the post-major combat phase. Wolfowitz responded in defense of the Office of the Secretary Defense (OSD): "There have been none of the record in Iraq of ethnic militias fighting one another that produced so much bloodshed and permanent scars in Bosnia along with a continuing requirement for large peacekeeping forces to separate those militias."[12]

Secretary of Defense Donald Rumsfeld "remained convinced that the Revolution in Military Affairs (RMA) had made massive ground forces unnecessary."[13] As a general principle in terms of the ends-means alignment, military forces must possess the needed capabilities and resources (means) to accomplish their assigned mission (ends). This is the basic logic behind effective strategy and can be alternatively phrased in the following manner: If a country is not in possession of the capabilities or resources necessary for victory or does not have a reasonable expectation of obtaining them in a timely and propitious manner, that operation, campaign, or war ought to be avoided. If massive ground forces are required to prevail in a particular conflict or theater, it is the responsibility of the executive branch (in particular the secretary of defense) to work cooperatively with the U.S. Congress to provide the combatant commander with every resource needed to secure the campaign's objectives.

The problem for U.S. leadership during the Bush administration was that the United States was prepared to fight and win in terms of major conventional operations but was unprepared to manage effectively the conditions that would secure the peace. Secretary of Defense Rumsfeld—who had a long and distinguished career spanning military service in Korea, government service in several administrations, and as an effective executive in the private sector—came from a tradition of American defense intellectuals who believed the reason for the existence of the U.S. military was to fight and win the nation's wars. Consequently, nation-building, social engineering, and other lofty projects were areas that would only serve to refocus the military's attention away from deterring and if necessary defeating any adversary toward tasks that would impact a military unit's time for training and preparing to complete its primary mission—to fight and to win. As a result of the time and focus taken away from preparing for combat by being required to train for "humanitarian" missions such as nation-building or other social and political projects, combat effectiveness is directly degraded by draining resources and in requiring combat forces to train for administrative and civil activities—time not available for preparing combat forces to fight and win.

For Rumsfeld, the U.S. military was prepared to fight OIF and win and to accomplish this critical task quickly, decisively, and without wasting a significant amount of taxpayers' dollars. With Saddam and his military and security apparatus defeated and disbanded, the post-conflict phase according to this perspective should be much easier and certainly less intense than the actual combat operations to prepare for a new Iraq. Moreover, Rumsfeld was locked in a struggle between the U.S. military and the OSD in the Pentagon to move away from what he perceived to be a cultural tendency to reject new ideas and new ways of doing things. For Rumsfeld, both Operation Enduring Freedom (OEF) and OIF were opportunities to showcase the leaner, more agile, and more lethal U.S. military and to put the argument as to what vision of the future would prevail to rest.

A military with a focus on "mass" (heavy armor, large numbers of troops) is, in general, expensive to maintain and even more difficult to lift through sea or air to crises regions around the world. Such a military also becomes vulnerable as it "masses" for an attack. In an age of nuclear proliferation, a future war may see a massing of forces met with a tactical nuclear device from any number of sources. In such environments, massing of forces as traditionally accomplished prior to operations becomes highly problematic. If, however, the military seeks to focus on "effects" by leveraging technology, speed, agility, accuracy, and lethality to impair an enemy's will to resist, a lighter and less expensive footprint becomes possible.[14] The debate within the Department of Defense while necessary was, during the lead-up to OIF, an unfortunate distraction that undermined unity of effort and caused both sides of the argument to push concepts and expectations best left for debate during a more propitious and stable time.

In terms of the first phases of both OEF (Afghanistan) and OIF (Iraq), Rumsfeld was proven correct. The U.S. military was prepared to fight and win, and it did so in what can only be described in both OEF and OIF as extraordinary displays of military competence and cutting-edge technology integrated with forward-leaning doctrine.[15] Conversely, by adopting strategic priorities that locked the secretary of defense into a prepackaged concept of what *must* transpire—a rapid campaign with a small footprint followed abruptly by a vanishing U.S. military presence—while ideal, did not match the realities or the necessary requirements of adaptability for effective regime change within Saddam's Iraq in 2003.

Thus, in the overall campaign, which required security and stability operations in addition to the initial lightning fast "network-centric" and "shock and awe" takedown of the regime, the United States did not meet the ends-means alignment requirement. The immediate responsibility lies with the civilian leadership of the Department of Defense, Rumsfeld, Wolfowitz, and Undersecretary of Defense for International Policy Douglas Feith. Additional responsibility rests with Vice President Richard Cheney who strongly backed Rumsfeld's OSD in the face of criticism from other members of the president's national security team.

However, within the political system of the United States, there is only one commander in chief of the military—the president—and his or her office must approve decisions regarding the initiation of war as well as the prosecution of that war. Additionally, in matters involving the declaration of war, the U.S. Constitution requires the executive branch to seek the approval of the Congress. As a declaration of war was not sought by the president—the argument goes—no approval from Congress was needed. Bush, however, sought Congressional consent for OIF and subsequently received it. This places an obligation or responsibility on the Congress to ask the difficult questions before providing its consent. In particular, this places a duty on the applicable committees, particularly the chairs and the ranking members, to ask hard questions, to question assumptions, and to inquire as to what happens *after* kinetic military operations succeed and security and stability operations begin. Finally, since the armed forces of the United States exist as an extension of the will of the American citizenry, as does its government, the ultimate responsibility for the use of force in the United States rests upon the people of the nation. In sum, authority, responsibility, and sovereignty rest with the people, and they exercise all three by holding their elected representatives and their appointed political operatives to account through regular and fair elections.

The requirement was largely met by the U.S. Congress in the case of OIF, with Wolfowitz assuring the appropriate committees that sufficient forces would be in place. The assumption was that post-major combat operations would not require large numbers of U.S. military personnel. If the Iraqi army had not been disbanded and government personnel had not been fired (a decision that rested with the civilian leadership of the Pentagon in conjunction with the president and vice president), Wolfowitz may have been proven correct. As it was, he was not.

> The first, the supreme, the most far-reaching act of judgment that the statesman and commander have to make is to establish by that test the kind of war on which they are embarking neither mistaking it for, nor trying to turn it into, something that is alien to its nature.
>
> —Carl von Clausewitz, *On War*,
> edited and translated by Michael Howard and Peter Paret
> (Princeton, NJ: Princeton University Press, 1976), pp. 88–89

Two months before the invasion, President Bush transferred responsibility for postwar stabilization from the U.S. State Department to the Department of Defense when he issued National Security Presidential Directive 24 (NSPD-24) on January 20, 2003. U.S. Central Command (USCENTCOM) chief, General Tommy Franks, assumed that the State Department had the capacity to coordinate postwar stabilization procedures in Iraq. For the Pentagon, the tough job would be removing the 800-pound gorilla from the room (Saddam and his military, intelligence, and security forces); once this threat was removed, U.S. planners, it seems, asked the hypothetical question: "How hard could it be, once Saddam and his regime are removed, to manage a country with the vast resources that would be available as oil production came back on line?" The answer, it would turn out, was, "So hard that you will not be able to accomplish the mission, given present competence, capabilities, and resources." Frankly, Rumsfeld was ultimately proven consistent on this issue, as well, as he rejected the concept that the Department of Defense could become effective nation-builders while possessing the primary mission of prevailing in armed conflict with its requirements of resources, competence, and focus.

Unfortunately, logical consistency is not the overriding metric of success in war and politics, as both are typically permeated with paradoxes, complexities, uncertainty, and fog. In terms of Iraq, the basic planning assumptions for a post-combat environment included the expectation that oil would fund reconstruction, Iraqi troops would help keep the peace, and the resistance would fade quickly.[16] Discussions at the U.S. Army War College during the informal "Noontime Lecture" (NTL) posited the following prewar planning assumptions: a rapid establishment of a new Iraqi government, expected viability of surviving Iraqi security forces, volume of international assistance available, a rapidly resuscitated economy, and a welcoming, in general, of Iraqi attitude toward "liberation."[17]

General Franks had disagreed with the decision to open a new front in Iraq when operations in Afghanistan had not yet, as of March 2003, been completed. Now, not only would CENTCOM need to fight on a second front, but it now, on the eve of a second war, was suddenly given the responsibility of postwar stabilization and security in Iraq. The complexities of the ongoing insurgency in Afghanistan were difficult enough—no foreign army in history had ever met with *lasting* success in the austere and hostile environment that was Afghanistan (Alexander the Great's and nineteenth-century Britain's temporary successes, notwithstanding).

THE UNITED STATES ISSUES SADDAM AN ULTIMATUM

The Bush administration began ratcheting up the pressure on the Iraqi regime in the fall of 2002, and on October 8, 2002, the UNSC voted (through UNSC Resolution 1441) to find Iraq in "material breach" of previous Security Council resolutions. On March 7, 2003, Britain submitted a March 17, 2003, deadline for Iraqi compliance with UNSCR 1441. On March 17, the United States demanded the departure of Saddam from Iraq and gave him 48 hours to leave the country or face a military campaign designed to remove him and his government from power. On March 19, U.S. Special Operations Forces entered Iraq in preparation for the launching of OIF.[18]

On March 19, 2003, communications intercepts suggested that Saddam would be staying at a facility known as Dora Farms. Bush, apprised of the information but not wanting to strike since he had offered a set time for Saddam to step down, waited until the 48-hour deadline passed, then ordered the strike on Dora Farms with one caveat: women and children were said to be at the presidential palace located on the property and the U.S. military was ordered not to strike where innocent civilians would be.

While U.S. Special Operations Forces entered Iraq on March 19 for targeting and special mission purposes, officially, OIF was initiated on March 20, 2003, as the United States fired more than 40 tomahawk cruise missiles at the buildings of Dora Farms and sent two U.S. Air Force (USAF) F-117A stealth fighter bombers, each armed with two one-ton bunker busters bombs, to attack tunnels and underground bunkers.[19] Saddam was not at Dora Farms during the strike, but later upon his capture he admitted to interrogators that he had been there only hours before the attack. While the attack on Dora Farms was followed by a select number of strikes elsewhere in Iraq, on March 21, the air campaign began in earnest with 1,700 air sorties, 504 of those cruise missile strikes. During March 23–25 missions against command and control, weapon storage facilities, and weapons systems believed to be related to WMD were accelerated.

The news and public discourse following the end of the war with Iraq centered on a belief that the Bush administration had deceived the American people and the world in presenting the threat of WMD in Iraq. In direct opposition to this argument is the fact that during the first few weeks of OIF, the United States was actively attempting to stop the potential use of WMD by Saddam's regime. The actions in the initial phase of OIF were indicative of a government extremely worried about Saddam's threats and the potential release of WMD. The rubble was still being cleared in New York and at the Pentagon, following the September 11, 2001, attacks, and internal debates raged within the Bush administration regarding courses of action against the Iraqi regime.

OPERATION HOTEL CALIFORNIA

Technically, OIF began with the attacks on Dora Farms; however, eight months prior, U.S. and coalition aircraft were systematically taking down Saddam's air-defense network (radar, batteries, and missiles) by virtue of Suppression of Enemy Air Defenses (SEAD) air operations under the auspices of Operation Northern Watch and Operation Southern Watch (enforcing a no-fly zone in northern Iraq flying protective cover for the Kurds and over southern Iraq flying air patrols to protect the Shiites).

The concept of both air and ground operations during OIF was reflected in what came to be known as *Rapid Dominance*. Additionally, in the summer of 2002, the United States launched Operation Hotel California, which sent CIA-U.S. Special Forces teams into Iraqi Kurdistan (northern Iraq) to coordinate with the Kurdish Peshmerga (paramilitary infantry) and their intelligence and special security section, the *Asayish*. The combined U.S. teams eventually challenged the American assumption that Turkey would cooperate with the United States in the 2003 Iraq War. Remarkably, their collected intelligence was not provided to the U.S. Army Brigade Combat Team (BCT) that was eventually assigned to Iraqi Kurdistan.[20]

Rumsfeld led a transition away from the "decisive force" (overwhelming force of the Weinberger Doctrine) that drove Operation Desert Storm, arguing not only was it too expensive to embrace in perpetuity and, given expected diminishing future defense budgets, it was also simply unsustainable. Moreover, the "mass" involved in Desert Shield/Desert Storm (1990–1991) required lift by sea and air, and the United States simply did not have sufficient strategic lift capabilities, and much of what was needed for Shield/Storm was moved by a very expensive use of civilian assets.

Although fortunate to have a friendly host in Saudi Arabia with excellent facilities, the conditions that allowed the United States to overcome the deficiencies in lift during Desert Shield/Desert Storm simply could not be assured during future operations. Decrease mass and you decrease the need for strategic lift, which also lowers costs; decrease mass and you also make your forces less of an inviting target for WMD as they assemble, or mass, in a forward-staging area. While sound logic, and consistent in a general sense, applied to operations in Iraq in 2003–2011, which required mass to control the country, the unanticipated expense of $2 billion a week for a number of years destroyed the argument that less mass was, over the long haul, less expensive—in that particular campaign and at that particular moment in history.

Thus, Rapid Dominance came to be the model upon which OIF was based. If the Iraqi theater of operations could have been controlled as planned, and *if* the planning assumptions had held, the war in Iraq would have been heralded as one of the most remarkable military campaigns in history. Indeed, the initial advance out of Kuwait and the subsequent drive into Baghdad to take down Saddam's government was one of the most decisive and swift movements of ground forces in human history. The success of that advance, while historic, was tempered by the fact that the war did not end with the fall of the regime and the occupation of Iraq, but it gave rise to a violent and burgeoning insurgency in which the United States, to include the Departments of Defense and State as well as the U.S. intelligence community, struggled.

As it turned out, Rapid Dominance was both rapid and dominant—for a month. Unfortunately, for Rumsfeld and his civilian lieutenants in the Pentagon in 2003, the Iraq War was less of a hundred meters "sprint" to a victorious finish and more like a grueling marathon that dragged on for 26 miles (or rather, eight years). Still, the first three weeks exceeded expectations, as high-performance ordnance was directed at air defense, leadership, and command and control in order to stop Iraq's commanders from being able to communicate or from receiving information from troops in the field regarding battle space developments. Once the arrayed enemy forces were cut off from headquarters, unable to adequately "see" what was happening around them—electronically and signals blinded— the sum total of these effects created a disorienting dynamic. U.S. and co-alition airpower, following the debilitating blows to air defense, leadership, and command and control, then set about attacking the arrayed enemy ground units.

By the time U.S. and coalition airpower abruptly transitioned the enemy from "being disoriented" to "departing in desperation," U.S. and coalition ground forces attacked from multiple directions. It is through lightning strikes both from the air and swift movement to contact on the ground that a military force achieves "rapid dominance." Thus, one masses effects rather than forces in achieving surprise, speed, maneuver, accuracy, and lethality, all aimed primarily at destroying the enemy's willingness to stand and fight. Or, as Clausewitz argued, "The objective is not, necessarily, to kill the enemy's soldiers but rather to kill their cour-age to resist." Rapid Dominance and what became referred to as shock and awe were aimed at destroying Saddam's troops' will to resist.

As this unfolded in real time, and as word spread among Iraqi units regarding the level of accuracy and lethality of the American arsenal, tens of thousands of Iraqi soldiers' weapons were cast aside, uniforms were discarded, and attempts were made to blend in with the civilian popula-tions. Many Iraqi units were destroyed where they stood or, opting to stay alive, vanished into thin air. Rapid Dominance in the early weeks of OIF had been able to manage enemy perceptions through the generation of "shock and awe" to the point where one Iraqi commander protested to his chain of command: "This is not combat, this is suicide." To destroy an enemy's will to resist and lead him to the rational calculation that he cannot achieve his aims were the sought after and achieved effects during the first month of OIF, as the Iraqi military vanished by either choice or force of arms.

Air strikes continued unabated against command and control, commu-nications, and large concentrations of Iraqi defensive positions, which were destroyed from the air or abandoned by Iraqi soldiers. Coalition air operations were under the command of USAF Lieutenant General

T. Michael Moseley serving as chief of U.S. Central Command Air Forces (CENTAF). The USAF monitored and controlled the air campaigns of both OIF and OEF from the Combined Air Operations Center (CAOC), originally located in Saudi Arabia but transferred to Al Udeid Air Base in Qatar in 2003.

After April 3, "there was little indication or response from Iraq units to any central direction. At about this time the outer defenses of Baghdad crumbled as soldiers fled back home, leaving equipment and uniforms behind."[21] Airpower was decisive in the rapid degradation of command and control and of Iraqi ground defenses and forces. This dynamic provided a window of opportunity for the ground campaign to rapidly (although later it would be shown to have been fleetingly) take control of the country.

Unlike Operation Desert Storm, which experienced a months-long air assault prior to moving in force on the ground, the ground campaign of OIF was initiated on March 20, 2003, concurrent with air operations. The initial thinking on OIF was to opt for a lengthy buildup of forces and, once a decisive force was fully in place, the ground phase would then proceed. This came to be referred to as the "standing start" plan and, given that Rumsfeld, Wolfowitz, and Feith disagreed with the standing start construct—describing it as "old think"—a "running start" plan was developed that envisioned beginning the invasion with a minimal force proceeded by deploying follow-on forces as required.[22] This was met with considerable resistance from ground force commanders, both army and marine, and a "hybrid" plan was created to increase forces on the ground before the start of the war while keeping a capacity to continue the deployment/employment cycle for the remainder of the apportioned forces.

Since Saudi Arabia had decided against allowing U.S. forces to launch an attack on Iraq in 2003 from Saudi soil, U.S. and U.K. land component commanders were confined to staging from Kuwait. U.S. and coalition partners fielded ground forces under CFLCC to attack north toward Baghdad on two axes of advance, with one grouping centered on U.S. V Corps and one formed on the I Marine Expeditionary Force (I MEF). The U.S. V Corps (U.S. Army Lieutenant General William Wallace, commanding) consisted of the following elements:

3rd Infantry Division (Mechanized)
101st Airborne (Air Mobile/Air Assault) Division
82nd Airborne Division
4th Infantry Division (Mechanized)[23]

Corps-level assets included:

17th Field Artillery Brigade
41st Field Artillery Brigade

214th Field Artillery Brigade
130th Engineer Brigade
205th Military Intelligence Brigade
18th Military Police Brigade
22nd Signal Brigade
28th Combat Support Hospital

I MEF (Lieutenant General James Conway, commanding) with the following subordinate commands:

1st Marine Division (Major General James Mattis, commanding)
2nd Marine Expeditionary Brigade (Task Force Tarawa)
1st (U.K.) Armoured Division (Lieutenant General Robin Vaughn Brims,
    general officer, commanding)
7th Armoured Brigade
16th Air Assault Brigade
3 Commando Brigade

In addition to the two large primary attack formations within the CFLCC (McKiernan, commanding) were:

Combined Joint Special Operations Task Force-North (TF Viking)

10th Special Forces Group
173rd Airborne Brigade (Separate)
1st BN, 508th Infantry Regiment (Airborne—ABN)
2nd BN, 503rd Infantry Regiment (ABN)
1st BN, 63rd Armor Regiment—Detached from 1st Infantry Division
D Battery, 319th Field Artillery Regiment (ABN) (105T)
2nd BN, 15th Field Artillery Regiment (105T)—Detached from 10th Mountain
    Division
26th Marine Expeditionary Unit (SOC)
1st BN, 8th Marines Regiment

TF Viking milestones:
Kirkuk liberation—April 10, 2003
Mosul liberation—April 11, 2003

Combined Joint Special Operations Task Force-West (TF Dagger)

5th Special Forces Group
1st BN, 124th Infantry Regiment—FLNG
2nd BN, 14th Infantry Regiment—Detached from the 10th Mountain Division
A Company, 1st Battalion, 19th Special Forces Group

The contingency operating plan for Iraq was OPLAN 1003-96, which had been formulated and fully reviewed in 1996. After President Bill Clinton authorized a policy of regime change in Iraq in 1998, the OPLAN was updated and transitioned to OPLAN 1003-98. The operational design called for an invasion force of more than 380,000 troops but, under pressure from Rumsfeld, General Franks reduced the number to 275,000 and provided it to President Bush on December 28, 2001. During 2002, the OPLAN was discussed and various recommendations were made regarding assumptions about international support varying from robust, reduced, or unilateral.[24]

POLO STEP

In the 1990s, the administration of U.S. President Clinton created a coded compartment for sensitive information regarding American covert actions and counterterrorism plans related to the activities of Saddam's regime in Iraq. By the mid-1990s this was expanded to include Osama bin Laden and his associates. This was code-named "Polo Step," and following the terrorist attacks on the U.S. homeland on September 11, 2001, CENTCOM and other U.S. military and national security components used the designation to include planning for the overthrow of Saddam should the necessity arise. At the time, any use of WMD or an invasion of any neighbor by Saddam would have most likely triggered a U.S. military response.

Table 9.1

Initial Planning, Code-Named "Polo Step"
"Running Start-Hybrid" Operational Timeline

Phase I
Preparation of the battlefield (30 days)
Complete posturing of initial force (60 days)

Phase II
Attack regime—flow follow-on forces
One heavy division—101st Air Assault—One heavy BCT
Two armored cavalry regiments (ACRs)—One division heavy or
light (20–45 days)

Phase III
Complete regime destruction (90 days)

Phase IV
Post-major combat hostilities
Phase IVa—Stabilization (2–3 months), Phase IVb—Recovery (18–24 months)
Phase IVc—Transition to security cooperation (12–18 months)
Achieve security cooperation within two years of initiation of Phase I

The basic operational concept was to conduct strategic, synchronized, simultaneous, and precision attacks against the Iraqi regime's support infrastructure, military centers, and communications systems and, through shock and awe, have them arrive at the assessment within their own strategic calculus that their capacity to resist as a functioning military had been destroyed and, as a result, their choices now revolved around two options: acquiesce or be killed. In essence, the United States and its coalition allies operationalized the entire breadth and depth of the battlefield, creating pressure at multiple points. Since the objective was the regime and its weapons rather than the Iraqi people, two weeks before the initiation of Phase I, U.S. and coalition aircraft dropped leaflets over Baghdad urging noninterference. The initial air operations would simultaneously then be joined by a rapid ground advance from coalition staging areas in Kuwait. Two supporting drives would sprint to Baghdad and seize control while displacing key individuals and elements of the Ba'athist government.

OIF GROUND OPERATIONS AGAINST REGIME-HELD BAGHDAD

Thus, V Corps advanced north just west of the Euphrates River in the first axis of advance, with the I MEF moving north just east of the river. Both groups would move to positions southwest and southeast of the city in a pincer movement advance essentially acting like dual hammers converging on a target from left and right. A key component was the anvil (the 4th Infantry Division), which would, at least theoretically, take up a position north of the city after transitioning through Turkey via ships in the Mediterranean Sea and moving south after securing key northern objectives in Iraq. Unfortunately, the anvil went missing as Turkey refused the initial financial incentives offered by the U.S. government and demanded greater compensation in order to allow American forces passage across Turkish territory to conduct military operations against Saddam's regime.Turkey had traditionally been a stalwart ally of the United States particularly in resisting attempts by the Soviet Union to expand its influence into the Middle East. However, in 2002, Recep Tayyip Erdogan founded the Justice and Development Party (AKP), which came to power in Turkey during the same year. The traditionally strong relations with the United States soon began weakening as the AKP, following 2002, began arresting Turkish military officers it deemed a threat to its rule.

THE "ANVIL" WENT MISSING

In 2003, in the lead-up to OIF, Erdogan as prime minister adopted a hardline vis-à-vis the United States and led the negotiations seeking an

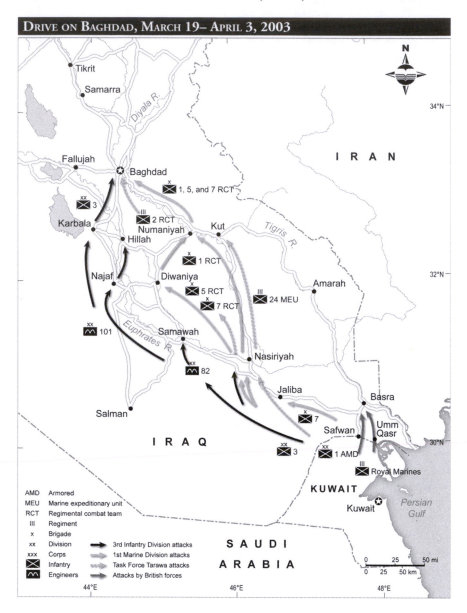

DRIVE ON BAGHDAD, MARCH 19– APRIL 3, 2003

extra $4 billion from the United States to allow the 4th Infantry Division (4th ID) to transit Turkish territory en route to Iraq. The United States had offered $6 billion in direct assistance, and Erdogan's government wanted $10 billion. The impasse meant that the 4th ID was not able to fulfill its expected role in descending south from Turkey and closing the backdoor for fleeing Iraqi forces exiting north upon the approach of U.S. and coalition forces. The "anvil" in the "hammer and anvil" in the operational design, as a result of the failed negotiations, was missing when the ground campaign of OIF was launched.

Other U.S. and coalition units moved to fill the vacuum in northern Iraq as a result of Erdogan's demands. On March 26, 2003, 954 paratroopers of the 173rd Airborne Brigade (Separate) conducted a combat jump from C-17 Globemasters of the USAF Air Mobility Command (62nd Airlift Wing, 728th Airlift Squadron, along with the 786th Security Forces Squadron) onto the Bashur Airfield in northern Iraq. The 173rd secured the airfield as U.S. Army armor was brought in, and within three days, the entire Brigade was on the ground and prepared to begin offensive operations. Joining up with Army Special Forces, the 173rd proceeded during Operation Option North to the vicinity of the northern Iraqi city of Kirkuk, home to the second largest oil reserves in Iraq (after the Rumaila fields in the South). The combined U.S. forces, operating in conjunction with Iraqi Kurdish fighters (Peshmerga), engaged and defeated the 2nd, 4th, 8th, and 38th Iraqi Infantry Divisions.

On April 24, 2003, a dozen Turkish Special Forces were arrested in Daquq—a village 45 minutes south of Kirkuk. Held for 24 hours, these soldiers were released by U.S. forces. Later that summer on July 4, 2003, troopers from the 173rd raided a safe house in the northern Iraqi Kurdish city of Sulaymaniyah, which housed members of Iraq's Turkmen Front and Turkish Special Forces (including a Turkish colonel and two majors). This situation subsequently became known as the "Hood Event," as these individuals had penetrated into Iraqi Kurdistan with orders to kill or capture local Kurdish civilian officials. A flurry of diplomatic activity ensued, and the Turkish soldiers were released to representatives of the Turkish military after being held in U.S. custody for 60 hours.

While Combined Joint Special Operations Task Force-North (TF Viking) and the 173rd did a superb job stepping in when the 4th ID had been rerouted, TF Viking or the "Sky Soldiers" of the 173rd simply did not have the resources or numbers to effectively block the back door for Iraqi regime elements escaping north and northwest from Baghdad, as V Corps and I MEF first approached from the South. The pincer movements by V Corps and I MEF in the approach to Baghdad were soon followed by operations inside the city; however, the four heavy brigades of the 4th ID were severely missed in the initial phase of OEF, arriving in theater from the Persian Gulf as follow-on forces in April 2003. The original mission by the 4th ID in northern Iraq was to hold in place 13 Iraqi divisions arrayed along the Green Line; in its absence this mission was accomplished by TF Viking.

The ability of V Corps and the I MEF to surround Baghdad and control the situation was ultimately degraded by both Turkey's ruling party AKP's hesitance in working with a NATO ally and the belief within the Bush administration that the additional $4 billion Ankara was demanding was simply too high a price and very likely result in setting an unwanted precedent for future operational needs. When costs associated with operations within the Iraqi theater later soared to $8 billion per month during the insurgency (for a period of years), paying an amount that seemed outrageous at the time may have been, in hindsight, the wiser and less expensive course of action.[25]

Moreover, the added miles and hours of operations required to move the 4th ID's M1A Abrams tanks and M2 Bradley fighting vehicles increased maintenance and repair issues—including downtime—and ultimately constrained the use of armor by American commanders. The 173rd was forced to secure areas that should have been cleared by U.S. armor. On several occasions, 173rd company-sized detachments were sent into high-threat situations, with a few unarmored M998 cargo "Humvees."

In the west of Iraq, U.S., U.K., and Australian Special Forces, many staging from Jordan as part of Combined Joint Special Operations Task Force-West (TF Dagger), secured key territories and installations. One of the more problematic threats during Operation Desert Storm was mobile Scud missile launchers. Saddam fired Scuds at Saudi Arabia as well as Israel in an attempt to draw Tel Aviv into the war and destroy the unity of the coalition aligned against him. Coalition Special Operations Forces during OIF entered Iraq from Jordan to eliminate the Scud missile threat against Israel.

The Australian Special Air Service Regiment secured the strategic Al Asad Air Base—the second largest airfield in Iraq—and then turned the base over to the U.S. 3rd ACR in May 2003. In March 2004, the 3rd ACR was relieved at Al Asad by elements of the I MEF. The Al Asad Air Base became one of the most important facilities for coalition operations in post-conflict stabilization efforts. As the insurgency grew following the close of major combat operations, Anbar Province in western Iraq—home to the majority of the country's Sunni Muslim population—became a critical area for U.S. and coalition counterinsurgency operations.[26] Al Asad Air Base provided the United States and its allies an invaluable resource in that fight.

In the ground advance north from Kuwait, the U.S. 3rd Infantry Division (the spearhead of V Corps) drove 150 miles into Iraq toward the city of Nasiriyah and its key bridges over the Euphrates River, while the I MEF and the British 1st Division advanced toward the southern city of Basra securing the Rumaila oil fields and the oil terminal at Umm Qasr.

Within three days, U.S. and coalition forces were within 100 miles of Baghdad, and air superiority had been achieved. The Iraqis continued to fire surface-to-air missiles, but its air force had, from the beginning of OIF, refused to engage in the air.

In the advance north, the first operational objective of OIF was seizing and controlling key bridges and military sites near the city of Nasiriyah with a population of approximately 250,000 people and strategically located on the Euphrates River, 225 miles southeast of Baghdad. The importance of Nasiriyah rested on the city's key position, as it guarded, through the presence of the Iraqi army's 3rd Corps and the Tallil Air Base, key supply routes to the North. The Iraqi 3rd Corps was composed of the 11th Infantry Division, the 51st Mechanized Infantry Division, and the 6th Armored Division, all at about a 50 percent strength level. The 51st was positioned in the South to provide security to the oil fields, while the 6th was in the North above the city near al-Amara. As a result, U.S. forces were faced with three brigade-sized formations of the 11th Iraqi Infantry Division positioned to defend the city. The Battle of Nasiriyah or, as it is often called, the Battle of the Bridges, lasted from March 23 to 29, 2003.

The overall operational plan for the ground component of OIF was rapid movement north by V Corps and the I MEF to secure Baghdad as swiftly as possible, effect regime change as soon as possible, and not become bogged down in battles along the way. The concept was to bypass many sites that would normally be seized and controlled in such an offensive campaign in order to protect the rear of the advancing army as well as secure landlines of communication (LLOCs)—particularly for resupply. However, due to the strategic location of the city, the air base, the headquarters of the Iraqi 3rd Corps, and the three brigades of the 11th Infantry Division, Nasiriyah would have to be secured in order to hold the bridges and keep the critical supply corridor open to U.S. and coalition forces as they advanced north and engaged Saddam's forces in the expected battle of Baghdad. Additionally, Marine Corps units would cross the river at Nasiriyah utilizing bridges taken and held by elements of V Corps.

THE DRIVE NORTH

On the night of March 20, the 3rd Brigade of the U.S. 3rd Infantry Division (3rd ID) advanced from positions in Kuwait into Iraq and drove 117 kilometers toward Nasiriyah. The mission was to contain the Iraqi 11th Division, while the remainder of the 3rd ID advanced northwest along and across the Euphrates River. On March 21 and 22, the U.S. Army 3rd ID engaged and defeated the Iraqi 11th Infantry Division southwest of

Nasiriyah and seized the Highway 1 Bridge across the Euphrates River. By March 23, the 3rd ID had passed control of the bridge off to the 2nd Marine Expeditionary Brigade (Task Force Tarawa), which had followed the 3rd ID into Iraq, protecting its flanks. TF Tarawa then attacked into Nasiriyah and captured additional bridges and river crossings.

In the South, after defeating the Iraqi 51st Mechanized Division and securing the oil fields near Rumaila, the U.S. 1st Marine Division transferred security responsibilities for the oil fields to the British 1st Armoured Division and then drove northwest to cross the bridges at Nasiriyah, continuing its march north to engage the Iraqi Republican Guard divisions then located outside Baghdad. With the United States in control of the bridges, the 1st Marine Division on its way north as the main striking force of the I MEF was able to cross the Euphrates River and proceed north on the east side of the river, while V Corps proceeded north on a parallel course west of the river. The Republican Guard divisions protecting the southern approaches to Baghdad would be hit nearly simultaneously by V Corps attacking from a northeast axis of advance west of the river and by I MEF attacking the Republican Guard from a northwest axis east of the river.

The plan was solid in formulation, but given the political problems that ensued with Turkey, it was less solid in execution. One remembers yet again the words of the Prussian general, Helmuth Graf von Moltke (the elder), who observed in the nineteenth century, "Strategy is the application of common sense to the conduct of war. The difficulty lies in execution."[27]

The pincer or double envelopment from the South required an attack from the North to block the escape routes out of the city. As the Turkish and U.S. governments failed in arriving at a mutually agreeable solution to allow the advance from Turkish soil to Baghdad, the U.S. 4th ID, instead of conducting an assault from the North, was still floating on ships, then rerouted through the Suez Canal to enter the theater of operations from Kuwait. The original plan for OIF had already been pared down from previous military recommendations in terms of ground forces, from 380,000 to about 160,000 in the initial phase, as it sought to maximize speed and maneuver and in the belief that technology had altered the basic dynamics of warfare, eliminating the need for heavy forces and overwhelming numbers and capabilities. A key aspect of this is that during the 1991 Gulf War, the United States committed overwhelming and decisive force and through superb diplomacy and political leadership received financial resources from allies, which eventually paid for a large portion of the bill.

In 2003, by eschewing both allies and military advice, the Bush administration pressed ahead and, after being unable or unwilling to secure Turkey's cooperation, entered ground combat in the heart of the Middle East, with objectives that included regime change to create long-term regional stability. After the United States took control of Baghdad, and the looting of shops and stores by Iraqis began, the United States with limited military resources in the theater was unable to act. The careful attention to detail that had accompanied the planning and execution of Rapid Dominance and shock and awe, effectively impacting the perceptions of Iraqi leaders, soldiers, and citizens in such a manner that they came to hold the belief that resisting was futile, was now dissipating in the emerging belief throughout Iraq that the United States and its allies were incapable or unwilling of stopping largely unarmed citizens rampaging through the streets. The aura of extreme might and power that Rapid Dominance did in fact achieve in the first three weeks of the war now collapsed as the United States was seen as, if not completely powerless, at least not sufficiently capable of controlling the streets of Baghdad. This belief became widespread and eventually altered the strategic calculus of those contemplating resistance.

BATTLE OF NASIRIYAH

The Battle of Nasiriyah also provided a glimpse of the insurgency that ensued following the end of major combat operations at the end of April 2003. During Operation Desert Storm, the United States confined itself to liberating a nation that welcomed American and coalition forces. Thus, the strength of the U.S. military was brought to bear against Iraqi forces in the air, in open terrain, and in urban settings that did not require occupation among a population that was, at the very least, partially hostile. In the lead-up to the Iraq War of 2003, some U.S. leaders such as Vice President Cheney expressed that U.S. forces would be welcomed as liberators, as many Iraqis would welcome the removal of Saddam.

However, even if they were not out in the streets throwing flowers, the reasoning went, the Iraqi army and security services would survive the war sufficiently intact to provide stability and order. Much of this prewar thinking was obtained by Defense Department leaders as a result of multiple contacts with exiled yet charismatic Iraqis who argued that once they returned to Iraq and were supported by the United States, they would then be positioned to steer the country on a path to greater democratization and modernization. The belief among key leaders in the Bush administration was that an effective interim Iraqi government would be up and running in a very brief amount of time.

Nonetheless, the problems during the Iraq War of 2003 began as early as the Battle of Nasiriyah, when the Iraqis were able to move beyond the solid (or strength) and find the gaps (or weaknesses) in the then unfolding U.S. military operation. The regular Iraqi army fought U.S. forces at Nasiriyah and then slowly succumbed to superior military force in a conventional-on-conventional–style battle. However, U.S. planners had not adequately anticipated nor prepared for the rise of irregular paramilitary groups on a wide-scale basis such as the Fedayeen Saddam that took the place of conventional army units in resisting U.S. operations.

After the United States took control of the city, small groups of Fedayeen Saddam, wearing civilian clothing and hiding among the people throughout the city, subsequently launched attacks on U.S. Marine patrols with small arms and rocket-propelled grenades (RPGs). Iraqi fighters in civilian clothes exploited the urban terrain where high-tech U.S. systems could not be adequately brought to bear, engaging in hit-and-run tactics while also utilizing protected sites (at least from the U.S. perspective) such as hospitals and mosques from which to stage and in which to hide.

The leaders of the newly developing insurgency, by engaging U.S. forces on the ground and in close quarter range, developed insights, gained intelligence, and became acutely aware of the soft targets of the U.S. military, that is, noncombat arms units moving in support of combat operations and units that were less protected and less able to defend themselves. Thus, they searched, found, and began targeting the gaps in the solid. For instance, at Nasiriyah, a support unit, the 507th Maintenance Company, found itself making a wrong turn off Highway 8 and driving directly into enemy-held territory in the city. The U.S. Army supply convoy was soon ambushed, with 11 soldiers killed and 6 taken prisoners. A company of marines attached to the 2nd Marine Expeditionary Brigade (Task Force Tarawa) swiftly reacted and rescued the ambushed supply convoy.

In another incident during the Battle of Nasiriyah, Iraqi fighters using urban terrain unfamiliar to U.S. forces were able to ambush Charlie Company, 1st Battalion, and 2nd Marines, who were hit by RPGs, mortars, and artillery fires as well as four Iraqi tanks that were hidden behind a building. Adding to the lethality of the incident, two Pennsylvania Air National Guard A-10s (close air support jets) cleared by the battalion's forward air controller mistakenly strafed Charlie Company's position. In the "Ambush Alley" incident, 18 marines were killed and 8 amphibious assault vehicles were disabled, many of the casualties caused by the friendly fire incident.

While the United States ultimately prevailed in the Battle of Nasiriyah, the stories of U.S. misfortunes as well as accounts of Iraqi heroism—as it took a full week for U.S. forces to subdue pockets of resistance—led to the bolstering of Iraqi morale and the solidification of the mind-set that America and its allies indeed had weaknesses which could be, as "the brave fighters" in Nasiriyah had demonstrated, successfully exploited and attacked.[28] As the events in Nasiriyah unfolded, Saddam's propaganda machine was spinning out the narrative in Baghdad that the Americans and their British allies were being killed by the thousands in Nasiriyah and Basra.

In Basra, the British attempted to insert MI-6 (Military Intelligence, Department 6) officers into the southern port city to undermine the strength of the resistance; however, the Basra paramilitary resistance continued for two weeks and was defeated only by close combat inside the urban terrain.[29] Knowledge of that terrain, both geographical and human, was generated by many years of contact by Britain in the key southern Iraqi port. In clashes at As Samawah (March 21–23, 2003), the Battle of An Najaf (March 25–29, 2003), and the Battle of Karbala (March 31–April 2, 2003), Iraqi resistance continued long after U.S. and coalition forces bypassed the cities. Eventually, as in Basra, the insurgency was broken only after close quarter battle (CQB) in urban centers.

BATTLE OF BAGHDAD

Iraqi military commanders and intelligence personnel were able to identify weaknesses in U.S. operations during the clashes leading up to the Battle of Baghdad (April 4–8, 2003) as well. However, the ability of the American military to adapt to changing circumstances, then quickly continue operations at a largely unbroken pace following mid-battle adjustments continued to serve U.S. forces well. Iraqi leaders believed U.S. forces would surround Baghdad first with armor, artillery, and conventional infantry (backed by airpower and air mobile/air assault units) and, once the roads in and out of the city were cordoned off, send in airborne troopers and marines (backed by Special Operations Forces units) to conduct clearing operations within the city itself. After U.S. troops were inside the city, Iraqi commanders planned on utilizing many of the "ambush, hit-and-run, and then disperse" tactics that had been useful in attacking American units in the other cities and on open roads.

U.S. commanders had other ideas. Urban combat can take the initiative from an advancing force and place it in the hands of a well-ensconced insurgency. Eventually, this often leads to confining the advancing force to reasonably protected garrisons, leaving many of the streets of the city in the hands of the insurgents, as it simply becomes too dangerous to conduct patrols in insurgent-infested areas. In order to undermine Iraqi commanders' expectations, U.S. commanders extended the concept of Rapid Dominance and directed American forces to mount two armored raids—nicknamed *Thunder Runs*—into the heart of the city. The use of armor in a city surprised the Iraqis in that tanks and other armored vehicles are highly susceptible to ambush from the top and from the rear.

In an act of daring courage, and, ultimately, sound military judgment, at dawn on April 5, an armored battalion consisting of 50 M1A1 Abrams tanks and 15 Bradley fighting vehicles led by Army Lieutenant Colonel Rick Schwartz attacked swiftly up Highway 8 into the heart of Baghdad, firing and taking fire then, just as swiftly, withdrawing. Every Abrams had been hit, although superficially, by RPG fire, while one tank, hit by a round by either a recoilless rifle or RPG from the rear—which penetrated a fuel cell that then set fire to the engine—had to be abandoned. The crew was rescued unharmed and the USAF later bombed the tank to keep it from falling into the hands of the enemy.

The tactic was audacious and struck at the heart of Saddam's narrative that U.S. forces would never be able to enter the city. So audacious was the strike, most Iraqis did not believe the initial reports.

> They are sick in their minds. They say they brought 65 tanks into the center of Baghdad. I say to you this talk is not true. This is part of their sick mind.
>
> —Iraqi Information Minister Muhammad Saeed al-Sahhaf

(Al-Sahhaf often made incredulous statements throughout OIF. As a result, U.S. forces as well as the Western media began referring to him as "Baghdad Bob.")

Two days after the first Thunder Run, an entire heavy brigade of Abrams tanks and Bradley armored fighting vehicles stormed into the center of Baghdad, this time maintaining their positions and fighting off all counterattacks.

> We captured an Iraqi brigadier general in the raid. He was completely surprised there were American tanks in the city. He believed their propaganda that Americans were hundreds of miles to the south, dying by the thousands. All of the sudden he's coming to work and there is a tank battalion rolling down the center of Baghdad.[30]

Rapid Dominance was meant to shape the perceptions of decision makers, soldiers, and the people of Iraq from the early hours of the war when strikes were directed specifically against Saddam's palaces and ministries in an effort to persuade the Iraqi people that it was safe to rise up against the regime. The Thunder Runs drove the point home to the people and to the government bureaucracy that Saddam's regime, as the Ba'athist regime's propaganda would have it, was not all powerful nor invincible on the ground and that for years after portraying the United States as cowards fighting from the sky and with standoff weapons were now witnessing them blasting through Saddam's iron ring around Baghdad—and charging in to the city—*on the ground*. At that moment in time, had the United States been in a position to take control of the streets and suppress the looting that immediately followed in the aftermath of the collapse of the regime and to maintain the perception in the minds of the people of competence, strength, and compassion, the issue would have been much more readily contained.

On April 9, in the center of Baghdad at the Al-Firdos Square, an M-88 recovery vehicle (heavy-duty tow truck for armor) was directed to attach a chain to a massive statue of Saddam and, amid the cheers of an assembled and celebrating crowd of Iraqi civilians, yanked the statue to the ground. Broadcast around the world, this powerful event marked the end of Saddam's regime. Less well covered, in terms of the media, was what was happening a couple of blocks away where a U.S. Marine patrol was taking fire from several hidden snipers.

Following the fall of Baghdad on April 8–9, U.S. and coalition forces took control of Tikrit (Saddam's hometown) on April 21 and occupied the oil-rich town of Kirkuk on April 29. On May 1, 2003, with the press at the ready, President Bush made a well-documented and very public carrier landing (Bush, as a young man, trained as a pilot in F-4 *Phantom* jet fighters—this landing, however, was made as a passenger) aboard the nuclear-powered aircraft carrier USS *Abraham Lincoln*. Serving as a backdrop from where the president addressed the crew, America, and the world was a large sign that said, "Mission Accomplished." In his address, Bush stated that major combat operations of OIF had been successfully concluded.

The expectation from the administration was all that remained to be accomplished was to clear pockets of resistance, stand up an interim government in Baghdad, and prepare the Iraqi people for national elections designed to introduce representative democracy to a region with a 5,000-year history of totalitarian and authoritarian government—with zero experience in Jeffersonian Democracy. OIF planning under Polo Step assumptions was that all of this, including the apparent expectation of a transformative cultural revolution, which would have been required to support democratic institutions, would be accomplished in the next two years (2003–2005).

Just as the Iraqis had not read Jefferson or Madison, they also had not been apprised of the Western etiquette of war that stipulated a gentleman's accord at the end. The culture of the Middle East was that conflict was sewn into the fabric of relations between tribes and regions. These animosities were ongoing and a part of life and while major combat would cease, the continuing presence of non-resolved animosities dictated that some level of armed struggle or resistance would never end. It took different forms, but it was a continuous and ongoing process. In the twentieth century, the Arab states, unable to defeat Israel through conventional battles (1948–1967), instead changed tactics from primarily engaging the Jewish state in conventional campaigns by creating the Palestine Liberation Organization (PLO) and other groups to conduct irregular or ghazi war (and terrorist activities) against Israel. They would do the same in Iraq.

However, Bush was correct in announcing the successful end to major combat operations against Saddam's armed forces. In 16 days of fighting, V Corps under U.S. Army Lieutenant General Wallace, advanced more than 540 miles from Kuwait on the Persian Gulf to Baghdad decisively defeating Iraqi army and bringing about the fall of the Ba'athist regime. It was arguably one of the most remarkable military advances in world history, certainly among the finest campaigns in the modern era.

When President Bush issued the NSPD-24 on January 20, 2003, and postwar operations were vested in the Department of Defense, Rumsfeld established the Office of Reconstruction and Humanitarian Assistance (ORHA) on the same day. The office was headed by retired Army Lieutenant General Jay Garner who created an initial team of 200 former military, foreign service, academic, and corporate individuals tasked with making the transition from war to stability and insuring steady progress toward modernization and democratization.

As Saddam's regime collapsed in mid- and late April 2003, Garner's ORHA was dissolved when the Coalition Provisional Authority (CPA) was created on April 21, 2003, following the establishment of a military occupation within Iraq. Garner was subsequently appointed as its first chief executive. The CPA was established as an interim government and based on UNSC Resolution 1483 adopted the powers of a transitional government in Iraq, including executive, legislative, and judicial authority. Garner reported directly to Rumsfeld. The CPA essentially served as the government in Iraq from its inception in April 2003 until its dissolution on June 28, 2004.

DE-BA'ATHIFICATION AND DISBANDING THE IRAQI ARMY

General Garner was instructed by Rumsfeld to disband the Iraqi army and to issue a "de-Ba'athification" order aimed at removing all Ba'ath party members from Iraqi government and nullifying any future employment with the central government. A great deal of controversy surrounded these issues particularly in the following months and years, as Iraq's political cohesion as a state descended into what can only be described as sectarian violence bordering on political chaos. The decision to disband the military and disqualify the Ba'athists from serving in the government was based on the intent of the Bush administration to remove Saddam from power. Thus, one of the key political objectives of OIF and COBRA II was to effect regime change within Iraq, as Saddam's government had been a continuing source of agitation, conflict, and regional instability since at least the invasion of Kuwait in 1990. This problem ran unabated throughout the 1990s and threatened a range of U.S., Western, and regional interests.

Once the decision was made for regime change (made during the Clinton administration in 1998), and blood and treasure expended yet again in dealing with Saddam's regime, U.S. leaders in April 2003 were not the least interested in removing Saddam while his tools of repression, that is, the military, security services, and key governmental agencies remained in place. There can be no doubt that key members of the Bush administration completely misread the consequences of disbanding the military and ruling out positions of power and authority for Ba'ath Party members. The historical evidence is difficult to refute. However, in April 2003 and given what had been ongoing for 13 years, including the use of chemical weapons against his own people, U.S. leaders wanted not only Saddam removed from power but also sought to dissolve the institutions and tools by which his authoritarian rule was supported.

The United States shared in the empowerment of Saddam in at least two instances. In the 1960s, Saddam became part of a CIA-sponsored six-man kill squad, which (eventually) aided in the assassination of the leader of Iraq, Abd al-Qasim. In the middle of ongoing Cold War dynamics, Qasim had increasingly followed policies that would have aligned Iraq as well as its vital geographical position in the Middle East and its oil reserves with the Union of Soviet Socialist Republics (USSR). Additionally, the United States supported Iraq in the 1980s when radical militant forces within Iran attempted to overrun Iraq, which would have then placed the radical clerics in Tehran in a position to directly threaten Saudi Arabia and seize control of the largest oil reserves in the world. The U.S. Department of Defense and the American intelligence community provided military and intelligence expertise that, while directly related to the Iranian threat to expand across the Middle East, was supportive of the government in Baghdad.

By 2003, however, the United States wanted Saddam and any supporting structures or organizational entity that could be used to bring him back into power within Iraq permanently removed. However, Garner argued that while the overall concern was valid, the disbanding of the military and the removal of government employees who were Ba'athists would create a very difficult situation in postwar Iraq. In Saddam's regime, to be a part of the government, one had to be in the Ba'ath Party. Hence, everyone who was experienced in running a government in Iraq was going to be told that their services were no longer needed. Garner also pointed out that many government employees were Ba'ath Party members because it was seen as necessary for government service, and many were not radicalized nor seized of intent for fighting or agitating for the return of Saddam. Senior-level Bush administration officials were adamant and communicated their determination to Garner: "Give the orders to disband the army and disqualify the Ba'athists." Knowing what would most likely occur given those actions, Garner refused.

This led to Garner's dismissal and his replacement by L. Paul Bremer, who took the title of U.S. presidential envoy and chief administrator, CPA. Bremer immediately issued CPA Order No. 1—the disqualification of any Iraqi from government service who was or had been, under Saddam, a member of the Ba'ath Party. On May 23, 2003, Bremer issued CPA Order No. 2, which formally disbanded the Iraqi army. As a result, 750,000 Ba'athists who had formed the core of the Iraqi political system had been fired by CPA Order No. 1. They went home and attempted to find jobs in a war-torn Iraqi society. Distraught and, in many instances, desperate, they were soon joined by 400,000 former Iraqi soldiers who were now left to fend for themselves in communities that offered very little gainful employment. While the "body" of Saddam's regime had been killed, the 1.15 million disenfranchised formed what could be described as the "ghost" of the former regime. It was this "ghost" that subsequently haunted U.S. efforts at stability and security operations.

> Military planners for OIF assumed that the coalition would be greeted as liberators and that the Iraqi Army would be able to assist in reconstruction efforts. Much of Iraq did treat the coalition as liberators, but the appreciative feeling dissolved when the CPA removed Baathists from consideration for employment in the new Iraq, and when the Iraqi Army was dissolved. Within two weeks of arrival in Iraq, the head of the CPA, Paul Bremer negated both planning assumptions. The arguments "for" and "against" dissolving the Iraqi military both had merits and consequences. Dissolving the Iraqi military removed one of Saddam's tools of tyranny and would allow the new Iraq to begin with a more ethnically balanced security force. Conversely, eliminating the Iraqi military threw 400,000 veterans into unemployment, left the coalition under manned and changed the Iraqi liberation into occupation. Security is the foundation for support and stability. Therefore 150,000 U.S. ground forces had little chance of occupying and stabilizing a country of 25 million people.[31]

The United States had been communicating with a number of exiled Iraqis who had been driven out of Saddam's Iraq and were, in the spring of 2003, prepared to return and assist in the establishment of a new government. Unfortunately, some of these individuals, such as Ahmed Chalabi, while charismatic and persuasive—at least to U.S. officials— were less effective once back in Iraq. The CPA on July 22, 2003, formed the Iraqi Governing Council, granted the council limited governing powers, and appointed members, which included Mowaffak al-Rubaie, Chalabi, Adnan Pachachi, and Adil Abdul-Mahdi. The Iraqi Governing

Council became a key coordination cell regarding the Development Fund for Iraq that, from May 2003 until June 2004, under CPA administration, dispensed about $19 billion in direct aid. The fund was meant to provide capital and finance for large-scale reconstruction projects such as hospitals, power, water, sewage, and other basic services. Unfortunately, the prewar planning assumptions had envisioned a postwar Iraq with substantial receipts from oil sales that were to assist in the day-to-day expenses of running the government. The fund was not designed for covering the day-to-day operating expenses of the transitional Iraqi government or paying large sums for security operations. The resources of the fund, however, were diverted to cover a range of contingencies, and subsequent auditing by U.S. government organizations found that vast sums were unaccounted for.

The CPA announced, however, on December 14, 2003, that U.S. forces operating jointly under Operation Red Dawn and led by elements of the 1st Special Forces Operational Detachment-Delta, with support from the 4th ID, and working in close cooperation with Iraqi sources, had captured Saddam on December 13. American troops had found him hiding in an underground makeshift shelter and took him into custody.[32] Thus, from April to December 2003, the United States was focused on hunting down Saddam and his top lieutenants, and over 200 were captured or killed, including his two sons, Uday and Qusay, on July 22, 2003. While this insured there would be no return of Saddam and his key supporters—which the United States deemed necessary in order for Iraqis to be able to transition to a new Iraq—Saddam's capture and subsequent trial and execution by an Iraqi court also served to crystallize a nascent insurgency that was being formed among the Sunni tribes. The fact that Shiites were coming into the new government in increasing numbers also served to alienate the Sunni population, particularly in Anbar Province.

In June 2004, a caretaker government was created and designated the Iraqi Interim Government, and preparations were made to conduct elections in order to introduce a government that, from a Western point of view, would be seen as legitimate by the people of Iraq. When one is without clean water, without electricity, has limited food supplies, and is uncertain about the future, the results of a Western-constructed election process, involving what were viewed as corrupt and foreign-supported Iraqi aspirants to leadership posts, were viewed with suspicion across Iraq. However, to the Sunni tribal leadership, with Sunnis being a minority in a Shiite-majority Iraq, the outcome of the January 2005 parliamentary elections was of acute interest, as they then led to the creation of the Iraqi Transitional Government and the installment of the Maliki government in 2006.

The empowerment of the Shiite-oriented Maliki government and its subsequent inability to bring Iraqis together led to a crackdown not only on the Sunni tribes but also on Shiite elements that Nouri al-Maliki could not convince to abide by his decisions. The efforts at creating an effective and representative government as well as the provision of basic services, including longer-term reconstruction and development projects, were hindered by a violent Iraqi insurgency. The nascent political environment was further endangered by the perception of an inept and corrupt government, as problems with electricity and clean water and other basic services caused substantial levels of frustration with the U.S.-backed government.

The harder Maliki and his government cracked down on provincial leaders and forces, the less willing they became to acquiesce in the face of central government orders and more determined they became in lending support to those engaged in a virulent insurgency. Many of the Sunni tribes viewed Iraqi Shiites as being closely aligned with Iranian policy preferences. Consequently, Maliki, an Iraqi Shiite, was widely seen by the Sunnis as a vassal of Iran and beholden to the United States. For millions of Sunnis, these facts and the nature of Maliki's support made the Shiite politician completely unacceptable as the leader of the new Iraq.

COUNTERINSURGENCY OPERATIONS

An insurgent is "one who rises in revolt against constituted authority; a rebel who is not recognized as a belligerent."[33] Thus, a counterinsurgency campaign involves "those political, economic, military, paramilitary, psychological and civic actions taken by a government to defeat an insurgency."[34] In its counterinsurgent activities in both Afghanistan and Iraq, the United States continually refined its counterinsurgency (COIN) strategy.

By 2013, Joint Doctrine for Counterinsurgency extended beyond the defeat of the insurgent to a broader appreciation that one cannot, generally, kill or capture one's way to victory in today's fourth generation warfare (4GW) environment.[35] This recognition is captured in the more expansive perspective on effective COIN operations, which "redefines the definition of counterinsurgency as comprehensive civilian and military efforts designed to simultaneously defeat and contain an insurgency *and address its root causes*" [Italics mine].[36]

During the Cold War era, the United States and its allies relied on, in many instances and circumstances, strong, authoritarian governments—some clearly best described as dictatorships—to frustrate the attempts by the Soviet Union at undermining the U.S.-led democratic coalition of nations. Intent on the destruction of Western democracies, Moscow attempted to undermine the United States around the world, in general, and in the undeveloped countries or "Third World," in particular.[37] This included the Middle East. After the demise of the Soviet Union and in the face of increasing violence associated with terrorist activities, most notably the attacks on the American homeland on September 11, 2001, the United States sought to change the dynamics wherein it had supported specific authoritarian governments and all but ignored issues relating to the domestic repression activities of that government against its citizens.

The underdeveloped nature of the Third World relative to the modernizing and advanced nations has many causes. One of the most prominent causes for this is expressed within the argument that the traditional authoritarian ruler was less interested in seeing growth and development within his or her country than he or she was in maintaining power and control. If growth and development created power centers that the ruler could not effectively control, then such advances were looked on suspiciously in terms of creating dynamics that led to the undermining of the government.

During the Cold War, the West had a greater interest in forestalling the spread of Soviet influence and communism in the underdeveloped world than in the spread of democracy. As such, in the objective of frustrating Soviet attempts at taking over a society or exerting significant influence, the United States and its allies supported authoritarian leaders with the strength to forestall Soviet penetration—particularly within the Middle East.

However, the underdeveloped nature of great regions of the world led to frustration among a significant portion of the inhabitants, and this manifested itself in a number of ways, including the rise of terrorist activities and an increase in the frequency and intensity of insurgencies in critical and vital regions. Following the September 11 attacks, the U.S. government under President Bush began a process of reviewing U.S. policy, particularly in the Middle East. While the administration believed that many terrorist attacks were initiated not from a sense of economic deprivation but from a violent ideology intent on global domination, it decided that more must be accomplished in creating greater economic opportunity in North Africa, the Middle East, and South Asia, even at the risk of undermining traditional U.S. authoritarian allies.

Reflecting these views, the Bush administration created the Broader Middle East Initiative designed with a goal of eventually overcoming the problems of development and economic growth within the region. The situation can be summarized in the following (admittedly oversimplified manner): It recognized that in dealing with the problem of terrorism one cannot expect to kill or capture one's way to a lasting solution. Accordingly, the decision calculus of would-be terrorists would have to be influenced in a positive manner. For instance, at the time of the Broader Middle East Initiative following in the wake of September 11, 2001, a young man in many Muslim and Arab countries found that the lack of development and economic growth had created an environment in which he had two choices: live in poverty and watch as your family suffered, or, pick up an AK-47 (or suicide vest) and do something about it. The perception among many was the lack of jobs and financial opportunity were directly related to corrupt political leaders and their corrupt allies in the business community.

Moreover, these young people were fed a steady diet by the often corrupt politicians and their business associates that great international powers were truly to blame for the lack of opportunity within their countries. This was an attempt to deflect criticism away from them and onto others. Adding to this mix of anger and discontentment were the radical fundamentalists who blamed the "godless" West for all the troubles in the Middle East. The Broader Middle East Initiative, at its core, attempted to change that equation to include a third option: the opportunity for obtaining a reasonably well-paying job, perhaps buying a home, but most certainly providing one's family with the basic necessities of life.

THE INSTABILITY ATTRACTED ADDITIONAL ELEMENTS OF AL-QAEDA

Into this mix of dissatisfaction, foreign occupation, and a culture prone to violent reactions, came hard-core al-Qaeda operatives transplanted from training camps and hideouts from around the world. These individuals eventually congregated in Iraq under the name of *Jama'at al-Tawhid wal-Jihad* led by Abu Musab al-Zarqawi. Zarqawi fought in Afghanistan during the 1980s and 1990s and was eventually arrested in Jordan and imprisoned until 1999. After returning to Afghanistan and setting up operations in Herat, he reportedly began focusing on Islamist factions operating in the informal territory of Kurdistan (parts of Iran, Turkey, Syria, and northern Iraq). Zarqawi pursued a particularly violent campaign in both Syria and Iraq, with a specialty of targeting Iraqi government and military personnel for cooperating with the United States.

In October 2004, the Zarqawi group issued a statement acknowledging the subordination of the group to bin Laden and al-Qaeda, which had been forced from Afghanistan by the Americans during OEF and, while maintaining affiliates around the world, relocated to Pakistan. The Zarqawi group then took the name *Tanzim Qaidat al-Jihad fi Bilad al-Rafidayn* (also known as al-Qaeda in Iraq or AQI), and the Iraqi city of Fallujah became an al-Qaeda stronghold and headquarters. Operating against the U.S. occupation, AQI became part of the insurgency, particularly strong in what came to be known as the Sunni Triangle, a region north of Baghdad with Baqubah at the east point of the triangle, Ar Ramadi on the west, and the city of Tikrit marking the tip of the triangular shaped area in the north.

While insurgent activity took place across Iraq, the vast majority of violence was centered in two regions. Sunni insurgents were centered in Anbar Province and the Sunni Triangle (which includes the cities of Samara and Fallujah), while violence flared in the poor Shia sections of cities from Baghdad to the southern city of Basra. Along with the Sunni insurgency extending to the Syrian border in Anbar Province in western Iraq, another disgruntled Iraqi leader was Muqtada al-Sadr who operated in the South independently of his Sunni enemies. Sadr was Shiite and led what was called the Mahdi Militia or the Mahdi Army and in June 2004 put 1,000 armed men into the streets of Baghdad in a direct challenge to the U.S.-controlled CPA.

The United States and the provisional Iraqi government moved immediately to arrest Sadr, who fled into the holy city of Najaf. One of the most influential Shiites in Iraq, Al-Sayyid Ali al-Husseini al-Sistani a religious cleric revered for his simple life, modest material surroundings, and his devotion to the original meanings of the *Quran* (including peace, harmony, and the alignment of one's life with the divine will), brokered a peace agreement between the United States and Sadr wherein Sadr declared a cease-fire and became a participant in the political process. This was followed by the United States incorporating the Mahdi Army into the Iraqi security forces. It was at this time that Chalabi stepped down as the key Iraqi leader under CPA authority and was replaced by a more acceptable leader to the Shiites, Iyad Allawi. Following the compromise with the more powerful Shiite factions, the majority of insurgent attacks, while still occurring across Iraq, were centered in the western provinces of Anbar, Ninewa, and Salah ad Din.

The comparison of military operations in COBRA II (OIF major combat operations aimed at taking down Saddam's regime) and ECLIPSE II (OIF stability and security operations following the removal of Saddam's regime) indicates the supremacy of Western conventional military operations and the significant drop in capacity, as it relates to securing the gains of victory. In the "conventional" military campaign of OIF COBRA II, the network-centric model of warfare was remarkable in the swift and decisive nature of the initial phase of the war. However, the problem with network-centric warfare is that while it swiftly moved information regarding targeting, followed by the triggering of automated weapons systems in many instances, the insurgents quickly learned to avoid being caught out in the open. Intermingled with the civilian population, coupled with Western sensitivities in striking civilians, a strike then required interpretation of the intelligence and targeting. Higher echelon commanders, including political (elected and appointees), sought to weigh in on such decisions. This process could not be fully automated requiring additional time and human decision making.

Hence, the advantages generated by network-centric, information-age warfare that provided the United States the ability to operate inside an opponent's OODA-Loop and thereupon the ability to control the operational tempo of the engagement were and are obviated by insurgents utilizing irregular, unconventional, and asymmetrical warfare conducted against a conventional force operating within the parameters of the laws of war (avoid killing innocents) and when such insurgents are fighting and hiding "among the people." In short, the OODA-Loop advantage had been offset by the insurgents' use of a "war among the people" (Flaechen-und Luecken). Moreover,

> Major combat operations in OIF were characterized by speed, precision and lethality—but when you transition into a set of conditions where you have to control terrain, you have to control the will of the people, you have to rebuild institutions that are emerging in a power vacuum—technology doesn't do that for you.[38]

In the summer of 2006, a classified report by marine intelligence warned that the United States was in danger of losing the war and noted that the outlook was particularly dismal in the western provinces (chiefly Anbar) and in the Sunni Triangle. Colonel Peter Devlin (U.S. Marine Corps [USMC]) wrote in the report: "The social and political situation has deteriorated to a point that MNF [Multinational Force] and ISF [International Security Force] are no longer capable of defeating the insurgency al-Anbar . . . Underlying this decline in stability is the near collapse of the social order in al-Anbar."

At that point in time, the ability to rethink the approach being taken—to adjust, to adapt, and to overcome—which had become a hallmark of the most successful militaries in history, allowed U.S. and allied commanders the freedom and opportunity to look anew at the problem and be open to alternative courses of action. By being open to new information and being able to readily admit that what you are presently doing is insufficient for success are characteristics handed down by a Western intellectual tradition that began with the critical analysis and scientific approach taken by the ancient Greeks. In the early modern world, this tradition was carried by Europeans into the new world and served as a foundation for American intellectual activity both in war and in peace. Freedom of thought is a necessary condition for critical analysis and scientific investigation. Critical analysis and scientific investigation are necessary for the development of advanced military technology. This same tendency toward critical thought now must be utilized in understanding and coming to terms with how opponents are mitigating the advantages of superior military conventional convention by conducting "war among the people."

For instance, the extensive experience of Great Britain and the incomparable value derived from that nation's heritage in both theoretical and empirical pursuits cannot be overstated in terms of its contribution to the modern profession of arms, in general, or the American military, in particular.

> On every occasion that I have been sent to achieve some military objective in order to serve a political purpose, I, and those with me, have had to change our method and reorganize in order to succeed. Until this was done we could not use our force effectively. The need to adapt is driven by the decisions of the opponent, the choice of the objectives, the way or method force is applied, and all the forces and resources available, particularly when operating with allies. All of this demands an understanding of the political context of the operation, and the role of the military within it. Only when adaptation and context are complete can force be applied with utility.[39]

For the forces on the ground in the initial months of the insurgency—prepared and trained to fight conventional battles—the problem required a significant reassessment of the way forward. As the old adage observes, when one's only tool is a hammer, every problem looks like a nail. Thus, the U.S. military needed both to put the hammer aside and learn, in the field, to become skilled with a scalpel. Such an approach would require more effective human intelligence rather than a near-complete reliance on imagery, signals, or ELINT.

> During the early years of Operation Iraqi Freedom, too many units attempted to fight an emerging and eventually flourishing insurgency the wrong way. They over-emphasized kinetic operations against an adaptive insurgent hidden in a sympathetic or intimidated population. While there are examples of successful counterinsurgency efforts at various levels of command during the course of Operation Iraqi Freedom, those successes have been sporadic and short-lived at best. However, with the implementation of a new strategy in Iraq based on the tenets of FM 3-24, *Counterinsurgency*, our military has proven that it can effectively conduct counterinsurgency operations on a large scale. An increase in troop density at key locations in and around Baghdad, a significant effort to move away from large forward operating bases to combat outposts (to protect the people), and a relentless attack on Al-Qaeda in Iraq were critical to improved security levels across the country.[40]

The reformulation of the approach toward the insurgency included the recognition that while forces ensconced at large forward operating bases miles from population centers may have added to the security of the those forces, the distance from forces to the people negatively impacted COIN operations. Since the insurgents were using the population for hiding purposes in order to neutralize Western advantages, U.S. and allied operations would have to be adjusted and redirected in acknowledgment that the insurgents were involved in a "war among the people." Accordingly, U.S.-, Iraqi-, and coalition-deployed units moved out of their protective barriers and developed "forward combat outposts" in key locations in population centers.

This created several important dynamics. First, by engaging with the people directly and, in essence, living among them, more and more people came to interact with the counterinsurgents. With communication channels open and the opportunity for direct contact, the host country's population more readily came forward and often offered increasingly important intelligence on the locations and plans of insurgent forces. By being located at the outposts, the reaction time to intelligence received-to-operational mission was reduced, which provided an increased capacity to engage the insurgents before they could disappear. Moreover, one of the strengths of the insurgency was that it created the perception in the minds of the people that after the United States left, it would be the insurgents who the people would be forced to deal with. By moving into the forward outposts and being seen as training and supporting Iraqi security personnel, and personnel that would remain in Iraq over the long term, the United States vitiated the perception that the people must deal with the insurgents because they would be the only ones with weapons after U.S. forces departed.

The concepts utilized were nothing startling, revolutionary, or exclusive to modern warfare, as they were practiced by armies in the ancient world and perfected by the Romans. You cannot impact events sufficiently for control and security if you opt to garrison security forces at a distance, cut off from the people, while the insurgents enjoy, essentially, a monopoly on population interaction. Population interaction if conducted properly builds rapport, establishes trust, and—just as important, if not more in the heat and intensity of virulent insurgency—generates actionable intelligence. In the twentieth century, there were many treatises on the nature of the problem of violent insurgencies.

David Galula's 1964 treatise *Counterinsurgency Warfare: Theory and Practice* served as the primary source behind the development of chapter five of FM 3-24, "Executing Counterinsurgency Operations." The principles Galula emphasized stood the test of time in various theaters of operation. Unfortunately, his work has remained largely unknown to front-line soldiers, some of whom ventured into the Iraq insurgency relying primarily on previous experience and instinct rather than proven principles discussed by Galula. Writing from first-hand experiences on the counterinsurgency battlefields of the 1940s and 1950s, Galula emphasized the importance of collecting intelligence from the local population to identify and then purge the insurgents from their midst.[41]

Galula's concepts regarding COIN operations can be summarized in the following seven points:[42]

1. Make contact with the people.
2. Protect the population.
3. Control the population.
4. Collect intelligence.
5. Win the support of the population.
6. Purge the insurgent.
7. Involve the population in the long-term solution.

For American forces operating in Afghanistan and Iraq, these concepts were refined and operationalized in both the theaters as *Clear, Hold,* and *Build,* which unfolded in a five-stage process:

1. Preparation stage
2. Clear stage
3. Hold stage
4. Build stage
5. Completion and transition stage

The preparation stage included planning, training, organizing and equipping, and synchronizing both civil and military forces. Here, assessment of the overall situation took place along with what roles each unit would perform as well as joint training and rehearsals. Designing and initiating *Information Engagement* (IE) operations for connecting with the people and opening a two-way communication process would take place in the preparation stage as well as establishing way stations for basic services for civilians that may be displaced as a result of operations against the insurgents.

Following the preparation stage were "Clearing" operations, which sought to clear the designated area by destroying, capturing, or forcing the withdrawal of insurgent combatants. Once the target area was cleared, the "Hold" phase was conducted by security forces (ideally by host nation [HN] forces) in order to establish an HN government presence at the local level. The "Build" phase encompassed support for the HN government by protecting the population and improving economic, social, cultural, and medical needs. The completion and transition stage involved a measured and methodical withdrawal of COIN forces, as HN personnel were empowered to handle the situation on their own. The Clear, Hold, and Build concept was the stated policy and doctrine for the U.S. military in the conduct of COIN operations during ECLIPSE II in Iraq and was a vital part of what became known as the "surge" strategy.

The "surge" was a term applied to the Bush administration's recognition that operations in Iraq were meeting with suboptimal results particularly in light of an exceedingly violent 2006. On January 10, 2007, Bush announced to the nation that he had ordered an additional 20,000 troops into Iraq, many heading into Baghdad, while extending the tours of army personnel and marines already in the vicinity of Anbar Province. The president stated in his public address that the United States sought a "unified, democratic federal Iraq that can govern itself, defend itself, sustain itself, and is an ally in the War on Terror."[43] The major element in the surge strategy was a change in focus for the U.S. military that Bush indicated would "help Iraqis clear and secure neighborhoods, to help them protect the local population and to help insure that the Iraqi forces left behind are capable of providing security for the people."[44]

What ultimately became one of the more decisive elements in the surge strategy was in convincing the Sunni tribal sheikhs to turn against the al-Qaeda elements in their midst. This resulted in the United States being able to benefit through the efforts of a 103,000-man army referred to as the "Sons of Iraq," part of the Anbar Awakening. The Sons of Iraq were armed and paid by the United States ($360 per month per man) and succeeded in rooting out much of the al-Qaeda presence in Anbar Province. However, many of the al-Qaeda fighters who managed to stay in the country simply shifted north into Mosul and the Diyala Province.

Prior to the launching of the surge in June, the United States readied hunter-killer teams (overseen by Task Force 121 and other special mission units [SMUs]) that took the increase in human intelligence during the surge and put it to effective use in targeting key insurgent figures and other high value targets (HVTs).[45] The surge sent five U.S. combat brigades plus support units, approximately 30,000 troops, into Iraq during February to mid-June 2007. By the summer of 2007, the United States had positioned 170,000 troops within Iraq. One of the more troubling issues, contributing to the sense of instability within Iraq, was the intransigence of anti-U.S. Shiite cleric Sadr and his self-described Mahdi Army. With the arrival of surge forces and the willingness of U.S. commanders to use them, Sadr opted to order his militia to stand down and ordered a general cease-fire on August 29, 2007. This essentially secured the Shiite sections of the South and allowed the United States to focus on the unruly Sunni-populated Anbar Province.

The surge essentially lasted for 18 months (February 2007–July 2008) and in that time span the reduction in overall violence was significant. Moving forces "among the people" in order to separate out the insurgents and to gain the people's trust provided a significant increase in human intelligence, which proved exceptionally useful.

Prior to the outbreak of the insurgency, the United States was able to move inside the Iraqi military's OODA-Loop through superior technology and superior training of personnel in network-centric warfare in observing, orienting, deciding, and acting faster than the opponent. Once major conventional operations ceased and the United States moved in support of the various political entities within Iraq, the effort lost the integrated, combined, and synchronized operational excellence generated in conventional U.S. military operations.

Following the success of major combat operations during OIF, an intelligent and adaptive enemy dispersed, hid among the people, and frustrated U.S. attempts at creating a new and increasingly democratic political environment within the country. Advantages in information technology, precision strike, and rapid maneuver provided the United States and its coalition partners with an unprecedented level of conventional military superiority, which they swiftly utilized in deposing and replacing the authoritarian regime of Saddam.

However, the American model of Rapid Dominance through network-centric warfare, while obviously effective in open terrain against organized enemy formations, was neutralized by an intelligently led insurgency hiding and fighting in the shadows and among the people. The insurgency by virtue of superior knowledge of the terrain, both human and geographical, and with intelligence assets across Iraq, soon operated within the OODA-Loop of the Iraqi HN government in whatever form the United States and its coalition partners helped create. The Shiite and Sunni insurgents seized the initiative and forced the HN and its coalition supporters into a reactive capacity.

The success of the Iraqi insurgency and specific aspects of its tactics, particularly improvised explosive devices (IEDs) and explosively formed penetrators (or projectiles, aka EFPs) against supply convoys and other soft targets, were soon mimicked by the insurgents within the Afghanistan-Pakistan theater. With the U.S. advantage in conventional military operations—particularly in terms of controlling the tempo, maintaining the initiative, and operating within an opponent's OODA-Loop—parried, the United States was forced to draw from an additional competitive advantage to overcome the insurgents' strategy: that of resources and capital. Burning cash and attempting to create democratic institutions without the necessary culture conducive to modern democratic political systems, the United States was essentially left with a singular strategy: to put in place a military and security force sufficient to block the insurgency's ability to topple the government once U.S. forces departed.

Once the Iraqi armed forces failed in standing up to the advance of Islamic State of Iraq and the Levant (ISIL) forces, President Barack Obama's administration was forced to rethink its strategy to pull U.S. forces out of both Iraq and Afghanistan and instead take the advice of U.S. military commanders and keep an auxiliary force available to provide direct support for both Iraqi and Afghan national forces. Admittedly in Iraq, the administration was reliant on the acquiescence of the Maliki government for the continued U.S. presence and the implementation of the Status of Forces Agreement (SOFA), which proved unrealistic as the Shiite-dominated government, partially aligned with Tehran, sought the swift removal of all U.S. forces from Iraq.

The failure of Iraqi forces to hold against the advance of ISIL required rethinking on the part of both Baghdad and Washington and marked the recognition of a key component of U.S. COIN strategy that stipulated the necessary and perhaps critical transition stage that had to be allowed sufficient time and resources to jell in order to insure the viability of the newly organized and trained government forces. The United States was also forced to rethink its own decision-making process in the face of burgeoning insurgencies in both Iraq and Afghanistan. With its advantages in information operations/network-centric warfare parried by an enemy operating among the people, which also served to provide the networked insurgency the ability to operate within the U.S. OODA-Loop, the United States began adapting and moved toward a less synchronized, less integrated, and an increasingly hierarchical "top down" organizational structure in security and stability operations, which added time to the decision-action process. This added time provided the insurgents the ability to move within the U.S. OODA-Loop, because their own decision-action cycle was quicker and swifter.

Thus, U.S. efforts, moving from the integrated and synchronized military operations that so successfully defeated Saddam's military, fell back to an earlier bureaucratic and glacially slow procedure that required the addition of political components for implementation. The U.S. military was built to conduct maneuver operations with lightning speed and lethal kinetic precision. While synchronized and integrated joint operations in combat had been honed to a level that was arguably the finest the world had ever seen, this unparalleled force was then tasked with security and stability operations in conjunction with political entities where the combined operation of military and political components, having been created ad hoc, never achieved the degree of unity of effort, unity of command, and cohesive bonding among units that come from a common training regime and extensive joint maneuvers.

In the fall of 2008, Obama won the U.S. presidential election after campaigning to end the Iraq war effort and refocus attention on the Afghan insurgency. Unable to come to an agreement with the Maliki government regarding SOFA to insure the protection of U.S. troops staying on in Iraq, the Obama administration began pulling out U.S. troops in 2009. However, actions taken by the United States, Iraqi security forces, and their coalition partners from the beginning of the surge in 2007 to mid-2008 when U.S. military commanders stated that American and coalition forces had wrested the initiative from the insurgent groups until mid-2010 when the United States was in the process of withdrawing had significantly quelled the insurgency and allowed an orderly withdrawal of U.S. and allied forces.

After Zarqawi was killed in June 2006, AQI created an umbrella organization designated as the "Islamic State in Iraq" (ISI) in October of the same year. With the advent of the surge, this latest manifestation of AQI was steadily weakened by both the U.S. troop surge and the creation of the Sahwa (Awakening) councils. On April 18, 2010, ISI's two top leaders, Abu Ayyub al-Masri and Abu Omar al-Baghdadi, were killed in a joint U.S.-Iraqi operation near Tikrit. U.S. Army General Raymond Odierno announced at a press conference held in June 2010 that 80 percent of ISI's top 50 leaders, including those involved in financial operations and recruiting, had been killed or captured, with only 8 remaining at large. Odierno also stated that ISI had been effectively cut off from the al-Qaeda leadership then operating out of Pakistan.

On May 16, 2010, a new leader was appointed as head of ISI—Abu Bakr al-Baghdadi—who immediately set about replenishing the group's ranks by joining forces with former Ba'athist military and intelligence officers who had been employed by the regime of Saddam. Two of these individuals, Samir al-Khlifawi and Izzat Ibrahim al-Douri, were key members of the Ba'athist security establishment. Al-Douri had long been one of Saddam's most trusted and valued lieutenants, and following the demise of Saddam's regime, he created the Army of the Men of the Naqshbandi Order, a Sunni/Sufi Islamist organization. But Al-Douri was strictly a Sunni nationalist Arab and a hard-line enforcer of Saddam's edicts in the old regime. Former Colonel al-Khlifawi, also known as Haji Bakr, became the overall military commander of ISI's operations.

As ISI regenerated itself, the U.S. military continued to withdraw forces from Iraq. On December 18, 2011, all U.S. forces had been withdrawn from Iraq, and the war came to an end. The key test of the Iraqi security forces came shortly thereafter. In the Clear, Hold, and Build COIN strategy, the critical element was after the Clear, Hold, and Build stages and resided in the completion and transition stage. It was in this stage where, theoretically, the Iraqi military and security personnel were sufficiently empowered to handle the situation on their own. When the new version of the radical elements of the Sunni insurgency manifested itself in the ISIL and attacked with several thousand fighters, an Iraqi army of some 30,000 troops dropped their weapons and exited quickly in what might charitably be described as an extremely swift retrograde movement.

While this retreat in the face of the enemy casts a negative light on the U.S. military and its vetting and training process in preparing those 30,000 troops, the complete story encompasses much more. The Iraqi government under Maliki mistakenly believed that they did not need the United States to ensure that the completion and transition stage of the COIN strategy had sufficiently prepared the Iraqi security forces to handle the insurgents on their own. U.S. military commanders believed that a residual U.S. presence was necessary to continue training the Iraqis for handling their own security over the long term and providing them backup in any short- or mid-term challenge. Instead, the Maliki government refused to provide the standard SOFA safeguards that U.S. allies around the world had extended to a U.S. military presence on their soil, as the Maliki-led government sought the immediate departure of American troops—a demand that was made without a complete under-standing of the tenuous nature of the security environment. Both Iraqi and American commanders warned the neophyte political leaders of the strong possibility of losing the gains made if U.S. troops were withdrawn in a manner that undercut the completion and transition stage of the COIN strategy prior to the full completion of the necessary steps called for in COIN doctrine.

Six months after the departure of U.S. forces from Iraq, ISI leader al-Baghdadi, in July 2012, released an audio recording online in which he announced that ISI would be returning to the former strongholds that U.S. forces and their Sunni allies had driven them out of in 2007 and 2008. Al-Baghdadi further declared the initiation of a new offensive cam-paign in Iraq called *Breaking the Walls*, with the objective of overrunning prisons that held captured ISI members. From mid-2012 to the summer of 2013, violence returned to Iraq, and monthly fatalities exceeded 1,000 in July 2013 for the first time since the spring of 2008.

In June 2014, ISI (referred to in the press and by Western leaders and commanders as ISIL or ISIS) overran the northern Iraqi city of Mosul and after securing other towns in the vicinity announced a further name change to the Islamic State, or simply IS, as the organization broadcast its declaration as the new Islamic Caliphate and demanded the Muslim community recognize al-Baghdadi as their rightful and legitimate ruler. On October 11, 2014, the terrorist group sent 10,000 fighters drawn from Syria and Mosul south to seize control of Baghdad.

It was here on the approach of 2,000 ISIL fighters that approximately 30,000 Iraqi troops trained by the United States dropped their weapons and retreated toward Baghdad. With a residual U.S. force in Iraq backed by U.S. airpower behind them, Iraqi forces would have been provided the confidence that they could, indeed, stand, fight, and win against ISIL. Instead they withdrew and left their weapons and those U.S.-supplied weapons, along with armored Humvees and other armor and weapons systems, became part of the ISIL's arsenal. By October 2014, ISIL fighters had advanced to within 15 miles of the Baghdad Airport. By year's end in 2014, ISIL was in control of Mosul, Fallujah, Tikrit, and Tal Afar. By the spring of 2015, the group was threatening to seize Ramadi. When ISIL made simultaneous moves against the city of Irbil in the north against Iraqi Kurdistan and the advance south against Baghdad in 2014, the U.S. military, upon request by the Iraqi government, began supporting the Iraqi military by conducting air strikes against ISIL units then caught out in open terrain.

By mid-2016, ISIL (also known as Daesh or the IS) was driven out of territory seized within the Sunni Triangle and was preparing to make a stand in the city of Mosul, its last remaining large stronghold in Iraq. Concurrent to Iraqi and coalition operations against ISIL within Iraq was the campaign in Syria aimed at eliminating ISIL's presence, as its fighters were being pushed back to their main base of operations in the city of Raqqa. Most likely the battles of Mosul and Raqqa will be ongoing as this book is released in the spring of 2017. The battle to eject ISIL from Mosul is instructive and revealing. Upon approach to the city and backed by U.S. and coalition airpower, the Iraqi army rolled back ISIL units caught out in the open. Once entering the city with ISIL utilizing a network of tunnels and rooftop snipers, the Iraqi army lost its competitive advantage, as the insurgents fought "among the people." By November 2016, the Iraqi leadership requested U.S. and British Special Operations Forces to lead the fight raging within the city. Both the United States and Britain responded in the affirmative.

While many commanders and analysts believe that once ISIL has lost the territory it controls in Iraq and Syria, it will, in effect, cease to be a "caliphate" and will become "just another garden variety terrorist group." There can be no doubt that the loss of territory will severely degrade any legitimate claim by ISIL as the Islamic Caliphate. However, even with victory in defeating the threat from ISIL in both Raqqa and Mosul, the spread of ISIL to other areas is ongoing. Much more robust than al-Qaeda with a larger network and greater financing, ISIL's ability to rejuvenate itself following the loss of territory in the Middle East will insure a continuing challenge to global security.

Thus, ghazi warfare (asymmetric, irregular operations) will continue until resources and capabilities can be aggregated sufficiently enabling successful Islamic jihadist conventional operational challenges. The principal targets of that warfare are secular democracy and competing religious schools of thought; in essence, those who refuse to submit to the Islamic jihadists' view of divine will and intention—and both principal targets serving as constituents within the domain referred to by the militant jihadists as the Darul Harb. War against the Darul Harb is perpetual until it is absorbed into the Darul Islam, or, until those within the Darul Harb recognize the supremacy of Islam and acquiesce to a special tax for "nonbelievers." Those refusing to recognize the supremacy of Islam or refusing to pay the special tax must be killed.

In short, this dualistic and militant perspective on human civilization posits political authority as being based on the ancient and medieval concept of the divine right of kings and clerics where that authority is presented as legitimate, being divinely ordained, for the strategic objective of control. The reoccurring pattern, recognizable throughout human history, unfortunately remains intact well into the modern world: armed violence and coercion utilizing a compelling ideology for the centuries-old stratagem enabling a small elite effective control over people, resources, markets, and trade routes. Such religious/ideological dynamics joined with great power competition for the same components of power, influence, and economic advantage have driven the military history of the ancient, medieval and, now, modern Middle East.

Chapter 10

Summary

No group or nation should mistake America's intentions: We will not rest until terrorist groups of global reach have been found, have been stopped, and have been defeated.

—U.S. President George W. Bush, November 6, 2001

To inquire if and where we made mistakes is not to apologize. War is replete with mistakes because it is full of improvisations. In war, we are always doing something for the first time. It would be a miracle if what we improvised under the stress of war should be perfect.

—Vice Admiral Hyman Rickover, U.S. Navy

The aggregation of power—the control of people, resources, markets, and trade routes—was seen in the Middle East by the world's earliest civilizations as a necessary means in achieving security and economic advantage in a dangerous and often violent world. Complementing efforts in achieving those ends was effective political leadership capable of establishing and utilizing a compelling ideology that served as the foundation upon which societal cohesion and unity of effort were achieved. Accordingly, political leadership and a unifying ideology, both underpinned by military competence, became the core tools by which the aggregation of power, security, and economic advantage was achieved in the ancient civilizations of the Middle East.

In the ancient world, the most effective ideologies evoked the most powerful supernatural dynamics whose nature, meaning, and "will," generally left to the interpretation of clergy elite, served as a religion-oriented justification for political authority, economic rules and prohibitions, and military security. In the Middle East, this process initially involved a multitude of "gods," or polytheism, where a plurality of local and regional deities was worshipped. However, in the process involving the accumulation of power, the clash of competing religious paradigms eventually led to the search for an all-encompassing power capable of overcoming the lesser deities and their relative and limited domains of action.

Hence, just as the authority and scope of the political organization were expanded during the power aggregation process, so arose the need to extend its authority through the alignment with an increasingly powerful deity capable of trumping its local and regional competitors. The ensuing strategic narrative argued that the regional and local deities were far less powerful than the "one-god" blessed with universal jurisdiction whose omnipotence and omniscience insured and comforted his or her followers that their earthly political, economic, and military activities were indeed backed by the most powerful force in the universe. Such concepts not only contributed to social cohesion, unity of purpose, and unity of effort among the citizenry but also served in instilling within the soldiers of an army a moral or psychological ascendancy anchored in a steadfast belief in ultimate victory.

In the late Middle Ages and continuing into the early modern world, the Ottoman Empire leveraged its political organizational skills and military effectiveness, both underpinned by a unifying religion-based ideology (Islam) in the aggregation of power leading to one of history's great empires. However, following a rebirth of learning, discovery, and critical thinking during the European Renaissance and the centuries that proceeded it, significant advances in technology followed, and the West began to rise, eventually transcending Ottoman economic and military advantage and by the late eighteenth century was positioned to directly challenge Turkish power.

Russia's wars against the Ottomans in the eighteenth century and Napoleon's 1798 Egyptian campaign marked the beginning of the loss of Turkish territory, as the initiative was seized by Western forces, and Ottoman armies and navies were forced to withdraw from previously held territory in the Black Sea region and in North Africa. Modern reforms throughout the Ottoman Empire in hopes of closing the technological gap with the West took on a new urgency in the nineteenth century and made their way into Ottoman provinces throughout North Africa and the Middle East, marking, in both regions, the beginning of the modern era.

Turkish power that had controlled the Middle East and North Africa during the fifteenth through the early nineteenth centuries, effectively suppressing local and regional infighting among tribes and religious groups, dissipated with the collapse of the Ottoman Empire following

World War I. The first half of the twentieth century was marked by Western efforts, particularly British and French, in filling the vacuum of power that arose from the Ottoman collapse and expanding their own influence. The second half of the century gave rise to a Cold War rivalry, and the United States replaced Britain as the primary military power in the Middle East and faced off against Soviet efforts at expanding its control and influence while simultaneously undermining Western interests in the region. The Cold War rivalry served as a backdrop for the Arab-Israeli Wars (in 1948, 1956, 1967, and 1973), with the last three bringing direct Soviet military involvement as Moscow attempted to support their clients in Egypt, Syria, and Iraq against Israel and its main proponent, the United States.

With the fall of the Soviet Union in 1991, the security paradigm of the Cold War relative to the Middle East and resting in part on America's backing of authoritarian rulers capable of resisting Soviet efforts at intrigue and "revolution" transitioned toward increased American efforts aimed at promoting greater democratization within the region. This relaxation of the Cold War security paradigm, that is, lessening support for authoritarian regimes in the Middle East, led to increased levels of protests, riots, and the occasional overthrow of governments, as the masses in the Middle East and North Africa demanded greater political participation and greater economic opportunity.

ARAB SPRING

These dynamics contributed to the most recent chapter of turmoil in the Arab world beginning in December 2010 with the precursors to the Arab Spring. Most riots or civil outrage turned violent are the manifestation of deeper unresolved issues within a society, and most, generally, erupt from an immediate cause associated with the actions of the police—actions that are seen by the population as unjust yet perceived as typical of the repressive and unfair nature of the government. In December 2010, a street fruit vendor in Tunisia was publicly slapped in the face by a police officer. After enduring years of indignities, abuse, and limited economic opportunity, this public act of humiliation by the forces of authoritarian repression led the fruit vendor to set himself on fire in protest.

As news spread, protests erupted across the country eventually leading to rioting and political unrest in a number of countries within the Arab League. Collectively these acts came to be known as the Arab Spring, with authoritarian governments being overthrown in Tunisia, Egypt, Libya, and Yemen. Significant violence also erupted in a range of countries, including Syria and Bahrain, with protests and rioting in Algeria, Iraq, Jordan, Kuwait, Morocco, and Oman. Relatively minor disruptions occurred in Sudan, Lebanon, Mauritania, and Saudi Arabia.

This environment of uncertainty and instability coupled with rapidly changing strategic dynamics as the United States loosened it support for strong authoritarian regimes was seized upon by factions and groups less interested in modern democracy and more in the advancement of their own claims to political power; claims based on a divine right to rule. The resulting turmoil, instability, and violence led to the further weakening of previously marginal national institutions. As national governments weakened, their power receded, and many of the "revolutionary" Islamist groups operated and expanded their reach in ungoverned spaces that resulted from failing or failed nation-states. Attempts at greater democratization by the West led to further weakening of existing institutions and a general rise in political instability, which provided the conditions for insurgent and terrorist groups to consolidate and proliferate.

LEADING FROM BEHIND

Attempting to withdraw from a strong military presence in the Middle East, in particular within Iraq, the United States announced its intention of leading from behind in the expectation that governments within the region would necessarily have to make the tough choices in creating inclusive political systems. Without a strong U.S. military presence, these governments were then faced with rising challenges from a number of groups, many developing into armed insurgencies. The Islamic State or Islamic State of Iraq and the Levant (ISIL) was such an entity.

While the U.S.-led West demonstrated unparalleled military superiority during conventional campaigns vis-à-vis opponents in the Middle East during the post–Cold War era, those opponents came to rely on insurgency campaigns or, war among the people, to blunt the effectiveness of the overwhelming nature of Western military advantages inherent in advanced technology and information dominance. The combined arms approach, one of the hallmarks of the armies of Alexander the Great, integrating and synchronizing operations across the spectrum of conflict provided the United States, with its network-centric approach to modern maneuver warfare, the ability to observe, orient, decide, and act (OODA-Loop) faster than its opponents.

Superiority within the OODA-Loop on the conventional battlefield provided the United States and its allies the ability to move inside an opponent's own OODA-Loop, seizing the initiate and forcing an enemy to react to events that had already occurred while denying him or her the ability to "see" and react to that which was actually occurring in real time.[1] Thus the aim became outpacing the reactive ability of an opponent's command and control while succeeding in achieving positional advantage. When both were achieved, both the enemy's ability and will to generate combat power became insufficient for determining events on the battlefield and in battlespace.

"WAR AMONG THE PEOPLE" NEUTRALIZES WESTERN ADVANTAGES

However, this military superiority so effective in kinetic operations against conventional military opponents in the open field was designed for major combat operations rather than the political warfare so common to modern insurgencies and those enemies conducting terror campaigns while hiding "among the people." In operations utilizing "Rapid Dominance," you may very well "shatter cohesion, produce paralysis, and bring about collapse," but it is in these conditions of ungoverned chaos that insurgencies and terrorist organizations find traction and generate the ability to proliferate. In short by collapsing an existing authoritarian regime and erecting weak institutions in its place, Western forces led by the United States created failing states and ungoverned territory and fostered the conditions in which virulent insurgencies and other violent militant groups found sustenance.

Additionally, with increased attacks by military forces against insurgent/terrorist groups and individuals hiding among the people, the greater the likelihood of collateral damage to innocents and the greater the alienation of the people whose support the counterinsurgent forces are attempting to influence. Thus, in the twentieth and early twenty-first centuries, the insurgents/terrorists effectively blunted the military advantages of the technologically superior West by insightfully exploiting its weaknesses in populated areas and by utilizing asymmetric operations. This asymmetric dynamic has been a pattern throughout military history and is summarized within the German concept of Flaechen-und Luecken.

In the contemporary era, the more effective insurgent and terrorist groups operating within the Middle East and around the world have neutralized the ability of the West to move within the insurgent and terrorist groups' OODA-Loop by hiding among the people and conducting a "people-centric" insurgent campaign. Such operations rely more on human intelligence and local knowledge (including religion-based ideological beliefs) than advanced munitions or high-performance platforms and weapons systems of precision engagement.

Many of these insurgent and terrorist groups have intelligent and well-educated leaders who are cognizant of the lessons of history and acutely understand the disaggregation of the Ottoman, British, and Soviet empires significantly impacted the nature of the modern Middle East and its associated military history. As the opening decades of the twenty-first century unfold, and with this acute understanding of history, the enemies of the West within North Africa, the Middle East, and in Afghanistan are actively attempting to disaggregate the power of the United States and its global allies. The specific target is the core group of secular democracies led by the United States and through a strategy utilizing asymmetric, terrorist attacks, undermining the sense of stability and peace within the target populations. Hence, the objective is not the military defeat of secular democracies; rather, to force the West into their paradigm of continuous or ghazi war, resulting in economic stagnation and paralysis while simultaneously altering the cohesion, unity, and social fabric of the target nations.

In his book, *Enhanced Interrogation: Inside the Minds and Motives of the Islamic Terrorists Trying to Destroy America* (Crown Publishing, 2016), CIA contractor James E. Mitchell writes about discussions with the mastermind of the September 11, 2001, attacks on the U.S. homeland, Khalid Sheikh Mohammed (KSM), during post-enhanced interrogation interviews. According to Mitchell, "KSM" spoke freely regarding al-Qaeda and its intentions and conveyed to Mitchell and others involved in the discussions that al-Qaeda did not expect to destroy the United States through sporadic terrorist attacks. Rather al-Qaeda expected to prevail by exploiting lax U.S. and European immigration rules and standards and by "outbreeding non-Muslims" and in the manipulation of the respective legal systems in order to install Sharia law.

Military proficiency, democratic values, and human rights serving as a unifying ideology in Western civilization and overwhelming economic power and advanced technology have reduced its opponents to strategies aimed at internal dislocation. The aggregation of power has provided the West with a range of capabilities, including the possession of one on the hallmarks of modern warfare: strategic endurance. "The key defining element of modern war is strategic endurance, and this quality is a function of the total integration of the social, economic, and political resources of the state in support of military operations."[2] The combination of aggregated power and strategic endurance contributed to the overwhelming conventional military capacity of the U.S.-led West vis-à-vis Middle Eastern militaries. At the core of this power is the secular, sovereign Western nation-state, particularly symbolized in the form of the United States. As such, the defeat of the Western nation-state and the dissipation of strategic endurance become an essential objective within the overall strategy of the violent jihadist insurgents, their associated terrorist groups, and their wealthy financial and often covert supporters.

Table 10.1

Al-Qaeda's 20-Year Plan (2000–2020)

Seven Stages
1. The "Awakening," began in 2001
2. "Eye-Opening," 2003
3. "Arising and Standing Up," 2010
4. Demise of Arab governments, 2010
5. Islamic Caliphate, 2013
6. "Total Confrontation," 2016
7. "Definitive Victory," ends in 2020

Source: U.S. Department of Defense

Both Sun Tzu in ancient China and Alexander the Great of Macedonia believed that it was essential understanding and then attacking an enemy's strategy. A key element in the success of Alexander was his ability to adroitly ascertain what his opponent was attempting to accomplish and then, just as swiftly, create a course of action effectively countering, followed by defeating, the enemy's strategy. In understanding the violent Islamic jihadists' strategy, it is first necessary to analyze the various components that both support and contribute to the jihadists' activities and undertakings. Accordingly, the phenomena of violent Islamic jihadism (VIJ) cannot be understood in isolation, as its ontological status—its existence—is not of an independent nature. Its longevity requires support from a range of other phenomena both within the Muslim world and from external sources.

It is from the moderate Muslim world that VIJ draws its recruits. and it is from a wide range of actors and groups within the moderate Muslim world from which it draws its sustenance. It should come as no surprise that tens of millions of "moderate" Muslims have an abiding preference to see their religious beliefs enshrined in nations around the world. This is not to say that the majority of Muslims are supportive of killing innocents or even infidels to achieve their objectives, as found within the ways and means of the VIJs. However, it is a simple matter for moderate Muslims to disavow the activities of the VIJs while claiming the high moral ground and in making the claim of acting in the direct support of God's or Allah's will. Publicly disavowing the tactics of the VIJs provides supportive moderates plausible deniability in terms of ways, means, and methods. And it is a fact that tens of millions of moderate Muslims around the world deplore the wanton murder and violence of the VIJs. Nevertheless the ends and the objectives remain the same for millions of moderates and VIJs: the proliferation of political Islam and the codification of Sharia law in institutions around the world. Consequently, the secular political system of Western democracies must be undermined and ultimately destroyed before a religion-based political ideology can be enshrined in governments throughout the world.

In terms of drawing recruits from the ranks of moderate Muslims, a critical element for acceptance within the wider Islamic world is that VIJs utilize a narrative that exploits the demographic dynamics currently under way in the Muslim world. With large segments of the population under 30, the "youth bulge" offers VIJ adherents a relatively soft target audience filled with youthful energy and visions of greatness unhindered by developed rational thought and mature experience. The book *The Quranic Concept of War* states that the primary purpose of Islamic warfare is population-centric aimed at defining the issues by the utilization of a simple but easily comprehendible narrative that posits good versus evil. The good versus evil construct has been enshrined in Middle Eastern culture since at least Zoroaster. The populist narrative enshrined in the young modern mind becomes the story of a heavenly ordained deliverance of the weak, the ill-treated, and the persecuted, from forces of tyranny and oppression.[3]

PSYCHOLOGICAL ASCENDENCY

Therefore, the strategy of VIJs is not about kinetic operations to challenge and defeat a conventional militarily superior West on the battlefield. However, just as the VIJ has drawn from ancient culture in framing its strategic narrative as good versus evil, weak and persecuted against the strong and oppressive, it also draws from the tradition of ghazi warfare and irregular operations—war among the people—to offset and neutralize an opponent's advantage in conventional military power. It relies on seizing the psychological ascendancy in the minds of its target audience found within the Muslim world (the Darul Islam) and those populating the Darul Harb or that part of the world not accepting Islam as dominant and the correct ideology.

Through the direction of a strategic information campaign, the VIJ seeks to create a conflict between Islam and those in the West. As U.S. President Barack Obama rightly stated in his address to the nation on December 6, 2015, "We cannot turn against one another by letting this fight be defined as a war between America and Islam." However, this should not blind us to the realities embedded in the preferences of tens of millions of Muslims promoting the expansion of Islamic Sharia law, which, by definition, seeks the elimination of secular legal institutions of the sovereign Western nation-state. After the elimination of Western society's legal foundations, it will, apparently, be left to an elite clergy to determine for us what God wills, followed by their translating the Lord's intentions into public policy.

The current strategy of the violent jihadists also involves dynamics operating at both a strategic and operational level. Strategically, the violent jihadists exploit a unifying ideology with claims to universal authority and jurisdiction. As such, the jihadists exploit the religion of Islam in generating a compelling "strategic narrative" and argue that the will of the most powerful God in the universe backs their activities. This is certainly not unique in the modern era and has been an integral aspect of military affairs for thousands of years.

STRATEGIC TRENDS AND THE DESTABILIZATION OF THE WESTERN NATION-STATE

The jihadists also rely on historical or "strategic trends" to undermine a major target of their operations—the modern Western secular, sovereign nation-state. These strategic trends include two key developments. The first is the process of "globalization" whereby transnational dynamics are largely beyond national control. Transnational threats to the Western secular and sovereign nation-state include terrorist groups operating in the shadows and often out of the reach of nation-states, and in many instances, such as in Afghanistan, Iraq, Syria, and Libya, these non-state actors thrive in failed and failing states and in ungoverned spaces.

Al-Qaeda is representative of the transnational movement of extremist organizations, networks, and individuals as well as their state and non-state sponsors. In the ghazi tradition of irregular warfare (IW), groups such as al-Qaeda represent no nation, wear no uniform, and do not mass armies or warships, as they operate in the shadows, conspire in secret, and attack without warning. They traditionally exploit the seams between legal jurisdictions and thrive in spaces where they are able to hide among the people in conditions of failing governance—which then allows them to install their own systems of governance while pursuing an active agenda of undermining other states in close proximity.

The process that has come to be known as globalization is contributing indirectly to the jihadist groups' intent on seeing the diminishment of the secular nation-state's authority, jurisdiction, and capacity to act in international affairs. Thus, the Islamic jihadist terrorist groups are empowered in their war against the Western nation-state by the forces of globalization, as both contribute to the diminishment of national power. In the following diagrams, the traditional power of the nation-state is being undermined by dynamics attributable to the globalization process, such as transnational relations beyond the authority of the nation-state and supranational authority being generated and deposited

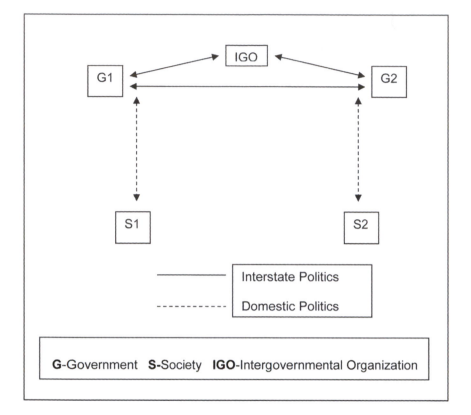

Figure 10.1   Traditional International System: A State-Centric Interaction Organization (Joseph S. Nye, Jr. and Robert O. Keohane, "Transnational Relations and World Politics: An Introduction," *International Organization,* Vol 25, No 3, Transnational Relations and World Politics, Summer 1971, 333. Used by permission of *International Organization.*)

in institutions beyond the nation's control such as intergovernmental organizations (IGOs) and nongovernmental organizations (NGOs).

In Figure 10.1, the traditional state relationship with its citizenry and the larger international environment is modeled and depicts the traditional state-centric international political system. In Figure 10.2, the forces of globalization, identified in these depictions as transnational relations and IGOs, are modeled depicting the loss of authority and control of the Western, sovereign nation-state.

While the violent jihadists actively exploit the trends and dynamics in the "globalization" phenomenon by undermining, in the hopes of ultimately destroying, the secular, sovereign Western-conceived nation-state, they enjoy at least the passive support or the quiet acquiescence of

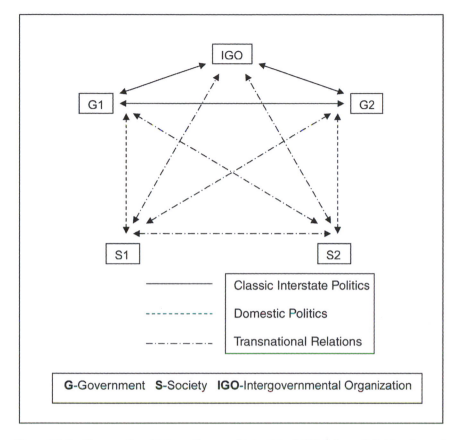

Figure 10.2 Transnational Interactions and Interstate Politics (Joseph S. Nye, Jr. and Robert O. Keohane, "Transnational Relations and World Politics: An Introduction," *International Organization,* Vol 25, No 3, Transnational Relations and World Politics, Summer 1971, 334. Used by permission of *International Organization.*)

countless millions of "moderate" Muslims wishing to see the institution of Sharia law and the adoption of Islam manifest itself on a worldwide basis. However, more directly, these jihadist groups also receive active support—funding and other access including safe conduct and safe harbor activities—from thousands of well-connected and well-endowed individuals and groups, including those from key and sympathetic governments.

The free flow of both people and information across national boundaries as well as the impact of the globalization of capital markets and the increasing power of the multinational corporation vis-à-vis national governments are creating new challenges to the capacity of states to meet the demands of their own societies or to effectively respond to transnational pressures. These challenges are significant to any nation—of any size. Add direct and indirect attacks from transnational terrorist organizations and the environment in the twenty-first century for state survival becomes increasingly problematic.

Moreover, the threat to the security and stability of the secular, sovereign Western nation-state is not confined to the forces of globalization or supportive Islamic groups around the world currently providing sustenance to jihadist terrorist groups. Most remarkable are the influential individuals and groups *within* Western nation-states themselves intent on the diminishment of national power and authority. The decision making and behavior of these actors are purposefully contributing to the demise of the traditional, sovereign nation-state, not in the intent of aligning with violent jihadist objectives but in support of their own agenda and beliefs regarding the nature of international politics. These actors and groups belong to a school of thought within the field of international relations that has become known as neoliberal institutionalism. It is important to understand how this ideology is undermining the vibrancy and capacity of the secular, sovereign nation-state.

The political beliefs held by many in the Obama administration regarding international politics in many ways reflected the views within the Clinton administration and permeate many of the universities in Europe and North America, particularly international affairs programs. This school of thought as it relates to international politics and military affairs borrows heavily from economic assumptions similar to those offered by the generation that was influential in the aftermath of the First World War. The ideas and developments during the interwar era were well chronicled and well critiqued in the thought of British historian Edward Hallet Carr and presented in the seminal book, *The Twenty Years' Crisis*.[4]

Throughout the nineteenth century and into the first decades of the twentieth century, an intellectual school of thought, collectively referred to as *idealism*, sought to eliminate the impact of power, struggle, and war on international politics—a worthy hope and a fine aspiration in the abstract. However, ignoring these dynamics in hopes that they might wither away by not discussing them in the halls of government or not addressing their continuing impact on international affairs in the colleges and universities was, and remains, unrealistic, incredibly naive and, as the empirical evidence indicates, dangerous. History has repeatedly shown tendencies to ignore empirical reality while substituting one's desires and personal preferences in the expectation that since "right" will automatically transform itself into "might" has instead laid the foundations for ineffective, and often, incompetent international institutions. Since political effectiveness, economic power, and military capacity have traditionally trumped "hope" as a strategy, these institutions have led to the imposition of structural conditions *increasing* rather than decreasing the likelihood of war. Moreover, in the 1930s when such naive beliefs animated Western diplomacy, the road to the Second World War was paved with good intentions and the destination, catastrophic.

While it would appear to be a self-evident proposition that a rational, objective observer would wish to see a more peaceful, stable, and prosperous world community including peace in the Middle East, war cannot be avoided nor violence and struggle minimized or suppressed through a process of blanket and mindless disarmament followed with wine toasts, handshakes, and signatures on paper. The lesson is reflected in the words of George Washington at Valley Forge, as his officers complained of the low quality of an arriving batch of new recruits, to which Washington responded, "We cannot have men as we would wish them, we must deal with them as they are."

The post–World War I generation took theoretical economic assumptions and utilized them as pragmatic political policy in the rough, violent, and often inconsistent world of international politics. For instance, Adam Smith, a key architect of economic liberalism—capitalism—argued that as everyone is freed toward pursuing their own self-interest in the economy, this will, in effect, serve in lifting up all others as the self-interested behavior will increase production and, in the aggregate, societal production will also be increased making the community richer and, theoretically, better off. As Smith argued, it is as if an "invisible hand" is created that lifts everyone—even as the original self-interested behavior is not intended or directed at making others better off. Economically, Smith's work has aided the rise in the wealth of Western nations.[5]

Western diplomats, politicians, and economists took these concepts and applied them to international politics in the 1920s and 1930s. The resulting policy was based on the following logic: allowing Chancellor Adolf Hitler to pursue Germany's self-interests will make, by virtue of an invisible hand, the entire international community better off. The idealists who adopted economic assumptions in order to present a consistent theoretical argument in support of their wishes and hopes to make the world more peaceful and conducive to their agenda, in fact, directly contributed to the violence and death that occurred during the Second World War—a war in which tens of millions perished.

While the George W. Bush administration has been rightfully criticized for its inept handling of post-major combat security and stability operations in Iraq during ECLIPSE II/Operation Iraqi Freedom (OIF), an understanding of the Obama administration's policies in regard to the Middle East and Afghanistan also warrant examination, as they were infused with assumptions from theoretical economics that have been forced into the inconsistent world of international politics and military operations—with suboptimal results.

NATIONAL SOVEREIGNTY AS A TARGET BY NEOLIBERAL INSTITUTIONALISM

Moreover, the school of thought that once was referred to as "idealism" has changed its name following the disastrous 1930s and 1940s and has since reinvented itself under the rubric of "neoliberal institutionalism." Neoliberal institutionalists believe that the secular, sovereign nation-state is one of the main problems, if not *the* main problem, in international politics. The neoliberal institutionalists argue that this system of independent and sovereign political entities interacting in an environment without central control is similar to the England of Thomas Hobbes where no central power was capable of enforcing the peace given an environment of a multitude of squabbling factions. For Hobbes what was needed was a powerful central government to insure order and to overcome a situation that amounted to political anarchy. The neoliberal institutionalists gained significant influence in the universities and government in the 1960s and 1970s and continue to argue that the international system is ensconced in anarchy due to the lack of centralized control, including problems arising from the sovereignty of independently, often unilaterally, acting nation-states.

From this view the following conclusion is reached: war and conflict are mainly the result of unilateral decisions and actions of sovereign nation-states operating in a system marked by political chaos and anarchy and permeated by what came to be known as the "security dilemma." Thus, the policy prescription from the neoliberal institutionalists' logic becomes: eliminate the power of the sovereign nation-state and create an international authority that has power and jurisdiction over the individual nation-state and can remove anarchy from the international political system and enforce peace and security and incentivize multilateral decision making.

CONFLUENCE OF AGENDAS IN TARGETING SECULARISM AND SOVEREIGNTY

In sum, from this viewpoint, international organizations and institutions are the remedy for struggle, conflict, and war in global affairs, and the slow but steady removal of sovereign national power is required before effective international institutions can become fully operational. Placing aside the range of criticism regarding the inefficient and often corrupt nature of international institutions, and the hopes, wishes, and associated demands of the idealists turned neoliberal institutionalists, the following reality has arisen: violent jihadists are actively involved in undermining, in the hopes of ultimately destroying, the secular, sovereign, Western-conceived nation-state. They enjoy at least passive support from countless millions of "moderate" Muslims, not necessarily in the violence wrought by the jihadists, but in the jihadist objective of seeing the institution of Sharia law and the adoption of Islam manifest itself on a worldwide basis. Simultaneous to these activities and preferences, within Western civilization, is a highly influential group in universities and national governments intent on undermining the sovereign power and authority of nation-states and transferring it into the hands of unelected "international institutions" and into the hands of their associated unelected committees.

Once that occurs, and once power and authority have been transferred from nation-states to these international entities, apparently the expectation is that peace, stability, and economic growth will miraculously overwhelm greed, corruption, struggle, and conflict in world affairs. If it were simply an innocuous exercise in creating a better world, the efforts would be applauded. The problem, arising from the agenda of destroying the viability and authority of nations, is that these are not innocuous exercises with zero adverse consequences; World War II stands as exhibit A in terms of consequences for superficial and naive thinking when it comes to international politics.

DARUL ISLAM ORDERS THE DARUL HARB: "CONVERT, PAY A TAX, OR DIE"

The concepts of Darul Harb, Darul Islam, and ghazi warfare emanating from ancient Arabia and Persia and animating the strategic thinking of the Ottoman Empire are important strategic considerations in the process as well. The demarcation of the world into a duality of good and evil, of light and darkness, provided the authorities the opportunity to cast their regime as the supporters of goodness and truth and in accord with the most powerful deity underpinning human reality. In doing so, the autocratic rulers were able to create a strategic narrative that was deployed against any individual, group, or tribe that threatened the ruler's authority, along with their associated societal and economic privileges. The original moral principles of Judaism and Christianity were also exploited, throughout history, in the same manner in order to justify authority, privilege, and advantage. In sum, this pattern of developing a strategic narrative for political advantage while basing it on religion is not confined to Islam.

War in the modern Middle East involves conventional kinetic operations aimed at *psychological dislocation*—through the application of decisive force (and effects) at the decisive point(s) and at the decisive time(s) aimed at convincing an enemy and his or her leaders that they cannot achieve their objectives through the application of military force. However, while perhaps necessary for success in major combat operations in winning the war, it has, during the modern era, proved insufficient in winning the peace.

Being able to prevail in winning both the war and the peace requires effective war termination involving *psychological ascendency* with a strategic narrative that is compelling and aligned with the interests, values, and belief of the people whose army has just lost the conventional campaign. Further, the peace accord must not be seen as overly humiliating, and the conditions for moving ahead must not be seen as overly or unjustly harsh. The conditions placed upon the German people following the First World War provided the environment for the rise of Hitler's Third Reich and the initiation of World War II. The arbitrary manner in which the United Nations established the State of Israel, which began seizing territory before the General Assembly vote established it as a recognized state, partially contributed to the conditions for continual conflict.

Operationally the violent jihadists have been able to blunt the overwhelming conventional military superiority inherent in network-centric warfare, which allowed the West, through information dominance, to move inside Middle Eastern and Afghanistan opponents' OODA-Loop, with the jihadists neutralizing the advantage by dispersing and conducting insurgent and terrorist operations among the people. Among the people, the violent jihadists were often seen as legitimate resistance fighters, fighting against an unjust set of circumstances that resulted in support and sustenance from much of the population. Accordingly, the efforts at the operational and tactical levels were supported strategically by the generation of a "moral" or psychological ascendancy through the utilization of a compelling strategic narrative based on a religion-based unifying ideology.

While the West enjoys superiority in achieving psychological dislocation through major combat operations, it has been frustrated in its attempts at arriving at psychological ascendency. Moreover, it has failed to appreciate the necessity of overcoming psychological *disruption* from external powers that attempt to generate influence and presence within the region. In the modern era, following the collapse of the Ottoman Empire, disruption was part of the policies and strategies of the Soviet Union from the 1920s until its collapse in 1991. In Vladimir Putin's Russia, in the first two decades of the twenty-first century, it has since been resurrected.

The Soviets have a deep interest in the Gulf area and would doubtless like to Balkanize it in some way to enable their influence to percolate more easily on the "divide and influence" principle.[6]

The Russians, like the Soviets before them would prefer their "resistance" to Western expansion and hegemony, avoid being settled at the strategic level in a general systemic war, particularly given the potential of such a conflict turning nuclear. Thus, since the advent of nuclear munitions at the end of the Second World War and in the decades that followed, modern warfare among great powers subsided to proxy wars and a general shift to substate violence, as "revolutionary" movements backed by the Soviets attempted to undermine the strong authoritarian governments backed by the United States and its allies. Low-intensity conflict became a specialization (Special Operations and Low Intensity Conflict [SOLIC]) for U.S. Special Forces, including Army Delta, Green Beret, Navy SEALs, and Central Intelligence Agency's (CIA) Special Activities Division (SAD). This involved actors with low-level political organizations, including war lords, insurgent groups, terrorists, and peasant revolts. Complexity of war at the high end and the risk of a nuclear exchange pushed conflict toward decentralized struggle in subnational conflict and violence. Intrigue and political warfare between the super powers and low-intensity proxy wars among their respective client states and subgroups took center stage during the Cold War.

Consequently the Soviets and the Russians became expert at undermining governments aligned with Western interests and in creating problems within a region while simultaneously inserting themselves as "indispensable" for any attempted solutions. As a result, the Russians forced their presence and influence by becoming both arsonist and fireman. If they do not have sufficient power for the classic "divide and conquer" principle, then Moscow settles for a "divide and influence" method of operation (MO), waiting patiently in the wings for the day Western power is successfully "disaggregated," by a combination of strategic and operational trends, forces, and events.

The requirements for successful military operations within the Middle East in the present era include an understanding and effective capabilities in dealing with the three psychological dimensions of warfare: *dislocation*, *disruption*, and *ascendancy*. The United States and its Western allies have mastered only psychological dislocation, while the Russians have become expert at disruption and funneling cash and support to those opposed to Western influence. The internal factions within the Middle East intent on opposing all external powers' attempts at controlling the region have mastered ghazi warfare and psychological ascendancy.

While cultural and historical dynamics have contributed to Middle Eastern factions and groups' expertise in asymmetric warfare (ghazi operations) and provided them with a competitive advantage in the creation and dissemination of a compelling strategic narrative, cultural and historical dynamics have also served to negatively impact their ability to conduct conventional military operations. Kenneth Pollack, a former CIA analyst and National Security Council Middle East expert, now at the Brookings Institution, argued in his exhaustive doctoral dissertation, "The Influence of Arab Culture on Arab Military Effectiveness," that problems for Arab conventional military competency include a tendency toward stifling initiative, lack of flexibility, and a general overcentralization, leaving those forces susceptible to disarray once leadership and command and control have been decapitated or neutralized.[7] This is one of the reasons the U.S. military immediately targeted command and control in Operation Desert Storm and OIF.

Pollack also found a tendency toward the manipulation of information in Arab culture. Negative information was hidden or selectively reported, while positive information was padded with inaccurate additions, often making the data unreliable. For example, Gamal Nasser, the president of Egypt during the 1967 Six-Day War, was not told for eight hours that his air force had been completely demolished by the Israeli Air Force. The tendency for overcentralization also resulted in what could only be described as "centralized isolation," stemming from an elitism that brought about a general discouragement of leadership, adaptability, and initiative at the junior levels. A significant gap and barrier to effective communication exists between the junior officer level of command and the enlisted ranks. DeAtkine (1999) argues that noncommissioned officers (NCOs) in the U.S. military have proven invaluable in bridging the gap between the officer corps and lower enlisted ranks. This has not been the case for most of the militaries in the Middle East. In the Middle East, there is a tendency for many in the officer corps (less within specialized and elite units) to involve themselves in social positioning and less with military proficiency and leadership. In the United States, the vast majority of the officer corps is focused on three primary concepts: mission-unit-country.

In the twentieth century and in the space of a disaggregated Ottoman Empire came Western-conceived nation-states.

Middle East and North Africa (MENA)
Era of Independence

- 1922: Egypt
- 1932: Iraq
- 1932: Arabia
- 1946: Syria
- 1946: Lebanon
- 1946: Jordan

- 1948: Israel
- 1951: Libya
- 1956: Morocco
- 1956: Sudan
- 1956: Tunisia
- 1961: Kuwait
- 1962: Algeria
- 1967: Yemen
- 1970: Oman

The various tribes, ethnic groupings, and factions within these "nation-states" provided loyalty to the family and other subnational groupings. While professional officer corps were created in all of the newly independent states, the vast majority of the people within the newly minted political organizations were slow to embrace nationalism and devotion to country. This provided "a disconnect" from the central government and its army and security forces on the one hand and the vast majority of the people on the other. This also provided conditions ripe for interfactional squabbling and Soviet intrigue. The Ottoman Empire for centuries enjoyed a monopoly over the exercise of psychological dislocation, disruption, and ascendancy in the Middle East and much of North Africa. While there were numerous outbreaks of violence, these were mostly contained by Ottoman central power.

The suppressive power of the Ottoman Empire, however, came with costs, as its subjects were not able to develop technology through freedom of thought and inquiry in order to compete effectively with the West. This was also the fate of China, which blocked exchanges with other countries beginning in the fifteenth century. Similarly, the Russian Empire blocked the ideas of the Renaissance, the Enlightenment, and the Industrial Revolution until battlefield losses during the Crimea War in the mid-nineteenth century convinced Moscow that the West's technological advances could no longer be ignored and scientific inquiry would have to be embraced.

The lack of trust exacerbating a lack of cooperation among the numerous tribes and factions within the Middle East negatively impacts coalition and alliance building, which in turn serves to stifle attempts aimed at the aggregation of power. This inability to aggregate sufficient power condemns the militaries of the Middle East and North Africa to suboptimal levels of strategic endurance vis-à-vis North America, Europe, Russia, and China. The lack of cooperation impacts military outcomes at the operational level as well. This lack among Arab militaries reduces their ability to synchronize and integrate combined arms operations, which are necessary to conduct war at the operational level. This requires the ability to act in a very complex environment with very complex instruments. This heightened complexity requires both operationalizing the entire battlefield and operating effectively in battlespace (space and cyberspace) where commanders apply pressure at multiple points, relying on both technology and decentralized battle where units must be led by officers skilled in adaptability and independent judgment (yet understanding and maintaining the overall integrity of the operational intent). Accordingly, "the ability to conduct simultaneous operations is the heart of operational art."[8]

> Operational synchronization is a difficult process because it requires nothing less than "the arrangement of battlefield activities in time, space, and purpose to produce maximum relative combat power at the decisive point."[9]

THE CLASH OF UNIVERSALISMS IN AN AGE OF WEAPONS OF MASS DESTRUCTION

However, while the West has succeeded in achieving military superiority in conventional military operations, it lacks an understanding and competence regarding the nature of ghazi warfare combined with psychological ascendancy, and it does not appear to understand the "clash of universalisms" in the competing strategic narratives.

The strategic and operational dynamics outlined unfold in an environment resembling Samuel P. Huntington's *The Clash of Civilizations*. However, more specifically than a general cultural clash of civilizations is the strategic problem arising from a clash of "universalisms," which is at the core of the multi-century conflict between Western democracy and Islamic fundamentalism. Both seek to advance a global expansion of their respective ideologies.

The two diametrically opposed political ideologies share in the belief that in order for their principles to be most effective, worldwide acceptance is necessary. Both possess large numbers of adherents following aggressive activities in the spread of their political views. The view within Islamic fundamentalism, including the view of millions of moderate Muslim supporters is that the Darul Harb—secular democracy—and other non-Islamic regions must be eliminated, and the expansion of the Darul Islam is the proper approach in doing so. Thus, the violent jihadists, in attempting to reduce the Darul Harb through terror and mass murder, if necessary, find intellectual justification from an expansionary view of political Islam. As noted, both the expansion of political Islam and Sharia law is supported by tens of millions of Muslims.

In the West, coercive democratization policies are being followed in order that traditional authoritarian rulers and government are replaced by representative democracy. Beginning with the French and American revolutions, the democratization process adopted armed violence along with its economic and political activities in order to insure the spread of democracy. Thus, Huntington argued that we can expect a "clash of civilizations"—the core of the clash between a secular Western view of government and that of political Islam is fundamentally a clash of universalisms. Since both perspectives believe that its reach and jurisdiction are universal, secular democracy and political Islam can be viewed as two competing and incommensurable intellectual frames of reference. In that each believes (and insists) that its perspective will and must prevail has led to the construction of strategic conditions for perpetual conflict. The key to the ultimate resolution of this historical impasse lies in understanding the nature of the dangerous trajectory of two violently and diametrically opposed ideologies followed by the creation of conditions, which will foster accommodation, stability, and development. Once a more rational and calm set of conditions is created, further opportunities for cooperation become possible as additional opportunities present themselves. The concepts of civil society, the elite pact strategy, and the Cartesian Compromise may offer insights into a potential way forward in crafting a grand strategy that over the long term may offer solutions for these ongoing issues.

In the contemporary era, the creation of civil society and the utilization of the "elite pact" strategy have become a focus. In authoritarian systems, a repressive government interacts directly with the citizen. In such a dyadic relationship, the government has an overwhelming preponderance of power over the individual citizen and uses the instruments of state policy—police, security services, the courts, prisons, and the like—to sanction citizens deemed as threats to the authoritarian government continued rule or existence. In order to lessen an authoritarian government's ability to isolate a citizen and apply pressure or sanctions, democratic activists attempt to create groups such as unions, civic groups, manufacturer associations, or any grouping that provides the citizen a voice among the many, which then possesses the ability to petition the government for redress of grievances and be less susceptible to individual coercion.

These groups that allow citizens to band together, interact, and make demands of their government create a buffer zone or space between the authoritarian government and the individual citizen. This space becomes a protective medium or even shield for increased political participation by a state's citizens and allows for increased leverage by a citizenry vis-à-vis its government. This is the main reason why Putin's government in Russia has begun to outlaw and coerce the groups attempting to expand civil society within Russia itself. An authoritarian government must first and foremost control its citizenry in order for entitled special interests to gain privilege. Civil society challenges that model of elite enti-tlement and thus becomes a danger for the special interest-coercive government model.

Active democratization in the modern era also utilizes the elite pact strategy. When Napoleon launched his Egyptian campaign in 1798, he believed that the French army would be widely hailed as a liberating force by the Egyptian people. But after taking military control of the coun-try, he and his officers were shocked that instead of jubilation and cries of joy among the people, they were met with a pervasive sadness and mel-ancholy among not only the elite but the masses as well. Part of the reason was that the privileged Egyptian elite, under the Mamluks, knew their people better than did the French. Thus, the special interest-coercive government model under the Mamluks formed and communicated a strategic narrative to the Egyptian people that appreciated and under-stood the nuances of Egyptian culture—their fears and hopes—and cre-ated the conditions that met the French not as liberators but as intruding occupiers.

Democratization activists in the twentieth century understood that, in general, the elite within an authoritarian society understood the nuances of a particular culture relative to the masses better than foreigners. Accordingly, those promoting democratization came to accept the follow-ing schemata.

Realizing the difficulties in effective communication with a population (masses) given a segment of an elite intent on countering any efforts toward democratization, the democratic activists, shown in Figure 10.3 as "international community," understood the need to enlist the assis-tance of others within an elite, less hostile to greater political and eco-nomic opportunities for the masses that would accrue, theoretically, in any democratization project. In general, within an authoritarian society, there are those who will oppose democratization either upon ideological grounds (Islamists) or upon self-interest grounds, as they stand to lose privileges and advantages with the creation of democratic institutions within the country. The elite that are intractably tied to the status quo within the authoritarian society and are prepared to fight to derail any changes can be referred to as the "hard-liner" elite.

Also within the elite are those who understand that the time for repres-sive government and the exploitation of the masses by a select few in the face of an increasingly literate, awakening, and socially connected popu-lation is coming to an end. This segment of the elite in understanding the awakening of people, including the generation of leidenschaft or col-lective energy combined with the decreasing utility of traditional government methods of control, find it their interest to proactively guide and shape this process for the betterment of their society as well as a

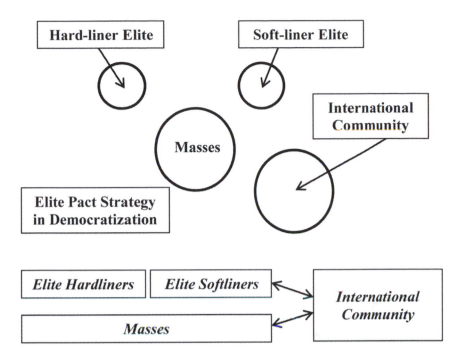

Figure 10.3 Democratization and the Elite Pact Strategy. Coalition of the Elite Soft-liners, Masses, and the International Community working jointly moves the country toward greater opportunity, openness, and democratization and in creating the ability for isolating and, if necessary, neutralizing the Elite Hardliners. Author's creation and interpretation from several sources including: Barrington Moore, *Social Origins of Dictatorship and Democracy* (Boston, MA: Beacon Press, 1993); Samuel P. Huntington, *Democratization in the Late 20th Century* (Norman, OK: University of Oklahoma Press, 1991); Guillermo O'Donnell, Philippe C. Schmitter, and Laurence Whitehead, *Transitions from Authoritarian Rule: Tentative Conclusions About Uncertain Democracies* (Baltimore, MD: Johns Hopkins University Press, 1986).

strong preference in maintaining a leadership role. As a result, these "softliners" are open to working with the democratic advocates within their own country and within the international community.

Accordingly, the elite pact strategy in the democratization process recognizes the invaluable contribution of an existing elite in an authoritarian society in leading that society toward developing conditions of greater political participation, protection, and rights among its citizenry. Thus, the international community, in recognizing the needed leadership role of the elite in any democratization process, enlists the support and assistance of the soft-liner elite in order to shape and guide the democratization process.

In order to seize the opportunities presented in the modern era vis-à-vis the authoritarian past, an alliance between the international community, the soft-liner elite, and the masses has the potential of being created in order to transition the society away from repression and the special interests-authoritarian political model. This alliance will be met, invariably, with resistance from the hard-liner elite, which will oppose any action that dissipates their traditional privileges or their views on the value of an authoritarian-totalitarian political ideology.

The softliners will need to be empowered with more than the promises regarding the advantages obtained from an open political system based on secular democracy in order to be successful in moving their societies forward toward greater economic and educational opportunities for the people. Lessons learned from the European historical experience with religious-political authoritarianism may prove insightful. Following the collapse of Antiquity and the demise of Rome in 476 CE, much of European political society rested upon the divine right of kings. Following the Renaissance (roughly the fourteenth to sixteenth centuries) and a generally awakening of the people, the divine right of kings to absolute rule based on religious authority came to be questioned. Violence and wars resulted and following a particularly violent episode of war from the mid-fourteenth century until 1648, peace was achieved (Treaty of Westphalia), as the Church of Rome came to the conclusion that its political power would now be limited in both degree and scope.

The Cartesian Compromise in the early seventeenth century aided in the end of the religious wars in Europe. Frenchman, mathematician, and philosopher Rene Descartes was a devout Catholic, but he sought to empower and unchain the "new science" arguing for it to be allowed to move forward without religious coercion or authoritarian constraints. Descartes essentially created the intellectual compromise that allowed the church to acquiesce in its demand for political, educational, and scientific control in Europe. Toward this, Descartes argued that reality was made up of dual substances—mind and body. The church, Descartes argued, should continue to enjoy preeminent oversight in the realm of mind and spirit, while science should be allowed to investigate matters freely relating to body or extension, that is, empirical reality in time and space.

Freed from religious dogma, scientific advances proliferated in the West eventually leading to the rise of military technology, which in the eighteenth century surpassed the long-standing military supremacy of the Ottoman Empire. Following the advances during the Industrial Revolution this intellectual freedom in the form of innovation and creativity generated the technology that was utilized successfully by Edmund Allenby and his British and Allied forces, as they pushed the Ottoman armies from Egypt, marched on Palestine, and entered Jerusalem in December 1917.

A TWENTY-FIRST-CENTURY CARTESIAN COMPROMISE

A compromise similar to that which effectively ended the power of the clerical establishment over government is required in terms of democracy and political Islam. Such a compromise, once in place, and once communicated effectively to the masses by the soft-liner elite, would move the process of greater opportunities for the citizenry forward in the face of those attempting to hold fast to traditional privileges and advantages in the special interest-authoritarian government era. As such, a coalition of the softliners, masses, and international community would move toward greater democratization and, as the hard-liner elite inevitably moved to forestall any progress, the coalition would be positioned to marginalize and, if necessary, neutralize the hard-liner attacks.

However, the necessary intellectual groundwork would have to be completed first, as T. E. Lawrence (Lawrence of Arabia) once remarked:

> We had to arrange their minds in order of battle, just as carefully and as formally as other officers arranged their bodies; and not only in our own men's minds, though them first, but the minds of the enemy, so far as we could reach them. And thirdly, the mind of the nation supporting us behind the firing line and the mind of the hostile nation awaiting the verdict, and the neutrals looking on.[10]

Since careful attention to the lining up the ideas in the minds should be conducted as meticulous as the arranging of bodies on the battlefield in terms of political warfare, more work is required in developing a compromise that would be effective. Perhaps useful in the deliberations were the strategies employed by the post–World War II generation. These leaders did not attempt to change Japan, Germany, or following the Korean War, South Korea overnight but took a long-term perspective that included educational policies and gradual social and political movement toward the institutions capable of supporting democracy. In these largely successful instances, they pressed first for the creation of a political culture more readily prepared to support the institutions of modern democracy. This serves in contrast to the present attempts at constructing the institutions of democracy within the modern Middle East without first creating the political culture that is necessary in supporting them.

While an in-depth expose on the potential ways forward in achieving a twenty-first-century Cartesian Compromise is beyond the scope of this book, there are fundamental points of convergence. Consider the ancient Arabic concept of *ihsan*—also referred to as *ehsan*—as well as the ancient

Greek concept of *arête*. The purpose of Sharia law is to promote the proliferation of ihsan in society, and the purpose of government in ancient
Greece (Plato, Aristotle) was to promote the conditions for the production
of arête, which maximizes *eudemonia*. Ihsan means human excellence;
arête also means human excellence. Both refer to the flourishing of the
human spirit by choosing and acting wisely and finding a proper balance
between excess and deficiency. This balance in the West is virtue in the
face of vice, and as Aristotle argued, acting in such a fashion man per-
forms his function, acting from rational principle, that is, dealing effectively with the phenomenal world and in doing so acting in accordance
with the natural order of things. In Islam, to act in such a fashion, the generation of ihsan, is to act in accord with the will of Allah. Such concepts
need to be explored.

In the coming decades, the United States and its allies have the opportunity of leading the rise of Middle Eastern populations long oppressed
by a series of authoritarian governments that predate Muhammad. It is
critical that the full range of issues, arguments, and ideas receive a full air-
ing under an objective light, which only comes into focus as a by-product
of the freedom of thought and the freedom of expression. Thus, the
United States and its allies need to recognize that the collective will or
energy of a people—leidenschaft—has taken a revolutionary trajectory
and can potentially be diverted for the narrow-minded purposes of the
violent jihadists seeking perpetual war. Instead, by providing
international leadership, America should assist the moderates within
the Middle East and across the Muslim world in providing assistance in
educational, economic, and political reform. Such reforms should reflect
the need for a patient, long-term process and avoid the jolts and uncertainty that have caused more harm than good.

The generation that led the way to victory in World War II did not
expect Japan or Germany to be a fully functioning democracy overnight
as the process took decades. In South Korea, the same patient, sustained,
long-term reform process brought forth tangible results, but this took
30 years and there remains a long distance still to travel, particularly in
regard to the North. Strategic patience, now less visible in American foreign and defense policy, needs to be reacquired, particularly as it relates
to the modern Middle East.

Accordingly, strategic patience in terms of sustained, long-term
reforms and development is needed. However, this patience cannot be
extended to the proliferation of weapons of mass destruction (WMD)
and terrorism. In short, while strategic patience is required for reforms,
zero tolerance in regard to counter-proliferation policy is absolutely
required given the nature of the threat arising from WMD and terrorism.
The reasons why this is absolutely necessary need to be brought vividly

to the attention of audiences in the West, in the Middle East, and around the world.

This is critical because the shock value on target audiences as envisioned by the terrorists if and when an attack involving WMD does occur will be lessened. Second, in order to conduct a robust counter-proliferation campaign, audiences need to be apprised as to why the United States and its allies are conducting what will appear to be preventive military strikes. The argument that WMD has altered the traditional lines between preemptive and preventive war has to be made. This includes a clearly articulated argument on how traditional nuclear deterrence has been conceived of in the past as occurring between two rational actors and the nature of deterrence in an age of suicidal terrorism, including aspects of plausible deniability.

While conventional military operations remain a competitive advantage for the West in relation to the armed forces and armed groups in the Middle East, the United States and its allies can ill afford to relinquish superiority in the practice of IW to its enemies and opponents operating in the Middle East or anywhere else in the world. Lessons learned from three American operations provide insight into a potential avenue forward: Eagle Claw, Anaconda, and ECLIPSE II.

Operation Eagle Claw was directed at rescuing the hostages held in Iran in the wake of the Iranian Revolution of 1979. The United States found that the newly established Delta force, while having trained extensively as a special operations unit, had scant integrated training with other units that were required in support of Eagle Claw. Thus sailors, airmen, marines, and other conventional army units were not provided the opportunity in training sufficiently for the operation into the Iranian desert. With lives lost and with mission failure came increased scrutiny that provided the integrated and synchronized training that U.S. Special Operations Forces came to epitomize in the years that followed.

Operation Anaconda during Operation Enduring Freedom (OEF) in Afghanistan highlighted additional problems for the U.S. military. In the early phases of the OEF, U.S. Special Forces and CIA special operators, working with the Northern Alliance in close coordination with U.S. airpower, drove the Taliban from power. Well integrated and highly synchronized, the operation was a remarkable exhibit of the application of military force. However, as the Taliban began to regroup after being scattered, the United States decided to attack a massing enemy formation before the Taliban and their al-Qaeda guests had the chance to organize and strike. The operation was placed in the hands of the 10th Mountain Division, and only a couple of weeks were provided in preparing Operation Anaconda.

Anaconda required the coordination of indigent forces (that were not Northern Alliance's soldiers), U.S. conventional forces, U.S. and allied Special Operations Forces, and U.S. airpower. The level of training and synchronized coordination that existed in the opening phases of OEF simply was not available for Anaconda, particularly between the disparate ground units and airpower. The United States rectified this weakness, and an integrated and highly synchronized combined military force was sent into Iraq during OIF, which drove Saddam from power in a decisive display of one of history's most remarkable offensives.

However, during post-combat security and stability operations referred to as ECLIPSE II in the follow-on stage to major combat operations of OIF, the insurgency that developed in opposition to the U.S. occupation created problems that the United States had difficulty in dealing with. While the United States achieved conventional military superiority through its ability (measured by technology, organization, leadership, education, and a unifying ideology) in moving inside an opponent's OODA-Loop, that superiority was largely neutralized once major combat operations ceased. By hiding among the population, the insurgents/terrorists placed the United States on the "horns of a dilemma," that is, providing an opponent with only bad options. Thus, the United States could strike at the insurgents hiding within the population. However, by doing so the United States would incur collateral damage as it was forced to strike in civilian areas, thus alienating the population and driving them closer to the insurgents. Or, refrain from such kinetic strikes, which allowed the insurgents effective sanctuary.

Once the war moved away from major combat operations, what was left was a weakened national government (host nation [HN]) whose task was to deal with the insurgents. Even with U.S. support, the HN faced an enemy that was able, through speed, agility, surprise, audacity, and superior intelligence, to move inside the U.S.-HN OODA-Loop.

In sum, during major conventional operations, the United States and its allies are able to move within an opponent's OODA-Loop. However, once major combat operations have concluded, the budding insurgencies outmaneuver and outpace the U.S.-HN coalition by turning the tables on the United States and the HN by moving inside *their* OODA-Loop.

In order to solve this dilemma where the United States and its allies, including moderate Arab and Muslim allies, are reacting slowly to insurgent operations, the following should be considered. General Stanley McChrystal, former head of Joint Special Operations Command (JSOC) and commander of U.S. operations in Afghanistan, argues in his book, *Team of Teams*, that the traditional top-down hierarchical approach to managing organizations is being outperformed by the networked, cellular (independent acting cells), and informal decision and action cycle of insurgent and terrorist groups.

The U.S.-HN organizational structural as it faces such an insurgency is a lumbering, slow-deciding, and even slower-acting dinosaur, while the insurgency moves with the agility of the lion or a pack of wolves. Accordingly, it became imperative to refine the U.S.-HN organizational structure when faced with a virulent case of insurgency. McChrystal recommends moving away from the slow moving OODA-Loop produced by the top-down hierarchical managerial approach to management and decision making, as they related to counterinsurgency (COIN) operations. In its place McChrystal recommends a flatter, more informal, less-hierarchical organizational structure capable of processing intelligence, information, and battlespace developments in order to, once again, operate inside the insurgents' OODA-Loop.

The lessons from Desert Claw, Anaconda, and ECLIPSE II should be examined closely, as they support the following observations. Joint operations, integrated and synchronized, have proven to be an effective attribute of the successful modern military armed force. While superior technology has provided an overwhelming competitive advantage to Western arms vis-à-vis their Middle Eastern counterparts, the critical aspect of that advantage is difficult to quantify. Technology, in and of itself, is not the key. If it were, Middle Eastern armies in possession of great wealth would be positioned to purchase military effectiveness and perhaps compete for superiority in the modern age.

The critical aspect of superior military technology lies within a society's culture. Advanced technology requires innovation and creativity, and those elements require a society that fosters and supports freedom of thought and freedom of expression. Islam as it is currently practiced demands subservience to an ideological belief system, wherein clerics determine the appropriateness of thought and action. This was precisely the state of affairs of medieval Europe when politics rested on the divine right of kings, to justify rule, authority, and obedience.

Freedom of thought and expression began accelerating during the Renaissance and with religious control of the nation-state reduced following the Treaty of Westphalia in 1648, innovation and creativity in the West eventually led to the Industrial Revolution, which drove Western arms past the power of the Ottoman Empire. Yet, with that rise of technology also came the expansion of "Auftragstaktik" in Western militaries. Independent and critical thinking fostered throughout the officer ranks allowed even junior officers to function in an environment cut off from central command. Arab and Muslim armies, once cut off from centralized command structures, lost the capacity for independent and effective decision making and action. However, Middle Eastern higher ranking officers,

Special Forces, and intelligence services received training in independent and critical analysis. An excellent example of this is OIF. Once command and control had been hit and lines of communications to the outer-lying formations disrupted, Iraqi units had difficulty in acting independently.

However, upon ceasing major conventional military operations, dismissing the Iraqi armed forces, as well as the Ba'athist government, the insurgency that rose was well stocked with high-ranking former military officers, Special Forces, and intelligence operatives. Simultaneously, the United States transitioned from a strictly U.S. military operation to one that included the HN, international groups, and U.S. civilian authorities, as it withdrew major combat elements. The Iraqi insurgency was then faced with an unintegrated, unsynchronized, and slower moving opponent, which it, in effect, ran circles around.

From historic events, Western special operations have learned to operate in an integrated fashion with conventional forces and vice versa. Both have learned to operate effectively in integrating and synchronizing air operations on the battlefield and in battlespace. Given that a successful insurgency incorporates important political aspects in their operations, particularly in the effective management of a strategic informational campaign, the United States needs to integrate political aspects that relate directly to its COIN strategy. What is needed is the integration and synchronization of operations across the political policy spectrum. Such that the political, diplomatic, economic, and informational capabilities needed in the spectrum can not only be trained and exercised to integrated and synchronized participation with military components of the spectrum, but an expeditionary capability with expertise across the political policy spectrum can also be readied for deployment. In short, we must integrate politics and governance with the spectrum of violence (low intensity conflict, conventional war, strategic great power war) to enable moving inside an opponent's OODA-Loop in any contested environment. The objective is a political policy and governance capability integrated and synchronized with the spectrum of force to overcome any challenge. Just as the United States found it difficult to coordinate the interagency process during Operation Eagle Claw (the failed Iranian hostage rescue attempt), it did, over the ensuing decades, vastly improve the process; we must now improve in order to neutralize the advantage of those conducting war among the people.

Essential in dissuading others as they contemplate uses of armed violence to further their objectives is to create, maintain, and be prepared to prevail, if necessary, across the political policy spectrum, including within the spectrum of conflict. This capability and the will to use it maximize the deterrent effect. The overall policy objective is to create the full range of capabilities in order that the chances that will require their use are minimized, that is, shaping the incentives and disincentives to conflict in ways conducive to its amelioration or resolution without having to resort to the use of compellent force.

Having such a capability available will not only improve the chances for success in COIN operations but will also provide a deterrent effect for those contemplating insurgency operations. As it stands in the aftermath of Iraq, Libya, and Afghanistan, too many groups are taking lessons from the less than optimal performances turned in by the United States and its allies (particularly HNs), and sensing opportunity for future courses of action, as the United States is deterred and even recoils from even the attempt at conducting effective COIN operations. We cannot cede the territory of failed states and ungoverned spaces to terrorists and violent jihadists as these areas are likely to expand given the fragility of the nation-state in the present era.

In the early nineteenth century, there were less than 30 nation-states in the international system. Now there are nearly 200. While many of these were well-intentioned creations, many also reflected scant recognition of the facts of the ground. In the aftermath of the collapse of the Ottoman Empire, many nation-states arose in the Middle East. Many of the borders drawn did not adequately reflect, or adequately respect, the cultures and societies that existed across the region. Many of the states that existed in 2000, including Iraq, Syria, Libya, Afghanistan, and others, will not, in all likelihood, remain intact in the coming years. It will be imperative to be able to operate effectively in failed states and ungoverned spaces, as both domains are likely to increase.

The aggregation of power provides the resources to maintain significant military forces and project that force or threat of force over great distances while sustaining them in the field and, when necessary, over time. While this is a necessary condition for military success, when dealing with great powers or great civilizations, particularly in the modern era, it is not sufficient. While power, force, and a unifying ideology provide the blunt foundations of military effectiveness, to be truly effective in the ancient and modern worlds, one needed and needs proficiency in two domains: psychological dislocation and psychological ascendancy.

Standing military forces can serve as a deterrent in order to dissuade potential adversaries from taking action in direct opposition to your interests. Thus, to deter an opponent requires sending a message—thus known in advance—that you possess both the capability and will to deliver to the opponent a set of circumstances that will vitiate any calculations of gain in taking the action you seek to deter. A compellent use of force is not attempting to deter specifically but rather compelling an opponent to cease or desist from a particular action already under way or force him or her to perform action you deem necessary. The application of military force is often required to compel behavior. However, compelling behavior can be achieved through a variety of means, including, but not limited to, the application of organized violence. Economic sanctions, for example, can be utilized in compelling an adversary or opponent to cease, desist, or take action you deem preferable.

In the application of military force to compel behavior, that is, warfare, one seeks to inflict upon an opponent's mind not necessarily a rational calculation regarding a cost-benefit analysis but rather an extreme psychological dislocation—a realization of being placed in a disadvantageous set of circumstances with the impression to the mind accentuated if such a realization occurs suddenly and violently and if he or she then feels that he or she is unable to counter your next move. Psychological dislocation in war, as B. H. Liddell Hart argued, springs from a sense of being trapped—suddenly, swiftly, and violently. Thus, the essence of success in military operations is the application of decisive force at the decisive point and at the decisive time in order to render to an opponent an extreme psychological dislocation and to sustain that shock and disequilibrium to both forces and leadership until surrender, force dissolution, or annihilation.[11] This is the nature of conventional military operations as practiced in both the ancient and modern worlds. The United States and its allies enjoy conventional military superiority over any opponent, in the Middle East, or in any other region of the world.

In the Middle East, beginning with the establishment of Israel in 1948, Arab nations challenged the Israeli Defense Forces (IDF) in series of essentially conventional wars. With the United States determined to provide Israel with a qualitative advantage over its regional enemies, the Arab nations were unable to destroy the Jewish state through conventional war. The Soviet Union intensified its military support in the late 1950s through to the 1973 October War, but its contributions were met by American arms and American weapons systems up to and including nuclear threats made by Moscow. Following the 1973 October War, enemies of Israel opted for irregular operations, terrorism, and ghazi warfare. Arab nationalism was surpassed by Iranian sponsorship of terrorism and the emergence of Islamic fundamentalism.

In a classic example of Flaechen-und Luecken, the advantage the United States and its allies enjoyed in conventional military operations has been muted or even neutralized by irregular operations characterized by British army general Rupert Smith as war amongst the people. As former U.S. Army colonel, Antulio Echevarria, has argued that the jihadi and violent Islamic fundamentalists are not involved in some new kind of warfare but rather "are subordinating their military operations to a well-crafted information campaign designed to exploit certain cultural and religious values."[12] They are using a unifying ideology in the same manner as it has always been used in both the ancient and modern worlds.

This instrument, utilized effectively while deploying a religious justification and evoking universal jurisdiction, has provided societies with the ability to cast themselves on the side of that which is not only right but also backed by the most powerful force in the universe. This provides such a society's soldiers and citizens with the belief in the righteousness of their cause and the solace and comfort in knowing (believing) their cause is directly supported by the overarching and most omnipotent force in the universe—that they are, in fact, on the right side of history. This, in turn, provides the society (both its soldiers and citizens) a sense of psychological ascendancy relative to their opponents—a sense of having seized the moral high ground vis-à-vis one's adversaries. This becomes the essence of effective political warfare, rendering to one's followers a sense of psychological ascendancy and a powerful expectation of ultimate victory.

Accordingly, in conventional military combat, one seeks to render to one's enemy an effective psychological dislocation by neutralizing his or her ability to generate effective combat power and doing so in a manner that delivers a sudden shock followed by a sense of helplessness in the realization that he or she will not be able to counter his or her adversary's next move. If, however, the enemy has an ideology and a culture that see warfare as continuous with setbacks expected in the ebb and flow of battle, then no matter how cataclysmically defeated tactically, that opponent will continue to resist and when able, fight.

In order to strategically defeat such an enemy, the psychological ascendancy provided by a well-crafted strategic narrative must be shown for what it is—a man-made ideology, a device in the service of the aggregation of power, that is, the strategy of controlling people, resources, markets, and trade routes for both security and economic advantage. When religion is exploited to control people, resources, markets, and trade routes for both security and economic advantage, it moves from divine revelation, peace, and harmony into the domain of political ideology, economic principles, and military affairs. When religion is exploited to aggregate power in order to advance narrow elite interests, whether Western, Middle Eastern, or Eastern, this moves from the will of God into the domain of potential crimes against humanity. Exploitation by a nefarious few pursuing narrow interests is countered by the free exchange of ideas and degrading their ability to control and monopolize violence and strategic coordination goods. In the Middle East and around the world, well into the modern era, exposing the charlatans for what they are and what they are attempting to get away with remains a work in progress. In an era of WMD, the clash of universalisms—historically an effective strategy to advance narrow self-interests—is simply too costly and too onerous an enterprise for the modern era.

Notes

Introduction

1. U.S. Army General Douglas MacArthur, "Statement on Aid to Great Britain in Response to a Request from William Allen White, Chairman of the Committee to Defend America by Aiding the Allies," September 16, 1940, in *General MacArthur Speeches and Reports 1908–1964*, Edward T. Imparato, ed. (Paducah, KY: Turner Publishing, 2000), p. 122.

2. Samuel P. Huntington, *The Clash of Civilizations and the Remaking of the World Order* (New York: Touchstone Books, 1998).

3. Peter Paret's introductory comments in Carl von Clausewitz, *On War*, edited and translated by Michael Howard and Peter Paret (Princeton, NJ: Princeton University Press, 1989), p. 34.

4. Canadian Security Intelligence Service, "2018 Security Outlook: Potential Risks and Threats," Occasional Papers (2016-06-03), June 2016, see pages 7 and 27. https://www.csis-scrs.gc.ca/pblctns/ccsnlpprs/2016/2016-06-03/GLOBAL_SECURITY_POST-CONFERENCE_ENGLISH.pdf, accessed June 20, 2016.

5. The term, "Middle East," is believed to have found its way into the public discourse through the writings of Alfred Thayer Mahan, an American naval officer and geopolitical analyst who argued in 1890 that sea power was key to Britain's rise to arguably the most influential nation in the world by the closing decades of the nineteenth century; see A. T. Mahan, *The Influence of Sea Power upon History 1660–1783* (1890; Gretna, LA: Pelican Publishing, 2003).

6. Martin Van Creveld, *Technology and War: From 2000 BC to the Present* (New York: The Free Press, 1989), p. 320.

7. This is not to disparage the ethical aspects of any of the world's major religions (Judaism, Christianity, Islam, Hinduism, Buddhism, etc.) or the joy that

has been brought to millions as a result of following many of their respective precepts and principles. It is to say, however, that religion was and continues to be utilized for the creation of effective political and economic ideology, which then transformed and transforms the original moral and spiritual foundation into an instrument of coercive control and for the manipulation of the behavior of entire societies and civilizations. Much of human history is permeated by religion-based ideological exploitation and, far too often, directed for the purpose of armed conflict and the realization of narrow and nefarious self-interest. This process continues in the modern era.

    8. Egyptian early 12th dynasty, circa 1991–1789 BCE.

Chapter 1

    1. Dror Ze'evi, "Back to Napoleon? Thoughts on the Beginning of the Modern Era in the Middle East," *Mediterranean Historical Review*, Vol. 19, No. 1 (June 2004), p. 77.

    2. Orville T. Murphy, "Napoleon's International Politics: How Much Did He Owe to the Past?" *The Journal of Military History*, Vol. 54, No. 2 (April 1990), pp. 165–166.

    3. The term "Mamluk" originates from Arabic meaning "slave." The Mamluks were forged into a fighting unit of unsurpassed quality defeating the Mongols at the Battle of Ain Jalut on September 3, 1260. They were also responsible for ejecting the last crusader kingdoms from the Middle East. They eventually came to rule in Egypt and in Syria. However, they, unlike the Ottomans, refused to incorporate the new gunpowder weapons into their arsenals. This allowed the Ottomans to defeat them during the Ottoman-Mamluk War of 1516–1517. As Ottoman vassals in control of Egypt at the close of the eighteenth century, they faced the French army under Napoleon in 1798, subsequently being cut to pieces by artillery and French infantry.

    4. John Keegan, *Intelligence in War: Knowledge of the Enemy from Napoleon to al-Qaeda* (New York: Alfred A. Knopf, 2003), p. 62.

    5. Napoleon Bonaparte, "Proclamation to the Troops Entering Toulon, May 1798," in *Napoleon's Addresses: Selections from the Proclamations, Speeches and Correspondence of Napoleon Bonaparte*, Ida M. Tarbell, ed. (Boston, MA: Joseph Knight, 1896).

    6. O'Brien Browne, "Napoleon's Desert Storm," *MHQ Military History Quarterly*, Vol. 25, No. 1 (Autumn 2012), p. 32.

    7. Anthony Brandt, "French Fiasco in Egypt," *Military History*, Vol. 27, No. 3 (September 2010), p. 40.

    8. Browne, "Napoleon's Desert Storm" (2012), p. 35.

    9. Nicholas Harris, ed., *The Dispatches and Letters of Vice Admiral Lord Viscount Nelson*, 7 vols. (London: Henry Colburn Publisher, 1844–1846), 3:37.

    10. J. C. Hurewitz, "The Beginnings of Military Modernization in the Middle East: A Comparative Analysis," *Middle East Journal*, Vol. 22, No. 2 (Spring 1968), p. 146.

    11. "In all the major Muslim states in the nineteenth century *Nizam* came to mean the 'modernized' regular or standing army, as opposed to the tribal army

and other irregulars on whom Muslim rulers had traditionally relied." Hurewitz, "The Beginnings of Military Modernization in the Middle East: A Comparative Analysis" (1968), p. 145.

12. See Charles Allen, *God's Terrorists: The Wahhabi Cult and the Hidden Roots of Modern Jihad* (Boston, MA: Da Capo Press, 2006).

13. After Action Report on Naval Engagement at Navarino Bay, October 20, 1827, to John Wilson Croker, secretary of the Admiralty, from Vice Admiral Sir Edward Codrington, October 21, 1827.

14. Hurewitz, "The Beginnings of Military Modernization in the Middle East: A Comparative Analysis" (1968), p. 148.

15. Carlo M. Cipolla, *Guns, Sails, and Empires* (New York: Minerva Press, 1965).

16. Hurewitz, "The Beginnings of Military Modernization in the Middle East: A Comparative Analysis" (1968), p. 150.

Chapter 2

1. Edward Erickson, "Strength against Weakness: Ottoman Military Effectiveness at Gallipoli, 1915," *The Journal of Military History*, Vol. 65, No. 4 (October 2001), p. 997.

2. Ibid., p. 996.

3. See John Keegan, *The First World War* (New York: Alfred A. Knopf, 1998), pp. 246–247. Many analysts and historians argue that Kemal's actions during fighting on April 25, 1915, represent the "vital moments of the campaign." Kemal's contribution to victory was significant, but additional factors beyond the range of one man's actions were arguably more decisive, particularly Britain's lack of understanding of the terrain upon which it would fight and in the underestimation of Ottoman military capabilities reinforced at Gallipoli by German technology and military advice.

4. Erickson, "Strength against Weakness: Ottoman Military Effectiveness at Gallipoli, 1915" (October 2001), p. 985.

5. Quoted in Erickson, "Strength against Weakness: Ottoman Military Effectiveness at Gallipoli, 1915" (October 2001), p. 982.

6. Germany's advance in 1918 would have been much more powerful and effective if not for the sacrifices of Britain, France, and Allied forces during the period 1914–1917. It was the effectiveness of the British navy that provided convoy protection to those 1.5 million U.S. soldiers, as they transited the Atlantic to the European theater of operations.

7. James D. Scudieri, "Iraq 2003–4 and the Mesopotamia, 1914–1918: A Comparative Analysis in Ends and Means," Master's Thesis, Center For Strategic Leadership, U.S. Army War College, Carlyle Barracks, PA, March 19, 2004. See also: Major General Charles Vere Ferrers Townshend, *My Campaign*, 2 Vols. (New York: James A. McCann Co., 1920), 1:298, 2:7–8; *British Official History* 2:134; and A. J. Barker, *The Bastard War: The Mesopotamian Campaign of 1914–1918* (New York: Dial Press, 1967).

8. Edmund Allenby, "Dispatch to the British War Cabinet," December 16, 1917.

9. For an in-depth look at cavalry operations in Palestine during World War I, see Jean Bou, "Cavalry, Firepower, and Swords: The Australian Light Horse and the Tactical Lessons of Cavalry Operations in Palestine, 1916–1918," *The Journal of Military History*, Vol. 73 (January 2007), pp. 99–125.

10. Herbert Rosinski, *The German Army* (London: Pall Mall Press, 1966), p.310. For more on the concept of *auftragstaktik* see: Fritz Hoenig, *Inquiries into the Tactics of the Future*, 4th ed., translated by Carl Reichman (Kansas City, MO: Hudson-Kimberly Publishing Company, 1898), pp. 25–27, 43, 220, 232–234, and 311; Tim Lupfer, *The Dynamics of Doctrine: The Changes in German Tactical Doctrine during the First World War, Leavenworth Papers, No. 4* (Fort Leavenworth, KS: Combat Studies Institute, USACGSC, July 1981), pp. 15–21, 44–46; John T. Nelson II, "Auftragstaktik: A Case of Decentralized Battle," *Parameters* Vol. 17, No. 3 (September 1987), pp. 21–34; and Michael J. Gunther, "Auftragstaktik: The Basis for Modern Military Command" (Fort Leavenworth, KS: School of Advanced Military Studies (SAMS), USACGSC, August 8, 2012).

11. Paul M. Kennedy, "The First World War and the International Power System," *International Security*, Vol. 9, No. 1 (Summer 1984), p. 25.

12. Roger Chickering, "Introduction: The Era of Total War 1914–1945," in *Cambridge Histories Online* (Cambridge, U.K.: Cambridge University Press, 2003), p. 188.

13. Mustafa Kemal Attaturk, quoted in Dankwart A. Rustow, "Ataturk as Founder of a State," *Daedalus*, Vol. 97, No. 3, *Philosophers and Kings: Studies in Leadership* (Summer 1968), p. 800.

14. See Maryanne A. Rhett, *The Global History of the Balfour Declaration: Declared Nation* (New York: Routledge, 2015); and Jonathan Schneer, *The Balfour Declaration* (New York: Random House, 2012).

15. In a speech delivered to the U.S. Congress on January 8, 1918, President Woodrow Wilson outlined American peace terms for ending the First World War and in establishing a new world order in its aftermath which came to be known as the "Fourteen Points." This was partially aimed at convincing the German leadership to end the war as the United States would seek to moderate any harsh terms demanded by the victorious European powers. Wilson spoke of the lofty goals of open agreements, free trade, human rights, democracy, and self-determination. Britain, France, and Italy, after suffering immensely from the war, were less prone to forgiveness and less aligned with Wilson's version of idealism. France's Georges Clemenceau, in reaction to Wilson's "Fourteen Points," sarcastically observed, "The good Lord only had ten," in reference to the Ten Commandments.

16. Sir Clarmont Percival Skrine, *World War in Iran* (London: Constable and Company Ltd., 1962) p. 56; see also Harold Nicholson, *Curzon: The Past Phase, 1919–1925: A Study in Post War Diplomacy* (London: Constable and Company Ltd., 1934), pp. 139–140.

17. Wahhabism is a school of thought within Sunni Islam, more accurately referred to as *al-Muwahhidun* or Unitarianism, seeking to purify the Islamic community and to purge it of progressive reforms that this school of thought argues have led the people astray and into moral decline and, in the process, have lost the original principles and power of true Islam as envisioned by the Muslim

prophet, Muhammad. The founder of al-Muwahhidun, Muhammad bin Abd al-Wahhab (1703–1791), eventually joined in alliance with Muhammad bin Saud the original ancestral link to present-day Saudi Arabia and, armed with the political and military effectiveness of the Saudi clan, coupled with the power of the al-Muwahhidun religious-legal ideology, conquered and unified the disparate tribes in the Arabian Peninsula, beginning in the eighteenth century.

18. N. Masalha, "Faisal's Pan-Arabism, 1921-33," *Middle Eastern Studies*, Vol. 27, No. 4 (October 1991), p. 684.

19. Considered the most aggressive of Haganah commanders, a former Russian army sergeant-major, Yitzhak Sadeh, was selected to lead FOSH, an elite special forces unit of 300 men tasked with preemptive and reprisal action aimed at Arab irregulars. When Orde Wingate was transferred out of Mandatory Palestine in 1939, FOSH was disbanded and its soldiers folded into other Haganah units such as HISH, HIM, and Palmach.

Chapter 3

1. Quoted in Andrew McGregor, "From Rommel to Qaddafi: Petrol Supplies Still Key to Military Success in Libya," *Terrorism Monitor*, Vol. IX, Issue 21 (May 27, 2011), p. 6.

2. Major Lawrence Rucker Snead (U.S. Army-Armor), "Wavell's Campaigns in the Middle East: An Analysis of Operational Art and the Implications for Today," Masters' Thesis, School of Advanced Military Studies (SAMS), U.S. Army Command and General Staff College, Fort Leavenworth, KS, 1994, p. 4.

3. Snead, "Wavell's Campaigns in the Middle East: An Analysis of Operational Art and the Implications for Today," 1994, p. 13.

4. Bruce I. Gudmundsson, "Tactical Exercises: Allenby's Turning Tactics," *Military History Quarterly*, Vol. 19. No. 4 (Summer 2007), p. 83.

5. Ibid.

6. James J. Schneider and Lawrence L. Izzo, "Clausewitz's Elusive Center of Gravity," *Parameters* (September 1987), p. 55.

7. John North, "Lessons of the North African Campaign," *Military Affairs*, Vol. 8, No. 3 (Autumn 1944), p. 164.

8. Carl von Clausewitz, *On War*, trans. Michael Howard and Peter Paret, eds. (Princeton, NJ: Princeton University Press, 1976), Book I, Chapter VII. Both Clausewitz and the Chinese philosopher of war, Sun Tzu, believed that the ultimate goal of strategy was to destroy an opponent's will to fight. However, Clausewitz argued that the destruction of his armed forces would, in most cases, be necessary to create the conditions where the goal of strategy would be obtained. Tzu, however, argued that the most effective strategy was to prevail, that is, to "de-spirit" the enemy without having to fight; see Sun Tzu, *The Art of War*, trans. Samuel B. Griffith (Oxford, U.K.: Oxford University Press, 1971).

9. "Frederick [the Great], liked to say that three men behind the enemy were worth fifty in front of him," said Colonel Ardant du Picq. Ardant du Picq (1821–1870) served in the French Army (1844–1870) and wrote *Combat Antique* (ancient battle), which was subsequently expanded into his *Etudes sur les Combat: Combat*

Antique et Moderne, published in English under the title of *Battle Studies*. See Colonel Ardant du Picq, *Battle Studies*, translated from the 8th edition in French by John Greely and Robert C. Cotton (New York: Macmillan, 1920). Also available online through the Project Gutenberg. Ardant du Picq was concerned with many aspects of battle; his focus, however, was on the moral and psychological dimensions of warfare.

10. Robert Satloff, "Lessons from a Forgotten War," *Foreign Policy*, November 2, 2012.

11. The Atlantic Wall was a massive undertaking by Nazi Germany between 1942 and 1944, which erected a coastal defense system on the sea coast of Europe to defend against an expected invasion by Great Britain and its allies, including the United States.

12. Dwight D. Eisenhower, "Report on Operation Torch," June 21, 1965. http://www.american-divisions.com/doc.asp?documentid=138, accessed May 14, 2013.

13. David Walker, "OSS and Operation Torch," *Journal of Contemporary History*, Vol. 22, No. 4 (1987), p. 667.

14. Shah letter to Roosevelt, August 25, 1941.

15. Kenneth Allred, "The Persian Corridor: Aid to the Soviets," *Military Review* (April 1985), p. 14.

16. Ibid., p. 20.

17. Ibid., p. 18.

18. T. H. Vail Motter, *The Persian Corridor and Aid to Russia* (Washington, DC: Center of Military History, U.S. Army, 2000), p. 6.

Chapter 4

1. David S. Painter, "Oil, Resources, and the Cold War, 1945–1962," Chapter 23, *Cambridge Histories Online* (Cambridge, U.K.: Cambridge University Press, 2010), p. 486.

2. See Magnus Persson, *Great Britain, the United States, and the Security of the Middle East: The Formation of the Baghdad Pact* (Lund, Sweden: Lund University Press, 1998). Persson's analysis includes an insightful discussion regarding the Egyptian hesitancy in aligning itself in a military pact led by Britain or the United States. That it ultimately opted out of CENTO (MEDO) reflects the influence of Soviet intrigue and the independence preferences of the Nasser government.

3. John W. Spanier and Steven W. Hook, *American Foreign Policy since WWII* (Washington, DC: CQ Press, 1995), p. 39.

4. Stephen E. Ambrose, *Rise to Globalism*, 5th ed. (New York: Penguin Books, 1988), p. 79.

5. Benny Morris, "Lashing Back: Israel's 1947–48 Civil War," *Military History Quarterly*, Vol. 21, No. 3 (Spring 2009), p. 32.

6. Quoted in David Harris, *The Crisis: The President, the Prophet, and the Shah— 1979 and the Coming of Militant Islam* (New York: Little, Brown, and Company, 2004), p. 19.

7. Daniel Yergin, *The Prize: The Epic Quest for Oil, Money & Power* (New York: Simon & Schuster, 1991), p. 411.

8. Ellen Jenny Ravndal, "Exit Britain: British Withdrawal from the Palestine Mandate in the Early Cold War, 1947–48," *Diplomacy and Statecraft*, Vol. 21, No. 3 (2010), p. 417.

9. Yoav Gelber, "The Israeli-Arab War of 1948," *Israel Studies: An Anthology*, Jewish Virtual Library Publications, July 2009. http://www.jewishvirtuallibrary.org/jsource/isdf/text/gelber.html, accessed March 1, 2014.

10. As Zionists agitated against British authorities and the mainstream Jewish establishment (Yishuv), militant organizations were created to force Jewish independence. Avraham Stern was symbolic of the individuals populating these movements. Stern served in the Haganah before becoming one of the leaders of the paramilitary group Irgun from which he split off by forming Lehi. Born in Poland in 1907, then part of Russia, as a child, Stern experienced the suffering of World War I and the difficulties of the average Jews in Europe during times of the great upheaval. He was determined to establish a national homeland for the Jewish people.

11. Morris, "Lashing Back, 1947–1948" (Spring 2009), p. 30.

12. Yoav Gelber, "The Israeli-Arab War of 1948."

13. Free Officer El-Sadat read the first statement of the revolution in the name of General Naguib to the Egyptian people on July 23, 1952. Egyptian State Information Service (SIS), Executive Department, Presidency of the Republic. http://www.sis.gov.eg/newVR/rev/english/1e.htm, accessed November 13, 2014.

14. Note by the executive secretary, National Security Council, "United States Policy Regarding the Present Situation in Iran," November 20, 1952, National Security Council NSC 136/1.

15. "Memorandum of Discussion at the 135th Meeting of the National Security Council," March 4, 1953, U.S. Department of State, *Foreign Relations of the United States, 1952–1954*, Volume X, *Iran 1951–1954* (Washington, DC: U.S. Government Printing Office, 1989), p. 699.

16. Richard H. Immerman, *John Foster Dulles: Piety, Pragmatism, and Power in US Foreign Policy* (Wilmington,DE: Scholarly Resources, 1998), p. 98.

17. Wilfred P. Deac, "Suez Crisis: Operation Musketeer," *Military History,*Vol, 18, No. 1 (April 2001), p. 58.

18. For more on Blue Bat see: Major General David W. Gray, U.S. Army (ret.), *The US Intervention in Lebanon, 1958: A Commander's Reminiscence* (Fort Leavenworth, KS: U.S. Army Command and General Staff College, August 1984); and, Lieutenant Colonel Gary H. Wade, U.S. Army, *Rapid Deployment Logistics: Lebanon 1958: Operation Blue Bat* (Fort Leavenworth, KS: U.S. Army Command and General Staff College, October 1984).

19. Stewart to Hadow (Tel Aviv), March 29, 1966, E1051/13 PRO PREM 13/1617, British Policy towards the Arab/Israel Dispute, The National Archives of the UK (TNA), quoted in Robert McNamara, "Britain, Nasser, and the Outbreak of the Six Day War," *Journal of Contemporary History*, Vol. 35, No. 4 (October 2000), pp. 620–621.

20. Ibid., p. 621.

21. Ofra Benjio, *The Turkish-Israeli Relationship: Changing the Ties of Middle Eastern Outsiders* (New York: Palgrave, 2004), pp. 52–53. Benjio argues that Turkish-Israeli ties were extensive although secret, including joint plans for war in Syria in the 1960s.

22. Brian McCauley, "Hungary and Suez 1956: The Limits of Soviet and American Power," *Journal of Contemporary History*, Vol. 16, No. 4 (October 1981), p. 777.

23. Associated Press, "Saudi Arabia Tells of Russian Offer of Arms," *Chicago Tribune*, October 9, 1955.

24. Oles M. Smolansky, "Moscow-Cairo Crisis, 1959," *Slavic Review*, Vol. 22, No. 4 (December 1963), p. 713.

25. Oles M. Smolansky, "Moscow and the Suez Canal, 1956: A Reappraisal," *Political Science Quarterly*, Vol. 80, No. 4 (December 1965), p. 581.

26. "During the 1956 Sinai-Suez Crisis a Soviet nuclear threat directed at Israel, Britain, and France halted their offensive against Egypt. This experience was a major factor in impelling Israel, as well as France, to seek a nuclear deterrent." Avner Cohen, *Israel and the Bomb* (New York: Columbia University Press, 1999), pp. 54–55.

27. Moshe Gat, "Nasser and the Six Day War, 5 June 1967: A Premeditated Strategy or an Inexorable Drift to War?" *Israeli Affairs*, Vol. 11, No. 4 (October 2005), p. 610.

28. M. M. El Hussini, *Soviet-Egyptian Relations, 1945–1985* (New York: Palgrave Macmillan, 1997), p. 179.

Chapter 5

1. Andre Beufre, "Une Guerre Classique Moderne: La Guerre Israelo-Arabe," *Strategie* (July–August 1967), p. 19, quoted in George W. Gawrych, "The Egyptian Military Defeat of 1967," *Journal of Contemporary History*, Vol. 26, No. 2 (April 1991), p. 277.

2. Warden quoted in Lieutenant Colonel Rita A. Springer, U.S. Air Force, "Operation Moked and the Principles of War," Department of Joint Military Operations, Naval War College, May 19, 1997, Abstract.

3. Curtis F. Jones, *Divide and Perish: The Geopolitics of the Middle East* (Bloomington, IN: AuthorHouse, 2010), p. 79.

4. O. Bull, *War and Peace in the Middle East: The Experiences and Views of a UN Observer* (London: Leo Cooper, 1976).

5. Jones, *Divide and Perish*, p. 80.

6. Eyal Zisser, "June 1967: Israel's Capture of the Golan Heights," *Israeli Studies*, Vol. 7, No. 1 (Spring 2002), pp. 168–169.

7. Ibid.

8. Zeev Elron and Moshe Gat, "Remarks on the Six Day War [And Response]," *The Journal of Military History*, Vol. 69, No. 3 (July 2005), p. 817.

9. Galia Golan, "The Soviet Union and the Outbreak of the June 1967 Six Day War," *Journal of Cold War Studies*, Vol. 8, No. 1 (Winter 2006), p. 3.

10. Gawrych, "The Egyptian Military Defeat of 1967" (April 1991), p. 278.

11. See Clive Jones, " 'Where the State Feared to Tread': Britain, Britons, Covert Action, and the Yemen Civil War, 1962–1964,"*Intelligence and National Security*, Vol. 21, No. 5 (October 2006), pp. 717–737.

12. Isabella Ginor and Gideon Remez, "The Spymaster, the Communist, and the Foxbats over Dimona: The USSR's Motive for Instigating the Six Day War," *Israeli Studies*, Vol. 11, No. 2 (Summer 2006), p. 88. See also: Anwar El-Sadat, *In Search of Identity: An Autobiography* (New York: Harper and Row, 1978), pp. 171–172. On May 13, 1967, Soviet Deputy Foreign Minister Vladimir Semyonov shared the information with Sadat in Moscow that Israel was planning to strike Syria and gave an expected attack window of May 18–22.

13. Elron and Gat, "Remarks on the Six Day War [And Response]" (July 2005), p. 817.

14. Major L. R. Mader, Canadian Army, "The 1967 Sinai Campaign: Some Lessons about the Manoeuvrist Approach," *The Army Doctrine and Training Bulletin* (Canada), Vol. 5, No. 3 (Fall 2002), p. 37.

15. C. Ernest Dawn, "The Egyptian Remilitarization of Sinai, May 1967," *Journal of Contemporary History*, Vol. 3, No. 3 (July 1968), pp. 201–224.

16. Lieutenant Commander Paul S. Grossgold, U.S. Navy, "The 1967 Arab-Israeli War: An Operational Study of the Sinai Campaign," Naval War College, June 1994.

17. Michael I. Handel, *Israel's Political-Military Doctrine*, Occasional Papers in International Affairs Number 30 (Cambridge, MA: Harvard University Center for International Affairs, July 1973), pp. 1–4.

18. Air supremacy is usually defined as permanent domination of an area where all contenders have been eliminated or so degraded that they cannot interfere or disrupt what you are trying to accomplish. Air superiority is a temporary domination of a specific air space or region where an opponent cannot oppose your actions; although he may still be capable of hurting your forces, when you have achieved air superiority, he cannot stop you.

19. George W. Gawrych, *Key to the Sinai: The Battles of Abu Ageila in the 1956 and 1967 Arab-Israeli Wars* (Fort Leavenworth, KS: U.S. Army Command and General Staff College, Combat Studies Institute Research Survey 7, 1990), p. 67.

20. Springer, "Operation Moked and the Principles of War," 1997, Abstract.

21. Ibid., p. 4.

22. Eliezer Cohen, *Israel's Best Defense* (New York: Crown), p. 195. The ordnance was based on the French company, MATRA's, BLU-107 Durandel.

23. John Warden, *The Air Campaign* (New York: Pergamon, 1989), p. 138. Since only 12 aircraft remained for the air defense of Israel, Major General Hod, IAF chief of the general staff, kept this information from Prime Minister Eshkol when he was asked to sign off on Operation Moked. In the planning discussions, Hod assured Eshkol that "not a single bomb would fall on Tel Aviv," Cohen, p. 186.

24. Leo Heiman, "Armored Forces in the Middle East," *Military Review*, Vol. 48, No. 11 (November 1968), p. 15.

25. Gawrych, *Key to the Sinai: The Battles for Abu Ageila in the 1956 and 1967 Arab-Israeli Wars* (Combat Studies Institute Research Survey 7, 1990), p. 123.

26. Heiman, "Armored Forces in the Middle East" (November 1968), p. 11.

27. "Message from Premier Kosygin to President Johnson," June 10, 1967, FRUS, 1964–1968, XIX, doc. 243.

28. Liberty would eventually be hit by torpedoes, rockets, white phosphorus, cannons, armor-piercing bullets, and napalm. Apparently someone wanted that

ship to sink and to sink with no survivors. However, while the attackers and those who sent them managed to kill 34 U.S. sailors, 117, although wounded, lived. Those survivors later recounted that they were attacked by aircraft with no markings. They further stated that clearly marked IAF aircraft overflew their naval vessel on several instances prior to the attack. These aircraft were close enough to the sailors to return the smiles that the Americans had sent to whom they believed their allies. When the attack began, the ship, the USS *Liberty*, dispatched a clear message to the fleet: "*Liberty* is under attack from unknown enemy air and surface units. Request assistance." Rescue aircraft dispatched by the Sixth Fleet were recalled by higher authority on two separate occasions.

29. L. Wainstein, "Some Aspects of the US Involvement in the Middle East Crisis-May-June 1976," Critical Incident No. 14, Institute for Defense Analysis Report R-132, prepared under contract with the Weapons Systems Evaluation Group, February 1968.

30. Albert Hourani, *A History of the Arab Peoples* (Cambridge, MA: Harvard-Belkap University Press, 1991), p. 411.

31. Yousef H. Aboul-Enein and Basil Aboul-Enein, *The Secret War for the Middle East: The Influence of Axis and Allied Intelligence Operations During WWII* (Annapolis, MD: Naval Institute Press, 2013), p. 52.

32. Chaim Herzog, *The War of Atonement, October 1973* (Boston, MA: Little, Brown and Company, 1975), pp. 8–9.

33. Yousef H. Aboul-Enein and Basil Aboul-Enein (2013), pp. 52–53.

34. Abraham Rabinovich, *The Yom Kippur War: The Epic Encounter that Transformed the Middle East* (New York: Schocken Books, 2004), p. 7.

35. W. Andrew Terrill, *Escalation and Intrawar Deterrence during Limited Wars in the Middle East* (Carlisle Barracks, PA: Strategic Studies Institute—U.S. Army War College, September 2009), p. 10: "The IAF was one of the finest air forces in the world, and was equipped with some of the best available US and French aircraft. Additionally, Israeli pilots routinely outperformed Arab pilots and had, on one occasion, even shot down Soviet pilots flying Egypt's Soviet made aircraft during the War of Attrition."

36. Ibid.

37. Uri Bar-Joseph, "The 1973 Yom Kippur War," *Israel Studies: An Anthology*, Jewish Virtual Library Publications, May 2009.

38. Michael B. Oren, *Six Days War: June 1967 and the Making of the Modern Middle East* (New York: Oxford University Press, 2002), p. 21.

39. "Middle East War: October 1973," *Military Review* Vol. 54, No. 2 (February 1974), pp. 48–49.

40. Joseph, "The 1973 Yom Kippur War," May 2009, p. 4. http://www.israel-studies.com/anth_pdf/Joseph.pdf, accessed June 2, 2012.

41. Ze;ev Schiff, *October Earthquake: Yom Kippur 1973* (Tel Aviv, Israel: University Publishing Projects, 1974), p. 113.

42. Joseph, "The 1973 Yom Kippur War," May 2009. http://www.jewishvirtual library.org/jsource/isdf/text/barjoseph.html, accessed June 15, 2012.

43. The term "kinetic," as it is utilized in military affairs, derives from kinetic energy as a phenomenon studied in the field of physics. Kinetic energy is produced by the motion of an object that provides striking power derived from

projectiles. In modern usage within the field of strategic studies, the phrase, "kinetic strike," is often used to describe interceptor missiles that physically hit their targets while defending against incoming ballistic missiles. In a non-kinetic event, interceptors are detonated near their targets destroying them or altering their course sufficiently resulting in the neutralization of the threat.

44. Terrill, *Escalation and Intrawar Deterrence during Limited Wars in the Middle East*, p. xi.

45. By the late 1950s, with the United States no longer in possession of a monopoly on atomic weapons, discussions centered upon how to keep an armed conflict between the Soviet Union and the United States from going "nuclear," and, if unsuccessful, "damage limitation." "Just preserving some choice for this contingency—just being able if we wish, to fight anything but a war of extermination—to keep open the possibility that we can demand his surrender or disarmament, limit the general war and bring it to a close, requires that we have the military ability to do more than go after the enemy in a single spasm, and the organizational ability to communicate something more than a quick "go" signal to our strategic forces at the instant war seems to be on. It requires that we be able to preserve some of our forces and control over them for hours, days, or longer." Trevor Gardner, "Organizing for Peace," *Bulletin of the Atomic Scientists*, Vol. 16, No. 7 (September 1960), p. 300.

46. Terrill, *Escalation and Intrawar Deterrence during Limited Wars in the Middle East*, p. 1.

47. Quoted in Bard E. O'Neill, "The October War: A Political-Military Assessment," *Air University Review*, Vol. 25 (July–August 1974), p. 28; see also Anwar Sadat, *In Search of Identity: An Autobiography* (New York: Harper Collins, 1978).

48. Terrill, *Escalation and Intrawar Deterrence during Limited Wars in the Middle East*, p. xii.

49. Aboul-Enein (2013), p. 56.

50. James A. Russell, "Extended Deterrence, Security Guarantees, and Nuclear Weapons: U.S. Strategic and Policy Conundrums in the Gulf," *Strategic Insights*, Vol. 8, No. 5 (December 2009), p. 2.

51. William B. Quandt, "Soviet Policy in October Middle East War II," *International Affairs*, Vol. 53, No. 4 (October 1977), p. 596. Quandt was on the staff of the U.S. National Security Council in 1973.

52. Cecil Brownlow, "Soviets Poise Three Front Global Drive," *Aviation Week and Space Technology*, November 5, 1973, p. 12.

53. Both Cold War antagonists imposed a cease-fire taking effect on October 28, 1973.

Chapter 6

1. Roham Alvandi, "Nixon, Kissinger, and the Shah: The Origins of Iranian Primacy in the Gulf," *Diplomatic History*, Vol. 36, No. 2 (April 2012), p. 348.

2. Charles G. Cogan, "Desert One and Its Disorders," *The Journal of Military History*, Vol. 67, No. 1 (January 2003), p. 204.

3. Cogan, "Desert One and Its Disorders" (2003), p. 211. The Holloway Report provided a catalyst for efforts aimed at reorganizing the Department of Defense, which was codified in the 1986 Goldwater-Nichols legislation that improved the Defense Department's ability to conduct joint and combined arms warfare, while the Cohen-Nunn Act consolidated Special Forces under U.S. Special Operations Command. See also Charles G. Cogan, "Not to Offend: Observations on Iran, the Hostages, and the Hostage Rescue—Ten Years Later," *Comparative Strategy*, Vol. 9, No. 1 (1990). Cogan spent 37 years with the CIA; see also Steve Smith, "Groupthink and the Hostage Rescue Mission,"*British Journal of Political Science*, Vol. 15, No. 1 (1984); to read the perspective and views of a key member of Carter's National Security Council, see Gary Sick, "Military Constraints and Options," in *American Hostages in Iran: The Conduct of a Crisis*, Paul H. Kreisberg, ed. (New Haven, CT: Yale University Press, 1985), pp. 154–155. For the views of the scene commander at Iranian desert rendezvous "Desert One," see James Lyle and John Robert Eidson, *The Guts to Try* (New York: Orion Books, 1990), as well as for the views of the Delta Force commander during Eagle Claw, see Charles A. Beckwith and Donald Knox, *Delta Force* (New York: Harcourt Brace and Jovanovich, 1983).

4. James A. Winnefeld, James A. Preston Niblack, and Dana J. Johnson, *A League of Airmen: U.S. Air Power in the Gulf War*, Project Air Force Report (Santa Monica, CA: RAND Corporation, 1994), p. 56.

5. An August 1977 presidential directive (Presidential Directive 18) announced the intent on forming a deployable force that was capable of rapid movement into the Middle East or onto the Korean Peninsula should a crisis warrant additional force projection. The discussions arose primarily in the wake of the 1973 October War when the United States was poised to send forces to defend Israel. Following the Iran hostage crisis in 1979, the intent (but no funding for a new force) became increasingly urgent for a RDF and planning for its creation was accelerated. When the Soviets invaded Afghanistan (Tehran's eastern neighbor and sharing a border with Iran), on December 26, 1979, and by early 1980 subsequently positioned next door to a turbulent, revolutionary Iran; the RDF became solely focused on the Middle East and the Persian Gulf. With the announcement of the Carter Doctrine on January 23, 1980, and the intent of the United States to repel any move against the Gulf by the USSR, on March 1, 1980, the Rapid Deployment Joint Task Force (RDJTF) was officially established with headquarters at MacDill Air Force Base in Tampa, Florida. The following year, on April 24, 1981, Reagan administration's secretary of defense, Caspar Weinberger, announced that the RDJTF would become an independent command with specific geographical parameters encompassing Central Asia and the Middle East. Under Reagan, the RDJTF officially became an independent command, the U.S. Central Command (USCENTCOM), on January 1, 1983. For further background, see: USCENTCOM, http://www.centcom.mil/ABOUT-US/HISTORY/, accessed November 3, 2016.

6. Matthew J. Ouimet, *The Rise and Fall of the Brezhnev Doctrine in Soviet Foreign Policy* (Chapel Hill, NC: The University of North Carolina Press, 2003), p. 95.

7. David Gibb, "Review Essay: Afghanistan: The Soviet Invasion in Retrospective," *International Politics*, Vol. 37, No. 2 (June 2000), p. 233.

8. National Security Council, The White House, NSDD-75, January 17, 1983, p. 1.

9. Ibid., p. 2.

10. In 1978, Iranian agents under the Shah, informed Saddam of a pro-Soviet coup d'état among a group of Iraqi army officers. Saddam executed the officers, and, to return the favor to Iran, the Iraqi leader had Khomeini removed from Iraq.

11. Colonel Maedh Ayed al-Lihaibi, Royal Saudi Air Force, "An Analysis of the Iran-Iraq War: Military Strategy and Political Objectives," Master's Thesis, U.S. Air War College, Maxwell Air Force Base, Alabama, May 1989.

12. Nebuchadnezzar II (634 BC–562 BC) was a ruler of ancient Babylon, reportedly endowed with "perfect wisdom" (*nam-ku-zu*) by the God, Marduk. Nebuchadezzar was responsible for the "Babylonian Exile of the Jews" as well as defeating the Egyptians and Assyrians, which provided control of Palestine and the trade routes across Mesopotamia (generally, present-day Iraq), from the Persian Gulf to the Mediterranean Sea.

13. William O. Staudenmaier, *A Strategic Analysis of the Gulf War* (Carlisle Barracks, PA: U.S. Army War College, 1982), p. 2. Note: prior to the Gulf War of 1991, the Iran-Iraq War (1980–1988) was referred in the literature as the "Gulf War."

14. One of the lessons learned and apparently adopted by the Iraqi army was reflected in its purchase of 2,000 heavy equipment transporters for mechanized and armor units. See David B. Lacquement, *Saddam Hussein's First War: An Assessment of Iraqi Operational Art in the Iran-Iraq War* (Fort Leavenworth, KS: School of Advanced Military Studies (SAMS), U.S. Army Command and General Staff College (CGSC), May 1991), p. 28, who cites S2, 177th Armored Brigade, and the Operations Group of the National Training Brigade of the National Training Center, *National Training Center Handbook: The Iraqi Army Organization and Tactics* (Fort Irwin, CA: National Training Center, January 3, 1991), pp. 124 and 136. In 1978, the Soviet Union agreed to completely reequip Saddam's armored forces with modern weaponry and support units. As a result of turning to the Soviets (and in the 1990s turning to the Russians), Saddam, who had worked with the United States in the 1960s, fell out of favor with the West.

15. Chris Bellamy, *The Future of Land Warfare* (New York: St. Martin's Press, 1987), p. 22.

16. al-Lihaibi, "An Analysis of the Iran-Iraq War: Military Strategy and Political Objectives," 1989, p. 17.

17. Rupert Smith, *The Utility of Force: The Art of War in the Modern World* (New York: Vintage Books, 2008), p. 3: "Consider this: the last real tank battle known to the world, one in which the armoured formations of two armies manoeuvered against each other supported by artillery and air forces, one in which the tanks in formation were the deciding force, took place in the 1973 Arab-Israeli War [1973 October War] on the Golan Heights and in the Sinai Desert."

18. Edgar O'Ballance, "The Iraqi-Iranian War: the First Round," *Parameters*, Vol. XI, No. 1 (March 1981), p. 57.

19. Iranian Revolutionary Guard commander, Morteza Rezai.

20. Robin Wright, *Dreams and Shadows: The Future of the Middle East* (New York: Penguin, 2008), p. 243.

21. Linda Malone, "The Kahan Report, Ariel Sharon and the Sabra-Shatilla Massacres in Lebanon: Responsibility under International Law for Massacres of Civilian Populations," *Utah Law Review*, Vol. 2 (1985), pp. 373–433.

22. These two separate weapons systems, HAWK and TOW, were sought by the Iranians as a result of lessons learned from the 1967 Six-Day War and the 1973 October War where Soviet-supplied SAMs similar to the U.S. HAWK's capability and Soviet-supplied ATGMs similar to the U.S. TOW achieved battlefield success against the IAF and armor formations of the IDF. This replication of success was unsuccessfully attempted by Saddam during opening stages of the Iran-Iraq War. Advanced weaponry has to be integrated within pragmatic and unifying doctrine and fielded by an integrated, synchronized, joint, and combined arms team. This capability is not limited to modern warfare, as superior military forces throughout history have prevailed over larger enemies by being relatively more proficient with a combined arms approach and fighting with highly disciplined, highly trained, integrated, and synchronized strike forces.

23. Michael Sterner, "The Iran-Iraq War," *Foreign Affairs*, Vol. 63, No.1 (Fall 1984), p. 129.

24. In Iran, the Marxist People's Mujahedin and the Kurdish minority, both supported by Iraq, took up arms against the Ayatollah's regime. Saddam in 1988 would launch the Anfal campaign, which targeted the Kurds in northern Iraq. By the end of the Iran-Iraq War, Saddam's forces, over a period of eight years, had killed tens of thousands of Kurdish men, women, and children.

25. R. K. Ramazani, "The Iran-Iraq War and the Persian Gulf Crisis," *Current History*, Vol. 87, No. 528 (February 1988), p. 63.

26. Report was a Defense Intelligence Agency analysis at the code-word level ("code word" security classification, i.e., above "Top Secret" classification) partially entitled: "At the Gates of Basra."

27. Alan Friedman, *Spider's Web: The Secret History of How the White House Illegally Armed Iraq* (New York: Bantam Books, 1993).

28. Kenneth R. Timmerman, *The Death Lobby: How the West Armed Iraq* (New York: Houghton Mifflin Company, 1991).

29. Classified report issued by the Office of the Director of Central Intelligence, "Is Iraq Losing the War?" Special National Intelligence Estimate SNIE 34/36.2-86, April 1986, p. 3.

30. See Zbigniew Brzezinski, *Power and Principle: Memoirs of the National Security Advisor, 1977–81* (New York: Farrar, Straus & Girou, 1983).

31. Dennis Showalter, "Introduction: Post-Total Warfare, 1945–2005," *Cambridge Histories Online* (Cambridge, U.K.: Cambridge University Press, 2013), p. 415.

Chapter 7

1. USCENTCOM, "Executive Summary: Operation Desert Shield/Desert Storm," July 11, 1991, p. 1. The contingency plan whose assumptions were being testing by "Internal Look 90" was OPLAN 1002-90 where CENTCOM simulated sending forces to the Middle East to deter an attack by "Country Red," to defend critical port and oil facilities, and to defeat enemy forces. The XVIII Airborne Corps had tactical command of U.S. forces.

2. Ibid., p. 2.

3. Later in 2003, following the close of major combat operations during Operation Iraqi Freedom, the United States, not fully understanding the implications, disbanded the Iraqi army, and hundreds of thousands of Iraqi troops were sent home in a war-torn economy; in essence, the fuse of national destabilization was lit.

4. Major Robert A. Nelson, "The Battle of the Bridges: Kuwait's 35th Brigade on the 2d of August 1990," *Armor*, Vol. 104, No. 5 (September–October 1995), p. 26.

5. Frank N. Schubert and Theresa L. Kraus (eds.), *The Whirlwind War: The United States Army in Operations Desert Shield and Desert Storm*, CMH-Pub 70-30-1, Center of Military History, U.S. Army, Washington, DC, 1995, "Creating the Shield," Chapter 3, p. 50.

6. Ibid., p. 62.

7. Ibid., p. 59.

8. See Robert H. Clemm, "Coalition Nations' Contributions to Desert Storm," in *The Encyclopedia of Middle East Wars: The United States in the Persian Gulf, Afghanistan, and Iraq Conflicts*, 5 Volumes, Spencer C. Tucker and Priscilla Mary Roberts, eds. (Santa Barbara, CA: ABC-CLIO, 2010), pp. 366–367.

9. Instant Thunder was based on the concepts from Colonel Warden's 1988 book; see John Warden, *The Air Campaign: Planning for Combat* (Washington, DC: National Defense University Press, 1988); also available from Pergamon Publishers, 1989.

10. David S. Fadok, "John Boyd and John Warden: Air Power's Quest for Strategic Paralysis," Masters' Thesis, School of Advanced Airpower Studies, Air University, Maxwell Air Force Base, Alabama, June 1994, p. 15.

11. PGMs served as a force multiplier with incredible accuracy and lethality reducing the numbers of air sorties required to effectively destroy targets as well reducing collateral damage to civilians. However, precision weapons accounted for only 9 percent of the munitions expended in Desert Storm. Comparatively, 10 years later in Afghanistan against al-Qaeda and the Taliban (Operation Enduring Freedom), PGMs accounted for nearly 70 percent of the expended ordnance.

12. Fadok, "John Boyd and John Warden: Air Power's Quest for Strategic Paralysis," June 1994, Abstract.

13. John R. Boyd, "Patterns of Conflict," unpublished briefing, 1986, p. 132. http://dnipogo.org/john-r-boyd/, accessed July 15, 2013.

14. See Kenneth Pollack, *Arabs at War: Military Effectiveness, 1948–1991* (Lincoln, NE: University of Nebraska Press, 2002).

15. Thomas R. Dubois, "The Weinberger Doctrine and the Liberation of Kuwait," *Parameters* (Journal of the U.S. Army War College), Vol. 21, No. 4 (Winter 1991–1992), p. 24.

16. See Caspar W. Weinberger, "The Uses of Military Power," *Defense*, Vol. 85, Armed Forces Information Service, Arlington, VA, December 1985, pp. 2–11.

17. James A. Winnefeld, James A. Preston Niblack, and Dana J. Johnson, *A League of Airmen: U.S. Air Power in the Gulf War*, Project Air Force Report (Santa Monica, CA: RAND Corporation, 1994), p. 118.

18. To accomplish this, *Louisville* conducted a 14,000-mile submerged, high-speed transit across the Pacific and Indian Oceans to the Red Sea, firing shortly

before noon on January 19, 1991. *Louisville* would return to combat operations in the Middle East in 2003 during Operation Iraqi Freedom where she made history as the only Pacific Fleet SSN to have twice launched cruise missiles in combat when the submarine fired numerous salvos into Iraq. See also https://www .navalhistory.org/2014/10/07/tomahawk-missiles-brought-power-to-the-punch -during-operation-enduring-freedom, accessed November 15, 2016.

19. James Titus, "The Battle of Khafji: An Overview and Preliminary Analysis," Air Power Research Institute, College of Aerospace Doctrine, Research, and Education, USAF Air University, September 1996, p. 3.

20. Center of Military History, *War in the Persian Gulf: Operations Desert Shield and Desert Storm, August 1990–March 1991*, CMH Pub 70-117-1, Center of Military History, U.S. Army Washington, DC, 2010, p. 27.

21. Lawrence Freedman and Efraim Karsh, "How Kuwait Was Won: Strategy in the Gulf War," *International Security,* Vol. 16, No. 2 (Autumn 1991), p. 18. Nationwide poll of 1,057 randomly selected adults conducted for the *Washington Post* and ABC on January 4–6 was reported in Richard Morris, "Gulf Poll: Most Americans Want Hill to Back Bush," *Washington Post,* January 8, 1991, p. A12.

22. Freedman and Karsh, "How Kuwait Was Won: Strategy in the Gulf War" (Autumn 1991), p. 6. Two centuries of combat between Persia and Greece had provided a treasure trove of intelligence to the Greeks and Macedonians regarding Persian strategy, tactics, and doctrine. When Alexander began the Persian campaigns beginning in 334 BCE, he was in command of what was arguably the finest army the world had ever known. Moreover, the Macedonian army had been specifically constructed by Philip (Alexander's father) with two specific objectives: take control of the Eastern Mediterranean world and destroy the Persian army's ability to conduct operations against Macedonia and its allies. Part of the military genius of Alexander the Great was the ability of obtaining information and intelligence on what an enemy's plans were for an upcoming battle, then quickly devising a plan that frustrated those objectives and aims, while controlling the battle and the initiative. By fielding a combined-arms approach army where infantry, cavalry, specialty units, and field technology were synchronized, integrated, and able to move more swiftly than its enemies, Alexander's forces were able to exploit the advantages inherent in understanding the opponent's movements—before the opponent made those movements. His army simply outmaneuvered and outfought its opponents. See specifically the Battle of Granicus in May 334 BCE and the Battle of Gaugamela (near present-day Irbil in northern Iraq). Both battles were against a Darius III-led Persian Empire, with victory at Gaugamela (also called the Battle of Arbela) leading to the end of the Persian Empire.

23. "Nine times out of ten an army has been destroyed because its supply lines have been severed"—General Douglas MacArthur, U.S. Army, August 1950, to the U.S. Joint Chiefs of Staff.

24. Lieutenant Colonel Jeffrey A. Kwallek (USAF), "OPDEC: The Operational Commander's Key to Surprise and Victory," Department of Joint Military Operations, Naval War College, Newport, RI, June 17, 1994, p. 24. OPDEC took as much as 20 percent of Iraqi forces out of the fight.

25. Center of Military History, U.S. Army, "Readying for the Storm," Chapter 7, p. 158. The British contribution to the coalition was significant, including

45,000 troops, 9 naval vessels, and 5 fighter squadrons. U.K. refueling tanker aircraft and bases also provided assistance to USAF operations, as the United States transited from America, Europe, and Asia into the KTO. Bulgaria opened its airspace, and Italy and Luxembourg made civilian aircraft transport available to CENTCOM. Pakistan sent the 7th Armored Brigade and an infantry battalion, and Afghanistan dispatched 300 mujahedeen fighters to the KTO, while Niger and Senegal troops served under Saudi command as well. The ability for Muslim nations to place their troops under Saudi leadership rather than Western command served the coalition well. Turkey's troops on the Turkish-Iraqi border forced Baghdad to located sizable forces in the North and away from the KTO. Denmark, Spain, Greece, Norway, Portugal, and Argentina all sent naval vessels, while South Korea contributed $355 million and sent a team of medical specialists. See also: *Conduct of the Persian Gulf War: Final Report to Congress.* United States, (Washington, DC: Department of Defense, April 1992), pp. 499–502.

26. "While in Saudi Arabia, VII Corps evolved into the largest most powerful tactical command ever fielded by the US Army: 3000 tanks, 700 artillery pieces, 142,000 soldiers organized into five heavy divisions, an armored cavalry regiment, aviation brigade and supporting organizations needed to execute the army's Air-Land Battle doctrine." Stephen A. Bourque, "Frederick Melvin Franks, Jr.," in *The Encyclopedia of Middle East Wars: The United States in the Persian Gulf,* Spencer C. Tucker, ed. (Santa Barbara, CA: ABC-CLIO, 2010). See also: Tom Clancy and Frederick Franks, *Into the Storm: A Study in Command* (New York: Putnam, 1997).

27. Center of Military History, *American Military History: 1991 Gulf War,* p. 32.

28. Iraq's command and control was considered the key center of gravity from both an operational and tactical-level perspective. Iraq's missiles and WMD along with the Republican Guard were also considered by Schwarzkopf and his staff to be centers of gravity.

29. Major Collin A. Agee, U.S. Army Intelligence, *Peeling the Onion: The Iraqi Center of Gravity in Desert Storm* (Fort Leavenworth, KS: School for Advanced Military Studies (SAMS), U.S. Army Command and General Staff College, July 4, 1992).

30. Peter S. Kindsvatter, "VII Corps in the Gulf War Ground Offensive," *Military Review,* Vol. 72, No. 2 (February 1992), p. 17.

31. Center of Military History, *American Military History: 1991 Gulf War,* p. 455.

32. Michael Green (ed.), *War Stories of the Tankers: American Armed Combat, 1918 to Today* (Minneapolis, MN: Zenith Press, 2008), p. 230.

33. Ibid.

34. See H. Norman Schwarzkopf and Peter Petre, *It Doesn't Take a Hero* (New York: Linda Grey Bantam Books, 1992) and Clancy and Franks, *Into the Storm: A Study in Command.*

35. Iraqi battalion commander, Republican Guard, Tawakalana Division, quoted in Stephen A. Bourque, *Jayhawk! The VII Corps in the Persian Gulf War,* Center of Military History, Special Publications CMH Pub 70-73-1, U.S. Army, Fort McNair (Washington, DC, 2002), p. 364.

36. Theodor W. Galdi, "Revolution in Military Affairs? Competing Concepts, Organizational Responses, Outstanding Issues," CRS Report to Congress 95-1170F, December 11, 1995. http://www.iwar.org.uk/rma/resources/rma/crs95-1170F.htm, accessed November 17, 2016.

37. Iraq possessed eight Republican Guard divisions. Two were kept up north, partly from the fear that the massed Turkish troops on the border may move south and partly to protect the leaders of the regime in Baghdad. Of the six that were in the KTO, Adan, Al Faw, Hammurabi, Medina, Nebuchadnezzer, and Tawakalna Divisions, only the Tawakalna and Medina Divisions received the ground campaign punishment Schwarzkopf had envisioned. The others escaped northward in what U.S. commanders described as "rather than the 'mother of all battles' as proclaimed would be the case by Saddam in the run up to the ground war, it became for the Iraqi Republican Guard divisions, the 'mother of all retreats.' "

38. Center of Military History, U.S. Army, "The Ground Campaign," Chapter 8.

39. Geoffrey Wawro, "The Sins of the First Gulf War," *The Daily Beast*, January 22, 2011.

40. Michael R. Gordon and General Bernard E. Trainor, *The General's War: The Inside Story of the Conflict in the Gulf* (Boston, MA: Little, Brown and Company, 1995), p. 302.

41. Final Report to Congress, "Conduct of the Persian Gulf War: Pursuant to Title V of the Persian Gulf Conflict Supplemental Authorization and Personnel Benefits Act of 1991 (Public Law 102-25)," April 1992, p. 21.

42. Schwarzkopf and Petre, *It Doesn't Take a Hero*, p. 381.

43. The main intent in establishing a no-fly zone in the North in 1991 was protecting the Kurdish population of northern Iraq from bombing, strafing, and chemical attack from the air by forces loyal to Saddam. The initial operations were designated Operation Provide Comfort and Operation Provide Comfort II, which were subsequently followed by Operation Northern Watch. Operation Southern Watch was established in 1992 to extend protection to the Iraqi Shia population in southern Iraq. Since the UN Security Council did not specifically authorize these measures, there were significant disagreements over the legality of the no-fly zones instituted in the skies above northern and southern Iraq. While the United States and its allies, principally Britain, France, and Turkey, had cited UN Security Council Resolution 688 as the basis in authorizing the no-fly zones, 688 does not contain an explicit authorization. The secretary-general of the United Nations at the time that Resolution 688 was passed, Boutros Boutros-Ghali, called the no-fly zones "illegal" in a February 2003 interview with John Pilger.

44. Alfred B. Prados, "Iraq: Post War Challenges and US Responses, 1991–1998," in *Iraq: Issues, Historical Background, Bibliography*, Leon M. Jeffries, ed. (New York: Nova Science Publishers, 2003), p. 83.

45. John Prados, *Keepers of the Keys: A History of the National Security Council from Truman to Bush* (New York: William Morris & Company, 1991), p. 550.

Chapter 8

1. David Bukay, "The Religious Foundations of Suicide Bombings: Islamist Ideology," *Middle East Quarterly*, Vol. 8, No. 4 (Fall 2006), pp. 27–36.

2. The White House, NSC, "National Strategy for Combating Terrorism 2006," Conclusion.

3. Arab coalition members with military or security forces (contributions): Saudi Arabia (60,000–100,000); Egypt (20,000); Syria (14,500); Morocco—Arab-Berbers (13,000); Oman (6,300); United Arab Emirates (4,300); Qatar (2,600); and Bahrain (400).

4. "An outcome of US intervention has been immense Arab pressure on the United States to settle the Palestinian question, something that worries Israel." Sheldon L. Richman, " 'Ancient History': US Conduct in the Middle East since World War II and the Folly of Intervention," Cato Institute, *Policy Analysis*, No. 159 (August 16, 1991). In an attempt to provide the rationale for the United States in refraining from being intervening when pressed, Richman quotes John Quincy Adams who wrote, "America goes not abroad in search of monsters to destroy. She is a well-wisher to the freedom and independence of all. She is the champion and vindicator only of her own . . ." Apparently, the use of American power to establish the State of Israel was an exception to Richman's reading of Adams.

5. In addition to the disenchantment of the jihadist crowd, the stark comparison of the Soviet's military performance in Afghanistan juxtaposed alongside the Western performance during the 1991 Persian Gulf War added to the disillusionment of key constituencies within the USSR and, combined with a multitude of internal problems, aided in the collapse of the empire by Christmas of 1991.

6. Sheikh Yusuf al-Qaradawi, February 2006, Chief Jurist, Muslim Brotherhood.

7. Bernard Haykel, Professor of Islamic Law, New York University, in "Two Views: Can the Koran Condone Terror?" *New York Times*, October 13, 2001.

8. The plans for the invasion of Afghanistan following the terrorist attacks in America on September 11, 2001, were developed by the CIA. This marked the first time in the U.S. history that such a large-scale military operation was planned by the CIA. Most personnel in CIA's Special Activities Division were and are seasoned veterans of the Special Operations Forces (SOF) community within the U.S. military. CIA recruits the very best from the SOF community and fields perhaps the finest special operators in the world; although British Special Air Service (SAS) personnel as well as other top-tier teams around the world would disagree with that assessment.

9. In order to obtain the use of the Uzbekistan base (K2) for the purpose of staging attacks in Afghanistan, the Uzbek government under Islam Karimov wanted U.S. assurances that it would destroy enemies of the Uzbek state and then maintaining camps within Afghanistan in order to neutralize any expected reprisals. Accordingly, several Islamic Movement of Uzbekistan (IMU) bases in Balkh and Kunduz provinces near the Uzbek border were among the first targets hit in Afghanistan by U.S. airpower.

10. See Gary C. Schroen, *First In: An Insider's Account of How the CIA Spearheaded the War on Terrorism in Afghanistan* (New York: Presidio Press, 2005). Schroen (CIA Special Activities Division) led the first U.S. personnel into Afghanistan, who were then followed by U.S. SOF. Schroen's experiences in Afghanistan before September 11, 2001, were featured in the Pulitzer Prize–winning book by Steve Coll, *Ghost Wars: The Secret History of the CIA, Afghanistan, and Bin Laden, from the Soviet Invasion to September 10, 2001* (New York: Penguin Press HC, 2004); see also Gary Bernsten and Ralph Pezzullo, *Jawbreaker: The Attack on bin Laden and al*

Qaeda: A Personal Account by CIA's Key Field Commander (New York: Crown Publishing, 2005). Bernsten went into Afghanistan in March 2000 as part of CIA team intent on capturing a senior al-Qaeda leader. U.S. national command authority (NCA) thought it would be too aggressive and might provoke unforeseen consequences. Bernsten returned to Afghanistan in late September 2001 and led the CIA's Operation Jawbreaker team at Tora Bora. See also Bob Woodward, "Secret CIA Units Playing a Central Combat Role," *Washington Post*, November 18, 2001, p. A1.

11. Roger Checkering, et al. (eds.), "The Era of American Hegemony, 1989-2005," in *The Cambridge History of War* (Cambridge, U.K., 2013), p. 582.

12. General Rupert Smith (ret.), *The Utility of Force: The Art of War in the Modern World* (New York: Vintage Books, 2008), see Part III, "War amongst the People," pp. 269–291. Smith spent 40 years in the British army and commanded the United Kingdom's 1st Armored Division during Operation Desert Storm and led coalition operations in Bosnia and Kosovo as well as commanding British forces in Northern Ireland.

13. For further reading (all by Peter F. Drucker), see *The Future of Industrial Man* (New York: The John Day Company, 1942); *The Age of Discontinuity* (New York: Harper and Row, 1969); *Management: Tasks, Responsibilities, Practices* (New York: Harper Collins, 1974); "The Age of Social Transformation," *The Atlantic*, December 1995; and *Innovation and Entrepreneurship: Practice and Principles* (Oxford, UK: Butterworth-Heineman, 2007).

14. U.S. Department of Defense, http://archive.defense.gov/transformation/about_transformation.html, accessed November 9, 2016.

15. Carl von Clausewitz, *On War*, Book I, Chapter III, trans. Michael Howard and Peter Paret, eds. (Princeton, NJ: Princeton University Press, 1989), p. 117.

16. Research Brief, RB-9148-CENTAF, RAND Corporation 2005, "Operation Enduring Freedom: An Assessment." The research brief, delivered to USCENTCOM Air Forces (CENTAF), describes work completed by the RAND National Defense Research Institute documented in *Air Power against Terror: America's Conduct of Operation Enduring Freedom*, by Benjamin S. Lambeth, MG-166-CENTAF, 2005. http://www.rand.org/pubs/monographs/MG166-1.html, accessed November 9, 2016.

17. Charles Duelfer, "What Saddam Hussein Tells Us about the Iran Nuclear Deal," Fox News, April 6, 2015. http://www.foxnews.com/opinion/2015/04/06/What-Saddam-Hussein-tells-us-about-iran-nuclear-deal.html, accessed April 7, 2015. Charles Duelfer was deputy executive chairman of UNSCOM from 1993 to 2000 and the head of CIA's Iraq Survey Group, which provided a critique of the intelligence community's reporting on WMD programs within Saddam's Iraq in 2004.

18. Ibid.

Chapter 9

1. Robert Taber, *War of the Flea: The Classic Study of Guerrilla Warfare* (Washington, DC: Brassey's Inc., 2002), p. 20.

2. Bernard Fall, "The Theory and Practice of Counterinsurgency," *Naval War College Review,* Vol. 51, No. 1 (Winter 1998, reprinted from April 1965), pp. 46–57.

3. The military objectives of OIF were: destabilize, isolate, and overthrow the Iraqi regime and provide support for a new broad-based government; destroy Iraqi WMD capability and infrastructure; protect allies and supporters from Iraqi threats and attacks; destroy terrorist networks in Iraq; gather intelligence on global terrorism; detain terrorists and war criminals and free individuals unjustly detained under the Iraqi regime; and support international efforts to set conditions for long-term stability in Iraq and the region. See Kevin Benson, "A War Examined: Operation Iraqi Freedom 2003: A Discussion with Kevin Benson, COL (USA Retired)," *Parameters*, Vol. 43, No. 4 (Winter 2013–2014), pp. 119–120.

4. For an excellent treatment of the issues surrounding preemptive and preventive uses of force, see Colin S. Gray, *The Implications of Preemptive and Preventive War Doctrines: A Reconsideration* (Carlisle Barracks, PA: Strategic Studies Institute—Army War College Press, July 2007).

5. See Robert Jervis, "War and Misperception," *The Journal of Interdisciplinary History,* Vol. 18, No. 4, *The Origin and Prevention of Major Wars* (Spring 1988), pp. 675–700; Robert Jervis, *Perception and Misperception in International Politics* (Princeton, NJ: Princeton University Press, 1976).

6. White House spokesman, Scott McClelland, on February 10, 2003, stated, "This is about an imminent threat." Ari Fleisher, also a White House spokesman, in answering a question from the media as to whether Iraq was an imminent threat, responded, "Absolutely, an imminent threat." Both quoted in Albert L. Weeks, *The Choice for War: The Iraq War and the Just War Tradition* (Santa Barbara, CA: ABC-CLIO, 2009), p. 42. Senior Bush administration officials, however, attempted to avoid the semantical difficulties and most often referred to Saddam's regime as a "serious threat."

7. Major General James A. Marks and Lieutenant Colonel Steve Peterson, "Lessons Learned: Six Things Every '2' Must Do—Fundamental Lessons of OIF," *Military Intelligence*, Vol. 29, No. 4 (October–December 2003), p. 5.

8. Lieutenant General David D. McKiernan, Commander, Combined Allied Land Forces, OIF, interview with PBS *Frontline*, February 26, 2004. http://www.pbs.org/wgbh/pages/frontline/shows/invasion/interviews/mckiernan.html, accessed January 3, 2017.

9. Barry McCaffrey, quoted in Vernon Loeb and Thomas E. Ricks, "Questions Raised about the Invasion Force," *Washington Post*, March 24, 2003.

10. Quoted in Nicolaus Mills, "Punished for Telling Truth about Iraq War," CNN, March 20, 2013. http://www.cnn.com/2013/03/20/opinion/mills-truth-teller-iraq/, accessed February 14, 2014. While Wolfowitz's assessment was ultimately shown incorrect, similar logic was utilized by Napoleon Bonaparte when he observed: "There are in Europe many good generals, but they see too many things at once. I see only one thing, namely the enemy's main body. I try to crush it, confident that secondary matters will then settle themselves."

11. Ibid.

12. Ibid.

13. Mark Moyar, "The Era of American Hegemony, 1989–2005," in *The Cambridge History of War*, Roger Chickering, Dennis Showalter, and Hans van de Ven, eds. (Cambridge, U.K.: Cambridge University Press, 2013), p. 585.

14. Desert Sabre, the ground campaign of Operation Desert Storm, emphasized mass, speed, and maneuver, largely conceived and conducted on a linear battlefield. OIF would be less inclined toward linearity and would trade mass for speed with a focus on massing effects rather than forces.

15. The United States and coalition forces during OIF were able to destroy Saddam's regime and his military forces in less than three weeks in what was one of the most decisive military operations in world history. While the U.S. military's performance was impressive, power in war and politics is nearly always relative; for a perspective on the nature of Iraq's weakness during initial combat operations in OIF, see: Stephen T. Hosmer, *Why the Iraqi Resistance to the Coalition Invasion Was So Weak* (Santa Monica, CA: RAND Corporation, 2007), p. iii.

16. Michael Elliot, "3 Flawed Assumptions about Post-War Iraq," *Time*, September 22, 2003, pp. 30–31.

17. Lieutenant Colonel James D. Scudieri, "Iraq 2003–4 and Mesopotamia 1914–18: A Comparative Analysis in Ends and Means," Master's Thesis, Center for Strategic Leadership, U.S. Army War College, Carlyle Barracks, PA, March 19, 2004.

18. In July 2002, Central Intelligence Agency's (CIA) Special Activities Division (SAD) teams became the first U.S. forces entering Iraq while preparing the groundwork for the arrival of U.S. Army Special Forces in northern Iraq for what became known as Operation Hotel California. Their mission was to link up with Kurdish Peshmerga fighters to conduct operations against an ally of al-Qaeda, Ansar al-Islam, which was then occupying territory in Northeast Iraq. Subsequently, Peshmerga, CIA Paramilitary Operations Officers (SAD), and Green Berets of the U.S. Army's 10th Special Forces Group (SFG) defeated Ansar al-Islam in northern Iraq and uncovered a chemical weapons facility at Sargat. The weapons facility at Sargat was the only (publicly declared) chemical weapons site of its type discovered in Iraq during the 2003 Iran War. See George Tenet, *At the Center of the Storm: My Years at the CIA* (New York: HarperCollins, 2007), pp. 388–389; and Mike Tucker and Charles Faddis, *Operation Hotel California: The Clandestine War inside Iraq* (Guilford, CT: The Lyons Press, 2009). Faddis was a CIA team leader in Iraq at the time.

19. Donald Rumsfeld, *Known and Unknown: A Memoir* (New York: Sentinel, 2011), p. 460.

20. See Tucker and Faddis, *Operation Hotel California*. Charles "Sam" Faddis was the leader of the CIA team that went into northern Iraq in the summer of 2002.

21. Timothy Garden, "Iraq: The Military Campaign," *International Affairs* (Journal of the Royal Institute of International Affairs, U.K.), Vol. 79, No. 4 (July 2003), p. 707.

22. "A War Examined: Operation Iraqi Freedom 2003: A Discussion with Kevin Benson, COL (USA Retired)" (Winter 2013–2014). Benson served as C/J-5 of the Coalition Forces Land Component Command (CFLCC) in the opening phase of OIF and coordinated COBRA II, the operational plan during the initial invasion, as well as ECLIPSE II, the follow-on plan for post-hostilities operations.

23. U.S. military planners had drawn up two sets of war plans: one that utilized Turkey as a key staging ground, moving approximately 80,000 U.S. troops (chiefly from the 4th ID) from ships in the eastern Mediterranean Sea through the NATO partner's territory and into northern Iraq, and one that did not. Being able to stage from Turkey would have threatened Iraqi forces from both the South (V Corps and the I MEF) and the North (4th ID, 173rd ABN, and Special Operations Forces). Simultaneously, this would have created a "hammer and anvil" effect, trapping any Iraqi forces wishing to resist between two axes of advance. However, the Turkish government sought $32 billion from the United States for it to allow American forces to transit the country for an attack on Saddam's regime. The Bush administration countered with an offer of $26 billion with $20 billion (USD) in loan guarantees and $6 billion in direct grants. Ankara sought at least $10 billion in direct grants. Unable to reach an agreement, the 4th ID was rerouted from waters off the coast of Turkey to the Persian Gulf where it moved into action by transiting Kuwait. Without the backdoor secured in OIF, former regime elements were more easily able to vanish and provided them the opportunity in serving as the foundation of the Iraqi insurgency following the close of major combat operations during OIF. See http://www.nytimes.com/2003/02/19/international/europe/19TURK.html, accessed March 5, 2015; Anthony H. Cordesman, *The Iraq War: Strategy, Tactics and Military Lessons* (Santa Barbara, CA: Praeger, 2003), p. 59.

24. See Michael Gordon and Bernard Trainor, *Cobra II: The Inside Story of the Invasion and Occupation of Iraq* (New York: Vintage Books, 2007); and Thomas E. Ricks, *Fiasco: The American Military Adventure in Iraq* (New York: Penguin Group, 2006).

25. The financial costs of military and stability operations within Iraq from 2003 to 2010 exceeded $757 billion in direct costs (Department of Defense [DoD] figure). The Congressional Budget Office (CBO) placed the direct costs at $815 billion (both DoD and CBO figures reported in Amy Belasco, *The Cost of Iraq, Afghanistan, and Other Global War on Terror Operations Since 9-11*, Congressional Research Service, CRS Report RL-33110 Prepared for Congress, December 8, 2014); while private analysts, including a study by Brown University, argue that total costs will be $1.1 trillion, others place the total costs, including interest, in that the war was financed at $3 trillion (Joseph E. Stiglitz and Linda J. Bilmer, *The Three Trillion Dollar War: The True Cost of the Iraq War* [New York: W.W. Norton and Company, 2008]).

26. Approximately one-third of the 4,486 American troops killed in Iraq perished in Anbar Province as the Sunnis, believing that their traditional influence in Iraq through the Sunni Ba'athist government of Saddam would slip away in a new Iraq, fought with fervor to maintain their influence. Al-Qaeda eventually made inroads in the Sunni Anbar Province, and many American deaths in Anbar were directly related to AQI activity (al-Qaeda in Iraq). One hundred U.S. servicemen lost their lives in the battle for control over the city of Fallujah, the site of the U.S. military's bloodiest confrontation since the Vietnam War and a location where AQI had taken root. From May 2003 until the departure of U.S. forces in December 2011, Fallujah was the center of anti-coalition violence. Three battles took place between 2003 and 2005 for control of the city. While more than 200 were

killed, nearly 2,000 coalition forces were wounded during operations in this vola-
tile site, part of what came to be known as the Sunni Triangle. Excellent sources for
further reading include: Bing West, *No True Glory: A Frontline Account of the Battle
of Fallujah* (New York: Random House/Bantam Books, 2005); Dick Camp, *Operation Phantom Fury: The Assault and Capture of Fallujah, Iraq* (Minneapolis, MN:
Zenith Press, 2009); William Head, "The Battles of Al-Fallujah: Urban Warfare
and the Growth of Air Power," *Air Power History*, Vol. 60, No. 4 (Winter 2013),
pp. 32–51.

27. Field Marshall Helmuth Graf von Moltke, *Instructions for Superior
Commanders*, quoted in Colin S. Gray, *Strategy and History: Essays on Theory and
Practice* (New York: Routledge, 2007), p. 77.

28. For greater detail on this important battle, see: Rod Andrew Jr., *The Battle of
An-Nasiriyah*, U.S. Marines in Battle (Washington, DC: History Division, U.S.
Marine Corps, 2009); Mark K. Snakenberg, "An Nasiriyah: America's First Battle
in Operation Iraqi Freedom," *Army History*, No. 76 (Summer 2010), PB 20-10-3,
Washington, DC, pp. 33–42; Richard S. Lowry, *Marines in the Garden of Eden: The
Battle for An Nasiriyah* (New York: Penguin Publishing, 2006); Tim Pritchard,
Ambush Alley: The Most Extraordinary Battle of the Iraq War (New York: Presidio
Press, 2006); and Gary Livingston, *An Nasiriyah: The Fight for the Bridges*, 2nd ed.
(Snead's Ferry, NC: Caisson Press, 2004).

29. For a critical view of British operations in Basra, see: "The Iraq Inquiry," an
in-depth critique of both the United Kingdom and the United States during the
2003 Iraq War, http://www.iraqinquiry.org.uk/the-report/, accessed August 1,
2016.. Led by Sir John Chilcot, the report also criticizes the United States and the
United Kingdom arguing that the war was unnecessary in that all peaceful alternatives had not been explored.

30. Colonel David Perkins, commander, 2nd Brigade, 3rd ID, quoted in Jim
Garmone, "Remembering the 3rd Infantry Division's Thunder Runs," *American
Forces Press Services*, March 18, 2004. On April 4, 2003, Perkin's unit was ordered
to make a demonstration into the heart of Baghdad. In response, Perkins sent
Lieutenant Colonel Schwartz and Task Force 1-64 into Baghdad for the first Thunder Run on March 5. On March 7, Colonel Perkins took the entire 2nd Brigade into
the heart of Baghdad and pierced the false narrative of Saddam's propaganda and
shocked his defense, security, and intelligence personnel into the realization that
the government could not stand in the face of a U.S. military campaign designed
to take Saddam and his regime down. For more on the Army's Thunder Runs
during OIF, see: David Zucchino, *Thunder Run: An Armored Strike to Capture
Baghdad* (New York: Grove Press, 2004); and Jason Conroy, *Heavy Metal: A Tank
Company's Battle to Baghdad* (Sterling, VA: Potomac Books, 2006). Captain Conroy
commanded Charlie Company assigned to Task Force 1-64, 2nd BCT, and 3rd
Infantry Division and was in the vanguard of Task Force 1-64's strike into
Baghdad on March 5, 2003.

31. Major Robert S. Weiler (USMC), "Eliminating Success during ECLIPSE II:
An Examination of the Decision to Disband the Iraqi Military," Master's Thesis,
U.S. Marine Corps Command and Staff College, Marine Corps University, Quantico, VA, 2009. However, in late April 1999, CENTCOM, then led by Marine General Anthony Zinni, conducted a war game, code-named "Desert Crossing," to

examine the opportunities and difficulties of taking military action against Saddam's regime and seeking to better understand the main war contingency planning of OPLAN 1003-98. The after-action reporting identified a range of difficulties arising from such a campaign particularly regarding post-major combat stabilization and governance problems. "When it looked like we were going in, I called back down to CENTCOM and said, 'You need to dust off Desert Crossing.' They said, 'What's that? Never heard of it.' " —General Zinni (ret.), 2004. National Security Archive (George Washington University). "Post-Saddam Iraq: The War Game, 'Desert Crossing' 1999," National Security Archive Electronic Briefing Book No. 207. http://nsarchive.gwu.edu/NSAEBB/NSAEBB207/, accessed January 15, 2012.

32. Saddam was captured after he was extracted from a hole in the ground in which he was hiding located near a farmhouse at ad-Dawr in the vicinity of Tikrit, Saddam's hometown. This event was the culmination of Operation Red Dawn conducted by Task Force 121 in a capture or kill mission against the former Iraqi dictator. Task Force 121 was supported by the 1st BCT, led by Colonel James Hickey of the 4th ID. The 4th ID was commanded at the time by Major General Raymond Odierno who later became chief of staff, U.S. Army.

33. *Oxford English Dictionary*, 2nd ed., 1989.

34. Ibid.

35. "Fourth generation warfare" is a term used by supporters and detractors. It is meant to describe conflict characterized by a blurring of the lines between war and politics on one hand and combatants and civilians on the other. The term was first used by analysts in the United States in 1989 to reflect warfare's return to a decentralized form. "In terms of generational modern warfare the fourth generation signifies the nation-state's loss of near-monopoly on combat forces, returning to modes of conflict common in pre-modern times. The simplest definition includes any war in which one of the main participants is not a state but rather a non-state actor." See William S. Lind, "Understanding Fourth Generation Warfare," *Military Review* Vol. 84, No. 5 (September–October 2004), pp. 12–16; Del Stewart, "De-constructing the Theory of Fourth Generation Warfare," *Military Intelligence*, PB 34-04-04, Vol. 30, No. 4 (October–December 2004), pp. 35–38; H. John Poole, *Tactics of the Crescent Moon: Militant Muslim Combat Methods* (Emerald Isle, NC: Posterity Press, 2004); Antulio J. Echevarria III, "Fourth Generation Warfare and Other Myths," Strategic Studies Institute, U.S. Army War College, November 2005.

36. Department of Defense, U.S. *Counterinsurgency*, Joint Publication (JP 3-32), Washington, DC, November 22, 2013, p. iii.

37. During the Cold War era (1947–1991), analysts spoke of the word being made up of three parts: The First World: whose constituents included the United States and the industrialized democracies of the free world (free from Soviet control), essentially the developed and modernized world—at least from the perspective of the United States and its allies; The Second World: the USSR and its satellites or allies; and the Third World: made up of the many nations across the world that had not yet modernized, democratized, that is, traditional governments with authoritarian rule and underdeveloped economies.

38. David McKiernan, interview, PBS, 2004.

39. General Rupert Smith (British Army, ret.), *The Utility of Force: The Art of War in the Modern World* (New York: Vintage Books, 2008). In 1990–1991, then Major-General Smith commanded the British 1st Armored Division in the 1991 Gulf War. Smith was subsequently involved in operations in the former Yugoslavia as deputy supreme allied commander, Europe, and was in Northern Ireland as general officer, commanding. In his seminal work, *The Utility of Force*, General Smith analyzes why competent modern militaries often win their battles while losing the war. A fundamental cause is the shift from industrial warfare to what Smith describes as "war amongst the people." In such an environment, a favorable outcome cannot be achieved through purely military means. Smith argues that strategies for war amongst the people should be analyzed as fighting and winning not a series of battles but rather fighting and winning a series of *confrontations*.

40. Lieutenant Colonel James R. Crider (U.S. Army), "A View from inside the Surge," *Military Review*, Vol. 89, No. 2 (March–April 2009), p. 81; see also: FM 3-24 Marine Corps Warfighting Publication 3-33.5, *Counterinsurgency* (Chicago, IL: University of Chicago Press, 2002).

41. Crider, "A View from inside the Surge" (2009), p. 81.

42. David Galula, *Counterinsurgency Warfare: Theory and Practice* (Westport, CT: Praeger, 2006).

43. President's address to the nation, January 10, 2007.

44. Ibid.

45. Bob Woodward, "Why Did the Violence Plummet? It Wasn't Just the Surge," *Washington Post*, September 8, 2008.

Chapter 10

1. Moving through the OODA-Loop faster than the opponent creates the conditions in which your forces change the combat situation more rapidly (Rapid Dominance) than the opponent can comprehend. "Generate uncertainty, confusion, disorder, panic, chaos ... to shatter cohesion, produce paralysis, and bring about collapse." John R. Boyd, "Patterns of Conflict," unpublished briefing, 1986, p. 5 and p. 132. http://dnipogo.org/john-r-boyd/, accessed July 15, 2013.

2. Richard A. Gabriel and Karen S. Metz, *A Short History of War: The Evolution of Warfare and Weapons, Professional Readings in Military Strategy, No. 5* (Carlisle Barracks, PA: Strategic Studies Institute—U.S. Army War College, 1992).

3. Colonel Mark W. Lukens, "Strategic Analysis of Irregular Warfare," Master's Thesis, U.S. Army War College, Carlisle Barracks, PA, January 2010, p. 5.

4. Edward Hallett Carr, *The Twenty Years' Crisis 1919–1939: An Introduction to the Study of International Relations* (New York: Harper Perennial, 1964).

5. Adam Smith, *An Inquiry into the Nature and Causes of the Wealth of Nations*, Edwin Cannan, ed. (Chicago, IL: University of Chicago Press, 1977). Smith's seminal achievement was originally published in 1776.

6. Edgar O'Ballance, "The Iraqi-Iranian War: The First Round," *Parameters*, Vol. XI, No. 1 (March 1981), p. 55.

7. Kenneth Pollack, *Arabs at War: Military Effectiveness, 1948–1991* (Lincoln, NE: University of Nebraska Press, 2002), pp. 259–261.

8. James J. Schneider, "The Loose Marble—and the Origins of Operational Art," *Parameters*, Vol. 19, No. 1 (March 1989), p. 87.

9. U.S. Army FM 100-5 Operations, quoted in William J.Bolt and David Jablonsky, "Tactics and the Operational Level of War," *Military Review*, Vol. 68, No. 2 (February 1987), p. 10.

10. T. E. Lawrence, "The Evolution of Revolt," *Army Quarterly and Defense Journal*, Vol. 1, No. 1 (Devon, U.K.: October 1920), p. 11. Also available through Praetorian Press LLC, 2011.

11. "[The] aim is not so much to seek battle as to seek a strategic situation so advantageous that if it does not of itself produce the decision, its continuation by a battle is sure to achieve this. In other words, dislocation is the aim of strategy." Sir Basil H. Liddell Hart, *Strategy*, 2nd rev. ed. (New York: Meridian Penguin Books 1991), p. 325.

12. Antulio J. Echevarria II, *Wars of Ideas and the War of Ideas* (Carlisle Barracks, PA: Strategic Studies Institute—U.S. Army War College, June 2008), p. 37.

Selected Bibliography

Adamsky, Dima. "Jihadi Operational Art: The Coming Wave of Jihadi Strategic Studies," *Studies in Conflict and Terrorism*, Vol. 33, No. 1 (2010): 1–19.

Adan, Avraham. *On the Banks of the Suez: An Israeli General's Personal Account of the Yom Kippur War*. Novato, CA: Presidio Press, 1991.

Agee, Major Collin A. *Peeling the Onion: The Iraqi Center of Gravity in Desert Storm*. Fort Leavenworth, KS: School for Advanced Military Studies (SAMS), U.S. Army Command and General Staff College, July 4, 1992.

Ajami, Fouad. *The Arab Predicament: Arab Political Thought and Practice since 1967*. Cambridge, U.K.: Cambridge University Press, 1993.

Allen, Charles. *God's Terrorists: The Wahhabi Cult and the Hidden Roots of Modern Jihad*. Boston, MA: Da Capo Press, 2006.

Al-Lihaibi, Colonel Maedh Ayed (Royal Saudi Air Force). "An Analysis of the Iran-Iraq War: Military Strategy and Political Objectives." Master's Thesis, U.S. Air War College, Maxwell Air Force Base, Alabama, May 1989.

Allison, Robert J. *The Crescent Obscured: The United States and the Muslim World 1776–1815*. New York: Oxford University Press, 1995.

Alvandi, Roham. "Nixon, Kissinger, and the Shah: The Origins of Iranian Primacy in the Gulf," *Diplomatic History*, Vol. 36, No. 2 (April 2012): 337–372.

Andrew, Rod, Jr. *The Battle of An-Nasiriyah*, U.S. Marines in Battle. Washington, DC: History Division, U.S. Marine Corps, 2009.

Ardant, Charles-Jean-Jacques-Joseph. *Battle Studies*. Whitefish, MT: Kessinger Publishing, 2010.

Ashkar, Riad, and Haythem al-Ayyubi. "The Middle East: The Military Dimension," *Journal of Palestinian Studies*, Vol. 4, No. 4 (Summer 1975): 3–25.

Athanassopoulou, Ekavi. *Turkey-Anglo-American Security Interests, 1945–1952: The First Enlargement of NATO*. London: Frank Cass, 1999.

Atkinson, Rick. *An Army at Dawn: The War in North Africa, 1942–1943*. New York: Henry Holt, 2002.

Aziz, King Abdul (Ibn Saud). Information Resource Data Base, "Battle of Sibilla." Accessed September 15, 2012. http://ibnsaud.info/main/3374.htm.

Baker, Raymond W. *Egypt's Uncertain Revolution under Nasser and Sadat*. Cambridge, MA: Harvard University Press, 1978.

Bani-Sadr, Abol Hassan. *My Turn to Speak: Iran, the Revolution & Secret Deals with the U.S*. Sterling, VA: Potomac Books (Brassey's), 1991.

Bar-Joseph, Uri. "The 1973 Yom Kippur War," *Israeli Studies: An Anthology*, Jewish Virtual Library Publications, May 2009. Accessed May 14, 2014. http://www.jewishvirtuallibrary.org/jsource/isdf/text/barjoseph.html.

Barker, A. J. *The Bastard War: The Mesopotamian Campaign of 1914–1918*. New York: Dial Press, 1967.

Bartholf, Colonel Mark. "The Requirements of Sociocultural Understanding in Full Spectrum Operations," *Military Intelligence*, Vol. 37, No. 4 (October–December 2011): 4–10.

Bass, Warren. *Support Any Friend: Kennedy's Middle East and the Making off the US-Israel Alliance*. New York: Oxford University Press, 2003.

Bawer, Bruce. *While Europe Slept: How Radical Islam Is Destroying the West from Within*. New York: Doubleday, 2006.

Beckwith, Charles A., and Donald Knox. *Delta Force*. New York: Harcourt Brace and Jovanovich, 1983.

Be'eri, Eliezer. *Army Officers in Arab Politics and Society*. Jerusalem: Israel University sities Press, 1969.

Ben-Horin, Yoav, and Barry Posen. *Israel's Strategic Doctrine*. Santa Monica, CA: RAND Corporation, 1981.

Benson, Kevin. COL (USA ret.). "A War Examined: Operation Iraqi Freedom 2003," *Parameters*, Vol. 43, No. 4 (Winter 2013–2014): 119–123.

Bermudez, Joseph S., Jr. "Iraqi Missile Operations during 'Desert Storm'—Update." *Jane's Soviet Intelligence Review*, Vol. 3, No. 5 (May 1991): 225.

Bernsten, Gary, and Ralph Pezzullo. *Jawbreaker: The Attack on bin Laden and al Qaeda: A Personal Account by CIA's Key Field Commander*. New York: Crown Publishing, 2005.

Birtle, Andrew J. *U.S. Army Counterinsurgency and Contingency Operations Doctrine, 1860–1941*. Center of Military History, Special Publications CMH Pub 70-66-1, U.S. Army, 1998.

Blackburn, Donald S. "Collision of Faiths," *Military History*, Vol. 11, No. 2 (June 1994): 62–68.

Bolger, Daniel. Why We Lost: A General's Inside Account of the Iraq and Afghanistan Wars. New York: Houghton Mifflin Harcourt, 2015.

Boot, Max. *Invisible Armies: An Epic History of Guerrilla Warfare from Ancient Times to the Present*. New York: Liveright Publishing, 2013.

Borum, Randy, and Michael Gellas. "Al Qaeda's Operational Evolution: Behavioral and Organizational Perspectives," *Behavioral Sciences and the Law*, Vol. 23, No. 3 (2005): 467–483.

Bostom, Andrew, ed. *The Legacy of Jihad*. Amherst, NY: Prometheus Books, 2005.

Bostom, Andrew G. *Shariah versus Freedom: The Legacy of Islamic Totalitarianism.* Amherst, NY: Prometheus Books, 2012.

Bou, Jean. "Cavalry, Firepower, and Swords: The Australian Light Horse and the Tactical Lessons of Cavalry Operations in Palestine, 1916–1918," *The Journal of Military History,* Vol. 71, No. 1 (January 2007): 99–125.

Bourque, Stephen A. "Frederick Melvin Franks, Jr." In *The Encyclopedia of Middle East Wars: The United States in the Persian Gulf, Afghanistan, and Iraq Conflicts,* 5 vols., edited by Spencer C. Tucker and Priscilla Mary Roberts, 366–367. Santa Barbara, CA: ABC-CLIO, 2010.

Bourque, Stephen A. *Jayhawk! The VII Corps in the Persian Gulf War.* Center of Military History, Special Publications CMH Pub 70-73-1, U.S. Army, Fort McNair, Washington, DC, 2002.

Brandt, Anthony. "French Fiasco in Egypt," *Military History,* Vol. 27, No. 3 (September 2010): 40–47.

Breitenbach, Daniel (Lt. Col). "Operation Desert Deception: Operational Deception in the Ground Campaign." Master's Thesis, U.S. Naval War College, Newport, RI, June 1992.

Browne, O'Brien. "The Enigmatic Lawrence of Arabia," *Military History,* Vol. 20, No. 4 (October 2003): 26–33.

Browne, O'Brien. "Napoleon's Desert Storm," *MHQ Military History Quarterly,* Vol. 25, No. 1 (Autumn 2012): 30–35.

Brownlee, Jason, and Tarek Masoud. *The Arab Spring: Pathways of Repression and Reform.* Oxford, U.K.: Oxford University Press, 2015.

Bukay, David. "The Religious Foundations of Suicide Bombings: Islamist Ideology," *Middle East Quarterly,* Vol. 8, No. 4 (Fall 2006): 27–36.

Butler, Daniel Allen. *Shadow of the Sultan's Realm: The Destruction of the Ottoman Empire and the Creation of the Modern Middle East.* Washington, DC: Potomac Books, 2011.

Camp, Richard. *Operation Phantom Fury: The Assault and Capture of Fallujah, Iraq.* Minneapolis, MN: Zenith Press, 2009.

Canadian Security Intelligence Service. "2018 Security Outlook: Potential Risks and Threats," Occasional Papers (2016-06-03), June 2016. Accessed June 20, 2016. https://www.csis-scrs.gc.ca/pblctns/ccsnlpprs/2016/2016-06-03/GLOBAL_SECURITY_POST-CONFERENCE_ENGLISH.pdf.

Capaccio, Tony. "A Barrage of Commando Missions Crippled Saddam," *Defense Week,* Vol. 12, No. 1 (April 8, 1991): 1.

Cary, Brian. "Debacle at Manzikert, 1071: Prelude to the Crusades," *Medieval History,* No. 5 (2004): 16–23.

Casais, Major Kenneth W. (USMC [Reserve]). "Israel's Wars in Lebanon, 1982–2006: An End/Means Mismatch." Master's Thesis, USMC Command and Staff College, AY 2008–209, Quantico, VA. Accessed November 12, 2013. http://handle.dtic.mil/100.2/ADA470727.

Cate, Alan. "Historical Perspectives of the Operational Art," *The Journal of Military History,* Vol. 70, No. 1 (January 2006): 288–289.

Catignani, Sergio. *Israeli Counter-Insurgency and the Intifadas: Dilemmas of a Conventional Army.* New York: Routledge, 2009.

Central Intelligence Agency. National Intelligence Estimate No. 11-6-63, "The Soviet Role in the Arab World," April 24, 1963.

Chami, Joseph G. *Days of Wrath: Lebanon 1977–82*. Beirut: Arab Printing Press, 1983.

Charters, David A. *The British Army and Jewish Insurgency in Palestine 1945–1977*. London: Routledge, 1986.

Chickering, Roger. "Introduction: The Era of Total War 1914–1945." In *Cambridge Histories Online*, edited by Roger Chickering, Dennis Showalter, and Hans van de Ven, 181–191. Cambridge, U.K.: Cambridge University Press, 2003.

Cicero, Marcus Tullius. *The Republic and the Laws* [47 BCE]. Edited and translated by N. Rudd. Oxford, U.K.: Oxford University Press, 1998.

Cipolla, Carlo M. *Guns, Sails, and Empires*. New York: Minerva Press, 1965.

Citino, Robert M. "The Throwback War," *Military History*, Vol. 29, No. 6 (March 2013): 26–37.

Clancy, Tom, and Frederick Franks. *Into the Storm: A Study in Command*. New York: Putnam, 1997.

Clausewitz, Carl von. *On War* [1832]. Edited and translated by Michael Howard and Peter Paret. Princeton, NJ: Princeton University Press, 1989.

Clemm, Robert H. "Coalition Nations' Contributions to Desert Storm." In *The Encyclopedia of Middle East Wars: The United States in the Persian Gulf, Afghanistan, and Iraq Conflicts*, 5 vols., edited by Spencer C. Tucker and Priscilla Mary Roberts, 366–367. Santa Barbara: CA, ABC-CLIO, 2010.

Cleveland, William. *A History of the Modern Middle East*, 5th ed. Boulder, CO: Westview Press, 2012.

Clews, Graham T. *Churchill's Dilemma: The Real Story behind the Origins of the 1915 Dardanelles Campaign*. Santa Barbara, CA: Praeger, 2010.

Coates, Kristian. *The First World War in the Middle East*. London: Hurst, 2014.

Cogan, Charles G. "Desert One and Its Disorders," *The Journal of Military History*, Vol. 67, No. 1 (January 2003): 201–216.

Cohen, Avner. *Israel and the Bomb*. New York: Columbia University Press, 1998.

Cohen, Eliezer. *Israel's Best Defense: The First Full Story of the Israeli Air Force*. New York: Crown, 1993.

Coll, Steve. *Ghost Wars: The Secret History of the CIA, Afghanistan, and Bin Laden, from the Soviet Invasion to September 10, 2001*. New York: Penguin Press HC, 2004.

Collins, Joseph J. *Understanding War in Afghanistan*. Washington DC: National Defense University Press, 2011.

Cordesman, Anthony H. *The Iraq War: Strategy, Tactics, and Military Lessons*. Santa Barbara, CA: Praeger, 2003.

Cordesman, Anthony H. "The Lessons of the Israel-Hezbollah War: A Briefing," Center for Strategic and International Studies, March 12, 2008. Accessed November 14, 2016. https://www.csis.org/analysis/lessons-israel-hezbollah-war.

Coyne, James P. *Airpower in the Gulf*. Arlington, VA: Aerospace Education Foundation, 1992.

Craig, Simon. "Battle of Ankara," *Military History*, Vol. 19, No. 3 (August 2002): 58–62.

Crider, Lieutenant Colonel James R. (U.S. Army). "A View from inside the Surge," *Military Review,* Vol. 89, No. 2 (March–April 2009), 81–88.

Davis, Paul K., and John Arquilla. *Deterring or Coercing Opponents in Crisis: Lessons from the War with Saddam Hussein.* Santa Monica, CA: RAND Corporation, 1991.

Dawn, C. Ernest. "The Egyptian Remilitarization of Sinai, May 1967," *Journal of Contemporary History,* Vol. 3, No. 3 (July 1968): 201–224.

Dayan, Moshe. *Diary of the Sinai Campaign.* New York: Schocken Books, 1966.

Deac, Wilfred P. "Duel for the Suez Canal," *Military History,* Vol. 18, No. 1 (April 2001): 58–63.

DeAtkine, Norvell B. "Why Arabs Lose Wars," *The Middle East Quarterly,* Vol. 7, No. 4 (December 1999). Accessed November 14, 2016. http://www.meforum.org/441/why-arabs-lose-wars.

Delong, Michael, and Noah Lukeman. *Inside CENTCOM: The Unvarnished Truth about the War in Afghanistan and Iraq.* Washington, DC: Regnery Publishing, 2014.

Delong-Bas, Natana J. *Wahhabi Islam: From Revival to Global Jihad.* New York: Oxford University Press, 2004.

Department of Defense, U.S. *Conduct of the Persian Gulf War: Final Report to Congress.* Washington, DC: U.S. Department of Defense, April 1992. Accessed July 29, 2015. http://www.globalsecurity.org/military/library/report/1992/cpgw.pdf.

Department of Defense, U.S. *Doctrine for Joint Operations.* Washington, DC: Joint Publications, 3-0, February 1, 1995. Accessed January 1996. http://www.dtic.mil/doctrine/new_pubs/jp3_0.pdf.

Department of Defense, U.S. *National Training Center Handbook: The Iraqi Army, Organization and Tactics.* Fort Irwin, CA: National Training Center, January, 3 1991.

Department of Defense, U.S., and David H. Petraeus. *U.S. Army Counterinsurgency Handbook.* New York: Skyhorse Publishing, 2007.

Department of State, U.S. "Memorandum of Discussion at the 135th Meeting of the National Security Council," March 4, 1953, U.S. Department of State, *Foreign Relations of the United States, 1952–1954,* Volume X, *Iran 1951–1954.* Washington, DC: U.S. Government Printing Office, 1989.

Devereux, David R. *The Formation of British Defence Policy towards the Middle East, 1948–56.* London: Palgrave Macmillan, 1990.

Dobson, Alan P. "The Reagan Administration, Economic Warfare and Starting to Close down the Cold War." *Diplomatic History,* Vol. 29, No. 3 (May 13, 2005). Accessed June 3, 2005. http://onlinelibrary.wileycom/doi/10.1111/j.1467-7709.2005.00502.x/pdf.

Dodge, Toby. *Inventing Iraq: The Failure of Nation-Building and a History Denied.* New York: Columbia University Press, 2003.

Doran, M. "The Pragmatic Fanaticism of al Qaeda: An Anatomy of Extremism in Middle Eastern Politics," *Political Science Quarterly,* Vol. 117, No. 2 (Summer 2002): 177–190.

Dowty, Alan. *Middle East Crisis: US Decision Making in 1958, 1970, and 1973.* Berkeley, CA: University of California Press, 1984.

Drucker, Peter F. *The Future of Industrial Man*. New York: The John Day Company, 1942.

Dubois, Thomas R. (Lt. Col). "The Weinberger Doctrine and the Liberation of Kuwait," *Parameters*, Vol. 21, No. 4 (Winter 1991–1992): 24–38.

Dunlap, Charles J., Jr. (Lt. Col). "There Was Reason behind Saddam's Air Strategy," *Air Force Times*, Vol. 5, No. 8 (September 6, 1993): 33.

Dupuy, T. N., and P. Martell. *Flawed Victory—The 1982 War in Lebanon*. Fairfax, VA: Hero Books, 1985.

Echevarria, Antulio J., III. "Fourth Generation Warfare and Other Myths," Strategic Studies Institute, U.S. Army War College, November 2005.

Eden, Anthony. *The Suez Crisis of 1956*. Boston, MA: Beacon Press, 1960.

Ehteshami, Anoushirvan. "Arms Transfers and the Search for Security in the Persian Gulf," *Strategic Studies*, Vol. 14, No.1 (January–March 1992): 5–22.

El Hussini, Mohrez Mahmoud. *Soviet-Egyptian Relations, 1945–1985*. London: Macmillan, 1987.

El-Rewany, Hassan Ahmed. *The Ramadan War: End of Illusion*. Carlisle Barracks, PA: U.S. Army War College, 2001.

Elron, Zeev, and Moshe Gat. "Remarks on the Six Day War [And Response]," *The Journal of Military History*, Vol. 69, No. 3 (July 2005): 811–820.

El-Sadat, Anwar. *In Search of Identity: An Autobiography*. New York: Harper and Row, 1978.

El-Sawah, Ossama M. *Deception in Ramadan War, October 1973*. Carlisle Barracks, PA: U.S. Army War College, 1999.

Engdahl, F. William. *A Century of War: Anglo-American Oil Politics and the New World Order*. London: Pluto Press, 2004.

Erickson, Edward J. "Strength against Weakness: Ottoman Military Effectiveness at Gallipoli, 1915," *The Journal of Military History*, Vol. 65, No. 4 (October 2001): 981–1011.

Eshel, Lt. Col. David (IDF). *Mid-East Wars: The Lebanon War 1982*. Israel: Eshel-Dramit Ltd., 1985.

Euben, Roxanne L., and Muhammad Qasim Zaman, eds. *Princeton Readings in Islamist Thought: Texts and Contexts from al-Banna to Bin Laden*. Princeton, NJ: Princeton University Press, 2009.

Fehrenbach, R. *This Kind of War: A Study in Unpreparedness*. New York: Macmillan, 1963.

Fenzel, John, III (Capt.). "Five Imperatives of Coalition Warfare," *Special Warfare*, Vol. 6, No. 3 (July 1993): 2–8.

Firestone, Reuven. *Jihad: The Origin of Holy War in Islam*. New York: Oxford University Press, 1999.

Ford, Roger. *Eden to Armageddon: World War I in the Middle East*. Cambridge, U.K.: Pegasus, 2010.

Fraser, T. G., Andrew Mango, and Robert McNamara. *The Makers of the Modern Middle East*. Milwaukee, WI: Haus Publishing, 2011.

Freedman, Lawrence, and Efraim Karsh. "How Kuwait Was Won: Strategy in the Gulf War," *International Security*, Vol. 16, No. 2 (Autumn 1991): 5–41.

Fregosi, Paul. *Jihad in the West: Muslim Conquests from the 7th to the 21st Centuries*. Amherst, NY: Prometheus Books, 1998.

Frisch, Hillel. *The Palestinian Military: Between Militias and Armies*. New York: Routledge, 2010.

Fromkin, David. *A Peace to End All Peace: The Fall of the Ottoman Empire and the Creation of the Modern Middle East*. New York: Henry Holt, 2009.

Gabriel, Richard. "The Warrior Prophet," *MQH Military History Quarterly*, Vol. 19, No. 4 (Summer 2007): 6–15.

Gabriel, Richard A., and Karen S. Metz. *A Short History of War: The Evolution of Warfare and Weapons, Professional Readings in Military Strategy, No. 5*. Carlisle Barracks, PA: Strategic Studies Institute—U.S. Army War College, 1992.

Galdi, Theodor W. "Revolution in Military Affairs? Competing Concepts, Organizational Responses, Outstanding Issues," CRS Report for Congress, 95-11-70F. Washington, DC: Congressional Research Service, December 11, 1995.

Galula, David. *Counterinsurgency Warfare: Theory and Practice*. Westport, CT: Praeger, 2006.

Garden, Timothy. "Iraq: The Military Campaign," *International Affairs* (Journal of the Royal Institute of International Affairs, U.K.), Vol. 79, No. 4 (July 2003): 701–718.

Garmone, Jim. "Remembering the 3rd Infantry Division's Thunder Runs," *American Forces Press Services*, March 18, 2004. Accessed November 17, 2016. http://archive.defense.gov/news/newsarticle.aspx?id=27039.

Gat, Azar. *A History of Military Thought: From the Enlightenment to the Cold War*. New York: Oxford University Press, 2001.

Gat, Moshe. "Nasser and the Six Day War, 5 June 1967: A Premeditated Strategy or an Inexorable Drift to War?" *Israeli Affairs*, Vol. 11, No. 4 (October 2005): 608–635.

Gates, Robert M. *Duty: Memoirs of a Secretary at War*. New York: Knopf, 2014.

Gawrych, George W. *Key to the Sinai: The Battles for Abu Ageila in the 1956 and 1967 Arab-Israeli Wars*. Leavenworth, KS: Combat Studies Institute Research Survey 7, U.S. Army Command and Staff College, 1990.

Gehring, Stephen P. *From the Fulda Gap to Kuwait: US Army in Europe and the Gulf War*. Center of Military History, Special Publications CMH Pub 70-56-1, U.S. Army, 1998.

Gelvin, James L. *The Israeli-Palestinian Conflict: One Hundred Years of War*, 3rd ed. Cambridge, U.K.: Cambridge University Press, 2014.

Gelvin, James L. *The Modern Middle East: A History*, 3rd ed. Oxford, U.K.: Oxford University Press, 2011.

Gibb, David. "Review Essay: Afghanistan: The Soviet Invasion in Retrospective," *International Politics*, Vol. 37, No. 3 (June 2000): 233–246.

Gideon, T. W. "Sword of Saud and the Birth of a Nation," *Military History*, Vol. 14, No. 3 (August 1997): 50–57.

Gilchrist, H. L. *A Comparative Study of War: Casualties from Gas and Other Weapons*. Edgewood Arsenal, MD: Chemical Warfare School, 1928.

Ginor, Isabella, and Gideon Remez. *Foxbats over Dimona: The Soviet's Nuclear Gamble in the Six-Day War*. New Haven, CT: Yale University Press, 2007.

Ginor, Isabella, and Gideon Remez. "The Spymaster, the Communist, and the Foxbats over Dimona: The USSR's Motive for Instigating the Six Day War," *Israeli Studies*, Vol. 11, No. 2 (Summer 2006): 88–130.

Gluska, Ami. *The Israeli Military and the Origins of the 1967 War: Government, Armed Forces and Defense Policy, 1963–67.* New York: Routledge, 2009.

Golan, Galia. "The Soviet Union and the Outbreak of the June 1967 Six Day War," *Journal of Cold War Studies,* Vol. 8, No. 1 (Winter 2006): 3–19.

Goldstone, Jack A. *Revolution and Rebellion in the Early Modern World.* Berkeley, CA: University of California Press, 1991.

Goodson, Larry P., and Thomas H. Johnson. *US Policy and Strategy toward Afghanistan after 2014.* Carlisle Barracks, PA: Strategic Studies Institute—U.S. Army War College Press, October 2014.

Gordon, Michael R., and General Bernard E. Trainor. *The General's War: The Inside Story of the Conflict in the Gulf.* Boston, MA: Little, Brown and Company, 1995.

Grau, Lester W. *The Bear Went over the Mountain: Soviet Combat Tactics in Afghanistan.* New York: Oxford University Press, 2007.

Gray, Major General David W. (U.S. Army, ret.). *The US Intervention in Lebanon, 1958: A Commander's Reminiscence.* Fort Leavenworth, KS: U.S. Army Command and General Staff College, August 1984.

Grenier, Robert. L. *88 Days to Kandahar: A CIA Diary.* New York: Simon and Schuster, 2015.

Grip, Lina, and John Hart. "The Use of Chemical Weapons in the 1935–36 Italo-Ethiopian War." SIPRI Arms Control and Non-Proliferation Programme, October 2009.

Grossgold, Lieutenant Commander Paul S. (USN). "The 1967 Arab-Israeli War: An Operational Study of the Sinai Campaign." Naval War College Student Papers, June 1994.

Gudmundsson, Bruce I. "Tactical Exercises: Allenby's Turning Tactics," *MHQ Military History Quarterly,* Vol. 19, No. 4 (Summer 2007): 80–93.

Guilmartin, John, Jr. "Wars of the Ottoman Empire: 1453–1606." In *The Origin and Prevention of Major Wars,* edited by Robert I. Rotberg and Theodore K. Rabb, 149–179. Cambridge, U.K.: Cambridge University Press, 1998.

Haddad, George M. *Revolutions and Military Rule in the Middle East, Vol. 1—The Northern Tier.* New York: Robert Speller and Sons, 1965.

Haddad, George M. *Revolutions and Military Rule in the Middle East, Vol. 2—The Arab States, Part I—Iraq, Syria, Lebanon, and Jordan.* New York: Robert Speller and Sons, 1971.

Haddad, George M. *Revolutions and Military Rule in the Middle East, Vol. 3—The Arab States, Part II—Egypt, the Sudan, Yemen and Libya.* New York: Robert Speller and Sons, 1973.

Hahn, Peter L. "Containment and Egyptian Nationalism: The Unsuccessful Effort to Establish the Middle East Command, 1950–1953," *Diplomatic History,* Vol.11, No.1 (Winter 1987): 23–40.

Hallaq, Wael B. *An Introduction to Islamic Law.* Cambridge, U.K.: Cambridge University Press, 2009.

Hallion, Richard. *Storm over Iraq: Air Power and the Gulf War.* Washington, DC: Smithsonian Institution Press, 1992.

Hamid, Tawfid. "The Development of a Jihadi's Mind." In *Current Trends in Islamist Ideology, Vol. 5,* edited by Hillel Fradkin, Husain Haqqani, and Eric Brown,

11–23. Washington, DC: Center on Islam, Democracy and the Future of the Muslim World, Hudson Institute, 2007.

Hammes, Thomas X. *"The Sling and Stone: On War in the 21st Century.* St. Paul, MN: Zenith Press, 2004.

Handel, Michael I. *Masters of War: Classical Strategic Thought*, 3rd. ed. London: Frank Cass, 2003.

Harris, David. *The Crisis: The President, the Prophet, and the Shah—1979 and the Coming of Militant Islam.* New York: Little, Brown, and Company, 2004.

Head, William. "The Battles of Al-Fallujah: Urban Warfare and the Growth of Air Power," *Air Power History,* Vol. 60, No. 4 (Winter 2013): 33–51.

Heiman, Leo. "Armored Forces in the Middle East," *Military Review,* November 1968, 11–19.

Henkin, Yagil. *The 1956 Suez War and the New World Order in the Middle East: Exodus in Reverse.* Lanham, MD: Lexington Books, 2015.

Hertog, Steffen. "Rentier Militaries in the Gulf States: The Price of Coup-Proofing," *International Journal off Middle East Studies*, Vol. 43, No. 3 (August 2011): 400–402.

Hirschman, Ira. *Red Star over Bethlehem: Russia Drives to Capture the Middle East.* New York: Simon and Schuster, 1971.

Hoffman, Jon T., ed. *Tip of the Spear: US Army Small Unit Actions in Iraq, 2004–2007.* Center of Military History, Special Publications CMH Pub 70-113-1, U.S. Army, 2009.

Holland, Cecelia. "Heraclius Brings Persia to Its Knees," *MQH: The Quarterly Journal of Military History,* Vol. 21, No. 1 (Autumn 2008): 30–39.

Hopkins, B. D. *The Making of Modern Afghanistan.* New York: Palgrave MacMillan, 2014.

Hounam, Peter. *Operation Cyanide: Why the Bombing of the USS Liberty Nearly Caused World War III.* London, U.K.: Vision Publications, 2003.

Hourani, Albert. *Arabic Thought in the Liberal Age 1798–1939.* Oxford, U.K.: Oxford University Press, 1962.

Hourani, Albert. *A History of the Arab Peoples.* Cambridge, MA: The Belknap Press of Harvard University, 1991.

Huband, Mark. *Warriors of the Prophet: The Struggle for Islam.* Boulder, CO: Westview Press, 1998.

Hughes, Matthew. *Allenby and British Strategy in the Middle East, 1917–1919.* New York: Routledge, 2013.

Huntington, Samuel P. *The Clash of Civilizations and the Remaking of the World Order.* New York: Touchstone Books, 1998.

Hurewitz, J. C. "The Beginnings of Military Modernization in the Middle East: A Comparative Analysis," *Middle East Journal,* Vol. 22, No. 2 (Spring 1968): 144–158.

Inbar, Efraim. "How Israel Bungled the Second Lebanon War," *Middle East Quarterly,* Vol. 14, No. 3 (Summer 2007): 57–65.

Jastrow, Morris. *The War and the Baghdad Railway: The Story of Asia Minor and Its Relation to the Present Conflict.* Philadelphia, PA: J.B. Lippincott Company, 1917.

Johnson, David E. *Military Capabilities for Hybrid War: Insights from the Israel Defense Forces in Lebanon and Gaza.* Santa Monica, CA: RAND Corporation, March 30, 2010.

Johnson, Rob. *The Iran-Iraq War* (Twentieth Century Wars Series). New York: Palgrave Macmillan, 2011.

Jones, Clive. " 'Where the State Feared to Tread': Britain, Britons, Covert Action, and the Yemen Civil War, 1962–1964," *Intelligence and National Security*, Vol. 21, No. 5 (October 2006): 717–737.

Jones, Clive, and Sergio Catignani, eds. *Israel and Hizbollah: An Asymmetric Conflict in Historical and Comparative Perspective*. New York: Routledge, 2012.

Jones, Curtis F. *Divide and Perish: The Geopolitics of the Middle East*, 2nd ed. Bloomington, IN: AuthorHouse, 2010.

Jones, Jeffrey B. (Col). "Psychological Operations in Desert Shield, Desert Storm and Urban Freedom," *Special Warfare*, Vol. 7, No. 3 (July 1994): 22–29.

Jones, Martin. *Failure in Palestine: British and United States Policy after the Second World War*. London: Mansell, 1986.

Kahalani, Avigdor. *The Heights of Courage: A Tank Leader's War on the Golan* (Contributions in Military Studies). Westport, CT: Praeger, 1992.

Kahili, Reza. *A Time to Betray: The Astonishing Double Life of a CIA Agent inside the Revolutionary Guards of Iran*. New York: Threshold Editions, 2010.

Kamrava, Mehran, ed. *Beyond the Arab Spring: The Evolving Ruling Bargain in the Middle East*. Oxford, U.K.: Oxford University Press, 2014.

Karsh, Efraim. *The Arab-Israeli Conflict: The 1948 War*. New York: Rosen Publishing Group, 2008.

Karsh, Efraim. *Islamic Imperialism*. New London, CT: Yale University Press, 2007.

Karsh, Efraim, and Inari Karsh. *Empires of the Sand: The Struggle for Mastery in the Middle East, 1789–1923*. Cambridge, MA: Harvard University Press, 1999.

Keegan, John. *Intelligence in War: Knowledge of the Enemy from Napoleon to al-Qaeda*. New York: Alfred A. Knopf, 2003.

Keegan, John. *The Iraq War*. New York: Alfred A. Knopf, 2004.

Keithly, David M., and Stephen P. Ferris. "Auftragstaktik, or Directive Control, in Joint and Combined Operations," *Parameters*, Vol. 89, No. 3 (Autumn 1999): 118–133.

Kennan, George (X). "Sources of Soviet Conduct," *Foreign Affairs*, July 1947.

Kennedy, Paul M. "The First World War and the International Power System," *International Security*, Vol. 9, No. 1 (Summer 1984): 7–40.

Keohane, Robert O. *After Hegemony: Cooperation and Discord in the World Political Economy*. Princeton, NJ: Princeton University Press, 1984.

Keohane, Robert O., and Joseph S. Nye, Jr. *Transnational Relations and World Politics*. Cambridge, MA: Harvard University Press, 1973.

Kimmerling, Baruch, and Joel Migdal. *Palestinians: The Making of a People*. New York: The Free Press, 1993.

Kindsvatter, Peter S. "VII Corps in the Gulf War Ground Offensive," *Military Review*, Vol. 72, No. 2 February 1992, pp. 16-37.

Kinzey, Bert. *The Fury of Desert Storm: The Air Campaign*. Blue Ridge Summit, PA: TAB Books, 1991.

Knox, MacGregor, and Williamson Murray, eds. *The Dynamics of Military Revolution, 1300–2050*. Cambridge, U.K.: Cambridge University Press, 2001.

Kober, Avi. *Israel's Wars of Attrition: Attrition Challenges to Democratic States*. New York: Routledge, 2009.

Koontz, Christopher N., ed. *Enduring Voices: Oral Histories of the US Army Experience in Afghanistan, 2003–2005*. Special Publications CMH Pub 70-112-1, 2009.

Kuniholm, Bruce. *The Origins of the Cold War in the Near East: Great Power Conflict and Diplomacy in Iran, Turkey, and Greece*. Princeton, NJ: Princeton University Press, 1980.

Lambeth, Benjamin S. *Air Power against Terror: America's Conduct of Operation Enduring Freedom*. MG-166-CENTAF, 2005. RAND National Defense Research Institute. Santa Monica, CA: RAND Corporation, 2005. Accessed November 12, 2016. http://www.rand.org/pubs/monographs/MG166-1.html.

Laqueur, Walter. *The Struggle for the Middle East: The Soviet Union and the Middle East, 1958–1970*. Baltimore, MD: Penguin Books, 1972.

Latimer, Jon. *Alamein*. Cambridge, MA: Harvard University Press, 2002.

Lawrence, T. E. *Revolt in the Desert*. New York: George H. Doran, 1927.

Leffler, Melvyn P. "Strategy, Diplomacy, and the Cold War: The United States, Turkey, and NATO, 1945–1952," *The Journal of American History*, Vol. 71, No. 4 (March 1985): 807–825.

Leshem, Mati D. *Israel's National Security Strategy: Past and Future Perspectives*. Carlisle Barracks, PA: U.S. Army War College, 1998.

Lewis, Bernard. *The End of Modern History in the Middle East*. Stanford, CA: Hoover Institution Press, 2011.

Lewis, Bernard. *The Shaping of the Modern Middle East*. Oxford, U.K.: Oxford University Press, 1994.

Lewis, Bernard. *What Went Wrong: The Clash between Islam and Modernity in the Middle East*. New York: Oxford University Press, 2002.

Liddell Hart, B. H., ed. *The Rommel Papers*. New York: Da Capo Press, 1935.

Liddell Hart, B. H. *Strategy*, 2nd rev. ed. New York: Meridian-Penguin Books, 1991.

Lind, William S. Keith Nightengale, John F. Schmitt, Joseph W. Sutton, and Gary I. Wilson. "The Changing Face of War: Into the Fourth Generation," *Marine Corps Gazette*, Vol. 73, No. 10 (October 1989): 22–26.

Lind, William S. "Understanding Fourth Generation Warfare," *Military Review*, September–October 2004, 12–16.

Livingston, Gary. *An Nasiriyah: The Fight for the Bridges*, 2nd ed. Snead's Ferry, NC: Caisson Press, 2004.

Louis, William Roger. *The British Empire in the Middle East 1945–1951: Arab Nationalism, the United States, and the Postwar Imperialism*. Oxford, U.K.: Oxford University Press, 1984.

Lowenthal, Marvin, ed. *The Diaries of Theodor Herzel*. New York: Grosset and Dunlap, 1962.

Ludke, Tilman. *Jihad Made in Germany: Ottoman and German Propaganda and Intelligence Operations in the First World War*. London: Global, 2005.

Luttwak, Edward, and Dan Horowitz. *The Israeli Army 1948–1973*. Cambridge, MA: Abt Books, 1983.

Lynch, Marc. *The Arab Uprising: The Unfinished Revolutions of the New Middle East*. New York: PublicAffairs, 2012.

Maalouf, Amin. *The Crusades through Arab Eyes*. New York: Schocken Books, 1985.

Macdonald, James B. "The Russian Campaign in Turkey" In *The New York Times Current History: The European War,* Vol. 8, 1083–1088. New York: New York Times Company, July–September 1916.

Mackinder, Halford. "The Geopolitical Pivot of History," *The Geographical Journal,* Vol. 23, No. 4 (April 1904): 421–437.

Mader, Major L. R. (Canadian Army). "The 1967 Sinai Campaign: Some Lessons about the Manoeuvrist Approach," *The Army Doctrine and Training Bulletin* (Canada), Vol. 5, No. 3 (Fall 2002): 36–45.

Mahan, A. T. *The Influence of Sea Power upon History 1660–1783* [1890]. Gretna, LA: Pelican Publishing, 2003.

Mansoor, Peter R. *Surge: My Journey with David Petraeus and the Remaking of the Iraq War.* New Haven, CT: Yale University Press, 2013.

Marks, Major General James A., and Lieutenant Colonel Steve Peterson. "Lessons Learned: Six Things Every '2' Must Do—Fundamental Lessons of OIF," *Military Intelligence,* Vol. 29, No. 4 (October–December 2003): 5–14.

Marten, Kimberly. "The Danger of Tribal Militias in Afghanistan: Learning from the British Empire," *Journal of International Affairs,* Vol. 63, No. 1 (Fall/Winter 2009): 157–174.

Martin, Jerome V. *Victory from Above: Air Power Theory and the Conduct of Operations Desert Shield and Desert Storm.* Maxwell Air Force Base, AL: Air University Press, 1994.

Mason, M. Chris. *The Strategic Lessons Unlearned from Vietnam, Iraq, and Afghanistan: Why the ANSF Will Not Hold, and the Implications for the US Army in Afghanistan.* Carlisle Barracks, PA: Strategic Studies Institute—U.S. Army War College, 2015.

Matheny, Michael R. "The Evolution of Operational Art from Napoleon to the Present," *The Journal of Military History,* Vol. 75, No. 4 (October 2011): 1294–1295.

Maughan, Barton. *Tobruk and El Alamein. Australia in the War of 1939–1945,* Vol. 3. Canberra: Australian War Memorial, 1966. Accessed December 10, 2014. http://www.qattara.it/Documents/volume%20completo.pdf.

McCaul, Ed. "Iranian Tank Commander," *Military History,* Vol. 21, No. 1 (April 2004): 44–49.

McCauley, Brian. "Hungary and Suez 1956: The Limits of Soviet and American Power," *Journal of Contemporary History,* Vol. 16, No. 4 (October 1981): 777–800.

McCausland, Jeffrey. *The Gulf Conflict: A Military Analysis: A Military Analysis of the Lessons of the Gulf War with Recommendations for Future Security in the Region.* London: Brassey's for The International Institute for Strategic Studies, 1993. (Adelphi papers, 282).

McChrystal, Stanley A. *My Share of the Task: A Memoir.* New York: Portfolio, 2014.

McChrystal, Stanley A. *Team of Teams: New Rules of Engagement for a Complex World.* New York: Portfolio, 2015.

McCullough, David. *Truman.* New York: New York: Simon and Schuster, 1992.

McGregor, Andrew. *A Military History of Modern Egypt: From the Ottoman Conquest to the Ramadan War.* Westport, CT: Praeger, 2006.

McGregor, Andrew. "From Rommel to Qaddafi: Petrol Supplies Still Key to Military Success in Libya," *Terrorism Monitor,* Vol. IX, No. 21 (May 27, 2011): 6–8.

McMaster, H. R. "What We Learned from the Battle of 73 Easting," *Military History*, Vol. 28, No. 3 (September 2011).

McMeekin, Sean. *The Berlin-Baghdad Express: The Ottoman Empire and Germany's Bid for World Power*. Cambridge, MA: Belkap Press, 2010.

McNamara, Robert. "Britain, Nasser, and the Outbreak of the Six Day War," *Journal of Contemporary History*, Vol. 35, No. 4 (October 2000): 619–639.

McRaven, William. *Spec Ops: Case Studies in Special Operations Warfare: Theory and Practice*. Novato, CA: Presidio Press, 1996.

Meade, Earle Edward, ed. *Makers of Modern Strategy: Military Thought from Machiavelli to Hitler*. Princeton, NJ: Princeton University Press, 1944.

Mearsheimer, John. "The False Promise of International Institutions," *International Security*, Vol. 19, No. 3 (Winter 1994–1995): 5–49.

Meigs, Montgomery C. "Operational Art in the New Century," *Parameters* (Spring 2001): 4–14.

Meyer, K., and S. B. Brysac. *Kingmakers: The Invention of the Modern Middle East*. London: W.W. Norton, 2008.

Moberly, Frederick J. *Operations in Persia, 1914–1919*. London: H.M.S.O., 1987.

Moore, J., ed. *The Arab-Israeli Conflict: Readings and Documents*. Princeton, NJ: Princeton University Press, 1977.

Moore, Robin. *The Hunt for Bin Laden: Task Force Dagger—On the Ground with Special Forces in Afghanistan*. New York: Random House, 2003.

Moran, Daniel. *Strategic Theory of War*. Monterey, CA: Naval Postgraduate School, 2001. Accessed August 14, 2013. http://www.clausewitz.com/readings/Moran-StrategicTheory.pdf.

Morgenthau, Hans J. *Politics among Nations: The Struggle for Power and Peace*. New York: Knopf, 1948.

Morrell, Michael. *The Great War of Our Time: The CIA's Fight against Terrorism: From al Qaida to ISIS*. New York: Twelve Publishers, 2015.

Motter, T. H. Vail. *The Persian Corridor and Aid to Russia*. Washington, DC: Center of Military History, U.S. Army, 2000.

Moyar, Mark. "The Era of American Hegemony, 1989–2005." In *The Cambridge History of War*, edited by Roger Chickering, Dennis Showalter, and Hans van de Ven, 566–588. Cambridge, U.K.: Cambridge University Press, 2013.

Murphy, Orville T. "Napoleon's International Politics: How Much Did He Owe to the Past?" *The Journal of Military History*, Vol. 54, No. 2 (April 1990): 165–166.

Murray, Williamson, and Peter R. Mansoor, eds. *Hybrid Warfare: Fighting Complex Opponents from the Ancient World to the Present*. Cambridge, U.K.: Cambridge University Press, 2012.

National Security Council, U.S. Note by the executive secretary, National Security Council, "United States Policy Regarding the Present Situation in Iran," November 20, 1952, National Security Council NSC 136/1.

Naylor, Sean. *Not a Good Day to Die: The Untold Story of Operation Anaconda*. New York: Berkley Caliber, 2005.

Neiberg, Michael S. "Allenby Captures Jerusalem," *Military History*, Vol. 31, No. 4 (November 2014): 56–64.

Nelson, Horatio. *The Dispatches and Letters of Vice Admiral Lord Viscount Nelson.* Edited by Nicholas Harris Nicolas. Cambridge, U.K: Cambridge University Press, 2011.

Nelson, Major Robert A. "The Battle of the Bridges: Kuwait's 35th Brigade on the 2d of August 1990," *Armor,* Vol. 54, No. 5 (September–October 1995): 26–32.

Niderost, Eric. "Final French Triumph in Egypt," *Military History,* Vol. 16, No. 3 (August 1999): 34–41.

Niderost, Eric. "Peak for Moslem Tide," *Military History,* Vol. 5, No. 3 (December 1998): 34–41.

North, John. "Lessons of the North African Campaign," *Military Affairs,* Vol. 8, No. 3 (Autumn 1944): 162–163.

Norton, Augustus R. *Hezbollah: A Short History.* Princeton, NJ: Princeton University Press, 2007.

O'Ballance, Edgar. "The Iraqi-Iranian War: The First Round," *Parameters,* Vol. XI, No. 1 (March 1981): 54–59.

O'Ballance, Edgar. *The Sinai Campaign 1956.* Westport, CT: Frederick A. Praeger, 1960.

Office of the Director of Central Intelligence. "Is Iraq Losing the War?" *Special National Intelligence Estimate* SNIE 34/36.2-86, April 1986.

Oler, Adam. "An Islamic Way of War?" *Joint Forces Quarterly,* National Defense University Press, No. 61 (2nd Quarter 2011): 81–88.

Oliver, Roy. *The Failure of Political Islam.* Cambridge, MA: Harvard University Press, 1996.

Olsen, John Adreas. *Strategic Air Power in Desert Storm.* New York: Routledge, 2003.

Oren, Michael B. *Power, Faith, and Fantasy: America in the Middle East, 1776 to the Present.* New York: W.W. Norton and Company, 2007.

Oren, Michael B. *Six Days War: June 1967 and the Making of the Modern Middle East.* New York: Oxford University Press, 2002.

Organski, A. F. K., and Jacek Kugler. *The War Ledger.* Chicago, IL: University of Chicago Press, 1980.

Orlin, Louis L. *Life and Thought in the Ancient Middle East.* Ann Arbor, MI: University of Michigan Press, 2007.

Ouimet, Matthew J. *The Rise and Fall of the Brezhnev Doctrine in Soviet Foreign Policy.* Chapel Hill, NC: The University of North Carolina Press, February 2003.

Ovendale, Ritchie. *Britain, the United States and the End of the Palestinian Mandate 1942–1948.* London: Royal Historical Society; Woodbridge, Suffolk [England]; Wolfeboro, NH: Boydell Press, 1989.

Ovendale, Ritchie. *Britain, the United States, and the Transfer of Power in the Middle East, 1945–1962.* Leichester, U.K.: Leicester University Press, 1996.

Painter, David S. "Oil, Resources, and the Cold War, 1945–1962." In *Cambridge History of War. Cambridge Histories Online.* Cambridge, U.K.: Cambridge University Press, 2010.

Palmer, Michael A. *Guardians of the Gulf: A History of America's Expanding Role in the Persian Gulf, 1833–1992.* New York, Free Press, 1992.

Palmer, Michael A. "Storm in the Air: One Plan, Two Air Wars?" *Air Power History,* Vol. 39, No. 4 (Winter 1992): 24–31.

Pape, Robert A. *Dying To Win: The Strategic Logic of Suicide Terrorism*. New York: Random House, 2005.

Paret, Peter, Gordon A. Craig, and Felix Gilbert, eds. *Makers of Modern Strategy: From Machiavelli to the Nuclear Age*. Princeton, NJ: Princeton University Press, 1986.

Parker, Geoffrey, ed. *The Cambridge History of Warfare*. Cambridge, U.K.: Cambridge University Press, 2005.

Parsa, M. "Conversion or Coalition? Ideology in the Iranian and Nicaragua Revolutions," *Political Power and Social Theory*, Vol. 9, No. 1 (1995): 23–60.

Parsa, M. *States, Ideologies, and Social Revolutions: A Comparative Analysis of Iran, Nicaragua, and the Philippines*. Cambridge, U.K.: Cambridge University Press, 2000.

Patai, Raphael. *The Arab Mind*. New York: Charles Scribner's Sons, 1976.

Peral, Luis, and Ashley J. Tellis, eds. "Afghanstan 2001–2014 and Beyond: From Support Operations to Sustainable Peace," Joint Report, European Union Institute for Security Studies (ISS), June 2011.

Persson, Magnus. *Great Britain, the United States, and the Security of the Middle East: The Formation of the Baghdad Pact*. Lund, Sweden: Lund University Press, 1998.

Pollack, Kenneth M. *Arabs at War: Military Effectiveness, 1948–1991*. Lincoln, NE: University of Nebraska Press, 2002.

Poole, H. John. *Phantom Soldier: The Enemy's Answer to U.S. Firepower*. Emerald Isle, NC: Posterity Press,: 2001.

Poole, H. John. *Tactics of the Crescent Moon: Militant Muslim Combat Methods*. Emerald Isle, NC: Posterity Press, 2004.

Puchala, Donald J. "The Integrationist Theorists and the Study of International Relations." In *The Global Agenda: Issues and Perspectives*, edited by Charles W. Kegley and Eugene M. Wittkopf, 185–202. New York: Random House, 1984.

Quandt, William B. "Soviet Policy in October Middle East War II," *International Affairs* (Royal Institute of International Affairs), Vol. 53, No.4 (October 1977): 587–603.

Quilter, Charles J. *U.S. Marines in the Persian Gulf, 1990–1991: With the First (I) Marine Expeditionary Force in Desert Shield and Desert Storm*. Washington, DC: History and Museums Division, Headquarters, U.S. Marine Corps, 1993.

Rabinovich, Itamar. *Syria under the Ba'th, 1963–1966: The Army-Party Symbiosis*. Jerusalem: Israel Universities Presses, 1972.

Ravndal, Ellen Jenny. "Exit Britain: British Withdrawal from the Palestine Mandate in the Early Cold War, 1947–48," *Diplomacy and Statecraft*, Vol. 21, No. 3 (2010): 416–433.

Reagan, Ronald. *An American Life*. New York: Threshold Editions, 2011.

Record, Jeffery. "The Bush Doctrine and War with Iraq," *Parameters*, Vol. 33, No. 1 (Spring 2003): 4–21.

Rees, Simon. "The Long Road to Kandahar: Second Afghan War," *Military History*, Vol. 21, No. 5 (December 2004): 30–37.

Ricks, Thomas E. *Fiasco: The American Military Adventure in Iraq*. New York: Penguin Group, 2006.

Rid, Thomas, and Mark Hecker. *War 2.0: Irregular Warfare in the Information Age*. Westport, CT: Praeger Security International, 2009.

Roberts, Priscilla. *Arab-Israeli Conflict: The Essential Reference Guide.* Santa Barbara, CA: ABC-CLIO, 2014.

Rubin, Barry, ed. *Conflict and Insurgency in the Contemporary Middle East.* New York: Routledge, 2010.

Rumsfeld, Donald. *Known and Unknown: A Memoir.* New York: Sentinel, 2011.

Rustow, Dankwart A. "Ataturk as Founder of a State," *Daedalus*, Vol. 97, No. 3, Philosophers and Kings: Studies in Leadership (Summer 1968): 793–829.

Sachar, Howard M. *The Emergence of the Middle East: 1914–1924.* New York: Alfred A Knopf, 1969.

Salzman, Philip. *Culture and Conflict in the Middle East.* Amherst, NY: Humanity Books, 2008.

Schemmer, Benjamin F. "USAF MH-53J Pave Lows Led Army Apaches Knocking Out Iraqi Radars to Open Air War." *Armed Forces Journal International*, Vol. 128 (July 1991): 34.

Schroen, Gary C. *First In: An Insider's Account of How the CIA Spearheaded the War on Terrorism in Afghanistan.* New York: Presidio Press, 2005.

Schwartz-Barcott, Timothy P. *Terror and Peace in the Qur'an and in Islam: Insights for Military and Government Leaders.* Falls Church, VA: U.S. Army War College Foundation Press, 2004.

Schwarzkopf, H. Norman, and Peter Petre. *It Doesn't Take a Hero.* New York: Linda Grey Bantam Books, 1992.

Scott, James M., ed. *Deciding to Intervene: The Reagan Doctrine and American Foreign Policy.* Durham, NC: Duke University Press, 1986.

Scudieri, Lieutenant Colonel James D. "Iraq 2003–4 and Mesopotamia 1914–18: A Comparative Analysis in Ends and Means," Master's Thesis, Center for Strategic Leadership, U.S. Army War College, Carlyle Barracks, PA, March 19, 2004, pp. 1–39.

Sharp, Jeremy M. *Lebanon: The Israeli-Hamas-Hezbollah Conflict.* CRS Report for Congress, RL 33566. Washington DC: Congressional Research Service, September 15, 2006.

Shield, Ralph. "Israel's Second Lebanon War: A Failure of the Afghan Model of Warfare?" Newport, RI: Joint Military Operations Department, Naval War College, 2007. Accessed September 22, 2013. http://handle.dtic.mil/100.2/ADA470727.

Showalter, Dennis. "Introduction: Post-Total Warfare, 1945–2005." In *Cambridge History of War. Cambridge Histories Online.* Cambridge, U.K.: Cambridge University Press, 2013.

Sick, Gary, and Lawrence Porter, eds. *The Changing Face of the Persian Gulf at the 21st Century.* New York: St. Martin's Press, 1997.

Sicker, Martin. *The Pre-Islamic Middle East.* Santa Barbara, CA: ABC-CLIO/Praeger, 2000.

Silinsky, Mark. *The Taliban: Afghanistan's Most Lethal Insurgents.* Santa Barbara, CA: Praeger, 2014.

Sinkaya, Bayram. *The Revolutionary Guards in Iranian Politics: Elites and Shifting Relations.* New York: Routledge, 2015.

Smith, Rupert. *The Utility of Force: The Art of War in the Modern World.* New York: Vintage, 2008.

Smith, Steve. "Groupthink and the Hostage Rescue Mission," *British Journal of Political Science*, Vol. 15, No. 1 (1984): 117–123.

Snakenberg, Mark K. "An Nasiriyah: America's First Battle in Operation Iraqi Freedom," *Army History*, No. 76 (Summer 2010), PB 20-10-3, Washington, DC, 33–42.

Sobhy, Abouseada Hamdy. "The Crossing of the Suez Canal, October 6, 1973 (The Ramadan War)." Carlisle Barracks, PA: U.S. Army War College, 2000.

Solley, Major George C. (USMC). "The Israeli Experience in Lebanon, 1982–1985." Quantico, VA: Marine Corps Command and Staff College, February 16, 1987.

Springer, Lieutenant Colonel Rita A. (USAF). "Operation Moked and the Principles of War," Department of Joint Military Operations, Naval War College, May 19, 1997.

Spyer, Jonathan. "Lebanon 2006: Unfinished War," *Middle East Review of International Affairs*, Vol. 12, No. 1 (March 2008). Accessed January 3, 2017. http://www.rubincenter.org/2009/10/unfinished-war/.

Staudenmaier, William O. *A Strategic Analysis of the Gulf War*. Carlisle Barracks, PA: US Army War College, 1982.

Stewart, Del. "De-constructing the Theory of Fourth Generation Warfare," *Military Intelligence*, Vol. 30, No. 4 (October–December 2004): 35–38.

Stewart, Richard W. *Operation Enduring Freedom: The United States Army in Afghanistan, October 2001–March 2002*. Center of Military History, Special Publications CMH Pub 70-83-1, U.S. Army, 2004.

Stewart, Richard W. *War in the Persian Gulf: Operations Desert Shield and Desert Storm, August 1990–March 1991*. Center of Military History, Special Publications CMH Pub 70-117-1, U.S. Army, 2010.

Streusand, Douglas E. *Islamic Gunpowder Empires: Ottomans, Safavids, and Mughals*. Boulder, CO: Westview Press, 2010.

Summers, Harry G., Jr. *On Strategy II: A Critical Analysis of the Gulf War*. New York: Dell, 1992.

Sykes, Christopher. *Wassmuss: "The German Lawrence."* London: Longmans, Green, 1936.

Taber, Robert. *War of the Flea: The Classic Study of Guerrilla Warfare*. Washington, DC: Brassey's Inc., 2002.

Tamkin, Nicholas. "Britain, the Middle East, and the 'Northern Front', 1941–1942," *War in History*, Vol. 15, No. 3 (2008): 314–336.

Tse-tung, Mao. *Selected Military Writings*. Beijing: Foreign Languages Press, 1968.

Tuchman, Barbara W. *The Guns of August*. New York: Macmillan, 1962.

Tucker, Spencer, ed. *Persian Gulf War: A Political, Social, and Military History*. Santa Barbara, CA: ABC-CLIO, 2014.

Tzu, Sun. *The Art of War*. Translated and annotated by Samuel B. Griffith. Oxford, UK: Oxford University Press, 1963.

U.S. Army. *US Army in World War II: The Middle East Theater, the Persian Corridor and Aid to Russia*. Center of Military History. Accessed November 17, 2016. http://wwwhistory.army.mil/html/bookshelves/collect/ww2-mideast.html.

Uyar, Mesut, and Edward J. Erikson. *A Military History of the Ottomans: From Osman to Attaturk*. Santa Barbara, CA: Praeger, 2009.

Van Creveld, Martin L. *Air Power and Maneuver Warfare*. Maxwell Air Force Base, AL: Air University Press, July 1994.

Van Creveld, Martin L. *Technology and War: From 2000 BC to the Present*. New York: The Free Press, 1989.

Vernon, Alex, and Neal Creighton Jr., Greg Downey, and Rob Holmes. *The Eyes of Orion: Five Tank Lieutenants in the Persian Gulf War*. Kent, OH: Kent State University Press, 1999.

Walker, David. "OSS and Operation Torch," *Journal of Contemporary History*, Vol. 22, No. 4 (1987): 667–679.

Ward, Steven R. *Immortal: A Military History of Iran and Its Armed Forces*. Washington, DC: Georgetown University Press, 2014.

Warden, John. *The Air Campaign: Planning for Combat* (Washington, DC: National Defense University Press, 1988).

Warden, John (Col). "Profile: Col. John A. Warden III—Air Force Veteran Battles for New World Order." *Government Executive*, Vol. 24, No. 2 (February 1992): 46.

Watts, Martin. *The Jewish Legion and the First World War*. New York: Palgrave Macmillan, 2004.

Weiler, Major Robert S. (USMC). "Eliminating Success during ECLIPSE II: An Examination of the Decision to Disband the Iraqi Military." Master's Thesis, U.S. Marine Corps Command and Staff College, Marine Corps University, Quantico, VA, 2009.

Weinberger, Caspar W. "The Uses of Military Power," *Defense*, Vol. 85, Armed Forces Information Service, Arlington, VA, December 1985: 2–11.

Weinberger, Naomi. *Syrian Intervention in Lebanon: The 1975–76 Civil War*. New York: Oxford University Press, 1986.

Welch, Captain Ryan (U.S. Army). "Operation Anaconda: The Battle for the Shah-i-kot Valley," *Armor*, Vol. 62, No. 6 (November–December 2003): 36–41.

West, Bing. *No True Glory: A Frontline Account of the Battle of Fallujah*. New York: Random House/Bantam Books, 2005.

Westermeyer, Paul W. *US Marines in Battle: al-Khafji, 28 June–1 February 1991*. Washington, DC: History and Museums Division, Headquarters, U.S. Marine Corps, 1993.

Wickham, Carrie Rosefsky. *The Muslim Brotherhood: Evolution of an Islamist Movement*. Princeton, NJ: Princeton University Press, 2013.

Williamson, Colonel Steven C. "From Fourth Generation Warfare to Hybrid War," Strategic Studies Institute, U.S. Army War College, Carlisle, PA, 2009.

Winnefeld, James A., Preston Niblack, and Dana J. Johnson. *A League of Airmen: U.S. Air Power in the Gulf War*. Project Air Force Report. Santa Monica, CA: RAND Corporation, 1994.

Woodward, Bob. "Secret CIA Units Playing a Central Combat Role," *Washington Post*, November 18, 2001, A1.

Woodward, David R. *Hell in the Holy Land: World War I in the Middle East*. Lexington, KY: The University Press of Kentucky, 2006.

Yergin, Daniel. *The Prize: The Epic Quest for Oil, Money and Power*. New York: Simon & Schuster, 1991.

Zabecki, David T. "Is the IDF Invincible?" *Military History*, Vol. 25, No. 6 (February 2009): 28–37.

Ze'evi, Dror. "Back to Napoleon? Thoughts on the Beginning of the Modern Era in the Middle East," *Mediterranean Historical Review*, Vol. 19, No. 1 (June 2004): 73–94.

Zimmick, Steven M. *US Marines in the Persian Gulf, 1990–1991: Combat Service Support in Desert Shield*. Washington, DC: History and Museums Division, Headquarters, U.S. Marine Corps, 1999.

Zisser, Eyal. "June 1967: Israel's Capture of the Golan Heights," *Israeli Studies*, Vol. 7, No. 1 (Spring 2002): 168–194.

Zucchino, David. *Thunder Run: An Armored Strike to Capture Baghdad*. New York: Grove Press, 2004.

Zurcher, Erik J., ed. *Arming the State: Military Conscription in the Middle East and Central Asia, 1775–1925*. New York: St. Martin's Press, 1999.

Index

About the Author

JAMES BRIAN McNABB, PhD, is adjunct professor with Troy University's Master of Science in International Relations (MSIR) program. He has taught in the Middle East at the American University in Sulaimania, Iraq; in Central Asia at the Kazakhstan Institute of Management, Economics, and Strategic Research; and at California State University, San Bernardino's National Security Studies MA program. His published works include contributions to ABC-CLIO's *World at War: Understanding Conflict and Society*; the paper "The Unanticipated Utility of U.S. Security Structures: Avoiding Cold War II in Central Asia," published in the journal *Comparative Strategy*; and "Parallels between the Crusades and OEF and OIF? Major Differences, Marked Similarities." McNabb holds a master's degree in national security studies from California State University, San Bernardino, and a doctorate in international politics from Claremont Graduate University.